Living
a Life of
Value

Living a Life of Value

A Unique Anthology of Essays
on Values & Ethics by
Contemporary Writers

Edited By

JASON A. MERCHEY
Creator of THE VALUES OF THE WISE SERIES

Living a Life of Value:

A Unique Anthology of Essays on Values & Ethics by Contemporary Writers

First Edition

Library of Congress Cataloging-in-Publication Data

Merchey, Jason A.

   Living a life of value: a unique anthology of essays on values and ethics by

   contemporary writers / Jason A. Merchey.-- 1st ed.

   p. cm. -- (Values of the wise series ; v. 2)

   Includes bibliographical references and index.

   ISBN 0-9773412-0-8

     1. Values--Quotations, maxims, etc. 2. Ethics--Quotations, maxims, etc.

     3. Conduct of life--Quotations, maxims, etc. 4. Wisdom--Quotations, maxims, etc.

     I. Title. II. Series: Merchey, Jason A. Values of the wise series ; v. 2.

2006925518

VALUES
of the WISE™
PRESS

Printed and bound in the United States of America on recycled paper

Cover and book design by Jason Gerboth

Production by Pueblo Indexing and Publishing Services

In honor of Katherine Martin, she who dared.

Dedicated to the philosophers, who, at their best, are lovers of wisdom.

Taking steps now to become wise is not another elitist retreat from the problems experienced by the majority of the world's people. It is, in fact, the most effective possible long-term attack on those problems.

Copthorne Macdonald

Be the change you wish to see in the world.

Mohandas K. Gandhi

CONTENTS

Living a Life of Value

CONTENTS

Contents

FOREWORD

Catherine Ryan Hyde

This is where it all began for me.

Nearly twenty-five years ago I was driving in Los Angeles late at night. I was in a bad neighborhood, and I was driving a bad car.

The fact that it was a bad car was nobody's fault but my own. I had this theory when I was younger. I thought that it was cheaper if you just drove the car and never took it to the mechanic. People laugh when I say it, but it made perfect sense to me. Mechanics charge money. If you don't go to them, you save money. What could be simpler and more obvious than that? It's one of those theories that work perfectly until the day it doesn't anymore. This is a story about that day.

I got to the bottom of the freeway ramp and stepped on the brake. The engine died—not out of the ordinary, I should mention. When you never take your car to the mechanic, the engine usually dies the minute you take your foot off the gas. But before I could start it again, something unusual happened. All electrical power to the car died. Headlights, dash lights, everything. Out. That was the minor problem. The major problem was the curl of smoke (smoke is almost never good news in any driving story) coming up from under the dashboard. It seemed to be coming through the firewall from the engine side. It was threatening to fill up the passenger compartment where I sat.

Now, when you're in your locked car in a bad neighborhood late at night, there's a strong motivation to stay there. But now the car is filling up with smoke, which I think is something like the textbook definition of being between a rock and a hard place.

Just so you don't have to do your own research, I'll tell you. The smoke wins.

I jumped out.

I thought I was alone out there. I hadn't seen anyone else around. But when I looked up, I saw two men—two total strangers—running very fast in my direction. One of them was carrying a blanket.

Of the many thoughts that danced in my head—and oh, there were many—would you believe that not a single one had anything to do with being rescued? I think my first thought was that I'd never made out a will. The second was that it didn't matter anyway, because I had nothing of value except my car, which was on fire. In any case, I definitely thought I was dead. At no time did it occur to me that total strangers might be running to my aid.

One of the men pushed past me and popped my hood release from the inside. The other opened the hood of my car, leaned his entire upper body into my flaming engine compartment, and smothered the fire with his bare hands and his own blanket.

About the time the fire was out, the fire department came roaring up. I think that's interesting to note, because I didn't call them. These two men didn't call them. Who called them? The only logical explanation is that someone going by on the freeway behind me, someone I never even saw, stopped at a call box (this was long before cell phones) and phoned it in for me.

Even before this experience I would have definitely called the fire department for anyone who needed them...it wouldn't have mattered if it was a total stranger; I would do that much for anybody. I think most of us would. But what about the bit where you lean into a burning engine compartment and smother the flames by hand? Would you do that for a total stranger? Key question.

The fire was out, so it was anticlimactic. There wasn't much left for the firefighters to do. They just helped get my car over to the side of the road. They showed me how the fire got started, which isn't a very interesting story. Then they told me what would have happened if these guys hadn't put it out.

We don't like to think about it as we drive (and I don't suggest you do), but a car is built much the way a Molotov cocktail is built. It's a big container of flammable liquid with a fuse running into it. The only real difference is that you don't pick up a car and throw it. Otherwise, the effect is the same.

That's when I realized that these two men may have saved a lot more than my car—and they put their own safety on the line to do it. I turned to thank them, knowing this had better be good. But they had already packed up and driven away.

I never even got to say thank you.

I got the car put back together. Amazingly. And I got back out on those freeways. But something had changed. This time I had one eye on the side of the road, looking for someone in trouble. Anyone. Didn't matter who it was. This time I was going to stop and help.

I got a few opportunities, too. And I did my bit a few times. More importantly, I started examining how much we do for each other and why. Why did those two men do more for me than most strangers would? Why did that change me into someone willing to do more for the next stranger?

We all want a kinder world. Right? But it's so easy to be kind. We can wake up on any given day and decide to do more for those around us and probably have a better day for it. So, if we all want a kinder world, and it's easy enough to be kinder, why aren't we doing it?

That, in a nutshell, is why I wrote the book *Pay It Forward*, the story of a boy named Trevor who changes the world with a simple idea. He does a big favor for three people and asks them to pay it forward to three more people—each—charging each of them with paying it forward to three more. I didn't write the book to change the world or start a real-life movement, because I never thought I could. I just wanted people to ask the question with me. Why don't we treat each other better? It would be so easy.

Deeper into this book, *Living a Life of Value,* many brilliant and well-educated individuals will shed light on far more complex aspects of social responsibility. They will speak to complicated issues in ways I never could.

But it all boils down to the same heart of the same issue. It's all about the way we treat each other.

At the risk of being perceived as overly simplistic and idealistic (a danger I already wholeheartedly embraced when I wrote *Pay It Forward*) I'd like to refer to the simplest, most perfect, most all-encompassing manifesto on values ever offered: The Golden Rule. "Do unto others as you would have others do unto you." It was probably the first lesson we all learned in school, and possibly the only one to speak to the subject of how we conduct ourselves in the world.

If we really practiced the Golden Rule, all human problems would essentially disappear. The only remaining problems would be pretty much weather-related. There would be no crimes, because no one wants to be the victim of one. We really couldn't attack or invade any foreign countries, since we don't desire to be attacked ourselves. We could fire all the newscasters (except we'd have to retrain them, because we wouldn't want to be fired) and just keep the weatherman and the sports guy. It's that perfect.

But obviously it doesn't work, right? After all, we have plenty of newscasters.

I don't agree that it doesn't work. I don't think it's fair to leave a tool sitting in the drawer and claim it doesn't work. It wasn't designed to work while sitting in the drawer. You have to pick it up and use it.

The Golden Rule works to the extent that we use it.

This is the point, I'm afraid, where we get hung up in the cold hard fact that we can't change anybody else. This is the point at which some say, "*I* would. But *they* won't. So why should *I* if *they* never will? Why even bother? Never mind."

Wow. Amazing. They talked themselves out of even starting.

This is why I made Trevor—the fictional inventor of the Pay It Forward movement—a twelve-year-old boy. I didn't have a lot of faith in grownups to get this job done. I pictured a grownup taking out a sheet of paper and listing all the reasons why it would never work, thereby talking himself (or herself) out of even trying.

Fortunately, shortly after the release of the book, I realized I had underestimated grownups. Lots of them came through with flying colors.

Others, like a few reviewers, not so much. Generally the book was well reviewed, but in a few instances it met with stinging criticism (though I can't claim to have been all that deeply stung). Here are the dreadful adjectives they used to insult it: They said it was idealistic. Worse yet, they said it was...sentimental.

Now, I don't know about you, but I must have been asleep or absent on the day the word sentimental became a mortal insult. Out of curiosity, I even looked it up. Sentiment would appear to mean a thought, a belief, or an emotion. Sentimental apparently means maudlin, mawkish, and sappy. Now, I work with words for a living, and I know of no other instance where a simple two-letter "al" suffix can change a word so drastically. Maybe it's not the suffix that did it. Maybe it was our attitudes that changed that word.

I mention this because it helps me make a point about another word: Values.

When I was first approached to be part of this book on values...well, let's just say I was guarded. Because it seems to me that in this country, over the last few decades, the word values has been co-opted by a group at the very radical right of things.

Family values. Remember that? But, as the bumper sticker so eloquently pointed out, hate is not a family value. Neither is anything that causes more war, poverty, or destruction of the environment. Not in my family, anyway.

This is what I value: Honest communication, emotional courage, kindness, open-mindedness, tolerance.

Too bad that puts me at odds with the people who seem to be shouting the loudest about values. Oh, that's another thing I value: A soft speaking voice. If you're comfortable in your beliefs, what is there to shout about?

Over the past six years I've had the opportunity to talk to thousands of schoolchildren on behalf of the Pay It Forward Foundation. More importantly, I've had the opportunity to listen to them.

We don't listen to our kids enough. That is my considered opinion. We spend a lot of time telling them to sit down, shut up, and listen to the grownups. But they have eyes and ears, thoughts, and observations. They look at the world and ask why. Why are so many people starving? Why is there war? Why are we polluting the earth?

We tell them that's just the way it is. Maybe we tell them it can't be changed because we're afraid they'll ask why we don't change it. Then what would we say?

I ask the kids what they don't like about the world. They tell me. We talk about it until we boil it down to that basic premise: It's all about how we treat each other.

Then I ask them how they treat each other. I ask how many kids think there's teasing and bullying going on at their school every day. The hands go up slowly at first. But they always go up. Then I ask how many of the kids like it that way. "How many of you *like* teasing and bullying and want to hang onto it?" No hands.

Now for the really important question: "If you all agree it's here, and none of you wants it, why do you have it?"

A lot of silence and blinking.

I know that no one of those kids alone could stop the physical and emotional brutality that is life at school. But they all could. All they would have to do is agree that there would be no more tolerance for it. It's absolutely within their hands.

I'm not as much of an idealist as people sometimes take me to be. I never said a simple idea like Pay It Forward is going to catch on and completely change the world. But it sure isn't going to make it any worse. How much it helps depends on the extent to which we leave it in the drawer or pick it up and use it.

No one can convince me that a simple resolve to treat each other better would not change the world. If one person commits to it, the world is better by one committed person. If thousands do (and by the way, thousands have) we are making a little more progress. What's wrong with small to medium world change? To sidestep a chance to change the world modestly because you can't change it completely strikes me as lunacy. Worse yet, it's lazy. And cowardly.

Yes, cowardly. I have a theory about cynicism. Cynics don't like it. And I don't really care. I think cynicism is a subtle form of cowardice. And I think optimism is a courageous act. And, as I said before, I value courage.

As to whether or not people will really pay it forward, I'll give the same answer that Reuben, my protagonist (I know, you only saw the movie, and that's not nearly the same) gave at the end of the book. He said, "Don't ask me if people will really pay it forward. Tell me. Will you?"

You're a person. If you will, that's a start on an answer.

I purposely made Trevor an ordinary boy. Or at least I thought I did. I meant to. Some mistakenly see him as a messiah, but I had something quite the opposite in mind. We don't need divine intervention to accomplish this. We don't even need a remarkable visionary. This is not rocket science. It's kindness. It's easy.

Chris Chandler, the reporter character, makes the following observation: "Knowing it started from unremarkable circumstances should be a comfort to us all. Because it proves that you don't need much to change the entire world for the better. You can start with the most ordinary ingredients. You can start with the world you've got."

So let's get started.

About the Author

Catherine Ryan Hyde is the author of story collection *Earthquake Weather*, and the novels *Funerals for Horses, Pay it Forward, Electric God*, and *Walter's Purple Heart. Pay It Forward* was adapted into a major motion picture. *Electric God* is also optioned for film and in development, with Nicolas Cage slated to play the lead role of Hayden Reese.

Her newer novels are *Becoming Chloe* (Knopf, March 2006), *Love in the Present Tense* (Doubleday, May 2006), and *Broken People* (Knopf, Spring 2007).

More than forty-five of her short stories have been published in *The Antioch Review, Michigan Quarterly Review, The Virginia Quarterly Review, Ploughshares, Glimmer Train* and many other journals, and in the anthologies *Santa Barbara Stories* and *California Shorts*. Her story "Bloodlines" was reprinted in the bestselling anthology *Dog is my Co-Pilot*. Her stories have been honored in the Raymond Carver Short Story Contest and the Tobias Wolff Award and nominated for Best American Short Stories, the O'Henry Award, and the Pushcart Prize. Three have been cited in Best American Short Stories.

She is founder and president of the Pay It Forward Foundation. As a professional public speaker she has addressed the National Conference on Education, twice spoken at Cornell University, and shared a dais with Bill Clinton.

She lives in Cambria, California, and writes full time.

INTRODUCTION

This is the second anthology in the series exploring the idea of "a life of value." The concept is a very old one, and has for centuries been sought by the wise for the rewards it brings. Yet, perhaps paradoxically, this lifelong pursuit of a shapeless construct that exists only in our heads is evidenced too by young children. Indeed, kings and thieves, persons from here and from there, free thinkers and shackled slaves, musicians and corporate leaders, generals and peacemakers, the dying and the healthy, the progressive and the conservative, and the inspired and the atheistic have lain their unique stones upon the road on which we are now walking. Fascinatingly, it is at once built, yet forever under construction. It is perfect, and at the same time in need of refinement. We grasp the ideas, and then lose them after a sleep.

There are certain values that those who are wise make their own, and though there is no true clarity about what it means to be wise—unlike having a college degree or possessing a certain number of dollars—we know wisdom when we see it. For example, kindness is better than meanness, honor is better than deceitfulness, and so on. But these values are not defined by some deity for our digestion. How do we come to know what honor is? What does it mean to be kind? Humans have been writing about, talking about, and living their values for centuries. Indeed, each of us has a story to tell; some part of wisdom is known to every person. No one has every element, as it is not a puzzle that one ever "finishes." We never "arrive" at our values like we do a travel destination, or grasp them like a trophy. Each day brings new challenges to us all. But if we study wisdom, and pursue our values, we can gain some understanding. And likely, we will enjoy the process, as a bee is naturally drawn to the flower or a kite loves the wind. Humans are unique in their pursuit of wisdom and are inseparable from their values; it is why we read, why we invent, why we love, why we cry. You can see it in our libraries and aeronautics, and feel it when you look at an ancient pyramid or a cave painting.

Quotations were the mode of the book *Building a Life of Value*, which used an architecture metaphor to communicate how we can use our values to build a life that we value—and that has some objective value as well. Following its publication, I thought it would be fun and rewarding to ask a diverse group of folks what they value, what has led them, what they are moved by, what their lives are about. Some were too busy. Others were uninterested. Some were reticent about writing specifically about their values, as though they had forgotten that everything they do is somehow related to what they value. I encountered many priorities besides writing about values, and even some gun-shyness. Perhaps I was asking people who did not normally exercise those muscles, as those in the driver's seat of the political right have been for decades. But some said they would share a piece of what they subjectively perceive values to mean. Indeed, one hundred agreed to participate—some by permitting me to include their snapshot of values in action in the book though it had been previously published. By the deadline, seventy-five had followed through.

It is similar to the previous book in that it is a compilation of "very long quotations" by a grouping of contemporary writers that is remarkable for its diversity. It includes millionaires and folks who live modestly, those with many degrees and those who've never graduated, men and women, people of various colors and creeds, the progressive and the moderately conservative, inventors and innovators, believers and skeptics, and so on. Everyone has a story to tell, a point to make, a perspective from which their values can be understood. For us to read what they write is like sitting on our grandfather's lap for a lesson; it is a communication about wisdom.

Living a Life of Value is a book that I am proud to have orchestrated, and I thank Gina Gerboth for her industry and loyalty along the way. I also am appreciative that each person contributing to this anthology has joined me in the search for wisdom (and trustingly offered their insights and illustrations for free!). And to you, the reader, thank you for supporting my dream of pursuing my values and communicating with you about them. I share a kinship with, and a respect for, you. May we find what we are looking for.

Jason A. Merchey

INGENUITY

THINKING LIKE CATHEDRAL BUILDERS
Outrageous Behavior, Freedom, and Hope

John Abrams

These are interesting times. I suppose that is so of all times, but somehow these seem pivotal. The question, as the artist Bruce Mau so succinctly says, is "Now that we can do anything, what will we do?"

A friend of mine tells a story about her youth. Drunk and crazy, she and her friends were out driving on Cape Cod late at night. They came to a rotary and they just kept driving around and around. Someone said, "Let's go backwards." They did, several times around, and then, sure enough, slammed into a car coming the other way. They were moving slowly, as was the other car, so it was just a minor fender bender. Both cars pulled to the side; the kids sobered themselves and gravely considered their predicament. A cop immediately showed up, and went to the rear car first. Another officer arrived and the first one came forward to their car. He said, "Everybody okay here?"

"We're fine sir," they replied.

Have you been drinking?"

"No, we haven't been drinking."

"That's lucky," he said, "the guy behind you is so drunk he says you were going backwards."

I don't suggest that we should all drive drunkenly, backwards, on rotaries. But I do propose that, sometimes, if we're outrageous enough, nobody can believe it. These are times, I think, that call for outrageous behavior. "A ship in harbor is safe," said the theologian William Shedd, "but that is not what ships are built for."

We may do well to keep this in mind—now that we can do anything—because we can't keep doing what we've been doing if we are to solve the problems we are faced with. These issues—the approach of Peak Oil (the time when the planet's people and economies demand more oil than suppliers can provide), the progression of global climate change, and the concentration of wealth, to name a few—are outrageously complex. They cry out for bold solutions, and they will not go away if we continue to disregard them. Government is not doing the job, especially our current one, which doesn't even believe in government. Businesses and communities must step up with local solutions that meet the challenges head on. Big business has taken big knocks in recent years, for good reason. Meanwhile, small, socially responsible businesses have become a beacon and a breath of fresh air. In many cases they are thriving, gaining strength, and beginning to make an impact. But we must do more, and we must do it for a long, long time.

Danny Hillis, the inventor of massive parallel computing, recently designed an immense clock that will tick once a year, bong once a century, and chime once a millennium. The clock is being built in the California mountains; its purpose is to illustrate a different way to think about time. It is designed to work for 10,000 years, the span of human civilization to date. In Stewart Brand's book about the project, called *The Clock of the Long Now*, he says:

> Civilization is revving itself into a pathologically short attention span. The trend might be coming from the acceleration of technology, the short-horizon perspective of market driven economics, the next election perspective of democracies, or the distractions of personal multitasking. All are on the increase. Some sort of balancing corrective to the short-sightedness is needed: some mechanism or myth that encourages the long view and the taking of long-term responsibility, where the long term is measured at least in centuries.

This view of time is squarely at odds with conventional short-term business thinking.

Thirty years ago I co-founded a design/build firm, South Mountain Company. Today I share ownership of the company with fourteen others. My fellow owners and I expect that the work of South Mountain will not be finished in our lifetimes; it will continue for generations. We think of our work as the cathedral builders of the Middle Ages thought of theirs. British business philosopher Charles Handy gives this perspective:

> Cathedrals inspire. It is not only their grandeur or splendor, but the thought that they often took more than fifty years to build. Those who designed them, those who first worked on them, knew for certain that they would never see them finished. They knew only that they were creating something glorious which would stand for cen turies, long after their own names had been forgotten...We may not need any more cathedrals but we do need cathedral thinkers, people who can think beyond their own lifetimes.

Problems take on a different cast when we assign them a long-term perspective. Hillis points out that difficult problems become impossible if you think about them in two- or five-year terms, as we usually do, but they become easier if you think in fifty-year terms.

The big problems, he says, "...were slow to arrive, and they can only be solved at their own pace."

Perhaps we will have the ability to overcome the staggering problems and tackle the tremendous opportunities we are faced with if we combine the patience of the cathedral builders with a willingness to behave outrageously.

The fifteen owners of South Mountain Company are committed to

Problems take on a different cast when we assign them a long-term perspective.

both approaches. For three decades we have practiced our craft, run our business, and based our decisions primarily on values and only peripherally on profit. Profit is a tool to serve our expectation that we can, over time, be a restorative force, at least in some modest way. The outrageous part is the principles on which our business is based: to use shared ownership and workplace democracy, limited growth by intention rather than response to demand, commitment to place, and long-term thinking in the pursuit of craftsmanship and service of the highest quality. These principles should hardly be outrageous, but I am finding that they are, for now anyway. That may be changing.

In 1987 we re-structured from a sole proprietorship to an employee-owned cooperative corporation. It was a dramatic hinge point in the history of the company. Ownership has become available to all employees, enabling people to own and guide their workplace. Nearly half of our employees share ownership, and the rest are headed there. The responsibility, the power, and the profits all belong to the group of owners. There are no outside investors and no non-employee owners. We decide what kind of business ours will be. The decisions are partly economic and partly philosophical, and the people making them have well-aligned interests.

Some people have a hard time believing that I gave up sole ownership and control, but they may not understand the tremendous rewards and benefits that derived from that decision, for me and for the company.

A key element of our approach is hiring "future owners" as opposed to employees. We envision people who enter the company staying and leading it forward. We don't know what they, as the perpetuators, will do or produce, but the essence of our collective enterprise will survive in them as they travel into a future we cannot even imagine. So we are not looking for people with specific skill sets—we can teach what we need to. We are looking for the kind of people we wish to share ownership with. Ownership is a big deal; it inspires commitment and responsibility. As Tom Friedman once said, "In the history of mankind, nobody has ever washed a rented car."

Many ecologists and a few intrepid economists question whether the planet can sustain a global economy that enjoys perpetual growth, but the advantage of individual enterprise growth is rarely challenged in the world of business. It is equally unusual to consider the concept of optimal size. In fact, conventional wisdom suggests that small businesses are just those that haven't yet achieved greater success.

For many years we have examined growth rigorously and evaluated the benefits and detriments that come with it. We suspect that we could not retain many of the qualities we value if we were significantly larger. We grow to achieve specific goals, but we are aware that when we choose to increase in size, we may disrupt and endanger treasured attributes, and limit good things like invention, personal fulfillment, and the quality of our workplace and our products. Careful control of growth has become a prominent link in South Mountain's chain of values. It's a tug on the sleeve that has our full attention; the gospel of unrestrained growth is not for us.

To forego expansion opportunities means the employees of this company choose to value the quality of their work life over the size of the potential compensation that might come with growth. But that doesn't mean we don't struggle with our values.

There's a story about Abe Lincoln when he was still practicing law in Springfield, Illinois. He represented a client who was fighting the railroad. A friend approaching Lincoln's office saw a man come flying out of the window, hit the ground, brush himself off, and run down the street. The friend rushed in to see what had happened.

"I threw him out the window," Lincoln said.

"Why? What did he do?" asked the friend.

"He's the lawyer for the railroad, and he offered me $5,000 to betray my client, but I turned him down. Then he offered me $10,000, and I turned him down again, and finally he offered me $15,000 and I tossed him out the window." The friend asked why he had chosen that moment to throw him out.

"Because," Lincoln answered, "he was getting close to my price."

The lure of greater financial success is strong and hard to forego. Sometimes it comes close to our price.

We have a long-term investment in the small island community we work in. All our eggs are in this one geographical basket. With its strengths and weaknesses, assets and issues, this is the place we know best—the place that serves as a laboratory for all our experiments, successes and failures alike.

Making expensive homes in a rural resort community, which is part of what we do, has many significant returns: freedom to explore craft, opportunities for the pursuit of quality, relationships with interesting people, and financial rewards. By itself, however, it does not directly serve a broad social purpose—beyond that of providing good jobs to those who do the work and good homes to a fortunate few—no matter how socially purposeful we are in the way we do it. In fact, if that is all that we do, we are part of the problem. We address this reality by using the financial resources and the web of relationships that derive from our work to help solve regional problems, to create desperately needed affordable housing, to limit our environmental impact, and to encourage—in many ways—a better future for the place where we live and work.

For two six-month periods, during the winters of 2003 and 2004, I left my company and took a sabbatical. The purpose was twofold: to write a book called *The Company We Keep: Reinventing Small Business for People, Community, and Place*, and to give the company an opportunity to emerge from the shadow and constraints imposed by my leadership. The thrilling part—the part the book doesn't cover, because it happened after the writing was done—was to come back to a far better company than the one I'd left. It's a different company, a new company.

Managing in my absence gave people in the company a new sense of legacy. It brought visceral meaning to the idea that this company will endure far beyond my tenure, and the people who truly stepped up and took the reins realized (especially the younger ones) that they are the people who will shoulder this task. When we build a business, we build a landscape. Landscapes take time to mature, and we are still, quite clearly, a work-in-progress. We are only at the beginning of a long journey. A new company is perpetually under construction. Thanks to a remarkably dedicated and competent group of co-owners, I was able to do something I'd wanted to do for a long time, and the company was able to undergo a period of deep organizational learning.

The great reward of writing the book has been hearing the stories of others, a diversity of extraordinary small projects and business experiments that are underway in many places. With our new abilities to communicate and share information, we are more able to find out what's happening in far-flung communities of interest (like my company or yours) and communities of place (like my island or your town). A mosaic of new institutions and approaches is emerging. Although optimism is not the currency of the day, I look around me and see wonderful ideas and forces stewing at the edges of our society. As we unpack these tools and concepts and use them in new ways, we may, ultimately, change the chemistry of our culture.

Some of the stories I hear are about principled and outrageous behavior in the face of adversity. The ability to behave in this way must derive from a robust sense of freedom—the idea that we are at liberty to create our own destiny. I heard Garrison Keillor do a monologue about growing up when he did, before parents were "involved" and before they read books about child rearing. He said: "Children were free and wandered in this magical land of childhood, beyond the notice of their parents. This was before kids needed to take entrance examinations to get into kindergarten. Back then we did wonderful, horrible things that our parents never knew of." He talked about the freedom to learn and experience that kids may have less of these days. He and his friends made a clubhouse out of an abandoned railroad station that hadn't been used in many years. He said: "This wasn't the 'Railway Recreation Center' fixed up for the kids on successive Sundays by a bunch of fathers who later had an awards dinner to congratulate themselves. This was just a place that nobody wanted full of wondrous things that nobody cared about. So we got it. We liked it that way, and we did what we wanted. And we learned the things we needed to. And we knew the feeling of freedom."

Most kids don't grow up that way today. But in small communities they still can, and often do. The other day I was at my son's house, and my grandson and two friends wanted a ride toward town. I was headed there and took them. They had skateboards with them, as usual. "Where do you want to go?" I asked.

They conferred amongst themselves and finally Kalib said, "The ramp."

"The skate park?" I asked.

"No, the ramp. It's on Lambert's Cove, just past the cemetery."

"What is it?" I asked.

"Oh, it's a ramp some guy built for his son, but now the kid is off at college and he lets us use it."

"He just lets you use it and doesn't worry?"

"Yeah, he's cool. He said if we get hurt don't sue him. We told him okay."

By this time we were on Lambert's Cove. "Right up here on the right," Kalib said. I stopped. They got out and walked down a dirt track into a field below the road.

From where I was I couldn't see the ramp. I watched them chatting as they strolled around a bend and disappeared from sight. They were unconfined and on the loose. I am glad for them, because they are learning that sense of freedom that may be an essential ingredient for us to take the risks that will be required to solve the problems of our times. It's the feeling of knowing that we can do anything,

It was exciting to come back from my sabbatical and lend a hand. It has now been eighteen months.

My fear, upon returning, is described beautifully by a story I read in the book *Presence*, written by Peter Senge and three collaborators. A Jamaican man was diagnosed with a terminal disease. After consulting a number of doctors, all of whom concurred with the diagnosis, he went through the usual period of denial. But gradually, with the help of friends, he came to grips with the fact that he would only live a few more months. "Then something amazing happened," he said. "I simply stopped doing everything that wasn't essential, that didn't matter. I started working on projects with kids that I'd always wanted to do. I stopped arguing with my mother. When someone cut me off in traffic, or something happened that would have upset me in the past, I didn't get upset. I just didn't have the time to waste on any of that." Near the end of this period, he began a new relationship with a woman who thought he should get more opinions about his condition. He consulted some doctors in the US. Soon after, he got a phone call saying, "We have a different diagnosis." The doctors told him he had a rare form of an entirely curable disease.

Here's the part of the story I love.

He said, "When I heard this over the telephone I cried like a baby, because I was terrified that my life would go back to being like it was before."

That's how I was feeling about the company. In my absence it had changed. Now I was afraid we would go back to being like we were before. But we haven't. Not yet anyway.

We continue to decentralize management, and we sense new urgency and great progress in new endeavors we've begun. We seem to have new determination to honor our long-term commitment to restoration and improvement of the region where we work and live. At this point in our sometimes ragged and thorny history, we seem to be more willing to take risks, to venture out onto limbs we may previously not have, to behave, on occasion, outrageously, and we are beginning to recognize that the frame of the cathedral is slowly emerging.

Along with outrageous behavior, long-term thinking, and a sense of freedom, another essential ingredient for making change might be unshakeable hopefulness (and even optimism).

In an essay called "The Death of Environmentalism," activists Michael Shellenberger and Ted Nordhaus condemn the cynicism, ineffectiveness, gloominess, and narrow thinking of the environmental movement. They compare it to the movement built by Martin Luther King that was broad, inclusive, non-threatening, and effective. They say, "Martin Luther King, Jr.'s 'I have a dream speech' is famous because it put forward an inspiring, positive vision that carried a critique of the current moment within it. Imagine how history would have turned out had King given an 'I have a nightmare' speech instead."

It makes no sense to me to dwell on all that is so wrong unless we recognize equally all that is so right. I believe in the essential goodness of people. I have a deeply embedded sense that if we are encouraged sufficiently, we will choose to care about the common good. There's nothing to keep us from building those cathedrals. We only need to be certain where we're headed, so we don't climb the ladder and find that it's leaning against the wrong building.

I don't pretend to know how much we can build on the foundations we have created, or to what extent our experience in business can help others toward a path to economic democracy, environmental restoration, and local community commitment. But maybe, just maybe, we can combine bold behavior, patience, freedom, and hopefulness into a uniquely potent combination that will prove that Gandhi's words were true when he said, "First they ignore you, then they laugh at you, then they attack you. Then you win."

© John Abrams

About the Author

John Abrams is the president and CEO of South Mountain Company, Inc., a thirty-year-old employee-owned design and building company located on the island of Martha's Vineyard, Massachusetts, and the author of *The Company We Keep: Reinventing Small Business for Community, People and Place* (Chelsea Green Publishing, 2005). John has grown children and grandchildren and lives with his wife Chris in a cohousing neighborhood that was designed and built by his company.

It's exhilarating to be alive in a time of awakening consciousness; it can also be confusing, disorienting, and painful.

Adrienne Rich

The surest way to corrupt a youth is to instruct him to hold in higher esteem those who think alike than those who think differently.

Mohandas K. Gandhi

We have to be able to say what kind of world we want. Protest just isn't enough - we need a vision...

Anita Roddick

What is life worth if we don't strive to build something that is bigger than we are and lasts longer than we do? For too long, we've not worried about future generations or met our obligations to each other. Instead, we have lived for ourselves, and for today. Such a world is simply not sustainable.

Bill Bradley

A values-based culture that encourages employee creativity is becoming the number one attribute for success. Building this culture demands a new and radically evolved management approach.

Richard Barrett

The problem is never how to get new, innovative thoughts into your mind, but how to get old ones out. Every mind is a building filled with archaic furniture. Clean out a corner of your mind and creativity will instantly fill it.

Dee Hock

To be a man is to feel that one's own stone contributes to building the edifice of the world.

Antoine de Saint-Exupery

When you do the common things in life in an uncommon way, you will command the attention of the world.

George Washington Carver

Originality is the essence of true scholarship. Creativity is the soul of the true scholar.

Nnamdi Azikiwe

Any authentic creation is a gift to the future.

Albert Camus

We take our shape, it is true, within and against that cage of reality bequeathed us at our birth, and yet it is precisely through our dependence on this reality that we are most endlessly betrayed.

James Baldwin

Two stonecutters were asked what they were doing.
The first said, "I'm cutting this stone into blocks."
The second replied, "I'm on a team that's building a cathedral."

Ancient Proverb

Only when man succeeds in developing his reason and love further than he has done so far, only when he can build a world based on human solidarity and justice, only when he can feel rooted in the experience of universal brotherliness, will he have found a new, human form of rootedness, will he have transformed his world into a truly human home.

Erich Fromm

He who will not apply new remedies must expect old evils.

Francis Bacon

Keeping an eye toward twenty-five years from now is an important example of broadening our vision. Increasingly, we understand that we both inherit a history and create one.

Eboo Patel

Without new visions we don't know what to build, only what to knock down.

Robin D. G. Kelley

VISION

AMERICA BEYOND CAPITALISM
What a "Pluralist Commonwealth" Would Look Like

Gar Alperovitz

The United States is the wealthiest nation in the history of the world. By the end of the 21st century it will have the technological capacity to increase the income of all its citizens many times over or to radically reduce work time and thereby allow a new flowering of democracy, liberty, and personal and community creativity. The new century could be—should be—one of innovation, hope, even excitement.

Few Americans approach the century this way. The future is clouded by problems rather than opportunities; it appears as an era of great political difficulty and danger. At the most obvious level is the threat posed by terrorism and war—and the many challenges to liberty that overly zealous responses to both have produced. At another are a whole series of worsening social, economic, racial, and other predicaments. Critically, confidence that the great traditional values at the very heart of the American experience can be sustained has been declining rapidly.

A political-economic system can continue to violate the values it affirms for a very long time without major consequences. It is unlikely, however, to be able to do so forever. Over time, ever greater cynicism is sure to develop; and with it, an ever deepening sense that American society has lost its moral compass, that government policies are merely the result of power-plays and brokering between interested parties which do not and cannot claim any deeper democratic or moral legitimacy. The question is: Can a meaningful, morally coherent, and ultimately positive politics be constructed in the emerging era of technological abundance?

Can a new direction be set which acknowledges the systemic nature of our problems and openly posits a concrete alternative and a process that might move in a new direction? Can the system be changed?

It is possible to define the underlying structural building blocks of a model political-economic system which differs in fundamental ways from both traditional capitalism and socialism.

The schematic model outlined here is termed a "Pluralist Commonwealth"—"pluralist" to emphasize the priority given to democratic diversity and individual liberty; "commonwealth" to underscore the centrality of new public and quasi-public wealth-holding institutions.

Neither traditional socialism nor traditional capitalism deals well with the power problems presented by large-scale enterprise.

At the heart of this model is a robust vision of community democracy as the necessary foundation for a renewal of democracy in general. The model prioritizes a variety of strategies to undergird local economies, thereby creating conditions favorable to the growth of local civil society associations and an increase in the power of local government to make meaningful decisions.

The model also projects the development over time of new ownership institutions, including locally anchored worker-owned and other community-benefiting firms, on the one hand, and various national wealth-holding bodies, on the other. These ultimately take the place of current elite and corporate ownership of the preponderance of large-scale capital.

At the national level, a major new institution—call it a "Public Trust"—is projected to oversee the investment of stock on behalf of the public as state and other pension boards commonly do today. The proceeds could

14

flow to individuals, to states, to municipalities, to the federal treasury—or perhaps to fund such basic public services as education or medical care for the elderly.

A fundamental shift in the ownership of wealth over time slowly moves the nation toward greater equality: directly, for instance, through worker-owned enterprises, and also indirectly, through a flow of funds from the large-scale public investments. (Capital would likely be assembled both by the taxation of elite income and wealth and through new loan guarantee strategies to finance the broadened public ownership of new investments.) Over time, these flows of funds are allocated to finance a reduction in the work week so as to permit more free time, which in turn bolsters both individual liberty and democratic participation. In addition, ownership structures and strategies that stabilize the local economy strengthen the traditional entrepreneurial foundations of liberty while also enhancing individual job security.

Finally, the emerging model implicitly moves in the direction of, and ultimately projects, a radical long-term devolution of the national political system to some form of regional reorganization and decentralization. The region is the most logical locus for economic planning aimed at securing jobs in particular communities and for handling ecological, transportation, and other issues in a rational and democratic fashion.

Neither traditional socialism nor traditional capitalism deals well with the power problems presented by large-scale enterprise. Significant economic actors in the socialist state are commonly unaccountable either to market forces or to the public; they are power systems within a power system. The modern for-profit corporation under capitalism is for the most part unaccountable to the public—and, contrary to traditional theory, in most cases unaccountable to its shareholders as well. As the Enron and other scandals have shown (and many scholarly studies demonstrate), managers and top executives largely run the system, dominating boards and annual meetings alike. Rarely are challenges to their power successful, even by major shareholders.

Taken together, the basic elements of the Pluralist Commonwealth's political-economic architecture offer an integrated approach for dealing with these fundamental problems of power.

First, over time the model steadfastly attempts to nurture and rebuild democratic experience by supporting policies and institutions designed to make democratic practice real in the lives of citizens. The development of a meaningful democratic culture is foundational: Without attention to nurturing an active and engaged citizenry, very little can be done to achieve larger democratic goals.

Second, the model opens a steadily expanding wedge of time for individuals to participate in democracy. This is one of the Pluralist Commonwealth's most important elements: Without time to participate, authentic democratic processes to constrain economic actors (be they private or public), and to monitor a revitalized public sector, are simply not possible.

Third, the model's financial mechanisms also aim to translate technological gains into greater equality—thereby offering long-term possibilities for equality of democratic participation in general and for challenging and containing the power of large-scale enterprise in particular.

Fourth, as in the case of modern public pension fund management, the change in ownership legitimizes the public's inherent right to ensure that major firms are made accountable to larger concerns—even as competitive practices are encouraged through a variety of well-established techniques. New ownership forms also facilitate greater openness, transparency, and accountability in enterprise management and governance.

Fifth, the Pluralist Commonwealth vision ultimately reduces the scale of the public institutions that hold firms to account. It is increasingly difficult to achieve effective continent-wide political associations; units at a regional scale (as exist now in certain large states) offer important strategic possibilities for greater political control of corporate practices.

It is commonly held that free enterprise capitalism is the most efficient of all systems—certainly more efficient than traditional socialism—and that other possibilities must inevitably also be inefficient. Even at this stage of development, however, there are reasons to believe the Pluralist Commonwealth could equal or possibly surpass the efficiency of real-world capitalism.

First, although some of the inefficiencies and wastes of capitalism are occasionally highlighted in the media, we are just beginning to grasp just how vast these may be. The electricity crisis in California in 2000 and 2001

16

cost the state tens of billions of dollars. A conservative estimate is that over $10 billion was directly attributable to market manipulations by private firms. Corporate scandals in 2001-2003 cost New York state alone an estimated $13 billion. The Enron scandal cost workers and pension-holders $1 billion. Lobbying by the oil, pharmaceutical, insurance, television, banking, and other industries regularly generates further billions of dollars of questionable federal subsidies.

Second, various quasi-public and public firms (e.g., worker-owned firms, municipal electric utilities) have been shown to be at least as efficient as traditional corporations—and in many instances more efficient. Public pension management strategies have also been shown to be as efficient or more efficient than those of private pensions.

Third, salaries paid to public managers in comparable positions are far lower. For instance, William J. McDonough, then president of the Federal Reserve Bank of New York, received $297,500 in 2001, while William Harrison, CEO of J.P. Morgan Chase, took home over $21 million. Top executives managing large state-run pension investments (e.g., CalPERS) received average compensation of less than $450,000 in 2001, while William Foley, chairman and CEO of Fidelity, garnered more than $13 million.

Fourth, additional strategies to achieve economic efficiency are already being developed. Louis Kelso, John Roemer, James Meade, and Leland Stauber have all suggested ways to combine the public's interest in important economic activity with strategies to insure the independence of strictly business decisions and the use of market discipline; new variations and refinements are likely to be put forward as time goes on.

Critics of public involvement in economic matters often implicitly compare new approaches with the efficiency properties of an abstract and rarefied free market model. The result is a self-serving "heads-I-win, tails-you-lose" argument: Traditional political-economic practices are evaluated as if they were (or should be) purely efficient free market operations, ignoring what everyone knows to be the actual dynamics of corporate political-economic behavior. Meanwhile, alternatives involving proposed public strategies are evaluated as if they must inherently involve grave political-economic market distortions—ignoring studies that demonstrate the measured efficiencies of a wide range of available alternative practices.

The truth is, various forms of market manipulation are central to the current corporate-dominated political-economic system, not peripheral to it.

They come with the territory—as everyone knows full well when they shift their gaze away from abstract theory to the real world of oil company lobbying, drug company political pay-offs, Microsoft anti-competitive maneuvering, Enron corruption, and Andersen accounting complicity.

The Pluralist Commonwealth model breaks the logic of the traditional argument, first, by challenging the utopian idea that most firms keep away from government in the current system; second, by developing various strategies which allow for both competition and increased citizen accountability; and third, by structurally changing ownership patterns in ways that achieve greater transparency so that when the inevitable problems arise, in either public or private settings, they can be openly debated and corrected. Finally, of course, the model's shift to new ownership forms inherently recaptures for broader public use excessive funds which might possibly be garnered through corporate political maneuvering.

We may add that to the extent the political-economic system defined by the Pluralist Commonwealth is able to achieve greater equality, it would likely also achieve much greater efficiencies in the development and use of human resources. Leaving aside the morality of the implicit choices of the present system, countless studies demonstrate that we currently throw away literally millions of productive people whose contribution to the economy could be enormous.

It is important to stand back from the difficulties of the current moment to consider underlying issues of principle which will frame the politics of the coming era—through times of war and terrorism and beyond. Four quite fundamental contentions are suggested by evolving political-economic developments.

First, that there is no way to achieve movement towards greater equality without developing new institutions which hold wealth on behalf of small and large publics.

Second, that there is no way to rebuild democracy with a big "D" in the system as a whole without nurturing the conditions of democracy with a small "d" in everyday life—including in economic institutions which allow and sustain greater stability of local community life.

Third, that there is no way to achieve democracy in a continental-scale system moving towards 400 million people, and possibly a billion or beyond, without radical decentralization, ultimately in all probability to some form of regional units.

Fourth, that there is no way to achieve meaningful individual liberty in the modern era without greater individual economic security and greater amounts of free time—and that neither of these, in turn, is possible without a change in the ownership of wealth and the income flows it permits.

These four contentions stand on their own. Indeed, at this point in American history, the ball is in the court of those who hold that equality, liberty, and meaningful democracy can be achieved without meeting the challenges suggested by the four basic points. Further related questions are whether there is any other way to achieve gender equality, ecological sustainability, and sustained, meaningful community.

The Pluralist Commonwealth model holds, beyond this, that democratic control of large economic enterprise, a central problem confronting all political-economic systems, can never be achieved without transforming and making public the ownership of large-scale wealth and without developing a new culture—and, further, that this can only be done by building on the four key elements: Without local democracy there can be no culture of democratic practice; without security and time, there can be only a weak citizenry; without decentralization it is difficult to mobilize democratic practice and accountability; and without major and far-reaching new forms of wealth-holding, there can never be adequate support for the conditions and policies needed to build a more egalitarian and free democratic culture in general.

Finally, the model is based on the judgment that greater equality, greater individual economic security, greater amounts of free time, and—upon this basis—the reconstitution of a culture of common responsibility are ultimately required if we are ever to reorient our community and national priorities in general.

The prospects for near-term change are obviously not great, especially when such change is conceived in traditional terms. Indeed, although there may be an occasional "progressive" electoral win, there is every reason to believe that the underlying trends will continue their decaying downward course. In many ways times are likely to get worse before they get better.

On the other hand, for precisely this reason we are likely to see much deeper probing, much more serious political analysis, and much more fundamental institutional exploration and development. Already states and municipalities in all sections of the country have moved forward to create—and systematically build political support for—many new political-economic experiments and strategies. Federal fiscal and other decisions are now producing pain and reassessment at every level.

In fact, just below the surface of conventional reporting, literally thousands of on-the-ground efforts which illuminate new principles have been quietly developing for the last several decades. In California, the state pension fund plays a significant role in state development. In Glasgow, Ky., the city runs a quality cable, telephone, and Internet service at costs far lower than commercial rivals. In Harrisonburg, Va., a highly successful company owned by the employees makes and sells cable television testing equipment. In Alaska, every state resident as a matter of right receives dividends from a fund that invests oil revenues on behalf of the public at large. In Alabama, the pension fund directly helps finance worker-owned firms.

Traditionally, a distinction has been made between "reform," on the one hand, and "revolution," on the other. The former implies nonviolent improvement in the outcomes of a given system, with no fundamental change in its basic institutional structure: It cleans up around the edges of the existing system, as it were, sometimes slowly, sometimes in major political outbursts. The latter, revolution, commonly implies abrupt and often violent change—above all of the fundamental institutional structures of the system.

The kind of change suggested by these emerging efforts involves an unusual combination of strategic approaches. Like reform, in the main it involves step-by-step nonviolent change. But like revolution, the process is oriented to the development of quite different institutional structures to replace traditional corporate forms over time. It might appropriately be called "evolutionary reconstruction."

A politics based on evolutionary reconstructive principles does not abandon reform when it can achieve important gains. On the other hand, such a politics explicitly seeks to understand and to foster the longer-term foundational requirements of the values it affirms. It is not satisfied with, nor misled by, occasional electoral gains that do little to alter the direction of long-term trends. It is a politics of historical perspective and commitment to the long haul.

Institutional restructuring, we tend to forget, is exceedingly common in the long sweep of world history. The difficulty lies in pulling ourselves out of the present moment to consider our own possibilities in broader historical perspective.

There have been five large-order political realignments over the course of American history, from before the Civil War to the Progressive era and beyond. Each has occurred in the face of arguments that nothing of great political significance was feasible. Further realignments over the course of the 21st century are not only possible, but likely.

Long before the civil rights movement, there were many years of hard, quiet, dangerous work by those who came before. Long before the feminist explosion were those who labored to establish new principles in earlier decades. It is within the possibilities of our own time in history that—working together and openly charting an explicit new course—this generation can establish the necessary foundations for an extraordinary future and for the release of new energies.

It may even be that far-reaching change will come much earlier and much faster than many now imagine.

Adapted from America Beyond Capitalism: Reclaiming Our Wealth, Our Liberty, and *Our Democracy (Wiley & Sons, 2005), www.americabeyondcapitalism.com. Reprinted by permission of* Dollars & Sense, *a progressive economics magazine based in Boston, MA. For subscriptions call 877-869-5762. For other inquiries, call 617-447-2177, or visit www.dollarsandsense.org.*

About the Author

Gar Alperovitz has had a distinguished career as a historian, political economist, activist, writer, and government official. He is currently the Lionel R. Bauman Professor of Political Economy at the University of Maryland and is a former Fellow of Kings College, Cambridge University; Harvard's Institute of Politics; the Institute for Policy Studies; and a Guest Scholar at the Brookings Institution.

He is the author of critically acclaimed books on the atomic bomb and atomic diplomacy and his articles have appeared in the *New York Times*, the *Washington Post*, the *Los Angeles Times*, the *New Republic, The Nation,* and *The Atlantic* among other popular and academic publications. He has been profiled by the *New York Times*, the *Associated Press, People, UPI,* and *Mother Jones*, and has been a guest on numerous network TV and cable news programs, including "Meet the Press," "Larry King Live," "The Charlie Rose Show," "Cross Fire," and "The O'Reilly Factor."

[America has] incredibly difficult issues and an honest search for solutions can only come from a sustained effort by the broadest array of America's brightest and wisest men and women. What the U.S. really needs is leadership that could marshal that effort.

Bob Herbert

We must take the responsibility for the life of all men, and develop on an international scale what all great countries have developed internally – a relative sharing of wealth and a new and more just division of economic resources.

Erich Fromm

When you look at the world perched on heights of arrogant, blind power, separated and disconnected from those who have lost their livelihoods, lifestyles, and lives - farmers and workers everywhere - it is easy to be blind both to the valleys of poverty and the mountains of affluence.

Vandana Shiva

Let America be America again. Let it be the dream it used to be.

Langston Hughes

I found that once you had changed the language of business from one which is purely economic to one of reflection and care and a dedication to social justice, people felt they could bring their heart to the workplace.

Anita Roddick

[On September 11, 2001], the second strong feeling I had was hope - hope that the United States would use the shock of this tragedy to reassess our economic, environmental, and military strategies.

Robert Chatterley

Industry only has the right to succeed where it performs a real economic service and is a true social asset...It is to the enlightened self-interest of modern industry to realize that its service to customers comes first, its service to its employees and management second, and its service to its stockholders last.

Robert Wood Johnson

The issue of economic justice, the issue of poverty, is the basis of most of the rest of the problems we have.

Ben Cohen

I observe God's Golden Rule: treat others the way you want to be treated. If you want healthcare, ensure that every man, woman, and child has healthcare. If you want a home to call your own, ensure that everyone in the United States has home. You want to have enough to eat, then you have to ensure that every person has enough to eat. If this sounds like Socialism, it is not, it is Christianity at its core.

Donna Reuter

The theory that business can and should be a force that aggressively promotes greater environmental and social good has its roots in the social transformation of the 1960s. Though that era was marked by a certain innocence, it was also a time of meaningful idealism. The explosion of social and environmental awareness that defined a generation led to a willingness to explore possible new paradigms.

Jeffrey Hollender

In an economic order centered on private property...rather than seeing relationships with others as essential to human existence and fulfillment, other people become potential obstacles to the taking of profits from one's property. In such a world, it is not surprising that the possibilities for meaningful communities are limited.

Prasannan Parthasarathi

Vision without action is a daydream. Action without vision is a nightmare.

Japanese proverb

This crippling of individuals I consider the worst evil of capitalism. Our whole educational system suffers from this evil. An exaggerated competitive attitude is inculcated into the student, who is trained to worship acquisitive success as a preparation for his future career.

Albert Einstein

MORALITY

BIG IDEAS NEED SHARP ELBOWS

Eric Alterman

We may never reach a consensus on just what it was about George W. Bush that led so many millions of Americans to ignore his Administration's dishonesty, incompetence, ideological fanaticism and corruption and vote for the guy. Early exit poll analysis put a premium on "moral values," but that explanation evaporated with even rudimentary scrutiny. Clearly the most significant advantage Bush enjoyed came in the various national security categories, despite the fact that this is the area where the Bush Administration's myriad failings, both personal and professional, ought to be most obvious.

Evidently, thirty years of attacks on liberals' national security credentials have taken their toll. Given both his experience as a senator and his heroism during the Vietnam War, abroad and at home, John Kerry should have easily trumped Bush here, but he didn't even come close. During the brief post-cold war/pre-"war on terror" interregnum, Bill Clinton could squeak past George H.W. Bush with a largely economic argument, but Osama bin Laden put an end to those days together with the Twin Towers. Unless liberals find a way to reverse this trend, they will forfeit election after election, notwithstanding the increasing extremism and irresponsibility of Bush & Co. in virtually every area of public policy.

We didn't always have this problem. From FDR's victory in 1932 through the election of 1968, liberals were viewed as "tougher" on national security than skinflint—frequently isolationist—conservatives, and the Democrats were the natural party of government. This does not mean they were always right; indeed, there is much in the conduct of US foreign policy under liberal leadership that turned out quite badly. (Nation readers hardly require a lesson in those misadventures.) The point is that, like it or not, the perception of "strength" is the sine qua non of American politics. As Bill Clinton famously observed, it is politically safer to be perceived to be "strong and wrong" rather than weak and right.

> Evidently, thirty years of attacks on liberals' national security credentials have taken their toll.

Not long ago at New York's Plaza Hotel, a few hundred people came together to salute two liberals who played a crucial role in creating what historian Kevin Mattson terms a "fighting faith"—one that appealed to the main currents of American political discourse while simultaneously inspiring a sense of solidarity and common purpose among middle-class and poor Americans. At the age of 96 and 87 respectively, John Kenneth Galbraith and Arthur Schlesinger Jr. have participated in as many of the great political and intellectual battles of postwar US history as any two men alive. Political comrades and intellectual allies, both men have pursued careers that, for a time, involved combining political combat and intellectual disputation. Remarkably—though it was not always apparent at the moment these disputes were taking place—neither has allowed the demands of politics to compromise his intellectual work. Nor, at the same time, have they held themselves to be above painful but necessary compromises that define political effectiveness.

This is no easy task. Mattson's invaluable new study, *When America Was Great: The Fighting Faith of Postwar Liberalism*, quotes Galbraith at a Congress of Cultural Freedom gathering in Milan in 1955, attacking intellectuals who treat their ideological constructs as reality. The goal for both men, as Mattson defines it, was a "tough-minded realism that saw intellect

26

in service to the world of politics, a world of messy compromise and inevitable failures." This is not to argue that political involvement is the only appropriate role for intellectuals. Schlesinger, who remains almost the ideal example of the intellectual engagé, greatly admired Richard Hofstadter and Lionel Trilling, who always retained their detachment. At the same time, Mattson notes, he praised Murray Kempton for offering an "antidote to the danger that those with influence might take themselves too seriously."

Of course, both men made their share of mistakes, political and intellectual. But they were not the most costly kind, thanks to an unyielding commitment of both the economist and the historian to battling the effects of extremism of all stripes. A lifetime of loyalty to intellectual inquiry helped to infuse each man's career—both inside and outside the political arena—with an abiding respect for the difficulties involved in remaking men and women according to ideological precepts, as well as with a strong sense of modesty about just how much mere politics could accomplish. Galbraith once explained that he always sought "a measure of detachment. I've felt that one should hold some part of one's self in reserve, never be completely sure of being right." Schlesinger concurred, noting that "democratic politics, as Orwell has observed, permits the participant 'to keep part of yourself inviolate.'" Both men lived up to what Mattson identifies as the "classic tenet of the liberal state," which acknowledges "many limitations in its demands upon men, [while] the total state acknowledges none."

At the event at the Plaza—organized by William vanden Heuvel in support of the Franklin and Eleanor Roosevelt Institute, at Hyde Park—friends, family and admirers of all political persuasions paid tribute to the numerous moments in each man's life when their actions contributed to the common good by demonstrating the kind of toughness, both moral and intellectual, that liberals are perceived to lack today. I have my biases, but I thought Bill Moyers best captured the combination of passion, intellect and political smarts both men helped pass down to a younger generation of liberals, qualities sorely needed today if liberals are ever again to exercise national power:

"Ken Galbraith and Arthur Schlesinger engaged in the passions of our times and brought to the liberal project the fire of deep conviction, the gravity of fierce intellect and the temperament of the tested warrior of ideas who accepts that the achievable is possible while the perfect can only be imagined...The hopes of common people rest not with saints but with flawed champions who understand that in a world where bad ideas wear brass knuckles, big ideas need sharp elbows."

Amen. Now, the hard part.

Reprinted by permission of The Nation *magazine and Eric Alterman.*

About the Author

Termed "the most honest and incisive media critic writing today" in the *National Catholic Reporter*, and author of "the smartest and funniest political journal out there," in the *San Francisco Chronicle*, Eric Alterman is a professor of English at Brooklyn College of the City University of New York, media columnist for *The Nation*, the "Altercation" weblogger for MSNBC.com, and a senior fellow at the Center for American Progress, where he writes and edits the "Think Again" column. Alterman is the author of the national bestsellers, *What Liberal Media?, The Truth About Bias and the News* (2003, 2004), and *The Book on Bush: How George W. (Mis)leads America* (with Mark Green, 2004). His newest book is *When Presidents Lie: A History of Deception and its Consequences,* (September, 2004). His *Sound & Fury: The Making of the Punditocracy* (1992, 2000), won the 1992 George Orwell Award and his *It Ain't No Sin to be Glad You're Alive: The Promise of Bruce Springsteen* (1999, 2001), won the 1999 Stephen Crane Literary Award. A senior fellow of the World Policy Institute at New School University, and former Adjunct Professor of Journalism at NYU and Columbia, Alterman received his BA in History and Government from Cornell, his MA in International Relations from Yale, and his PhD in US History from Stanford. He lives with his family in Manhattan where he is at work on a history of postwar American liberalism.

You've got to get people to believe that change is possible... You have to show them that you can fight things successfully even if you don't win.

Winona LaDuke

Yes, I'm a liberal, and I'm proud of it. It's a term we need to reclaim. Because I believe most Americans are liberals just like me. Most Americans believe in helping people. And most Americans believe that government has a role to play - to create opportunity, to protect our environment, to provide for the common good.

Al Franken

Women have been trained to speak softly and carry a lipstick. Those days are over.

Bella Abzug

Honor is much dearer than money.

Yiddish proverb

One reason for my hope lies in the tremendous energy, enthusiasm, and commitment of a growing number of young people around the world. As they find out about the environmental and social problems that are now part of their heritage, they want to fight to right the wrongs.

Jane Goodall

If the strong were good, society's problems would begin to disentangle immediately.

Jason Merchey

Progressives have to do more than oppose. We have to develop compelling arguments for moving the country in a different direction: What should America's role in the world be? How can we create a fairer economy? What kind of society do we want to be? This requires new, big ideas...

Robert L. Borosage & Katrina vanden Heuvel

Alone we can do so little; together we can do so much.

Helen Keller

DEVELOPMENT

GROWING MY WAY

Judith Barad

One of the earliest values I can remember forming came from my response to the *Robin Hood* television series. I related to the series because my early childhood was filled with experiences I perceived as unfair. My younger sister was seen as all-good while my parents treated and talked about me to others as all-bad. Very sensitive to this injustice, I readily empathized with Robin Hood's concern for helping the poor and reapportioning wealth from the affluent. After all, I reasoned, this distribution of wealth was unfair. Not only did I form a lifelong political belief based on my early reflections when viewing *Robin Hood*, but I also defended other children in school who, it seemed to me, were being treated unfairly by teachers. I clearly recall standing up in class one day and telling a teacher to "stop picking on Jeff" because he did nothing to warrant her attack.

Not all of my teachers appreciated my budding concern for justice. Attempting to wield their authority over me in ways I perceived as unjust, they seemed to be as unworthy of respect as my parents. I became suspicious of their teachings. When I was assigned a book report on the Mexican-American War in fourth grade, I learned that, contrary to the view the teacher wanted me to accept, the Americans were clearly at fault due to their unjustified aggression. I thought of Manifest Destiny as a pernicious doctrine and, much to my teachers' and parents' consternation, I sided with the American Indians over the US military. I was getting in the habit of standing up for my beliefs, even though my parents were often called to school and I was subsequently berated and punished.

Undeterred, my habit of standing up for my beliefs expressed itself one day in sixth grade during a demonstration of dissection or, at least, an attempted demonstration. Paul held up a goldfish, which he had just taken out of a fishbowl. Before he cut it open he wanted to make sure it was dead. As I watched the goldfish gasping for breath, the full horror of the action impelled me out of my seat. This act of "murder" was unjust and violated the principle of "do no harm," which was beginning to take root in me. I demanded that the experiment stop. When the students and teacher merely looked at me in amazement, I screamed for the experiment to stop. At last, Paul put the still-living fish back into the bowl, but the incident meant another call to my unsympathetic parents.

My courage in saving the fish at school was partially motivated by my empathetic love for my pets. My first pets were parakeets, whom I exchanged kisses with. When I was seven years old, my father brought home our first puppy, a boxer. I soon related to her as my sibling. My sister and I taught our youngest sibling to play the card game Old Maid and we often dressed her in our clothes. Glad to be the center of so much attention, she took it in good humor, although my mother didn't.

Living by your own lights isn't easy, especially for children.

Living by your own lights isn't easy, especially for children. Much of the time, I despaired over not being accepted by my family or at school. However, I did have indirect help. In fifth grade, all the students in class were supposed to go to the library and select a poem to memorize. For some reason, I was immediately attracted to "Hope" by Emily Dickinson. Having memorized this poem for my assignment, I kept repeating it to myself, both at the time and for many years afterward. It not only uplifted my spirit, but by clinging to hope, I was able to survive the emotional and physical abuse at home and the ostracism at school.

My pre-teen years also yielded some ethical insights. The first of these was a reaction to one of my mother's teachings. She had always insisted that there was a big difference between a "white" lie, which was permissible, and a "black" lie, which was impermissible. I understood that she was basing this moral distinction on the liar's intention, yet it seemed to be an artificial distinction. A lie, I reasoned, is dishonest regardless of the liar's motivation. Dishonesty is morally impermissible. Moreover, telling one lie often generates more lies, becoming so complicated one couldn't keep track of them. Years later, I expressed this insight by saying, "Lying creates a habit of dishonesty." I also recognized that "white" lies destroy trust between people. Finally, they can harm the person being lied to by encouraging them to think that they don't need to change something when perhaps they really should. For instance, suppose Sue asks me whether her dress looks nice, and I respond it looks fine even though I'm aware it's loud and gaudy. As a result of my lie, she wears the dress in public and people make fun of her within her range of hearing. I have harmed her far more than if I had said that the other dresses she has worn look better on her.

"Hope" is the thing with feathers—
That perches in the soul—
And sings the tune without the words—
And never stops—at all—

And sweetest—in the Gale—is heard—
And sore must be the storm—
That could abash the little Bird
That kept so many warm—

I've heard it in the chilliest land—
And on the strangest Sea—Yet,
Never, in Extremity,
It asked a crumb—of Me.

Emily Dickinson

Another belief my mother tried to teach me was that God would punish me if I didn't obey her. For several years, I feared that this was true. However, when I was twelve years old, I decided to investigate this teaching for myself since I was both suspicious of the belief and suspicious of my mother. My investigation prompted me to read the whole of Genesis and Exodus. Oh, oh! My reading suggested that God is indeed judgmental, demands that parents be obeyed, and doesn't hesitate to punish people. Not seeing anything to worship about a god of this nature, I became an atheist.

The same sort of thing happened when I entered high school in 1962. A teacher kept discoursing about the dreadfulness of communism. During one of these harangues, I asked her, in front of the class, whether or not she had read the *Communist Manifesto*. She confessed she hadn't read it. Under my continued questioning, it became clear that she had no basis on which to make an informed judgment about communism. Due to this incident I acquired a short-lived but widespread reputation in high school of being a communist. However, the ethical insight I gleaned both from this exchange and my biblical examination was that a person should investigate the basis for one's judgments about politics or religion, or else these judgments should be withheld.

Given my conclusions about my mother's and teacher's erroneous beliefs, I became an ethical relativist for a few years. Since the judgments of such "authorities" couldn't be trusted, I reasoned that no one person could know moral truths. Whatever anyone thought was right, was right. No one should tell another person what to believe since no one is an authority on the matter. I still think this is a stage everyone should go through on their way to becoming an independent thinker.

My independent thinking was greatly stimulated when *Star Trek* first appeared on television in 1966. Reflecting on the thinly disguised moral messages in each episode, I realized that freedom and responsibility go hand in hand, that altruism is admirable, the humans must do no harm, and that all individuals should be treated justly. I had already experienced these principles as lived values, but *Star Trek* helped me to articulate them. Thirty-three years later, I wrote *The Ethics of Star Trek*. As the black sheep of my family, I naturally related to the character of Spock. From Spock, I understood why moral decisions should be made by reason—not emotion or tradition. I deeply appreciated the character's use of logic, as well as his inner war between his emotions and his reason. I began to think of myself from a more universal perspective as an earthling, rather than as an American.

As the war in Vietnam waged on, I stood strongly against our country's involvement despite my father telling me to "Love it or leave it." Since I didn't have the resources to leave the country, I could at least leave my family. At eighteen years old, I married a physically and emotionally abusive man, repeating the same cycle of abuse I suffered as a child. My belief in ethical relativism went out the window, having realized that spousal abuse and the abuse of children is wrong, regardless of what anyone else thinks. A year after marrying this man, I divorced him despite my mother's admonition, "You made your bed, now lie in it!"

For years afterward, I lived in fear that my former husband would learn where I lived and harm me. This was my initial motivation to take karate lessons, which I continued for three years. As I advanced in rank, I regained the courage I had in my childhood. Controlling my karate movements also taught me discipline and concentration. Another television series, *Kung-Fu*, complemented my daily karate practice. Spurred on by learning the history of karate and the issues raised in the show, I began to read Buddhist philosophy. One of the most important insights that I internalized from this reading is the importance of living in the moment, of being mindful of my surroundings and actions.

After starting karate, I had an opportunity to learn transcendental meditation. Upon arriving at the Transcendental Meditation Center, a representative, who was assigned to give me my mantra, asked why I wanted to learn meditation. I responded, "To know myself." Knowing myself through introspection had become very important to me since I didn't think other people's image of me was credible. Also, I reasoned, providing I was honest, who could know what was going on in my mind better than I? I meditated twice a day, twenty minutes each day, for three years. I had several mystical experiences and alternative states of consciousness brought on by my daily meditation. Some mystical experiences occurred spontaneously, outside of meditation. Although most of the insights I achieved in these experiences were spiritual rather than ethical, a couple of them overlapped both areas. Two such realizations were that all conscious beings are interconnected and that God exists. The latter realization didn't relate in any way to my childhood belief in a judgmental, angry, vengeful god. To the contrary! I experienced God's presence as a completely loving one, a presence that cared far more about each conscious being than any of us could care about each other.

The discipline, focus, and concentration I acquired from three years of practicing karate and meditation led to my enrolling in at Oakton Community College at twenty-seven years of age. Initially, I approached college with some trepidation, hearing in the back of my mind my mother's insistence that I was "dumb." Oddly, I started out wanting to be a police officer in order to transform the institution, which I perceived as replete with legal thugs. However, I was fortunate to meet a wonderful philosophy professor who showed me that philosophy could help me to know myself more deeply and discover my place and relation to the universe. I began to desire wisdom, a desire that has stayed with me to this day.

Sitting in this great professor's "Introduction to Philosophy" course, I had a number of realizations that deeply affected my life. As he exposed the class to stoic ethics, I became aware that no one makes me feel angry, sad, or happy. No one forces me to feel or do anything. I am fully responsible for my actions and feelings. Blaming others is a copout.

My teacher also showed a film that made me aware that being indirectly responsible for an action is much the same as having direct responsibility. Often the person who directly performs a dastardly deed has been supported in their act by others, who hypocritically stay behind the scenes. This ethical belief led me to become a lacto-ovo vegetarian for the rest of my life. During the five years previous to this decision, I had been uncomfortable about eating the flesh of other animals. This discomfort was exacerbated when I realized that all conscious beings are interconnected. But I rationalized that someone else was killing them—not I. Now, confronted with the realization that indirect responsibility and direct responsibility are almost the same thing, and that indirect responsibility supports direct responsibility, I could no longer hide behind this excuse. I faced up to the fact that I couldn't kill an animal simply to satisfy my taste preferences when healthy alternatives are available. But if I couldn't kill an animal, how could I support an industry that kills to satisfy my selfish desires? I would be very selfish indeed to say that a conscious individual should be killed merely to become "meatballs" for my spaghetti dish when I could easily substitute spaghetti with marinara sauce.

Enrolling in the same outstanding teacher's "Philosophy of Religion" course, I had another life-changing experience. One of his requirements for the course was that students attend a religious service that differed from the religion of their family. Since he was getting to know me as a person, he suggested that I attend a service at the Buddhist temple. Sure enough, I loved it! However, one time wasn't enough so I kept attending each Sunday for six months, learning and practicing Zen meditation and Buddhist chant.

The Buddhist practices helped to clear my mind, except for one pressing problem. After reading Plato's "Allegory of the Cave" in my teacher's

"Introduction to Philosophy" course, I developed a deep desire to teach philosophy. Plato made it clear that the enlightened person has a duty to share what he or she learns with others. Although I wasn't sure about being enlightened, I did think I had some valuable insights that should be shared. My parents, on the other hand, wanted me to be an attorney when they saw I was capable of making straight As. Since I now had a young daughter to support, the seemingly lucrative prospect of being a lawyer beckoned to me. I was torn between the two professions. As I was sitting alone in a classroom pondering this problem, an old custodian I had befriended asked me to share what so obviously troubled me. After I told him about my dilemma, he responded that he advised his older son, who once had the same problem, to attend business school in order to make more money. But his son, the custodian continued, later regretted his decision to follow his father's advice. Learning from this experience, he wisely advised me to pursue the career that I love. The Buddhists, in their eightfold path, call this "right livelihood."

I continued my philosophical education at Loyola University in Chicago. Although I had earlier worked as a volunteer to extend the deadline for passing the Equal Rights Amendment and I had written letters of protest to institutions that used animals in research, my activism really proliferated at Loyola. During this two-year period, I was a volunteer in a soup kitchen, visited an elderly lady who requested company through the University, helped match reports of missing pets with animals who had been picked up by the Anti-Cruelty Society, participated in projects to raise money for shelter animals, and I sponsored a couple of orphaned children in India, through a Catholic agency. The Jesuit University had a philosophy of education that involved educating the entire person, not just the intellect. I appreciated that kind of education, and I still do. It helped me to understand that in helping others, I am helping myself. I also stopped making hasty judgments of other people, after reflecting that these judgments were often mistaken and I later regretted forming them. During my time at Loyola, I converted to Catholicism since it seemed the path best suited for my spiritual needs.

I temporarily discontinued my volunteer work when I entered graduate school at Northwestern University since the competitive atmosphere and my concern for being a good mother took all my time. After four years, I finished my dissertation entitled "The Means to an Active Faith According to St. Thomas Aquinas." The central point of this dissertation, which later became a book, is that there are two levels of faith and the more developed level issues in ethical actions. Naturally, I deeply believed that faith requires more of us than lip service or going to church each week. Faith, should issue in compassionate actions and a commitment to higher values.

A year after graduating from Northwestern, I was offered a philosophy position at Indiana State University in Terre Haute. Within a couple of years, I started a community organization named "Friends for the Ethical Treatment of Animals." Subsequently, I also sponsored a student animal rights organization by the same name. Filing a Freedom of Information Act request, I learned about ISU's dog lab. Informing the community about this lab, I spearheaded a demonstration against it. At this time, I was an untenured professor whose position was jeopardized by these activities. Yet, as I had known since the time I voiced opposition to dissection in sixth grade, I knew I had to act on my beliefs. Having the courage to stand by one's convictions entails that neither risking failure in school or facing the possibility of losing one's career should prevent anyone doing what they think is right. Related activities included hosting PETA's "Animal Rights 101" at ISU and developing an "Ethics and Animals" course, which is still being offered. Further, since I was in charge of the speaker's program for the department, I invited a number of famous animal rights leaders to campus.

Under my leadership, the community animal rights' group held a hunt sabotage event, rescuing a deer trapped in barbed wire. The group protested a fur coat fashion show, passed out literature exposing the horrors of vivisection, exposed Eli Lilly's dog lab, and encouraged people to seriously consider vegetarianism. We also informed the community about product testing on animals and how to live cruelty-free. One intensive effort involved a series of protests on behalf of Mr. T, a lion held in a small cage next to a railroad track. I was present when the owner allowed boys to throw stones at him. A woman from another state offered to buy the lion and send him to a sanctuary for mistreated wild animals. Despite the fact that these protests attracted a lot of media attention, the attempt to free Mr. T. was unsuccessful.

My activism culminated in my eight-year endeavor to build West Central Indiana's first no-kill shelter for stray dogs and cats. It became my mission. I envisioned a state-of-the-art building in which strays would be housed, neutered, and socialized until they were adopted into good homes. The shelter would also serve as a public education center on animal related issues. In order to realize this dream, I began an organization dedicated to building the shelter and opening the shelter organization. Over the years I served as president of this 250 member organization, I wrote many successful grants and, (along with other board members) wrote regular newsletters, organized fund raising, and acted in a public relations capacity. I also forged a good relationship with the local traditional shelter and spoke before many community organizations and elementary schools about responsible pet care. Eventually, $300,000 was raised to build and open the shelter on a large tract of donated land.

At the same time that I worked to realize my dream, I formulated an animal control ordinance for the county I lived in, which incorporated the best parts of other animal control ordinances I had researched. While working on both community-related projects, I wrote my second book, entitled *Aquinas on the Nature and Treatment of Animals.*

Although the shelter is still operating, I resigned as president shortly after it opened. A local television station, needing to increase its ratings, started airing sensationalist stories that insinuated I used my position to commit sundry crimes. Their charges had no basis in truth and the police never bothered to investigate their highly imaginative claims. Half of the board wanted me to bow out since, in their view, I had become a liability to the organization. With great sadness, I complied.

After a long period of mourning, I again engaged in some ethical decision-making that profoundly impacted my life. I decided to forgive other people, even those who wronged me at the animal shelter. My reasoning process, if given dialogue form, proceeded in the following way:

"Do you want to be happy?"

"Yes, of course!"

"Does holding on to and reliving past wrongs done to me by other people contribute to my happiness?"

"Obviously, the answer is no."

"So let your injured feelings go. Remember what you learned while a student at Oakton: 'no one makes me feel angry or hurt. I am fully responsible for my feelings.'"

Rather than feel angry and hurt, feel sad for the person who has acted so badly. They haven't harmed you if you don't allow yourself to feel harmed. Actually, they have harmed themselves."

Years later, the former board members asked for my forgiveness and I responded quite honestly that I had already forgiven them. The act of forgiving freed me from the emotional burdens I had shackled myself with. Accompanying this freedom was a marked increase in happiness.

The notion that I'm responsible for my happiness was important in forming another moral principle. Being a thin-skinned person, I often felt hurt when students scowled at me or sent rude remarks my way. In order to unblock my happiness from this kind of hurt, I turned my attention to the fact that these students (or other people) probably don't share my beliefs and values. They judge me based on their own beliefs and values, which I would probably reject based on how they act. So why should I pay attention to people who judge me based on beliefs and values I would not be willing to adopt? Further, they probably have their own issues that have nothing to do with me. I was learning not to take anything personally.

One last ethical value deserves mention. Although I've tried hard to love other people I encounter, I almost always failed. The reason, I came to realize, is that I didn't love myself enough. Being in control of my feelings, I can direct them toward happiness, gratitude, and love. This is for my own sake. Yet as I focus on perceiving in other people and in my environment things that arouse my happiness, gratitude, and love, I am becoming the sort of person I have always wanted to become. I can love others and feel compassion for them as an act of love and compassion for myself.

The process of growing as an ethical person is one that continues as long we live. It's a remarkable adventure of both the mind and the spirit. To summarize this adventure, I suggest the following four steps:

1. **Know yourself.** Honestly observe your thoughts, words, and actions. Become aware of your beliefs and assumptions, your strengths and weaknesses, your attitudes and natural reactions.

2. **Put yourself in the place of others.** Try to experience what they must be feeling; use your imagination to put yourself in someone else's shoes. Anticipate how some of your actions make others feel. Imagine how people feel when you see them interact.

3. **Observe other people, or even television characters, paying attention to the qualities you admire in them.**

A. Compile a list of qualities you respect in anyone: for instance, do you admire honesty, objectivity, compassion, generosity, and courage?

B. Based on this list, think of the ideal person who exemplifies these qualities.

4. **Practice these qualities on a daily basis until they become a habitual way for you to act.** Use your model of an ideal person as a guide for how to act. The more you practice your values, the easier it becomes. In this respect, practicing values is just like running or learning to play piano. It takes time and repetition to get used to an ethical way of decision-making and living.

Keep in mind that you will sometimes fail to act in a way that meets your approval. Don't be disheartened. This doesn't mean you're a failure. Just start again to live the life of the kind of person you want to be. It's worth it!

© *Judith Barad*

About the Author

Judith Barad is both Professor of Philosophy and Women's Studies at Indiana State University. After graduating magna cum laude from Loyola University of Chicago in 1980, she attended Northwestern University. She received her PhD in Philosophy from Northwestern in 1984. In 1985 she accepted a position in Philosophy at Indiana State, where she eventually served as the chairperson for nine years. She is the author of three books and numerous articles on ethics, including such topics as feminist ethics, the role of emotion in moral judgments, the treatment of animals, the philosophy of Thomas Aquinas, and *The Ethics of Star Trek*. She has given dozens of national and international scholarly presentations, and has recently been an ethics consultant for Boeing.

My reality is my reality. I'm not going to deny it. I'm not going to deny it at all. I stand in front of people. Behold my reality.

Carlos Santana

Only in growth, reform, and change, paradoxically enough, is true security to be found.

Anne Morrow Lindbergh

Confidence doesn't come out of nowhere. It's a result of something...hours and days and weeks and years of constant work and dedication.

Roger Staubach

You've got to do your own growing, no matter how tall your grandfather was.

Irish proverb

The path to our destination is not always a straight one. We go down the wrong road, we get lost, we turn back. Maybe it doesn't matter which road we embark on. Maybe what matters is that we embark.

Barbara Hall

Let us leave every man free to search within himself and lose himself in his ideas.

Voltaire

A path to take is always ours to make; strengthening the soul and breaking the mold will set a mind free; how wonderful to breathe.

Trish Gomez

When you feel in your gut what you are, and then dynamically pursue it, don't back down and don't give up. You're going to mystify a lot of folks.

Bob Dylan

To dare to live alone is the rarest courage; since there are so many who had rather meet their bitterest enemy in the field, than their own hearts in their closet.

Charles Caleb Colton

There is but one success - to be able to spend your life in your own way.

Christopher Morley

Jade requires chiseling before becoming a gem.

Chinese proverb

My great mistake, the fault for which I can't forgive myself, is that one day I ceased my obstinate pursuit of my own individuality.

Oscar Wilde

Nothing splendid has ever been achieved except by those who dared to believe that something inside them was superior to circumstance.

Bruce Barton

It is never too late to be what you wanted to be.

George Eliot

I'm still growing up; we all are. I'm still finding Fish.

Antwone Fisher

The art of living lays less in eliminating our troubles than in growing with them.

Bernard M. Baruch

Character builds slowly, but it can be torn down with incredible swiftness.

Faith Baldwin

It is an open question whether any behavior based on fear of eternal punishment can be regarded as ethical or should be regarded as merely cowardly.

Margaret Mead

Growing is the reward of learning.

Malcolm X

RESPONSIBILITY

CERTAIN UNALIENABLE RESPONSIBILITIES

Wendell Berry

If we are responsible older people, we try to teach the young to read, write, speak and think with care and with due respect for the complexity of issues and events. We try to give them the knowledge that informs and enables care, believing that such knowledge and such care will lead to understanding and to a sufficient measure of truth.

But if we aren't careful we will imply to our children and students that the present world of politics, industry and commerce is eagerly awaiting the arrival of young people who are able to read, write, speak and think with care—and that would be wrong. As we are aware ourselves, we need to warn the young that the dominant mode of thought and speech in the present world is oversimplification, often gross oversimplification, leading to falsehood.

For example, the powers of the present world, "liberal" and "conservative" alike, have been assuming for a long time:

That economic value originates in "the market" or "the economy," not in the earth or in human need for the earth's products.

That the economy, having thus no natural limits, is therefore limitless.

That therefore the "global economy," being merely the logical result of limitless economic growth, involves no natural or cultural penalties, and is a "win-win situation" for everybody.

That the profitability of this economy is the result of altruism and compassion, but its destructiveness is merely "inevitable."

That the "inevitable" inequities, injustices and damages of this economy, and the consequent anger, require it to be protected militarily by the world's most powerful nation in the interest of its own security.

That the result of this more or less constant warfare will certainly be national security and world peace.

> As we are aware ourselves, we need to warn the young that the dominant mode of thought and speech in the present world is oversimplification, often gross oversimplification, leading to falsehood.

I don't have time here to construct an argument against this remarkable set of assumptions, but will only point out that it is invalidated by its oversimplifications and its internal contradictions.

It is invalidated, furthermore, by its indifference to some of the fundamental principles of our culture and politics:

That the earth belongs to God, who loves it and has enjoined us to "keep it"—that is, to take proper care of it.

That we are to love our neighbors as ourselves, and that we must not exclude from this love even our enemies.

That since God has imparted His spirit and His breath to all the living world, we are not permitted to exclude any of it from our love and care.

That, for those reasons, colonialism in any of its forms is wrong and justly to be opposed.

That it is "self-evident...that all men are created equal" and are "endowed by their Creator with certain unalienable rights," among which are "life, liberty, and the pursuit of happiness."

That governments derive "their just powers from the consent of the governed."

These great principles are not "problems" to be "solved" by some hotshot intellectual or politician. They are not going to be easily or quickly understood by anybody. They are instructions to be suffered, lived with, struggled with, learned from, for the lifetime of a civilization—and, we must hope, for longer than that.

How are we to "keep" this world? Who are our neighbors? Who are ourselves? How are we to enlarge the practical and effective reach of our love? What is the meaning of political equality? What, properly, may we consider to be our rights? On what conditions may we properly consent to be governed? What is security? What is patriotism? What is peace?

My dear children, don't let anybody else answer those questions for you. Keep them vital, never finally answered, in your thoughts. Beware the establishment. Beware the anti-establishment establishment. Stay responsible, stay alive, all your life.

Reprinted with permission by the Land Institute.

About the Author

Wendell Berry, essayist, novelist and poet and the author of *The Unsettling of America*, gave this commencement talk to Highlands Latin School in Louisville, Kentucky. His granddaughter was one of the two graduates. Berry farms in Kentucky and is a member of the Land Institute's Prairie Writers Circle, Salina, Kansas.

If we value the pursuit of knowledge, we must be free to follow wherever that search may lead us. The free mind is not a barking dog, to be tethered on a ten-foot chain.

Adlai Stevenson

...having a morality must at least imply the acknowledgement of principles as impartially applying to one's own conduct as well as to another's, and moreover, principles which may constitute a constraint or limitation upon the pursuit of one's own interests.

John Rawls

Our responsibility as privileged human beings is to pay back for the opportunities we've received.

Kathryn Anastos

The things taught in school are not an education but the means of an education.

Ralph Waldo Emerson

You cannot escape the responsibility of tomorrow by evading it today.

Abraham Lincoln

Plato equates wisdom not merely with good judgment but also with the ability to plan and deliberate in accordance with policies that are framed for the good of the community, in a way that goes beyond self-interest.

Judith Barad

When they turn the pages of history,
When these days have passed long ago,
Will they read of us with sadness,
For the seeds that we let grow?

Neil Peart

As we move toward a global society, becoming ever more aware of the sufferings and struggles of the peoples of the Earth, there is more and more reason to recognize the social responsibility each of us has and respond to it.

Justine Willis Toms & Michael Toms

The future will not belong to those who stand on the sidelines.

Paul Wellstone

You are what you do.

Bill Maher

Conscience...is the impulse to do right because it is right, regardless of personal ends.

Margaret C. Graham

Few things can help an individual more than to place responsibility upon him, and to let him know that you trust him.

Booker T. Washington

Hyperindividualism is what, in the end, drives global warming: the sense that we each should have a big car and a big house and a big life, that it is an imposition in any way to share with others (share our mobility with others in a bus, for instance). Hyperindividualism is also what drives so much of our social evil.

Bill McKibben

True character arises from a deeper well than religion. It is the internalization of moral principles of a society, augmented by those tenets personally chosen by the individual, strong enough to endure through trials of solitude and adversity. The principles are fitted together into what we call integrity, literally the integrated self, wherein personal decisions feel good and true. Character is in turn the enduring source of virtue. It stands by itself and excites admiration in others.

Edward O. Wilson

Make no mistake: change is coming, and it will simply force itself upon us in the name of survival if we sit idly by during its approach. If we're wise, we'll avoid such and eleventh-hour response and its reactionary dangers and make change while time remains to make it thoughtfully. We'll realize as a business community and as a society that the question really isn't why we should do it. The question is why on earth we would do anything else.

Jeffrey Hollender

INTEGRATION

NORMATIVE WORLDVIEW

Michael Boylan

O ur ability to value anything is inextricably tied to our personal
worldview. This is because worldview forms the context for all of
our normative and factual judgments. It is only through an exploration of worldview that we can come to know fundamentally what valuation is all about and how it can be used correctly or not. This process forms
the basis of intersubjective dialogue about value. Thus, we begin with: (a)
individual investigation into the foundation of valuation itself, and then
move to (b) group consensus about such standards of valuation. These
standards, in turn, allow social groups to discuss individual values of ethics,
religion, and aesthetics along with their resultant social institutions.

This essay will be a brief snapshot on how normative worldview is connected both to a theory of ethics and a general theory of social justice. For
those who want to explore this relationship in more detail, I would suggest
my book, *A Just Society*[1]. What this short overview means to accomplish is
to set out the topography of this author's vision of ethics and social philos-

ophy. In the appendix, there are key jargon words that are given further specification. The entire intent is to entice further exploration.

Though my approach does advocate a particular normative position (based upon my metaethical approach), it is certainly possible for others to use the same normative worldview methodology and come up with different results. This is because the Personal Worldview Imperative and the Shared Community Worldview Imperative are metaethical principles that may support several (though a limited number of) theories. I have offered an outline of one sort of response that I have put forward as grounded by these principles. This initiative concentrates upon the areas of ethics and social/political philosophy. As such it is developed in the two major sections of my approach.

Ethics

Ethics as a field can be parsed into: metaethics, normative ethics, and applied ethics[2]. One begins with normative ethics because it is here that norms for action are determined. There are different normative theories that prescribe various actions and rationales for such. This is one major problem in ethics. Which normative theory is correct? Is it one theory or a medley of theories? In order to answer this question philosophers have often taken to more theoretical examination of the foundations of the theories themselves. Such examination is the province of metaethics. Much of twentieth-century ethics was devoted to metaethics as philosophers struggled with abstract problems meant to give clarity concerning the status of normative theories.

The third area of ethics is applied ethics. Applied ethics began to gain popularity in the early 1980s with increased work in business ethics, medical ethics, environmental ethics, and problems in social and political philosophy. One of the principal criticisms of applied ethics was that it often seemed that practitioners jumped to intuitive judgments that lacked theoretical grounding (normative ethics and metaethics). This criticism continues to be the weak point in applied ethics. In an effort to answer real life problems, it often seems that practitioners ignore the other branches of ethics all together. (A similar sort of attack is made against those who solely practice metaethics, viz., that they ignore practice all together.)

One way around the "connection" problem in applied ethics is to find a link integral to normative and applied ethics. One candidate for a link between the various branches of ethics is Normative Worldview.

Every person lives with her own worldview. Among those who practice anthropology and sociology, it has been dogma to assert that all worldviews are on a par. That is to say that the worldviews of Martin Luther King, Jr. and the Adolf Hitler are on a par. This way of confronting worldviews is mistaken. A better way is to set out normative criteria in order to evaluate worldviews. In this way, the worldview of an individual could be shown to be good or shown to be bad. As I demonstrate in *A Just Society*, a flawed worldview ought to be changed. In this sense we may not adopt whatever worldview we want. Only a proper worldview will do. Because worldview has normative features this approach connects to normative ethics. Because we all live in the context of a worldview, this approach connects to applied ethics. Because the criteria upon which normative worldview is based must be theoretically tested, it connects to metaethics. In this way, the normative worldview approach unifies ethics.

The normative theory that this author employs is a "rights-based" deontological approach based upon the necessary conditions for human action. These goods are ranked according to their primacy to action (entitled "embeddedness"). All agents will claim first those goods most necessary to action and then subsequently those that are less embedded. The moral turn occurs when agents accept the duty to provide others the basic goods necessary for action. This duty is correlative to the authentic claim of others for these goods. So many people disregard this part of the

> Every person lives with her own worldview.

equation. They are "free riders" who want what they can get without regard for others. In the appendix there is the key argument for the "Moral Status of Basic Goods." In this argument (if it is correct), the logical duty is set out for everyone to respect the rights of others on the basis of a purely rationalistic understanding of the nature of action. This argument suggests that what is most primary in our understanding of ourselves as human is that we want to be good (whatever that means). Each of us thinks of being good differently. Some of us think of it as being very powerful and having lots of money. Others think of it as just having their own way with things. Be that as it may, we all should agree that before all this we need certain goods to make this happen. Since none of us are, by nature, above anyone else, then all of us have an interest in supporting the fundamental principles of action.

These goods are set out in the Table of Embeddedness (see appendix). When we think of public policy, we need to support the basic goods of a group of people over the less embedded (according to foundational principles of action) claims of others. Thus, tax policy that supports food stamps and public housing trumps high income tax breaks. The way that this begins is with public discourse that encourages diverse opinions (see the common body of knowledge and the shared community worldview imperative in the appendix).

The acceptance of the relative embeddedness of the goods described in the Table of Embeddedness is augmented by two moral imperatives: the Personal Worldview Imperative and the Shared Community Worldview Imperative (see appendix). These imperatives connect all the values an agent holds, and enjoin him or her to put them into an order through which they work together. Because these two imperatives and the ranking of goods are heavy on empirical content, the ease in application is far greater than other accounts that are more abstract in their exposition. It is the supposition of this approach that increasing empirical content in the expression of a normative theory makes the application easier for everyone. This is because the individual is able to imagine just what it would be like to live in such a world informed by the theory. This ability to project the theory into one's life is not unlike literary theory that often cites such projectability as a positive feature of a poem, play, or novel. Keats called it "negative capability." Shelley termed it "the willing suspension of disbelief." In literature or in ethical theories, this capacity refers to how readily a theory is imaginable such that it might be brought forth to one's worldview for inspection. The only way change occurs is when an individual or a group of individuals confront a new theory that overlaps their own worldview yet makes a persuasive (empirically rich) reason for alteration.

In the realm of ethics, the approach of normative worldview commands not only an examined life according to certain principles (coherence—inductive and deductive—completeness, and applicability) that give rise to certain dispositions of the will: sympathy, care, openness, and love. Together these dispositions create a good will. It is only through the creation of a good will via the structures of the Personal Worldview Imperative that a person can fulfill a basic human desire to be good.

Social/Political Philosophy

The transition to the social/political realm involves an analogous move. Just as there is a Personal Worldview Imperative governing the conduct of the individual, so also there is a Shared Community Worldview Imperative governing the formation of micro and macro communities in which we all reside. The way to move from the individual to the community is first by setting out a model of intersubjective agreement. One such candidate is what I call the common body of knowledge. The common body of knowledge describes a social event in which certain understandings about the world (factual and normative) are set forth and agreed upon. This allows all members of the community to use language in the same way and to limit differences to real disputes (rather than talking at cross-purposes in purely verbal disputes). From this perspective other understandings emerge. Among the most important (from this perspective) are those concerning the shared values among members of the community. These are holistically understood through ethics, aesthetics, and religion (among others). Once the community comes to an understanding on the shape of the amalgam, it is in a position to create a shared community worldview. Only those shared community worldviews that fit the imperative should be adopted. Again, not all worldviews will do. If there is a sub-group that advocates child sacrifice to the god, Baal, the larger community must hold up the practice to the Personal Worldview Imperative to illustrate its error. Only values that meet the criteria of the Personal Worldview Imperative will be allowed into the community worldview.

When the periodic process of community exploration and renewal is complete, the general community must create public policy that is driven by the resultant values and tempered by an understanding of distributive and retributive justice that refers back to the Table of Embeddedness for its relative structure. At the end of the book I illustrate through several examples how such public policy can be formulated under this rubric.

The concept of normative worldview transcends idiosyncratic preference and creates equality among every individual's personal worldview (that meets the Personal Worldview Imperative).

In this way normative worldview examines both the personal perspective and the community perspective. The exploration of normative worldview creates a vantage point that unites ethics and points to a general theory of social and political philosophy. Together, these two normative frameworks constitute a united theory of the right and wrong of all human action.

Appendix: Key Terms

Personal Worldview Imperative: All people must develop a single, comprehensive, and internally coherent worldview that is good and that we strive to act out in our daily lives.

Shared Community Worldview Imperative: Each agent must contribute to a common body of knowledge that supports the creation of a shared community worldview (that is itself complete, coherent, and good) through which social institutions and their resulting policies might flourish within the constraints of the essential core commonly held values (ethics, aesthetics, and religion).

Common Body of Knowledge: A set of factual and normative principles about which there is general agreement among a community or between communities of people. This includes (but is not limited to) agreement on what constitutes objective facts and how to measure them. It also includes (but is not limited to) what counts as acceptable values that will be recognized as valid in the realms of ethics, aesthetics, and religion.

Moral Status of Basic Goods and The Table of Embeddedness: The basis for the outlines of my theory of distributive justice.

A. The Moral Status of Basic Goods

All people, by nature, desire to be good—Fundamental Assumption

In order to become good, one must be able to act—Fact

All people, by nature, desire to act—1, 2

People value what is natural to them—Assertion

What people value they wish to protect—Assertion

All people wish to protect their ability to act—3-5

Fundamental interpersonal "oughts" are expressed via our highest value systems: morality, aesthetics, and religion—Assertion

All people must agree, upon pain of logical contradiction, that what is natural and desirable to them individually is natural and desirable to everyone collectively and individually—Assertion

Everyone must seek personal protection for her own ability to act via morality, aesthetics, and religion—6, 7

Everyone, upon pain of logical contradiction, must admit that all other humans will seek personal protection of his or her ability to act via morality, aesthetics, and religion—8, 9

All people must agree, upon pain of logical contradiction, that since the attribution of the basic goods of agency are predicated generally, that it is inconsistent to assert idiosyncratic preference—Fact

Goods that are claimed through generic predication apply equally to each agent and everyone has a stake in their protection—10, 11

Rights and duties are correlative—Assertion

Everyone has at least a moral right to the basic goods of agency and others in the society have a duty to provide those goods to all—12, 13

B. The Table of Embeddedness

These are the goods that any agent may claim in hierarchical order according to their proximity to the possibility of action. The justification for their observance is found in "The Moral Status of Basic Goods" argument.

Basic Goods

Level One: Most Deeply Embedded[3] (that which is absolutely necessary for Human Action):

Food

Clothing

Shelter,

Protection from Unwarranted Bodily Harm

Level Two: Deeply Embedded (that which is necessary for effective basic action within any given society):

Literacy in the language of the country

Basic mathematical skills

Other fundamental skills necessary to be an effective agent in that country, e.g., in the United States some computer literacy is necessary

Some familiarity with the culture and history of the country in which one lives

The assurance that those you interact with are not lying to promote their own interests

The assurance that those you interact with will recognize your human dignity (as per above) and not exploit you as a means only

Basic human rights such as those listed in the US Bill of Rights and the United Nations Universal Declaration of Human Rights

Secondary Goods

Level One: Life Enhancing, Medium to High-Medium on Embeddedness:

Basic societal respect

Equal opportunity to compete for the prudential goods of society

Ability to pursue a life plan according to the Personal Worldview Imperative

Ability to participate equally as an agent in the Shared Community Worldview Imperative

Level Two: Useful, Medium to Low Medium Embeddedness:

Ability to utilize one's real and portable property in the manner she chooses

Ability to gain from and exploit the consequences of one's labor regardless of starting point

Ability to pursue goods that are generally owned by most citizens, e.g., in the United States today a telephone, television, and automobile

Level Three: Luxurious, Low Embeddedness

Ability to pursue goods that are pleasant even though they are far removed from action and from the expectations of most citizens within a given country, e.g., in the United States today, a European Vacation

Ability to exert one's will so that she might extract a disproportionate share of society's resources for her own use.

© Michael Boylan

Notes

[1] *Michael Boylan,* A Just Society *(Lanham, MD, NY, Oxford: Rowman and Littlefield, 2004).*

[2] *For those readers wishing an introduction to philosophical ethics, see: Michael Boylan,* Basic Ethics *(Upper Saddle River, NJ: Prentice Hall, 2000). I might note that this book spawned a series of books entitled* Basic Ethics in Action *with accessible books covering Business Ethics, Medical Ethics, Environmental Ethics, and Social/Political Ethics.*

[3] *"Embedded" in this context means the relative fundamental nature of the good for action. A more deeply embedded good is one that is more primary to action.*

About the Author

Michael Boylan (PhD, University of Chicago) is professor of philosophy and philosophy department chair at Marymount University. His most recent book, *A Just Society* (August, 2004), is his manifesto on ethics and social/political philosophy (and the most complete depiction of his normative worldview theory). He is also the author of *Basic Ethics* (2000), an essay on normative and applied ethics, *Genetic Engineering: Science and Ethics on the New Frontier* (2002, with Kevin E. Brown), *Ethics Across the Curriculum: A Practice-Based Approach* (2003, with James A. Donahue), and *Public Health Policy and Ethics*, (ed. 2004) along with thirteen other books on philosophy and literature and over seventy articles. He is the general editor of a series of trade books on public philosophy with Basil Blackwell Publishers and another series of books with Prentice Hall, as well as the co-editor in ethics for the *Internet Encyclopedia of Philosophy*.

For every man who lives without freedom, the rest of us must face the guilt.

Lillian Hellman

Moral excellence comes about as a result of habit. We become just by doing just acts, temperate by doing temperate acts, brave by doing brave acts.

Aristotle

Man is now able to soar into outer space and reach up to the moon; but he is not moral enough to live at peace with his neighbor.

Sri Sathya Sai Baba

The greatest responsibility an individual assumes is to oneself.

Madeline Bartosch

Better a little with righteousness than much gain with injustice.

Proverbs 16:8

The imperative is to define what is right and do it.

Barbara Jordan

It is truly said: It does not take much strength to do things, but it requires great strength to decide what to do.

Chow Ching

There is a higher court of justice and that is the court of conscience. It supercedes all other courts.

Mohandas K. Gandhi

For evil to flourish, the good need stand by and do nothing.
Many "good Christians" and so-called ethical leaders deserve shame.
They turned their heads and turned in their friends to the king,
Rendering the lofty principles of their god and philosophers lame.

(First line an adapted quote from Edmund Burke)
Jason Merchey

There is no such thing as ethical truth. However, those committed to humane-egalitarian ideals can make a truth-claim rare and precious: they can look reality and the truths of science in the face and find nothing that makes them flinch.

James R. Flynn

The most important human endeavor is the striving for morality in our actions. Our inner balance and even our very existence depends on it. Only morality in our actions can give beauty and dignity to our lives.

Albert Einstein

...we have to validate our own existence, our own morality, our own life. And that comes by taking a stance, by standing up and remaining human. And there are times when remaining human is the only resistance possible.

Chris Hedges

Wisdom, compassion, and courage are the three universally recognized moral qualities of men.

Confucius

Moral theories can be compared to road maps. A good theory offers guidance or signposts for thinking about and resolving moral issues.

Judith A. Boss

I have no idea of submitting tamely to injustice inflicted either on me or on the slave. I will oppose it with all the moral powers with which I am endowed. I am no advocate of passivity.

Lucretia Mott

While conscience is our friend, all is at peace; however once it is offended, farewell to a tranquil mind.

Mary Wortley Montagu

To care for anyone else enough to make their problems one's own, is ever the beginning of one's real ethical development.

Felix Adler

RESPONSIBILITY

REFLECTIONS ON THE ETHICS OF SELFLESSNESS

Nathaniel Branden

T his essay is offered not as a full treatise on ethics but rather as a stimulant to new thinking about some old issues. It challenges some conventional notions about morality and invites a reexamination of certain ethical precepts often associated with spirituality, religion, and mysticism. It is an exercise in what, in *The Six Pillars of Self-Esteem*, I call "the practice of living consciously," applied to the field of values. The focus of these reflections is the traditional identification of goodness with "selflessness."

In an ethical context, "selflessness" means devoid of, or untainted by, self-interest. To behave selflessly is to act without concern for any benefit to oneself. This is commonly regarded as the essence of morality, especially in mystical traditions. It is held to be the way that spiritually evolved people behave. Indeed, such behavior is sometimes taken as evidence of one's spirituality.

By contrast, selfishness is commonly regarded as evidence of one's non-spirituality.

Observe, first of all, that in equating unselfishness with morality, the implication is that self-interested actions are either immoral or nonmoral. That is, they are either bad or without moral significance. If, for instance, I protest paying taxes to support welfare programs of which I do not approve, then according to this code I am being selfish and therefore immoral. If I work to support myself, that is not immoral but neither is it admirable; it is ethically neutral.

This doctrine takes for granted as self-evident a clash between self-interest and morality: We can pursue our self-interest or we can be moral, but we can't be both. And it upholds self-sacrifice as the ideal. Sometimes this ideal is expressed as "a life of selfless service."

As one transpersonal psychologist puts it: "As [spiritual] awakening begins, motivations inevitably shift from the egocentric toward the desire to serve others. This kind of service is seen as absolutely necessary if the awakening and development are to continue; [spiritual] growth requires a life of service."

What is significant about this viewpoint concerning the evil of "selfishness" is in how many versions it has appeared throughout human history. Don't be selfish—subordinate your interests to those of the tribe. Don't be selfish—subordinate your interests to those of the family. Don't be selfish—sacrifice for the pharaoh, emperor, king, church, country, race, state, proletariat, society, or globe. Remember: service is your noblest goal; selfishness is the root of all evil.

In this doctrine, selfishness is presumed to be narrow, petty, small-minded, materialistic, immature, narcissistic, anti-social, exploitative, mean-spirited, arrogant, ruthless, indifferent, cruel, and potentially murderous. These traits are evidently regarded as being to one's self-interest, since they are labeled as expressions of selfishness. It is interesting to speculate about the psychology of those who believe this. By my own understanding I would say that these traits are self-destructive and that self-destruction is not to one's self-interest.

If one's goal is a happy and fulfilling life, self-interest is best served by rationality, productivity, integrity, and a sense of justice and benevolence in dealings with others. It is served by learning to think long-range and to project the consequences of one's actions, which means learning to live responsibly. Irresponsibility is not to one's self-interest—and neither is mindlessness, dishonesty, or brutality.

In taking for granted a conflict between morality and self-interest, exponents of self-sacrifice and selfless service assume, first of all, that no one could have a selfish interest in being moral, and second, that the purpose of morality is not to serve the individual's well-being but to subordinate it to allegedly higher ends. These are the necessary presuppositions of the idea that morality equals selflessness. This doctrine says to the individual: your life does not belong to you; you are not an end in yourself but only a means to the ends of others; you are here to serve; you have no right to exist for your own sake. What is remarkable is that when this moral vision is offered in a religious context, it is identified as an expression of "love for humankind."

By way of clarifying the confusion surrounding the issue of selfishness and unselfishness, consider the following example. A young woman—I will call her Marny—decides she would like to become an architect. Her father is deeply disappointed, because he had always dreamed that after college she would join him in the dress business. "Must you be so selfish?" Marny's mother says to her. "You're breaking your father's heart."

"If I don't study architecture," Marny answers, "I'll break my own heart."

So Marny goes to college to become an architect. While at college, she dates a young man who falls in love with her. He begs her to marry him, give up architecture, and become the mother of his children. "In the first place," Marny tells him gently, not wishing to cause pain, "I don't love you. And in the second place, I don't plan to have children, at least not in the foreseeable future."

"Not have children?" the young man cries. "How can you be so selfish? And don't you care at all about my happiness?"

"Don't you care at all about mine?" she responds, smiling.

A few years later, now a practicing architect, she meets a man with whom she falls in love. Marny sees in him the embodiment of the traits she most admires: strength, self-confidence, integrity, and a passionate nature unafraid of love or intimacy. To marry him, share her excitement and joy with him, nurture him at times, support him in his struggles as he supports her in hers—join with him in fighting for causes in which they both believe—is experienced by her as selfish in the most natural and benevolent sense of the word. She is living for her values. Her life is productive, stimulating, and filled with love.

So when her husband becomes ill, for a long time she curtails many of her activities to take care of him. When friends praise her for her "unselfishness," she looks at them incredulously. "I love him," is her only answer. The thought of selfless service would not occur to her. She would not insult what she feels for her husband by calling her caretaking self-sacrifice. "Not if you hold the full context," she explains. "What would I do if I were 'selfish?' Abandon him? Whose notion of self-interest is that?"

Later, when her husband recovers and life has stabilized again, she returns to work with great passion. She is eager to make up for lost time. When certain of her friends call to discuss personal problems, she accommodates them for a while, but when she realizes how much of her energy is being drained by them she finally calls a halt. "Sorry," she says. "I don't want to disappoint you, but right now I've got more urgent priorities."

"God, but you're selfish," she is told.

When she deals with other human beings, she respects the legitimacy of their self-interest and does not expect them to sacrifice it, any more than she would sacrifice her own. And she cannot understand why other people do not necessarily feel this way.

She notices that "selfish" is what some people call her when she is doing what she wants to do rather than what they want her to do. She also notices that while she is not intimidated by this accusation, many others are.

Question: Is Marny a virtuous woman or an unvirtuous one? Is she moral or immoral? Clearly, she is not an altruist, since altruism, in its literal meaning, is not merely kindness or benevolence but the subordination of self to others. But then what is Marny? What can we say about her?

The first thing I would say about her is that she operates consciously. And the next thing I would say is that she stands outside traditional moral categories: she is an exponent of rational or enlightened self-interest—a possibility not even acknowledged by those who talk about self-sacrifice as the moral ideal, and imply that the only alternative to sacrificing self to others is sacrificing others to self. Marny does neither; she does not believe in the practice of human sacrifice. She does not believe that masochism and sadism exhaust our moral possibilities.

Observe that everything she does is motivated by loyalty to her values. She acts on her judgment. And her judgment is thoughtful, not impulsive. For her husband, whom she loves most in the world, there are almost no limits on what she is prepared to do (within a rational framework). For her friends, there are many more limits; she is generous, but not to the point of ignoring her higher values. If she supports certain causes, it is because they concern values that are important to her and to the kind of world she wishes to live in. She respects self-interest but understands that what is or is not to one's self-interest is not necessarily self-evident—it requires thought. And her range of concern is a lifetime, not the convenience or inconvenience of this moment. That is why I say she operates consciously.

The philosopher Immanuel Kant would tell her she is immoral, since everything she does is by selfish inclination. Kant taught that any action contaminated by self-interest to even the smallest degree can make no claim to moral merit—only that which is done out of duty can be virtuous. Hitler would tell her she has no right to live for herself, that her life is owed to the German race, and that the pursuit of personal happiness leads only to suffering. Stalin would tell her that her petty bourgeois preoccupations are absurd, that her egoistic inclinations are subversive, and that her life belongs not to herself but to the Proletariat, meaning the State. Mao would tell her it is evil and irresponsible for her to imagine that her person is her property—she must accept that she is to be disposed of as the People see fit. The Pope would tell her that her practice of birth-control is sinfully egocentric. A New Age psychologist enamored with the wisdom of the East might tell her she is retarded in her spiritual development because she still thinks of her happiness in terms of the narrowly personal. And a mystic would tell her that if she dedicates unknown years of her life to meditation, prayer, and study, eventually the veil of ignorance will fall away and she will grasp that selfishness is indeed the root of all evil and that only through selfless service can her soul fully awaken.

Now, if we want to talk about evil, I will say that these teachings are what I regard as evil—because of the consequences to which they lead for human life on earth.

No one inveighed against "selfishness" or advocated "selfless service" more passionately than the leaders of Nazi Germany, the Soviet Union, Communist China, or Cambodia. Take a look at what those "ideals" mean when translated into political reality. More people have been tortured and murdered in this century than any other in history, and the justification was always "in the name of a higher good to which the individual must be subordinated." Hitler, Stalin, Mao, and Pol Pot taught their people a lot about "selfless service."

It could be argued that whatever may be true about the cases just cited, it does not apply to Buddhists, who are probably the most peaceful, non-violent people on the planet. This is correct, and it is a fair point to raise. However, consider this: if we teach that individuality is an illusion and that service to others is the essence of morality, what kind of cultural and intellectual climate do we help create? One that serves a society built on the principles of individual freedom and individual rights—or a society that proclaims duty to the collective above all? Is the doctrine of selfless service more likely to protect an individual when freedom is threatened, or make the individual more vulnerable to manipulation and control?

> In the course of everyday life, we are bombarded in a thousand ways with messages to the effect that "service" is the highest mark of virtue and that morality consists of living for others.

Anyone who practices psychotherapy almost certainly knows how frightened many people are of even the most appropriate acts of self-assertiveness—they do not know how to answer the charge that they are being selfish. How many people die in insane wars because they do not want to admit that they care more about their own lives than about some abstract cause that may make no sense to them? How many people give up their dreams and aspirations in deference to the needs and demands of others because they dread the charge of being egocentric? This is an open secret: almost everyone knows it and almost no one talks about it. Instead, we go on insisting that ego is the cause of all our misery.

In the course of everyday life, we are bombarded in a thousand ways with messages to the effect that "service" is the highest mark of virtue and that morality consists of living for others. We are told that the intelligent, the enlightened, the able, the competent, the strong must exist for the sake of those who lack those traits; that those who suffer or are in need have first claim on the lives and energy of the rest of the human race, that theirs is the right superseding all other rights. We are told that an individual's mind and effort are the property of the community, the nation, the globe. We are told that those who have created wealth owe a particular debt to those who have not created it—including an apology. And all the while politicians, religious leaders, and intellectuals subtly or not so subtly chastise the electorate for being too reluctant to sacrifice for the greater good.

Most people do not try to practice the code of self-sacrifice consistently in their everyday choices and decisions. That would not be possible. But to the extent that they accept it as right, they are left in confusion, if not in a moral vacuum. They have no adequate set of principles to guide their actions. In relationships, they do not know what demands they can permit themselves and what demands they can permit to others; they do not know what is theirs by right, theirs by favor, or theirs by someone's sacrifice. Under the pressure of conflicting personal desires and conflicting external injunctions, they fluctuate between sacrificing themselves to others and sacrificing others to themselves. They swing between the belief that self-surrender is a virtue and the knowledge that they must smuggle some selfishness into their lives in order to survive.

Small wonder that when some people do decide to be selfish, they are so often selfish in the narrow and petty sense rather than in the rational and noble sense. No one taught them that rational self-interest is possible—and that it is the obligation of a conscious human being to think carefully about what does in fact represent long-term self-interest. When they hear selfishness castigated as petty, cruel, materialistic, anti-social, or mean-spirited, these epithets strike a responsive chord within them: their own guilt feels like a validation of the charge.

If we are operating consciously, the most obvious question to ask, when someone proposes "a life of selfless service," is why?

Those who tend to associate spirituality with selfless service typically offer two answers to the question of why? The first is not really an answer. It consists of the assertion that at a certain level of spiritual evolution, one gains the mystical insight—as a self-evident fact, requiring no further explanation—that one should take the path of selfless service. It becomes as obvious as the sun hanging in the sky—one simply sees it. This is not an explanation likely to impress a thoughtful person.

The second, and by the far the more interesting explanation, is the statement that the value of such service lies not so much in the help given the beneficiaries as in liberation from ego on the part of the one who serves. A life of service, it is said, facilitates self-transcendence. In secular terms, this is dangerously close to an egoistic justification: I will serve others as a means to personal development.

I confess I am not really clear on what a life of selfless service literally means. I cannot find a plain definition anywhere. Do we ask people what they would like us to do and then do it (like a solicitous "pleaser")? Do we decide what we think is best for them and do that (like a totalitarian altruist)? Does it mean we abandon the life and work we chose before we attained liberation from ego and go searching the world for suffering to ameliorate (like anyone for whom self-surrender is glory)?

What also confuses me is that I have known a number of prominent intellectuals who became professors, wrote books, and then, at some point, saw the light and embraced the ideal of selfless service. They are still professors and they still write books, and in their books they talk about the ideal of service—but apart from that I cannot see how their lives has changed. Whom are they serving, and how are they doing it? (Some of them have become social activists dedicated to saving the world from capitalism, about which they know appallingly little.)

Perhaps I will be asked: But is not the justification for a life of service the fact that there is so much suffering in the world? Are not kindness and compassion virtues even in your morality?

The answer to the second question is yes, kindness and compassion are virtues. We cannot have a decent life without them. But why would anyone identify kindness or compassion with self-sacrifice? If it is in the name of one's values—such as regard for the value of a human life—kindness can be as much an act of self-assertion as any other act of self-expression. And yes, there is a great deal of suffering in the world. And one of the reasons for that suffering is the fact that most people have never been taught a code of ethical principles that would support a truly human form of existence on earth.

We can deepen our understanding of this last point by considering one of the greatest causes of suffering on the planet—poverty. If one is genuinely interested in relieving suffering and is disposed to approach the problem consciously, it is logical to assume one would wish to understand how poverty is eliminated. Fortunately, the answer is known.

Prior to the industrial revolution and the birth of capitalism, poverty was the natural condition of almost the entire human race. It was not perceived as an aberration but as the norm—98 percent of the world's population lived in conditions unimaginable to a twentieth-century citizen of the United States. That was poverty of a kind that makes what we call poverty today look like luxury. Then, dating from the time of the American Revolution, the ideas of individualism, human rights, and political-economic freedom—capitalism—began to sweep the Western world. To the extent that capitalism was accepted, which varied enormously from country to country, the result was an unprecedented rise in the standard of living of millions and millions of people that would have been inconceivable a century earlier. Infant mortality rates dropped and life expectancy leapt upward. In the brief span of less than two hundred years, the West witnessed a growth in material well-being unequaled by the sum of human progress up to that time. At every step of the way, the freer the country was, the faster the rate of progress and the more rapid the decline of poverty.

What compassionate mystic understood what he was seeing, above all in the United States, stopped talking about self-sacrifice, decided to rethink his code of values—and began proclaiming the glories that were possible when human intelligence is liberated and people are free to act on their own initiative? What compassionate mystic—hit by a this-worldly vision—got enlightenment and realized that there might an answer to suffering this side of Nirvana, and began to champion the right of life, liberty, property, and the pursuit of happiness?

Notice, even today, with the worldwide collapse of collectivist economies, how grudgingly the Vatican acknowledges the achievements of free minds and semi-free markets in raising the quality of our lives. Notice the resentment that still attaches to the word profit by glowering, cassocked Rip van Winkles who still think they are living in the year 1200 and have not yet discovered the industrial age, let alone the information age. Notice the arrogant presumptuousness of offering miserly recognition to entrepreneurs who have transformed the world—and immediately following it by scolding reminders that they are, after only, only servants of humanity and should not be allowed to forget it.

To carry this point still further: a major part of the world that, for a very long time, fiercely resisted the incursion of "Western ideas" is Asia, and this is an area where the influence of mysticism has been at its strongest and where, for centuries, poverty has been at its worst. But in the years following World War II, the situation began to change. Slowly the ideas of entrepreneurial capitalism caught fire in the Asian mind. Men (and women!) of courage, initiative, and ambition began to challenge old traditions and think about the possibilities of this world, if governments would cede them even a modest degree of economic and political freedom. They got a little freedom, and then they pressed for a little more and a little more. The battle is still going on and is far from over. But what has happened has been described as a miracle.

To quote from John Naisbitt's *Megatrends Asia:*

From 1945 to 1995, half a century, Asia went from rags to riches. It reduced the incidence of poverty from 400 million to 180 million, while its population grew by 400 million during the same period. The World Bank has pronounced that nowhere and at no time in human history has humanity achieved such economic progress, and concluded that the East Asia story is an economic miracle.

A significant aspect of this story is the cultural transformation in the role of women. An increasing number of Asian women have become entrepreneurs, against thousands of years of tradition. And more and more women are pouring into the workplace. (In Japan, for example, virtually all the currency traders are women.) To be sure, there is still much resistance to these changes, and there are still efforts to integrate Asia's semi-capitalism into "the old ways," resulting in some rather incongruous mixtures of practices and principles. That is culturally inevitable. But an extravagant source of human energy has been released by such freedom as has been permitted and is not likely to be bottled up again.

In an age in which few achievements seem to impress us and the most extraordinary triumphs of human intelligence often leave us blasé, take a moment to meditate on the meaning of the quote from Naisbitt. And then ask yourself:

Why aren't the apostles of kindness, compassion, and concern for human suffering shouting about this historic achievement from the rooftops?

Why are they not celebrating the nobility of the entrepreneurial spirit and the power of the liberated mind to accomplish "miracles"?

Why are they not championing such life-serving virtues as independence, productive ambition, competence, self-responsibility, self-assertiveness, integrity, perseverance, and the drive to innovate?

Instead, they still talk as if we lived in preindustrial times, before anyone grasped that wealth could be created, when all one could do at best was share one's meager subsistence with a fellow sufferer, and the first traders and businessmen were looked on with scorn because of their concern with "material" reality. Perhaps, then, in the darkness and despair of the times, kindness and compassion were just about all human beings could offer one another. Certainly they could not project new industries that would offer employment to millions of people, build communities, heal poverty, and create undreamed of possibilities of survival and well-being. But today the evidence is all around us—and if it is not acknowledged and appreciated then we have to wonder whether the amelioration of suffering is really the primary agenda of these exponents of enlightenment, or whether other agendas are operating within them that enjoy a higher priority. With the best will in the world, I am unable to believe that blindness of this magnitude can be innocent.

It is not kindness, compassion, or selflessness that lift people out of poverty. It is liberated human ability—combined with perseverance, courage, and the desire to achieve something worthwhile and (sometimes) make money in the process. But of course, such motives are not unselfish. And that is why they can accomplish "miracles."

Kindness and compassion are virtues, to be sure, but what has carried the world and moved it forward, lifting humankind out of the cave and beyond a life expectancy of twenty-four—what has conquered disease and steadily lightened the burden of human existence—what has created and goes on creating new possibilities for fulfillment and joy on earth—is the rational, self-assertive egos of audaciously imaginative men and women who refuse to accept suffering and stagnation as our destiny.

If you doubt it, drop all our selfless politicians, social activists, and mystics into some jungle where people still live as they lived hundreds of thousands of years ago, barely able to scratch out subsistence and at the helpless mercy of every upheaval of nature, and invite these visiting humanitarians to create abundance.

"Even if everything you say is true," I am sometimes asked, "hasn't our progress generated new problems, new dislocations, instabilities, and dangers?" The answer is that every step of human progress creates new difficulties and challenges, and they can and will be overcome, but not by cursing the virtues that made the progress possible, not by curtailing the freedom that allows intelligence to function.

"But isn't there more to life than mere material reality?" The short answer is, of course. For a slightly longer answer, I will quote a favorite passage of mine from *Atlas Shrugged:*

> You, who claim that you long to rise above the crude concerns of the body, above the drudgery of serving mere physical needs—who is enslaved by physical needs: the Hindu who labors from sunrise to sunset for a bowl of rice, or the American who is driving a tractor? Who is the conqueror of physical reality: the man who sleeps on a bed of nails or the man who sleeps on an inner-spring mattress? Which is the monument to the triumph of the human spirit over matter: the germ-eaten hovels on the shorelines of the Ganges or the Atlantic skyline of New York?

I will add: and if India has become economically more developed than it was forty-plus years ago, when the above passage was first published—if, for example, once-starving India has now become an exporter of food— who are the persons responsible: those who preached the renunciation of ego or those who fought for greater freedom for the individual? Those who lead ashrams or those who lead research institutes and business enterprises? Those who stare at another dimension or those who work to transform this one?

If ego is the unifying center of consciousness, the faculty within us that thinks, judges, wills, and drives the process of achievement, then—before embracing selflessness as an ideal—reflect on the nature of a world from which ego has vanished and consider whether it is a world in which you would wish to exist.

Right here, right now, is an opportunity to live consciously.

© Nathaniel Branden

About the Author

With a PhD in psychology and a background in philosophy, Nathaniel Branden is a practicing psychotherapist and life coach in Los Angeles, and, in addition, does corporate consulting and offers seminars, workshops, and conferences on the application of self-esteem principles and technology to the problems of modern business.

The name Nathaniel Branden has become synonymous with "the psychology of self-esteem," a field he began pioneering over four decades ago. He has done more, perhaps, than any other theorist to awaken America's consciousness to the importance of self-esteem to human well-being.

His many best-selling works include: *The Psychology of Romantic Love, The Six Pillars of Self-Esteem, Taking Responsibility, The Art of Living Consciously*, and *My Years With Ayn Rand*.

His writings have been translated into eighteen foreign languages and, worldwide, have sold over four million copies. He may be contacted through his website, www.nathanielbranden.com.

There is a fine line, that if crossed, turns self-confident to egotistical; one needs to remain conscious of that to make sure he/she does not cross to the dark side.

Shellie Clack

Be wisely selfish.

Tenzin Gyatso

Honor is self-esteem made visible in action.

Ayn Rand

They can, because they think they can.

Virgil

Live your life as you see fit. That's not selfish. Selfish is to demand that others live their lives as you see fit.

Anthony De Mello

Our betters, religious and secular, like to instruct us on the virtues of universal brotherhood. But it is hard enough to overcome selfishness; harder still to overcome the ties of family and tribe and nation. How are we to feel for all humanity?

Charles Krauthammer

A bar of iron costs $5, made into horseshoes its worth is $12, made into needles its worth is $3500, made into balance springs for watches, its worth is $300,000. Your own value is determined also by what you are able to make of yourself.

Unknown

Never violate the sacredness of your individual self-respect.

Theodore Parker

In nothing do humans approach so nearly to the gods as doing good to others.

Cicero

One of the greatest struggles in modern times is self-confidence.

Tom Morris

There is only so much time in a day, and there are only so many people whom I can directly impact without sacrificing something valuable to myself. However, caring for myself does not obviate the humane and humanistic ideals that make up a significant part of humanity's potential: caring for the young, for our neighbor, for our community, for our country, and for the planet. Simply: I would want my eulogy to reflect my self-esteem and my individual accomplishments, but I would be remiss if I lived my life such that they were the entirety of my legacy.

Jason Merchey

Disciplining yourself to do what you know is right and importance, although difficult, is the highroad to pride, self-esteem, and personal satisfaction.

Margaret Thatcher

Men with faith can face martyrdom while men without it feel stricken when they are not invited to dinner.

Walter Lippmann

We cannot each single-handedly cure all of society's ills, but we can contribute more kindness, more caring, and more consciousness to what is happening inside of us and around us. And that will begin to make a difference.

Barbara De Angelis

Ayn Rand's rejection of the moral code that condemns selfishness as the ultimate evil and holds up self-sacrifice as the ultimate good is a radical challenge to received wisdom, an invitation to a startlingly new way to see the world.

Cathy Young

Without the help of selfishness, the human animal would never have developed. Egoism is the vine by which man hoisted himself out of the swamp and escaped from the jungle.

Blaise Cendrars

RESPONSIBILITY

ACCOUNTABILITY

Arthur Charchian

I recently spent four days in a training workshop focused on developing strong management skills in handling "problem" employees. For the last eight years I have worked for one of America's top companies, and every year it seems the company spends tens of millions of dollars on training programs that try to get managers, and ultimately employees, to do the right thing. These millions are spent with the intention of holding people accountable for their actions, for their work products, in customer relations, and to the company. Unfortunately, just like pork-barrel spending, these millions achieve very little in results. The reason: accountability is a value and values are learned, not trained.

Case in point: I have an employee who completely lacks accountability. At first it was amusing hearing excuses as to why something was not done. I felt like an elementary school teacher with a student who had an awful lot of neighborhood dogs hungry for homework assignments. Now, I am sickened each time the phone rings and I see her name appear on the screen, because it will never be a call affirming accountability for the latest screw up, but rather another baseless excuse.

Why have I not fired her? Ask the Human Resource folks who have me bound and gagged. The lack of accountability is so intolerable that I find myself being pulled into a cycle where I too would stop taking accountability. I try to fight the strong pull, but it takes more and more energy to stay out. Like a small planet, once the gravitational pull of a black hole has you, it's almost impossible to not to be dragged in.

> Our society has low expectations both of people and their value systems.

Luckily, when it comes to employment, another option exists. After eight years with what I had thought could be my "career company," I am the one who will be leaving. There is more honor in living a life of value than there is in trying to make six figures.

How did it come to this? Why would a company spend millions to train employees on values and accountability, only to provide safe haven for employees who run afoul of their training? Answer: The Lowest Common Denominator.

Our society has low expectations both of people and their value systems. When I was young, I was taught respect, honor, honesty, and, most of all, accountability. Now, respect is what will get you killed if a gang member thinks you did not show him any. Honor is only brought up in recruitment ads for the Army. Honesty disappeared with Internet profiles. Accountability does not exist when you don't have a solid base of values. It becomes a catch phrase used by the overpaid consultant sharing long-ago stories of being accountable to his client and what great results were had.

But I still have hope, because there is magic in being accountable and living in accord with one's values. Amazing things happen when people singularly and collectively show accountability. Accountable parents raise happy and healthy children. Accountable entrepreneurs run companies and model values that are emulated by their employees. Accountable customer service representatives make your day when you try for the third, and you swear last, time to get an issue resolved or question answered.

Here's to accountability!

© *Arthur Charchian*

About the Author

Arthur Charchian is a born again entrepreneur. After eight years battling in the corporate rat race, he has set out to complete a long list of life goals he had drafted in his youth. Among Arthur's goals is to complete his attorney licensing requirements, become a restaurateur, own a bar, run a charity, travel to Cuba, become a father, and live long enough to enjoy it all.

Arthur holds a Bachelor of Arts in Political Science and a Bachelor of Science in Biology from the University of California, Irvine. Arthur completed his Juris Doctorate at the University of San Diego.

Arthur most recently worked in the tobacco industry and has also ventured into diverse fields such as: real estate development, medical technology, internet start-ups, import/export, and asset recovery.

Arthur lives in Sierra Madre, California with his wife, Rena.

Nothing so completely baffles one who is full of trick and duplicity himself, than straightforward and simple integrity in another.

Charles Caleb Colton

Successful people are those who are clear about their values and who make choices and commitments consistent with them.

Jan Phillips

The political leaders - and the people who vote for them - have decided that it's a bigger priority to build another bomber than to educate our children. They would rather hold hearings on the depravity of a television show called Jackass than about their own depravity in neglecting our school and children and maintaining our title as Dumbest Country on Earth.

Michael Moore

Victim status is the modern promised land of absolution from personal responsibility.

Laura Schlesinger

Good words do not last long unless they amount to something. Words do not pay for my dead people.

Chief Joseph

When your goal is remaking the Middle East, you don't want to get stuck making it up as you go along.

Maureen Dowd

The church is only open on Sunday. And you can't keep asking Jesus to keep doing things for you.

Bill Cosby

You are responsible for your place in the culture, and you must make a contribution, and you must accept responsibility for what goes down on your watch. You have no excuse if you are a conservative not to be concerned about the environment. You are equally responsible. Future generations are not going to ask what political party you were in. They are going to ask, "What did you do about it?" when you knew the glaciers were melting.

Martin Sheen

What is virtue? It is to hold yourself to your fullest development as a person and as a responsible member of the human community.

Arthur Dobrin

Our national debt is at an all-time high – currently surpassing $8 trillion – and your personal share of that debt totals more than $27,000. While I would like to tell you that Congress is working overtime to remove that undeserved burden from the shoulders of American taxpayers, I am disappointed to report that Congress recently approved legislation that would raise our deficit (and your share of our skyrocketing debt) even more.

Susan Davis

If you like things easy, you'll have difficulty. If you like problems, you'll succeed.

Laotian proverb

My mother's bottom line was truth to her values. It meant bringing your heart and your humanity to work. I learned at an early age that these are as essential for business as they are for life.

Anita Roddick

My grandfather once told me that there were two kinds of people: those who do the work and those who take the credit. He told me to try to be in the first group; there was much less competition.

Indira Gandhi

Sometimes the best helping hand you can get is a good firm push.

Joan Thomas

You're not obligated to win. You're obligated to keep trying to do the best you can every day.

Marian Wright Edelman

FULFILLMENT

THE VALUE OF LIFE ITSELF

Janet Clemento

The morning I left for Naples, I woke before dawn and sat at the kitchen table as the sun rose over our lovely garden. I will never forget this moment. I watched in awe as a brilliant ray of golden light illuminated the limb of a tree…splashed itself on just one little dew-drenched section of the tree. I was so struck by this vision, so grateful for this "miracle" that I'd witnessed, sitting there in my kitchen, as I'd done on so many other mornings. But this day was different; this was my "Aha Moment," a moment in time when I actually saw the simplicity and splendor of life, a moment when I truly understood the profound gift of life, a moment when I experienced the natural order of things with my entire being. And I thought, *I am a very lucky woman, to have this life, this body, this vision, this awareness, this one moment in time.* I felt so much joy and gratitude that I forgot I was dying.

In the last ten years I have journeyed to places within myself I never knew existed.

To journey into one's self is to know your source. To face your own mortality is a terrifying and liberating experience. I've found that the process of self-exploration, the search for truth and knowledge is precisely what drives me to survive. And survive I have. Three go-rounds with cancer have led me to death's door and beyond. I've stepped over the threshold and come back to life again and again, stronger and more informed, each time. Each time it has been a choice. Each time, I've realized that when I fully accept responsibility for my life, my choices, and my thoughts, I can create a different set of circumstances. I've learned that when I am fully present in body, mind, and spirit and am willing to objectively take a look at and merge all three, a shift in thinking and dramatic cellular changes occur. I've also learned that what I choose to think directly affects my physical being; my physical being directly affects other beings and the entire ecological system...I, as do all of us, directly affect the whole. I've learned that healing is about being whole.

Now, more than ever, our world requires a fierce reality and mind shift, a different way of looking at life, looking at our lives and making the internal changes that will naturally create the changes necessary for global survival.

Now, more than ever, our world requires a fierce reality and mind shift, a different way of looking at life, looking at our lives and making the internal changes that will naturally create the changes necessary for global survival. Sustainability on the earth, evolutionary intelligence, creating peace and abundance, ending hunger and poverty, it all has to come from each and every one of us.

One Friday evening as I was walking home, I noticed the sky was absolutely apricot. This vibrant, electric apricot sky which made the greens in the palm trees look almost fluorescent. *Now this is a painting,* I thought. And then I realized that the sun was setting and part of the sky was that true sky blue. Blue, blue, blue with bright white clouds, and as I spun around to get the full effect of every inch of the sky that I could see from my place on the planet, right next to the apricot, right to the left of it, there was a deep purple cloud with a brilliant rainbow in the foreground. The colors were breathtaking; I just couldn't believe my eyes. All this color, all this beauty, right here in my parking lot, right here between the buildings. It was all right there and all I had to do was look up.

Just then a man and a woman were walking towards me and they said, "Hello." I just pointed up and said, "Did you see the rainbow?" The man said, "No, but thank you for calling it to our attention." I realized how easy it would have been to miss, if not for the turn of our heads. We all just stood there for a few moments until the setting sun took all the color home with it.

By western medical standards, I'm a walking miracle, but the real miracle is life itself. We decide to live it or not, to be a part of it or not, to accept responsibility for it or not.

It's so simple. So easy to miss.

© Janet Clemento

About the Author

Janet Clemento has over thirty years experience as a marketing, advertising, and branding consultant. Janet founded Creative Concepts by Clemento, an advertising and marketing firm in Chicago serving a wide variety of national and international clients. She is a gifted strategist and marketing visionary. Diagnosed with end-stage cancer in 1995, Janet orchestrated a remarkable recovery by using art therapy, expressive arts, complementary and allopathic medicine in her holistic approach to living with a life threatening disease.

If your compassion does not include yourself, it is incomplete.

Siddhartha Gautama

Look solely for happiness, and I doubt you'll find it. Forget about happiness, seek wisdom and goodness, and happiness will probably find you.

M. Scott Peck

If a physical fact can produce a psychological state, a psychological state can produce a physical fact.

Neville

I am a part of all I have met.

Alfred Tennyson

Your time or my time might be for hire, but time itself is not. Hence time is our most precious asset – and how we decide to use our time is the most important decision we can make.

Lou Marinoff

I will be conquered; I will not capitulate.

Samuel Johnson

You need to claim the events of your life to make yourself yours. When you truly possess all that you have been and done...you are fierce with reality.

Florida Scott Maxwell

I have learned that success is measured not so much by the position one has achieved in life as by the obstacles he has overcome.

Booker T. Washington

Spirituality, which inspires activism and similarly, politics, which move the spirit - drawing from the deep-seated place of our greatest longings for freedom - give meaning to our lives.

Cherríe Moraga

Whether we worship the sun or the "son," we always worship life itself; we worship ourselves.

Wes Nisker

Let him who would move the world first move himself.

Socrates

That old, bald cheater: Time.

Ben Jonson

Read not books alone, but man also; and chiefly thyself.

Thomas Fuller

These are times in which a genius would wish to live. It is not in the still calm of life, or the repose of a pacific station, that great characters are formed.

Abigail Adams

The grass isn't greener on the other side, it's greener where you water it.

Shawn Miller

In those first hours when I realized I had cancer, I never thought of my seat in the Senate, of my bank account, or of the destiny of the free world. My wife and I have not had a quarrel since my illness was diagnosed. I used to scold her about squeezing the toothpaste from the top instead of the bottom, about not catering sufficiently to my fussy appetite, about making up guest lists without consulting me, about spending too much on clothes. Now I am either unaware of such matters, or they seem irrelevant.

Richard Neuberger

Every hour we invest on the job is an hour not invested directly in our children, our mates, our community, our health, our spiritual development, our search for meaning, or our contribution to the larger life.

Vicki Robin

I love my life; if not, it would not be worth dying for.

Looking Glass

RESPONSIBILITY

BUY LOCAL MONTH
Thanksgiving to the New Year

Kevin Danaher

There is a growing grassroots movement focused on strengthening local economies and defending them against large corporations. This movement manifests itself on diverse tactical fronts: the anti-sprawl movement is increasingly effective at stopping WalMart and other corporate box stores from entering their communities; the local economy movement is passing a wide array of local legislation that brings greater control of the economy into local hands; the fair trade movement is channeling consumer spending in the global North into the hands of low-income producers in the global South; and the green economy movement is shifting more and more capital into enterprises that believe in doing business without harming nature.

Now imagine the popular power that would be unleashed if we could find a theme that would unite all these efforts and combine them with the mobilizing power of the global justice and peace movement that has proven its ability to mobilize millions of people to protest war and institutions such as the World Bank and the World Trade Organization. Is there a campaign that could unite these forces but express itself in a positive way that would gain support from mainstream Americans? Is there a campaign theme that could be decentralized around the country, and have an inherent critique of corporate power, yet be largely positive in its message, actions and impact?

Now imagine the popular power that would be unleashed if we could find a theme that would unite all these efforts and combine them with the mobilizing power of the global justice and peace movmements...

The answer to these questions is yes, if we can develop mass support for designating the month between Thanksgiving and Christmas as "Buy Local Month." During that month, individuals and organizations will pledge to shop only at locally-owned stores. The campaign can be decentralized in a viral way by spreading the ideas and organizing tools like shareware. Groups such as Global Exchange can produce educational materials explaining why it is important to fortify local economies by preventing money from being siphoned away by transnational corporations. The organizing for such a campaign can be decentralized and customized to local conditions and capabilities. More progressive areas can stress ecological and fair trade products; more conservative areas can focus on local ownership.

We would start a tradition that could grow each year and possibly spread around the world. It would show people the economic power of community organizing. Local merchants would love it and we could recruit them to help with publicity and donated materials. We would get support from associations of small enterprises (e.g., Hemp Industries Association, www.sprawl-busters.com, Co-op America Business Network).

In an election year, the campaign would have a positive impact no matter who wins the presidential election: if a Republican wins, the next month his corporate pals get hit with a big shift in Christmas spending away from the big corporations toward the "little people" (it favors Main Street over Wall Street); if the Democrat wins, it sends a shot across their bow economically to remind them who elected them. And it influences a new administration's thinking at the best time—right at the outset when they are formulating initial policies. If the Republican wins, people will need something positive to focus their political energies on. If the Democrats win, the Buy

Local Month gets people focused on a positive way to resist corporate power, and reminds them that the real mainstream issues are close to home and economic, not political in far-away Washington.

For the radicals out there: yes, we want to reduce consumption in general (the US constitutes 4.5 percent of the world's population, and we consume about 25 percent of the world's resources). But people do shop, whether we like it or not, and if we can get them to keep their money in the local economy instead of it going to large corporations, we can strike a blow for economic democracy—local enterprise is easier to control than transnational enterprise.

We would reach out to large constituencies such as the AFL-CIO and MoveOn.org, but we would also appeal to local Chambers of Commerce and small business sectors that have been hammered by the double whammy of economic recession and the invasion of the large box stores. We would promote it at the Green Festivals and try to get as much national publicity as possible. We would promote it at all the big demonstrations and political conventions. And, because it is a decentralized model, it does not need much money. Existing organizations can incorporate the pledge into their ongoing work with little additional effort or expense.

© *Kevin Danaher*

About the Author

Distinguished by his sense of humor and eloquence, Kevin Danaher is an exceptionally dynamic speaker. *The New York Times* calls him the "Paul Revere of globalization's woes."

As co-founder and director of public education for the human rights organization Global Exchange, Dr. Danaher has spoken at universities and for community organizations throughout the US, encouraging people to expand their political vision and providing viable ideas for action. He also emphasizes that a renewed commitment to social justice and human rights are essential for eliminating terrorism. A longtime critic of the so-called "free trade" agenda, Danaher explains how the US must work harder than ever with other countries to reduce poverty and inequality if we want the cooperation of the world's people in ending terrorism.

Having traveled worldwide, Danaher is familiar with the problems and prospects of economic development in many developing countries.

He conducts regular workshops on topics ranging from contrasting elite globalization with people's globalization, to organizing to replace the corporate economy with a locally controlled, green economy. Dr. Danaher is also the author and/or editor of eleven books, including his latest, *Insurrection: Citizen Challenges to Corporate Power* (with Jason Mark), and *Ten Reasons to Abolish the World Bank and the IMF*. Dr. Danaher is the co-executive producer of the Green Festivals (www.greenfestivals.org) and the executive director of the Global Citizen Center (www.globalcitizencenter.org).

There is no greater satisfaction for a just and well-meaning person than the knowledge that he has devoted his best energies to the service of the good cause.

Albert Einstein

We have four billion people on this planet who aren't getting two meals a day. None of us, no matter what our resources are, can cure that problem, but each of us can make a difference. Pick your spot where you want to make a difference.

Mark S. Albion

We're all born into this mess. We're not responsible for it. We're only responsible for every day we let it go on without changing things.

Gloria Steinem

Native Americans used to make decisions based on how it would affect seven generations ahead. How many of our politicians who vote against environmental protection are thinking of their children? Their grandchildren? Either they are stupid or they do not care about children.

Jane Goodall

If you don't run your own life, somebody else will.

John Atkinson

Few will have the greatness to bend history itself, but each of us can work to change a small portion of events, and in the total of all those acts will be written the history of this generation.

John F. Kennedy

We know what we need to do. We may not know all the answers, but we know enough of them that we have no excuse not to act. Too many focus on the difficulty of the problem merely as a means of evading responsibility.

Paul Wellstone

Every day I wake up and use my morals in every decision, action, and thought - just as my friends in red AND blue states do. No one party has "ownership" of these things.

Pat Maliff

WHAT ABU GHRAIB TAUGHT ME

Barbara Ehrenreich

The sight of women soldiers gleefully participating in the torture of Iraqi detainees taught this feminist a difficult but important lesson: A uterus is no substitute for a conscience. Even those people we might have thought were impervious to shame, like the secretary of Defense, admit that the photos of abuse in Iraq's Abu Ghraib prison turned their stomachs.

The photos did something else to me, as a feminist: They broke my heart. I had no illusions about the U.S. mission in Iraq—whatever exactly it is—but it turns out that I did have some illusions about women.

Of the seven U.S. soldiers now charged with sickening forms of abuse in Abu Ghraib, three are women: Spc. Megan Ambuhl, Pfc. Lynndie England and Spc. Sabrina Harman.

It was Harman we saw smiling an impish little smile and giving the thumbs-up sign from behind a pile of hooded, naked Iraqi men—as if to say, "Hi Mom, here I am in Abu Ghraib!" It was England we saw with a naked Iraqi man on a leash. If you were doing PR for Al Qaeda, you couldn't have staged a better picture to galvanize misogynist Islamic fundamentalists around the world.

Here, in these photos from Abu Ghraib, you have everything that the Islamic fundamentalists believe characterizes Western culture, all nicely arranged in one hideous image—imperial arrogance, sexual depravity...and gender equality.

A certain kind of feminism, or perhaps I should say a certain kind of feminist naiveté, died in Abu Ghraib.

Maybe I shouldn't have been so shocked. We know that good people can do terrible things under the right circumstances. This is what psychologist Stanley Milgram found in his famous experiments in the 1960s. In all likelihood, Ambuhl, England and Harman are not congenitally evil people. They are working-class women who wanted an education and knew that the military could be a stepping-stone in that direction. Once they had joined, they wanted to fit in.

And I also shouldn't be surprised because I never believed that women were innately gentler and less aggressive than men. Like most feminists, I have supported full opportunity for women within the military—1) because I knew women could fight, and 2) because the military is one of the few options around for low-income young people.

Although I opposed the 1991 Persian Gulf War, I was proud of our servicewomen and delighted that their presence irked their Saudi hosts. Secretly, I hoped that the presence of women would over time change the military, making it more respectful of other people and cultures, more capable of genuine peacekeeping. That's what I thought, but I don't think that anymore.

A certain kind of feminism, or perhaps I should say a certain kind of feminist naiveté, died in Abu Ghraib. It was a feminism that saw men as the perpetual perpetrators, women as the perpetual victims and male sexual violence against women as the root of all injustice. Rape has repeatedly been an instrument of war and, to some feminists, it was beginning to look as if war was an extension of rape. There seemed to be at least some evidence that male sexual sadism was connected to our species' tragic propensity for violence. That was before we had seen female sexual sadism in action.

But it's not just the theory of this naive feminism that was wrong. So was its strategy and vision for change. That strategy and vision rested on the assumption, implicit or stated outright, that women were morally superior to men. We had a lot of debates over whether it was biology or conditioning that gave women the moral edge—or simply the experience of being a woman in a sexist culture. But the assumption of superiority, or at least a lesser inclination toward cruelty and violence, was more or less beyond debate. After all, women do most of the caring work in our culture, and in polls are consistently less inclined toward war than men.

I'm not the only one wrestling with that assumption today. Mary Jo Melone, a columnist for the St. Petersburg (Fla.) Times, wrote on May 7: "I can't get that picture of England [pointing at a hooded Iraqi man's genitals] out of my head because this is not how women are expected to behave. Feminism taught me 30 years ago that not only had women gotten a raw deal from men, we were morally superior to them."

If that assumption had been accurate, then all we would have had to do to make the world a better place—kinder, less violent, more just—would have been to assimilate into what had been, for so many centuries, the world of men. We would fight so that women could become the generals, CEOs, senators, professors and opinion-makers—and that was really the only fight we had to undertake. Because once they gained power and authority, once they had achieved a critical mass within the institutions of society, women would naturally work for change. That's what we thought, even if we thought it unconsciously—and it's just not true. Women can do the unthinkable.

You can't even argue, in the case of Abu Ghraib, that the problem was that there just weren't enough women in the military hierarchy to stop the abuses. The prison was directed by a woman, Gen. Janis Karpinski. The top U.S. intelligence officer in Iraq, who also was responsible for reviewing the status of detainees before their release, was Major Gen. Barbara Fast. And the U.S. official ultimately responsible for managing the occupation of Iraq since October was Condoleezza Rice. Like Donald H. Rumsfeld, she ignored repeated reports of abuse and torture until the undeniable photographic evidence emerged.

What we have learned from Abu Ghraib, once and for all, is that a uterus is not a substitute for a conscience. This doesn't mean gender equality isn't worth fighting for for its own sake. It is. If we believe in democracy, then we believe in a woman's right to do and achieve whatever men can do and achieve, even the bad things. It's just that gender equality cannot, all alone, bring about a just and peaceful world.

In fact, we have to realize, in all humility, that the kind of feminism based on an assumption of female moral superiority is not only naive; it also is a lazy and self-indulgent form of feminism. Self-indulgent because it assumes that a victory for a woman—a promotion, a college degree, the right to serve alongside men in the military—is by its very nature a victory for all of humanity. And lazy because it assumes that we have only one struggle—the struggle for gender equality—when in fact we have many more.

The struggles for peace and social justice and against imperialist and racist arrogance, cannot, I am truly sorry to say, be folded into the struggle for gender equality.

What we need is a tough new kind of feminism with no illusions. Women do not change institutions simply by assimilating into them, only by consciously deciding to fight for change. We need a feminism that teaches a woman to say no—not just to the date rapist or overly insistent boyfriend but, when necessary, to the military or corporate hierarchy within which she finds herself.

In short, we need a kind of feminism that aims not just to assimilate into the institutions that men have created over the centuries, but to infiltrate and subvert them.

To cite an old, and far from naive, feminist saying: "If you think equality is the goal, your standards are too low." It is not enough to be equal to men, when the men are acting like beasts. It is not enough to assimilate. We need to create a world worth assimilating into.

© Barbara Ehrenreich

About the Author

Barbara Ehrenrcich is a widely published essayist and author. She received the Sydney Hillman Award for Journalism for her bestseller, *Nickel and Dimed* (Owl Books, 2002).

Ms. Ehrenreich is a columnist for *The Progressive* and a frequent contributor to *Time, Harper's Magazine, The New Republic, The Nation*, and *The New York Times Magazine*. She has authored and co-authored the following books: *Blood Rites: Origins and History of the Passions of War* (Metropolitan, 1997), *The Worst Years of Our Lives: Irreverent Notes from a Decade of Greed* (Random House Inc., 1990). *Fear of Falling: The Inner Life of the Middle Class* (Pantheon Books, 1989), *The Snarling Citizen* (Farrar, Straus & Giroux, 1995), *The Hearts of Men: American Dreams and the Flight from Commitment* (Anchor Books/Doubleday, 1983), T*he American Health Empire: Power, Profits and Politics* (Vintage Books, 1971), *Witches, Midwives and Nurses: A History of Women Healers* (Feminist Press, 1972), *For Her Own Good: 150 Years of the Experts' Advice to Women* (Anchor Press, 1978), *Re-Making Love: The Feminization of Sex* (Random House Inc., 1986), *The Mean Season: The Attack on Social Welfare* (Pantheon Books, 1987), and the novel, *Kipper's Game* (Farrar, Straus & Giroux, 1993). She has most recently co-edited a collection of essays with Arlie Russell Hochschild called *Global Woman* (Metropolitan, 2002).

Ms. Ehrenreich has a PhD in Biology as well as honorary degrees from Reed College, the State University of New York at Old Westbury, the College of Wooster in Ohio, John Jay College, University of Massachusetts-Lowell, and La Trobe University in Melbourne, Australia.

All that is necessary for the triumph of evil is for good men to do nothing.

attributed to Edmund Burke

We women have great influence, and we need to become warriors of peace, guardians of love, and agents of kindness. The result can only be the great satisfaction of creating happiness, and this is contagious.

Adriana de Gaspar de Alba

Whatever happens to one people affects all people; I plead against in difference.

Elie Wiesel

In addition to the "CYA mentality" that so many in the military are taught from the earliest days in boot camp or the war college, it is a diminishing of the enemy that makes Abu Ghraib possible. The paucity of respect, tolerance, and kindness that marks our treatment of prisoners in this so-called "war on terror" makes me feel like this is more like a "war on civility," "war on honor," and "war on our image abroad."

Jason Merchey

If Democrats aren't going to stand up to an executive who disdains the other branches of government and doesn't worry about trampling on the rights of innocent Americans, what do we stand for?

Russ Feingold

Why were we able to put hundreds of thousands of troops and support personnel in Saudi Arabia within a few months to fight Saddam Hussein when we are unable to mobilize hundreds of teachers or doctors and nurses and social workers for desperately underserved inner cities and rural areas to fight the tyranny of poverty and ignorance and child neglect and abuse?

Marian Wright Edelman

The dilemma of Abu Ghraib is an old and pervasive one: Do we set aside the restraints of chivalry and honor in order to "get the job done" in the most effective way possible?

Scott Farrell

We can conceive of a world in which God corrected the abuse of free will by his creatures, so that a wooden beam became soft as grass when used as a weapon. But such a world would be one in which wrong actions were impossible, and therefore freedom of the will would be void.

C. S. Lewis

The other day I drove by a car that had the bumper sticker IF YOU'RE NOT OUTRAGED, YOU'RE NOT PAYING ATTENTION. The question is where outrage leads you. Destroying people to save mankind is not an option.

Anna Quindlen

Injustice anywhere is a threat to justice everywhere.

Martin Luther King, Jr.

It is our choices that show what we truly are, far more than our abilities.

J. K. Rowling

Moral maturity entails making our own well-reasoned moral decisions rather than simply following the dictates of the crowd or going with our selfish desires.

Judith A. Boss

Let's create a world in which, when people see the Stars and Stripes, they will think of us as the people who brought peace to the world, who brought good-paying jobs to all its citizens and clean water for the world to drink. In anticipation of that day, I am putting my flag out today, with hope and with pride.

Michael Moore

This country's constitution never stated that we would over throw regimes, nor conquer countries. Nor ought we to kill and maim innocent women, children, and destroy their livelihood, their homes. Until the warlords in our government leave office, there can be no peace in this world.

Gil Haimson

RESPECT

SPARE THE ROD

Riane Eisler

What is the link between intimate violence and war? Why do societies that treat women with respect fare better? A movement challenges traditions of violence in the family.

Every day, the headlines assault us with death and destruction. We read of brutal attacks that maim and kill civilians and even target children. The torture of prisoners and beheading of hostages in Iraq. The carnage in Sudan and the Congo. Despite anti-war protests by millions of people, despite promises by politicians that preemptive wars will bring security, despite a global peace movement teaching nonviolent conflict resolution, war and terrorism continue unabated. What fuels this firestorm of violence—and how can we stop it?

We're sometimes told violence is "human nature." But findings from sociology, psychology, and neuroscience show that a major factor in whether people commit violence is what happens during a child's early formative years. As research from Harvard University and Maclean Hospital shows, the brain neurochemistry of abused children tends to become programmed for fight-or-flight, and thus for violence.

When children experience violence, or observe violence against their mothers, they learn it's acceptable—even moral—to use force to impose one's will on others. Indeed, the only way they can make sense of violence coming from those who are supposed to love them is that it must be moral.

Terrorism and chronic warfare are responses to life in societies in which the only perceived choices are dominating or being dominated. These violent responses are characteristic of cultures where this view of relations is learned early on through traditions of coercion, abuse, and violence in parent-child and gender relations.

It's not coincidental that throughout history the most violently despotic and warlike societies have been those in which violence, or the threat of violence, is used to maintain domination of parent over child and man over woman. It's not coincidental that the 9/11 terrorists came from cultures where women and children are terrorized into submission. Nor is it coincidental that Afghanistan under the Taliban in many ways resembled the European Middle Ages—when witch-burnings, public drawings and quarterings, despotic rulers, brutal violence against children, and male violence against women were considered moral and normal. Neither is it coincidental that, in the U.S. today, those pushing "crusades" against "evil enemies" oppose equal rights for women and advocate harshly punitive childrearing.

For much of recorded history, religion has been used to justify, even command, violence against women and children. The subjugation of women and children is still the central message of many fundamentalist religious leaders today—leaders who, not coincidentally, also advocate "holy wars."

Many religious and secular leaders have spoken out against international terrorism and wars of aggression. But we urgently need to hear their voices raised also against the intimate violence that sparks, fuels, and refuels international violence. Far too many customs and public policies still accept, condone, and even promote violence against women and children.

I'm passionately involved in an initiative to change this. The Spiritual Alliance to Stop Intimate Violence (SAIV) aims to end violence against women and children by engaging the moral authority of spiritual and religious leaders. More than 80 percent of the world's people identify with a religious faith and look to religious leaders for guidance. SAIV was formed to encourage enlightened spiritual and religious leaders to speak out against intimate violence as strongly as they do against terrorism and war. This is essential, not only for the many millions whose lives are taken or blighted by terror in the home, but for us all, because intimate violence teaches that it is acceptable to use force to impose one's will on others.

SAIV has gathered a council of leaders who are prepared to break the silence on this pivotal issue.

Among them are Prince El Hassan bin Talal of Jordan; A.T. Ariyatne, the leader of the Sarvodaya peace movement of Sri Lanka; Ela Gandhi, granddaughter of Mohandas Gandhi; Betty Williams, Irish Nobel Peace Laureate; Bill Schulz, director of Amnesty International; Janet Chisholm, chair of the Episcopal Peace Fellowship; Irfan Ahmad Khan, president of the World Council of Muslims for Interfaith Relations; Kalon Rinchen Khando, Tibetan Minister of Education for the Dalai Lama; Harvey Cox, professor at the Harvard Divinity School; Jane Goodall; and Deepak Chopra. Under the direction of Jim Kenney, former director of the Council for a Parliament of the World's Religions, SAIV is reaching out to religious and spiritual leaders, health professionals, policy makers, teachers, and parents to discuss the link between intimate and international violence.

Cultures of war or peace

Surprisingly, none of our conventional social categories takes the relationship of intimate violence and international violence into account. Indeed, classifications such as religious versus secular, right versus left, East versus West, and developed versus developing do not tell us whether a culture's beliefs and institutions—from the family, education, and religion to politics and economics—support relations based on nonviolence and mutual respect, or rigid rankings backed up by fear and force.

In studying societies across cultures and epochs, looking at both the public and personal spheres, I discovered configurations that transcend conventional categories. Since there were no names for these configurations, I coined the terms partnership model and dominator or domination model.

Hitler's Germany (a technologically advanced, Western, rightist society), Stalin's USSR (a secular leftist society), fundamentalist Iran (an Eastern religious society), and Idi Amin's Uganda (a tribalist society) were all violent and repressive. There are obvious differences between them. But they all share the core configuration of the domination model. They are characterized by top-down rankings in the family and state or tribe maintained through physical, psychological, and economic control; the rigid ranking of the male half of humanity over the female half; and a high degree of culturally accepted abuse and violence—from child- and wife-beating to chronic warfare.

How a society structures the primary human relations—between the female and male halves of humanity, and between them and their children—is central to whether it is violent and inequitable or peaceful and equitable

The partnership model, on the other hand, is based on a democratic and egalitarian structure in both family and state or tribe and on equal partnership between women and men. There is little violence, because rigid rankings of domination, which can be maintained only through violence, are not part of the culture. Because women have higher status, stereotypically feminine values have social priority.

(When I say stereotypically, I mean traits stereotypically classified by gender to fit the domination model. In this model, "masculine" traits and activities, such as toughness and "heroic" violence, are more valued than nonviolence and caregiving, which are associated with the half of humanity barred from power.)

Prosperity and rights

Where the rights of women and children are protected, nations thrive. In fact, a study of 89 nations by the organization I direct, the Center for Partnership Studies, shows that the status of women can be a better predictor of the general quality of life than a nation's financial wealth. Kuwait and France, for example, had identical GDPs (Gross Domestic Product). But quality of life indicators are much higher in France, where the status of women is higher, while infant mortality was twice as high in Kuwait.

The social investment in caring for children characteristic of the partnership model actually contributes to prosperity. Finland is a good example. Like other Nordic nations, Finland's economy is a mix of central planning and free enterprise. In the early 20th century, Finland was very poor. That changed as the country invested in its human capital through childcare (both daycare and allowances for families), healthcare, family planning, and paid parental leave. Like other Nordic nations, Finland ranks near the top in United Nations Human Development Reports—far ahead of the United States, Saudi Arabia, and other wealthier nations. In all the Nordic nations, a much higher than average percentage of legislative seats are filled by women (35 to 40 percent), strong men's movements disentangle "masculinity" from violence, and governments discourage or legally prohibit physical discipline of children in families. These nations also pioneered education for peace, have low crime rates, mediate international disputes, and invest heavily in aid to developing nations.

We see similar patterns of nonviolence coupled with respect for women and children among the Minangkabau, an agrarian culture of 2.5 million people in Sumatra, where, anthropologist Peggy Sanday reports, violence isn't part of childrearing, women aren't subordinate to men, and nurturance is part of both the female and male roles. The Teduray, a tribal culture in the Philippines, also don't discipline children through violence, nor is violence integral to male socialization. As anthropologist Stuart Schlegel writes in Wisdom from a Rain Forest, the Teduray value women and men equally, and elders—both female and male—mediate disputes.

An important lesson from these cultures is this: How a society structures the primary human relations—between the female and male halves of humanity, and between them and their children—is central to whether it is violent and inequitable or peaceful and equitable.

Countering domination and violence

The "culture wars" launched in the U.S. by the fundamentalist right give special attention to relations between women and men and parents and children. Their fully integrated political agenda centers on reimposing a male-headed family where women must render unpaid services (with no independent access to income) and children learn that orders must be strictly obeyed on pain of severe punishment.

Progressives urgently need a social and political agenda that takes into account both the public sphere of politics and economics, and the personal sphere of family and other intimate relations. Only through an integrated progressive agenda that takes into account both the personal and public spheres can we build foundations for cultures of peace rather than war.

Reprinted from Yes! A Journal of Positive Futures, PO Box 10818, Bainbridge Island, WA 98110. Subscriptions: 800-937-4451 Web: www.yesmagazine.org.

About the Author

Riane Eisler is author of the international bestseller *The Chalice and The Blade*. Her newest book, *The Power of Partnership*, won the Nautilus Award in 2003. She is president of the Center for Partnership Studies (www.partnershipway.org) and co-founder of the Spiritual Alliance to Stop Intimate Violence (www.saiv.net).

When you carry out acts of kindness you get a wonderful feeling inside. It is as though something inside your body responds and says, yes, this is how I ought to feel.

Harold Kushner

For a nation to be thoroughly respected, the perception of its strength needs to be matched by a perception of its goodness. It helps to be thought of as just, generous, conscientious, mindful of the opinion of others, even a little humble.

Robert Wright

Competition and individualism appear to be basic human needs, and society benefits from them. But they need to be tempered and balanced by care.

Pearl M. Oliner & Samuel P. Oliner

All the bloodshed, all the anger, all the weapons, all the greed, all the armies, all the missiles, all the symbols of our fear – there is a deeper wave than this rising in the world...Love is the seventh wave.

Gordon Sumner

Violence attempts to constrain the other's freedom, to force him to act in the way we desire, but with ultimate lack of concern, with indifference to the other's own existence or destiny.

R. D. Laing

The most fundamental kind of love, which underlies all types of love, is brotherly love. By this I mean the sense of responsibility, care, respect, knowledge of any other human being, the wish to further his life. This is the kind of love the Bible speaks of when it says: love thy neighbor as thyself.

Erich Fromm

A man, to be greatly good, must imagine intensely and comprehensively; he must put himself in the place of another and of many others; the pleasures and pains of his species must become his own.

Percy Bysshe Shelley

My interest in respect is fueled by powerful memories of my parents' empathy and compassion.

Sara Lawrence-Lightfoot

MODESTY

THE GARDEN OF SIMPLICITY

Duane Elgin

Simplicity of living is not a new idea. It has deep roots in history and finds expression in all of the world's wisdom traditions. More than two thousand years ago, in the same historical period that Christians were saying "Give me neither poverty nor wealth," (Proverbs 30:8), the Taoists were asserting "He who knows he has enough is rich" (Lao Tzu), Plato and Aristotle were proclaiming the importance of the "golden mean" of a path through life with neither excess nor deficit, and the Buddhists were encouraging a "middle way" between poverty and mindless accumulation. Clearly, the simple life is not a new social invention. What is new are the radically changing ecological, social, and psycho-spiritual circumstances of the modern world.

The push toward simpler ways of living was clearly described in 1992 when over 1,600 of the world's senior scientists, including a majority of the living Nobel laureates in the sciences, signed an unprecedented "Warning to Humanity." In this historic statement, they declared that, "human beings and the natural world are on a collision course...that may so alter the living world that it will be unable to sustain life in the manner that we know." They concluded that: "A great change in our stewardship of the earth and the life on it is required, if vast human misery is to be avoided and our global home on this planet is not to be irretrievably mutilated."

Roughly a decade later came a related warning from 100 Nobel Prize winners who said that "the most profound danger to world peace in the coming years will stem not from the irrational acts of states or individuals but from the legitimate demands of the world's dispossessed." As these two warnings by the world's elder scientists indicate, powerful adversity trends (such as global climate change, the depletion of key resources such as water and cheap oil, a burgeoning population, and a growing gap between the rich and poor) are converging into a whole-systems crisis, creating the possibility of an evolutionary crash within this generation. If we are to create instead an evolutionary bounce or leap forward, it will surely include a shift toward simpler, more sustainable and satisfying ways of living.

> Most people are not choosing to live more simply from a feeling of sacrifice; rather, they are seeking deeper sources of satisfaction than are being offered by a high stress, consumption-obsessed society.

Although the pushes toward simpler ways of living are strong, the pulls toward this way of life seem equally compelling. Most people are not choosing to live more simply from a feeling of sacrifice; rather, they are seeking deeper sources of satisfaction than are being offered by a high stress, consumption-obsessed society. To illustrate, while real incomes doubled in the US in the past generation, the percentage of the population reporting they are very happy has remained unchanged (roughly one-third) and, at the same time, divorce rates have doubled and teen suicide rates have tripled. A whole generation has tasted the fruits of an affluent society and has discovered that money does not buy happiness. In the search for satisfaction, millions of people are not only "downshifting" or pulling back from the rat race, they are also "upshifting" or moving ahead into a life that is, though materially more modest, rich with family, friends, community, creative work in the world, and a soulful connection with the universe.

In response to the unique pushes and pulls of modern conditions, in the United States and a dozen or so other "postmodern" nations, a trend toward simpler living has evolved from a fringe movement in the 1960s to a respected part of the mainstream culture in the early 2000s. Now glossy magazines tout the simple life from the newsstands across the US while it has become a popular theme on major television talk shows. Surveys show a distinct subpopulation—conservatively estimated at 10 percent of the US adult population or 20 million people—is pioneering a way of life that is outwardly more sustainable and inwardly more spiritual.

Importantly, the simple life is not simple. Many, diverse expressions of simplicity of living are flowering in response to the challenges and opportunities of our times. To present a more realistic picture of the scope and expression of this way of life for today's complex world, here are ten different approaches that I see thriving in a "garden of simplicity. " Although there is overlap among them, each expression of simplicity seems sufficiently distinct to warrant a separate category. So there would be no favoritism in listing, they are placed in alphabetical order based on the brief name I associated with each.

1. **Choiceful Simplicity:** Simplicity means choosing our path through life consciously, deliberately, and of our own accord. As a path that emphasizes freedom, a choiceful simplicity also means staying focused, diving deep, and not being distracted by consumer culture. It means consciously organizing our lives so that we give our "true gifts" to the world—which is to give the essence of ourselves. As Emerson said, "The only true gift is a portion of yourself."

2. **Compassionate Simplicity:** Simplicity means to feel such a sense of kinship with others that we "choose to live simply so that others may simply live." A compassionate simplicity means feeling a bond with the community of life and drawn toward a path of reconciliation—with other species and future generations as well as, for example, between those with great differences of wealth and opportunity. A compassionate simplicity is a path of cooperation and fairness that seeks a future of mutually assured development for all.

LIVING A LIFE OF VALUE

3. **Ecological Simplicity:** Simplicity means to choose ways of living that touch the Earth more lightly and that reduce our ecological footprint. This life path remembers our deep roots in the natural world. It means to experience our connection with the ecology of life in which we are immersed and to balance our experience of the human-created environments with time in nature. It also means to celebrate the experience of living through the miracle of the Earth's seasons. A natural simplicity feels a deep reverence for the community of life on Earth and accepts that the non-human realms of plants and animals have their dignity and rights as well the human. This is an ecological simplicity that appreciates our deep interconnection with the web of life and is mobilized by threats to its well-being (such as climate change, species-extinction, and resource depletion).

4. **Economic Simplicity:** Simplicity means there are many forms of "right livelihood" in the rapidly growing market for healthy and sustainable products and services of all kinds—from home-building materials and energy systems to foods. When the need for a sustainable infrastructure in developing nations is combined with the need to retrofit and redesign the homes, cities, workplaces, and transportation systems of "developed" nations, then it is clear that an enormous expansion of highly purposeful economic activity can unfold.

5. **Elegant Simplicity:** Simplicity means that the way we live our lives represents a work of unfolding artistry. As Gandhi said, "My life is my message." In this spirit, an elegant simplicity is an understated, organic aesthetic that contrasts with the excess of consumerist lifestyles. Drawing from influences ranging from Zen to the Quakers, it celebrates natural materials and clean, functional expressions, such as are found in many of the hand-made arts and crafts from this community. Simplicity is a path of beauty.

6. **Family Simplicity:** A growing number of people are opting out of the fast track of life out of concern for the well-being of their children and the integrity of the family. In seeing our consumer society trying to take possession of our children's minds from an early age,

people are seeking to reduce some of the clutter and complexity they are otherwise bombarded with each day.

7. **Frugal Simplicity:** Simplicity means that, by cutting back on spending that is not truly serving our lives, and by practicing skillful management of our personal finances, we can achieve greater financial independence. Frugality and careful financial management bring increased financial freedom and the opportunity to more consciously choose our path through life. Living with less also decreases the impact of our consumption upon the Earth and frees resources for others.

8. **Political Simplicity:** Simplicity means organizing our collective lives in ways that enable us to live more lightly and sustainably on the Earth which, in turn, involves changes in nearly every area of public life—from transportation and education to the design of our homes, cities, and workplaces. The politics of simplicity is also a media politics as the mass media are the primary vehicle for reinforcing—or transforming—the mass consciousness of consumerism. Political simplicity is a politics of conversation and community that builds from local, face-to-face connections to networks of relationships emerging around the world through the enabling power of television and the Internet.

9. **Soulful Simplicity:** Simplicity means to approach life as a meditation and to cultivate our experience of intimate connection with all that exists. A spiritual presence infuses the world and, by living simply, we can more directly awaken to the living universe that surrounds and sustains us, moment by moment. Soulful simplicity is more concerned with consciously tasting life in its unadorned richness than with a particular standard or manner of material living. In cultivating a soulful connection with life, we tend to look beyond surface appearances and bring our interior aliveness into relationships of all kinds.

10. **Uncluttered Simplicity:** Simplicity means taking charge of a life that is too busy, too stressed, and too fragmented. An uncluttered simplicity means cutting back on trivial distractions, both material and non-material, and focusing on the essentials—whatever those

may be for each of our unique lives. As Thoreau said, "Our life is frittered away by detail...Simplify, simplify." Or, as Plato wrote, "In order to seek one's own direction, one must simplify the mechanics of ordinary, everyday life."

As these ten approaches illustrate, the growing culture of simplicity contains a flourishing garden of expressions whose great diversity—and intertwined unity—are creating a resilient and hardy ecology of learning about how to live more sustainable and meaningful lives. As with other ecosystems, it is the diversity of expressions that fosters flexibility, adaptability, and resilience. Because there are so many pathways of great relevance into the garden of simplicity, this cultural movement appears to have enormous potential to grow—particularly if it is nurtured and cultivated in the mass media as a legitimate, creative, and promising life-path for the future.

Our evolutionary intelligence is now being tested. The choices made within this generation will reverberate into the deep future. Although human societies have confronted major hurdles throughout history, the challenges of our era are genuinely unique. Never before have so many people been called upon to make such sweeping changes in so little time. Never before has the entire human family been entrusted with the task of working together to imagine and then consciously build a sustainable, just, and compassionate future. Seeds growing for the past generation in the garden of simplicity are now blossoming into the springtime of their relevance for the Earth. May the garden flourish!

© Duane Elgin, Revised 9/05

About the Author

Duane Elgin has more than twenty-five years of experience in exploring the broad sweep of human evolution and in working for a sustainable and soulful future. This has taken various forms, including work as an author, speaker, researcher, and media activist. Duane is the author of *Awakening Earth* (Morrow, 1993) and *Voluntary Simplicity* (Morrow, 1981, revised 1993).

I believe we can accomplish great and profitable things within a new conceptual framework...one that values our legacy, honors diversity, and feeds ecosystems and societies...It is time for designs that are creative, abundant, prosperous, and intelligent from the start.

William J. McDonough

In order to achieve true sustainablility for all life forms, we must put our primary needs of fresh air, clean water, and biological and cultural diversity above corporate profit.

Julia Hill

Humanism, in all its simplicity, is the only genuine spirituality.

Albert Schweitzer

Does anyone really need a Hummer for city traffic? What's next, "Honey, let's take a tank to the P.T.A. meeting tonight."

Bill Maher

The simple fact is that our current unsustainable, "more-is-better" culture undermines any hope of achieving justice - at home or abroad. We often hear about how the United States consumes a vastly disproportionate amount of resources relative to the rest of the world. Americans are building bigger houses, driving bigger cars, and consuming more and more of everything than just about anyone else anywhere.

Nydia M. Velázquez

As the country that benefits most from global economic integration, it is our job to make sure that globalization is sustainable, and that advances are leading declines for as many people as possible, in as many countries as possible, on as many days as possible.

Thomas L. Friedman

When we recognize that we are dependent on other species - the oxygen from the trees, the food that earthworms and millions of soil organisms provide for us sustainably, our paradigms shift to taking care of biodiversity instead of wiping it out in the name of progress and development.

Vandana Shiva

Life is enriched by aspiration and effort, rather than by acquisition and accumulation.

Scott Nearing

SELF-AWARENESS

ACHIEVING SELF-ACTUALIZATION

Albert Ellis

A chieving emotional health and self-actualization are goals that over-lap but are not quite the same. As REBT shows, when you are anx-ious, depressed, enraged, and self-hating, you strive for certain healthy goals, such as unconditional self-acceptance, unconditional other-acceptance, and high frustration tolerance. But even if you achieve these aims and are hardly ever miserable, you may be far from happy or self-actu-alizing. So REBT usually helps you, first, to be less disturbed, and second, to discover what you really enjoy in life. It then helps you to get more of that and to discover what you really dislike, and helps you to get less of that. Seems simple, but it has, as this paper points out, its complications. Other authorities on self-actualization—including Abe Maslow, Carl Rogers, S.I. Hayakawa, and Ted Crawford—have given imperfect answers to solving this problem. So here is the imperfect REBT answer!

Critique of Self-Actualization Theories

The self-actualization theories of Abraham Maslow, Carl Rogers, and other authorities have been seriously questioned by a number of critics. I shall now consider some their major objections to see how Rational Emotive Behavior Therapy theory and practice deals with them.

Is self-actualization too individualistic, self-seeking, and indulgent? Maslow's concept of self-actualization has often been attacked for these reasons. This is partly true, but the REBT theory includes both self-interest and social interest. Because humans choose to live with others, their morality, emotional health, and self-actualization had better always include their being quite concerned about the present and future welfare of others and their entire social group. Their very survival—especially in a nuclear age—seems to require a great deal of social interest.

M. Daniels questions whether deciding to pick self actualizing goals defeats people's spontaneous ways of living in a more fully-functioning manner. No, says REBT, not if people adopt an and/also and not merely an either/or approach. One of the main goals of actualizing can be to seek more spontaneous ways of living, and one main by-product of spontaneously (and risk-takingly) trying new pursuits is to discover new enjoyments and then to make re-achieving them a future goal. Experimentation partly is goal-seeking, and goal-seeking partly is spontaneously experimenting with new endeavors. They can both be spontaneous and planned. I once planned to unspontaneously force myself to speak in public in order to overcome my public speaking phobia, and as I did so, I began to spontaneously enjoy what I was doing. As a teenager, I spontaneously had my first orgasm without ever realizing that I was about to bring it on, and thereafter I plotted and schemed to bring on more and more of them!

Do people have an essential "real self" which they can discover and actualize? Maslow, Karen Horney, and to some extent Carl Rogers hold that people have an underlying biological or transpersonal "real" or "true" self that they can discover and actualize. But, as Daniels points out, their biological real self is somewhat restrictive, and REBT holds that it is quite different for all individuals and that, with experimentation and hard work, it can even be significantly changed. Thus, people with strong biological tendencies to be weak-willed, undisciplined, or irrational can learn and work hard to overcome their unfulfilling handicaps.

REBT holds that several human aspirations and goals—such as sex, love, gustatory, and meaning-oriented desires—are at least partly (and individualistically) motivated but that they are also strongly socially and environmentally influenced; and, they can also be distinctly—and consciously—self-developed and modified. REBT is highly skeptical that humans have any "true" transpersonal, transcendental, or mystical selves, though they are certainly often born and reared with strong propensities to think or experience that they do. REBT acknowledges that a belief in religion, God, mysticism, Pollyannaism, and irrationality may help people at times. But it also points out that such beliefs often do much more harm than good and block a more fully functioning life. Daniels rightly observes that the biological "real" self of Horney, Maslow, and Rogers is supposed to be "truer" and "better" than a socially acquired conforming self, but that this idea "leads to the denial of constructive social involvement, to existential isolation and social involvement—not either/or. It says that because people choose to live in a social group (family, community, nation) and not to be asocial hermits, they need to learn to care for themselves and for others, and preserve—and help actualize—themselves as well as their sociality. They can choose—or not choose—to put themselves first in some respects, but preferably should put others—particularly some selected other—a close second.

Maslow held that self-actualizing people are biologically and personally motivated (have a "real" self), and somewhat contradictorily, held that they are also motivated by nonpersonal, objective, and universal "values of being."[1] He also saw self-transcendence as altruistic and socially interested, and devoted to mystical pathways that transcend human consciousness and have a nonbodily, "spirituals" aspect. REBT holds that people can be biologically-inclined to be self-altruistic and also biologically and sociologically inclined to be altruistic and socially involved. So it unites or integrates Maslow's and Roger's individualistic and socialized goals.

REBT, however, sees no evidence that humans ever truly transcend their humanity and develop a transpersonal, transcendental, or superhuman "self" that achieves "higher, miraculous states of consciousness." They frequently aspire to such mystical states, and devoutly believe that they experience them. But they are probably self-deluded and do not really achieve Absolute Truth, godliness, or completely nonhuman consciousness. So, however much human mystics experience Nirvana, selflessness, unity with the Universe, or similar "transpersonal" states, it is unlikely (though not impossible) that they really have superhuman powers and very unlikely that their special state of altered consciousness is "better" than the usual state of consciousness. In some ways it appears to be a deficient, Pollyannaish, unauthentic state!

A. McIntyre partly concurs with L. Geller that moral consensus and agreed upon self-actualization are based on conflicting premises that are mainly emotive and include assertions of personal preferences or imply some more arbitrary ideal that should be achieved but is never really agreed upon. Again, this seems to be true, but mainly means that no single "ideal" set of characteristics will suffice for all people at all times, but that they can still select "ideal" (or "nonideal") traits and then experiment (which is almost the REBT essence of health and actualization) to determine whether they are suitable.

McIntyre says that because self-actualization involves a goal, as we search for progress in achieving it we discover more about it and change it. Daniels agrees that "a theory of self-actualization . . . can therefore only be particularly accurate; it is forever vague and incomplete."[2] REBT adds that not only the theory but also the practice of self-fulfillment is almost by necessity experimental, changing, and incomplete.

Gellar holds that it is meaningless to speak of general self-actualization, because it is highly multidimensional and involves the pursuit of excellence or enjoyment in whatever ways each individual chooses to desire and emphasize. This argument has much truth to it, since both "healthy" and "enjoyable," not to mention "maximally enjoyable" pursuits, differ from culture to culture and from individual to individual in each culture. "Self-actualizing," in fact, implies to some degree being chosen and actualized by each individual self. However, because almost all humans have many similar biological tendencies (e.g., to like to perform well and be approved of by others) and because most cultures abet many of these tendencies (though, of course, in different ways), the REBT hypothesis is that much of the time most contemporary people will lead both a "healthier" and "more enjoyable" life if they achieve several of the "self-actualizing" characteristics listed in this chapter.

Does self-actualization mean "peak experiences" and "altered states of consciousness"? Maslow sometimes implied that maximum self-actualization is achieved by what he called "peak experiences," though at other time he said that they "can come at any time in life to any person." Other writers have identified self-actualization with "altered states of consciousness." Both "peak experiences" and "altered states of consciousness," however, have several different meanings, and none seem to be intrinsically involved with self-actualization, as I shall now indicate.

Both Maslow and S.R. Wilson identify "peak experiences" and altered states of consciousness" with the "real self" and its somatic-experiential element. They hold that people can learn to minimize their rational, symbolic interactional, or judging selves and become aware of somatic states and feelings that they otherwise ignore, and thereby achieve "peak" or "altered" experiences and become more self-actualizing. I (and REBT) hold that this is partly true, but that most humans only occasionally achieve this "unconsciousness" state; that they usually achieve it by consciously, philosophically striving for, interpreting, and defining it; that they almost always achieve it very briefly and keep flitting back to regular evaluative consciousness; and the "peak experiences" are both cognitive and somatic-experiential, as Maslow also said. Seymour Epstein, a well-known psychologist, has a view of the experiential part of our personality as being both cognitive and emotional that is illuminating in this respect.

Some authorities, such as the Zen Buddhists, identify "peak experiences" and "altered states of consciousness" with nonego, allegedly nonjudgemental, pure contemplative states (which, paradoxically, are judged to be "better" than ordinary states of consciousness). Such states probably can be—again, occasionally and briefly—achieved. REBT partly goes along with this view, since it encourages people to never judge nor measure their selves, essence, totality, or being, for that will lead them to overgeneralize and self-defeatingly deify or devil-ify themselves. But REBT favors people still rating their deeds, acts, and performances as "good" or "bad" for certain chosen values and goals, and I think that humans would not survive if they did none of this kind of rating.

Moreover, even if people could often achieve pure egolessness, zero judging, and a Zen state of no-mind, and even if that state helped them (at least temporarily) give up feelings of depression, panic, and damnation, they would then throw away the baby with the bath water, probably achieve little or no pleasure, and therefore be dubiously self-actualized. They could define egolessness (and it concomitant, desirelessness) as self-actualization. But in any usual sense of the word, would it really be that?

Psychologist Sid Wilson identifies people's "real," "somatic" self and "altered states of consciousness" with what Mihali Csikszentmihalyi calls flow experiences—that is, activities in which people become so intensely or flowingly involved that they derive unusual fun or joy because, as Wilson puts it, their "self-sustaining, self-protective thought processes that characterize ordinary consciousness are minimized."[3] This "flow experience" is similar to what REBT calls a "vital absorbing interest" and indeed often adds to people's enjoyment.

However, as Wilson notes, most flow activities include rational thought and also include people's evaluating their performances but only minimally evaluating their selves or personhoods. I would call them a somewhat different but hardly an altered state of consciousness. Flow activities are definitely encouraged in REBT, but REBT also encourages and teaches people how to nondamn and nondeify their selves in innumerable nonflow, as well as in flow, activities. Flow may well lead to reduced self-judgment, but conscious, philosophic use of REBT will lead to even less self-judgment. What is more, flow is almost always temporary, and flowing individuals then return to self-evaluation—unless they use REBT or some other highly conscious thinking to permanently minimize it.

Maslow, Charles Tart (a transcendental psychologist), and others identify "peak experiences" and "altered states of consciousness" with mystical, transcendental experiences. This may well be an illegitimate connection, as it can easily be argued whether transcendental experience really exists. Thus, I can believe and feel that I am God, the Center of the Universe, the Devil, an Eternal Force, or what I will. But am I truly what I say and feel I am? Or am I deluded? Even if we call mystical, transcendental experiences "real" (and in one sense we may because my belief that I am God or the Center of the Universe itself is some kind of experience), is it good, is it enjoyable, is self-actualizing for to have this mystical feeling? Only if I (and my fellow mystical-minded individuals) think it is, for I could feel terrified by my believing myself to be the Devil—or God! And I could be delighted to be my all-too-human self who has no transcendental experiences. So mystical "altered states of consciousness," or "peak experiences," can be anti- instead of self-actualizing.

Rational Emotive Behavior Therapy, like most other therapies, has a dual goal: first, to help people overcome their emotional blocks and disturbances; and second, to help them become more fully functioning, self-actualizing, and happier than they otherwise would be. I have elsewhere outlined the REBT goals of nondisturbance, so let me now describe some of the goals that presumably would desirable for a more fully functioning or self-actualizing person.

I take my main outlook in this respect from my friend Ted Crawford, who has been working on a theory of the fully functioning person and finds that most people are split or fragmented and think, feel, and act in terms of either/or rather than and/also. They need to go beyond the acceptance of an integrated wholeness that helps them accept and cope with meaning that has logic and consistency but that also acknowledges ambiguity, paradox, inconsistent "truths," and other troublesome cognitions that seem to block individuals from becoming fully functioning. To achieve this integrated wholeness, they can choose to accept the principles and practice of and/also many, many times "until the skills and attitudes that enable one to successfully go beyond 'and/also' are a stable habit."[4]

Actively Choosing Self-Actualization

I have worked with Ted Crawford for a number of years on his theory of self-actualization and its linkage with Rational Emotive Behavior Therapy, so let me now state his latest, succinct version and then expand on it. To make a stable habit full functioning, Ted states that one had better "consciously choose the goal or purpose of becoming fully functioning."[5]

Yes, REBT holds that people are born as well as reared with strong tendencies both to defeat themselves, and to ignore their capacity to function more fully and to change their self-destructive thoughts, feelings, and behaviors to achieve fuller functioning. To a large degree, they choose emotional-behavioral disturbance (or health) and choose restricted (or fuller) functioning. Therefore, to more fully actualize themselves, they had better choose to work at achieving more growth, development, and happiness.

More specifically, to make themselves more fully functioning, people need to ask themselves, "What do I really like and dislike?" "How can I experiment and discover what I truly prefer and prefer not to feel and do?" "Which of my likes (e.g., smoking) and dislikes (e.g., exercising will probably be self-harming as well as enjoyable?" "What am I likely to prefer and abhor in the future?" "What do I do to enhance my preferences and decrease my dislikes?" "How can I align my opinions more closely to the data of my experiences?"

By discovering the answers to relevant questions like these, and then by acting on this information, most people can push themselves toward greater self-actualization.

Ted Crawford advises that people who want to achieve greater self-actualization had better "dispute or otherwise let go of shoulds and musts." This is a cardinal theory and practice of REBT. More specifically, REBT holds that people usually make themselves needlessly anxious, depressed, self-hating, and self-pitingly and needlessly dysfunctional when they take their healthy preferences for achievement, approval, and comfort and change them into dogmatic, extreme musts, demands, and commands on themselves, others, and the environment. In so doing, they almost always sabotage their self-fulfilling urges and potentials. Therefore, as Crawford advises, they had better dispute or otherwise let go their shoulds and musts.

How? By using a number of REBT cognitive, emotive, and behavioral methods. Thus, they can cognitively question and challenge their own absolutist demands and commands, reframe them, convince themselves of rational coping statements, read and listen to REBT materials, talk others out of their musts, use problem-solving methods, and otherwise acquire a basic philosophy of tolerance, self-acceptance, and long-range hedonism. Emotively, people can surrender their self-sabotaging, musts by using strong coping statements, rational emotive imagery, shame-attacking exercises, role-playing, and other REBT dramatic evocative techniques. Behaviorally, non-actualizing people can act against and dispel their musts by making themselves use the REBT (and other cognitive-behavioral) methods of in vivo desensitization, forceful homework assignments, reinforcement and penalizing procedures, and skill-training techniques.

As Crawford points out, self-actualizing solutions can be better achieved if people "join the problem without the requirement of a solution or the promise of a solution. The requirement that a solution should and must be available blocks the development toward self-actualization."[6] When People join a self-actualizing problem in an and/also way, they flexibly observe, guess, invent a theory, revise their guesses, and grow an emergent "solution" or new possibilities.

More concretely, people don't absolutely have to find a solution to the problem of actualizing themselves. If they tell themselves, "I must actualize myself! I must not fail to achieve perfect self-actualization!" that is akin to saying, "I must not think of a pink elephant!" Then they most probably will think of a pink elephant—and will block their actualizing themselves. The thought that it is necessary to achieve actualization will interfere with their asking and answering the kinds of questions mentioned above that will lead to their individually discovering what it is, how to achieve it, and how to work at achieving it.

Crawford notes that people who want to actualize themselves had better "explore the problem as a system without blaming anyone for the status quo or for resisting the 'solution' one has, and thereby redesign the system. When there is a problem, all participants contribute to the situation (or system) that creates the problem—even when they are innocent of wrongdoing. They are responsible for what they do but not blameworthy or damnable as persons."[7] In more concrete REBT terms this means:

Don't blame anyone, including yourself, for anything. Acknowledge that you (and others) may behave ineffectually and thereby defeat yourself and others about many important goals and values. But only negatively rate or assess what you and they do, and actively refrain from measuring your self— or their selves—for poor performances. Work at unconditionally accepting your self, your youness, your humanity, whether or not you perform well or are approved of by others.

At the same time, measure or rate what your problem in actualizing yourself is; how well you are working at "solving" it; how good your "solutions" probably are; and how you can keep working to improve them. But don't evaluate, nor especially damn, yourself (or other people) for the poor "solutions" you or they devise. You (and others) may act badly about your (and their) self-actualization, and you may use your "bad" solutions to work for "better" ones—but not if you denigrate yourself and them for both of your responsibility for low-level self-actualization.

> Don't blame anyone, including yourself, for anything.

Because you refrain from condemning people, your self-actualizing plans and accomplishments will very likely remain perpetually open-ended and revisable—which is one of the main characteristics (one might almost say requisites) of a more fully-functioning person. According to REBT, rational people consider and utilize alternate, nonrigid paths to happiness, and are therefore open to endless reactualization.

Ted Crawford notes that fully functioning individuals "meet the challenge of a situation as soon as feasible in contrast to procrastination. Procrastination delays, usually significantly, the development of such a stable habit."[8] More specifically, REBT adds to his anti-procrastination stance.

You additionally sabotage your emotional health and maximum fulfillment, after doing so by damning yourself and others, by indulging in low frustration tolerance (LFT). When you keep believing that life is too hard, that it must not be that hard, and that you can't stand the hassles and efforts required to enjoy it, you add discomfort, anxiety, and depression to ego disturbance, and thereby increase your frustrations and annoyances.

Procrastination and low frustration tolerance not only make you dysfunctional and miserable, but also enormously block your ability to learn and use REBT and other effective therapies. Catch-22: Whining about life's unniceties creates LFT and the LFT augments whining and sabotages self-actualizing change!

Characteristics of Self-Actualizing Persons

The REBT view of self-actualization overlaps with views from other schools of thought, such as those of Carl Rogers and Abraham Maslow, which at times differ significantly from REBT. But the REBT view also mirrors the ideas of Alfred Korzybski, the founder, and S.I. Hayakwa, the promulgator, of general semantics, a school of thought that is close to and which has significantly influenced REBT. As Hayakawa points out, some of the characteristics of the more fully-functioning individual that are endorsed by Maslow, Rogers, and general semantics, and with which REBT agrees, are these:

Nonconformity and individuality. Fully-functioning persons (FFPs) are not "fully adjusted" to nor outrightly rebellious against the social group. "The semantically well-oriented person is primarily concerned with the territory and not with the map, with social reality rather than the social façade."[9] REBT has always endorsed sensible nonconformity and individuality in sex, love, marital, vocational, recreational, and other aspects of life. It has, from its start, also been a highly unconventional form of psychotherapy and has only recently been accepted as a leader in the more conventional cognitive-behavioral movement.

Self-awareness. FFPs are aware of their own feelings, do not try to repress them, often act upon them, and even when they do not act upon them are able to admit them to awareness. In REBT terms, they acknowledge their negative feelings (e.g. anxiety and rage) but do not necessarily act out on them. They often make efforts to change their feelings when they are unhealthy and self-defeating. They "know themselves" but also know how little they know about themselves.

Acceptance of ambiguity and uncertainty. FFPs accept ambiguity, uncertainty, the unknown, approximateness, and some amount of disorder. "Emotionally mature individuals accept the fact that, as far as has yet been discovered, we live in a world of probability and chance, where there are not, nor probably ever will be, absolute necessities nor complete certainties. Living in such a world is not only tolerable but, in terms of adventure, learning, and striving, can even be very exciting and pleasurable."[10]

Tolerance. FFPs are extensional—responding to similarities and differences, rather than intentional—tending to ignore differences among things that have some name. They do not see all tress as green, all education as good, nor all modern art as silly. The REBT version: "Emotionally sound people are intellectually flexible, tend to be open to change at all times and are prone to take an unbigoted (or, at least, less bigoted) view of the infinitely varied people, ideas, and things in the world around them."[11]

Acceptance of human animality. FFPs accept their and others' physical and "animal" nature, and rarely disgust themselves about body products, odors, or functions. In REBT terms, they may not like various sensations and feelings but refrain from "awfulizing" about them.

Commitment and intrinsic enjoyment. FFPs tend to enjoy work and sports as ends or pleasures in themselves and not merely as means toward ends (e.g., working for money or playing sports to achieve good health). As REBT puts is, commitment to people, things, and ideas, mainly because people want to be absorbed and committed, is one of the main aspects of emotional health and happiness. Robert Harper and I have particularly endorsed people's throwing themselves into a long-term vial and absorbing interest in order to achieve maximum fulfillment and happiness.

Creativity and originality. Maslow, Rogers, and Hayakawa, as well as many other authorities, show that fully functioning personalities are usually innovative, creative, and original about artistic as well as commonplace problems. In REBT terms, they tend to be self-directed rather than other-directed, original rather than conformist, flexible rather than rigid, and "seem to lead better lives when they have at least one major creative interest."[12]

Social interest and ethical trust. S.I. Hayakawa, endorsing Alfred Korzybski, Abraham Maslow, and Carl Rogers, holds that FFPs are deeply ethical, trustworthy, constructive, and socialized. TEBT, following Alfred Adler, puts the same point of view this way: "Emotionally and metally healthy people tend to be considerate and fair to others; to engage in collaborative and cooperative endeavors; at times to be somewhat altruistic; and to distinctly enjoy some measure of interpersonal and group relationships."[13]

Enlightened self-interest. Healthy and enjoying people are true to themselves as well as to others, often put themselves first, usually put a few selected others a close second, and the rest of the world not too far behind. Their self-interest is mainly directed toward enjoying, and not to proving, themselves.

Flexibility and scientific outlook. Science not only uses empiricism and logic, but as Karl Popper, Bertrand Russell, Ludwig Wittgenstein, and other philosophers of science have shown, it is intrinsically open-minded and flexible. As REBT emphasizes, people largely neuroticize themselves with rigid, imperative musts and shoulds, and, conversely, are significantly less neurotic and self-actualizing when they scientifically dispute their dogmatic, unconditional musts and change them to preferences and alternative-seeking desires.

Unconditional self-acceptance. Carl Rogers and Paul Tillich emphasize unconditional self-acceptance, and from the start REBT has held that humans will rarely be undisturbed and self-fulfilling unless they rate only their deeds and performances and not their global "selves." Instead, they can choose to accept "themselves" whether or not they perform well, are approved by significant others, or have deficits and handicaps. Many other psychotherapies, for example, that of Nathaniel Branden, encourage people to strive for self-esteem or self-efficacy, accepting themselves because they perform well and predict that they will continue to do so. But REBT tries to help them not rate their selves, their totality, at all, but rate only their behaviors, or, less elegantly, rate themselves as "good" or "worthy" just because they exist, because they choose to do so. Using REBT, self-actualizing people can reframe their "failures" as feedback rather than as self-damnation. This feedback provides important information about what does not work, and therefore calls for a change in approach to a situation rather than giving up on it.

Risk-taking and experimenting. Self-actualization without risk-taking and experimenting is almost unthinkable. People had better experiment with many tasks, preferences, and projects in order to discover what they really want and don't want, and to keep risking new defeats and failures in order to achieve better enjoyments.

Long-range hedonism. As REBT has noted since its inception in 1955, short-range hedonism—"Eat, drink, and be merry, for tomorrow you may die!"—has its distinct limitations, for tomorrow you will probably be alive with a hangover! Therefore, maximum self-actualization can largely be achieved by aiming for intensive and extensive pleasures today and tomorrow, and where the former (as in many addictions) sabotage the latter, immediate gratification has often better been avoided and long-range hedonism sought out and abetted.

Work and practice. As noted above, the three major insights of REBT are: (1) take responsibility for disturbing yourself and do not cop out by blaming others; (2) face the fact that your early disturbances do not automatically make you disturbed today; (3) understand that no magical forces will change you, but only your own strong and persistent work and practice—yes, work and practice. Similarly with self-actualization: Only by working at planning, plotting, scheming, and steadily acting at are you likely to become a fully-functioning person.

Conclusion

The REBT view of human nondisturbance and self-actualization agrees with other therapeutic outlooks in many respects. Thus, a study of 610 clinical psychologists showed that all five major groups—psychoanalytic, behavioral, humanist-existential, eclectic, and cognitive—reported substantial agreement on the importance of self-system development, self-examination, and exploratory activities in personal change.[14]

The self-actualizing characteristics that REBT emphasizes perhaps more than many other leading psychotherapies are flexibility and a scientific outlook, self-acceptance instead of self-esteem, and long-range hedonism. In regard to achieving, and not merely endorsing, a more fully functioning personality, it advocates the points that Ted Crawford and I outlined at the beginning of this paper:

- Actively choosing self-actualization.
- Disputing absolutist shoulds and musts that block its achievement.
- Preferring, but not requiring, the solving of self-actualizing problems.
- Tolerance of oneself and others.
- Overcoming procrastination and low frustration tolerance.
- Framing the problem as a systemic problem to be redesigned.
- Moving from either/ors toward and/alsos—including ambiguity, paradox, inconsistency, and confusion and then working toward an integrated wholeness.

In this manner, Rational Emotive Behavior Therapy not only strongly endorses a self-actualizing, action-oriented philosophy, but also actively encourages some important way in which it may be achieved. Above all, it stresses that the views outlined in this paper are its current formulations that had better be experimentally tried, and, when and if falsified, be quickly revised or abandoned.

© Albert Ellis

Notes

[1] A. H. Maslow, Toward a Psychology Being (New York: Van Nostrand Reinhold, 1968), p. 97.

[2] M. Daniels, "The Myth of Self-Actualization," Journal of Humanistic Psychology 28, no. 1 (1988): 13.

[3] S. R. Wilson, "The 'Real Self' Controversy: Toward n Integration of Humanistic and Interactionistic Theory," Journal of Humanistic Psychology, 28, no. 1 (1988): 49.

[4] T. Crawford and A. Ellis, "A Dictionary of Rational-Emotive Feelings and Behaviors," Journal of Rational-Emotive and Cognitive Behavioral Therapy 1, no. 7 (1989), pp. 3-5.

[5] Ibid.

[6] Ibid.

[7] Ibid.

[8] Ibid.

[9] S. I. Hayakawa, "The Fully Functioning Person," Symbol, Status, and Personality (New York: Harcourt Brace Jovanovich, 1968), p. 57.

[10] A. Ellis, The Case Against Religiosity (New York: Institute for Rational Emotive Therapy, 1983), p. 2-5.

[11] Ibid.

[12] Ibid.

[13] Ibid.

[14] M. J. Mahoney et al., "Psychological Development and Optimal Psychotherapy: Converging Perspectives Among Clinical Psychologists," Journal of Integrative and Eclectic Psychotherapy, 8 (1989): 251-63.

About the Author

Albert Ellis was born in Pittsburgh in 1913 and raised in New York City. He made the best of a difficult childhood by using his head and becoming, in his words, "a stubborn and pronounced problem-solver." A serious kidney disorder turned his attention from sports to books, and the strife in his family (his parents were divorced when he was twelve) led him to work at understanding others.

Developed by Ellis, Rational Emotive Behavior Therapy is a direct and efficient problem-solving method, well suited to Ellis' personality.

The Art and Science of Love, his first really successful book, appeared in 1960, and he has now published fifty-four books and over 600 articles on REBT, sex and marriage. He is currently President Emeritus of the Albert Ellis Institute in New York, which provides professional training programs and psychotherapy to individuals, families, and groups.

There is little room for wisdom left when one is full of judgment.

Malcolm Hain

Most people live, whether physically, intellectually, or morally, in a very restricted circle of their potential being. They make use of a very small portion of their possible consciousness...We all have reservoirs of life to draw upon, of which we do not dream.

William James

What man actually needs is not a tensionless state but rather the striving and struggling for some goal worthy of him. What he needs is not the discharge of tension at any cost, but the call of a potential meaning waiting to be fulfilled by him.

Viktor Frankl

Freedom is man's capacity to take a hand in his own development. It is our capacity to mold ourselves.

Rollo May

What is necessary to change a person is to change his awareness of himself.

Abraham Maslow

I do not have a Pollyanna view of human nature. I am quite aware that out of defensiveness and inner fear, individuals can and do behave in ways which are incredibly cruel, horribly destructive, immature, regressive, anti-social, and harmful. Yet one of the most refreshing parts of my experience is to work with such individuals and to discover the strongly positive directional tendencies which exist in all of them, as in all of us, at the deepest levels.

Carl Rogers

Humanism definitely places the destiny of human beings within the very broad limits of this natural world. It submits that we can find plenty of scope and meaning in our lives through freely enjoying the rich and varied potentialities of this luxuriant earth; through preserving, extending, and adding to the values of civilization; through contributing to the progress and happiness of humankind during billions and billons of years; or through helping to evolve a new species surpassing Homo sapiens.

Corliss Lamont

DEDICATION

PERSPECTIVE

Anita Endrezze

I have MS. I can walk with some effort, but I'm relatively lucky. For many years I had no symptoms beyond some occasional and confusing flare-ups (like partial blindness, numbness, and voice slurring). In fact, I wasn't diagnosed until four years ago after I had an MRI. Since then, the disease has progressed to affect my walking and leaves me feeling weak. I have the plaques in my brain as well as in my spine. In addition, I've been going through menopause, with hot flashes that have left me feverish and weak. To top that off, I take Coumadin, a blood-thinning medication, because I had numerous strokes due to hormone replacement therapy, which was meant to stop the hot flashes!

Enough already!

All of my life I've dealt with a fragile body, but I always ignored it and tried to make my spirit stronger. I was born crippled. The doctors put me in a cast for a year and straightened my foot and leg, but it was never normal. I was thin and spindly—definitely not athletic material.

I developed in another direction. I'm an artist and a writer. I'm used to looking for symbols, shades of meaning, the substance below the surface, the unusual, and I've embraced the power of the intellect to overcome obstacles. I've challenged myself to see things from different perspectives than the ordinary.

Then I was hit with this disease.

I wondered: what is the meaning of my life at this point?

In the past, my writing has helped people to understand and see things in a new way. My paintings have given people pleasure. Now I can't write or paint as much as I'd like to because my right side is weak and tires easily. I'm right-handed.

I've always wanted to create. To make something new out of what materials I have. To see in a different way and to find the words or colors to let other see, too. And I have wanted to help people. I begged the universe to let me help.

But in my dark moments, I asked myself, how can I help others when I can't even help myself?

Last year, I decided to tutor through the local school district. I had tried subbing and ab-so-lutely hated it! But I enjoy teaching, so I thought one-on-one would be better. At least, I wouldn't have thirty out-of-control kids.

My first assignment was to teach a little eight-year-old girl who was a quadriplegic. When I found that out, I was nervous. What did I know about teaching someone that ill? And I was a high school and university teacher, not an elementary-level instructor. What could I teach her? How would I teach her? I had no materials beyond a pad of paper and some pencils. What was I supposed to do?

I barely slept the night before I was to meet her. Then, in the middle of the night (when so many revelations often come to us), I realized this wasn't about me. It was about helping her.

The next day, I met Ramona (not her real name). She had been a quadriplegic since she was three and hurt in a car accident. Her parents weren't in the picture. She'd been fostered out or in hospitals for five years.

Now she had a good foster mother and two foster siblings with their own physical problems.

I introduced myself and sat down to get to know her. Ramona was hooked up to the chair, her life support system, but I soon looked past that restriction. I saw a beautiful girl with dark curly hair. Her eyes sparkled. She was Hispanic, with creamy brown skin, and a great sense of humor.

She knew some of the alphabet so I thought I'd start there. After all, I'd taught my own kids to read, even though I'd never done it as a professional.

I found a new use for my creativity. I was puzzled at first on how to write the letters of the alphabet. You see, I tutored in her home, a very tiny apartment, and there was no blackboard or whiteboard. The school district gave me a pack of alphabet flash cards but that wasn't useful for writing words.

Ramona needed to use a mouth gripper to manipulate objects, since she couldn't move her arms. I tried paint. I couldn't use acrylic or tube watercolors since they contained toxins. So I mixed water with the little ovals of paint for kids. We used her prop board, but the paint ran too much. So then I tried felt tip pens. The felt pens were clumsy and skipped on the paper as the gripper wobbled in her mouth. A whiteboard wouldn't work well, either.

Then I thought of magnetic letters. I scrounged the thrift stores until I had several sets to work with. I brought my cookie baking sheet. We found something that worked!

She had some memory problems due to the accident, but she stuck with it. She had spirit and determination. For weeks we went over letters. I read stories to her and found out she had a sweet tooth. I never left home without a sucker or some cookies for her as a reward for her hard work.

Soon we were arranging sentences, and changing the meaning by switching a word or two. She got the idea of grouping numbers according to color, so we practiced making sets. She learned to read several sentences. A humble start, but something she'd never done before. I wanted her to feel good about learning.

In the middle of our tutoring, she had an operation on her back. Almost two dozen pins were inserted in order to straighten and strengthen her spine. I wasn't able to teach her for a couple of weeks. When I returned, she'd forgotten some words. We started all over again and she picked it up right away. Finally, over two months later, she was able to attend a real classroom for the first time in her life at a local elementary school. She has friends now and ways to see the world beyond her physical disabilities.

I like the army slogan "an army of one." It implies that within each of us is the potential ability to be more than ourselves, or what we think of as "self." It also suggests that if all of us unite, we can be an army, a force of good, because each of us has strengths that support each other.

I learned that I can't be Oprah and reach millions. I can only help the world one person at a time. And that one person has the chance to help others, so that, eventually, you do help hundreds of people. You learn to read one letter at a time, after all.

I still have the disease. I still get depressed at times. I still hope for a cure or a better treatment than I'm now taking. Somewhere, a research doctor is working on it. He or she is trying to help, too.

At the beginning of this essay I wrote that I wondered how I could help others when I couldn't even help myself. I was looking at it backwards. It is when I help others that I help myself.

© Anita Endrezze

About the Author

Anita Endrezze is a writer and an artist. She is half-Yaqui Indian and half-Caucasian (Slovenian, Saxon-German, and north Italian). Her most recent book is *Throwing Fire at the Sun, Water at the Moon* (University of Arizona Press, 2000), a book of tribal history told by myths, poetry, fiction, historical accounts, and family stories. An earlier book of poems, *At the Helm of Twilight*, (Broken Moon Press, 1992) won both the Governor's Writers Award for Washington State and the Seattle Bumbershoot/Weyerhaeuser Award. She lives in Everett, Washington with her family.

Circles in the Sky
for Aaron, age fourteen

After you were born,
hawks soared
weightless
in my dreams,
their feathers full of fire
and dark air.

Then one fell
from the sky,
breaking its neck
on our roof.
Your father brought it to me
while I cradled your head
to my breast.

We called you *Sunhawk*
and wished for you:
insight, quickness.

When you were six,
you asked me skyfuls
of questions:
When was the first reality?
I held a feather of wisdom.
When the first man or tree,
woman or bird,
was aware of its own existence.
I tucked the feather behind my ear,
proud of my answer.
But then you asked:
Wouldn't the first reality be
in the mind of the creator?

Now you shave half your hair, dye it
red-gold
so that it looks like a nest of flames.
You listen to rap, instead of the wind,
and girls phone you at midnight,
hanging up when I say hello.
I caw: *turn down your music,*
get off the phone, clean your room!

We argue, staring wildly at each other,
our mouths twisted in anguish.
You insist I never understand
anything,
I'm suffocating you, clipping your wings.
Then I remember nights I rocked you to
sleep
and days I stood lost in a forest
of your needs. You remember
your first nest, under my ribs,
and you take a deep breath.
Mom, I'm still the same.
I haven't changed.

And you're half-right, my fledgling
in baggy pants and size 10 shoes.
You're still the same
and you have changed.
Son, we circle each other
in widening spirals,
my wings outspread,
hovering over you,
while you stretch your wings
for the dizzying dive
into adulthood,
that journey as immense
and endless as the sky.

Anita Endrezze (1994)

Basically, human beings want satisfaction and fulfillment, and we especially want to feel a sense of accomplishment in what we are doing. Being of service and achieving something of value to others while feeling balanced and healthy are the essential reasons for working.

Justine Willis Toms & Michael Toms

What is it you plan to do with your one wild and precious life?

Mary Oliver

Every child comes with the message that God is not yet discouraged of man.

Rabindranath Tagore

All work is empty, save when there is love.

Kahlil Gibran

I always liked to chase the girls. Parkinson's stops all that. Now I might have a chance to go to heaven.

Muhammad Ali

The value of life can be measured by how many times your soul has been deeply stirred.

Soichiro Honda

There's nothing like giving to someone else and realizing you are strengthening the fundamental fabric of society.

Diana Aviv

Time is limited, so I better wake up every morning fresh and know that I have just one chance to live this particular day right, and to string my days together into a life of action, and purpose.

Lance Armstrong

We draw the circle of our family too small.

Agnes G. Bojaxhiu

May there be enough clouds in your life to make a beautiful sunset.

Rebecca Gregory

You have not lived until you have done something for someone who can never repay you.

John Bunyan

Psychology and sociology aside, there is a final reason why money can't buy happiness: the things that really matter aren't sold in stores. Love, friendship, family, respect, a place in the community, the belief that your life has purpose—those are the essentials of human fulfillment, and they cannot be purchased with cash.

Gregg Easterbrook

Who I am in this moment between life and death is what I believe I am, and what I believe I am allows some room for choice.

Arnold R. Beisser

Minds are not conquered by arms, but by love and magnanimity.

Baruch Spinoza

The best time to plant a tree is twenty years ago. The second best time is now.

Chinese proverb

Give a little love to a child, and you get a great deal back.

John Ruskin

I am in the world to change the world.

Muriel Rukeyser

A man without ambition is dead. A man with ambition but no love is dead. A man with ambition and love for his blessings here on earth is ever so alive. Having been alive, it won't be so hard in the end to lie down and rest.

Pearl Bailey

HONOR

THE HORSE YOU RODE IN ON
Heroes, Chivalry, and Beasts of Burden

Scott A. Farrell

How is a hero like a horse? Sounds like the beginning of a rude joke, doesn't it? Yet surprisingly, as we explore the ways in which one can lead a life of value in the today's world, maybe that comparison deserves some serious consideration rather than just a witty punch line.

When we think of animals to associate with heroes and champions, we usually imagine fearsome, powerful creatures like hawks, lions, or wolves. We think that heroism requires the kind of strength, ferocity, and spirit that are embodied by such creatures.

We also associate heroes with dragons and other mythical beasts. After all, heroes are supposed to fight monsters, aren't they? The hero is the one who rescues the helpless maiden from the jaws of a fire-breathing lizard, or slays the troll that lurks within the depths of the dark, primeval forest.

But we don't usually make a connection between a hero and a horse. A horse is a beast of burden, after all. Horses are for herding cattle, for pulling wagons, for drawing plows—not exactly the sorts of activities that call to mind the image of a glorious hero.

Yet there is a long tradition of worthy ideals that springs from the connection between the horse and the hero; ideals that are important to anyone seeking a life of value in today's world. Those ideals are known as "chivalry."

Although we often think of chivalry as a slightly absurd (but mostly harmless) demonstration of manners and etiquette, the concept really runs much deeper than that. Chivalry is a warrior's code of honor. It is the code of the hero, and it literally would not exist without the horse. "Cheval" is an old word for "horse," and hundreds of years ago, when warriors rode on horseback, "chevalerie" became the way of the warrior.

Bear in mind, however, the warrior who lived by the "code of chevalerie" was not a plundering barbarian or a mighty conqueror pursuing glory, riches, and fame. The person who adhered to this code was known as a knight, a word that means not "victor," "adventurer," or some other aggrandizing epithet, but "servant." The knight—the greatest hero of an age—was proud to be called a servant.

In times of trouble, the knight's job was to step into harm's way to protect those who could not defend themselves. In times of peace, the knight's duty was to serve as an arbiter of justice and fairness. Chivalry dictated that a knight should set ego and vanity aside, and put the needs of others ahead of his own. As the fourteenth-century knight Geffroi de Charny wrote in his book *La Livre de Chevalerie*: "It is the duty of great knights to place the people's profit (i.e., 'welfare') before their own, to strive with all their might for the defense of the people and the land, and to maintain the rights of the humble as well as the mighty...The knights of greatest worth are those who give help and comfort in many good and needful ways." This notion of the knight as "the warrior who works for the benefit of others" was simply revolutionary. Rarely before in history had warriors with swords and armor been anything but a force for destruction, pillage, and subjugation. Never before had the principles of compassion and duty been codified with such noble idealism. While not every knight lived up to the high ideals of chivalry, the role of "the good servant" became forever associated with the knights who followed the code of chivalry.

Apart from riding on horseback, the knight also presented an image of a hero who was literally a "workhorse" for worthy causes and people in need. In the early fifteenth century, the Spanish knight Diaz de Gamez, in his chronicle of *The Unconquered Knight*, observed: "Knights are not chosen

146

from feeble or timid souls, but from among men who are strong and full of energy, bold and without fear; and for this reason there is no other beast that so befits a knight as a good horse…Horses are so strong, swift and faithful that a brave knight, mounted on a good horse, may do more in an hour than a hundred others could have done afoot."

No wonder, then, that the symbol of knights and chivalry was not the sword, the shield, or the lance, but the spurs. Urged forward by a sense of duty and honor, like a horse put to the spur, the knight never faltered in seeking ways to be of service, to help, to defend, to be of benefit to those in need.

The code of chivalry is sometimes criticized as being outdated, sexist, bombastic, and superfluous. Chivalry has been blamed for dulling the competitive edge of personal initiative with unattainable ideals of fair play and quixotic equanimity. But the ideals of chivalry, far from being dead or obsolete, remind us of what is truly valuable and honorable in a world that sometimes seems awash in indulgences of vanity, ego, and conceit. Chivalry reminds us that knights in shining armor are those who spur themselves forward to help and work and serve.

> While not every knight lived up to the high ideals of chivalry, the role of "the good servant" became forever associated with the knights who followed the code of chivalry.

How is a hero like a horse? Sometimes the world needs heroes who are ferocious lions, soaring hawks, lone wolves and fire-breathing dragons, but more often than not, heroes are simply beasts of burden. More often than not, heroes are the ones who are willing to shoulder the load and keep moving forward, whatever the cost. More often than not, the knight in shining armor is the parent or teacher, the coach or the manager, the doctor, the police officer, the mechanic, or the hundreds of others who step forward every day to be the honorable workhorses of today's world by simply putting the needs of others ahead of their own in the spirit of valiant service that is still defined by the "code of chevalerie."

© Scott Farrell

About the Author

I became interested in the history of knights in armor when my high-school social studies class took a field trip to a Renaissance Faire. I joined a local chapter of a living history group that puts on armored jousting tournaments—not exactly the typical hobby for a fifteen-year-old. But something about this image intrigued me: the warrior-knight whose job it is to protect and serve, rather than attack and conquer. Now, twenty-five years later I still enjoy exploring medieval history. I enjoy seeing how this wonderfully colorful period is similar to our own time: conflicting loyalties, political complexities, and a variety of ways to use power, wealth, and authority for either beneficial or self-serving ends. Seeing chivalry as a warrior's code of honor, not just as a synonym for romance and courtesy, and using that code in an environment of real competition, aggression, and conflict has given me an interesting perspective of value ethics in action. Being a champion and living up to the standard of a knight in shining armor is a challenging and rewarding goal in life. Visit www.chivalrytoday.com to learn more.

The age of chivalry is never past, so long as there is a wrong left unredressed on earth.

Charles Kingsley

I cannot and will not cut my conscience to fit this year's fashions.

Lillian Hellman

Chivalry need not be awesome, heroic acts. Simply "being of service to someone else" when you'd rather be taking a nap is simple, safe, wonderful thing to do.

Jason Merchey

I'm really glad that our young people missed the Depression, and missed the great big war. But I do regret that they missed the leaders that I knew. Leaders who told us when things were tough, and that we would have to sacrifice, and these difficulties might last awhile.

Ann Richards

There is just one way to bring up a child in the way he should go, and that is to travel that way yourself.

Abraham Lincoln

It's a matter of taking the side of the weak against the strong, something the best people have always done.

Harriet Beecher Stowe

We will not relocate [from the South] to San Francisco; we will not move somewhere more accommodating to our tastes; we will stay and fight to improve things, like honorable men and women should. We will not accept defeat at the hands of an unworthy enemy. We will proudly wear what we believe on our chests to show the non-believers the flame of truth that burns inside our hearts.

Kevin Anderson

Conscience...is the impulse to do right because it is right, regardless of personal ends.

Margaret C. Graham

PROGRESSIVISM

DEMOCRACY'S NEXT STEP
Building a Dignitarian Society

Robert W. Fuller

Fundamental political change, in contrast to business-as-usual incre-mentalism and stagnation, depends upon two things: a vision with the power to effect political realignment and the identification of something to fight. Franklin D. Roosevelt's New Deal and Martin Luther King's dream of racial equality met both criteria.

A moral vision that could bring political realignment today is that of a "dignitarian" society. The basic tenet of a dignitarian—in contrast to an egalitarian—society is that although we are unequal in rank, we are equal in dignity. The goal of a dignitarian society is to structure our personal rela-tions and our social institutions so that rank is not abused and human dig-nity is universally protected.

In the last four decades, Americans learned to look at themselves through the lens of color. What we saw was the injustice of racism. Similarly, when we looked through the lens of gender, we saw the inequities of sexism. Looking at ourselves through the lens of rank is no less illuminating and transformative.

Whether your title reads president or citizen, boss or employee, doctor or patient, teacher or pupil, rank defines your authority. When it's a badge of excellence, rank is not a problem. On the contrary, we admire and emulate those who've earned their rank and exercise the power it signifies to serve their employees, students, patients, or fellow citizens.

But when those with higher rank use their power to exploit those of lower rank, we're speaking not of rank, but of its abuse.

We don't have a ready name for rank-based abuse, but it needs one. When abuse and discrimination are race-based, we call it racism; when they're gender-based, we call it sexism. By analogy, abuse of the power inherent in rank is "rankism."

> Recent front-page examples of institutional rankism include corporate corruption, sexual abuse by clergy, elder abuse, and the undue political influence of special-interest groups.

Rankism lies at the root of much of the dysfunction now plaguing America and its democracy. Like other forms of discrimination, it occurs at both interpersonal and institutional levels. For example, when a boss harasses an employee or a teacher humiliates a student, that's interpersonal rankism. "Somebodies" with higher rank and more power in a particular setting can maintain an environment that is hostile and demeaning to "nobodies" with lower rank and less power in that setting, much as most everywhere whites used to be at liberty to mistreat blacks.

Thirty-five years of affirmative action have put racists and sexists on notice. But far less attention has been paid to the rankist abuses that occur within a race or gender. Blacks insult and exploit other blacks of lower rank, whites do the same to whites, and women to women, all with confidence that it will pass as business as usual.

Recent front-page examples of institutional rankism include corporate corruption, sexual abuse by clergy, elder abuse, and the undue political influence of special-interest groups. At the societal level, rank-based discrimination afflicts none more inescapably than those lacking the protections of social rank—the working poor. Two recent books chronicle this widening fissure. In *Nickel and Dimed*, Barbara Ehrenreich argues that the working poor are in effect unacknowledged benefactors whose labor subsidizes the more advantaged. In *The Working Poor: Invisible in America*, David Shipler describes the economic black hole into which the poor can fall with scant hope of ever extricating themselves.

To produce political realignment, a vision must be for something and against something. For example, King's vision was for "equality and justice" and against racism. Likewise, a dignitarian society is for equal dignity and against rankism. Rankism is invariably experienced as an abridgement of dignity.

Rankism is the illegitimate use of rank, and, equally, the use of rank illegitimately acquired or held. When the high-ranking aggrandize themselves at the expense of subordinates, that's rankism. It's the opposite of service. Good leaders eschew rankism; bad ones indulge in it. When leaders are perceived by subordinates as condoning rankism, it spreads like a virus through the ranks. Photos of the humiliation of Iraqi prisoners by their American guards exposed the arrogant face of rankism to the world.

In the workplace, rankism destroys morale, stifles initiative, and taxes productivity. In the schools, defending against the indignities of rankism takes precedence over learning. Everywhere, rankism takes a terrible toll, as do racism and sexism where they're not disallowed. In international relations, the rankism that is perceived by weaker nations as unilateralism, exceptionalism, and bullying incites anti-Americanism and fuels a passion for revenge.

A majority of eligible voters are not locked into the positions championed by either conservative or progressive elites. What could engage these voters is a dignitarian agenda, committed to proactively rooting rankism out of our civic and social institutions. By focusing attention on the abuse of power, a politics of dignity can sidestep the culture wars and reinvigorate democracy.

A dignitarian society that provides health care to some but not to others is inconceivable. Likewise, wealth would not be a precondition for getting a quality education. Without these basics, the American dream is a mirage. In a dignitarian society respect for the environment would be a corollary of respect for human dignity. And, candidates would not have to command a fortune to run for office. If we continue to tolerate rankism in civic affairs, it will corrode American democracy as did our long sorry accommodation of racism.

Building a dignitarian society to overcome rankism is democracy's next step.

© *Robert Fuller*

About the Author

Robert W. Fuller taught at Columbia University and served as president of Oberlin College. He is the author of *Somebodies and Nobodies: Overcoming the Abuse of Rank* (2003) and *All Rise: Somebodies, Nobodies, and the Politics of Dignity* (2006).

154

The essence of immorality is the tendency to make an exception of myself.

Jane Addams

We must build a new world, a far better world – one in which the eternal dignity of man is respected.

Harry S. Truman

Whoever debases others is debasing himself.

James Baldwin

You can stand tall without standing on someone. You can be a victor without having victims.

Harriet Woods

He who does not have the courage to speak up for his rights cannot earn the respect of others.

Rene G. Torres

One's dignity may be assaulted, vandalized and cruelly mocked, but it cannot be taken away unless it is surrendered.

Michael J. Fox

There will be no peace if there is no justice-no justice if there is no equity-no equity if there is no progress-no progress if there is no democracy-no democracy if there is no respect for the identity and dignity of the peoples and cultures in today's world.

Rigoberta Menchu

There but for the grace of God go I.

1 Corinthians 15:9-10

MEANING

A HOME-BASED LIFE

Gina Gerboth

Becoming a parent changes most people in profound and significant ways. When I was expecting my first baby I had visions of our lifestyle changing, but superficially to be sure. I thought that we would go about our days as we always did—working, dining out, and vacationing pretty much as we had before. I knew we would have to make adjustments. I was expecting to have to leave restaurants quickly when Junior had had enough. I knew that trips to Disneyland would probably replace trips to the spa. I knew that I would need job flexibility so that I could be there for sick days and special events. But what I didn't know was that our whole world was to turn upside down.

My first son was born while I was employed by the federal government. As employers go, they were pretty progressive. Flex-time and an on-site day-care were established to provide parents with family-friendly options. I returned to work when he was three months old and went down to the child care center to visit him frequently throughout the day. It was supposed to be an ideal situation, but it left me longing. I didn't want someone else being the first to see his milestones. I felt torn while I was up at my desk. And his tears when I left each time broke my heart.

After a little more than a year back on the job, my husband and I decided to make the leap to being a one-income family. I quit my job and became a full-time mother. Those days when I was first at home were almost decadent with leisure.

We were able to live comfortably on one income for several more years. I had another baby, and he added to the joy and delight I found in mothering. I kept busy in various ways: writing, volunteering, visiting with friends, keeping home. I figured this was a temporary arrangement until the kids went to school and I went back to work. I wanted to soak up every minute of it. But as my children grew, I knew I didn't want this to be only a chapter in our family's story. I wanted this to become our lifestyle.

As my older son grew, I knew that I wanted him and his brother to have a home-based education. That is not to say only in the home (for learning takes place everywhere, every minute of the day), but in the arms of the family. I'd met many homeschooled children and was impressed by the variety of experiences each day brought to them, as well as the range of skills and talents they were able to develop when they weren't interrupted by schedules or bells. They were confident because of those abilities—not because a test score or grade told them they were capable or not. That is what I wanted for my kids.

Most of the homeschooling families I knew were one-income families, and when my husband lost his job during the recession of 2001, I was afraid that homeschooling might not be an option for us. We decided to move to a smaller town, in hopes of curbing living expenses. Living simply was not a hardship for us; it was an adventure. My husband found another job in his previous field, though it was clear it would be hard to support any family on his income alone, no matter how frugal we could be. We were in a holding pattern, but began a long dialogue about what we wanted. We didn't want to just exist. We wanted to live. We wanted to be present.

I came to sense that society somehow encourages parents and adults to compartmentalize child-raising. Kids move from daycare during the work hours to the educational system. The schools that were once established to keep kids safe while their parents were in the factories seem, in many ways, to provide the same function to parents who are now at the office. Before- and after-school programs provide child care for those hours in between, when the parents need to start work and when the school session begins. Sports, classes, lessons only add to the time that kids spend away from their families. Since nothing gave us greater satisfaction than to see those light bulbs illuminate in our children's heads, we realized that if we were to be available to them, we needed to be there.

And so, we soon knew that neither one of us really wanted to work in an office, away from the kids. The birth of our third son really cemented our decision to pursue self-employment. Because I believe deeply in a baby's need for his mother's constant presence—for food, warmth, security, and love—we knew that we were at least delaying economic security for another five years, which was something that was going to be a real hardship under our new circumstances. We needed more income. We needed to find a way to do that while still allowing us to create the family life we wanted for ourselves. We knew it would not be an immediate change, but we seemed to set out down a path, perhaps unconsciously to a large extent, that led us to working from home.

Meeting a family's financial and social needs should not be mutually exclusive. We live in a culture where children are still to be seen and not heard to a great extent. We sigh with annoyance when a co-worker brings their kids into the office on a no-school day. We relegate our children to planned activities so that we can have some "me time" in every aspect of daily living—from work to worship. We squirm when we see a baby nurse in a restaurant, and we glare without empathy when that same baby cannot be comforted easily. Everyone agrees that children are great—most people want them—but they want them on their terms. Somewhere along the way we've forgotten to ask, "What do the children want?"

Jesse Jackson said it most profoundly: "Your children need your presence more than your presents." This does not end with infancy. Nor does it even end with early childhood. It is commonly sited that most teenage pregnancies occur between the hours of three o'clock and six o'clock in the afternoon—after school is over but before parents return home from work. And yet even teenagers will gravitate toward the "Kool-Aid house," that house where an adult is available to be a sounding board and unobtrusive role model.

People say, "Being a stay-at-home mom isn't an option for everyone." And that's true; it's not. But neither is it only an option for the independently wealthy or upper middle-class, one-income families. On one hand, it is possible to take a hard look at what what's really important and tailor your lifestyle to meet your one income. But it is also possible to change the face of what it means to be an employed parent. Working at home is one way to earn money while being available to your children, but there are many other possibilities. Many parents are now taking babies to work with them or working on alternating schedules so that one parent is available to the children at any given time.

> Meeting a family's financial and social needs should not be mutually exclusive.

There are many ways bring in money without outsourcing our children, and all have advantages and disadvantages on a personal level. Our family's choice for everyone to be home most of the time certainly falls well outside of the mainstream. There are less radical ways to implement the critical changes that our going to bring our children into the foreground of culture and society.

And truly, working, schooling, and living at home can be a challenge. The way that we have chosen to create a home-based life will look different from what others might choose. Some might work at home, but send the kids to the neighborhood school, others might have one parent employed outside of the home, and still others may just prefer to do what they can after work and school hours to make family life more rich and rewarding. What has worked for my family may not be effective for others, but here are some things that we have done that help our family lifestyle become a fulfilling one:

* Give everyone, including (perhaps especially) the littlest, the same respect that we want for ourselves. This means hearing what everyone has to say and eliciting input from everybody on those things that can be decided by the group. Where to take the next vacation and even which book to read next may be negotiable, but respecting personal space may not be.

* Establish some sacrosanct family rituals. One meal a day together and no business calls during evening family time are some ways that we try to keep the inevitable flow of work from running into all aspects of our lives.

* Don't forget that taking care of the individual means that the group functions more cohesively. For the parents this may mean getting some exercise or fresh air—a walk, a trip to the gym, or a yoga class is welcome. For

the kids in families with more than one child, spending time with each child separately (even if it a simple trip to the grocery store or post office) fosters their sense of individuality and those interpersonal relationships.

● Be predictable, but flexible. Kids do thrive on rhythm and routine, but everyone in the family needs to understand that sometimes work or family will have to take priority over the schedule. One of the most liberating things for parents is learning to say, "I've changed my mind." And working during unfavored hours will allow you to take kids to lessons or take daytrips now and then.

● Remember to savor the little things. Sometimes you might wonder why you're taking the long way around. Try to bring your focus back to why you've consciously chosen this lifestyle: to put your family first.

The details of my story are not important—they are only illustrations of how one family is living a home-based life. What is important is that, over time, children come to be seen as part of the fabric of our society, rather than as accessories to be included or not, as convenient. As for me, I don't want to look back, sixteen years from now, and say, "Where did the years go? It all went so fast!" I want to be here, now.

© Gina Gerboth

About the Author

Gina Gerboth is a freelance writer, editor, and indexer who works from her home in Southern Colorado. When not busy working, learning alongside her three young sons, volunteering, or researching her latest project, Gina enjoys reading, movie-watching, knitting, and practicing yoga.

The aim of college, for the individual student, is to eliminate the need in his life for the college; the task is to help him become a self-educating man.

C. Wright Mills

Understanding the atom is a childish game in comparison with the understanding of the childish game.

Albert Einstein

Literature is strewn with the wreckage of those who have minded beyond reason the opinion of others.

Virginia Woolf

I'm talking about these people who cry when their son is standing there in an orange jumpsuit. Where were you when he was two? Where were you when he was twelve? Where were you when he was eighteen, and how come you didn't know he had a pistol? And where is his father, and why don't you know where he is? And why doesn't the father show up to talk to this boy?

Bill Cosby

If you are planning for one year, grow rice. If you are planning for twenty years, grow trees. If you are planning for centuries, grow men.

Chinese proverb

Most want the wealth of this country to be used for human needs-health, work, schools, children, decent housing, a clean environment-rather than for billion-dollar nuclear submarines and four billion-dollar aircraft carriers.

Howard Zinn

I trust the time is coming, when the occupation of an instructor of children will be deemed the most honorable of human employment.

Angelina Weld Grimke

... the most important thing you can learn in this era of heightened global competition is how to learn.

Thomas L. Friedman

I think back on my father's example of responsibility; when a spider was frightening me by crawling up the wall, he would be called. He would come quickly, wearing a serious and dutiful expression on his face. My dad would actually trap the spider with a little cup and a piece of stiff paper, and then release it outdoors. As I saw the objectionable thing crawl away, not much registered except for relief that I would not be traumatized by that wicked little arachnid after all! However, unbeknownst to me, my mind was being taught; I was learning some deep lessons about how to be in the world.

Jason Merchey

How many times have we heard that our children are "the future of our country?" How seriously do we take that? We must ensure that the youngsters of this country and all other countries start out on the right foot and that these children have the right values and beliefs instilled in them from the beginning. We must strengthen our schools and communities, fostering a stronger environment for learning for our nation's youth.

Max Cleland

Thank goodness I was never sent to school; it would have rubbed off some of the originality.

Beatrix Potter

Once I knew how to read, I was off on my own.

Dennis Kucinich

What the mother sings to the cradle goes all the way down to the coffin.

Henry Ward Beecher

I saw the angel in the marble and I carved until I set him free.

Michelangelo

A child is not a vase to be filled, but a fire to be lit.

François Rabelais

How is it that little children are so intelligent and men so stupid? It must be education that does it.

Alexandre Dumas

TRUTH

PURSUING TRUTH THROUGH SUFFERING

Sean Gonsalves

It may seem odd that a paid-member of the "liberal" media, which, for many, implies a commitment to undermining religious life, would acknowledge publicly that religion is the very foundation of my journalism.

And not just any religion, but a particular, historically-conditioned, Bible-centered religious tradition; namely, the black Baptist Church.

Within that tradition, despite its deep homophobia and sexism, I was nurtured to identify with what Jesus called "the least of these my brethren"—the despised, the dispossessed, the disenfranchised, the despairing.

I didn't shout "amens" or "Thank you, Jesus!" during church services, but the seeds of wisdom embedded in that environment were planted deep within my soul as an adolescent.

It's only recently that I've begun to truly appreciate the depth of wisdom imparted.

Though the elderly women in the church of my youth had little, if any, formal education, I recall one "church mother" pulling me aside one day after Sunday School. She inquired as to why I had a sour expression on my face. I don't remember my response but I remember hers.

She quoted the gospel of Luke, in which Jesus says: "The Kingdom of God is within you." Based on that scripture, she said, "If the Kingdom of God is within us, that means we ought to leave a little heaven behind wherever we go."

One Sunday, a scholarly preacher, whose name I cannot recall, visited our church. He brought our attention to three familiar biblical descriptions of Jesus—that he is called "the Suffering Servant," "the Truth," and "the Word." Based on that formulation, the preacher said, if our Lord is all these things, then it is a condition of truth to allow suffering to speak.

Elaborating, he said, you can't know the truth about racism until you've heard from those who have suffered under its yoke. You can't know the truth about sexism, until you hear the cries of its victims. And you can't know the truth about economics until you've given due consideration to the plight of the poor.

These, and other, bits of ethical wisdom, handed down through generations of black folks seeking both spiritual and political freedom in a capitalist society built on white skin privilege, has left its indelible stamp on me.

It just so happens that the ideals of journalism in the United States parallels, in many important ways, my own religious values.

Values-parallel

The most prestigious award given to journalists, the Pulizter Prize, was named after Joseph Pulitzer, editor of *New York World* and the *St. Louis Post-Dispatch*. In his statement of policy, he implored journalists to: "always oppose privileged classes and public plunderers, never lack sympathy with the poor, always remain devoted to the public welfare, never be satisfied with merely printing the news; always be drastically independent; never be afraid to attack wrong, whether by predatory plutocracy or predatory poverty."

In my ten years as a syndicated columnist and reporter for a daily newspaper, I have begun to learn the inherent limits of being a single individual working amidst a long-standing corporate culture as well as the various challenges that environment holds for those committed to the standard that Joseph Pulitzer held up as a benchmark.

The inherent limits of individual values

Much has been written about this subject by others with far more clarity and insight than I could possibly provide here—one of the most accurate analyses having been done by Noam Chomsky and Edward Herman in their classic work, *Manufacturing Consent.*

As Chomsky has observed, and as I've seen first hand, US corporate media outlets are inherently conservative. For one thing, news organizations' source of revenue comes from "the privileged classes" of which Pulitzer spoke. And, we're not talking about newspaper or cable subscriptions. We're talking about revenue from advertisers, which means that a news organization functions, to significant degree, as a tool by which a business sells audiences to other businesses.

In practice, though, newsrooms tend to be insolated from the business departments, every editor, reporter, publisher, and pundit knows what side of the bread the butter is on.

In practice, though, newsrooms tend to be insolated from the business departments, every editor, reporter, publisher, and pundit knows what side of the bread the butter is on.

Also, news organizations tend to have a bias in favor of institutions (i.e. businesses, government, and law enforcement agencies)—institutions that primarily seek to conserve or expand power.

There's also the inherent limitation of space and time. Again, applying Chomsky and Herman's observations are helpful. If, for example, I am writing about the Iraq War debate and stated that according to UNSCOM, the first team of weapon inspectors in Iraq from 1991 to 1998, had qualitatively disarmed Iraq and that whatever insignificant elements of a WMD program remained intact afterward didn't constitute a regional threat, let alone a global one.

Most, if not all, of the institutional authorities before the war, claimed Iraq did indeed have a viable WMD program and had just been keeping it secret. After the war, reality forced them to concede the WMD intelligence was "mistaken."

Mistaken? I interviewed UNSCOM's chief weapons inspector, former US Marine Captain Scott Ritter several times and he explained in great detail why Iraq couldn't possibly have a viable WMD program after the work that UNSCOM did.

Those interviews were conducted three years before the US-led invasion. I spoke to Ritter again during the Senate hearings on the "threat" posed by Iraq. He told me, and I reported, that he contacted the committee co-chairman, Senator Joseph Biden, informing the committee of his availability to testify. I called Biden's office myself and asked them why Ritter wasn't asked to testify. A Biden spokesperson told me, they were aware of Ritter's expert, on-the-ground knowledge of Iraq's WMD capabilities, or lack thereof, but still hadn't decided whether to invite him.

They never did and to this day pundits, reporters and editors continue to believe that "everyone" thought Saddam had WMD and so the eventual confirmation of Ritter's pre-war observations are said to be an instance of "mistaken" intelligence.

Of course, the reality was and is that not "everyone" was "mistaken" — especially not the guy who has more knowledge of Iraq WMD than 99.9 percent of everyone in America.

To do justice to this topic, one needs more time and space than talk shows and newspaper columns allow.

The art of truth-telling

When donning my columnist hat, given these limitations, I endeavor to take easy answers and conventional wisdom and turn them into more difficult questions—to paraphrase Professor Cornel West, another child of the black Baptist church

To put it in the religious-ethical language of my church tradition, this process of writing is a form of "iron sharpening iron," or putting received wisdom through the refiner's fire. It is an act of faith as expressed in the African proverb: to ask well is to know much.

It is my hope that such work contributes to the public good insofar as it enhances readers' intellectual self-defense skills. After all, as J.S. Mill said, "He who knows only his own side of the case, knows little of that."

More specifically, and taking a cue from George Orwell's famous essay "Politics and the English Language," I've taken to critically analyzing mealy-mouthed and misleading words and phrases we all encounter in the news. Orwell writes:

> One ought to recognize that the present political chaos is connected with the decay of language, and that one can probably bring about some improvement by starting at the verbal end. If you simplify your English, you are freed from the worst follies of orthodoxy. You cannot speak any of the necessary dialects, and when you make a stupid remark, its stupidity will be obvious, even to yourself.

> Political language—and with variations this is true of all political parties, from Conservatives to Anarchists—is designed to make lies sound truthful and murder respectable, and to give an appearance of solidity to pure wind.

From there, Orwell suggests, and I agree, that these things cannot be changed all at once but, "if one jeers loudly enough" it is possible to "send some worn-out and useless phrase into the dustbin where it belongs."

When I'm about the business of doing straight news reporting, again I call on the church values instilled in me as boy: empathize, especially with those whose views oppose your own personal preferences or frames of reference, and be honest. Go out of your way not to misrepresent a particular view or event. What is produced will not, and I would argue cannot, be completely objective. But it will be honest, fair, and inclusive of both Pulitzer's predatory plutocrats and the victims of predatory poverty; "the least of these," allowing "suffering to speak."

© Sean Gonsalves

About the Author

Formerly with Universal Press Syndicate and now self-syndicated, columnist Sean Gonsalves' work has appeared in the *Seattle Post-Intelligencer, Boston Globe, Kansas City Star, Oakland Tribune, Washington Post* and *USA Today.*

Over the past ten years, Sean's weekly column—particularly popular among progressives, liberals, and staunch conservatives blogging and web-surfing in cyberspace—has become a platform for examining the intersection of language, politics, and culture.

With the soul of a biblical prophet, Sean is a fierce critic of what Joseph Pulitzer called "predatory plutocracy and predatory poverty." His column-writing is complemented by ten years of experience as a daily reporter for the *Cape Cod Times*, where he's done everything from investigative reporting and feature-writing to covering municipal government and murders.

His reporting on the Mashpee Wampanoag Indian tribe's quest for federal recognition won first place honors from the New England Press Association in 2000 and his coverage of the tribe's dealings with indicted lobbyist Jack Abramoff, as well as his reporting on the Hurricane Katrina evacuee village set up last fall on Cape Cod's Otis Air Force Base has garnered national attention.

A father of three children, Sean is also a regular guest on *New England Cable News* morning news show in his capacity as a reporter for the Cape Cod Times. In 2000, he did a segment for Emily Rooney's popular WGBH show *Greater Boston.*

A frequent lecturer and radio-talk show guest, he has made frequent appearances on the *Michael Medved Show*, NPR, alternative radio stations, and the BBC.

When the press is free, and every man is able to read, all is safe.

Thomas Jefferson

[The early Christians illustrate] how a steadfast and heroic moral minority undermined the world's greatest empire and eventually came to power. Faced with relentless and spectacular forms of repression, they kept on meeting over their potluck dinners (the origins of later communion rituals), proselytizing and bearing witness wherever they could. For the next four years and well beyond, liberals and progressives will need to emulate these original Christians, who stood against imperial Rome with their bodies, their hearts and their souls.

Barbara Ehrenreich

A free press is one where it's OK to state the conclusion you're led to by the evidence.

Bill Moyers

We are all capable of believing things which we know to be untrue... and then, when we are finally proved wrong, impudently twisting the facts so as to show that we were right. Intellectually, it is possible to carry on this process for a long time, until sooner or later these false beliefs bump up against reality - often on a battlefield.

George Orwell

Nothing contributes so much to tranquilize the mind as a steady purpose - a point on which the soul may fix its intellectual eye.

Mary Wollstonecraft

The only theology worth doing is that which inspires and transforms lives, that which empowers us to participate in creating, liberating, and blessing the world.

Carter Heyward

The chief characteristics of the liberal attitude are human sympathy, a receptivity to change, and a scientific willingness to follow reason rather than faith.

Chester Bowles

PEACE

CITIZEN SOLDIERS
A Counter to Military Adventurism

John Greeley

Four years after our retaliatory invasion of Afghanistan, we are still there. After using the military to drive the Taliban from power, we find that in our haste to do something about the awful events of 9/11, perhaps the swift use of war was not the best possible approach to the problem. We did not defeat them. They simply scattered. Today, Afghan opium production has never been higher, nor has the influence of the regional warlords ever been stronger; due in large measure to increased profits from the drug trade they control.

Our government sustained and supported these same groups against the Russians because it suited our strategic, international purposes. And today, Afghan "democracy" is mostly illusory, no matter how much we may congratulate ourselves for making it happen. It is a form of government in name only. As to the question of its eventual success, it will depend on the people and on how much America interferes in their destiny. The attempt to force a military solution, although initially dramatic and apparently decisive, in the end proves to be far too simplistic and temporary.

In Iraq, the Bush administration's invasion to prevent the possibility of a tyrant attacking us—or even thinking of doing so—has done nothing positive except to depose Saddam Hussein, disband the civil service, disband the army, and allow the ancient city of Baghdad to be looted after our air attacks destroyed the sewage, electric, and water purification plants. As these issues remain unaddressed, the possibility of civil war grows with each passing day. Whether the constitution, formulated by, through, and seemingly for the benefit of the occupiers is or is not supported in the next referendum, there may already be enough politically seismic activity in motion to throw the entire country into chaos. What is important to note is that we are powerless to stop it, even though we started it.

Iraq is not so much a work of political compromise in progress that we can be proud of as much as it is an uncontrollable force of nature like a volcano near eruption. Democracy does not come easily under any circumstances and it especially does not come out of the business end of a rifle. How can an army of occupation "spread democracy"? Especially under conditions such as these, where there is not even a Status of Forces agreement in place. We are free to conduct whatever operations we choose because we are the army of occupation and have the power to do so.

And as if this were not enough, the Bush administration talks from time to time about using "the military option" against Iran, Syria, North Korea, Columbia, or indeed any other country foolish enough to oppose our international hegemony. It is clear that we no longer utilize the diplomatic corps as our primary instrument of conducting foreign policy. It is said that dealing "military to military" is more efficient based on the theory that, in lesser developed nations, the military is often the only organized institution available. If the Bush administration were to place the emphasis on more traditionally oriented international relationships, then third world diplomatic corps would be up to the task. They are there, but remain overshadowed by the military dictatorships we keep in place for strategic reasons.

This also creates opportunities for our government to lend them countless millions of dollars to finance the purchase of our military hardware so we can send technicians and military personnel to instruct and maintain the equipment. It also gives the government a way to create legally binding attachments and riders to the sales contracts favorable to our corporate business interests.

Of course, all of this is done in the name of the American people, yet no where is there an opportunity for discussion or even fewer attempts at public disclosure. We are presented after the fact with decisions made because of what is called military and strategic necessity. We are asked to accept the inevitability of the global militarization of international relations. But there is a counterbalance.

We have succeeded thus far in addressing world problems by using an all-volunteer army. We now field hand picked, dedicated people who would never think of questioning orders. They are loyal, professional and willing to expose themselves to impossible dangers in the name of patriotism and brotherhood. They are a truly admirable group of men and women in whom we can and should take a great deal of pride, but at the same time the danger to misuse their immense power is very great. One might even say it is a temptation far too great to resist. This administration certainly hasn't.

The value of creating such a fighting force became apparent after several administrations witnessed the successes of the protest movements of the 60s in swaying public opinion. "Hell no, we won't go," rang in the ears of our leaders in Washington, DC and turned their defense of the Vietnam War into the butt of a joke. To the protesters who might be drafted, this was a matter of life or death. It was seen as a serious deterrence to the will of national leadership and had to be thwarted. Universal service was abolished in 1973.

Today, those who protest our presence in both Afghanistan and Iraq are mostly limited to those whose lives are most directly affected by it; the parents, spouses, and the veterans themselves of those conflicts. They are the ones who best understand the stakes of this game. They are the ones who now question the loudest why we are there and why they must obey increasingly more absurd commands to return to combat yet again.

In large measure, most Americans are undisturbed by these events. They are too busy just trying to make a living in what has become a two-income family survival economy. And it is at this level that an entry point to the debate must be made. We all must understand that the Army is not "them." Even in the modern context of an all-volunteer service, it is still "us," but we have been led to believe that somehow it is a higher calling for which only a few are qualified to be chosen.

This is understandable, to a point, since rarely is the average person called on to offer the sacrifice of his or her life in a cause larger than themselves. Modern marketing techniques have been employed to tell us that only the best people can do that, but history tells us differently. Historical momentum comes from determined individuals who refuse to be denied what they have chosen as their goal. The same sources insist that only a few can master the highly technical aspects of modern warfare. Tell that to the jihadists carrying rocket launchers and AK-47's.

What really counts the most is the existence of strong beliefs in the rightness of the cause for which the potential sacrifice of life on the battlefield is offered. This, in turn, is conditioned on the value attached to the preservation of a particular way of life and thus intimately tied to the protection of loved ones. Presumably, all citizens everywhere want that at a minimum. The general population, especially here in America, is quite capable of being mobilized into action if they understand the gravity of the situation, and that is what we must do. We, the people, are the counterpoint, the deterrent. We are the only force big enough to dissuade an administration hell bent on ever more military adventures (for which the Congress has no political will to oppose) from pursuing them.

> We are the laborers who operate the machines of death.

We are the laborers who operate the machines of death. To go to war, any administration first has to make a coherent, credible case for its necessity. So to insure that the voice of the people is heard, we must do two things. First, we must enroll every citizen at the age of eighteen in a universal draft and require two years' service from them. That will accomplish several things. It will get everyone from every region in the nation into the program, get them a medical exam and all requisite treatment necessary to have a healthy population, and proper education as to habits, diet, and exercise to maintain that health. It also identifies other basic problems such as literacy and poverty. After basic military training, that percentage already so inclined will enter the armed forces. If more are needed, they are at hand for inclusion.

As for the rest, their training is far from having been a waste of tax revenue. They will go on to fulfill the remainder of their service either in additional job training, or field work on national projects benefiting every county in the nation, and thus, the nation as a whole. They will be our network of first responders complete with newly-learned communications skills and the equipment necessary to organize a society fractured and confused by national disasters, economic downturns, and threats from terrorists or any other source. We, the people, trained by us, the government, will never again be at a loss for what to do because living among us will be those trained in what to do and how to do it. The people will lead themselves.

The real enemy America faces has never been something out there, ready to do us harm. It has always been our fear of "it." That is the single most significant social factor threatening to tear the fabric of our society apart. We are our most important resource. Not oil, not cash accumulation. We must not let any administration teach us we are stronger by remaining divided amongst ourselves. By dispelling fear of the unknown and replacing it with basic skills and equipment to be self-reliant, at least on an emergency basis, a whole new generation of independent Americans will truly be born.

The people of New Orleans, for example, have been portrayed as having run wild because there was no government there to provide the proper supervision. What nonsense! The stories of pillage and worse were fabrications for the most part. People were desperate for water and food, so they took it. Never mind the racism inherent in much of the reporting. If working radios had been pre-positioned along with small boats, medical supplies, food and water, etc., and if there with properly trained graduates of the newly instituted draftee program armed with the knowledge to cope with the situation instead of johnny-come-lately, swat-team uniformed, M-16s-at-the-ready stormtroopers (without water, food, etc.), things would certainly have been different.

A universal draft can provide the basis for all future capabilities in war-making, the handling of natural disasters, organizing for epidemics, and for anything else the future may throw at us. United is the way we must stand because divided we surely will fall. The reason such a law will never pass is that our lawgivers recognize too much power when they see it, and they will never relinquish it. Maybe it is time for us to insist they do.

© John Greeley

About the Author

John Greeley served in the Marine Corps from 1963 to 1967 and returned from one tour of duty in Vietnam in 1966 with the rank of Captain. He used the GI Bill to attend St. John's University Law School at night, graduating in 1975. Since then, he practiced law for a few years after which he went into business in the real estate and construction industries where he remains to this date.

After years of studying international relations and domestic policy, he went to work for the Vietnam Veterans of America Foundation in Washington, DC and spent several years focusing in on the relationship between waging war and foreign policy. He was a contributing editor for *Interventionmag* and currently writes for his own blog, Thoughtfulcitizen.blogspot.com. He has recently formed Thoughtfulcitizen, Inc. where he continues to write on current events, occasionally offering op ed pieces to various publications.

One is left with the horrible feeling now that war settles nothing; that to win a war is as disastrous as to lose one.

Agatha Christie

War on nations changes maps. War on poverty maps change.

Muhammad Ali

I am thinking about violence and intolerance a lot these days. The human desire for vengeance is so deep that one wonders how the cycles of violence can ever by stopped. I fear humans become immune to violence after awhile. Violence becomes routine and, as Max Weber would say, "takes on the appearance of being rational." We are in desperate need of progressive and humane values spreading as far and wide as possible.

Gary E. Kessler

There must be civil disobedience of laws which are contrary to human welfare. But there must be also an uncompromising practice of treating everyone, including the worst of our opponents, with all the respect and decency that he merits as a fellow human being. We can expect to face tear gas, clubs and bullets. But we must refuse to hate, punish or kill in return...

Dave Dellinger

The next great advance in the evolution of civilization cannot take place until war is abolished.

Douglas MacArthur

Peace may never come to pass until little boys everywhere are encouraged by their parents and develop the desire to play with toy peacemakers rather than toy soldiers.

Jason Merchey

It is exactly when you're in the midst of a war, or about to go into a war, that you need your freedom of speech; lives are at stake. If you are put in fear of speaking out, then democracy has been severely crippled.

Howard Zinn

RESPONSIBILITY

APOLLO NOW

William Greider

T he tragedy of New Orleans provides Americans with an ominous metaphor for understanding our future. We did not fix the levees, though we were warned. That is a simple way of expressing the national predicament in this new century. As a society, we are engulfed by similar vulnerabilities—forms of ecological and economic deterioration that are profoundly more threatening than an occasional hurricane. And we have been told. Yet we are not "fixing the levees." Preoccupied with current desires and discontents, this very wealthy nation has lost sight of its future.

The levee metaphor, vividly dramatized by the Gulf Coast disaster, has the potential to move the country in a new direction—to inspire a generational shift in thinking that could launch a new era of fundamental reforms. But the imperative to act requires nothing less than a reordering of American life—a result that seems most unlikely. Given the corrupted condition of representative democracy, politicians are seldom punished for keeping the hard truth from voters. The mass culture marinates American citizens in false triumphalism.

Events, nevertheless, have delivered a teachable moment—an opportunity to reframe and reargue many long-neglected matters. The wheels are coming off the right-wing bus. The President of Oil and War is no longer much believed. The vast suffering and physical destruction in New Orleans have made all too visible what ecologists and social critics have been trying to explain for years. Their warnings once seemed too abstract or remote to require public action. New Orleans announced, for those who will listen, that the future is now.

Oceans are warming, the Arctic ice cap is shrinking. The deep topsoil of Iowa is draining into the Mississippi River, leaving behind chemical swamps. Good drinking water, once freely available to all, has become a scarce commodity for commercial exploitation. Much of the population, dispersed farther and farther from urban centers, is pole-axed by soaring gasoline prices. Meanwhile, the gorgeous abundance of consumer goods continues to poison earth, air and water. This year, Americans will throw away something like 100 million cell phones, pagers, pocket PCs and portable music players, interring their toxic contents in the "dump" called nature.

> The vast suffering and physical destruction in New Orleans have made all too visible what ecologists and social critics have been trying to explain for years.

Should we blame the farmers? The oil and chemical companies? The teenagers who love their gadgets? The politics of blame-and-shame was brilliantly perfected thirty years ago by the environmental movement but gradually lost its effectiveness, partly because it framed the contest as a righteous struggle between good guys and bad guys—virtuous citizens versus dirty industrial polluters (and often their workers). It felt good to identify the culprits, but moral indignation eventually loses its power to enforce. Plus, the enormity of what we face is too all-encompassing. Not many of us can truly claim innocence.

The predicament is fundamental and universal: It is the collision between industrial society and nature. Politicians and environmental activists can be forgiven for not wishing to take on the "American way of life," but essentially that is what's required. Eliminating this collision, before it destroys the very basis of modern prosperity and life itself, calls for nothing less than the transformation of the American industrial system and mass-consumption economy. Among other things, it means reinventing the processes of production and redesigning virtually every product. It means taking responsibility for what we make and consume—recovering what is now discarded in landfills, dumped in rivers or vaporized in air and atmosphere. It means remanufacturing components and materials into new products.

Daunting and radical as that all might sound, the good news is that these great changes are technologically feasible. The transformation will take decades, even generations, to complete, but industrial experts affirm that it is doable. Starting promptly on this historic commitment will avoid (or at least mitigate) the larger catastrophes ahead.

The real obstacle is political, not scientific, because reform depends on the choices society makes (or fails to make). Who is the "we" responsible for these choices? One way or another, it is all of us. Virtually every institution of capitalism—manufacturers and merchants and, above all, the financiers who discipline them—will be compelled to alter routine functions in deep ways. But so will consumers and workers. As with other aspects of American life, the burden will not fall evenly on every citizen. Sacrifices and disruptions are typically maldistributed downward on the ladder of income and status. The goals of environmentalism often sound preciously elitist because the most severe costs usually fall on the working class or poor, people with limited margins. Not surprisingly, they sometimes resist.

It will be essential to recognize that inequality is an ecological issue. If this sweeping transformation proceeds, the impact on work, wages and living standards has to be a central component of the reform agenda—not just necessary for political support but also to insure that a healthier society emerges from the deep changes. In fact, the logical promise of industrial transformation is that it will lead to better lives for all—improved circumstances and health, greater economic security and brighter prospects for the future. Every ordinary American wants that, and every ordinary American is entitled to expect it.

Making it happen requires a new progressive perspective that fuses the ecological imperative with economic outcomes. We need a synthesis that replaces fear with hope—not as rhetoric but bolstered with proof that this goal is attainable for all. Inventive minds are already working on it.

Washington isn't going to enact such a bold program while oil-based Republicans remain in power. But the Apollo agenda is generating forward momentum on state and local levels, field-testing the politics of fusion as blue-green partners argue out their differences. In California a plan for homeowner tax breaks to finance a "million solar roofs" temporarily stalled (and rightly so) on labor's demand for prevailing wage rates for the workers who will do the installation. When Washington State was enacting its green building code, the paper industry initially persuaded machinists and carpenters to oppose the higher standards for timbering as a threat to local jobs. But the unions reversed themselves when the alliance demonstrated that the industry's job claims were false. (In fact, the legislation gives preference to regionally produced lumber.)

"We have a lot of examples where we have gotten rid of the wedge, a few cases where we failed," Rickert said. "It's still the beginning, but I think we've gotten past the toughest patch." In one notable example, the United Mine Workers Union, whose coal miners are the most directly threatened by climate-change reform, has officially acknowledged that global warming must be addressed. That might seem like a small step, but it puts the UMW out in front of ExxonMobil.

Meanwhile, a new coalition of Christian conservatives—Set America Free—has launched its own campaign to reduce US oil consumption with reform ideas that parallel the Apollo Alliance. Unfortunately, both left and right efforts are embracing the utterly illusory, soothing-sounding goal of "energy independence" within the next decade or two. But the two efforts demonstrate the potential for new alliances that leap across the usual barriers of party and ideology.

Even so, the struggle for industrial transformation advances here on many fronts. Activist campaigns are encouraging American companies and sectors to adopt higher ecological standards in their products and purchasing, covering everything from wood to hamburgers. Other efforts are developing enterprises that embrace the new values.

The concept of take-back laws is slowly gaining traction at the state level for consumer electronics and packaging, though not yet for cars. Local governments, which bear the financial burden of waste disposal, are beginning to think seriously about shifting some of the cost to manufacturers, through fees or taxes on sales—giving companies a strong reason to produce less waste in the first place. Xerox and other industry leaders are developing take-back and reuse programs, anticipating the legal responsibility that will someday be the standard. The ultimate goal is producing waste-free products.

California—first in the nation as usual—has enacted a take-back law for computer monitors and television sets; the customer pays a fee of about $10 up front, financing the eventual recycling and recovery costs when these items are discarded. Maine's new law on recycling electronics is much closer to the European approach, however, because it compels the manufacturers to internalize these costs on their balance sheets. The companies, not the consumers, will either pay pound-for-pound for recycling their worn-out products or do the work themselves. Either way, the cost pressure is on them to reduce waste and harm—a concept known as "extended producer responsibility."

A potential breakthrough exists in a consortium of legislators from ten Northeastern states. The consortium members are developing a model state law based on the Maine example. If they get it right, we could see rapid political advances at the state level. (Bush's Environmental Protection Agency, meanwhile, studied the matter for four years—and then punted.)

When industrial transformation does finally come to our shores, Americans will discover a wonderful wrinkle—it creates jobs, many millions of them. The consuming public will be more enthusiastic about serious reform once folks recognize that industrial reordering delivers good jobs with good wages for Americans—not more bucket-shop employment that exploits workers.

If the United States takes the high road, every level of our society can benefit from the economics of doing what we need to do anyway. The metaphor of the New Orleans levees poses the question: Will we decide to reshape the future in positive terms, or sit back and let the bad stuff happen to us?

Reprinted by permission from The Nation *and William Greider.*

About the Author

William Greider, a prominent political journalist and author, has been a reporter for more than thirty-five years for newspapers, magazines and television. Over the past two decades, he has persistently challenged mainstream thinking on economics.

For seventeen years Greider was the National Affairs Editor at *Rolling Stone* magazine, where his investigation of the defense establishment began. He is a former assistant managing editor at the Washington Post, where he worked for fifteen years as a national correspondent, editor, and columnist. While at the Post, he broke the story of how David Stockman, Ronald Reagan's budget director, grew disillusioned with supply-side economics and the budget deficits that policy caused, which still burden the American economy.

He is the author of the national bestsellers *One World, Ready or Not, Secrets of the Temple* and *Who Will Tell the People.* In the award-winning *Secrets of the Temple,* he offered a critique of the Federal Reserve system. Greider has also served as a correspondent for six *Frontline* documentaries on PBS, including "Return to Beirut," which won an Emmy in 1985.

Greider's next book will be *The Soul of Capitalism: Opening Paths to A Moral Economy.* In it, he untangles the systemic mysteries of American capitalism, details its destructive collisions with society, and demonstrates how people can achieve decisive influence to reform the system's structure and operating values.

Raised in Wyoming, Ohio, a suburb of Cincinnati, he graduated from Princeton University in 1958. He currently lives in Washington, DC.

We know more about war than we know about peace, more about killing than we know about living. We have grasped the mystery of the atom and rejected the Sermon on the Mount.

Omar Bradley

Now is the time to think like poets, to envision and make visible a new society: a peaceful, cooperative, loving world without poverty and oppression, limited only by our imaginations.

Robin D. G. Kelley

We're not trying to fight the old system. We're trying to build a new one.

Susan Collin Marks

While it is true that without a vision the people perish, it is doubly true that without action the people and their vision perish as well.

Johnetta Betsch Cole

Ultimately, having a world that endures means reducing both the average individual's consumption and aggregate rates of population growth, as well as applying technological change to reduce human impacts on the environment. Having a world that is equitable and peaceful means ending gross disparities in income, power, and consumption.

Robert Engelman

Great movements in the past have arisen from small movements, from tiny clusters of people who have gotten together here and there. If you've got a movement that's strong enough, it doesn't really matter who's in the White House; what really matters is what are people saying, what are people doing, what are people demanding.

Howard Zinn

From the positive perspective, our species is going to survive, evolve, and eventually we will look back on the problems of today and wipe our collective brows, exclaiming: "Whew! We were mired in some deep moral, environmental, and societal problems, but we made it! Peace abounds; justice reigns; truth flourishes!"

Jason Merchey

JUSTICE

VIOLENCE

Laurent Grenier

Flashes of memory stream into my consciousness. They take me back thirty years plus. I was a boy then, a newcomer to a poor and tough neighborhood. My parents, of moderate means and daring to a fault, had decided to move there after my father had accepted an editing job in the federal government. They had taken a lease on a low-rent brick house, which was also run-down, covered in filth, and littered with trash. I do not mince my words: Previous tenants had been pigs that got along with bugs and rats.

"The house has potential," my mother had said to reassure me, seeing that I was aghast at its sordid aspects. Its one redeeming feature, besides its solid construction, was a large woody front yard, neglected, allowed to become a large dumping ground, as weedy as it was woody, but potentially attractive and pleasant, to be sure.

My mother was a hard worker with a great deal of stamina, creativity, and tastefulness. She mastered the art of doing wonders with little money. After three months of intense labor—which for the first week involved a carpenter and two garbage collectors plus two dump trucks—the house was transfigured, quite presentable, even nice, much to my amazement. It now contrasted sharply, cuttingly, with the slums at the rear of the house and on the left of it. On the right was a school and at the front, across the street, was a nunnery on a large piece of land. My parents had conveniently focused their attention on these establishments, as if the good education and good disposition of their teachers and sisters could shield us from the evils of the slums.

Needless to say, they did not. Violence was rampant in this neck of the woods and I was elected punchbag with only one dissenting vote: mine! At the root of this violence was malevolence, which grows from resentment, after one has been subjected to mistreatment. As much as my family projected an image of distinction, the neighborhood boys were malevolent and violent toward me. To them this image of distinction was an act of humiliation; their feelings were hurt and it was natural for them to hurt me. Of course it is a lot worthier to elevate oneself than to abase someone else. It is also a lot harder, and nature spontaneously levels everything the easy way. Moral excellence relates to culture, is an acquired trait, by virtue of which a human is courageous and just, worthy of praise.

One winter evening, I was crossing the field next to the rink where I had played hockey, when a gang of hoodlums encircled me like a pack of wolves. There were six of them, one of whom—a weakling who always relied on others to feel powerful—lived three doors down, east of my house, across the back street. The leader stepped forward and turned around with a snicker. "Hey shithead, come and kiss my ass." I was tempted to kick it, not kiss it. "No thanks. Please let me go; I don't care for trouble." As I was finishing my sentence, one of the boys lunged toward me from behind and shoved me forward. I dropped my hockey equipment and braced myself to fight and suffer. I was big for my age, but big is small when outnumbered by six to one.

Again the leader took the initiative; the fight was on. With several thrusts, punches, and kicks, I repelled my assailants momentarily, until I was knocked and wrestled to the ground. Fists and feet hit me everywhere, non-stop, from all directions. Suddenly I heard a menacing shout and everyone slipped in a last blow before fleeing. A brave and kind man had caught sight of their misdeed and chosen to intervene, armed with a hockey stick. I was hurt but saved.

A few days later, still aching all over, I saw the weakling, alone by his house—his hovel to be exact, which was covered with old imitation brick, torn in places, and infested with cockroaches, rats, and woodworms. His face was bruised and wet from weeping, as he screamed with rage, "Fucking bastard, fucking bitch, fucking life, fuck, fuck, fuck!" My anger was now tempered with compassion. I unclenched my fists, prompted by a desire to spare him. I could not demean myself to add pain to his pain, already so excessive that it overflowed in streams of tears and curses.

His father was an illiterate and idle drunkard who collected welfare and spent considerable time and money at the tavern. At home, slouching in an armchair, he forever watched TV and drank beer or liquor. When grossly intoxicated, he sometimes vomited before reaching the bathroom and, without cleaning up his mess, fell unconscious on his bed, the armchair, the floor, or wherever. He was also vulgar and brutal. He often battered his son and his wife, and heaped insults on them.

His wife was an abusive and sluggish woman who had grown obese from attempting to fill her inner void with chips, cookies, and pop. Day after day she wore the same tattered nightgown and constantly found reasons for bawling out her son and swiping him. She drove him insane, then used this insanity as another reason for persecuting him.

These two loathsome and pitiful parents rendered his life at home unbearable. He usually roamed the streets with fellow-sufferers from similar—miserable and violent—backgrounds. Together they ganged up and took their resentment out on other kids such as me. My aggressors, first, were victims.

My insight into the origin of violence came to me at that time and has never left me. I saw then and still see a victim in every aggressor. Some say there is such a thing as gratuitous violence, committed by individuals whose youth was favorable to all appearances. Violence for the sake of violence, an exercise in brutality at the expense of others, without provocation, past or present? I beg to differ.

Appearances are not a valid means of assessing someone's youth, whose favorableness or unfavorableness is a subjective, not objective, matter. Circumstances have no value in themselves, but in relation to people who consider them favorably or not. Attitude is here the only relevant concept. Also, brutality cannot be exercised at the expense of others unless these others are viewed heartlessly as expendable. This heartlessness is greatly suspicious, unlikely to belong to someone who regards humans with favor, thanks to a feeling of solidarity, of mutual benefit.

In my opinion, aggressiveness is triggered by hostility, without which it is dormant: a mere potentiality incapable of harm. It may include an abnormal sensitivity or intellect that intensifies or alters someone's perception of the environment. The fact remains hostility, as perceived by someone who feels painfully antagonized and proportionally victimized, is always a factor. Therefore, aggression cannot be dissociated from victimization, not only that of the victims but also that of the aggressors. These aggressors are victims of their sick minds or of the ill treatment they have endured. They deserve compassion, besides indignation.

They are liable to a punishment that ought to be effective and exemplary, not vengeful. Vengeance and violence are one and the same thing. Both are resentful and harmful. Both are reprehensible. The harm inflicted does not remedy the harm suffered; it simply compounds one harm with another, and invites yet another harm. It lengthens the chain of savagery from x (a frightening number of savage links) to x+1, potentially +2, +3, +4, etc., instead of breaking it and helping to free humanity from it. There is no worse slavery than savagery. The best course is to make every effort to get over a wrong and forgive it, while bringing the wrongdoer to justice.

In sum, justice should not serve to avenge people. It should serve to prevent crime and protect the public, by intimidating or incarcerating those who are a menace to others except under threat or behind bars. It should never push the severity of this mandate to the point of cruelty, in which case it would be a perversion of justice, an ominous sign of barbarity. On the contrary, it should be a jewel in the crown of civilization and foreshadow the coming of a better humanity, more consistent with its true nature and purpose—in a word, more humane.

The difference between severity and cruelty is radical yet subtle; it must be emphasized. Cruel law enforcers delight in the punishments they inflict and readily overstep the mark. They are vicious and blameworthy, like the criminals they punish. Law enforcers who are severe, but not cruel, administer punishments reluctantly or regard them as a necessary evil they would gladly forgo if they could. They deplore the criminal element in society and strive to neutralize it through intimidation, or incarceration as a last resort, and preferably through reformation, a fundamental change of the criminal mind for the better. Their ideal, as unattainable as it is elevated, is the supremacy of justice without the institution of justice: no threats, no prisons, only people who deeply understand and freely exercise the principle of justice.

Impossible as this supremacy is, it is usefully pursued. The institution of justice can become less and less necessary for the manifestation of justice, which can become more and more customary. This progress depends on the wisdom and willpower of its proponents who make it their duty to educate, assist, and encourage potential followers. It also presupposes that these potential followers take an active part in this endeavor. They cannot be actual followers unless they welcome this education, assistance, and encouragement, and display intelligence and determination of their own.

> Generally, in a loving environment, human beings show humanity as naturally as fruit trees give fruit in the summer.

How much can we collectively be civilized—that is, mutually respectful and helpful, in the knowledge that this high goal can unite our wills toward a common good of colossal proportions? In other words, what is the ceiling of our possible civilization, which implies responsibility and solidarity, an elevation of life to love? Nobody knows the limit, so none should be set but the sky!

Generally, in a loving environment, human beings show humanity as naturally as fruit trees give fruit in the summer. Love is to these beings as sunshine is to these trees. It helps them grow into what they are meant to grow into (unless their nature is flawed from the start, which is an exception to the rule): beautiful and bountiful creations, as opposed to ugly and puny aberrations. Yet, beware of love; it can be possessive and manipulative, selfish and devilish! Yes, some angels have horns, unnoticeable at first sight under their pretty hair; their paradise is hell.

True love is in the image of God (by God I simply mean the fundamental cause of everything. It brings us into existence and, within the limits of its might, supports us in our quest for fulfillment). It is a desire to nurture, not to capture. Under its divine rule, one always has the other's best interests at heart. No one, however, should be supportive to the point of being an accomplice in someone's oppressive or destructive acts of egocentricity, folly, or injustice. These evils should not be loved and served; they should be hated and combated.

Hate is legitimate toward them, whereas the people who embody them are worthy of love because they exceed them by their ability to do good. They are indeed greater than the sum of their evil ways; they include the power to improve them. Therefore hate is directed at these ways, and love at this power: It promotes the people's ability to do good. What if a person who is oppressively or destructively egocentric, foolish, or unjust never responds to this love? In that case it is lost and the life of this person shamefully amounts to a waste of soul.

By a stroke of luck, my parents were bright and warm people who helped me blossom into a joyful and respectful individual. Their love was true and so was the love of many others who took part in my life. I was also lucky enough to be a good seed. I was a strong and healthy boy, extremely lively and moderately clever, cheery and gentle-natured, though impatient and self-assertive. In my eyes, until my family moved to the poor and tough neighborhood, civility was the norm among the members of society; it made sense. Barbarity, on the other hand, was a stupefying rarity. The abused weakling gave me an understanding of barbarity—which was common in this neighborhood—and replaced my stupefaction with commiseration.

Excerpted from the book A Reason for Living, *by Laurent Grenier,*
http://laurentgrenier.com/ARFL.html.

About the Author

Laurent Grenier's career as a full-time writer and philosopher spans over twenty years. He has released various articles in art and philosophical magazines. He has also written some philosophical essays, a collection of memories and thoughts, and a compendium of physiology and nutrition, still unpublished.

As the twig is bent, the tree is inclined.

Virgil

True strength is delicate.

Louise Nevelson

It is essential and useful to introduce in the minds of children whenever they face some conflict [that] the best way, the most realistic way, to solve the conflict is dialogue, not violence. Violence means one side [wins a] victory, [and] one side [must face] defeat.

Tenzin Gyatso

The direction of cultural evolution - including whether a social system is warlike or peaceful - depends on whether we have a partnership or a dominator social structure.

Riane Eisler

We'll never stop the cycle of violence unless we stop the violence at home and unless we invest in the health and the skills and the intellect and the character of young people of America. That is part of what liberalism is about.

Paul Wellstone

Try trusting that love is in our genetic code, that we are meant for it, and that it is our ultimate source of wisdom. It involves surrendering to not knowing while hungering to know. And perhaps this reconnection to what matters - through nature, human relationships, and the sacred dimension in life - will be the true source of power that takes us from here to there.

Betsy Taylor

Peace is possible around the world, and children are the answer.

Quincy Jones

We humans have the capacity to change the world with acts of love and kindness. Let's start by teaching our children the importance of compassion.

Goldie Hawn

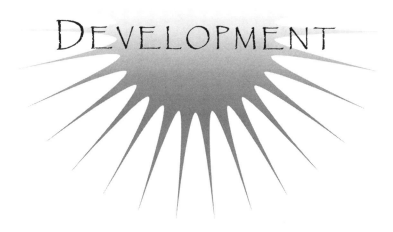

DEVELOPMENT

THE GREAT EXODUS
From the Horror and Darkness
of the Human Condition

Jeremy Griffith

The human condition is the underlying issue in all human affairs and finding understanding of it delivers a whole new, utterly fulfilling, world-saving, and almost unbearably exciting way for humans to live.

The human condition is not, as some think, the state of inequality or warring or globalized greed or environmental devastation or racial and gender oppression in the world, although these problems are all products of it. It is the issue of our species' non-ideal, corrupted, "fallen" state.

The real, fundamental question about humans is why are we so competitive, aggressive and selfish when the ideals are to be cooperative, loving and selfless? Are humans essentially good and if so, what is the cause of our evil, destructive, insensitive and cruel side?

The difficulty however has been that whenever we tried to think about this fundamental question we couldn't find an answer and, not finding one, were left feeling insecure, uncertain about our goodness and worth. In fact, so deeply depressing has the underlying issue of our human condition been that we learnt, from a very early age, not to think about it. Indeed, while there has been an infinite amount written on the subject of humans' capacity for good and evil, only a rare few individuals have been able to engage the core issue and fear in being human of whether or not we are at base evil, meaningless, worthless beings—even, for the believing, unGodly. The twentieth-century philosopher Nikolai Berdyaev was one who was brave enough to write of an "ancient, primeval terror" in facing the issue of "the fallen state of the world," elaborating that "the very distinction between good and evil is a bitter distinction, the bitterest thing in the world…There is a deadly pain in the very distinction of good and evil, of the valuable and the worthless."[1] The philosopher Søren Kierkegaard was another who dared to articulate the "deadly" depression caused by trying to confront the "tormenting contradiction" of our condition, saying the depression is so great it is equivalent to living death and, as a result, we learn not to "even dare strike up acquaintance with" it, so much so we are able to "only now and then" "glimpse" "its presence." In his suitably titled book, *The Sickness Unto Death*, Kierkegaard wrote:

> Human alienation is at base our denial, or block out, of the issue of the human condition.

> …the torment of despair is precisely the inability to die…that despair is the sickness unto death, this tormenting contradiction, this sickness in the self; eternally to die, to die and yet not to die…there is not a single human being…in whose innermost being there does not dwell an uneasiness, an unquiet, a discordance, an anxiety in the face of an unknown something, or a something he doesn't even dare strike up acquaintance with…he goes about with a sickness, goes about weighed down with a sickness of the spirit, which only now and then reveals its presence within, in glimpses, and with what is for him an inexplicable anxiety.[2]

Human alienation is at base our denial, or block out, of the issue of the human condition. The psychiatrist R.D. Laing recognised that "the condition of alienation…is the condition of the normal man"[3], emphasising the extent of it when he said that "between us and It [our true self and the issue that resides there] there is a veil which is more like fifty feet of solid concrete. Deus absconditus. Or we have absconded."[4] Laing, like Kierkegaard, also pointed out that we have so blocked out the issue of the human condition we hardly know it exists, saying, "We are so out of touch with this realm [where the issue of the human condition resides] that many people can now argue seriously that it does not exist," summarising in the next sentence that "it is perilous indeed to explore such a lost realm."[5] We can appreciate how "perilous" it has been and thus how important the "fifty feet of solid concrete" block out is when we consider that if we were to suddenly remove the block out and fully confront the issue of the human condition we would, at that moment, die from suicidal depression—or at least go mad.

In his poem, "No Worst, There is None" (like Kierkegaard's *The Sickness Unto Death*, another apt title) Gerard Manley Hopkins summarised the suicidally deep depression that faced anyone who dared plumb the terrifying depths of the issue of our corrupted condition with the words, "O the mind, mind has mountains; cliffs of fall/Frightful, sheer, no-man-fathomed.[6]

It is true that until now this riddle of riddles of the existence of good and evil in our human make-up hasn't been able to be understood, or "fathomed," and that near total denial of the issue has been the only means to cope with it. What has happened to change all this is that science has finally made it possible to explain this ultimate of riddles; science enables us to understand that when humans became fully conscious and able to wrest management of our lives from our instincts, our instincts resisted this takeover and that it was this opposition that unavoidably led to the upset angry, egocentric and alienated state of our human condition.

A simple analogy helps explain what happened. We all know that many bird species are perfectly instinctively orientated to migratory flight paths. Of course this is not a conscious understanding of where they should or shouldn't fly, rather it's an instinctive orientation their species acquired over generations of natural selection. What then would happen if we placed a fully conscious brain, such as humans have, in the head of one of these migrating birds? With its newly acquired conscious mind this bird now needs to understand where it should and shouldn't fly. Not having any understandings it has to find this knowledge through experimentation. Looking down from its migratory flight path, it sees an apple tree on an island and thinks, "why not fly down for a feed?" Not knowing any reason why it shouldn't, it goes ahead with this, its first experiment in self-management, and flies toward the island. As soon as it does so however its instinctive self tries to pull it back on course. It is in fact inadvertently trying to stop its search for knowledge. The bird's instinctive self in effect criticizes it because the instinctive self is unaware or ignorant of the conscious self's need to search for knowledge. The bird is in a dilemma—it is experiencing the equivalent of the human condition. If it obeys its perfectly orientated instinctive self it will remain perfectly on course but it will never find understanding. If it defies its instinctive self it will find understanding but it will have to live with the ignorant criticism from its instinctive self. Unable to discard its brain the bird has no choice but to persevere with its experiments in understanding and battle the criticism. Not able to refute the criticism with explanation of why these mistakes were necessary all the bird could do was retaliate against the criticism, try to prove it wrong or simply ignore it. It did all three: it became angry towards the criticism; it tried to demonstrate its worth, prove it was good and not bad; and it blocked out the criticism. The conscious bird became angry, egocentric and alienated—in a word, upset.

This is similar to the Biblical account of the Garden of Eden where Adam and Eve take the fruit from the tree of knowledge—go in search of understanding—except in this presentation Adam and Eve are not the banishment-deserving evil, worthless villains they are portrayed as in Genesis but immense heroes. They had to go in search for knowledge and defy ignorance. Upset was the price we had to pay to find understanding. As it says in the song "The Man of La Mancha," we had to be prepared "to march into hell for a heavenly cause."

The fearfully depressing so-called "burden of guilt" has finally been lifted from the human race by science because, after centuries of discovery, science is now able to reveal that while the gene-based learning system can give species orientations only the nerve-based learning system is capable of insight, and therein lies the explanation of the human condition.

Finding the understanding of the fundamental goodness of humans ends the unjust criticism that has so upset us. Our anger, egocentricity and alienation can now subside. To draw on the analogy once more, our conscious bird would not have become upset if it could have explained why it was not bad to fly off course.

The real need on Earth has been to find the means to love the dark side of ourselves, to bring understanding to that aspect of our make-up—because that is where the inability to love others comes from. As psychoanalyst Carl Jung emphasized, "wholeness" for humans depended on the ability to "own their own shadow"—or as philosopher Laurens van der Post said, "True love is love of the difficult and unlovable."[7]

While the arrival of the dignifying and thus liberating biological understanding of our human condition is the ultimate breakthrough in the human journey to enlightenment—the Holy Grail of the whole Darwinian revolution—there is an immense problem with its acceptance. While humans couldn't explain our corrupted, fallen state we sensibly coped with it by denying it and creating contrived, artificial forms of reinforcement to sustain our sense of self-worth. However, with the arrival of this ameliorating truth about why we became so upset, all the artificial, fabricated denials, delusions and evasions that we have been using to cope are suddenly exposed. The truth destroys the lies, as it must, but we are now so adapted to the lies we find the truth hard to face. Honesty day, truth day, revelation day is also exposure day, transparency day, in fact the "judgement day" many mythologies have long anticipated. While "judgement day" is actually a day of great compassion—as an anonymous Turkish poet once said, it is "not the day of judgment but the day of understanding"[8]—having the truth about our false selves revealed can feel like the foundations of our whole existence are being taken from under us. When the all-precious reconciling, humanity-saving understanding of the human condition arrives, rather than it feeling like the long sought-after liberating fulfillment and reward for all our species' accumulated efforts, it feels like a hurtfully exposing, vicious, even punishing attack. Again our mythologies have foreseen this problem. In the Bible the prophet Isaiah spoke of a time when the truth arrives, which "gives you relief from suffering and turmoil and cruel bondage…[that it] will come with vengeance; with divine retribution…to save you. Then will the eyes of the blind be opened and the ears of the deaf unstopped…Your nakedness will be exposed."[9]

The essential problem that occurs when understanding of the human condition arrives is that the generation present at that junction are faced with too much change to have to adjust to. Alvin Toffler anticipated this crisis in his book *Future Shock*, writing, "Future shock…[is] the shattering stress and disorientation that we induce in individuals by subjecting them to too much change in too short a time."[10]

The question then is, how are we to cope with the sudden exposure the liberating understanding of the human condition inevitably brings? To answer this question we must first context how humans have, up until now, coped with their extremely upset angry, egocentric and alienated state.

The thirteenth-century Mongol conqueror Genghis Khan could be described as someone who lived out his upset to the full. Every day he satisfied his anger with bloodletting, his egocentricity through the domination of others, and his mind or spirit by blocking out any feelings of guilt or remorse. There would have been no peace in his world or in his own life.

The need to manage excessively upset behaviour led to the establishment of the first major social form of control, "Imposed Discipline"—a series of rules and laws enforcing social behaviour through threat of punishment. For example, at the time of the arrival of Europeans to North America a grand union of Indian tribes, known as the Iroquois Confederacy, was formed by two Indian prophets, Hiawatha and "The Great Peacemaker." These prophets realised that the endless rounds of payback warfare between and within the tribes could only be stopped by everyone agreeing to a set of restraining rules that were to be enforced by punishment. So effective was the resulting imposed discipline that the Confederacy rapidly emerged as one of the strongest forces in northeastern North America during the 17th and 18th centuries. Parallels can be drawn with the way in which the Jewish prophet Moses effectively brought order to the Israelite Nation through his Ten Commandments.

The limitation however of imposed discipline is that restraining your upset through fear of punishment is a negative, oppressive way to have to live. As immensely successful it has been in constraining upset, complying with laws out of fear is not a very spiritually inspiring existence. What was needed was a more personally satisfying form of restraint, and the solution that arose was religion.

The essential premise of religion is that it requires individuals to defer to the soundness and integrity of thought of a great prophet, or prophets. Rather than live through your upset self you place your faith in the soundness and truth of the prophet, and in doing so you are effectively "born again" from your upset angry, egocentric and alienated state to that of a well behaved, "good" person. The benefit of religion is that you are actively participating in goodness rather than having it forced upon you; you feel you are on the side of right at last, that you are righteous, and, as a result, gain immense relief from the guilt of being so upset.

Possibly the best sales pitch ever given for religion was by the apostle St. Paul when he wrote:

> Now if the ministry that brought death, which was engraved in letters on stone, came with glory…fading though it was, will not the ministry of the Spirit be even more glorious? If the ministry that condemns men is glorious, how much more glorious is the ministry that brings righteousness! For what was glorious has no glory now in comparison with the surpassing glory. And if what was fading away came with glory, how much greater is the glory of that which lasts![11]

Thus, in coping with the human condition the first "glorious" improvement on destructively living out our upset was that of discipline enforceable by punishment. But since discipline provided little in the way of joy for the mind or spirit it was hard to maintain, it didn't "last," it was "fading," especially in comparison to the immensely guilt-relieving, "righteous" way of living offered by the next "surpassing glory," religion. Through our support of the religion's prophet we could participate in idealism.

However, as the search for knowledge continued and the resulting upset state of anger, egocentricity and alienation increased, so too did the need to find more effective ways to cope—in particular escape the increasing levels of suicidally dangerous depressing guilt. This ever increasing need to find ways to feel good and not bad about ourselves did however have an extremely dangerous potential. Eventually it could stop the search for knowledge and if that were to occur then the ultimate knowledge we had to find, namely self-knowledge, understanding of the human condition, would never be discovered and humanity would be condemned to terminal upset—specifically, unbearable levels of self-estrangement or alienation from having to adopt excessive amounts of psychological denial and delusion. Ultimately, only the reconciling, dignifying understanding of the human condition could liberate humanity from its insecure state and stop our species' march to extinction from excessive alienation.

To explain how finding relief from the ever-growing sense of guilt could stop the search for knowledge we have to return to the analogy of the bird that became fully conscious and flew off course. At any time the bird could fly back on course, obey its instinctive orientation and, in so doing, stop and thus relieve the criticism emanating from its instinctive self for having flown off course, but that meant abandoning the all-important search for knowledge.

As the need grew in more and more people to give up the corrupting quest for knowledge and take up guilt-relieving support of an expression of the cooperative, loving, selfless ideals of life, the danger of humanity entering a state of terminal alienation also increased. If we graph the growth of upset in the world it follows an exponential path, eventually entering a stage of almost vertical ascent where the levels of alienation in society double every few generations. At this point a crisis stage in the human journey occurs where there is an extreme danger of the search for knowledge ending. It is precisely this crisis point that has now arrived.

The following documents the different ways of coping that humans have had to adopt during the final stages of the march of upset—when the graph of upset climbs vertically—and which have now culminated in this crisis situation.

To derive the sense of guilt-relieving righteousness that religions supplied involved living in denial of the need to participate in humanity's heroic but corrupting search for knowledge, however given humanity's inability to clearly explain the search such denial hasn't been too difficult. In *The Simpsons* TV cartoon series, Ned Flanders is the born again religious character who is typically portrayed as having a self-satisfied, "I-occupy-the-moral-high-ground" attitude over the still-human-condition-embroiled Homer Simpson. This drives Homer crazy with frustration because he intuitively knows Ned is deluding himself in thinking he has the moral high ground, is the more together, sound person and is on the right track, but Homer can't explain why Ned is so extremely deluded and totally dishonest in his view of self.

It was this delusion and dishonesty that made giving up the battle particularly dangerous because its maintenance required constantly persuading yourself, and others, that you are right—even Ned has an intuition he is practicing delusion so he has to work hard at maintaining it. There has always been much talk of the need for freedom but it is only now that we can clearly explain what we needed to be free from—namely, free from the condemning oppression of idealism in order to search for knowledge and, to a degree, be non-ideally behaved. Dogmatic insistence on idealism oppressed the job at hand, and the associated denial and delusion destroyed the honesty that the effective pursuit of truth so depends upon.

In fact the great value and indeed beauty of religion was that while you personally had abandoned the upsetting battle of searching for knowledge, the battle continued indirectly through the honesty of the prophet your religion was founded around. The prophet's soundness was an indirect acknowledgment of your lack thereof. Religions provided a way for humans to be, to a degree, honest about their corrupted, false state without having to openly admit and therefore confront it and, in so doing, helped minimise the truth-destroying levels of denial and delusion in the world. As Carl Jung was fond of saying about Christianity, "the Christian symbol is a living being that carries the seeds of further development within itself."[12]

However, as upset increased and the need for relief from guilt grew this great benefit of religion, of its degree of honesty, became its liability. As people became more upset the honesty in religion became too confronting, guilt-inducing and dangerously depressing. By retaining a presence of soundness and truth in the form of the prophet, religion reminded us of our own corrupted state and alienation from truth, which in turn accentuated our sense of guilt. As author Mary McCarthy once wrote about religion, "Only people who are very good can afford to become religious; with all the others it makes them worse."[13]

Eventually the increasing need for a more guilt-free form of idealism to live through gave rise to socialism or communism, movements that didn't involve the condemning recognition of the world of soundness that religions were based upon. These movements avoided the whole issue of soundness and denied the depressing notion of a perfecting God. Instead they simply, dogmatically demanded an idealistic social or communal world and, in doing so, denied and oppressed the whole reality of the knowledge-finding, creative, egocentric, corrupting, unavoidably-variously-upset, individualistic, competitive, combative, materialism-compensation-needing, self-distraction-hungry, human-condition-afflicted world. As Karl Marx, whose theories underpinned socialism and communism, said, "The philosophers have only interpreted the world in various ways; the point is [not to understand the world but] to change it."[14] By "change it" he meant just make it cooperative or social or communal. The attraction—and inherent lie—of socialism or communism was that you could support and have the ideals without acknowledging the reality of humans' knowledge-finding struggle and resulting human condition. It can be seen from this that both movements were far more sophisticated than religion in their degree of evasion, superficiality and dishonesty.

The limitation of socialism or communism is that while there is no confronting prophet present, there is an obvious acknowledgment of the condemning cooperative, sound ideals. In time, as levels of upset and thus insecurity rose, the need developed for an even more guilt-free form of idealism to live through. This was supplied by the New Age Movement (the forerunners of which were the Age of Aquarius and Peace Movements). In this movement all the realities and negatives of our corrupted condition were transcended in favour of taking up a completely escapist, think-positive, human-potential-stressing, self-affirming, motivational, feel-good approach. The truth is the new age movement was not leading humanity to an aquarian new age of peaceful freedom from upset, but to an even more heightened state of deluded, dishonest alienation than that espoused by socialism. As the philosopher Thomas Nagel recognised, "The capacity for transcendence brings with it a liability to alienation, and the wish to escape this condition…can lead to even greater absurdity."[15]

The limitation of the new age movement was that while it did not remind humans of the cooperative ideals, its focus still remained the issue of humans' variously upset, troubled, estranged, alienated state—a problem the next level of delusion dispensed with by simply denying its existence. The Feminist Movement maintained that there is no difference between people, especially not between men and women. In particular it denied the legitimacy of the exceptionally egocentric, combative male dimension to life that we can now understand was taking on the heroic front role in fighting ignorance. Based on extreme dogma, the feminist movement could not and has not produced any real reconciliation between men and women, rather, as this quote points out, "What happened was that the so-called Battle of the Sexes became a contest in which only one side turned up. Men listened, in many cases sympathetically but, by the millions, were turned off."[16] Only by winning the battle to champion the ego—that is, explain the human condition and establish that our egocentric conscious thinking self is good and not bad—could the polarities of life of "good" and "evil," that women and men are in truth an expression of, be reconciled.

Where feminism falls down is in the fact that while it superficially dispensed with the problem of humans' divisive reality, we still remain the focus of attention and that is confronting. The solution that emerged to this limitation was the Environmental or Green Movement which removes all need to confront and think about the human state since all focus is diverted from self onto the environment—as this quote acknowledges, "The environment became the last best cause, the ultimate guilt-free issue."[17] Of course the truth is that by not addressing the cause of the destruction of the natural world, namely the issue of our human condition's angry, egocentric and alienated state, there has been no real let up in the pace of the devastation of our world.

Yet, for all its guilt-relieving benefits there is still a condemning moral component to the environment movement. If we are not responsible with the environment, good, we are behaving immorally, bad. Moreover, the purity of nature exists in stark contrast to humans' corrupted condition. At this stage in the march of upset a form of pure idealism had to be manufactured whereby any confrontation with the, by now, extremely confronting and depressing truth of the dilemma of the human condition was totally avoided. This need for a totally guilt-stripped form of idealism was met by the development of the Politically Correct Movement and its intellectual equivalent, the Post-modern Deconstructionist Movement. These are pure forms of dogma that fabricate, demand and impose ideality or "correctness," in particular that of an undifferentiated world, in complete denial of the reality of the underlying issue of the existence of and reasons for the different levels of alienation between individuals, sexes, ages, generations, races and cultures. In his 2001 book, *The Liar's Tale: A History of Falsehood*, Jeremy Campbell described "postmodern theory" as having elevated "lying to the status of an art and neutralised untruth." It has "neutralised untruth" because by denying the existence of the whole issue of humans' variously upset state it made any discussion of such differences—any pursuit of insight—impossible. Instead of actually reconciling and thus "deconstructing" the good versus evil dialectic and, by so doing, taking humanity beyond or "post" the existing upset, "modern" world to a human-condition-ameliorated, upset-free, "correct" one, as these movements in effect claimed they were doing, they were in reality leading humanity further away from that state. The gloves are off now, the confidence of—and sheer anger and aggression underlying—the industry of denial and delusion was such that it was now prepared to go the whole hog and brazenly mimic the arrival of the true world at the actual expense of any chance it had of arriving. The fact is post-modernism represents the very height of dishonesty, the most sophisticated expression of denial and delusion to have developed on Earth. Terminal alienation was upon us.

The science historian Jacob Bronowski summed up the dangerous situation humanity had arrived at when he said:

I am infinitely saddened to find myself suddenly surrounded in the west by a sense of terrible loss of nerve, a retreat from knowledge into—into what? Into…falsely profound questions about, are we not really just animals at bottom; into extra-sensory perception and mystery. They do not lie along the line of what we are now able to know if we devote ourselves to it: an understanding of man himself. We are nature's unique experiment to make the rational intelligence prove itself sounder than the reflex [instinct]. Knowledge is our destiny. Self-knowledge, at last bringing together the experience of the arts and the explanations of science, waits ahead of us.[18]

We can now understand that the decision by many to quit the battle to find knowledge was not a cowardly "loss of nerve" but a necessary decision to avoid suicidally dangerous depression. As upset increased, ever more deluded and artificial guilt-relieving ways of living simply had to be adopted.

Of course this guilt-relieving aspect could not be admitted because without the explanation for upset we had to cope by denying we had anything to be guilty about. To avoid admitting that these new directions in ways of living were driven by guilt we justified them by saying that they were necessary means of countering the devastating levels of upset in the world. The truth is however that the procession of movements, from religion onwards, was entirely selfishly based upon finding better ways to avoid guilt because, as we can now see, from humanity's journey to enlightenment's point of view, religions offered an infinitely better way to support idealism and counter upset both in ourselves and in the world.

The danger for humanity's journey to enlightenment came from the increased levels of delusion and denial that we were having to employ to cope. To be truly free we humans had to confront and understand our condition, not escape it by adding more and more layers of denial. Denial blocked access to the truth, that being its purpose, but ultimately we had to find the truth. The purpose of a conscious mind is to understand; ultimately to understand ourselves—as Socrates said, "the only good is knowledge and the only evil is ignorance," and "the unexamined life is not worth living"—but in the end a preference for ignorance and the associated need to oppress any examination of our lives, oppress any freedom to think, question and pursue knowledge, threatened to become the dominant attitude in the world. As George Orwell famously predicted, "If you want a picture of the future, imagine a boot stamping on a human face [freedom] forever."[19] Of the great twin political problems of the age, of the brutality of the right and the dishonesty of the left, it is the dishonesty of the left that has the potential to, and is poised to, destroy the world.

This insight can come as a shock because until now we have been unable to explain the human condition and, as a result, see through all our denials and delusions. Now that we are able to explain the human condition we can at last understand that real idealism involved being prepared to "fly off course" in search of knowledge and that these movements that lacked religion's central element of honesty and truth were pseudo-idealistic. They were deluding their adherents that they were capable of bringing about real change in the world when the truth is they were leading humanity away from any meaningful change. Ever since its inception pseudo-idealism has been the art of creating the cooperative ideal state by denying the reality of the upsetting battle involved in achieving it. The litany of pseudo-idealistic causes served to relieve humanity of excessive guilt but, as Bronowski said, "They do not lie along the line of what we are now able to know if we devote ourselves to it: an understanding of man himself."

In truth, all these movements that have emerged since the advent of religion have been led by false prophets, merchants of denial and delusion, advocates of means to escape rather than pursue understanding of our condition. Mythologies contain extremely powerful warnings about the rise of pseudo-idealism and its rejection of religion. In the Bible the apostle Matthew recorded Christ's counsel about "the sign…of the end of the age"[20] when "many will turn away from the faith…and many false prophets will appear and deceive many people,"[21] concluding that "when you see standing in the holy place "the abomination that caused desolation," spoken of through the prophet Daniel—let the reader…flee to the mountains…For then there will be great distress, unequalled from the beginning of the world until now."[22] In Daniel's description of "the abomination that causes desolation,"[23] where "truth was thrown to the ground,"[24] he said, "a stern-faced king, a master of intrigue, will arise. He will become very strong…He will cause deceit to prosper, and he will consider himself superior,"[25] and he "will invade the kingdom [of honesty] when its people feel secure, and he will seize it through intrigue [deceit],"[26] clarifying that "With [truth-and-guilt-avoiding, feel good] flattery he will corrupt those who have violated the covenant [seduce those who have become extemely upset]."[27]

In the race between self-discovery and self-destruction from terminal alienation, it appeared the latter had won. R.D. Laing got the truth up about just how sick with alienation the human race has become when he wrote: "We are born into a world where alienation awaits us[28]…the ordinary person is a shrivelled, desiccated fragment of what a person can be. As adults, we have forgotten most of our childhood, not only its contents but its flavour; as men of the world, we hardly know of the existence of the inner world[29]…The outer divorced from any illumination from the inner is in a state of darkness. We are in an age of darkness. The state of outer darkness is a state of sin, i.e. alienation or estrangement from the inner light.[30] "We are dead, but think we are alive. We are asleep, but think we are awake. We are dreaming, but take our dreams to be reality. We are the halt, lame, blind, deaf, the sick. But we are doubly unconscious. We are so ill that we no longer feel ill, as in many terminal illnesses. We are mad, but have no insight [into the fact of our madness]."[31]

What has saved the day at this eleventh hour is the arrival of the dignifying, ameliorating, biological understanding of the human condition—that is, as long as we can overcome the final hurdle arrived at earlier of there being too much accumulated superficial and artificial denial and delusion in the lives of humans, as R.D. Laing made very clear, for us to have to suddenly confront. Understanding of the human condition is the all-precious, ameliorating, liberating truth we have always sought but when it arrives, rather than feeling wonderfully liberated by it, we feel damnably exposed.

The reality is that to solve this problem of the dangerously depressing exposure that the liberating truth brings, we have two choices. We can refuse to accept the liberating knowledge—attack and try to destroy it with all the misrepresentation and vitriol we can muster while building our wall of denial up even higher to block it out. However, since the accumulated efforts of all the humans who have ever lived have essentially been dedicated to finding this liberating knowledge that will secure the welfare of all future generations, this option is not really open to us.

The second option we have is to accept and support the liberating knowledge but avoid confronting it too deeply. Clearly it is this option that we must take up—and avoiding overly confronting the exposing information can be done. We each have to investigate the explanation of the human condition that is now available sufficiently to verify to our own satisfaction that it is the liberating explanation of the human condition and then support the information without pursuing our study of it and the truths it reveals beyond what we are personally capable of confronting.

The main concern has to be that the all-important insights into our human condition are made available to future generations so they don't have to grow up without understanding of the human condition as we did. With access to the reconciling explanation of the human condition they won't have to adopt all the denials and delusions we had to adopt to cope and which now make confronting the truth about ourselves so difficult.

The task of the current generations who have grown up in the dark as it were, without the ability to understand the human condition, is to hold this key understanding aloft, support it in every way possible. By doing so the upset state of the human condition will, over only a few generations, be brought to an end. We have to see ourselves as the conduit generation connecting the old world of denial with the new denial-free world.

What is so wonderful about this new way of living is that whereas only yesterday there seemed to be no hope for the human race and the world appeared to be spiralling to destruction, suddenly, today, a totally psychologically rehabilitated human race is only a step away.

There is still some artificiality in this new way of living whereby our old egocentric, competitive, individualistic way of living is abandoned in favour of living in support of the insights into the human condition that are now available. We are not living out our upset and we are to a degree transcending our upset state, but the level of dishonesty is minimal compared to all the aforementioned artificial ways of coping with the human condition.

Importantly this new way of living has no relationship to religion. There is no deity or central figure of worship or adoration, nor is there any mysticism or religiosity or abstract metaphysic involved. The focus is entirely on knowledge, albeit knowledge we can't always confront. Further there is no faith involved. Faith has been replaced by first-principle-based knowledge that is able to be verified through scientific investigation.

The big difference in this new way of living is that the "weakness" aspect of giving up the battle has gone because the battle to "fly off course" and find knowledge, ultimately self-knowledge, has been won. There is no longer any justification for anyone pursuing the upsetting, corrupting search for knowledge. The search for more knowledge goes on of course, but from here on it has to be conducted as much as possible from a secure, unevasive, denial-free basis, rather than from the insecure, evasive, denial-complying position from which it has been conducted in the past. The priority for the immediate future is not to attain more knowledge, but to expeditiously bring the human race, and indeed the world, back from the brink of destruction.

Giving up the battle is an extremely discredited strategy because it has for so long been perceived as weak and that misperception does take time to overcome. The truth however is this new way of living has virtually no negative aspects to it and as that fact dawns on people—that they can go to work for humanity now in a most extraordinarily effective way without there being any tainted aspect to doing so—it is going to lead to an almost unbearably excited state of being for humans. While we are not yet free of the human condition we are as good as free of it because the excitement of just being able to participate in this final great charge to freedom will carry all before it. The great exodus from the horror and darkness of the human condition is on. Soon an army in its millions will appear from horizon to horizon to do battle with human suffering and its weapon will be understanding. In St Paul's measures, if imposed discipline was considered "glorious" yet had "no glory now in comparison with the surpassing glory" of religion, where we participated in idealism through our support of the embodiment of the ideals, then this new way of living where we live in support of the understandings of the ideals is the beyond-comparison, culminating glory of all glories.

Many mythologies have anticipated this time when everyone is finally able to, and indeed now has the responsibility to go to work for humanity and not for themselves. In the Bible the prophet Joel provides this description: "Like dawn spreading across the mountains a large and mighty army comes, such as never was of old nor ever will be in ages to come…Before them the land is like the garden of Eden, behind them, a desert waste—nothing escapes them. They have the appearance of horses; they gallop along like cavalry…They charge like warriors; they scale walls like soldiers. They all march in line, not swerving from their course. They do not jostle each other."[32] There are similar portrayals elsewhere in the Bible, for instance in Isaiah 2 where Isaiah says, "They will beat their swords into plowshares and their spears into pruning hooks. Nation will not take up sword against nation, nor will they train for war anymore," and that "the earth will be full of the knowledge of the" truth and, as a result, "the wolf will live with the lamb."[33] Other entries can be found in Isaiah Chapters 5, 11 and 40; in Daniel Chapters 8 to 12; in Hosea Chapters 5 and 14; and in Hosea Chapter 6 where Hosea says the relieving truth, "will come to us like the winter rains, like the spring rains that water the earth."

In recent times other equally prophetic descriptions have appeared in popular culture, such as in the lyrics of Bob Dylan's songs "When The Ship Comes In"[34]and "The Times They Are A-Changin'";[35] Jim Morrison's "Break on Through";[36] "Aquarius"[37]from the rock musical *Hair*; Elvis Presley's "If I Can Dream";[38] Cat Stevens' "Peace Train"[39] and "Changes IV";[40] John Lennon's "Imagine";[41] Tracy Chapman's "Why";[42] and Hunters & Collectors' "Holy Grail."[43] In a similar vein, while the Rolling Stone's "I Can't Get No Satisfaction,"[44] Bob Dylan's "Like a Rolling Stone,"[45] Supertramp's "The Logical Song"[46] and U2's "I Still Haven't Found What I'm Looking For,"[47] don't anticipate the new human-condition-ameliorated world, they fully see through the existing one.

In conclusion, it can now be seen that there were three great steps in managing our upset state during our species' journey to enlightenment: first-ly, living in fear of punishment; secondly, living in support of the embodi-ment of the ideals through religion; and now, finally, living in support of the understanding of the ideals. In tenth-century Flora, Italy, an abbot named Joachim famously proposed that human history unfolds in three stages. He expressed his concepts in terms of the Trinity, with God the Father being the first stage of *authority* where humans obeyed the disciplining Ten Commandments of Moses. This was followed by God the Son, the stage where humans supported the *embodiment of the ideals* in Christ. The third stage, he said, would be the age of the Holy Ghost or Spirit, which we can now understand is the stage where humans support the *understanding of the ideals*. He predicted this final stage would occur at the end of the first mil-lennium, much to everyone's disappointment when that didn't eventuate. It turns out he was a millennium short in his prediction of when we would be able to live the ultimate life of value.

Author's Note: there are many questions not answered in this brief presentation, such as what was our species' original instinctive orientation that we were having to "fly off course" from. To read a more complete presentation of this new way of living, including the answer to this question and many more, visit www.humancondition.info.

Notes

[1] N. Duggington, The Destiny of Man (1931, 1955), 14–16.

[2] A. Hannay, (1849, 1989), 48–52.

[3] Ibid., 24.

[4] Ibid., 118.

[5] The Politics of Experience and The Bird of Paradise (1967), 185.

[6] Approximately 1885

[7] Journey Into Russia (1964), 145.

[8] National Geographic (November, 1987)

[9] 14:3; 35:4,5; 47:3

[10] (1970), 4.

[11] 2 Corinthians 3:7–11.

[12] The Undiscovered Self: Present and Future (1961).

[13] Memories of a Catholic Girlhood, (1957).

[14] "Theses on Feuerbach," written in German in 1845.

[15] The View From Nowhere, (1986).

[16] Don Peterson, Courier Mail, (June 1994).

[17] Time magazine (December 31, 1990).

[18] The Ascent of Man (1973), 437.

[19] Nineteen Eighty-Four (1949).

[20] 24:3

[21] 24:10-11

[22] 24:15-21

[23] 11:31

[24] 8:12

[25] 8:23-25

[26] 11:21

[27] 11:32

[28] The Politics of Experience and The Bird of Paradise (1967), 12.

[29] Ibid., 22.

[30] Ibid., 116.

[31] Self and Others (1961), 38.

[32] Joel 2

[33] 11:6,9

[34] 1964

[35] 1964

[36] 1966

[37] 1966, written by James Rado & Gerome Ragni

[38] 1968, written by Earl Brown

[39] 1971

[40] 1971

[41] 1971

[42] 1986

[43] 1993, written by Mark Seymour

[44] 1965

[45] 1965

[46] 1979, written by Richard Davies & Roger Hodgson

[47] 1987

About the Author

Jeremy Griffith is an Australian biologist who was born in 1945, raised on a sheep station in central New South Wales, and educated at Geelong Grammar School in Victoria. He played representative rugby football, making the trials for the national side, the "Wallabies," in 1966, and, prior to and after graduating from Sydney University in 1971, spent six years in the wilds of Tasmania undertaking the most thorough investigation ever into the plight of the Tasmanian tiger, concluding it was extinct. After creating a successful furniture manufacturing business based on his own simple and natural designs, Jeremy started writing about the human condition in 1975, and in 1983 established the Foundation for Humanity's Adulthood as a non-profit organization dedicated to promoting analysis of the human condition. He is the author of three books, *Free: The End of The Human Condition* (1988), *Beyond The Human Condition* (1991), and, in 2003, the Australian bestseller, *A Species In Denial*. In 2004 he wrote the four synopses for "The Human Condition Documentary Proposal" which has received endorsements from such leading scientists as Professors Stephen Hawking and Richard Leakey. Professor Harry Prosen, former president of the Canadian Psychiatric Association, has described Jeremy's account of the human condition as "one of, if not the most important contribution to both understanding and ameliorating the human condition written thus far."

The evil that is in this world almost always comes of ignorance, and good intentions may do as much harm as malevolence if they lack understanding.

Albert Camus

We have to dismantle the illusion that we're trying to become positive and perfect. That's the wrong approach. The approach is to become complete.

Jacquelyn Small

If it were all so simple! If only there were evil people somewhere insidiously committing evil deeds, and it were necessary to separate them from the rest of us and destroy them. But the line dividing good and evil cuts through the heart of every human being. And who is willing to destroy a piece of his own heart?

Alexandr Solzhenitsyn

Aristotle believed that virtue, which is essential to the good life, involves living according to reason. Only by living in accordance with reason, which is our human function, can we achieve happiness and inner harmony.

Judith A. Boss

Human beings can attain a worthy and harmonious life only if they are able to rid themselves, within the limits of human nature, of striving to fulfill wishes of the material kind.

Albert Einstein

For Plato, ethical thought is based not on culture, religion, or power, but rather on the development of the soul (that is, the mind). Only through the soul can we possibly contemplate such eternal realities as the Forms. Knowing these timeless ideals, we can then understand what it means to build a good society, become good individuals, and live our lives accordingly.

Judith Barad

Anything in life that we don't accept will simply make trouble for us until we make peace with it.

Shakti Gawain

LIBERTY

LIBERALISM'S BRAIN ON DRUGS
Where Does Drug Policy Fit into the Debate on Liberty?

Ryan Grim

At some point, everyone ought to throw his or her political theory—whatever it is—up against the wall of reality to see if it sticks. I ran smack into that wall when the state shackled Mark, one of my best friends, and hauled him off to a dank, violent, maximum-security prison for a seventeen-year stay. His crime: possession of a spoonful of cocaine, some of which they said he intended to distribute. The judge had recommended he be sent to a prison that focuses largely on drug treatment, but it is hopelessly overcrowded. So there Mark sits in Hagerstown, Md., his letters reflecting a mind slowly losing its tether as violence and mayhem swirl around him.

I've always believed that we live in a fundamentally liberal society that can trace its way back to enlightenment thinkers like Jefferson, Madison, Locke, Mill, and Rousseau. Sure, the past twenty-four years of the Reagan, Bush and even Clinton regimes haven't been kind, but one bedrock principle still seemed intact: If not equality and fraternity, we'll always have liberty. And so, as guards frogmarched my friend out of the courtroom shackled hands to feet, I wondered how confining that man for seventeen years jibes with my understanding of our nation's values. Is imprisoning hundreds of thousands of people an acceptable policy result of a liberal, pluralistic democratic society? Or, is the drug war proving libertarians correct about the potential for abuse of government power?

> I've always believed that we live in a fundamentally liberal society that can trace its way back to enlightenment thinkers like Jefferson, Madison, Locke, Mill, and Rousseau.

The principal disagreement between libertarians and liberals regarding the expansion and protection of liberty goes something like this. Libertarians argue that the state, broadly understood to include both state and federal governments, is the greatest threat to individual freedom. Therefore the best way to guard liberty is to restrict the power of the state to the greatest extent possible, leaving it only to protect two "freedom froms"—the freedom from force and the freedom from fraud. The rest, they say, will work itself out.

Liberals counterclaim that the libertarian critique ignores the reality of other organized forms of power—such as corporations, private militias and intractably racist state governments—that can infringe on an individual's freedom. They argue that freedom can only exist fully against the backdrop of some measure of equality and opportunity. Liberalism therefore calls for the expansion of state power based on the belief that such power should be used to create space for and protect individual rights and freedoms. In other words, liberals expect their elected government to provide freedom from oppressive nongovernmental forces and to help guarantee equal access to real opportunity.

But what if the government itself becomes the oppressor?

Eric Sterling, a Reagan-era-drug-warrior-turned-reformer who now heads up the Criminal Justice Policy Foundation, refers to what he calls the "drug war exception to the Bill of Rights." Unlawful searches and seizures are not permitted—unless cops are searching for drugs, which are not legal property and therefore not protected. No self-incrimination—unless it's a drug test. No cruel and unusual punishment—unless you were caught with cocaine. And so our two greatest bulwarks against tyranny, checks and balances and the Bill of Rights, are out the drug war window.

Today, one of every eight black men between the ages of 25 and 29—the cohort Mark falls into—is behind bars. The U.S. incarceration rate not only ranks number one in the world, but also some eight times higher than Western European nations.

In "An Analytical Assessment of U.S. Drug Policy," Peter Reuter, a conservative critic of the drug war and the director of the University of Maryland's Center on the Economics of Crime and Justice Policy, and David Boyum, a health policy consultant, have come to some radical conclusions.

"As currently implemented, American drug policies are unconvincing," Reuter and Boyum write. "They are intrusive...divisive...and expensive, with an approximate $35 billion annual expenditure on drug control...yet they leave the nation with a massive drug problem, greater than that of any other Western nation." Reuter and Boyum call for, among other proposals, eliminating criminal penalties associated with marijuana and drastically increasing emphasis on drug treatment instead of incarceration.

In an April essay in the Washington Monthly, William Galston, a leading philosopher of liberalism, challenged liberal thinkers to question how their conception of freedom might shape a liberal political view:

Edmund Burke famously observed that Americans "sniff the approach of tyranny in every tainted breeze." Even today, the extraordinary value Americans place on individual liberty is what most distinguishes our culture, and the political party seen by voters as the most willing to defend and expand liberty is the one that usually wins elections. Conservatives have learned this lesson; too many liberals have forgotten it. And as long as liberals fool themselves into believing that appeals to income distribution tables can take the place of policies that promote freedom, they will lose.

The questions before us are, what is the meaning of freedom in the 21st century, and what are the means needed to make it effective in our lives? Those of us who oppose the conservative answer cannot succeed by changing the question. We can only succeed by giving a better answer.

At some point, that better answer must take into account the scope of the state's authority to incarcerate its citizens. Imprisonment is the antithesis of individual freedom. With more than two million citizens locked up in American prisons and jails, the time for a better answer is long past due.

I asked Galston: Is this state of affairs an acceptable result of a pluralistic liberal system, or is there something fundamentally illiberal about American politics today?

"You could reasonably take the position that the current policies are badly flawed in principle and also leading to very negative consequences," he says. "Certainly it's the case that the more seriously you take liberty as the bedrock of a liberal society the more seriously you have to take the deprivation of liberty."

He blamed the lack of drug war dissension on "the political traumas inflicted on liberal Democrats in the '70s and '80s in the debate over drugs and crime, when the party and liberals were tarred with a brush—soft on crime, soft on drugs, maybe even encouraging a drug culture." But he suggests that these wounds may be healing, and that the public may be ready for a serious debate on drug and incarceration policy.

And none too soon. Silence from liberals in this debate is, in effect, an endorsement for the status quo. It is time to stand up in defense of liberty—not just equality and fraternity.

Following the publication of this essay in In These Times, *Mark was moved from the maximum-security prison to one with more of an emphasis on drug treatment. He was lucky; he had been told that the wait would be eleven years. It is hoped that he will be released from the prison within the next five years.*

© *Ryan Grim*

About the Author

Ryan grim writes for the *Washington City Paper* and trueblueliberal.com. His work has appeared in a number of progressive publications, including *Rolling Stone, The Nation, Slate, Salon*, and *The American Prospect*, among others. He is a contributor to the book *Under The Influence: The Disinformation Guide To Drugs*. Before pursuing journalism, Grim worked as an advocate for the marijuana policy project, which works to reduce the harm associated with marijuana—arguing that the greatest harm is prison. He is also a fellow with dc writerscorps, a nonprofit organization that teaches poetry to inner-city middle school students.

When they took the fourth amendment, I was silent because I don't deal drugs.
When they took the sixth amendment, I kept quiet because I know I'm innocent.
When they took the second amendment, I said nothing because I don't own a gun.
Now they've come for the first amendment, and I can't say anything at all.

Tim Freeman

It is not heroin or cocaine that makes one an addict, it is the need to escape
from a harsh reality. There are more television addicts, more baseball and
football addicts, more movie addicts, and certainly more alcohol addicts in this
country than there are narcotics addicts.

Shirley Chisholm

The issue of the criminal justice system is deeper than simply the death
penalty. There is unequal justice in this country, not only racial profiling, not
only crack cocaine, but also in terms of kids getting mandatory sentences for
first-time non-violent drug use and being put away twenty years. That should
not happen.

Bill Bradley

Look, the role of government is to protect us from other nations and other
people; the government has no business protecting me from me. But we refuse
to accept that you can't save someone who doesn't want to be saved. I have
come to the realization that America doesn't have a drug problem, some
Americans do. And it is their personal responsibility to fix it, not mine.

Dennis Miller

With the solitary exception of the Eskimos, there isn't a people on Earth that
doesn't use psychoactive plants to effect a change in consciousness, and there
probably never has been.

Michael Pollan

American bankers are laundering huge amounts of drug money, everybody
knows it: how many bankers are in jail? None; but if a black kid gets caught with
a joint, he goes to jail.

Noam Chomsky

INGENUITY

TOOLS WITH A LIFE OF THEIR OWN

Richard Heinberg

Nearly everyone complains from time to time that our tools have become Sorcerer's Apprentices; that we have come to serve our machines instead of the other way around; and that, increasingly, our lives are regimented as if we ourselves were mere gears in a vast mechanism utterly beyond our control.

We are not the first people to feel this way: criticism of technology has a history. The Luddites of early nineteenth-century England were among the first to raise their voices—and hammers!—against the dehumanizing effects of mechanization. As industrialization proceeded decade-by-decade—from powered looms to steam shovels, jet planes, and electric toothbrushes—objections to the accelerating, mindless adoption of new technologies waxed erudite. During the past century, books by Lewis Mumford, Jacques Ellul, Ivan Illich, Kirkpatrick Sale, Stephanie Mills, Chellis Glendinning, Jerry Mander, John Zerzan, and Derrick Jensen, among others, have helped generations of readers understand how and why our tools have come to enslave us, colonizing our minds as well as our daily routines.

These authors reminded us that tools, far from being morally neutral, are amplifiers of human purposes; therefore each tool carries its inventors' original intent inherent within it. We can use a revolver to hammer nails, but it works better as a machine for the swift commission of mayhem; and the more handguns we have around, the more likely it is for inevitable daily personal conflicts to go ballistic. Thus, as clashes over human purposes form the core of ethical and political disputes, technology itself, as it proliferates, must inevitably become the subject of a widening array of social controversies. Battles over technology concern nothing less than the shape and future of society.

In principle, those battles—if not the scholarly discussions about them—reach all the way back to the Neolithic era, even to our harnessing of fire tens of thousands of years ago. Mumford drew a through-line emphasizing how modern megatechnologies are externalizations of a social machine that originated in the pristine states of the Bronze Age:

> The inventors of nuclear bombs, space rockets, and computers are the pyramid builders of our own age: psychologically inflated by a similar myth of unqualified power, boasting through their science of their increasing omnipotence, if not omniscience, moved by obsessions and compulsions no less irrational than those of earlier absolute systems: particularly the notion that the system itself must be expanded, at whatever the eventual cost.[1]

Zerzan goes further, asserting that it is the human tendencies to abstract and manipulate, which are at the heart of our tool-making ability, that cut us off from our innate connections with the natural world, and therefore obscure our own inherent nature.

This effort to show how our current technological crisis is rooted in ancient patterns is certainly helpful. But it is important also to keep in mind the fact that the discussion about mechanization's collateral damage has intensified relatively recently, due to the fact that the scale of technology's intrusion into our lives and its toll upon the environment have grown enormously in just the past two centuries.

Some techno-critics have sought to explain this recent explosion in the power and variety of our tools by tying it to developments in philosophy

(Cartesian dualism) or economics (capitalism). Strangely, few of the critics have discussed at any length the role of fossil fuels in the industrial revolution. That is, they have consistently focused their attention on tools' impacts on society and nature, and on the political conditions and ideologies that enabled their adoption, rather than on the fact that most of the new tools that have appeared during the past two centuries are of a kind previously rare—ones that derive the energy for their operation not from muscle power, but from the burning of fuels.

Mumford, one of my favorite authors, devoted only one comment on one page of his seven-hundred-page, two-volume masterpiece *The Myth of the Machine*, to coal, and neither "petroleum" nor "oil" appears in the index of either volume. My own 1996 book *A New Covenant with Nature*, which was mostly devoted to a critique of industrialism, does no better: "coal," "oil," and "energy" are absent from its index.

And yet it appears to me now that, in assessing technology and understanding its effects on people and nature, it is at least as important to pay attention to the energy that drives tools as to the tools themselves and the surrounding political-ideological matrix. In short, we who have been criticizing the technological society, using the methods of historical analysis, have missed at least half the story we are attempting to weave when we fail to notice the energetic evolution of tools.

This essay is a brief attempt to make up for this oversight. It will also discuss why the impending peak in global oil production will pull the plug on the kind of "progress" we have come to expect over the past two centuries, providing an historic opportunity to reshape humanity's relations with technology and with nature.

Classy Tools

It is helpful for our purposes to have a way of classifying tools according to their energy inputs. The following four categories, outlined in my book *The Party's Over*, correspond very roughly to four major watersheds in social evolution:

A. Tools that require only human energy for their manufacture and use. Examples include stone spearheads and arrowheads, grinding tools, baskets, and animal-skin clothing. These sorts of tools are found in all hunter-gatherer societies.

B. Tools that require an external power source for their manufacture, but human power for their use. Examples: all basic metal tools, such as knives, metal armor, and coins. These tools were the basis of the early agricultural civilizations centered in Mesopotamia, China, Egypt, and Rome.

C. Tools that require only human energy for their manufacture, but harness an external energy source. Examples: the wooden plow drawn by draft animals, the sailboat, the fire drill, the windmill, the water mill. The fire drill was used by hunter-gatherers, and the wooden plow and sailboat were developed in early agricultural societies; the windmill and water mill appeared at later stages of social evolution.

D. Tools that require an external energy source for their manufacture and also harness or use an external energy source. Examples: the steel plow, the gun, the steam engine, the internal combustion engine, the jet engine, the nuclear reactor, the hydroelectric turbine, the photovoltaic panel, the wind turbine, and all electrical devices. These tools and tool systems are the foundation of modern industrial societies—in fact, they define them.

For thousands of years, human beings have engaged in a constant struggle to harness extrasomatic energy (that is, energy sources outside the human body). Until recently, such energy came mostly from the capture of work performed by animal muscles. In the US, as recently as 1850, domesticated animals—horses, oxen, and mules—were responsible for about 65 percent of the physical work supporting economy; today the percentage is negligible: virtually all work is done by fuel-fed machines. Slavery was a strategy for capturing human muscle power, and the end of most overt slavery during the nineteenth century was more or less inevitable when Class D tools became cheaper to own and keep than human slaves—or domesticated animals, for that matter.

In early civilizations, agricultural workers sought to capture a surplus of solar energy on a yearly basis by plowing and reaping. It always takes energy to get energy (it takes effort to sow seeds, build a windmill, or drill an oil well). For agricultural societies, the net-energy profit was always moderate and sometimes nonexistent (hence recurrent famines): in most cases about 90 percent of the population had to work at farming in order to provide enough of a surplus so as to support the rest of the social edifice—including the warrior, priestly, and administrative classes. The extraction of coal, and especially of oil and natural gas—substances representing millions of years of accumulation of past biotic energy—has often provided a spectacular net-energy profit, sometimes on the order of fifty to a hundred units obtained for every one invested. As a result, with fossil fuels and modern machinery, only two percent of the population need to farm in order to support the rest of society, enabling the flourishing of a growing middle class composed of a dizzying array of specialists.

Increasing specialization was also enabled by a flourishing of differing types of machines, and that differentiation was itself in turn fueled (quite literally) by the availability of cheap energy to make them go. Labor productivity increased relentlessly, not because people worked longer or harder, but because they had access to an increasing array of powerful extrasomatically powered tools.

The availability of Class D tools produced excitement and wonder—initially among the few people wealthy enough to own them, and also among the crafty and highly motivated inventors available for hire. These were tools that were, in a sense, alive: they consumed a kind of food, in the form of coal or oil (indirectly so in the case of electrical power), and had their own internal metabolism. Gradually, as mechanized production showed itself capable of producing more goods and gadgets than could possibly be soaked up by the wealthy elites, the latter devised the strategy of creating a consumer society in which anyone could own labor-saving machinery. The rank and file was soon persuaded of the dream of eliminating drudgery. And, due to the scale of the energies being unleashed, the fulfillment of that dream seemed well within reach.

That scale is difficult to comprehend without using familiar examples. Think for a moment of the effort required to push—for only a few feet—an automobile that has run out of gas. Now imagine pushing it twenty miles. This is, of course, the service provided by a single gallon of gasoline, and it represents the energy equivalent of at least a month of human labor (much more than this by some accounts). The amount of gasoline, diesel, and kerosene fuels used in the US in one day has roughly the energy equivalence of 20,000,000 person/years of work. If the building of the Great Pyramid required 10,000 people working for 20 years, then the petroleum-based energy used in the US on an average day could—in principle, given the necessary stone and machinery—build over one hundred Great Pyramids. Of course, we don't use our oil for this purpose: instead we use it mostly to push millions of heavy metal cars along roadways so that we can get to and from jobs, restaurants, and video rental stores.

With computers and cybernetics, we managed to create tools with not just a life, but a mind of their own. Now our tools not only "breathe," "eat," and do physical work; they also "think." Increasingly we find ourselves in synthetic, self-regulating (if not yet self-replicating) environments—shopping malls, airports, office buildings—in which non-human multi-celled biota are present only as ornaments; in which human work consists only of doing the few tasks for which we have not yet succeeded in inventing profitable automatic surrogates. The wonder of seeing drudgery eliminated is accompanied by the nuisance of being managed and bossed about by machines, and of being rendered helpless by mechanical failures or—horror of horrors—power outages.

> The machines themselves have become so sophisticated, their services so seductive, that they are equivalent to magic.

What does it take to do all of this? It takes eighty-four million barrels of oil per day globally, as well as millions of tons of coal and billions of cubic feet of natural gas. The supply network for these fuels is globe-spanning and awesome. Yet, from the standpoint of the end user, this network is practically invisible and easily taken for granted. We flip the switch, pump the gas, or turn up the thermostat with hardly a thought to the processes of extraction we draw upon, or the environmental horrors entailed.

The machines themselves have become so sophisticated, their services so seductive, that they are equivalent to magic. Few people fully understand the inner workings of any modern Class D tool, and different tools require their own unique teams of specialists for their design and repair. But what is more important, in the process of becoming dependent upon them, we have become almost a different species from our recent ancestors.

Infrastructure Matters

To understand how we have become so different, how different we have become, and also how the end of cheap extrasomatic energy is likely to impact us and the society in which we are embedded, it is helpful to draw a lesson from cultural anthropology.

Comparative studies of human societies have consistently shown that the latter are best classified on the basis of their members' means of obtaining food. Thus we commonly speak of hunting-and-gathering societies, horticultural societies, agricultural societies, fishing societies, herding societies, and industrial societies. The point is, if you know how people get their food, you will reliably be able to predict most of the rest of their social forms— their decision-making and child-rearing customs, spiritual practices, and so on.

Of course, from a biological point of view, food is energy. And so what we are saying is that understanding energy sources is essential to understanding human societies.

Anthropologist Marvin Harris identified three basic elements present in every human society:

- **infrastructure** (which consists of the means of obtaining and processing necessary energy and materials from nature—i.e., the means of production),
- **structure** (which consists of human-to-human decision-making and resource-allocating activities), and
- **superstructure** (consisting of the ideas, rituals, ethics, and myths that serve to explain the universe and coordinate human behavior).

Change at any of these levels can affect the others: the emergence of a new religion or a political revolution, for example, can change people's lives in real, significant ways. However, the fact that so many cultural forms seem consistently to cluster around ways of obtaining food suggests that fundamental cultural change occurs at the infrastructural level: if people switch, for example, from hunting to planting, or from planting to herding, their politics and spirituality are bound to shift as well, and probably in profound ways.

The industrial revolution represented one of history's basic infrastructural shifts; everything about human society changed as a result. This revolution did not come about primarily because of religious or political developments, but because a few prior inventions (steel, gears, and a primitive steam engine—i.e., Class B and C and simple Class D tools) came together in the presence of an abundant new energy source: fossil fuels—first coal, then oil and natural gas. Ideas (such as Cartesian dualism, capitalism, Calvinism, and Marxism), rather than driving the transformation, achieved prominence because they served useful functions within a flow of events emanating from infrastructural necessity.

What Hath Hydrocarbon Wrought?

What have been the structural and superstructural impacts of industrialism?

Because only a reduced portion of the population is required to work the land (now with tractors and harvesters rather than oxen) in order to produce food-energy, a large majority of the populace has lost direct connection with the land and with the cycles of nature. If hunters get their food-energy from hunting, we get ours from shopping at the supermarket.

The ensuing proliferation, at first of factory work, and later of specialized occupations, has led to the development of universal compulsory public education and the idea of the "job"—a notion that most people today take for granted, but that seems strange, demeaning, and confining to people in non-industrial cultures.

With the expansion of the educated middle class, simple monarchial forms of government soon ceased to be defensible. By the latter part of the eighteenth-century, a trend was well established, within industrial nations, of revolution and the widespread and growing expectation of democratic participation in governance—though of course that expectation was quickly hijacked by the nouveau mercantile elites. Somewhat later, the economic exploitation of labor that typified both previous agricultural civilizations and the new industrial states also became the target of revolution; once again, the effect of revolution was primarily merely to rearrange deck chairs: people's actual daily work and psychic life were still being shaped by machines, and, at a deeper level, the energy sources that propelled them.

We must remember that industrialism followed on the heels of the European takeover of the resources and labor of most of the rest of the world during centuries of conquest and colonialism. Thus the experience and expectation of economic growth had already insinuated themselves into the minds of members of the European merchant class before industrialism took hold. After the commencement of the fuel revolution, with vastly more energy available per capita, economic activity achieved seemingly perpetual logarithmic growth, and economic theories emerged not only to explain this growth in terms of "markets," but to affirm that now, because of markets, growth was necessary, inevitable, and unending: world without end, amen. Fractional-reserve banking, based on the wonder of compound interest, served as the financial embodiment of these new expectations. In effect, within the minds of society's managers and policy makers, faith in technology and markets supplanted previous religious faith in the hallucinated agricultural and herding deities that had presided over Western civilization for the previous couple of millennia.

In the early twentieth century, as mechanized production mushroomed to swamp existing demand—among people who mostly still lived rurally and fairly self-sufficiently—for manufactured products, elites began experimenting with mass propaganda in the form of advertising and public relations. Later, television would dramatically increase the effectiveness of these efforts, which amounted to nothing less than the regimentation of the human imagination according to the demands of the capitalist-industrial system.

Since women were now needed both as consumers and workers in order to continue the perpetual expansion of that system, feminism (via the destruction of old domestic roles and the promotion of new ambitions and consumer tastes) became an inevitable byproduct.

In short, just as we would predict on the basis of the theory of infrastructural determinism, when fossil fuels deeply altered humanity's means of obtaining sustenance from the earth, everything about human society changed—from child rearing to politics; from cultural myths to personal dreams.

Of course, many—though not all—of these changes were destructive both of people and nature. And so, while most of the political struggles of the twentieth century centered on questions of the distribution of power and wealth (as had been the case since the first agricultural surpluses were laid aside ten thousand years ago), many of those struggles also grew from efforts to control technology's caustic impacts, which were linked by the social critics both to tools themselves and to people's attitudes toward them. Technological politics focused on a range of issues: nuclear weapons and nuclear power, polluting chemicals, ozone-destroying chlorofluorocarbons, greenhouse gases, and the genetic engineering of food, to name only a few familiar examples.

Meanwhile, the most radical of the techno-critics drew inspiration from the trend toward cultural relativism that had won over mid-twentieth century anthropologists such as Stanley Diamond, who evinced profound admiration for the world's remaining hunter-gatherers. For the anarcho-primitivist philosopher John Zerzan, all technology is damaging, debauched, destructive, and demeaning, and only a return to our primordial, pre-linguistic, pre-technic condition will enable us to recover fully our innate freedom and spontaneity.

But all of the techno-critics, from the mildest to the most extreme, tended to assume that, for decades hence, barring intervention, humanity will pursue a continued trajectory of technological change: the only thing that can thwart this ongoing "progress" will be the awakening of a new moral sensibility leading humans to reject technology, entirely or in part.

Peak Oil and the Limits of Technology

With the discourse on Peak Oil that has commenced mostly since the beginning of the new millennium has come a focus on energy as a determining factor in social evolution, at least as important as technology per se, or ideas, or political struggles. And with that shift has also come the sense that it is resource limits that will probably eventually drive basic cultural change, rather than moral persuasion, mass enlightenment, or some new invention.

As oil and gas prices rise, signaling the commencement of the peaking period, we continue to see the rollout of new inventions in the form of the latest iPod, the next generation of nuclear bombs, improved surveillance tools, and so on. However, there is also evidence that this stream of new inventions, like the global stream of oil, is starting to dry up.

Physicist Jonathan Huebner of the Pentagon's Naval Air Warfare Center in China Lake, California, has for several years been studying the pace of technological change and invention, as catalogued in the publication *The History of Science and Technology*. After applying some elaborate mathematics, he has concluded that the rate of invention of significantly new and different tools peaked in 1873 and has been dwindling gradually since then. Huebner calculates our current rate of innovation at seven important technological developments per billion people per year—which is about the same rate as prevailed in Europe in 1600. If the trend continues, by 2024 the innovation rate will have declined to that of the Dark Ages.

Assuming that Huebner is right, it would seem that the nineteenth-century adoption of fossil fuels led to an early-peaking wave of invention, on whose trailing edge we are living today. As fossil fuels likewise peak and decline, we are unlikely to see another such burst of similar kinds or degrees of innovation; instead, we will see adaptation to a lower-energy cultural environment. And that adaptation may occur by way of versions of older cultural patterns that flowed from previous generations' responses to similar levels of available energy.

Peak Oil will be a fundamental cultural watershed, at least as important as the industrial revolution or the development of agriculture. Yet few mainstream commentators see it that way. They discuss the likelihood of energy price spikes and try to calculate how much economic havoc will result from them. Always the solution is technology: solar or wind and maybe a bit of hydrogen for green-tinged idealists; nuclear, tar sands, methane hydrates, and coal-to-liquids for hard-headed, pro-growth economists and engineers; Tesla free-energy magnetic generators for the gullible fringe dwellers.

But technology cannot solve the underlying dilemma we face as a result of our application of fossil fuels to every human problem or desire: we are growing our population, destroying habitat (and undermining global climatic stability), and depleting resources in ways and at rates that are incapable of being mitigated by any new tool or energy source. The only way forward that does not end with the extinction of humanity and millions of other species is a scaling back of the entire human project—in terms both of human numbers and of per-capita rates of consumption.

And that is exactly what Peak Oil implies.

How dramatic a pull-back are we talking about? No one knows. It depends to a large degree on how we manage the inevitable collapse in financial and governance systems, and whether the countries of the world can be persuaded to adopt a global Oil Depletion Protocol; or whether instead nations merely fight mercilessly over the last petroleum reserves until even the "winners" are utterly spent and the resources in dispute have been used up or destroyed in the conflict itself.

In the worst case, Zerzan's ideal of a return to hunting and gathering may be realized—though not by moral choice, but by cruel fate.

If Class D tools fueled by cheap oil eliminated drudgery, life without abundant extrasomatic energy will imply more labor—certainly for food production. The return of slavery is a frighteningly real possibility. Such nightmare scenarios can only be averted by careful, hard, cooperative work.

Staring at Techno-Collapse

In the meantime, what should we expect, and what should we do?

Realistically, I think we can expect to see some of the worst excesses of human history, but perhaps only briefly and in certain places. Within a few decades the governmental and corporate structures capable of perpetrating such outrages will have crumbled for lack of fuel. We can also anticipate—and participate in—localized cooperative attempts to reorganize society at a smaller scale.

Under the circumstances, efforts to try to bring industrialism to ruin prematurely seem to me to be pointless and wrongheaded: ruin will come soon enough on its own. Better to invest time and effort in personal and community preparedness. Enhance your survival prospects. Learn practical skills, including the manufacture and use of Paleolithic tools. Learn to understand and repair (as much as is possible) existing Class B and C tools that are likely still to be useful when there is no gasoline or electricity.

Preserve whatever is beautiful, sane, and intelligent. That includes scientific and cultural knowledge, and examples of human achievement in the arts. Nobody can preserve it all, or even a substantial portion; choose what appeals to you. A great deal of this knowledge is currently captured on media with dubious survival prospects—magnetic disc or tape, compact laser disc, or acid-soaked paper. If someone doesn't make the effort, the best of what we have achieved over the past centuries and decades will disappear along with the worst.

In the best instance, the next generations will find themselves in a low-energy regime in which moral lessons from the fossil-fuel era and its demise have been seared into cultural memory. Maybe they will be able to maintain local, renewables-based electrical grids, and maybe also some powered transportation, so that they will still have access to a few tools with lives of their own. Perhaps not. In either case, we can hope that, like the Native Americans, who learned from the Pleistocene extinctions that over-hunting results in famine, they will have discovered that growth is not always good, that modest material goals are usually better for everyone in the long run than extravagant ones, and that every technology has a hidden cost. One hopes that, like the Haudinausaunee, who long ago concluded that fighting over scarce land and resources only means the endless perpetuation of violence, they will also have learned the methods and culture of peacemaking.

We humans tend to learn really tough lessons only by bitter experience. These are tough lessons indeed. If we learn them, perhaps the initially exhilarating but now bitter experience of addicting ourselves to fossil fuels and then having to go cold turkey will not have been entirely pointless.

© *Richard Heinberg*

Note

[1] *Quoted in* Questioning Technology, *ed. by Zerzan and Carnes.*

Recommended Reading

John Zerzan and Alice Carnes, eds., Questioning Technology: Tool, Toy or Tyrant? *(New Society, 1991).*

Bryan Appleyard, *"Waiting for the lights to go out,"* The Sunday Times, *October 16, 2005.*

MuseLetter #160, *"How to Avoid Resource Wars, Terrorism, and Economic Collapse," www.museletter.com.*

About the Author

Richard Heinberg is the author of six books including *The Party's Over: Oil, War and the Fate of Industrial Societies* (New Society, 2003, 2005), and *Powerdown: Options and Actions for a Post-Carbon World* (New Society, 2004). He is a journalist, educator, editor, lecturer, and a Core Faculty member of New College of California, where he teaches a program on "Culture, Ecology and Sustainable Community." His monthly *MuseLetter* was nominated for an Alternative Press Award and has been included in *Utne* magazine's annual list of Best Alternative Newsletters. His essays and articles have appeared in many journals including *The Ecologist, Z Magazine, The Futurist, European Business Review, Earth Island Journal, Yes!, Wild Matters, The Proceedings of the Canadian Association of the Club of Rome, Alternative Press Review,* and *The Sun;* and on Web sites including Alternet.org, EnergyBulletin.net, ProjectCensored.com, and Counterpunch.com.

Either the human being must suffer and struggle as the price of a more searching vision, or his gaze must be shallow and without intellectual revelation.

Thomas De Quincey

We do not inherit the earth from our ancestors, we borrow it from our children.

Haida proverb

We are all afraid – for our confidence, for the future, for the world... Yet every man, every civilization, has gone forward because of its engagement with what it has set itself to do.

Jacob Bronowski

The eyes of the future are looking back at us, and they are praying for us to see beyond our own time.

Terry Tempest Williams

Given our civilization's increasing technological prowess, there's no reason to believe we can't identify a host of economically viable, biobased alternatives to unsustainable fossil fuels and petrochemicals.

Jeffrey Hollender

The power to question is the basis of all human progress.

Indira Gandhi

Many historians, sociologists, and psychologists have written at length, and with a deep concern, about the price that Western man has to pay for and will go on paying for technological progress.

Aldous Huxley

Our earlier, technologically and socially less-advanced partnership societies were more evolved than the high-technology societies of the present world, where millions of children are condemned to die of hunger each year while billions of dollars are poured into ever more sophisticated ways to kill.

Riane Eisler

The most exciting breakthrough of the twenty-first century will occur not because of technology, but because of an expanding concept of what it means to be human.

John Naisbitt

No issue is more pressing than the havoc we are wreaking on our planet.

Anita Roddick

We once had an Iron Age, and after that a series of intervening ages we have come to the Age of Irony. The rapid changes of the last hundred years show us that there may be no such thing as progress, that for every step forward, we take at least one step backward.

Wes Nisker

Without moral progress, modern Buddhists warn, our rapid technological advances could lead us down the path to disaster.

Judith A. Boss

The world has achieved brilliance without wisdom, power without conscience. Ours is a world of nuclear giants and ethical infants.

Omar Bradley

If we don't turn around now, we may just get where we're going.

Navajo proverb

I am not afraid of tomorrow, for I have seen yesterday and I love today.

William Allen White

You can still fight a war over oil, but where do you drop the bombs if you want to tackle climate change? That's a problem that can only be solved through international cooperation. So climate change could very well turn out to be the match that ignites the transformation.

Marilyn Ferguson

PROGRESSIVISM

BEYOND ECONOMISM

Hazel Henderson

The human family numbering now over six billion is clearly the most biologically successful species on planet Earth. We have evolved from our birthplaces on the African continent to colonize every part of Earth, consuming 40 percent of all its primary photosynthetic production—leading to the current and mass extinction of other species. We have conquered the oceans, the moon, and outer space, and have now set our sights on Mars. To continue our spectacular technological success and preserve the options for our grandchildren's survival, we must now face ourselves and fearlessly diagnose our major failures: the fragmenting of human knowledge, the persistence of violent conflicts, wars, and poverty. The UN Millennium Development Goals provide an initial agenda. Fulfilling these goals and shifting from fossil fuels to renewable resources and their sustainability can employ every willing man and woman on earth and expand global prosperity. Reintegrating human knowledge, systems thinking, and multidisciplinary approaches to public and private decisions are widely recognized as necessary to address the human condition in this new century. A preeminent example of such new consciousness is the Earth Charter (www.earthcharter.org).

Reappraisals of the work of Charles Darwin, together with new evidence from historians, archeologists, and anthropologists, now clearly point to the evolution of human emotional capacity for bonding, cooperation, and altruism (www.thedarwinproject.com). Competition, territoriality, and tribalism, rooted in the fears of our past, served humans well in our early trials and vulnerability. So did cooperation and the ability to trust and bond with each other—influenced in all humans by the hormone oxytocin. Higher levels of this hormone during pregnancy and lactation bond women to their children, over the extended developmental period to maturity.[1] Today, research by scientists from many fields—neurosciences, endocrinology, psychology, physics, thermodynamics, mathematics, and anthropology—have invalidated the core assumptions underlying economic models, which dominate public and private decision-making in most countries and multilateral agencies, including the World Bank, the International Monetary Fund (IMF), and the World Trade Organization. This new research reveals economics as a profession, not a science. Yet today, as privatization and technological evolution speed change and globalization, economists and their general equilibrium models still drive these processes. While competition remains a key driver in evolution and all human affairs, cooperation and co-evolutionary processes are equally important. Social sciences study the full range of human behavior—with the exception of economics, which assumes competition and self-interest are rooted in human nature. Political economy studies, as they were originally termed, rose to academic prominence after the publishing in 1776 of Adam Smith's great work *An Inquiry Into the Nature and Causes of the Wealth of Nations*. Invoking the scientific knowledge of the day, Smith related his famous theory of an "invisible hand" that guided competition among self-interested individuals to serve the public good and economic growth. Smith drew parallels ascribing this pattern of human behavior to Sir Isaac Newton's great discovery of the physical laws of motion. Economists of the early industrial revolution based their theories not only on Adam Smith's work, but also on Charles Darwin's *The Descent of Man* and *The Origin of Species* (www.thedarwinproject.com). They seized on Darwin's research on the survival of the fittest and the role of competition among species as additional foundations for their classical economics of "laissez faire." Yet, in class-ridden Victorian Britain, economists and upper-class elites espoused theories known as "social Darwinism." Charles Darwin also saw the human capacity for bonding, cooperation, and altruism as an essential factor in our successful evolution.[2]

In retrospect, how otherwise could we have gone from the experience of over 95 percent of our history lived in roving bands of twenty-five people or less[3] —to today's mega cities: Sao Paulo, Shanghai, Mexico City, or Jakarta? These improbable metropolises—along with global corporations and governance institutions such as the United Nations and all its agencies and the European Union, now expanded to embrace twenty-five formerly warring countries—could never have emerged without humanity's capacities for bonding, cooperation, and altruism.

> So as we have evolved into our complex societies, organizations, and technologies of today we need to re-examine our belief systems and the extent to which they still may be trapped in earlier primitive stages of our development.

So as we have evolved into our complex societies, organizations, and technologies of today we need to re-examine our belief systems and the extent to which they still may be trapped in earlier primitive stages of our development. Why, for example, do we underestimate our genius for bonding, cooperation, and altruism—seemingly stuck in our earlier fears and games of competition and territoriality? Why do we over-reward such behavior and still assume in our economic textbooks and business schools that maximizing one's individual self-interest in competition with all others is behavior fundamental to human nature? Scientific research is now revealing excessive individualism as dogma, while systems views, including those of Ken Wilber, Richard Slaughter, Fritjof Capra, Elisabet Sahtouris, Riane Eisler, Jane Jacobs, myself, and many others seek a balance in acknowledging society, culture, and the planet's ecosystems.

Why is our equal genius for bonding and cooperative behavior—even altruism—not taught in business schools as the true foundation of all human organizations and our greatest scientific and technological achievements? In reality, as every business executive knows, competition and territoriality are channeled *within* structures of cooperation and networks of agreements, contracts, laws and international regulatory regimes that allow airlines, shipping, communications, and other infrastructure to undergird global commerce and finance. This reality is now recognized as "co-opeti-tion,"[4] but has not supplanted the competition model in economic theory. Thus, the formula for humanity's success has always rested on cooperation while embracing competition and creativity.[5] Yet, shocking evidence documents[6] that the very methods and curricula still taught in most business schools encourages managers in the kind of behavior that produced the wave of corporate scandals and crimes at Enron, Worldcom, Parmalat, Tyco, and Arthur Andersen.[7] This debate in academia can be followed by accessing the publications of Sweden's Dag Hammarskjold Foundation (www.dhf.uu.se) and the French movement for "post-autistic economics," covered in the *LeMonde* and at www.paecon.net.

What do deep, primitive beliefs about the primacy of competition and territoriality have to do with poverty, conflicts and wars? All are rooted in ancient human fears—of scarcity, of attacks by wild animals or other fear-ful bands of humans. Rooting out these fears—deeply coded in our "us-ver-sus-them" political and economic textbooks—is the essential task of our generation. We must move beyond this economics of our early reptilian brains to include the economics of our hearts and forebrains! These old fears underlie today's continuing cycles of oppression, poverty, violence, revenge, and terrorism. Indeed, if we humans do not root out these now-dysfunctional old fears, we will destroy each other. Politicians frequently use fear to manipulate consent. Yet fear can be counterproductive. Franklin D. Roosevelt, during the Great Depression in the US, proclaimed that we have nothing to fear but fear itself!

Meanwhile, the fantastic potential humans have created for further suc-cesses through pursuing the UN Millennium Development Goals and build-ing prosperous, equitable, sustainable human societies is now within our grasp. The new "superpower" of global public opinion is already rejecting the old dysfunctional dogmas. Over ten million people demonstrated peace-fully worldwide against the preemptive war on Iraq. Yet as Thomas Kuhn described in his *Structure of Scientific Revolutions* old dysfunctional beliefs often persist long after they have been disproved.[8] Dysfunctional beliefs are deeply entrenched in many of the models of economics that dominate our decision and public policies. This malfunctioning source code underlying economics focused on money circulation, is still replicating behaviors and organizational structures that imperil human survival under twenty-first-century conditions. The creation of money—from clay tablets to coins to electronic data—was a vital social innovation to track transactions beyond barter in early markets. Yet, money does not equate to wealth, and today's high-tech electronic barter reminds us that money is merely one form of information—no longer needed in today's electronic barter transactions.[9]

Echoes of obsolete theories are still heard today and propounded in mainstream economic textbooks as theories of "efficient markets," rational human behavior as "competitive maximizing of individual self-interest," "natural" rates of unemployment (codified as the NAIRU rule of central bankers), and the ubiquitous "Washington Consensus" formula for economic growth (free trade, open markets, privatization, deregulation, floating currencies, and export-led policies). Lately, the US Federal Reserve Board's use of "neutral" interest rates has been exposed by the Levy Institute as convoluted and favoring asset owners above workers' wages (www.levy.org). Central banks' theoretical money-circulation models must be scrutinized because these institutions have won independence from political control and wield enormous power over societies. Monetary policy and money-creation are now widely understood as political, not scientific.[10] Such unaccountable, obscure theories still underpin today's economic and technological globalization and the rules of the World Trade Organization, the International Monetary Fund, the World Bank, stock markets, currency exchange, as well as central banks. The policy drumbeats of economists and market players supported central banks. They were buttressed by their claims that economics, with its increasing use of mathematical models, had matured into a science, matching the feats of natural sciences since Newton and Darwin in discovering the laws of nature. Economists' theories from Smith's "invisible hand" to Vilfredo Pareto's "optimality" were elevated from theories to the status of scientific principles. Many debates over categories and indicators derived from such theories involve basic questions of causality. For example, why is education a "cost" not an "investment"?[11]

In 1969, the Central Bank of Sweden put up US$1,000,000 to create a prize to confer scientific status and legitimacy on the academic discipline and widespread policy advocacy of the economics profession. Thus, the Bank of Sweden named its economics prize "in memory of Alfred Nobel" and lobbied this designation onto the Nobel Prize Committee. As his descendant, Peter Nobel put it, "The Bank of Sweden, like a cuckoo, laid its egg in the nest of another very decent bird, infringing on the name and trademark of Nobel." Since 1969, most of the Bank of Sweden Prizes in Economic Science have been awarded to US economists espousing the Chicago School policies of laissez faire "free markets" typical of its most prominent prize winner Milton Friedman (who is often erroneously described as a "Nobel laureate"). Peter Nobel added, "These economists use models to speculate in stock markets and options—the very opposite of the humanitarian purposes of Alfred Nobel."[12] Chicago School doctrine holds that if individuals and private business make money that this process will eventually "lift all boats" in a rising tide of prosperity, thus confusing money with wealth—a much broader concept. While controversies have often surrounded Nobel awards, arguably the Bank of Sweden prize should be properly named, since economics is central to public policies in all countries and multi-lateral agencies.

In December 2004 many scientists revolted, including members of the Nobel Committee and Peter Nobel himself, demanding that the Bank of Sweden's economics prize either be properly labeled and de-linked from the other Nobel prizes or abolished. The reason was the awarding of the economics prize to two more Chicago School economists Edward C. Prescott and Finn E. Kydland for their 1977 paper purporting to prove by use of a mathematical model, that central banks should be freed from the control of politicians—even those elected in democracies. The mathematicians pounced, pointing to the many misuses of their models by Prescott and Kydland and other economists to "dress up" their questionable theories and unscientific assumptions.[13] Yet economics is an honorable profession, like law, medicine, engineering, architecture, and other such applications of knowledge. Lawyers are known as advocates. Economists have always been advocates of various government policies, regulations or deregulation, and of the interests of their clients (most often bankers, financial firms, and corporations in general). These advocates, whether lawyers, economists, or lobbyists, have legitimate roles in policymaking. Transparency requires that the public is fully informed—and the issues are argued honestly.

The globalization of finance and technology, the spread of privatization, and deregulated markets have produced a range of unanticipated consequences. For example, today's global Information Age has already become The Age of Truth—where careless corporate actions can destroy a global brand in real time. Business leaders worldwide have responded by embracing the idea of good corporate citizenship, both at home and globally. Two thousand companies have signed on to the ten principles of Global Corporate Citizenship of the Global Compact, launched by the United Nations in 2000, covering human rights, workplace safety, justice and ILO standards, as well as the environment and anti-corruption. Civic groups worldwide now monitor all the companies who have engaged with the Global Compact, to see if they are walking their talk. Backsliders are publicly exposed hundreds of Web sites. The World Social Forum has successfully linked hundreds of thousands of civic activists and organizations and made the beautiful city of Porto Alegre, a mecca of innovative thought. My TV series "Ethical Markets" on US public broadcasting stations benchmarks higher standards, corporate ethical performance, and socially-responsible investing worldwide (www.ethicalmarkets.com). Contrary to *The Economist*'s editorial skepticism about such corporate social responsibility, [14] 77 percent of CEOs of major corporations surveyed by KPMG and the World Economic Forum in 2005 said that such higher ethical behavior was "vital to profitability."

Capitalism's great proponent, Adam Smith, argued that markets could only work efficiently if all buyers and sellers had equal power and information, and if no market transactions harmed others. Smith might hardly recognize today's evolution of global markets or companies moving toward social and environmental responsibility. Similarly, such changes in corporate behavior have been driven by trillions of pension funds' dollars and millions of investors who care about their children's future and the state of our planet. Students and prospective employees also ask about companies' performance on human rights and the environment, while new auditing standards of the Global Reporting Initiative (GRI) prescribed "triple bottom line" accounting for people, profit, and environment. Six hundred global corporations now comply with GRI accounting in their Annual Reports. (www.gri.org). Sustainability has become a buzzword and even Wall Street's venerable Dow-Jones now has its Sustainability Group Index. The surprise to economists, mainstream financial players, and media is that these new indices: London's FTSE4Good, the US Calvert Social Index, and Domini Social 400 Index, as well as Brasil's New BOVESPA, regularly out-perform the mainstream Dow-Jones and Standard and Poors 500 (www.ethicalmarkets.com). Are we witnessing an evolution of human collective behavior toward moral sentiments and altruism? Or is cooperation for the common good now a condition of our survival? I submit that both are involved.

We are also entering the Age of Light. As we humans shape this current global stage in our development, our new awareness of our beautiful planetary home is calling forth an expanded identity, which I explored with Japanese Buddhist leader, Daisaku Ikeda of Soka Gakkai (with some twenty million members worldwide) in our *Planetary Citizenship*.[15] This larger identity enfolds and gives deeper meaning to our identity with our family, our community and companies, and the country of our birth. We are enriched by the unique expressions of so many other cultures in our world. We savor their art, dance, music, literature, and, especially, their cuisine! This human mutual appreciation for diversity is the starting point for planetary citizenship and the necessary transition to global sustainability, as the online global debates of the Global Transition Initiative illustrate (www.gti.org). Fundamentally, we humans have three basic resources at our disposal for this transition: information, matter, and energy. Of these, information is primary, since the quality of information drives our use of matter and energy.

In every country where industrialism took hold, the "tortoise" of social innovation lagged behind the "hare" of technological innovation. The history of the Industrial Revolution with all its good and bad news has included the lagging response of social rules to distribute the fruits of mechanized production and steer technological development and regulations to ameliorate its social costs and environmental damage. The very notion of an "invisible hand" inhibited broader views and visions of how economic systems could be steered to foster the common good, shared prosperity and protect nature's wealth. In the USA, lawyer Louis O. Kelso and philosopher Mortimer Adler challenged economists' panglossian model of "frictionless" technological change. Kelso recognized that if a machine took over a worker's job, then the worker would need to own a piece of that machine. Employee Stock Ownership Plans (ESOPs) now exist in eleven thousand US employee-owned companies.[16] A few industrialists evolved from their single-minded accumulation of money and material goods into philanthropists promoting wider access to education, health. and other global public goods.

In my *Politics of the Solar Age*,[17] I documented the ideological biases of neoclassical economics and the unreality of many of the inaccurate assumptions underlying even today's economics textbooks. I documented their critiques of economics, building on the 1971 classic by Nicholas Georgescu-Roegen, *The Entropy Law and the Economic Process*, which I reviewed in the *Harvard Business Review*.[18] Other scientists, including physicist Professor Dr. Hans Peter Durr of Germany's famed Max Planck Institute, agree that economics is not a science. Durr says "economics is not even bad science because its core assumptions are incorrect." I had previously asked Professor Durr "how could such a scandalous misuse of other sciences have continued unchallenged for over forty years?" Durr replied that academic etiquette usually restrained scholars from other fields from straying into other disciplines, especially with such criticisms. Austrian physicist, systems theorist, author of *The Web of Life*, Fritjof Capra asserts, "The dimension of meaning, purpose, values and conflicts is critical to social reality. Any model of social organization that does not include this critical dimension is inadequate. Unfortunately, this is true for most theoretical models in economics today."[19]

Neither have economists been held to the same standards of accountability as other professions. If a doctor makes a patient sick, a malpractice suit can be filed. Economists' bad advice can make whole countries sick—with impunity, as, for example, IMF economists' advice worsened Indonesia's economic woes in 1997. Today, economists from the IMF and central banks to those serving financial firms all bemoan the trend toward spending rather than saving. They refuse to acknowledge that this behavior is shaped by advertising, credit cards and the constant barrage of consumerism on global mass media.[20]

Neuroscientists, biochemists, and those studying the role of hormones, as well as psychologists, anthropologists, behavioral scientists, and evolutionary biologists are now dealing death blows to economics' most enduring error. This lies in its model of "human nature" as the "rational economic man" who competes against all others to maximize his own self-interest. This fear- and scarcity-based model is that of the early reptilian brain and the territoriality of our primitive past. Neuroscientist Paul Zak at Claremont University, California, has linked trust, which enables humans to bond and cooperate and is crucial to markets, to the reproductive hormone, oxytocin.

Indeed, we now know from brain science why people are susceptible to behavior change via mass media, advertising, and other forms of persuasion and lures to instant gratification. Brain researchers, using MRIs (magnetic resonance imaging), have explored how the "reptilian" portions of the human brain (associated with the limbic system) are susceptible to irrational urges, instant gratification and short-sightedness. The discovery of "mirror" brain cells enabling humans to empathize with each other also accounts for human suggestibility and the power of persuasion in mass media and advertising. Now that economists' competitive self-interest models of human behavior are under attack by such brain research, this field is being colonized as "neuro-economics" or "behavioral economics" in the same way that economists captured other disciplines as "ecological economics" and "environmental economics." This tendency to colonize other disciplines with false claims of universality was due to the power and financial advantages of economists as apologists for the powerful interests of business and finance. Humans are always "of two minds" about the signals in their lives and environments. They shift back and forth between their pre-frontal cortex (the seat of rational decision-making) and their reptilian, limbic brains. As yet, few have focused on the implications of this new brain research for the crucial role and responsibility of the advertising and commercial media industries. Over $400 billion is spent annually on advertising to override our rational pre-frontal cortex and its longer-term decisions "to save for a rainy day" and tempt us to run up credit card debts to buy goods on impulse through sophisticated manipulation of our senses and limbic brains. Advertising in the USA is a pre-tax cost for companies in order to promote mass-consumption. Today, mass-consumption of goods as an engine of economic growth is unsustainable.[21]

The critique of economics by mathematicians is that people don't behave like atoms, golf balls, or guinea pigs. Unlike the economists' "rational economic man," people are often irrational and their motivations are complex, with many, especially women, enjoying caring, sharing, and cooperating often as unpaid volunteers. Mathematics is now employed by some economists, by programming "agents" in computer models that are supposed to mimic human behavior. One recent model "Sugarscape" funded by gullible foundations, simply recreated poverty gaps and trade wars. Clearly, if they had programmed half of their "agents" with the behavior females so often exhibit (by choice, or involuntarily in patriarchal societies) they might have produced different results. Economics is patriarchal to its core, which accounts for the rise of feminist economics.[22]

Today, all economies are still mixtures of public and private sectors, two sides of the same coin with markets created by human rules and laws—a major social innovation. The two top layers of the "cake" of total productivity, the private and public sectors, rest on two lower layers ignored by economists: the Love Economy of unpaid work and Nature's Productivity. Mass communications and the Internet enlarged the new Third Sector: the citizen non-profit groups, charities, and foundations of global civic society. The World Social Forum, launched in Porto Alegre, in 2000, has focused the global debate about new paths to sustainable human development. The "cultural DNA" of societies always determines the size and scope of public, private and civic society sectors: based on their unique history, values, goals and beliefs that energize their people. The one-size-fits-all economic theories of development, such as the "Washington Consensus" have been discredited as they encountered the realities of the unpaid Love Economy, informal sectors, diverse cultures, topography, climate, agriculture, and the basic productivity of ecosystems.

Today, the chinks in economists' armor are becoming widely evident, including the game of preempting the work in other disciplines. Psychologists won recent Bank of Sweden Memorial Prizes in Economics for challenging simplistic economic models of human behavior. Even Harvard University may soon allow a new course in its economics department that challenges the orthodoxies still undergirding the policies of the IMF and the decisions of Wall Street and the world's bourses. A few economists borrowing from psychologists and real world observation now admit that we humans are not always competitively maximizing our own self-interest—the standard economic view of *homo economicus*. Many people enjoy giving as well as receiving, care about what kind of world we are leaving our children—"irrational" behavior to an economist.

A recent experiment at Baylor College of Medicine in Houston, Texas involved two women who were observed with the use of a $2.5 million brain scanner as they interacted in a game involving financial and investing behavior. The brain researcher's goal was to test, and hopefully discover, the secret of trust, the crucial human behavior that makes markets possible—and the variable missing from the mathematics used by economists in their models. Neuroscientist, Paul Glimcher of New York University explained that "we have started looking for pieces of economic theory in the brain." After monitoring the many moves between the two young women, it turned out that, contrary to economic theory and many game theorists, these two female players trusted each other. Economics and traditional game theory predict that lack of trust on the part of both players would cause both to lose (the Prisoner's Dilemma). The outcome of the women's game was that both won. Such optimal outcomes are termed "win-win" games, as opposed to the "win-lose" games of economic theory and the "lose-lose" outcome of the Prisoner's Dilemma game.

This outcome also challenges game theorist, John Nash's famous equilibrium, for which he won a Bank of Sweden Prize in Economics, and which "predicts" that in economic transactions between strangers predicting each other's responses—that the optimal level of trust is zero! Because economics is based on patriarchal values, it devalues the work of women in child rearing, caring for the old, and community volunteering as "uneconomic" in terms of the GNP. Economics did not predict the rise of socially-responsible investing (now at $2.2 trillion in the USA alone)[23] and textbooks still imply that trusting, caring, sharing, volunteering, and cooperating are irrational unless self-serving.

The best-known economists in the USA are admitting these and other errors, including Paul Krugman, Joseph Stiglitz, John B. Perkins, and Jeffrey Sachs. Unsung women economists revealed the patriarchal bias of economic theories and led the way in pinpointing these and other errors. They devised more realistic models – from Sweden's Alva Myrdal, India's Devaki Jain, Denmark's Esther Boserup, to Argentina's Graciela Chichilnisky, Brazil's Aspasia Camargo and futurist Rosa Alegria, Germany's Inge Kaul, New Zealand's Marilyn Waring, myself, and many others in the USA and other countries.

Statistical revisions, including those to overhaul GNP and GDP national accounts were pledged by 170 governments at the Rio de Janeiro Earth Summit in 1992. They were also recommended by the largest-ever global convening of statisticians of sustainable development and Quality of Life (ICONS) in Curitiba, Brazil October 2003.[24] Such statisticians have also repeatedly recommended that GNP and GDP record national assets: the value of public infrastructure investments in roads, public health facilities, sewage-treatment, ports, airports, schools, and universities that underpin the productivity of modern economies. In too many countries, these asset accounts, which properly balance the public debts undertaken to construct such vital infrastructure, are not recorded. Such public works, buildings, and facilities are immensely valuable and should be amortized over their lifetime of use—often over a hundred years. Try running a company like this, where your balance sheet could not include the value of your factories and capital assets! The USA made some of these needed corrections in January 1996 and these "stroke of the pen" corrections accounted for one third of the budget surplus of the Clinton administration. Canada followed suit in 1999 and went from a deficit to a $50 billion budget surplus.[25] The investments called for in the Millennium Development Goals, the Monterrey Consensus, and other proposals, such as the Global Marshall Plan, must be properly accounted as assets, since they will also produce dividends for societies as they transition to sustainability.

Today, in our Information Age, we acknowledge the value of investments in research and development, management education, and employee training programs. Accountants are learning to account for intangible assets, goodwill, brands, and other reputational risks and benefits.[26] Risk-analysis models, such as those of Innovest Strategic Value Advisors, Inc. (New York, London, Toronto, Hong Kong), now calculate social and environmental risks overhanging a company's balance sheet, which, if not recorded, can be overlooked and lead to sudden loss of shareholder value. Multi-billion dollar US public pension funds now require companies in their portfolios to disclose their plans to mitigate risks of climate change. Similar disclosures are mandatory in the European Union. Another area is corporate advertising, which is coming under increasing public criticism. I founded the non-profit EthicMark Institute, which will be based at Case Western University at the Center for Business as Agent of World Benefit, founded by David Cooperrider and Judy Rodgers. The EthicMark Institute will recognize advertising campaigns that inspire and enhance the human spirit with the "EthicMark" certification.

The World Bank is catching up with all these statistical innovations—beyond macroeconomic models to multi-disciplinary systems approaches—using all the multiple metrics beyond money to map these diverse aspects of human development and progress. I and my partner, The Calvert Group of socially-responsible mutual funds use the multi-discipline approach in our Calvert-Henderson Quality of Life Indicators, which are updated regularly at www.calvert-henderson.com. The World Bank staffing is more multi-disciplinary, replacing some of its macroeconomists with sociologists, anthropologists, epidemiologists, educators, and even civic society representatives.

In its 1995 report on the Wealth of Nations, the Bank acknowledged that 60 percent of this wealth is comprised of human capital and 20 percent ecological capital. Financial and built capital (factories and monetary assets) represented only 20 percent. For fifty years the Bank focused most of its attention on "economic" growth of this 20 percent of countries' wealth. Now, the Bank is shifting its focus to that 60 percent of human capital with more health and education investments.

Yet the Bank has not, so far, campaigned to add even public asset accounts to GNP/GDP. Neither the Bank nor the IMF require the addition of asset accounts, even for infrastructure assets, let alone for education and health—the most vital investments to maintain that 60 percent of the human capital comprising the wealth of nations. These accounting corrections will shift statistical focus to longer-term and sustainable investments. I, and other critics of the IMF's many mistakes over the past decades, am now calling for the permanent overhaul of their GNP/GDP and all other macro-economic models. The IMF should not only set up proper accrual accounting of assets for all investments in public infrastructure, but should re-categorize education and public health from "consumption" to "investment" in human capital. The World Bank and the UN System of National Accounts (UNSNA) should make similar corrections and add nations' public investments in education and public health to these asset accounts and amortize them over twenty years—the time it takes to raise a child to a healthy, well-educated, productive adult. It is these accounting corrections that can reveal the opportunities for long-term financial and social returns in the Millennium Development Goals, as Jeffrey Sachs shows in *The End of Poverty*.[27]

Even neoconservative economics recognizes that education is a "public good," a "positive externality" in economic jargon, i.e., activities that individuals and private business are unlikely to fund adequately since they cannot capture the full returns to such private investments. Economists still need to clarify the difference between markets ruled by competition and commons, which require cooperative rules. Educators, public health professionals, and the majority of citizens can support adequate taxes so crucial to their children's futures. In light of the new brain research, the current practices in US public schools of commercial sponsorship of TV news, sports and events, product advertising, junk-food vending machines, and curricula prepared by corporate PR departments—all to supplement budgets—may be ruled illegal. Research shows that children and adolescents have not yet developed forebrain capabilities to override such influences. Teachers should be better paid and schools should not have to fight in annual government budgeting with other expenditures for needed police, fire protection, and other public services, and even military weapons.

As all such new scorecards of real wealth and human progress are implemented, societies and companies can steer themselves on sounder paths toward order and prosperity. The new GNP/GDP asset accounts will end today's egregious overstating of public debts and the excuses it offered for excessive interest rates, sovereign bond yields and currency speculation. Developing countries in the HIPIC group are already being relieved of un-repayable, often odious debt under formulas agreed at the July 2005 G-8 Summit in Scotland. Former IMF chief economist Kenneth Rogoff suggested many reforms in his article in *The Economist*, July 24, 2004. I moderated five TV debates on "Reforming International Finance" between Kenneth Rogoff, John B. Perkins, author of best seller *Confessions of an Economic Hitman* and Sakiko Fukuda-Parr, lead author of the UN's Human Development Report.[28] Even before the G-8 Summit, the IMF's new President, Rodrigo Rato accepted the need to change many of its socially disastrous policies and to write off more un-repayable debt—largely due to pressure from global civic society and public opinion.

In this new century, long-held ideas are changing. The European Union is a new model of integration of formerly warring countries. Despite the "No" votes in France and Holland over the proposed EU Constitution and recent budget squabbles, negotiation, cooperation, and multi-lateral agreements are the way forward. The wars in Afghanistan and Iraq have revealed the many problems that, even politicians and military leaders now admit, require diplomatic solutions. New approaches to terrorism now favor funding education and building schools in countries where poor parents have no choice but to send their children to fundamentalist "madrassahs" where they are taught the ways of "jihad" and suicidal "martyrdom" to kill others in the name of God. Countries that pandered excessively to individual immigrants' rights to retain their own culture and language (multiculturalism) are rebalancing toward the needs of societies for inclusive, shared values, languages, and the "melting pot." Meanwhile, the search for balance between the rights of individuals and society continues.

In our age of weapons of mass destruction, wars are the most dangerous and ineffective options. We see already in our twenty-first-century that
the new weapons of choice are currencies, as well as better diplomacy, intelligence, and widely shared information. Investments geared toward the
Global Marshall Plan can help guide the reprioritizing needed to steer societies toward equitable resource-use and reduction of conflicts.[29] Insurance
policies for peace-keeping forces can reduce military budgets for countries
wishing to follow Costa Rica, which abolished its army in 1947. The proposed United Nations Security Insurance Agency (UNSIA),[30] a partnership
of the Security Council with insurance companies would assess country
risks and collect premiums that would be pooled to train standing UN
peacekeeping and humanitarian forces.[31] Reforming and expanding the
Security Council is now on the UN's agenda. The UN General Assembly
should take up all the alternative financing mechanisms, including those of
the 2002 UN Monterrey Consensus, the Global Marshall Plan, so as to
implement the Millennium Development Goals. The time has come for
global taxes on arms sales, currency trading, airline tickets, and e-mail to provide global public goods: education, health care, sounder international
financial architecture, and peacekeeping.

These human skills now have laid before us a rich array of potentials for
astounding, widespread, shared prosperity, peace, and restoring and our
planet's ecosystems. These new visions and values underlie in the United
Nations Millennium Development Goals, in the UN Global Compact, in the
Prague Declaration on Humanizing Globalization, the Global Marshall
Plan, the ILO's Report of the Commission on the Human Dimensions of
Globalization, and in the sixteen principles of the Earth Charter, now rati-
fied by hundreds of municipalities, companies, and thousands of NGOs in
over one hundred countries. The way forward and transition to peaceful sus-
tainable societies is possible.

© *Hazel Henderson, www.hazelhenderson.com, September 2005, paper for the*
World Wisdom Council Meeting, Tokyo, Japan, November 9-13, 2005.

Notes

[1] Hazel Henderson, "G-8 Economists In Retreat," InterPress Service, (Montevideo, NY, Rome: June 2003).

[2] David Loye, Darwin's Lost Theory of Love, (ToExel, New York: 2000).

[3] Joseph Tainter, The Collapse of Complex Societies, (Cambridge University Press, NY: 1988).

[4] Adam M. Brandenburger and Barry J. Nalebuff, Co-opetition (Currency Doubleday, Bantam Doubleday, Dell Publishing, New York: 1996).

[5] R. Axelrod, The Evolution of Cooperation, (Basic Books, NY: 1984); Hazel Henderson, Building A Win-Win-World, (Berrett-Koehler, San Francisco: 1996); James F. Moore, The Death of Competition, (Harper-Collins, NY: 1996); Robert Wright, Non-Zero (Pantheon, NY: 2000).

[6] "Bad For Business?" The Economist, (February, 17, 2005).

[7] Sumantra Goshal, "Bad Management Theories are Destroying Good Management Practices," Academy of Management Learning and Education 4, no. 1 (2005): 75-91.

[8] Thomaas S. Kuhn, The Structure of Scientific Revolutions, (University of Chicago Press, Chicago: 1962). As a friend, I had the pleasure of discussing his theories with him over many dinners at my home in Princeton.

[9] Hazel Henderson, "Information: the Great Leveler," World Affairs, 5, no. 2 (2001): 48-58.

[10] Bernard Leitaer, The Future of Money, (Random House, London, UK: 2001).

[11] Hazel Henderson, "Education: Key Investments in the Wealth of Nations," Boston Research Center Newsletter #23, (Fall-Winter 2004).

[12] Hazel Henderson, "Abolish the 'Nobel' in Economics?" InterPress Service, (Rome, Montevidao, Washington, DC: December 2004).

[13] Dagens Nyheter, (Stockholm: December 10, 2004).

[14] The Economist, (January 25, 2005).

[15] Hazel Henderson and Daisaku Ikeda, Planetary Citizenship (Middleway Press, Los Angeles: 2004).

[16] Corey Rosen and John Case, Martin Staubus, Equity, (Harvard Business School Press, Boston: 2005).

[17] 1981, 1986

[18] 1971

[19] Hazel Henderson, "Abolish the Nobel Prize?" InterPress Service, (Rome, Montevidao, Washington, DC: December 2004).

[20] "The Shift Away From Thrift," The Economist, (April 7, 2005).

[21] Hazel Henderson and Alan F. Kay, "Proposal for a Truth in Advertising Assurance Set-Aside," Human Development Report, (NY: 1998). Outlines a way to reduce the volume of advertising fairly and without curbing freedom of speech.

[22]Hazel Henderson, "L'Imposture," LeMonde Diplomatique, (February 2005).

[23]http://www.socialinvst.org

[24]Hazel Henderson, "Statisticians of the World Unite," InterPress Service, (November 2003),and
http://www.sustentabilidade.org.br.

[25]Hazel Henderson, Beyond Globalization: Shaping a Sustainable Global Economy,
(Kumarian Press: 1999).

[26]Verna Allee, "Increasing Prosperity Through Value Networks," (2003).

[27]Jeffrey Sachs, The End of Poverty, (Penguin Books, London: 2005).

[28]Available on DVD from http://www.ethialmarkets.com.

[29]Franz Josef Radermacher, "Global Marshall Plan: A Planetary Contract," Global Marshall Plan
Foundation, (Hamburg, Germany: 2004).

[30]See http://www.hazelhenderson.com, click on UNSIA.

[31] Hazel Henderson

References

Ackerman, Frank and Heinzerling, Lisa, Priceless, The New Press, New York, London, 2004.
Allee, Verna, Increasing Prosperity Through Value Networks (2003).
Altman, Daniel, Neoconomy, Public Affairs, New York 2004.
Axelrod, R. , The Evolution of Cooperation, Basic Books, NY (1984).
Batra, Ravi, Greenspan's Fraud, Palgrave, Macmillan, New York, 2005.
Brandenburger, Adam M., Nalebuff, Barry J., Co-opetition, Currency Doubleday, Bantam
Doubleday, Dell Publishing, New York, 1996.
Goshal, Sumantra "Bad Management Theories are Destroying Good Management Practices,"
Academy of Management Learning and Education, 2005, Vol. 4, #1, pp 75-91.
Henderson, Hazel and Ikeda, Daisaku, Planetary Citizenship, Middleway Press, Los Angeles,
2004.
Henderson, Hazel and Kay, Alan F., Human Development Report, "Proposal for a Truth in
Advertising Assurance Set -Aside" outlines a way to reduce the volume of advertising fairly and
without curbing freedom of speech, United Nations Development Program, 1998, NY.
Henderson, Hazel, Beyond Globalization: Shaping a Sustainable Global Economy, Kumarian
Press (1999).
Henderson, Hazel, Building A Win-Win-World, Berrett-Koehler, San Francisco (1996).
Henderson, Hazel, The UN Policy and Financing Alternatives, FUTURES, Elsevier, UK 1995.
Kuhn, Thomas S., The Structure of Scientific Revolutions, University of Chicago Press, Chicago
(1962).
Landes, David, The Wealth and Poverty of Nations, New York, Norton, 1998.
Leitaer, Bernard, The Future of Money, Ramdon House, London, UK, 2001.

Loye, David, Darwin's Lost Theory of Love, *ToExel, New York, 2000.*

Moore, James F., The Death of Competition, *Harper-Collins, NY (1996).*

Nadeau, Robert and Kafatos, Menas, The Non-Local Universe: the New Physics and Matters of the Mind, *Oxford University Press, UK, 1999.*

Nadeau, Robert The Wealth of Nature *(Columbia University Press, 2003).*

Perkins, John B., Confessions of an Economic Hit Man, *Berrett-Koehler, San Francisco (2004).*

Polanyi, Karl, The Great Transformation, *Beacon Press, Boston (1945).*

Radermacher, Franz Josef, Global Marshall Plan: A Planetary Contract, *Global Marshall Plan Foundation, Hamburg, Germany (2004).*

Rosen, Corey; Case, John; Staubus, Martin, Equity, Harvard Business School Press, Boston, 2005.

Sachs, Jeffrey, The End of Poverty, *Penguin Books, London (2005).*

Schumpeter, Joseph A., Capitalism, Socialism and Democracy, *Harper and Row, New York, 1942, 1947.*

Tainter, Joseph, The Collapse of Complex Societies, *Cambridge University Press, NY (1988).*

Wright, Robert, Non-Zero, Pantheon, NY (2000).

About the Author

Hazel Henderson, founder, Ethical Markets Media, LLC and Series Creator and Co-Executive Producer of its TV series, is a world renowned futurist, evolutionary economist, a worldwide syndicated columnist, consultant on sustainable development, and author of *Beyond Globalization*, and seven other books. Her editorials appear in twenty-seven languages and more than 400 newspapers syndicated by *InterPress Service*, Rome, New York, and Washington DC. Her articles have appeared in over 250 journals, including (in USA) *Harvard Business Review, New York Times, Christian Science Monitor,* and *Challenge, Mainichi* (Japan), *El Diario* (Venezuela), *World Economic Herald* (China), *LeMonde Diplomatique* (France) and *Australian Financial Review.* Her books are translated into German, Spanish, Japanese, Dutch, Swedish, Korean, Portuguese, and Chinese.

She sits on several editorial boards, including *Futures Research Quarterly, The State of the Future Report*, and *E/The Environmental Magazine* (USA), *Resurgence, Foresight* and *Futures* (UK). She co-edited, with Harlan Cleveland and Inge Kaul, *The UN: Policy and Financing Alternatives*, Elsevier Scientific, UK 1995 (US edition, 1996). Since becoming a full-time TV producer, Hazel has stepped down from her many board memberships, including Worldwatch Institute (1975-2001), Calvert Social Investment Fund (1982-2005), and other associations, including the Social Investment Forum and the Social Venture Network. She remains on the International Council of the Instituto Ethos de Empresas e Responsabilidade Social, Sao Paulo, Brasil. Hazel remains a Patron of the New Economics Foundation (London, UK) and a Fellow of the World Business Academy. The first version of her Country Futures Indicators (CFI), an alternative to the Gross National Product (GNP), is a co-venture with Calvert Group, Inc.: the Calvert-Henderson Quality-of-Life Indicators (Desk Reference Manual, 2000), updated regularly at www.calvert-henderson.com.

The ability to think straight, some knowledge of the past, some vision of the future, some skill to do useful service, some urge to fit that service into the well-being of the community- these are the most vital things education must try to produce.

Virginia Gildersleeve

If this life is our sole opportunity for self-enjoyment, it is also our sole opportunity to make our actions count on behalf of social good, to contribute significantly to the more lasting human values, and to leave a name behind us that will be honored and beloved by the community.

Corliss Lamont

How wonderful it is that nobody need wait a single moment before starting to improve the world.

Anne Frank

I have taken pains to show that financial markets left to their own devices don't tend towards an equilibrium that assures an optimum allocation of resources. The theories of efficient markets and rational expectations don't stand up to critical examination.

George Soros

The first duty of a human being is to assume the right relationship to society - more briefly, to find your real job, and do it.

Charlotte Perkins Gilman

He that plants trees loves others besides himself.

Thomas Fuller

How can one not speak about war, poverty, and inequality when people who suffer from these afflictions don't have a voice to speak?

Isabel Allende

Act as if what you do makes a difference. It does.

William James

DEDICATION

SERVANT LEADERSHIP

Robert H. Hertel

With genuine leadership, there are no secret weapons, no special formulas, nor any magic bullets. With servant leadership, this is especially true. It is paradoxical in the context of asking how can one both serve and lead simultaneously. Genuine leadership is not something you can just go out and buy, but something you must work toward continually. Don Frick states in his essay in *Insights on Leadership* from the Greenleaf Center for Servant Leadership that Robert Greenleaf observes "that rewarding, challenging, risky growth is often uncomfortable and seldom neat. Servant leadership simply is not easy. Most meaningful things seldom are!" How true this is, but it also a personal investment in oneself.

The concept of servant leadership has long fascinated and captivated me since I was initially introduced to it several years back by a colleague at Chapman University. I first read the original essays of Robert Greenleaf, *On Becoming a Servant Leader* when I began teaching eleven years ago in the Organizational Leadership program at Chapman's San Diego campus. Having studied through three management degrees and having had more of a managerial perspective as an original framework for leadership, I was truly fascinated by the utter simplicity and high potential of Robert Greenleaf's concept.

Greenleaf Center CEO Larry Spears identified ten characteristics for servant leadership. They are: listening, empathy, healing, awareness, persuasion, conceptualization, foresight, stewardship, commitment to the growth of people, and building community. I'm confident that there are really more we could add to this list, but that will come in time.

With genuine leadership, there are no secret weapons, no special formulas, nor any magic bullets.

I questioned this concept as, "How could something so simple and to the core not be the leadership model in practice in business today?" What conscious organization would not want to adopt this philosophy into their organizational culture? The more I researched servant leadership, the more I found myself identifying myself with it, and the more I wanted to learn about it and bring this into my personal leadership philosophy. It really boiled down to an inside out approach to leadership where genuine and true leadership is developed from within oneself. So why was something so logical, so pure, so simple not recognized as the leadership norm in organizations? After all, I felt organizations surely would see the simplicity and the raw effective beauty of this concept...or would they?

I must admit, and many of you may have shared this same experience, that the initial reading of Greenleaf's essays was not all that easy. Greenleaf's style was quite a bit different than what I was used to reading, but the essence of being so different intrigued me even more. I was enamored and I just wanted to keep reading them over and over! When I did, I discovered continually new and enriched meaning to his message.

This became increasingly more fascinating to me, and I think back to this being the beginning of my real servant leadership journey. These writings were dynamic, not merely something static in nature that you may read again and get the same concept from! The next significant experience was with the *Insights to Leadership* book edited by Larry Spears and Michelle Lawrence. It was much more traditional in reading style and maybe even more impacting on me. The opportunity to now see the concepts of

Greenleaf's original writings now being interpreted by so many amazing people lit the fire in me.

When talking about leadership theories, concepts, and philosophies amongst colleagues, friends, faculty, as well as my organizational leadership students at Chapman, so very many diverse leadership theories always surface and the plethora of definitions of what is perceived as leadership are soon to follow. Many of these theories are even quite manipulative in nature. So why do we then see so many of these styles still in practice in organizations?

Servant leadership, though simple in concept, requires a very significant commitment by both the organization desiring to implement servant leadership into their organizational culture and its people—those who will live and breathe it. As many of you know, servant leadership is very often misunderstood as some type of "touchy-feely" approach to leadership, and many organizations prefer to maintain the status quo of training its employees in management and supervision disguised as leadership, rather that taking the challenge or truly developing its leaders through servant leadership. I refer to this as a more peripheral approach, or better yet, training "counterfeit leadership."

Believers and practitioners of servant leadership intimately know that true and lasting leadership comes from within, and there simply is no "quick fix" to developing this leadership philosophy. The inner work of leadership, the time we spend looking within, is the most important work of leadership development. No way around it. Our success and effectiveness with accomplishing this important inner work, then, directly affects how well we work with others, and subsequently the overall success of the organization. It is a more effective, holistic approach to leadership through service to others. But initially as we begin our journey, I think we have to serve ourselves once we make the conscious choice to pursue the servant leadership philosophy. Not self-serve, but serve ourselves through our own development that is ongoing in nature.

Servant leadership is a living process. It's a process that has no real ending point and requires continuous learning and practice. This is a whole-life philosophy that we use and apply in virtually all areas of our lives. True and genuine leaders do not shut off the "leadership switch" when they leave work, but rather adopt it as a part of living the philosophy. It is not necessarily easy, nor is it overly difficult. It is a real commitment. Mistakes will be made along the way of this continuous journey, but servant leaders learn from them and move forward. Servant leadership is not something you can pretend to be practicing because of its inherent openness. Those who try to circumvent the process and simply call themselves "servant leaders" are easily identified.

There is an essential potpourri of leadership styles and programs that supposedly can be incorporated into our organizations in a few simple steps and with a relatively small investment in resources or changes in one's self to resolve the seemingly never-ending issues we encounter each day in our work environments. So why do we then believe that the simpler something is the better choice? Servant leadership is a simple philosophy, yet it requires time and commitment. Many organizations seek the more traditional "quick fix" approaches to leadership training by sending their people off to the infamous "one day" trainings with the hope that their people will come back with the necessary leadership skills. After all, these take merely a day, cost the organization relatively little money, and the employee gets a nice certificate for attending. How wonderfully simple! How realistically ineffective!

Buyer beware, because this tends to come back and sting us. How many times have our managers come back from seminars without any research beyond the seminar, now declaring this new concept they have learned as gospel? How about the manager who reads the latest and greatest management book and comes into work and declares this as the panacea of leadership? This is most often called "Leadership by Best Seller." And what happens when little effort beyond laying out a few key concepts begins to disappoint our workers and is perceived as shallow or without substance? There is a lot of counterfeit leadership out there, so again, buyer beware!

We have seen leadership taught in many of our schools disguised under management degrees. As Warren Bennis says, "Managers do things right, leaders do the right things." The focus being that the emphasis is first and foremost on the organizational aspects, followed by how we deal or work with others, and if there is any time left, we may touch a bit on the development of the self. It's no real wonder we are where we are in so many ways. Look at the Enrons and the MCI's out there. What went wrong? Who allowed it to happen? Just when do so many good people make the decision or choice to compromise their ethics and values and let so much abhorrence happen that they negatively affected so many others, just to meet some arbitrary bottom line? How can so many misconstrue the basic business concept of business being in business to make money as being a license to do whatever it takes to make a buck? Can business thrive and survive without these techniques? Absolutely yes, it can!

Being keenly aware of the management framework from my past education, I know schools have addressed leadership in more management concept and terminology. We were often, as they called it, "taught" leadership. We were taught systems and processes from traditional management perspectives. We were taught from a mostly organizational perspective, with little time addressing our relationships with others who we worked with. The biggest void was that we really never had any effort or time for the most important work—that of developing ourselves as leaders.

It is quite the opposite in servant leadership where the focus is first and foremost on developing the self, and then examines how we develop skills for working and developing others, and finally how we take this fabulous knowledge and work within this framework to serve our organizations. This is a more whole approach. You may even say this servant leadership concept is selfish in its development of the self first. There really is no other way. How can we best be able to serve others if we have not invested in ourselves first?

This is a bit contrary to the many and frequent attempted practices we see fumbled each and every day in business, in our schools, on boards of directors, in our government, as well as in many other areas around us. So the magic questions: why is there so much of this out there? Why are there so many misconceptions as to what servant leadership really is and what it is not?

So the fundamental question arises, "Just how do we take this seemingly impossible leadership concept into the real world of bottom line management?" "Just how do we get the rules to change in business from writing the rules to protect their business rights to that of writing the rules to do the right thing?" The concept of servant leadership will never be a quick-fix approach. The very essence of servant leadership is that of genuineness, service to others, giving of oneself from the heart, empathy, and significant substance. It in itself is a path that literally does not have a specific end, but is a continual and ongoing journey. How can we connect with and launch other people on this journey? Servant leadership is the genuine article, and it requires that a conscious choice be made and a commitment to invest the time to develop our servant leadership skills.

In 1998, the opportunity landed in my lap to develop a special topics course in our graduate Organizational Leadership program at Chapman University. Naturally, and without a doubt, I wanted to, or shall I say, I had a calling to share what I have discovered about servant leadership. Dr. Mark Maier, who was the founding chair of this unique program, was dedicated to the principles of servant leadership and facilitating organizational transformation within a values-centered framework. How could one not absolutely love to be a part of such a progressive leadership degree program?

I began doing web and library searches to find out all I could about servant leadership with the goal of creating a course that would focus on the self, the other, and how these are integrated to have profound and lasting effects on our organizations. Needless to say, the course was so successful that it was difficult each night to end the class and we would regularly run well over the class closing time! Never has this happened in my teaching and training experiences. Other courses soon followed, and we soon introduced servant leadership to our undergraduate organizational leadership program. Once again we saw amazing success and an increased thirst by all to find out more about servant leadership! Never have I found so much interest in the study of leadership.

So again, this amazing concept takes things to another level in my life. Those who serve give of themselves with nothing expected in return. Nothing expected, but yet absolutely amazing things began to happen as I continued to practice servant leadership throughout my life. Opportunities began to literally drop right in front of me and I began to meet so many wonderful people, I could not believe it. My calling to serve became a call to action, something I have always believed leadership is all about.

Leadership is not merely something we sit and discuss as definitions. Leadership can be anything anybody says it is until you have to go make something happen. Leadership is essentially getting out and making something good happen. It can be at home or at work. It can be in any part of your life, but it definitely is all about making good things happen, serving others, and helping them grow too. It is an everlasting leadership as well, because those you serve will likely find that same calling and urge to serve. Contagiously positive leadership!

While reading an article in the *San Diego Union Tribune* on September 28th, 2000 by Neil Morgan, another life-changing moment took place. It was like a shot in the arm! The article was about Dr. Ken Blanchard, world renowned author, speaker, and leadership guru and how he was making a pro bono investment in San Diego by creating the San Diego Leadership Initiative. He invited a cross section of the community leadership in and about the San Diego area to meet and discuss what was good, as well as not so good, in San Diego leadership.

It was impressive that such an instrumental figure in leadership, someone who I had read about throughout my formal education and author of so many well known books, would be giving so much of himself to a community he genuinely cared about. He was putting servant leadership into practice. Indeed, it is contagious!

The fact is that people take Blanchard very seriously, and when the call went out to the community leadership, it was answered. Blanchard stressed his goal to the community. His goal is to create a culture in San Diego of servant leaders moving the greater San Diego area not only from a success mentality, but to significance mindset in place of what he called self-serving leaders.

Blanchard asked them if his vision for San Diego could work; and he asked for their ideas. He thought it would be great to have those coming to San Diego for whatever reason discover just how San Diego became a servant leadership town and show how it could work in their town as well. He also stressed that San Diego could become a destination of choice, a provider of choice, and an employer of choice. He wants San Diego to be known for a leadership process that generates a true and genuine commitment which enhances the lives of its greatest asset—its people.

As each of you assesses "Living a Life of Value," consider reading about servant leadership. Don't let the title of the philosophy scare you off. That would be a mistake. Keep an open mind, look at this, and give it a chance to sink in. It is often said that it can take up to a year to begin to fully understand the concepts of this model and to begin putting them into practice, but I assure you it is well worth it.

For more information on your journey of discovering the values of servant leadership, look to www.greenleaf.org and www.leadershipinitiative.org.

© Robert Hertel

About the Author

Robert Hertel is a highly respected leadership training specialist, educator, and community leader. He has been lecturer and academic program manager at Chapman University for the past eleven years, facilitating in the award-winning Organizational Leadership degree program. Mr. Hertel also facilitates in the business disciplines at San Diego Mesa College and has taught over 240 college courses at a variety of colleges and universities. Professor Hertel has also guest lectured at United States International University, National University, San Diego State University, and University of San Diego. He has a unique passion for servant leadership and organizational development, bringing current research and theory into practical real-world application.

Previously, Mr. Hertel worked as an external consultant to the Ken Blanchard Companies with their "Office of the Future" think tank project and has worked with the management team from the Ken Blanchard Companies and other national and San Diego business leaders and organizations. Mr. Hertel serves on the San Diego Leadership Initiative Board as the Executive Director and on the executive board of directors for the American Red Cross of San Diego and the Imperial County Chapter.

A true leader is someone who is here to be of service.

David Friedman

May we, as image-makers and shapers of the culture, set our sights on things we value and rituals we engage in that heal and serve.

Jan Phillips

My mother's bottom line was truth to her values. It meant bringing your heart and your humanity to work. I learned at an early age that these are as essential for business as they are for life.

Anita Roddick

Most of the MBA students [I interviewed] admire people for their hearts more than their heads – they admire people who do good. But why, if you greatly respect one way of life, would you feel compelled to pursue an entirely different course? It isn't easy to give yourself permission to pursue your dreams, follow your heroes, and seek your inner truth.

Mark S. Albion

If it is true that love is the only sane and satisfactory answer to the problem of human existence, then any society which excludes, relatively, the development of love, must in the long run perish of its own contradiction with the basic necessities of human nature.

Erich Fromm

We can't solve the problem of corporate irresponsibility by imposing volumes of laws and regulations that try to restrain the system, because the system is designed not to be restrained. I believe the solution lies in redesigning the corporation itself to build in some self-restraint.

Robert C. Hinkley

I think many people assume, wrongly, that a company exists simply to make money. While this is an important result of a company's existence, we have to go deeper and find the real reasons for our being.

David Packard

RESPONSIBILITY

WHAT MATTERS MOST

Jeffrey Hollender

About two years ago, I started writing a book about the true nature of business responsibility. It was going to be a book written in response to the climate of scandal caused by the whole sordid Enron/Worldcom/ImClone mess. I was sure this atmosphere was going to result in companies of all kinds jockeying to look like good corporate citizens even as they continued practicing bad business-as-usual behind the scenes. I wanted to expose the coming fraud.

I wanted my new book, *What Matters Most*, to be about exposing another dose of corporate greenwashing. I was going to take companies to task for making it look like they were doing the right thing when, in fact, they were doing the same old wrong things beneath the thinnest veneer of social and environmental responsibility. I was raring and ready to go. Primed to play the muckraker and unmask the evildoers; but the more I dug, the more I discovered a single fact that surprised even me. Namely, that some of the changes occurring in America's corporate culture are not window dressing at all, but are actually important, substantive changes rooted in a sincere desire to make the world a better place. It turned out there are companies taking responsibility to heart and changing the way they did business.

As I continued to write, what emerged was a much different book than the one I set out to create. I kept discovering businesses that really are changing and businesspeople legitimately thinking beyond bottom line mentality. A book that I thought would likely end with no small sense of hopelessness, instead ended up imbued with tremendous optimism; the further I dug, the more I saw a light at the end of a very long tunnel. Companies were coming to the conclusion that they did not want to end up shattered wrecks like Enron and Worldcom. They were beginning to engage in the fundamental processes of change necessary to ensure their sustainability and, perhaps more importantly, our own as well.

I must admit I also wrote the book because my whole life has been a dance with issues about values and responsibility. I felt that through my experience as president and CEO of Seventh Generation, the nation's leading brand of natural household products, I could help explain the history of social responsibility—where it has come from, where it is today, and, most importantly, how we as businesses, as employees, as customers, and as investors can engage and help move the rest of the business community forward in a direction that will maximize its positive impact on the world.

Of course, every company has its own timetable for such developments. And by many measures and in many opinions, businesses today are not moving fast enough. But make no mistake: they are moving, and this is overwhelmingly positive news. Corporate responsibility has become a very widespread movement. Some twenty-five hundred companies around the world, including many of the largest multinationals, have voluntarily decided to start looking at their social behavior, articulating the types of commitments they want to make, and creating corporate social responsibility reports that place this commitment in black and white for all the world to see.

Beyond this voluntary participation, countless other companies have been forced into being more responsible whether they like it or not. The largest insurance company in Britain, for example, now requires every firm that it insures to make disclosures about environmental risks, human rights risks, risks in relationships with communities, and so on, because as an insurer they know that these things matter. More to the point, they can refuse vital insurance coverage to companies whose excessive wrongdoing is cause for concern. Since the businesses this company insures represent over

25 percent of the total value of the British Stock Exchange, this policy has had a significant impact on the behaviors of many companies.

There also appears to be a populist sentiment of sorts at work here. Underneath the senior management at most companies, I found vast ranks of employees who have a tremendous desire to take the high road and do the right thing. In most cases, when things go seriously wrong, it is poor leadership that sends the company in the wrong direction, not thousands of employees who conspire to do the wrong thing. Workers and managers are seeking opportunities to do good and are waiting for someone to structure an activity that they can participate in that will allow them to make positive contributions to their community.

The most frequent obstacle to this "will of the people" is a lack of enlightened corporate leadership. However, in researching my book, I also found that far more corporate leaders than I would have imagined have "gotten religion" and have made becoming responsible a fundamental part of where they want to take their company. There are the well-known examples like Ray Anderson at Interface Carpets in Atlanta, Georgia, but there are also thousands of unknowns, from Chiquita to Intel, who have made many of Interface's same changes without seeking or receiving the same level of publicity.

While many of these CEOs have had a legitimate change of heart, others have simply finally begun to see the purely practical light and decided to make changes, not necessarily for altruistic reasons, but because they make good economic sense. Many have now seen how their competitors' financial performance has been significantly improved by better practices. And though I am happiest with purer means of motivation, I am glad that businesspeople are at last grasping the fundamental truth that by being more responsible they can quite simply make more money. They can mitigate financial risks they would otherwise encounter, retain their best employees, build stronger and more respected brands, live in greater harmony with the communities in which they do business, and boost the bottom line. Whether it is a CEO that realizes his or her company's contribution to global warming is an increasing legal liability or one who understands that such pollution is inefficiency and inefficiencies cost money. The result is better behavior that benefits us all.

I recently read a report from the German sustainability rating company Oekom Research and Morgan Stanley Dean Witter having completed a study indicating that companies with higher sustainability ratings outperform their counterparts who score lower on sustainability practices. The study, which examined the 602 companies in the Morgan Stanley Capital International World Index that have received Oekom's Corporate Responsibility Ratings, found that the 186 highest-ranked companies in terms of sustainability outperformed the remaining 416 companies by 23.4 percent between January 2000 and October 2003.[1]

> Like a giant, lumbering tanker in the cumbersome process of adjusting its course, the corporate world is slowly turning itself around and heading in the right direction—because it has to; because truly, if profits are going to survive in any meaningful form, the engines that create them are going to have to become fundamentally involved with the problems that we face as a global society.

I think this represents a fundamental shift that is occurring in society and business that is making responsible corporate behavior an imperative rather than something a handful of businesses choose to do. I also think this shift is fundamentally raising the expectations that the public has of the role business should play in society. There are a number of signs that the public will not tolerate the kind of behavior that they tolerated in the past. There is a new level of expectation, and it is going to change the unspoken guidelines under which commerce operates. It does not mean that every business is going to become a good business, but we are in the process of setting the bar higher than it has ever been set before, and these new standards are going to force some level of change on even the most reticent companies. Public opinion, public relations and public pressure from an increasingly enlightened citizenry are already starting to see this change.

Add all these factors together, and it is clear we can be optimistic about the changes taking place. Like a giant, lumbering tanker in the cumbersome process of adjusting its course, the corporate world is slowly turning itself around and heading in the right direction—because it has to; because truly, if profits are going to survive in any meaningful form, the engines that create them are going to have to become fundamentally involved with the problems that we face as a global society.

The key to change is to keep up the pressure, and while many of my motivations for writing this book changed as it unfolded, I did not set out to write a book that was just for people in the business community. Though I wanted it to be useful to them, I wanted to write it for the rest of us because it is our responsibility as consumers, employees, investors, and individuals to help the companies we buy from and work for become conscious of the bigger picture and attuned to the future we are creating. I also wrote the book for those who work in the nonprofit sector who want to better understand how they can constructively and strategically engage with businesses and find ways to work collaboratively rather than in constant conflict.

The role of NGOs has changed as dramatically as the role of businesses has changed. We think of Greenpeace as this endlessly combative organization, casting a bright light on all the corporate misdeeds around the world, and yet today, you have Greenpeace in England working in deep collaboration with a company like Shell not over a few months, but over many years. This collaborative relationship is helping Shell find a way to change, creating a positive impact on the environment. This is a tremendously important and positive change. It does not mean that those relationships are without conflict, the book articulates how difficult and strained those relationships often can be, but in the end those relationships are responsible for producing positive change. At BP and Shell, at Chiquita, at Starbucks, at Nike, at almost every company I can think of, some significant part of the positive change has come about because of a relationship with a NGO.

Another important challenge is that corporate responsibility issues are not black and white. There is no such thing as a perfectly responsible company. You can find something wrong with every business on the face of the earth including Seventh Generation. Even those companies like Patagonia, Tom's of Maine, and Ben & Jerry's that you might think are "walking the walk," have issues of responsibility that they need to deal with. That is a challenging picture for the public, because once the consumer comes to terms with the fact that every company is somewhat good and somewhat bad, the question for them becomes "how good is good enough?" How good does a company have to be for the consumers and shareholders and investors to feel like "this is a company I want to support"? This is one of the most challenging questions both the corporate world and the public face.

You have many companies like Nike who became very well known for mishandling one significant aspect of their business, in their case labor relations and supply chain management, and who is not known, in fact has failed to effectively communicate, many of the positive things they have accomplished on the environmental front. This challenge is compounded by the fact that the media tends to publicize the bad and largely ignore the good. Often companies are reluctant to promote their positive accomplishments for fear that by holding themselves up for doing something good will only attract more criticism—which then becomes part of a never-ending spiral of confrontation, positive change, followed by closer examination, followed by more confrontation.

Of course, I do think it is through the concept of transparency and disclosure that we as employees, consumers, and investors can get enough information to come to those conclusions ourselves. Today, thankfully, there are an increasing number of third parties who read and evaluate these corporate disclosers, much the way financial analysts attempt to decode corporate financial statements, and who can help draw conclusions with which we can agree or disagree. What is so hard is that the playing field does not yet have defined and agreed upon boundaries. There is no consensus about what is an acceptable balance between the positives and negatives, or a rate of change that is fast enough and deep enough to clearly conclude that a business is doing a "good" job in fulfilling its obligation to be a responsible corporate citizen. This is a new world that business has to navigate through, and why they need help.

I am continually asked what key issues a company must address to become a socially responsible. I think it all starts with values. First, you have to develop and build consensus and understanding around a clear set of values and operating principles. This does not mean a list that is mounted on a plaque and hung on the wall; it must live in the hearts and minds of every employee. Second, commitment from the top of the company is key because if the head of the company is not committed to being open and honest, how can you expect anyone else to be? Once you are clear on your values, you then move into a more formal process of determining what structure, benchmarks, and measurements are needed to evaluate your progress toward achieving a set of goals based on your values. There are a whole variety of structures. Most of them are framed in the kind of Corporate Social Responsibility (CSR) reporting companies do to determine and disclose their socially responsible activities. The benefit of these reports is that they ask you a series of questions that force you to address different aspects of your business. Next, you need to decide how operationally change will happen: who is responsible for what, where are the conflicts, challenges, roadblocks, etc.

I also think the notion of transparency and disclosure is something you have to come to terms with early on, because the kind of transparency and disclosure that is required of a responsible business is very different than what most businesses are used to. Most businesses are used to only disclosing financial information, or positive news about new products, new customers, or new hires. They are not used to having to report, how much pollution they are creating, what the impact of that pollution is on the environment, and what the health impacts of the pollution might be. There could be other issues that pertain to their products' safety, problems with quality control, conflicts with local community groups, or allegations from other businesses of unfair competition that are all within the appropriate scope of disclosure and transparency. Companies need to understand and come to terms with what is required from a transparency and disclosure perspective because if you don't, you will never create trust, which I think is the fundamental part of being a socially responsible business.

As I noted, businesses are looking for nonprofit partners to help them in the process. If you are operating in a third world country and you are extracting natural resources, it is probably not on your agenda to build constructive community relations with the indigenous people in the area. You may not have the experience needed to develop those relationships so you create partnerships with NGOs who can help you address those challenges in a responsible manner.

I think it is important to remember that we are in the middle of this fundamental change and while we have learned many lessons on what works and what doesn't, there are many unresolved questions that we are still in the process of seeking answers to. It is a messy process. And, it is a new process. It is also a process that has poorly defined boundaries—when we talk about responsibility, what exactly are we responsible for, how broadly does that responsibility extend, where does it start, where does it end?

We have seen how difficult it is for businesses to live in a time of such rapid change, where the expectations of their stakeholders can change from month to month. A company's responsibility often seems to grow ever wider in concentric circles, bringing greater territory and increasing the tension between what they are obligated to account for and what critics feel is fair to take aim at. If you think about a company like Nike, everyone today can say they should have been responsible for the way the laborers employed by the contract manufacturers and who made their products were treated; however, ten years ago there were thousands of American companies who did not think twice about this and would never have considered it part of their responsibility. Our whole economy was built in part upon goods and services provided by third world countries at very cheap prices. We, as consumers, have benefited from that structure and no one asked the question "why is it so cheap to get things made in China?" Today, I think that most businesses that sell a consumer product that bears their brand name understand risk and the responsibility equation that goes along with third world manufacturing. What they don't understand is what is next, what will they be accountable for tomorrow that they have not thought about today.

I have done a lot of thinking about the ways we have put such principles in motion here at Seventh Generation, and how others can use the lessons we have learned at their company.

I should probably start by saying that Seventh Generation is far from perfect and that a core part of corporate responsibility is being open about our failures and shortcomings. We do practice a whole variety of techniques to help ensure that we behave in a manner that is in keeping with our values—it all starts with those values. Developing a culture that both understands and is committed to those values is essential. Articulating the behaviors that are consistent with those values and creating benchmarks to monitor your behavior against your values is a discipline we are just learning to master.

We started the process long ago by clearly defining our values, our mission, and our operating principles. Once we established who and what we wanted to be as a company, we made those values a benchmark against which we could measure our actions and decisions, and ultimately, determine whether or not we are accomplishing our objectives. While excellent

employee benefits, community involvement, charitable donations, outstanding customer service and products that exceed customer expectations are all
important, if not critical, we practice corporate responsibility based upon a
new set of metrics: how honest and complete is the communication
between staff members, as well as with customers and other stakeholders;
how safe is it to challenge your boss (how many people are willing to show
up and sit across from me and let me know that they feel that my own
behavior seems to conflict with our stated values); what is happening with
employee turnover, and why are people leaving; to what extent do our products and our entire company deplete the planet of non-renewable resources,
create greenhouse gasses, or produce solid waste, and so on. These are just
a few of hundreds of questions we ask and track on a daily basis.

We do a variety of other things, too. Every year we take several days and
have a staff retreat where we explore what our values mean, how well we are
doing at living them, and in what ways can we make changes to better live
those values. We just completed our first corporate social responsibility
report in 2004to publicly set forth how well we are doing, how we intend to
measure ourselves, what a good job means, and what goals we are setting for
ourselves in the future. We integrate personal, community, and value-based
goals into everyone's job description and performance expectations. How
well our employees do on dealing with their personal and community goals
impacts how much of a bonus they earn. We also use coaches to facilitate
interpersonal development, provide on site massages, take two days a year
to snow shoe, raft, or just walk through the woods together, insist that
everyone in the company serves on a committee like our "green team" or
"community service group," and a long list of other activities. We focus
pretty obsessively on the importance of work-life balance.

We also use 360-degree reviews, where everyone in the company evalu-
ates everyone else. This means that everyone at Seventh Generation gets the
opportunity to critique my job performance, the way I live our values, and
the degree to which I effectively provide leadership for the company's
vision. With a list of about fifty or so measures, it is not a process for faint
of heart CEOs or anyone else who is not deeply committed to their own
ongoing personal growth. However, it is as rewarding as it is interesting, and
it is most assuredly helped me become a better leader and a better person,
too. Does all this take away from our business success? Not at all—we have
been growing at about 25 percent a year for the past five years. We are prof-

itable and have become the nation's leading brand of natural, non-toxic household products.

Altogether, the business of bringing socially responsible goals to life is quite a process, and companies looking to do so should understand that there is nothing easy about it. Many things have to happen before you can even take the first step. I will say it again and again: it all starts with values. You have to become really clear about what your values are and also about what it means to live by them. On the road to social responsibility, a company is not going anywhere without this necessary map. Secondly, you have to have a commitment from the top of the company, because if the senior management is not ready to be brutally honest about what is working and what is not (and where they are in the process), you cannot really expect anyone else to be either. In my own case, I found I had to examine the way I led and managed people. As Gandhi once said, "Be the change you wish to see in the world." First and foremost, I needed to be an example of what I wanted Seventh Generation to be. I had to exemplify a certain level of honesty and disclosure. That does not mean I have to be perfect, just honest about where I am succeeding and where I am not. The trust that was going to be created within the company, and without, had to start with me. I have come to learn that if you cannot be an example of what you want your company to be, your company does not stand a chance of becoming a truly responsible business.

This transparency forms the foundation of trust, and it is very different from the kind of self-revelation that most businesses know. While companies commonly disclose their financial information, they are not used to reporting how much pollution they are creating or publicly considering what the health impacts of that pollution might be. Adopting this kind of behavior, whether it is on a personal level or on a corporate basis, can be very difficult because it is just not in the DNA of most executives. It is not what they have been taught to do. For the majority of both people and companies, it is uncharted territory littered with unknowns.

And that is perhaps the most important thing to remember about this whole business of transforming commerce into something that is fundamentally better for everyone: we are in the middle of the process, and while we have learned many lessons about what works and what does not work, there remain many lessons to be learned and many unanswered questions to be answered. Again, remember this whole process has very poorly defined boundaries. When we talk about responsibility, what exactly are we responsible for? How broadly does that responsibility extend? Where does it start? Where does it end? With so many questions, there are bound to be mistakes made along the way. I think it is very important for everyone to remember that it is okay to make mistakes during the journey as long as we admit it honestly, openly, and with the best intentions.

Fortunately, in spite of the challenges, I think corporate responsibility is something entirely possible to achieve on a broad scale. I also believe that there has never been a better time to bring about this type of fundamental change. Beyond the passion and commitment of many thousands of companies, the risks of being irresponsible have never been higher. Today, we as employees, customers, investors, community citizens, and interested nonprofits have the attention of the business community. Businesses understand like never before that they must not only listen to these other voices, but also seek them out.

Just look at the current landscape and you will find that many companies leading the charge are among the world's largest corporations. Look at a company like Intel, which employs sixty thousand people, and you will find a culture, a philosophy, and a structure that are in keeping with many of the ideas contained in my book. And you will find a great deal of hope in that simple fact. Big companies can no longer say that social responsibility is really only possible in small firms. Sure, it started with companies like The Body Shop, Ben & Jerry's, and Patagonia, but today that baton has been passed to far larger entities. Admittedly, these larger companies face decidedly different challenges, but I believe that any of these challenges can be overcome.

This is a unique moment because we have those companies' attention. We need to seize this moment and use it to insist that business be in it for more than the money. Insist that businesses also make a positive difference in addition to a buck. Business has the power to change the world and make it better for this generation and those to come. But that is only going to happen if we demand that each and every company we patronize commit to this new paradigm and all the possibilities it represents. After writing this book, I believe those possibilities are almost endless.

Finally, after having said all this, I personally believe that for all the talk of metrics and guidelines and benchmarks and indices, that the heart, as opposed to the head, may well be the best place to find the real drivers of change. Inspiring people to look inside themselves for the passions and the ideas, the mission and the beliefs that we can all make a difference is really what matters most.

© *Jeffrey Hollender*

Note

1 *http://www.socialfunds.com/news/article.cgi/1289.html*

About the Author

Jeffrey Hollender is president and corporate responsibility officer of Seventh Generation, the seventeen-year-old company that is the leading brand of natural household products in the United States.

Hollender is a member and former director of the Social Venture Network, he was a co-founder and a director of Community Capital Bank, a New York financial institution that invests in affordable housing and community development. He is also the former chairperson of Vermont Businesses for Social Responsibility, an almost five-hundred-member group, the largest state organization of its kind.

Jeffrey frequently addresses social and environmental responsibility at regional, national, and international venues. Speaking engagements have included such varied groups as the Harvard Environmental Forum, the Green Festival, the World Resources Institute, Nike Apparel Group, the Environmental Protection Agency, the United Nations Summit on Sustainable Growth, the Businesses for Social Responsibility national conference and many others.

He is the author of the best-selling book: *How to Make the World a Better Place: A Guide for Doing Good.* His new book, *What Matters Most* was released in December 2003. For more information, see the website www.whatmattersmost.biz.

A Director shall discharge the duties of the position of Director in good faith...but not at the expense of the environment, human rights, the public health or safety, the communities in which the corporation operates, or the dignity of its employees.

Robert Hinkley

Who among our business leaders will look beyond the quarterly profit sheet and take up the banner for programs that will make our country stronger, like health care for all, good public education, equality, clean air an water, a benevolent foreign policy, and living wages?

Joan Claybrook

Even if you work for one of the many millions of small businesses – you are part of that aggregated mass of business that can choose to be part of the problem – or a highly effective part of the solution. You can help your firm make the right choice.

Mallen Baker

There is no such thing as simply "doing business." No, there are six categories of acts, none of which is "just business." There are Right Acts for Profit; Inconsequential Acts for Profit; Wrong Acts for Profit; Right Acts for No Profit; Inconsequential Acts for No Profit; and Wrong Acts for No Profit.

Jason Merchey

Possessing material comforts in no way guarantees happiness. Only spiritual wealth can bring true happiness. If that is correct, should business be concerned with only the material aspect of life and leave the care of the human spirit to religion?

Konosuke Matsushita

Though the ethical challenges we face in the workplace may be different from those in our personal lives, the principles of ethical conduct that apply to those challenges do not change. There is no such thing as business ethics - there is only ethics.

Michael S. Josephson

WILL

MAKING A DIFFERENCE
A Daily Journey

Paul Jacobson

On November 6, 2003, while leaving work, Paul Jacobson was involved in a tragic car collision. In an instant, Paul's life was changed forever. Among his many injuries, Paul suffered severe damage to his spinal cord. After months in the hospital and intensive rehabilitation, Paul has returned home to face the challenges of life in a wheelchair.

In November 2003, I was involved in a car accident that left me paralyzed from the mid-chest down. I wound up in intensive care for one month and was in rehabilitation, in San Diego, for three more months. Over the course of the last two years, I've had an opportunity to learn a great deal about myself, about others, and about what really matters in life.

While in the hospital, I was fortunate to have visitors every single day who gave me their well wishes. It made me feel really good knowing that there are a number of people who cared and were willing to think about me and donate their time. Also, there were a number of folks who were able to help me out financially. The outpouring of emotion and resources to me was, and continues to be, incredibly overwhelming.

In that time, I was able to see the impact my accident had in other people's lives, particularly my friends'. In many ways, my accident was a wake up call to many of my friends, who now think twice before drinking while driving and are more cautious on the road. They have begun to realize what I realize: that life is very fragile and, without any fault of your own, things can change instantly. Without warning your life can be impacted in ways that you could have never imagined.

Prior to my accident, I was active in sports. I played baseball, basketball, and tennis almost every day. This accident, leaving me paralyzed, has moved me down a new path. I now have a new birth date, and that's November 5, 2003. I say that because I am now forced to find a new way to live. I am relearning everything. I have adopted the stance where I am prepared to make the best of my new life. I have accepted that there are a new set of cards, so I might as well play them.

But not everyone in similar situations can find a way to be positive. I have met others who have sustained a similar type of injury and are mired in depression and just don't know how to face their new lives. I am so fortunate to have a solid infrastructure that has supported me and has given me the courage to face my new reality. I am motivated to heal and get stronger for the people who have been there for me. They've given so much of themselves to me that, in some way, I feel obligated to improve and try to make the best life that I can.

I now go back to the hospital three times a week to do outpatient therapy. I still have many friends in the hospital, including social workers, doctors, and nurses. I continually ask them, "Who can I go see? Who can I talk to?" I want to tell new patients that things are going to be better so they can begin to put some perspective around their situation. I want new patients to know that I was in the exact same position, and I think that by seeing my improvements they can have some hope for the future.

Very early on, some friends of mine helped put together a foundation called the Paul Jacobson Spinal Cord Foundation. The mission of the foundation is to help other folks who have sustained spinal cord injuries with the difficult transition from the hospital to the home. There are many comforts in the hospital that you take for granted. You push a button and a nurse comes running. Once you leave the hospital, you leave that comfort zone. When you return home to what used to be your comfort zone, you find new challenges, such as finding assistance with your care, getting transportation, making adaptations to your home, getting medical supplies and medical equipment. So our foundation's aim, is to provide money, tools, and the information that new spinal cord patients need to make the smoothest transition possible. It's very exciting to me that we're able to help people make the best of their new life. Just that simple fact alone, making a difference in people's lives in a positive way, is incredibly meaningful to me, particularly for those who've had a similar injury as mine.

I've learned a number of very interesting lessons since my accident. First of all, I very much appreciate what I have today. This is especially true of my relationships. I try to foster those relationships so they can become better tomorrow than they are today. Secondly, I understand that time is a precious and fleeting resource that you don't get back. I am now very thoughtful about my time, and spend it where it generates the greatest return. Thirdly, and simply, I tell everyone to maximize their long-term disability insurance. Spend an extra five or ten dollars a month, because most people who sustain a serious injury will not have he coverage required to manage financially in the long term.

> I believe that making a difference in someone's life is really the ultimate contribution whether you're injured or not injured.

Prior to my accident, it was important for me to make others feel comfortable. I think I succeeded as people were able to be honest and talk to me about anything without fear of repercussion. Since my accident, I have stigmas attached to me, namely my injury and my wheelchair. There is a greater challenge in making people feel comfortable. I feel have to clear the hurdle of the stigma and work towards eliminating pity in order to maintain the type of relationships in which I was previously accustomed to. It's actually something I'm more aware of. I just want to feel normal and regular.

I believe that making a difference in someone's life is really the ultimate contribution whether you're injured or not injured. That is your legacy, your imprint, the mark that you leave on other people. By leaving my mark, I allow others to take my message and move it forward. With this injury, I'm afforded an amazing opportunity to share my perspective, my story, and my appreciation for life with other people—with people who may not be able to define how they are going to move forward in their new life. I've already been down this road two years now, and I can see where I'm going and where I've been. I can share my experiences through the foundation and through my own personal conversations with those who have sustained any kind of an injury, affliction, or negativity in their lives. I want people to know that the human is incredibly powerful.

If you would have told me before my accident, that I would sustain a spinal cord injury and not walk again in all likelihood, I would've told you, "I'm not going to make it. I'm not going to be able to survive this. I'm not going to have any interest in pursuing a life in this manner." However, what I learned was that the human spirit is strong and resilient. You find a way to make things work, you find a way to sustain and ultimately, in my case, to be productive. And that is the message I would want to share with others. Things may not look real good right now, but you're going to improve, you're going to find that your spirit is a lot stronger than you've ever suspected. You can make a difference, not only in your own life, but in other people's lives as well.

© Paul Jacobson

About the Author

A forty-year-old e-commerce professional and Internet marketing instructor, Paul now spends his time retraining his body in hopes of regaining his strength and independence. During Paul's recovery, he discovered that he was part of an underserved population whose fundamental needs were not being met by social service or nonprofit agencies. Under his guidance, the Paul Jacobson Spinal Cord Foundation was created to support recent victims of traumatic spinal cord injury. The Foundation gives financial assistance to new victims of spinal cord injury, easing their transition from hospital to rehabilitation to home. Today, two years since his injuries, Paul's energies are focused on rehabilitation and helping others as they begin the long and painful process of recovery.

A life of purpose is the purpose of life.

Deepak Chopra

God sells knowledge for labor, honor for risk.

Dutch proverb

Courage, it would seem, is nothing less than the power to overcome danger, misfortune, fear, injustice, while continuing to affirm inwardly that life with all its sorrows is good; that everything is meaningful even if in a sense beyond our understanding; and that there is always tomorrow.

Dorothy Thompson

I have learned that success is measured not so much by the position one has achieved in life as by the obstacles he has overcome.

Booker T. Washington

Life without challenges, without ups and downs, with everyone happy, in my opinion would soon pale. Hardships, setbacks, and disappointments are a necessary part of a rich life. It is true that sometimes they are not necessarily evenly distributed, and some crack under the strain, but a large number, perhaps most, overcome the obstacles and begin to thrive. I believe that life without unevenness would be like living exclusively on dessert.

Gene Lester

Continue searching harder, deeper, faster, stronger, and louder and knowing that one day, you'll be called upon to use all that you've amassed in the process.

Jodie Foster

He that wrestles with us strengthens our nerves and sharpens our skill. Our antagonist is our helper.

Edmund Burke

Many persons have a wrong idea of what constitutes true happiness. It is not attained through self-gratification but through fidelity to a worthy purpose.

Helen Keller

MORALITY

THREE PILLARS OF MORAL LEARNING
A Letter to a Young Cousin on Her High School Graduation

Bruce Jennings

Dear BC,

Congratulations on this important day in your life! I am so happy for you, and I wish I could be there in person to tell you so. But your parents have asked me to do something even more significant—to write something that attempts to celebrate the person you have been and are, and to call forth the person you have still to become.

I wish I could say more based on my knowledge of you and times we have spent together, but, of course, I can't write something like that because circumstances have kept me from watching you grow up, year by year. What I have before me is a snapshot of a very young girl, a little shy, as I recall, but bubbling with joy just beneath the surface. Perhaps we will come to know each other better in your adulthood and my old age. I hope so. For now, what I can offer are some thoughts and observations only about what you will encounter in your life and how you might think about the challenges and opportunities that lie in store.

I have spent nearly my whole adult life studying ethics and morality, and it is about leading a moral life that I want to share some ideas with you now. It is not advice that I have to offer, mind you. I have no reason to think you need such advice from me, and anyway, you have resources aplenty in your family, church, and friends for that. No, what I have to offer is not suggestions about what to do so much as a way of thinking about what it is you are doing and will do.

> Human moral experience is not made up entirely of clearly set forth matters of right and wrong and does not consist solely of obedience to specific injunctions and prohibitions.

What I have to say can be summarized in two thoughts. First, the moral life—the actions we take and the choices we make that importantly affect the lives of others and shape our own lives and identity—is not best understood as following a set of rules, but rather as a journey of human self-realization and self-discovery. Second, on that journey there are some moral capacities or moral senses that are essential if we are to make our way.

One very common and widespread way to understand ethics and morality is to think in terms of a set of beliefs, like a creed, or a set of authoritative rules and obligations, such as the Ten Commandments. Creeds and commandments provide rules and directions for living. And surely part of the moral life as we experience it involves the understanding of and obedience to such directives, imperatives, or commands.

As important as this perspective on ethics is, however, I suggest that the moral life is better understood as a journey or as a narrative of exploration and self-discovery. Human moral experience is not made up entirely of clearly set forth matters of right and wrong and does not consist solely of obedience to specific injunctions and prohibitions. Much of lived moral experience consists of the ongoing task of finding one's way; of taking one's bearings; and of locating oneself in relationship to others, in relationship to our own conscience, and in relationship to purposes broader, higher than our own.

Generalizations drawn from tradition, wisdom, and experience are necessary, even essential, but each life lived is unique; and so has yours been and will be. No one before you has walked exactly your path, and no one will again. Thus, the moral life is a journey of discernible destination, but unknown route. When exploring unfamiliar domains, one needs to use all of one's sense and each of one's senses. Just as there are five physical senses, there are (at least) three moral senses also. These are the three D's of the moral life: a sense of *direction*, a sense of *danger*, and a sense of *discernment*—what needs to be paid attention to and what does not.

I shall say something more about these moral senses in a moment, but first I wish to point out that the moral life has both a horizontal and a vertical dimension. What I mean by the horizontal dimension is quite straightforward: morality involves relationships with other human beings, who are on the same plane of being as ourselves.

The idea behind the metaphor of the vertical dimension of the moral life is somewhat more complex. First, consider the descending vertical dimension in the chain of being. To live a proper moral life, to have right relationships with other human beings horizontally, it is necessary to have the right vertical relation with nature, with the earth upon which we stand. Like Antaeus of ancient myth, our moral strength flows from our roots in the earth, the natural sphere that supports and sustains our very existence. Not to see our connection with nature as something that affects our connections with each other is a failure of the moral imagination, unhappily widespread in our own times.

Moreover, the vertical goes up as well as down. To have right horizontal relationships with others, it is also necessary to have a sense of something that is greater and higher than ourselves.

Does this mean that a person must be religious in order to be ethical? No, I do not think so. But what I do think is necessary in a moral life is the capacity of imagination that gives us the idea that there is something higher than our own self-centered perspective, something we cannot yet see, and that there is a destination we have not yet reached. This is not religion, perhaps, and it is not what many people nowadays call "spirituality." I would call it a feeling for the sacred. Anyway, let's return now to the three moral senses. I will say something more about the sacred at the end.

A sense of moral direction or reckoning. The moral life requires a sense of direction, a moral compass. And this sense changes your awareness of space and time. It alerts you to the fact that you are acting amid a web of feelings, expectations, vulnerabilities, and needs. And it alerts you to the fact that what you do today will affect who and where you will be tomorrow. Acting unethically is so often a function of being disoriented or lost; of forgetting or losing track of where we are and what is appropriate given where we are. We don't have anything to look up to because we have lost our orientation, and we don't know which way "up" is anymore.

A sense of moral danger and restraint. Morality requires an awareness of boundaries and limits. The moral life is anchored in the sense of going too far, a sense of trespass. All human cultures draw lines that must not be crossed, and when they are, not only the individual transgressor but the entire community is in danger. Boundaries are necessary because human beings are free-ranging creatures by nature; we are curious, even avaricious, in our desire to explore, to grasp, to appropriate. *Pleonexia*, the Greek word for taking what is not your own, for grasping and violating proper boundaries, is the prototype of all immoral conduct. We must sense danger before we reach it; we must be able to put on our moral brakes. Without a moral compass, we lose our way; without moral brakes we go over the edge into a yawning abyss.

A sense of moral discernment and responsibility. Discernment means to see and hear the proper things; to listen and to watch. The term "responsible" usually means that one can be relied upon to do what is expected and required—to be reliable, steadfast, loyal. It also means to be held accountable.

By moral responsibility I mean something else not fully captured in these meanings, namely, the *ability to respond*. The moral life is made up of encounters with difference and otherness. That otherness must be discerned, must be responded to. "Attention must be paid," laments Willie Loman's wife in Arthur Miller's great play, *Death of a Salesman*. I believe that the moral imagination is fundamentally rooted in this capacity to be moved by the recognition of the Other. Or, to put the point more precisely, the moral life is rooted in the recognition of the mutual "being-there" that one shares with the Other as human being; the mortality, the vulnerability, the sheer insufficiency.

The philosopher Emmanuel Levinas says that the moral life is made possible by the act of looking into the face of the Other. This alone saves us from solipsism and narcissism, and they are the negations of the moral life. In the story of Moses speaking to God in the sacred fire of a burning bush, at first, Moses hid his face because he was afraid to look at the face of God. (Exodus 3) But only at first. Even though the text does not say so, once God identifies himself and reassures Moses, then Moses does look God in the face. It is necessary to believe this. It is a morally essential hypothesis. We cannot hide our face if we are to be recognized, named, identified, transformed. And if we do not hide our own faces, we will not be able to hide from the face of the Other.

Moreover, in this way, discernment and the ability to respond teaches us to reach out to others, not because they are like us, but precisely because they are unlike us, at least temporarily: the weak, the needy, the oppressed, those who are afraid. Simone Weil refers to this reaching out as the capacity to be attentive. To attend: this suggests patience, listening, service. "The capacity to give one's attention to a sufferer," Weil observes, "is a very rare and difficult thing; it is almost a miracle; it *is* a miracle."[1] Figure out which way you are facing, because the direction you face will tell you who you are. Use your moral brakes precisely when the desire to accelerate is strongest. Cultivate your ability to respond when called out of yourself. These are not so much rules for living as discoveries one makes in living. They are linked, I believe, by the power of the imagination that takes us beyond ourselves, what I earlier referred to as the sacred. The sacred not only properly orients our vision, it expands it. The moral life has but a limited triumph over narcissism when it leads us to have regard for those most like us or those who have directly helped us. It is the Other as Stranger to whom we must bind ourselves; it is the Stranger who calls our name. The moral life consists largely in learning the Other's name. By encountering the sacred vertically, we are assisted in our calling to name and to be named by other people, and to be there, with and for them in the horizontal moral community.

There is no better time than on the day of your graduation, a day of going out, moving on, to reread Exodus 3:1-14, the narrative of Moses' encounter with God in the burning bush. I find this brief text immensely suggestive and vital for our understanding of the moral life because it contains a transformation of the greatest significance. So great in fact that it is God who appears to be transformed, although it is the moral growth and transformation of Moses—from an apolitical shepherd who only wants to mind his own business to the leader and conscience of a people—that the story is fundamentally about. Moses encounters sheer plenitude and complexity—a god that has no name, for names attach to pieces of being, except the name of being itself as a whole. But already we have a connection between that which is and those who are becoming. Not only is this a god of power and righteousness or justice—he can make fire that does not consume, turn sticks into snakes, he can lay waste the wicked, and all the rest. But this is a god who can also see, hear, and feel the vulnerability and suffering of *his* radical Other—the mortal, the weak, the fearful, and the slow. "Then the Lord said, 'I have seen the affliction of my people who are in Egypt, and have heard their cry…I know their sufferings, and I have come down…'"

The moral life is all about how well we can see, hear, and feel these things—seeing affliction, hearing cries, knowing suffering. We humans on the horizontal landscape of ethics don't come down, but because the sacred has come down to us, we can come out of ourselves and go out to one another. By going out, we also go up.

I extend my best hopes and highest expectations to you today.

Your loving cousin,

Bruce

© Bruce Jennings

Note
[1] George A. Panichas, Ed., *"Reflections on the Right Use of School Studies with a View to the Love of God,"* Simone Weil Reader *(Moyer Bell Ltd., NY: Moyer Bell Ltd, 1977)*, 51.

About the Author

Bruce Jennings is Director of the Center for Humans and Nature in New York, a private foundation dedicated to the study of ethics and values issues in the areas of health, the environment, and public policy. He is also a lecturer in ethics at the Yale School of Medicine and serves as a consultant to The Hastings Center, a leading organization in the field of bioethics. He has written and lectured widely on ethical and social issues.

You don't have to think about doing the right thing. If you're for the right thing, then you do it without thinking.

Maya Angelou

Humanism expresses a set of significant moral values, which focus on fulfilling the best in human beings and are positive contributions to human good...Humanist morality can provide a genuine basis for excellence and nobility.

Paul Kurtz

Moral principles, like the artist's palette, may provide the form of our final decision, but never the specific content.

Judith Barad

I think this is the first time in my life I ever voted alone in the United States Senate, and I have to tell you, I think it was the right thing to do.

Barbara Boxer

The Master said, "The gentleman understands what is moral. The small man understands what is profitable."

Confucius

There is a higher court of justice and that is the court of conscience. It supercedes all other courts.

Mohandas K. Gandhi

At the end of the day I sleep well, and in life there is nothing more important than that. What matters is doing the right thing and being true to yourself and standing up on principle.

Gavin Newsom

People think it's hard to do the right thing; it's not hard to do the right thing, it's hard to know what the right thing is. Once you know - once you know what's right - it's hard not to do it.

Sol Yurick

HONOR

HAPPINESS THROUGH HONORABLE ACTIONS

Julian Kalmar

D o you want to live with a strong sense of peacefulness, happiness, goodness, and self-respect? The collection of happiness actions broadly categorized as "honor" help you create this life of good feelings.

As the *American Heritage Dictionary* defines it, honor is "personal integrity maintained without legal or other obligation." It's a deep sense of rightness in our choice of actions. However, this sense of rightness does not display itself as ugly self-righteous behavior. It is a quiet personal experience of rightness that leads to a lasting sense of well-being.

Here's an example to show how honorable actions create happiness.

Say a store clerk fails to charge us for an item. If we don't say anything, we receive an immediate reward, don't we? We feel excited by our good fortune, and could leave the store with a sense of glee. We made no mistake and we made no effort to cheat them. So, why not allow the error to benefit us? It seems we would still be able to respect ourselves afterwards.

To discover why we should take honorable action, we need only play out each possible future.

If we keep silent, and profit from the clerk's mistake, we would leave the store with adrenaline coursing through our veins; we would get away with something. We would drive home with a sense of sneaky excitement. Later we might tell our spouses or friends about our good fortune.

On the other hand, if we tell the clerk about the uncharged item, the clerk would be grateful and thank us for our honesty. We would leave the store with a quiet sense of honor that we might never share with another soul.

In the first case, where we don't tell the clerk, a couple of things would happen. Deep down inside we would know ourselves as a type of thief, as evidenced by our sneaky excitement. In the process, we would lose some peace of mind and self-respect. We would also demonstrate that we cannot be trusted, since we advertise our dishonor by telling our spouses and friends. We tarnish our own reputations by telling others.

In contrast, bringing the error to the clerk's attention causes different things to happen. Immediately the clerk knows us to be honorable. They like us. They remember us thereafter and treat us well. Upon leaving the store, we reflect on our sense of goodness. We feel honorable and our self-respect is boosted. Our kindness to the clerk is reflected back to us immediately and over the long term when they see us again.

Whenever we take honorable action we gain the deep internal rewards of self-respect, peace of mind, goodness, and a sense of nobility. All of these greatly contribute to our sense of well-being. Honorable actions create happiness.

There is a beautiful positive cycle that is created by living a life of honorable actions. Honorable thoughts lead to honorable actions. Honorable actions lead us to a happier existence. And it's easy to again think and act honorably when we're happy.

Unfortunately, there is a negative version of this cycle. Dishonorable thoughts lead to dishonorable actions that lead to pain and unhappiness. Unhappiness leads to more dishonorable thoughts.

So, strive for the positive cycle. While it can be difficult to start, once it's started, it's easy to continue.

The opportunities for expressing honor—and thus for becoming happier—are all around us. In our work lives we express honor by always doing quality work, never leaving details unattended, working in the company's best interest, treating customers and employees well, never working in a divisive spirit, and striving to promote harmony.

In our larger lives we express honor through honest and ethical actions, being punctual, doing what we promise, holding ourselves accountable for our actions, treating others with respect, and so on. Although the list is endless, the common theme is a sense of quiet rightness. We feel quiet, at peace with our thoughts and actions.

> The opportunities for expressing honor—and thus for becoming happier—are all around us.

Many people look to books of laws or religious teachings to know what is honorable, but you can almost always tell honorable actions by consulting your inner spirit. Simply ask yourself which course of action creates the least internal and external turmoil in the long run. Predictions of your mental quietude are good guides.

Just as we did with the inattentive store clerk example, ask yourself if you would be more or less peaceful, happier or unhappier in the long run, more self-respecting or less, more honorable or not.

If you always choose the honorable route, you are never plagued by the fear of "being discovered" and no one can ever threaten to expose your past. That brings the peace of mind essential for genuine happiness.

© *Julian Kalmar*

About the Author

Julian Kalmar is part of a small think tank dedicated to spreading happiness throughout the world. More happiness teachings are available in his four CD audio collection, "Happiness: The Highest Gift." This collection won the June 2005 "Audio-of-the-month" award, an award also won by Nelson Mandela, Wayne Dyer, and Marc Allen in 2005. See www.thehappinessformula.com.

The most exhausting thing in the world is being insincere.

Anne Morrow Lindbergh

Many of the values I learned as a child, which could be boiled down to one simple phrase - doing the right thing - have shaped the kind of man I've become. Education and training helped me become a reporter, but character determines what kind of reporter I am.

Sylvester Monroe

All virtues spring from honor.

Albanian proverb

I am sustained by knowing that I am doing what is right.

Desmond Tutu

The more I practice truth-telling, the easier it becomes.

Angeles Arrien

It is my belief that the lack of understanding of the true cause of happiness is the principal reason why people inflict suffering on others. Some people think that causing pain to others may lead to their own happiness, or that their own happiness is of such importance that the pain of others is of no significance. But this is clearly shortsighted. No one truly benefits from causing harm to another being.

Tenzin Gyatso

When you know what you're doing you can do what you want.

Moshe Feldenkreis

Be as beneficent as the sun or the sea, but if your rights as a rational being are trenched on, die on the first inch of your territory.

Ralph Waldo Emerson

Reputation is what other people know about you. Honor is what you know about yourself.

Lois McMaster Bujold

It may be that religion is dead, and if it is, we had better know it and set ourselves to try to discover other sources of moral strength before it is too late.

Pearl S. Buck

The purpose of morality is to teach you, not to suffer and die, but to enjoy yourself and live.

Ayn Rand

I think we all have a little voice inside us that will guide us. It may be God, I don't know. But I think that if we shut out all the noise and clutter from our lives and listen to that voice, it will tell us the right thing to do.

Christopher Reeve

At the end of the day I sleep well, and in life there is nothing more important than that. What matters is doing the right thing and being true to yourself and standing up on principle.

Gavin Newsom

It's the tough decisions that really test our character, for character is revealed when the price of doing the right thing is more than we want to pay.

John Naber

Have the courage to say no. Have the courage to face the truth. Do the right thing because it is right. These are the magic keys to living your life with integrity.

W. Clement Stone

You will never be happy if you continue to search for what happiness consists of. You will never live if you are looking for the meaning of life.

Albert Camus

People spend a lifetime searching for happiness; looking for peace. They chase idle dreams, addictions, religions, even other people, hoping to fill the emptiness that plagues them. The irony is the only place they ever needed to search was within.

Baruch Spinoza

INTEGRITY

HOW SHOULD ONE LIVE?

Gary E. Kessler

I encountered Socrates as a mere boy. Perhaps I should say that, as with so many of the youth of ancient Athens, Socrates encountered me. Not, of course, the flesh and blood Socrates, but the literary Socrates; the Socrates Plato immortalized in his dialogs.

I recall three things from this early encounter. First, Socrates put a question to me that has haunted me all of my life. How should one live? This, he claimed, is the most important question a person can ask. Second, he admonished me to follow an argument wherever it may lead. Third, he claimed, "the unexamined life is not worth living."

How should one live? Note that even though many people interpret this as primarily an ethical question, it is not. It is a more general question, a question that can be asked about all areas of life. Socrates does not ask how *ought* one to live, only how *should* one live. His answer that a life pursuing virtue is the best way to live reinforces our tendency to think of this as a question about morality. However, the Greek word for virtue is better translated as excellence, and excellence can be pursued in all areas of one's life from sports and health to moral actions and relations. Striving for excellence as we negotiate the highways and byways of life is an important and worthwhile value. It has even achieved the status of an ad slogan that reminds us to be "all that we can be." Such platitudes, however, are not much help when it comes to the concrete situations of life in which we find ourselves. Socrates realized this when he admitted that, although the pursuit of virtue is an important value, and he thought it had something to do with wisdom, he was not at all certain what wisdom was.

> Striving for excellence as we negotiate the highways and byways of life is an important and worthwhile value.

The difficulties associated with finding an answer to Socrates' question as I lived my life did not, however, make the question go away. It stayed with me. I came to realize that there is no single or final answer to this question. Different answers are relevant to different stages of one's life. The answers of youth are not the answers of middle age. The answers of middle age are not the answers of old age. The key, at least for me, was the realization that the answers were far less important than the question. Just asking this question, not forgetting it, not putting it on the backburner of consciousness, but keeping it in mind and seriously asking it when making important decisions reveals its value for living. It reminds us that the human animal is not merely controlled by instincts or by the social forces of cultural circumstances, but that we have choices. This is one reason why Socrates calls it the most important question humans can ask. Just asking it reminds us of our power to choose and thereby empowers us to explore alternatives and take responsibility for our choices and for our lives. The question reveals our freedom—the freedom to reflect, to change, to override our instincts. It also reveals the importance and power of asking questions. How should one live? One should live by asking questions and examining the answers with all of one's critical faculties.

I have had in my life a lot of questions and still do. At times, that has been a burden. It requires living with uncertainty, something many people find uncomfortable. I remain convinced, however, that a life of asking questions is a good way to live. It is good not because it leads to wealth or to health or to happiness, but because it leads to truth. We mortals have a problem with truth. We are rightly skeptical when others claim that what they tell us is the Truth. We are rightly skeptical when philosophers and theologians tell us the Truth. There is no such thing as the Truth. But there are truths— little ones and big ones, uncomfortable ones and pleasant ones, past ones and future ones. Where can we find them? We can only find them, Socrates reminds us, by following an argument wherever it leads and by examining our beliefs and values.

Following an argument wherever it leads, the second Socratic idea that so impressed me in my youth, is not an easy thing to do. It demands a determination to be rational even when thinking about issues and ideas about which we have strong convictions. I soon discovered that my natural tendency was to believe what I had been taught, or what felt right, or what made me happy. I also discovered that prejudice, bias, and the idols of popular culture played a much larger role in my beliefs than I was willing to admit. We "fix our beliefs" (to borrow an expression from the philosopher Charles S. Pierce) in many ways. If we take the time to carefully discover how we came to hold a belief, we often discover that it was not the result of following the logic of an argument or the result of a careul weighing of the evidence. Of course discovering how we got to a belief does not necessarily tell us it is a wrong belief or one we should discard. But it can send up red flags. One red flag that tends to get my attention is when I find myself stopping short as it were. I follow an argument just so far, and when I fear it may be heading in a direction I do not like, a powerful feeling of inertia arises. I want to stop, to rest, to distract myself, to do anything but continue down a path that I fear will lead me to discard one of my dearly beloved myths about the world, or others, or about myself. We want to control the argument, to make it yield the conclusions we so dearly value, to manipulate the evidence so we get results that say what we want them to say.

It appears that not even Socrates always followed an argument wherever it led. At crucial points he listened to his "daemon" or inner voice, which he took to be divine, for advice about what to do and proudly announced that it had never let him down. A close examination of the Socratic literature reveals that Socrates may well have pulled a few logical tricks in order to get his dialog partner into the corner he desired. So Protagoras, the archetypal sophist, accuses him of violating the rule of logical distribution by construing his claim that the courageous are confident as equivalent to the claim that the confident are courageous.[1] I took heart when I realized that even my revered teacher might not have followed an argument wherever it leads, but only into territory he liked or at least Plato, his admiring student, liked. Plato, who created the Socratic dialogs that have so deeply influenced western culture, makes no secret of his dislike for all forms of sophistry, not to mention the sophists that prowled the streets of ancient Athens teaching what they called "wisdom" for a price. Even so, he could not totally disguise the fact that many of Socrates' contemporaries thought that Socrates was himself a sophist or little better than those who so misled, in Plato's opinion, the fine young men of the Athenian *polis*.

Part of growing up is the realization that those who gave us sage advice in youth were not always capable of following their own advice. It is easy to jump from there to the conclusion that the advice is no good, and we can ignore it. But the advice to follow an argument wherever it leads is good advice even if Socrates may not have always heeded it. It is good advice because it places on us the demand to be rational. This reveals our humanity just as the demand to ask how one should live reveals our humanity. The question about living tells us that we have freedom of choice and the demand to follow an argument to its conclusion reveals that we are or at least can be "rational animals" (to borrow a term from Aristotle).

The third thing I remember from my early encounter with Socrates is his notorious pronouncement in the *Apology* that the "unexamined life is not worth living." I say this is notorious because at first glance it seems wrong. Ignorance can often be bliss and who are we to say that a life of ignorance is a life totally devoid of value and worth?

In graduate school, I studied philosophy and comparative religions. When I decided to make teaching at the university level my career, I began to preach the gospel of the importance of critical thinking. Critical thinking is essential to the examined life. Without it we wander aimlessly through life following wherever the herd leads and worshiping the "idols of the tribe" (as Francis Bacon so aptly put it). When my students began to question Socrates' dramatic pronouncement that a life that is unexamined is not worth living, I jumped to my mentor's defense. For me, critical thinking crystallized the values of reflection on how one should live, a willingness to follow an argument wherever it may lead, and examining one's life. Slowly it dawned on me that this claim also had to be critically examined. Why is the unexamined life not worth living? Is there no value in bouncing through life in the manner of the proverbial airhead?

We need to keep in mind the context in which Socrates made his claim about the worth of the examined life. He had been sentenced to death by a jury of his peers for corrupting the youth of Athens and for denying the gods. Those who found him guilty and passed the sentence fully expected him to accept the lesser punishment of exile. He refused exile even though the alternative was death. He tried to explain why and. although he knew most of his peers would find it hard to understand, he insisted that a life of keeping quiet, not questioning those in authority, and not teaching the youth to engage in critical thinking about all manner of things was a life he would prefer not to live. Did he mean this to be true of him and not others? Did he mean that the unexamined life was not worth living for Socrates, but might well be worth living for others?

Whatever his intention, succeeding generations have taken his pronouncement as a recommendation for all human beings that have the capacity to think. All of us should critically and rationally examine our beliefs and actions. If we refuse this challenge then the value, worth, and quality of our lives is diminished. We are less than we might be. We are failing in our pursuit of excellence.

If asking how one should live reveals our freedom, and following an argument wherever it leads reveals our rationality, then examining our beliefs and values reveals our capacity for self-transcendence. A distinctive feature of being human is the ability to step back as it were and look at ourselves. Our self-consciousness allows us to make ourselves an object of our own thought. Without this capacity for self-transcendence, Socrates' assertion about the value of examining our lives makes no sense. We can, of course, lead an unexamined life. If we do, however, we are denying our full worth as human beings.

Critical thinking can, however, lead to problems. I have often been accused of being argumentative, even pugnacious. I plead guilty. It is too easy to slip from appropriate questioning to inappropriate questioning and cynicism. Yet questioning is what we must do if we wish to pursue wisdom. When our leaders wish to rush to war, which involves the horrendous destruction of life and the increase of suffering on this globe, when people wish to exploit the environment for profit, when those with power and influence wish to convince us that God is on our side and that they know with certainty the divine will, we must speak out. Voicing truth to power is not easy, nor is it something that will win friends and favors. The alternative is worse because it leads to the destruction of the only home (this lovely planet) that we have and to the suffering of present and future generations. Wisdom is not what some guru says, or some leader of stature, or some self-appointed spokesperson for the Almighty. Wisdom is, at least in part, critical thinking. It is the willingness to examine our own assumptions, our own narrow view of things, our own presuppositions and biases. Shift through the evidence. Ask: what does some supposed authority have to gain by these claims? Ask: what do I have to gain by believing them?

Asking how one should live, following an argument wherever it leads, and examining one's life make our lives more valuable by allowing our humanity—our freedom, our rationality, and our capacity for self-transcendence—to flourish. But not all humans can flourish. Not all humans are in a position nor do they have the luxury of living an examined life. Life for them is finding enough to eat. It is a matter of mere survival, of coping with extreme poverty, fear, illness, and living without hope for a better future. They are victims of dire circumstances. Sadly, all too many of our fellow humans find themselves in these straights. Preaching to them the virtues of examining one's values and beliefs is like discussing, as the Buddha said, abstract metaphysical issues with someone who is near death from a serious injury. It is not only irrelevant but also it woefully misses the point.

The plight of so many of our neighbors on our planet reminds us that living a life of value is not, nor can it be, an individual matter. We live in a world whose natural wonder and splendor we are rapidly destroying. We live in a world of war, terrorism, violence, and appalling suffering. Lives of value must acknowledge and deal with these social problems. Hence both the values of compassion and justice must accompany any personal quest for living the sort of life Socrates advocated.

In college I learned that Plato thought the three primary virtues humans need to cultivate are moderation, courage, and wisdom. If we mortals can manage that, our lives would be just, and if the citizens of the ideal state could manage that, the fourth virtue of justice would follow from the three primary virtues. For Plato justice was a by-product of his version of a life of value. He was wrong on two counts. First, justice should not be relegated to the status of a by-product. It needs to be central to a life of value because without it the application of critical thought to questions like how one should live cannot even get off the ground. Second, Plato left out compassion. Compassion, feeling with the suffering of others, must go hand and hand with the pursuit of justice.

How does living a life of value lead to compassion and justice? We might get there by persistently asking the question how one should live, but we might not. We might get there by exercising our powers of rational thought and critical examination of our beliefs, but we might not. Nothing logically compels us to include compassion and justice on our list of values. We must add other ingredients. We need to watch an eagle soaring on wind currents, waves striking a beach, a squirrel outside the window precariously balancing on the limb of a magnificent hemlock tree, awe inspiring cloud formations, and the realization that this planet on which we are privileged to live is also a precarious perch that will someday disappear into the cosmic dust. We need to experience the love of family and friends. We need to experience the kindness of a stranger, the joy of a child, and realize as we witness and try to alleviate human suffering that "there but for the grace of God go I."

I will be the first to confess that I have not always lived a life that incorporates the values Socrates recommended. Nor have I been as compassionate as I should be, and I have too often turned away from the demands of justice. These values are ideals for which I strive. Yet failure is no excuse. Failure is an opportunity for renewed commitment to both the environment and the living creatures that inhabit this wondrous world in which we live. It is an opportunity for exercising our freedom to choose, our rational ability to critically examine cherished beliefs, and our capacity for self-transcendence.

Socrates, in a classic example of Socratic irony, had to admit that he did not know what wisdom was and that was precisely why the Oracle at Delphi said that he was the wisest person in Athens. Unlike others who strutted around Athens proclaiming their wisdom, Socrates was wise because he knew he was not wise. This acknowledgement of fallibility is a key element in the pursuit of wisdom. Never doubt that you can be wrong about how you should live and about whether you have followed an argument to the end. It is doubt that keeps us examining our lives and beliefs. And, odd as it may seem, it is our willingness to admit that we can be wrong that sparks both our compassion and demand for justice.

Author's Note: My thanks to Dr. Jack Hernandez, Doug Dallam, and John Nesset for reading a first draft of this essay and making helpful suggestions.

Note

¹ *See* Protagoras *350.*

About the Author

Gary E. Kessler, BA, M Div, PhD, is Emeritus Professor of Philosophy and Comparative Religion at California State University, Bakersfield. He is a native of Wisconsin and received his PhD from Columbia University in New York City in 1970. He is the author/editor of over five books and many scholarly articles. The sixth edition of his best-selling *Voices of Wisdom: A Multicultural Philosophy Reader* (Wadsworth) will be published in 2006. The second edition of his book *Studying Religion: An Introduction Through Cases* was recently published by McGraw-Hill. He retired from teaching in 2004 and now devotes his scholarly time to writing and research. He is presently working on a book dealing with religion and violence, tentatively titled *The Dark Side of Religion*. He lives with his wife Katy in Bellingham, Washington.

We are never so certain of our knowledge as when we're dead wrong.

Adair Lara

Neither for the sake of oneself nor for the sake of another does a wise person do any wrong; he should not desire son, wealth, or kingdom (by doing wrong); by unjust means he should not seek his own success. Then only such a one is indeed virtuous, wise, and righteous.

Siddhartha Gautama

If we die in another war or if we continue being tense and neurotic and anxious in an extended cold war, then this is due to the fact that we don't understand ourselves and we don't understand each other. We need psychology.

Abraham Maslow

At the moment that you are most in awe of all there is about life that you don't understand, you are closer to understanding it all than at any other time.

Jane Wagner

Think freely and independently or you are a slave bound by imaginary shackles. These shackles may be wrought by tradition, emotion, neediness, or fear.

Jason Merchey

Make your values mean something.

Patrick Lencioni

Very few beings really seek knowledge in this world. Mortal or immortal, few really ask. On the contrary, they try to wring from the unknown the answers they have already shaped in their own minds – justifications, confirmations, forms of consolation without which they can't go on.

Anne Rice

Never mistake knowledge for wisdom - one helps you make a living; the other helps you make a life.

Sandra Carey

INTEGRITY

WHERE DO YOUR LOYALTIES LIE?

David Kim

Whether we like it or not, values are a part of our everyday decision-making process. Most of the time, we make decisions easily without having to search the depths of our morals and values, but every so often we might find ourselves in a moral dilemma. It is times like these when it pays to know what you value most.

I am a law enforcement officer and have been for the past eight years. Many of my experiences have led me to believe that generally people's views about law enforcement officers and the job we do is polarized or "black and white" if you will. However, this could not be further from the truth. I believe law enforcement officers operate in the so-called gray area. Keeping this in mind, it greatly benefits any law enforcement officer to know what his or her values are.

My first values check came quite early in my career. I had only been a law enforcement officer for about two years. I was invited to a private social gathering at an acquaintance's house and decided to attend. When I arrived nothing seemed inappropriate at the time. As the evening progressed, a fellow law enforcement officer I worked with regularly arrived. It seemed he was much more acquainted with the host than I. A short time later, the host started smoking pot and offering it to all of his guests. I politely declined to partake and decided it was time to leave. However, before leaving I tried to find my co-worker and give him the scoop. When I found him he was blazing up with the rest of the partygoers. I promptly pulled him aside and asked him what the hell he was doing. His answer was, "Relax man; it's just pot."

> We probably won't remember most of the good decisions we make, but we'll most definitely remember all of the bad ones.

I tried to remind him of his position, but he just smiled and took another hit as if in defiance. Disturbed at this point, I left.

All I could think about was how just a week or so before, this co-worker and I had arrested a man with a gallon freezer bag full of marijuana. It bothered me that this law enforcement officer would arrest someone with marijuana, but would use it himself. Now, in the big scheme of things, marijuana use and possession of personal use quantities is small change, but this was now challenging my values system.

Who did I owe my loyalty to? Do I say nothing, let it go, and compromise my belief that a public servant should not engage in any illegal activity? Do I report the incident and risk being labeled a rat? I contemplated this dilemma for two days before coming to my decision. I decided to take what I knew to my supervisor. Of course this kicked off an investigation which uncovered that twelve other officers were involved in drug use and distribution. I regularly received death threats at my house and even the guys that were not involved in the scandal did not really trust me anymore. I had broken the code of silence.

My life was miserable for about two months until I was transferred. Initially, I questioned whether I had made the right decision, given all the difficulties I was having with co-workers. I mean, who cares what the hell those other cops did, I didn't do anything wrong. However, I know that I made the right choice for me because if I had not reported it, I would still be dwelling on the whole situation today asking myself how I could have disgraced myself and my position. No, these days I rarely even think about the incident, my conscience is clear, and I upheld what I thought was right.

The thing I know for sure is that had I not been clear about what I thought was right and wrong, I would not have had a good reference point for making a decision I could live with. We probably won't remember most of the good decisions we make, but we'll most definitely remember all of the bad ones.

© David Kim

About the Author

David Kim is a Supervisory Border Patrol Agent, stationed along the Mexican-United States border. He is also a former member of the United States Coast Guard. He is a father of four, and expecting a fifth. He has earned the rank of Shodan in Sekiguchi-Do, a samurai sword art. He grew up playing Dungeons & Dragons with Jason, whom he has known for more than half his life.

God never ordained you to have a conscience for others. Your conscience is for you, and for you alone.

Henry Ward Beecher

I shall be honored to go to jail. Under a dictatorship, the detention cell is a place of honor.

Miriam D. Santiago

Fame is a vapor. Popularity an accident. Riches take wings. Only one thing endures, and that is character.

Horace Greeley

A warrior deems life a light thing when compared to honor.

Japanese proverb

Is honor an archaic concept?
Is it becoming the appendix of the human mind?
Those who do value it seem suspect.
Seeing a Catch-22 and a double-bind,
People fold instead of standing erect-
True honor is becoming difficult to find.

Jason Merchey

Character – the willingness to accept responsibility for one's own life – is the source from which self-respect springs.

Joan Didion

Ordinary riches can be stolen; real riches cannot. In your soul are infinitely precious things that cannot be taken from you.

Oscar Wilde

All fortune belongs to him who has a contented mind. Is not the whole earth covered with leather for him whose feet are encased in shoes?

Panchatantra

It matters not what you are thought to be, but what you are.

Publilius Syrus

What lies behind us and what lies before us are small matters compared to what lies within us.

Ralph Waldo Emerson

If the society today allows wrongs to go unchallenged, the impression is created that those wrongs have the approval of the majority.

Barbara Jordan

It is a blessed thing that in every age someone has had the individuality enough and courage enough to stand by his own convictions.

Robert G. Ingersoll

...a crisis is exactly what is required to shock people out of unaware dependence upon external dogma and to force them to unravel layers of pretense to reveal naked truth about themselves, which, however unpleasant, will at least be solid. Existentialism is an attitude which accepts man as always becoming, which means potentially in crisis.

Rollo May

Living by your ideals requires that strength and courage be your allies.

Jason Merchey

The least initial deviation from the truth is multiplied later a thousand fold.

Aristotle

When you come from a place of truth, and if you align yourself with that which is right, and true, and good - that which you know will serve to help other people - then nothing can stop you.

Brenda Reed

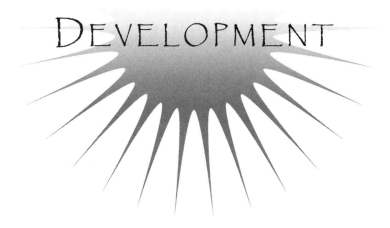

DEVELOPMENT

CITIZENS OF THE GREY AREA

Mark Kingwell

Winnipeg is a city that inevitably finds itself the butt of jokes. Frigid and dark in winter, hot and mosquito-swarmed in summer, it is not the sort of place one would choose to found a city, at least given world enough and time. A recent writing contest sponsored by the Brooklyn-based editors of the *McSweeney's Quarterly*, David Eggers et al., offered as a prize "a large sack of dirt from Winnipeg," which I can only presume was meant as a self-evident joke. (The other prizes included a complete set of Lemony Snicket books, a gift more straightforward in macabre appeal.)

At the same time, perhaps because of its climactic afflictions, Winnipeg has become a hotbed of creative activity. Magazines, art collectives, and independent publishers all thrive there now, taking up residence in abandoned downtown office buildings fashioned in a more prosperous era from red brick and smooth granite. The *Utne Reader*, alternative culture's bible, labeled the city one of the coolest places in North America—and not in the sense of temperature. The filmmaker Guy Maddin turned the unlikely trick of making the city hip enough through his quirky cinematic vision to get Isabella Rosellini to shoot on location (mostly interiors, to be sure).

I lived in Winnipeg for seven years in the 1970s, the crucial period, especially for a boy, of junior high and high school. Alas for me, not much of this sharp indie culture was up and running at the time. There were some memorable punk bands like The Fuse, The Pumps, and Les Pucks, not to mention Popular Mechanix, the guys who offered us a city-fond anthem called "Ice Box City." The winters were long, snowbound, and cold to the point of madness—minus forty degrees, the single place where the Fahrenheit and Celsius scales meet—was a regular visitor. In Winnipeg, cars need to be plugged in overnight so their engine blocks wouldn't crack from freezing.

I went to an all-boys Jesuit high school called St. Paul's, whose sports teams were called the Crusaders. The school motto, *Sicut Miles Christi*, means "like soldiers of Christ," and the school logo was, perhaps predictably, an armed-to-the-teeth mounted Christian warrior, possibly on his way to put infidels to the sword in the holy land. I always thought it a bit ironic that our patron, Paul, had been, famously, knocked off his mount on the road to Damascus. Saul was called by God and became Paul, the ablest and most eloquent of God's proselytizers. But Paul, if he was a warrior of the spirit, was also a prophet of compassion. Love, he told the Corinthians, is always patient and kind; it is never jealous; love is never boastful or conceited. Love does not come to an end.

Paul did not mean romantic or marital love, despite the overuse of this passage in wedding ceremonies every year and from coast to coast. He meant *caritas*, the general love of the other that is maybe better translated as care rather than charity, with its unfortunate connotations now of pity and even condescension. "When I was a child, I used to talk like a child, and think like a child, and argue like a child, but now I am a man, all childish ways are put behind me. Now we see as through a glass darkly; but then we shall be seeing face to face." Just as we grow up in this life, so shall we in the next.

I do not believe there is a next life, or that there exists the God Paul here claims to represent, though I did at the time. What I still hear in this call is the original blinding insight of Paul's conversion. We must be knocked from our horses, stopped on our way, to see the truth.

Care eludes us at every moment unless we are able, somehow, to halt the smooth childish exchanges of everyday life, with its ceaseless chatter of hawking and pandering.

In my senior year of high school, as part of a community service obligation, I joined a group of five students from the school who traveled every Tuesday afternoon to a distant suburb of Winnipeg. Here we volunteered in a program for what were then called "developmentally delayed" children—little guys, mostly between six and eight years old, who were not responding at the usual pace to external stimuli. None of them were Down's syndrome kids, nor suffering from any obvious brain damage or illness. They were, as our supervisor used to say, "citizens of the grey area." Maybe they would find the groove of normal at some future point. Maybe they would get worse. Some might have been autistic or otherwise comprehensively impaired. The one commonality was that none of them could talk.

Or, at least, none of them did. Our job was to take them swimming in the treatment center's indoor pool. I had been on a competitive air force base swim team in grade school and had just missed out on the standard lifeguard's qualification, called the Bronze Medallion. The swimming part was easy. Far harder was knowing how to handle the kids. They did not respond to questions or gestures. Their eyes would wander, their heads loll like little rag dolls. Though they didn't fear the water, they didn't jump or splash. It was never clear if this was the highlight of their week, something horrific, or any one of many degrees of indifference between. Being in the pool with them was eerie and disconcerting, the only sound a gentle lapping of water as it echoed in the tiled interior of the pool.

Most of us took to swimming backwards with the boys cradled in front. They were so little, most of them, that this meant they rested on our chests and floated as we tugged them along, kicking gently. Sometimes they made little sounds, moans or grunts, which we could not easily parse.

After half an hour, we took them back to the change room, put on their clothes, and returned them to whatever else the day had in store. We went home and, because we were naturally too cool to dry off properly, I always remember that feeling of being able to snap a strand of frozen hair between my fingers as we walked across the iron-hard ground to my friend John's car, his goalie equipment sharing space in the back seat.

One day I was swimming with one of our little guys, his tiny rib cage held between my hands as I swam, and he suddenly showed unmistakable signs of distress. He waved his arms around with more energy than I had ever seen before. His head thrashed from side to side. He made noises that were not speech and all they told me was that he was in trouble —not why. I was stricken. He had no words to tell me what was the matter. I had plenty of words, but they could not reach him. We were locked in a moment of intimacy, in a sense, but with no language at all to bridge the gap between us. My stomach began to turn as I ran quickly through the possible ways things could go. He wasn't drowning so my artificial respiration skills were irrelevant. He wasn't bleeding. His trouble was internal, and set to stay that way because he could not speak. And I felt, for the first time really felt, the drastic aloneness of consciousness. I could feel his panic, I could read it, but I could not address it because, floating there in the pool, there was no way to reach him through the mystery of who he was and what he was going through.

Lucky for him, and I guess for me, it was not as bad as it seemed.

Almost comical, actually, considering how frozen in dread to two of us briefly were. I wrapped my left arm around his skinny body and power-kicked over to the side of the pool — where he promptly vomited up his lunch in the gutter. No more than a bad case of indigestion, plus maybe a little cramp from entering the water too soon after eating. I shook with relief, and though I would like to be able to report that he smiled, he did not. He never smiled.

The Jesuits, ever masters of ratiocination since their founding by Ignatius of Loyola, taught me how to think. They showed me what makes an argument good or bad, the powerful concepts of validity and fallacy. When I left school and traveled east for university, I took with me a sense of how reason works. More important, though, I took away an awareness of when it does not. When language fails, we are set back in an almost animal condition. We cannot reach out with our minds, only, it somehow seems, our bodies. We feel that strange form of distress, which is pain at the pain of others. "I feel your pain," a president once said, but this is nonsense; nobody's feels anybody else's pain. What we can, and do, feel is the tug of compassion—sometimes mixed with fear and even panic—when we are confronted by the distress of another.

I have spent most of my adult life dealing in arguments. As an academic philosopher and a social critic, I teach and write about big questions using small-bore tools: precision in reasoning, rigor in criticism, accuracy in scholarship. Philosophy is an exacting vocation and one at which I always feel to some degree an impostor. This, I have learned, is a common feeling. Even the most learned scholars sometimes confess that they are often at sea, not quite certain—despite rhetorical self-presentations or collegial acclaim—of what they wish to argue. Even or especially. For it seems to me that the greatest gift a philosopher can possess is modesty in the face of tasks before him; and so the greater the scholar, perhaps the larger the measure of humility.

Of course, I imagine my colleagues, my students, and certainly my political opponents would find any claims about personal humility to be rather incongruous, coming from someone who has been so critical of the current arrangement. This, I think, is just par for the course. There is no contradiction, though there may well be irony, in feeling humble at one level while arguing without fear or compromise at another. I hope, or anyway I like to think, that no matter what kind of argument I may be making, I am engaging what scholars like to call the principle of charity.

Not, again, in the sense of pity or condescension, rather to mean that gesture of respect we extend to a text or an interlocutor, whereby we try, so far as we are able, to understand it in its own terms, to give it its due. Charity of this sort leads to civility in dialogue, and dialogue in turn becomes the first virtue of both scholars and citizens. Citizenly virtue, which is critical as well as charitable, is what alone may allow a social body to be just.

But I won't argue all that here. All of that is, in any event, a rather ideal picture, an optative theory of justice (as one of my more charitable colleagues calls it). Whenever I see public debate getting out of hand, or collapsing under its own weight, or being hijacked by special interests—including corporate or Christian ones—armed with claims of certainty or absolute knowledge, I think of my little friend in the swimming pool. Though he could not speak a word, he has two important things to say to us.

First, never take for granted the gift of communication. Even being able to disagree with another is a blessing beyond measure, because in disagreement there is shared far more than we sometimes think: of language and reason and shared future. We may not solve our disagreements by finding a single truth to adjudicate them, but we can always be confident that the communicative action of public discourse is an achievement of such a high level that even failures are really features of success.

Second, do not neglect those who cannot speak. Justice is not just for those with voices, not limited to those who can phrase their interests and make their claims in terms that others already understand. The silent, too, demand our attention and our care and also, sometimes, our advocacy. And the silent may not be confined to those who look like us.

> Language, that wispy link between two minds, is not always needed for communication.

In philosophy after Descartes we often refer to what is called the mind-body problem. The problem is that, if the mind is (as Descartes argues) an immaterial substance without location and dimension—an inner mystery—and the body a material substance without any mental aspect, how can the two manage to relate? How does a non-material desire (I wish for an orange) issue in a material movement (I reach for the orange)?

Philosophers have spent centuries grappling with this problem, and the details of the various solutions occupy many volumes. But the basic solution is simple: the mind is not immaterial, and the body is not without consciousness. Language, that wispy link between two minds, is not always needed for communication.

When I saw and felt his little body writhing in the water, my young charge taught me a lesson I am still trying to catch up with. It was a lesson both epistemological and political, and I often think that, even though I would not put away all childish things for some time to come, it marked the moment I became a philosopher. Not a soldier of Christ, but maybe one of hope, and so of justice. In the grey area.

© *Mark Kingwell*

About the Author

Mark Kingwell, Professor of Philosophy at the University of Toronto, was born in 1963 and educated at Toronto, Edinburgh, and Yale, where he completed a PhD in 1991. Kingwell has held visiting posts at Cambridge University, the University of California at Berkeley, and the City University of New York, where he was the Weissman Distinguished Professor of Humanities in 2002. His major awards include the Spitz Prize for political theory (1997), the Drummer-General's award for non-fiction (1998), and National Magazine Awards for essay-writing (2002) and columns (2004). In 2000 he was awarded an honorary DFA by the Nova Scotia College of Art and Design for contributions to theory and criticism.

Kingwell is the author of nine books of philosophy and cultural theory: *A Civil Tongue* (1995), *Dreams of Millennium* (1996), *Better Living* (1998), *Marginalia* (1999), *The World We Want* (2000), *Practical Judgments* (2002), *Catch & Release* (2003), *Nothing for Granted* (2005); and *Nearest Thing to Heaven* (2006). He is also co-author of the best-selling photographic history of the twentieth century, *Canada: Our Century* (1999).

He is a contributing editor of *Harper's Magazine* and, from 2001 to 2004, was chair of the Institute for Contemporary Culture at the Royal Ontario Museum.

Kingwell's articles and reviews have appeared in many leading academic journals, incuding *Journal of Philosophy, Ethics, Political Theory,* and *Yale Journal of Law and the Humanities*, as well as more than forty mainstream publications, including *Harper's, Utne Reader*, the *New York Times Magazine, Adbusters*, and *The Globe and Mail*, where he is a contributing book reviewer. Mark Kingwell's writing has been translated into eight languages, and he has lectured to popular and academic audiences around the world. He is currently at work on a book examining cities and consciousness.

I don't think much of a man who is not wiser today than he was yesterday.

Abraham Lincoln

To philosophize is to explore one's own temperament, yet at the same time to attempt to discover the truth.

Iris Murdoch

Stand by the traditional values of the left by being on the side of the weak, poor, and oppressed, but think very carefully about what will really work to benefit them. In some ways, this is a sharply deflated vision of the left, its utopian ideas replaced by a coolly realistic view of what can be achieved.

Peter Singer

What are a human being's greatest needs? As a spiritual being, he is primarily and inescapably concerned with values; as a social being, he is primarily and inescapably concerned with other people and also with other sentient creatures; as a person, he is primarily and inescapably concerned with developing himself.

E. F. Schumacher

The philosophers have interpreted the world; the point, however, is to change it.

Karl Marx

Just as Socrates felt that it was necessary to create a tension in the mind so that individuals could rise from the bondage of myths and half-truths to the unfettered realm of creative analysis and objective appraisal, so we must see the need for nonviolent gadflies to create the kind of tension in society that will help men rise from the dark depths of prejudice and racism to the majestic heights of understanding and brotherhood.

Martin Luther King, Jr.

To avoid situations in which you might make mistakes may be the biggest mistake of all.

Peter McWilliams

Nobody is bored when he is trying to make something that is beautiful, or to discover something that is true.

William R. Inge

Truth itself is immutable, even if we as humans in our thinking do not possess the truth immutably.

Mortimer J. Adler

One doesn't discover new lands without consenting to lose sight of the shore for a very long time.

Andre Gide

The principle goal of education is to create men who are capable of doing new things, not simply of repeating what other generations have done – men who are creative, inventive, and discoverers.

Jean Piaget

If we have the opportunity to be generous with our hearts, ourselves, we have no idea of the depth and breadth of love's reach.

Margaret Cho

We do not receive wisdom, we have to discover it for ourselves by a voyage that no one can take for us-a voyage that no one can spare us.

Marcel Proust

If you were all alone in the universe with no one to talk to, no one with which to share the beauty of the stars, to laugh with, to touch, what would be your purpose in life? It is other life – love – which gives your life meaning. This is harmony. We must discover the joy of each other, the joy of challenge, the joy of growth.

Mitsugi Saotome

The power to question is the basis of all human progress.

Indira Gandhi

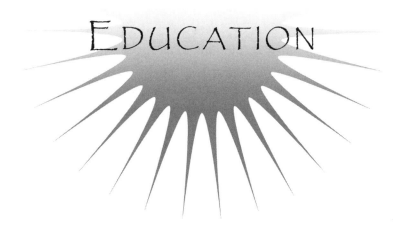

EDUCATION

UNCONDITIONAL TEACHING

Alfie Kohn

Has there even been a wider, or more offensive, gap between educational rhetoric and reality than that which defines the current accountability fad? The stirring sound bites waft through the air: higher expectations…world-class standards…raising the bar…no child left behind. Meanwhile, educators and students down on the ground are under excruciating pressure to improve test results, often at the expense of meaningful learning, and more low-income and minority students are dropping out.

Some of the results of that pressure are plainly visible to anyone who cares to look: You can see practice tests replacing student-designed projects, children appearing alternately anxious and bored, terrific teachers quitting in disgust. But there are also subtler effects. The current version of school reform is changing what we value. If the sole goal is to raise achievement (in the narrowest sense of that word), then we may end up ignoring other kinds of learning beyond the academic. It's exceedingly difficult to teach the whole child when people are held accountable only for raising reading and math scores.

Moreover, when some capabilities are privileged over others, and a broader approach to education is sacrificed, we begin to look at students differently. We come to lose sight of children "except as they distribute themselves across deciles," (Hogan, 1974, p. iii). That means that some kids—namely, the high scorers—are prized more than others by the adults. One Florida superintendent observed that "when a low-performing child walks into a classroom, instead of being seen as a challenge, or an opportunity for improvement, for the first time since I've been in education, teachers are seeing [him or her] as a liability" (Wilgoren, 2000). I've heard essentially the same rueful observation from teachers and administrators across the country.

Debilitating Effects of Conditional Acceptance

A diminution in what we value, then, may affect whom we value. But the damage isn't limited to those students who fail to measure up—that is, by conventional standards. If some children matter more to us than others, then all children are valued only conditionally. Regardless of the criteria we happen to be using, or the number of students who meet those criteria, every student gets the message that our acceptance is never a sure thing. They learn that their worth hinges on their performance.

That's more than distasteful—it's debilitating. Psychological theorists and researchers (e.g., Deci and Ryan, 1995; Kernis, 2003) are coming to realize that the best predictor to mental health may not be one's level of self-esteem but the extent to which it fluctuates. The real problem isn't self-esteem that's too low ("I don't like myself very much") so much as self-esteem that's too contingent ("I like myself only when..."). Conversely, kids who have an underlying sense of their own value are more likely to see failure as a temporary set-back, a problem to be solved. They're also less likely to be anxious or depressed (Chamberlain and Haaga, 2001).

In turn, the best predictor of whether children will be able to accept themselves as fundamentally valuable and capable is the extent to which they have been accepted unconditionally by others. As Carl Rogers (1959) argued half a century ago, those on the receiving end of conditional love—that is, affection based not on who they are but on what they do—come to disown the parts of themselves that aren't valued. Eventually they regard themselves as worthy only when they act (or think or feel) in specific ways.

In the course of researching a book on these issues, I discovered considerable empirical support for this theory. One summary of the research put it this way: "The more conditional the support [one experiences], the lower one's perceptions of overall worth as a person" (Harter, 1999; also see Assor et al., 2004). When children receive affection with strings attached, they do indeed tend to accept themselves only with strings attached. For example, investigators at the University of Denver (Harter et al., 1996) have shown that teenagers who feel they have to fulfill certain conditions in order to win their parents' approval often end up not liking themselves. That, in turn, may lead a given adolescent to construct a "false self"—in other words, to pretend to be the kind of person whom his or her parents will love. This desperate strategy to gain acceptance is often associated with depression, a sense of hopelessness, and a tendency to lose touch with one's true self. At some point, such teenagers may not even know who they really are because they've had to work so hard to become something they're not.

> Taking a stand against oppressive policies that are imposed from outside our schools may well be a necessary component of unconditional teaching, but it's not sufficient.

In short, unconditional acceptance is what kids require in order to flourish. And while it's most critical that they experience that kind of acceptance at home, what happens at school matters, too. "Unconditional parenting" (Kohn, 2005) is key, but what might be called "unconditional teaching" is also important. One study found that students who felt unconditionally accepted by their teachers were more likely to be genuinely interested in learning and to enjoy challenging academic tasks—as opposed to just doing things because they had to and preferring easier assignments at which they knew they would be successful (Makri-Botsari, 2001).

To provide this unconditional support, we must actively oppose the policies that get in the way, such as those that encourage us to value children on the basis of their academic standing—or, worse, merely on the basis of their test scores. Although there are risks involved, there may well be a moral obligation to participate in organized, active resistance to destructive mandates. "Putting children first" is an empty slogan if we watch passively while our schools are turned into test-prep centers.

Taking a stand against oppressive policies that are imposed from outside our schools may well be a necessary component of unconditional teaching, but it's not sufficient. Even if we succeeded in eliminating external pressures related to standards and testing, it's possible that some of our own practices also lead children to believe that we accept them only conditionally. Sometimes that acceptance seems to depend on their doing well and sometimes it depends on their being good. Let's look at each of these in turn.

Acceptance Based on Performance

All of us want our students to be successful learners, but there is a thin line that separates valuing excellence (a good thing) from leading students to believe that they matter only to the extent they meet our standards (not a good thing). Some people elevate abstractions like Achievement or Excellence above the needs of flesh-and-blood children. Thus, by steering extra resources to, or heaping public recognition on, students who succeed, we're not only ignoring the counterproductive effects of extrinsic motivators (Kohn, 1993), but possibly sending a message to all students – those who have been recognized and those who, conspicuously, have not – that only those who do well count.

Nel Noddings (1992) made a similar point in discussing the kind of teacher who pushes students relentlessly but also praises those who manage to live up to his high expectations ("You are the best!"). Such instructors are often admired for being both demanding and encouraging. However, if "You are the best!" just means "You can do A.P. calculus," then this suggests that only those who master differential equations are "the best." Surely, says Noddings, "a student should not have to succeed at A.P. calculus to gain a math teacher's respect."

Or consider those educators, particularly in the arts, whose professional pride is invested in the occasional graduate who goes on to distinguish herself as a well-known novelist or violinist. There is a big difference between trying to help as many students as possible cultivate a love of, and some competence at, one's field and trying to sift through many hundreds of students in search of the very few who will later become famous. The latter suggests a profoundly antidemocratic sensibility, one that sees education as being about winnowing and selecting rather than providing something of value for everyone. And, again, all students realize that they matter to such a teacher only if they measure up.

My point is not that we shouldn't value, or even celebrate, accomplishment. But paradoxically, unconditional teaching is more likely to create the conditions for children to excel. Those who know they're valued irrespective of their accomplishments often end up accomplishing quite a lot. It's the experience of being accepted without conditions that helps people develop a healthy confidence in themselves, a belief that it's safe to take risks and try new things.

Acceptance Based on Obedience

Sometimes the conditions placed on acceptance have more to do with compliance than with success. A case in point: temporarily ejecting a student from a class activity—or even from school—for misbehaving. This practice is sometimes rationalized on the grounds that it isn't fair to the others if one student is allowed to act badly. But those other students, the ones in whose name we are allegedly taking this action, are being told, in effect, that everyone is part of this community only conditionally. That creates an uneasy, uncertain, and ultimately unsafe climate.

Adele Faber and Elaine Mazlish (1995) ask us to put ourselves in the place of a child who has been subjected to the punishment known euphemistically as time-out: "As an adult you can imagine how resentful and humiliated you would feel if someone forced you into isolation for something you said or did." For a child, however, it is even worse, since she may come to believe "that there is something so wrong with her that she has to be removed from society."

Those who seem to accept students conditionally—requiring them to act in a particular way in order to be valued, or even in order to be allowed to stay—often see themselves as trying to reinforce or eliminate specific student behaviors. What they often don't see is that traditional classroom management techniques, along with the narrow emphasis on observable behaviors that underlies those techniques, make it very difficult to attend to the person who engages in those behaviors. In fact, I would propose the following rule of thumb: the value of a book about dealing with children is inversely proportional to the number of times it contains the word behavior. When our primary focus is on discrete behaviors, we end up ignoring the whole child.

That doesn't mean exemplary educators who avoid time-outs, detentions, and other punishments are simply ignoring misbehavior. The real alternative to making children suffer for their offenses (or dangling goodies in front of them for doing what they're told) is to work with them to solve problems. A "working with" approach (Child Development Project, 1996; DeVries and Zan, 1994; Kohn, 1996) asks more of the teacher than does a "doing to" approach, but it's a good deal more effective because even if the latter succeeds in imposing order temporarily, it does so by undermining students' moral development, compromising the relationship between teacher and students, and making it more difficult to establish a supportive environment for learning. In sum, giving the impression that we value children only when they're good doesn't promote goodness any more than giving the impression that we value children only when they succeed promotes success.

In an illuminating passage from her recent book *Learning to Trust* (2003), Marilyn Watson explained that a teacher can make it clear to students that certain actions are unacceptable while still providing "a very deep kind of reassurance—the reassurance that she still care[s] about them and [is] not going to punish or desert them, even [if they do] something very bad." This posture allows "their best motives to surface," thus giving "space and support for them to reflect and to autonomously engage in the moral act of restitution"—that is, to figure out how to make things right after doing something wrong. "If we want our students to trust that we care for them," she concludes, "then we need to display our affection without demanding that they behave or perform in certain ways in return. It's not that we don't want and expect certain behaviors; we do. But our concern or affection does not depend on it."

This is the heart of unconditional teaching, and Watson points out that it's easier to maintain this stance, even with kids who are frequently insulting or aggressive, if we keep in mind why they're acting that way. The idea is for the teacher to think about what these students need (emotionally speaking) and probably haven't received. That way, she can see "the vulnerable child behind the bothersome or menacing exterior."

The popular view is that children who misbehave are just "testing limits"—a phrase often used as a justification for imposing more limits, or punishments. But perhaps such children are testing something else entirely: the unconditionality of our care for them. Perhaps they're acting in unacceptable ways to see if we'll stop accepting them.

Thus, one teacher (quoted in Watson, 2003) dealt with a particularly challenging child by sitting down with him and saying, "You know what[?] I really, really like you. You can keep doing all this stuff and it's not going to change my mind. It seems to me that you are trying to get me to dislike you, but it's not going to work. I'm not ever going to do that." This teacher added: "It was soon after that, and I'm not saying immediately, that his disruptive behaviors started to decrease." The moral here is that unconditional acceptance is not only something all children deserve; it's also a powerfully effective way to help them become better people. It's more useful, practically speaking, than any "behavior management" plan could ever be.

Providing Unconditional Acceptance

Teaching in this way is not just a matter of how we respond to children after they do something wrong, of course. It's about the countless gestures that let them know we're glad to see them, that we trust and respect them, that we care what happens to them. It's about the real (and unconditional) respect we show by asking all students what they think about how things are going, and how we might do things differently, not the selective reinforcement we offer to some students when they please us.

Unconditional teachers are not afraid to be themselves with students—to act like real human beings rather than crisply controlling authority figures. Their classrooms have an appealing informality about them. They may bring in occasional treats for their students—all their students—for no particular reason. They may write notes to children, have lunch with them, respond from the heart to their journal entries. Such teachers listen carefully to what kids say and remember details about their lives: "Hey, Joanie. You said on Friday that your Mom might take you to the fair over the weekend. Did you go? Was it fun?"

It's not possible to like all one's students equally well, but unconditional teachers try hard not to play favorites. More than that, they do their best to find something appealing about each child and respond accordingly. They make it clear that, while there are certain expectations in the classroom—expectations that, ideally, the students themselves have helped to suggest—the teacher's basic affection need not be earned. Caring that has to be earned isn't real caring at all.

Accepting students for who they are—as opposed to for what they do —is integrally related to the idea of teaching the whole child. That connection is worth highlighting because the phrase "whole child" is sometimes interpreted to mean "more than academics," which suggests a fragmented education. The point isn't just to meet a student's emotional needs with this activity, her physical needs with that activity, her social needs with something else, and so on. Rather, it is an integrated self to whom we respond. It is a whole person whom we value. And to do so in any way that matters is to accept children unconditionally, even (perhaps especially) when they screw up or fall short.

It isn't easy to create these sorts of relationships when there's no time to know each student. Huge classes, huge schools, and short periods are impediments to more than academic achievement. That's why, once again, unconditional teachers understand the need to work for systemic change— for example, pressing for the demise of the factory-like American high school model, an impediment to good teaching if ever there was one. But in the meantime, within whatever structures we work, we need to think about whether our posture toward students really provides them with as much of the unconditional acceptance they need as possible.

Imagine that your students are invited to respond to a questionnaire several years after leaving the school. They're asked to indicate whether they agree or disagree—and how strongly—with statements such as: "Even when I wasn't proud of how I acted, even when I didn't do the homework, even when I got low test scores or didn't seem interested in what was being taught, I knew that [insert your name here] still cared about me."

How would you like your students to answer that sort of question? How do you think they will answer it?

© Alfie Kohn

References

Assor, A., Roth, G., & Deci, E. L. (2004). The emotional costs of parents' conditional regard: A self-determination theory analysis. Journal of Personality, 72, 47-89.

Chamberlain, J. M., & Haaga, D.A.F. (2001). Unconditional self-acceptance and psychological health. Journal of Rational-Emotive and Cognitive-Behavior Therapy, 19, 163-76.

Child Development Project. (1996). Ways we want our class to be: Class meetings that build commitment to kindness and learning. Oakland, CA: Developmental Studies Center.

Deci, E. L. & Ryan, R.M. (1995). Human autonomy: The basis for true self-esteem. In Efficacy, Agency, and Self-Esteem, edited by M. H. Kernis. New York: Plenum.

DeVries, R. & Zan, B. (1994). Moral classrooms, moral children. New York: Teachers College Press.

Faber, A., & Mazlish, E. (1995). How to talk so kids can learn. New York: Rawson.

Harter, S. (1999). The construction of the self: A developmental perspective. New York: Guilford.

Harter, S., Marold, D.B., Whitesell, N.R., & Cobbs, G. (1996). A model of the effects of perceived parent and peer support on adolescent false self behavior. Child Development, 67, 360-74.

Hogan, R. F. (1974). Foreword to Measuring growth in English by P. B. Diederich. n.p.: National Council of Teachers of English.

Kernis, M. H. (2003). Toward a conceptualization of optimal self-esteem. Psychological Inquiry, 14, 1-26.

Kohn, A. (1993). Punished by rewards: The trouble with gold stars, incentive plans, A's, praise, and other bribes. Boston: Houghton Mifflin.

Kohn, A. (1996). Beyond discipline: From compliance to community. Alexandria, VA: Association for Supervision and Curriculum Development.

Kohn, A. (2005). Unconditional parenting: Moving from rewards and punishments to love and reason. New York: Atria Books.

Makri-Botsari, E. (2001). Causal links between academic intrinsic motivation, self-esteem, and unconditional acceptance by teachers in high school students. In International perspectives on individual differences, vol. 2: Self perception, edited by R.J. Riding & S. G. Rayner. Westport, CT: Ablex.

Noddings, N. (1992). The challenge to care in schools: An alternative approach to education. New York: Teachers College Press.

Rogers, C. R. (1959). A theory of therapy, personality, and interpersonal relationships, as developed in the client-centered framework. In Psychology: A study of a science. Study I: Conceptual and systematic, vol. 3, ed. Sigmund Koch. New York: McGraw-Hill.

Watson, M. (2003). Learning to trust: Transforming difficult elementary classrooms through developmental discipline. San Francisco: Jossey-Bass.

Wilgoren, J. (2000, March 14). Florida's vouchers a spur to 2 schools left behind. New York Times, A1, A18.

About the Author

Alfie Kohn writes and speaks widely on human behavior, education, and parenting. His latest book is *Unconditional Parenting: Moving from Rewards and Punishments to Love and Reason,* just published by Atria / Simon & Schuster. Of his nine earlier books, the best known are *Punished by Rewards: The Trouble with Gold Stars, Incentive Plans, A's, Praise, and Other Bribes* (1993), *No Contest: The Case Against Competition* (1986), and *The Schools Our Children Deserve: Moving Beyond Traditional Classrooms and "Tougher Standards"* (1999).

Kohn has been described in *Time* magazine as "perhaps the country's most outspoken critic of education's fixation on grades [and] test scores." His criticisms of competition and rewards have helped to shape the thinking of educators—as well as parents and managers—across the country and abroad. Kohn has been featured on hundreds of TV and radio programs, including the *Today* show and two appearances on *Oprah*; he has been profiled in the *Washington Post* and *the Los Angeles Times*, while his work has been described and debated in many other leading publications.

Kohn lectures widely at universities and to school faculties, parent groups, and corporations. In addition to speaking at staff development seminars and keynoting national education conferences on a regular basis, he conducts workshops for teachers and administrators on various topics. Among them: "Motivation from the Inside Out: Rethinking Rewards, Assessment, and Learning" and "Beyond Bribes and Threats: Realistic Alternatives to Controlling Students' Behavior." The latter corresponds to his book *Beyond Discipline: From Compliance to Community* (ASCD, 1996), which he describes as "a modest attempt to overthrow the entire field of classroom management."

Test scores alone don't tell us whether we've educated a complete human being. We should be asking, "What strengths of character do young people need for human flourishing over a lifetime – in their roles as students, workers, community members, and democratic citizens?"

Thomas Lickona & Matthew Davidson

We should want more from our educational efforts than adequate academic achievement, and we will not achieve even that meager success unless our children believe that they themselves are cared for and learn to care for others.

Nel Noddings

The [United States] educational system is geared toward obedience.

Noam Chomsky

Most higher education is devoted to affirming the traditions and origins of an existing elite and transmitting them to new members.

Mary Catherine Bateson

The forces of change facing the world could be so far-reaching, complex, and interactive that they call for nothing less than the reeducation of humankind.

Paul Kennedy

No one has yet fully realized the wealth of sympathy, kindness, and generosity hidden in the soul of a child. The effort of every true education should be to unlock that treasure.

Emma Goldman

Establishing lasting peace is the work of education; all politics can do is keep us out of war.

Maria Montessori

What is needed to make democracy work as it is not now working- to bring into existence in reality a sound conception of democracy? The mass liberal education of the mass electorate. Not just schooling, but an education that involves moral training as well as training of the mind.

Mortimer J. Adler

COURAGE

COURAGE

Bernice Lerner

In June of 1944, my mother, then fourteen, was deported with her family, with all of the Jews from her hometown, Sighet, to Auschwitz-Birkenau. Within weeks of her arrival she was "selected" for the gas chamber. As the killing machinery was overburdened, she and hundreds of doomed others awaited their fate in a cordoned-off barracks. Her sixteen-year-old sister, Elisabeth, who had been "selected" to work, came to the barracks window to say good-bye to my mother. Sorrowful tears gave way to a plan. As Auschwitz law demanded that the "count" of inmates be exact, and as circumstances were such that two other sisters had also been separated in the last "selection," my aunt arranged to bring back into the barracks the pail (used for excrement) the other "condemned" sister brought out (to be emptied). In trading places, my aunt chose to share my mother's destiny. Be strong and of good courage. Act for the best, hope for the best, and take what comes…if death ends all, we cannot meet death better.

As the daughter of Holocaust survivors, my legacy includes numerous accounts of courage in extreme circumstances. My grandfather pointed out different types of cows as he and my mother peered through the slats of the cattle car that took them through the countryside en route to Auschwitz. His last words to her were that he had confidence she would make it. My Aunt Esther scolded Hungarian Gendarmes when she saw them torturing my father in a river near their home. My Aunt Ratzi, who worked in the kitchen of the Christianstadt labor camp, smuggled food out to starving inmates. (When caught, an "X" was carved into her shaven head and she was put in a cellar, in knee-deep water. When released, she continued her "illegal" activities.) My Uncle Irving risked his life to bring my father bread, when their Hungarian Labor Battalions crossed paths in Poland. My Uncle Hershu spoke on behalf of his war-weary comrades when they were imprisoned in Russia and in dire need of food. In acting humanely, in acting for the best, they each defied their oppressors.

> Life and death situations cast into bold relief the fact that our actions are, existentially and morally, of consequence.

Life and death situations cast into bold relief the fact that our actions are, existentially and morally, of consequence. We understandably hold as exemplars those who are not paralyzed by fear, who do not panic or despair, and who instead display courage, despite the dire circumstances in which they find themselves.

We are moved, for example, by individuals' deeds on a day now etched into our collective consciousness—September 11. Terri Tobin, a Police Department veteran, pulled three people out of the rubble. With concrete lodged in her skull, a shard of glass in her back, and multiple fractures, she gave up her spot on an ambulance for a photographer with multiple fractures. Kathy Mazza, a Port Authority police captain, blasted open glass walls at the World Trade Center allowing hundreds to escape before meeting her end in the inferno. While giving last rites to a victim, Reverend Mychal Judge was fatally injured. And Abe Zelmanowitz sacrificed his life by staying with his quadriplegic friend and colleague at Empire Blue Cross and Blue Shield, Edward Beyea. In the annals of this terrible day is, too, the heroism of Todd Beamer, one of the passengers aboard United Airlines Flight 93, who spoke words of prayer to a telephone operator before overpowering his plane's evil hijackers. It is not possible to reconstruct what happened in the final moments of the lives of every rescuer, helper, flight passenger, office worker, and ordinary citizen. We know only that courage—to act for the best, hope for the best, and take what comes—is a virtue to which decent people aspire.

Though we may be fortunate enough not to stand at the crossroads of a treacherous mountain pass, in the course of our daily lives, in normality, we must also make choices. We need to know when to be afraid, when to take decisive action, when to check personal tendencies toward recklessness or cowardice. We need to realize—as did Frank L. Baum's Cowardly Lion—that we have within us the capacity for courage; the ability to wisely assess situations, to figure out what the right thing to do is, and to act accordingly.

Courage can be practiced. At almost any age one can develop the habit of speaking out against injustice, asking for help when it is needed, and meeting difficult challenges. It is important to note, too, that courage may look different, depending upon individuals' inclinations and particular circumstances. For a teenager who longs to be accepted by his peers, it may take courage to abstain from a negative activity in which they invite him to participate; for a person suffering from depression, it may take courage to get out of bed in the morning to face the day; for a shy person, it may take courage to attend a social gathering, to strike up a conversation. For many of us, it takes courage to admit to having made a mistake, to forego or submit to medical procedures, or to make significant, called-for, changes in our lives. We must summon what wisdom we possess to discern a right path, though we may not certainly know whether there is any right one. In considering each day's demands, in acting courageously, we not only cannot meet death better, we give meaning to our lives.

© Bernice Lerner

About the Author

Bernice Lerner is director at the Center for the Advancement of Ethics and Character at Boston University's School of Education and the author of *The Triumph of Wounded Souls: Seven Holocaust Survivors' Lives* (University of Notre Dame Press, 2004).

My father said, "There are times to sit, or stand and be counted,"
When good people die, just laws are forsaken, banned books smolder, It is a
time when our steed must be armored and mounted; The balance of good and
evil rests on our collective shoulders.

Jason Merchey

Altruists have a particular perspective in which all mankind is connected
through a common humanity, in which each individual is linked to all others and
to a world in which all living beings are entitled to a certain humane treatment
merely by virtue of being alive.

Kristen Renwick Monroe

One isn't necessarily born with courage, but one is born with potential.
Without courage, we cannot practice any other virtue with consistency. We
can't be kind, true, merciful, generous, or honest.

Maya Angelou

Thou shalt not be a victim. Thou shalt not be a perpetrator. Above all, thou
shalt not be a bystander.

Holocaust Museum, Washinton DC

In every man's heart there is a sleeping lion.

Armenian proverb

The great, wonderful quality of human beings is that we can overcome even
absolute terror, and we do.

Isabel Allende

A new position of responsibility will usually show a man to be a far stronger
creature than was supposed.

William James

You cannot just decide or claim that you have honor - or loyalty, or courage.
You have to pay for it.

John A. Marshall

Fall seven times, stand up eight.

Japanese proverb

So many people walk around with a meaningless life. They seem half-asleep, even when they're busy doing things they think are important. This is because they're chasing the wrong things. The way you get meaning in your life is to devote yourself to loving others, devote yourself to your community around you, and devote yourself to creating something that gives you purpose and meaning.

Morrie Schwartz

I never made a moral decision to rescue Jews. I just got mad. I felt I had to do it. I came across many things that demanded my compassion.

Otto, last name withheld

There is a kind of virtue that lies not in extraordinary actions, not in saving poor orphans from burning buildings, but in steadfastly working for a world where orphans are not poor and buildings comply with decent fire codes.

Randy Cohen

Our prime purpose in this life is to help others. And if you can't help them, at least don't hurt them.

Tenzin Gyatso

I will permit no man to narrow and degrade my soul by making me hate him.

Booker T. Washington

You should never have your best trousers on when you go out to fight for freedom and truth.

Henrik Ibsen

The truth that many people never understand, until it is too late, is that the more you try to avoid suffering the more you suffer, because the smaller and more insignificant things begin to torture you in proportion to your fear of being hurt.

Thomas Merton

FULFILLMENT

A JEWISH PERSPECTIVE ON LIVING A LIFE OF VALUE

Pat Libby

In Judaism there is no word for "charity." *Tzedakah*, the word that most approximates that concept in English, translates as "righteousness" or "justice." I was raised to believe that as a Jew one of my primary responsibilities was *Tikun Olam*, which means, "to repair the world." I have embraced that sense of responsibility during my nearly thirty-year professional career (and before that, as a volunteer), and challenged myself to think about how I could create lasting change during my short time on earth. *Tikun Olam* has motivated me to work in a variety of settings for non-profit corporations which I will describe briefly in this essay.

But first, let me tell you a little bit more about this Jewish notion of change, because on the surface it can be an intimidating concept. You might think, "How does one go about repairing the world? That's a tall order! Where to start? Who am I to believe that I can make a difference?"

There is a part of the liturgy we read during our High Holy Day services that says, in essence, God does not ask "Why have you not been as great as Moses?" but instead asks "Why have you not been yourself? Why have you not been true to the best in you?"[1] To me those phrases speak volumes. They tell me I do not have to be Gandhi or Einstein to create change (a tremendous relief on both accounts since I am not interested in being that self-sacrificing and, sadly, am not brilliant). Those phrases assure me I can create change in a way and on a scale that is meaningful for me. All that is required is that I know in my mind and heart that I am being the best person I know how to be.

Personally, it is important that the change I create be much bigger than myself (I admit I am an overachiever). I want my work for change to continue well past the time when I am gone from this planet. It does not matter to me that people remember my name twenty years after I die, but I do hope the effort I have helped catalyze is still taking place in some form or another.

> I want my work for change to continue well past the time when I am gone from this planet.

For others, being a change agent might entail something much simpler: volunteering once a month at an animal shelter, testifying before a zoning committee about preserving a swath of open space, donating money for a cause, participating in a protest march, or just being as kind as one can possibly be to others. It does not matter what it is as long as the activity has real meaning for that person—as long as it is meaningful for you.

For most of my life I did not talk about the spiritual motivation for my work. I just lived it by helping develop a network of community gardens in low-income neighborhoods, supporting efforts to save family farms and promote organic agriculture, enabling community development corporations to get the resources they needed to build affordable housing and create jobs in low-income neighborhoods, and most recently, by teaching nonprofit management professionals how to create high performance organizations through a graduate program I designed and oversee at the University of San Diego.

Each opportunity has required incredibly hard work and has proven to be been tremendously rewarding. And each opportunity has been a blessing. To see produce bloom on former vacant lots gardened by people who need that food is a real joy. To work with banking executives on securing financing that will create new housing and commercial development in economically distressed communities is utterly fantastic (and to see those projects develop and affect people's lives is even better). To watch my students apply what they learn in the classroom to grow their own organizations, and to see them develop as individuals, is one of the greatest gifts I could ever receive.

I want to disabuse you of any notions you might have that I am driven only by creating good in the world. My home is full of lovely art purchased over the years (mostly, from artist friends), I love a good glass of wine (or two), shopping, and taking vacations when I can. My husband and I have not inherited any material wealth, we have just worked hard to build a nice life for ourselves by doing things that we care about deeply, and we have been fortunate to support ourselves doing those things.

I am often asked by people how they can go about making a change from working in the private sector to working in the nonprofit sector. These people come to me not because they view me as a spiritual person (there is no reason for them to have any idea about my beliefs); they seek me out because I direct an academic program that pertains to the nonprofit sector. Since you are taking the time to read this book, my guess is you are searching for how to create or enhance your own life of value and are perhaps asking yourself a similar question. If so, I hope the following will help guide you to a nonprofit career.

First, ask yourself what moves you. Is it dance, the environment, helping the poor, affordable health care? Before you can begin to affect change, you must know what type of change you wish to affect. Selecting an issue or a cause that you believe in is the first step.

Second, ask yourself an honest question: how much money do I need to earn? It is no secret that salaries in the nonprofit sector tend to be lower than those in the private sector. In addition, it is unlikely you will be able to work in a position that is parallel to your current one because you will be in a learning stage in your new career (the reverse would also be true; I am sure it would be very difficult for me to manage a restaurant even though I have overseen various nonprofit organizations). Be realistic about what you need to live on and whether or not you can be happy with that amount of income.

Third, educate yourself. There are tremendous differences between the for-profit and nonprofit sector of which the "bottom line" is only the most obvious. It is rare that a person can make a seamless transition from one sector to the other without understanding the differences and challenges that are inherent in nonprofit leadership and management. As an example, let us take a minute to look at the question of impact. If you are overseeing a program that is designed to encourage teens from low-income families to enroll in college so they will ultimately have more earning power, how do you assess your success? Do you simply count the number of youth you have persuaded to apply to college, do you look at what they major in after they matriculate, their graduation rates, the types of jobs they land once they finish or all of the above? If you are providing housing for low-income families with the objective of helping them become more economically stable, how can you be sure that the housing helps them achieve that goal? Measuring success in the nonprofit sector where organizations are in, but not of, the market[2] is much trickier than counting sales volume. Other stark differences include understanding how to attract and motivate a large voluntary workforce, learning the differences in financial accounting practices, mastering the art of leveraging resources through alliances and coalitions, acquiring advocacy skills, learning a whole host of fundraising practices, and understanding legal accountability and transparency issues. Learning the differences in the terrain is not an insurmountable task, but it is one that will make the journey much richer. It is analogous to learning a foreign language before traveling to a new country—one can get by knowing only a few phrases, however, the more fluent the traveler, the more worthwhile the experience.

To gain that baseline knowledge, read books on nonprofit management and attend some classes at your local college or nonprofit management support center. The book I often recommend is *Managing a Nonprofit Organization in the 21st Century*, by Thomas Wolf.[3] Wolf has done a terrific job writing a book that is fun to read yet contains lots of good, basic information about the third sector. It is so enjoyable I tell my students they should take it to the beach.

Fourth, ask yourself for what size organization you would like to work. The nonprofit sector is enormous (the third largest contributor to the gross domestic product in the United States, it is larger than the banking and technology sectors combined[4]). If your passion is education, you could choose to work for a large institution like a university or a hospital or, alternatively, select a charter school or community clinic. There is a big difference in the types of resources and support services that will be available through these various institutions and benefits will vary tremendously. Smaller institutions will likely afford you more creative freedom, larger ones, perhaps more security. So consider your choices wisely and in accordance with what you believe is the best fit for your personality.

I am not advocating that everyone work for a nonprofit. It is the path I have chosen as the most comfortable for living my own values and you will determine yours.

There is so much to do in the world and so many injustices that enrage me. Yes, enrage. According to the United States Census Bureau, poverty in America increased by 1.1 million individuals from 2003 to 2004 for a total of 37 million people.[5] Poverty in America is as great now as it was in 1965. Equally significant is the way our government calculates who is poor, which results in standards that are artificially low. For example, a family of three is considered poor if it has an annual income of $15,670, but what of the family that earns $16,000? Moreover, with the exception of Alaska and Hawaii, variations in regional living costs are not factored into US poverty standards.[6] As I write this essay, Congress has just passed enormous cuts in basic programs that serve the poor and is proposing yet another round of tax cuts for the wealthiest. I often ask how our country has developed a common consensus that government needs to be continually cut because it is so laden with waste. Where is the common sense and decency that mandates we provide our most vulnerable citizens, including children, the elderly and the disabled, the means to live as they deserve?

I could just as easily beat my breast about the horrific Sudan killings, illiteracy, nuclear proliferation, war throughout the Middle East, child labor, global warming, and a whole host of other issues. Reading the paper and taking stock of what is going on in the world can be overwhelming at times.

Yet, while I am not Moses (and do not pretend to be—not even close) I know I can make a difference in my own small way. I cannot solve all the problems that ignite my ire—not even a single one—but I can try to do something to make the world a little better, and I do. If you are not doing so already, I hope this essay has helped you realize that you can make a difference and that nothing you do will be too small to matter. If you are already living your values by contributing to goodness in the world, I want you to know that I am grateful for your efforts.

© *Pat Libby*

Notes

[1] Gates of Repentance: The New Union Prayerbook for the Days of Awe, *Central Conference of American Rabbis, (New York, 1978 [5738], revised 1996).*

[2] *Salamon McCambridge, "In but not Of the Market: The Special Challenge of Nonprofit-ness,"* Nonprofit Sector Quarterly, *10, no. 1, (Spring 2003).*

[3] *Published by Fireside Press.*

[4] *McKinsey & Company, "Not-for-profit management: The gift that keeps giving,"* McKinsey Quarterly, *2002.*

[5] *These are the most recently available statistics.*

[6] *United States Department of Health and Human Services, Annual Poverty Guidelines.*

About the Author

Pat Libby is a Boston native who learned the art of Tikun Olam by hearing her Jewish family describe their exploits over hundreds of animated Sabbath dinner discussions. A self-described "accidental academic" who was asked to translate her many years of nonprofit leadership experience into graduate course work, she now directs the Nonprofit Leadership & Management Program at the University of San Diego.

Greatness is not found in possessions, power, position, or prestige. It is discovered in goodness, humility, service, and character.

William A. Ward

I'm doing what I think I was put on this earth to do. And I'm really grateful to have something that I'm passionate about and that I think is profoundly important.

Marian Wright Edelman

Measure your greatness by the length of your reach, but also by the gentleness of your touch. For now, the world needs hands that love, not hands that conquer. Let your hands be among them.

Kent Nerburn

Relationships are all there is. Everything in the universe only exists because it is in relationship to everything else. Nothing exists in isolation. We have to stop pretending we are individuals that can go it alone.

Margaret Wheatley

Too often we underestimate the power of a touch, a smile, a kind word, a listening ear, an honest compliment, or the smallest act of caring, all of which have the potential to turn a life around.

Leo F. Buscaglia

Don't complain about what you don't have. Use what you've got. To do less than your best is a sin. Every single one of us has the power for greatness, because greatness is determined by service - to yourself and to others.

Oprah Winfrey

I have learned more about love, selflessness, and human understanding in this great adventure in the world of AIDS than I ever did in the cutthroat, competitive world in which I spent my life.

Anthony Perkins

WISDOM

PLAYING THE WISDOM GAME
Some Thoughts about the Nature and Development of Wisdom

Copthorne Macdonald

What is wisdom? Like stupidity, we know it when we see it. But because wisdom manifests in so many different ways, it can't be adequately defined in a few words. Short dictionary definitions highlight some of wisdom's characteristics such as "keen discernment," "a capacity for sound judgment," and "the ability to discern inner qualities and relationships," but they don't get to the heart of the matter.

Joseph W. Meeker's eloquent yet concise statement about wisdom is much more illuminating:

Wisdom is a state of the human mind characterized by profound understanding and deep insight. It is often, but not necessarily, accompanied by extensive formal knowledge. Unschooled people can acquire wisdom, and wise people can be found among carpenters, fishermen, or housewives. Wherever it exists, wisdom shows itself as a perception of the relativity and relationships among things. It is an awareness of wholeness that does not lose sight of particularity or concreteness, or of the intricacies of interrelationships. It is where left and right brain come together in a union of logic and poetry and sensation, and where self-awareness is no longer at odds with awareness of the otherness of the world. Wisdom cannot be confined to a specialized field, nor is it an academic discipline; it is the consciousness of wholeness and integrity that transcends both. Wisdom is complexity understood and relationships accepted.[1]

Wisdom is internal, embodied by persons. Words of wisdom arise from it. Wise behavior arises from it. But wisdom itself is not its products. Wisdom is a mode of cognition—one rooted in perspectives, interpretations, and values. Wisdom is not about facts per se, it is about the context-linked meaning of facts. It is about the significance of facts and their implications. Wisdom is a kind of meta-knowledge that helps us make better sense of the rest of our knowledge. Wisdom does this by relating our ordinary, everyday knowledge to a variety of contexts, and by viewing it from a variety of illuminating perspectives. Among those perspectives are:

> Wisdom is a mode of cognition—one rooted in perspectives, interpretations, and values.

The self-knowledge perspective: Wise people have a greater than ordinary understanding of themselves. They are aware of their strengths and weaknesses and have developed "workarounds" to stay out of trouble. Because they have paid attention to how their own minds work, they are better able to understand the mind processes of others.

Laws-of-nature perspective: We contemplate doing things in the physical world and ask ourselves: Will this work? What will be the consequences of doing this? In such circumstances an understanding of basic scientific laws can at times lead to better, wiser, decisions.

Laws-of-life perspectives: If we are observant, we eventually sense some general rules that apply in our relations with other people: Sexual infidelity almost always causes pain for someone. Angry words shut down communication. We rarely adopt other people's lists of dos and don'ts, but if we see these generally applicable truths for ourselves they can help guide our actions.

The system perspective: The system perspective on reality is a powerful tool for understanding the world around us. Complexity in the natural world emerges as a hierarchy of natural systems or "holons," which have the property of being a whole at their own systemic level and a part or component in a system at the next level up the hierarchy. The physical hierarchy of systems moves from subatomic particles to atoms to molecules to crystals and cells, to living organisms, then to ecosystems, the biosphere, the solar system, the galaxy, and the universe. In another branch of this hierarchy, human beings start communicating with each other and give birth to those systems we call societies, economies, and nations.

The evolutionary perspective: What is the universe up to? Where does humanity fit in? Have we become agents of the evolutionary process? Some wise people have developed an understanding of our cosmic and evolutionary contexts and found it helpful to look at the human situation from this "big picture" vantage point.

The complexity-of-causation perspective: There is a human tendency to simplify causation. We pick out some dominant element in a situation and call it "The Cause," when in fact there are myriad necessary elements— an entire causal matrix—with roots that go back to the origin of the universe.

Broadened-identity and "oneness" perspectives: As a person develops psychologically and spiritually, their sense of identity tends to broaden. Their circle of concern and identity widens from me, to us—and for a few, to the entire universe and its underlying ground.

The finiteness-of-life perspective: Time is the raw material of our life, and a conscious awareness of our eventual death helps us to keep our life on a meaningful track and avoid meaningless, life-wasting detours.

A host of "high-values" perspectives: The deeply-held values of wise people are vantage points from which to view life situations and the world: Is this just? Is this truthful? Is this caring and compassionate? Etc.

The Role of Values in Wisdom

Nicholas Maxwell has called wisdom "the capacity to realize what is of value in life for oneself and others."[2] The embracing of "high" or "superior" values is a hallmark of wisdom. High values have two roles in the lives of wise people. First, they provide those illuminating slants on the data of life. Second, they guide the decision-making process toward wiser decisions.

Human decision making is a largely unconscious process in which a constantly shifting hierarchy of internalized values interacts with a constantly shifting set of perceived circumstances and retrieved memories. Some values, such as survival and reproduction, are hardwired. Other values, and their position in the value hierarchy, are the products of life experience and the influences to which we have been exposed. At any given moment our decisions are made by the combined action of:

- The brain-mind process currently in charge
- The hierarchy of value priorities that exists at that moment
- The perceived nature of the situation calling for a decision
- Memories of similar or related situations

Regarding item one, above, there are three distinct brain-mind processes, each having its own hierarchy of values:

- The instinctive/reactive process located in the earliest parts of our brain to evolve—the structures of the brain stem and limbic system and their change-resistant programming
- The intellectual process: typically centered in the left hemisphere of the neocortex
- The intuitive process: less clearly understood, but generally associated with the right, nonverbal hemisphere

These processes and their values work together to make our decisions and control our behavior in the same way a computer's hardware and software work together to make the computer's decisions and control its outputs. We can look at the three brain-mind processes as the hardware of our behavioral control system. And the internalized values that each process utilizes constitute the heart of the software.

If you ask a person to list their personal values in order of relative importance, you are likely to get a list with some pretty impressive stuff on it. Yet if we look dispassionately at that person's behavior, it might soon become apparent that their deep-down, internalized, operational values are not the same as their professed values—or at least do not have the stated priority. People always do what seems best, and that "best" is determined by how their hierarchy of internalized values interacts with the brain/mind's assessment of past, present, and anticipated future circumstances. As Nobelist Roger Sperry put it, "Human values...can...be viewed objectively as universal determinants in all human decision making. All decisions boil down to a choice among alternatives of what is most valued, for whatever reasons, and are determined by the particular value system that prevails."[3] Superior values, "the values of the wise," produce superior decisions and superior behavior.

The self-actualizing and ego-transcending people that psychologist Abraham Maslow studied were wise people, and Maslow's reports on their behavior and mindsets tell us much about the nature of wisdom and the values that underlie it. Maslow's self-actualizers focused on concerns outside of themselves; they liked solitude and privacy more than the average person, and they tended to be more detached than ordinary from the dictates and expectations of their culture. They were inner-directed people. They were creative, too, and appreciated the world around them with a sense of awe and wonder. In love relationships they respected the other's individuality and felt joy at the other's successes. They gave more love than most people, and needed less. Central to their lives was a set of values that Maslow called the Being-Values, or B-Values: wholeness, perfection, completion, justice, aliveness, richness, simplicity, beauty, goodness, uniqueness, effortlessness, playfulness, truth, honesty, reality, self-sufficiency.

Wise values express themselves in wise attitudes and wise ways of being and functioning. Among the value-based expressions of wisdom that speak strongly to me are:

- Feeling fully responsible for one's life choices and actions
- A positive, "let's make the most of it" attitude
- A reality-seeking, truth-seeking orientation

- A desire to learn, and a feeling of responsibility for one's own learning
- A desire to grow, to develop, "to become all I am capable of becoming"
- Being attentive: aware of mind events and mental processes as well as what is happening around us
- Being creative: producing uniqueness and novelty that has value
- Being a two-brain-hemisphere person, with intellect and intuition working together
- Being self-disciplined: able to work now for a reward later
- Being courageous: able to face dangers and fears with clarity and skill
- Being aware of one's own eventual death to the degree that it helps guide one's life
- Being able to deal with situations appropriately, using a large repertoire of approaches and techniques. Choosing the approach that best fits each situation: appropriate planning, appropriate timing, appropriate problem-solving, dealing with commitments appropriately, etc.
- Being non-reactive: able to deal skillfully with powerful emotions
- Being deeply loving, and able to manifest love in appropriate ways
- Having a sense of wonder
- Being compassionate
- Behaving in ways that benefit others
- Possessing a deep happiness that is independent of externals
- Recognizing that there are limits to personal knowledge and to the ability of our species to know

The world is not divided into wise and unwise people. None of us is perfectly wise or totally unwise. We are wise to the degree that characteristics like those mentioned above are part of us, to the extent that we actually live them. The specific qualities developed will differ in kind and degree from person to person, and this results in each wise person's wisdom having a distinctive character or "flavor."

Developing Wisdom

The good news is that the acquisition of wisdom is not something we must leave to the whims of fate, as many in the past have assumed. If we want to become wiser people, we can develop the characteristics of wisdom and incorporate them into our lives. The bad news is that we're pretty much on our own in doing that. It would be nice if we lived in a wisdom-fostering culture—one in which every institution was dedicated to helping us become wiser. But we don't. So how do we become wiser people? In short, by exposing ourselves to wisdom-fostering influences, and by intentionally practicing, with effort, the behaviors and attitudes that we someday hope to become effortless expressions of our deepest, truest self.

The Role of Influences

If we don't like the values we have internalized to date or the particular mental process that is calling the shots, then we must change things. We are surrounded by influences that push us toward ordinary behavior and ordinary ways of thinking. But we need not be prisoners of ordinary; we can shift the balance of influences. We can intentionally increase our exposure to positive influences—influences that promote and reinforce the kind of changes we are trying to make. We can, for instance:

Hang out with people who are already living the values we'd like to make our own. Where do we find such people? Groups that focus on personal growth and doing good in the world are a likely bet. Among these are some open-minded, non-doctrinaire religious groups such as Unitarians, Quakers, and Buddhists. Local and online discussion and activist groups are another possibility. Some of these focus on psychological or spiritual growth. Others focus on various social issues. We can experiment, and when we find a group that feels right, get involved.

Find out more about the nature and development of wisdom. As a starting point you might want to visit The Wisdom Page, "a compilation of wisdom-related resources," at www.cop.com/wisdompg.html.

Read biographies of exceptional people. Your local library has many of these, and your librarian would be pleased to suggest some good ones.

Learn from the experiences of others. People all around us are struggling to up level their lives—some skillfully and successfully, others very unskillfully and unsuccessfully. The world's literature, and movies too, present us with countless additional life stories. What can we learn from them?

Can we pick out the strategies and behaviors that work and those that don't? Can we start to sense some general "laws of life" behind the specifics?

Be open to wise sayings that energize and motivate. Twice in my life sets of words have resonated so deeply with me that they initiated significant life changes. The first of these was a statement by Etienne de Grellet, a nineteenth-century Quaker, that I encountered as a university student:

"I shall pass through this world but once. If, therefore, there is any good thing I can do or any kindness I can show, let me do it now. Let me not defer it or neglect it, for I shall not pass this way again."

The second turning point, a decision to pursue my own psychological and spiritual development, was triggered by the words "become all you're capable of becoming" at a corporate seminar on Abraham Maslow's theory of motivation.

There was also a third set of words. It didn't change my life direction, but confirmed and clarified it. It is Goethe's admonition to "Go and dare before you die."

The Role of Practice

Becoming clear about the values we would like at the center of our lives—the values we want to make truly our own in a deep and powerful way—is the first step. The next challenge is to move these values from our head to our heart and our guts. In psychological terms, we must internalize them so they are not merely nice thoughts, but actually guide our behavior. Doing this takes effort, and, during one of his trips to North America, the Dalai Lama gave an example of what we need to do. He spoke to an audience about the need for everyone to internalize that key value of wisdom, compassion. His advice to those who wanted to develop compassion was to put themselves in challenging situations and then, despite the natural reluctance to do so, behave compassionately. By making the effort to engage in value-based action—again, and again, and again—we eventually internalize the value. Expressing the value in action gradually takes less and less effort until it becomes part of our outlook, part of our natural way of being, part of who we are.

Becoming a wiser person is an exercise in inner development, and there are activities that can help us along the way. Counseling and other forms of psychotherapy can, if needed, help us reach the starting point for advanced work which we might call responsible adulthood or mature ego. A person at this stage is free of psychoses and crippling neuroses and has developed emotional control and empathy to an ordinary degree. To help us move beyond this stage we need other resources. Many people start with writings that discuss the farther reaches of human development. The writings, in turn, lead us to do-it-yourself practices: mind-quieting practices, self-knowledge practices, ego-transcending practices, and oneness-realization practices. You can find many suggestions at www.cop.com/innerwork.html.

It is widely recognized that the fast track to self-knowledge and other important aspects of wisdom is meditation — particularly the kind devoted to exploring the mind/body process, variously called mindfulness, vipassana, or insight meditation. For more information about this and related practices read The Importance Of Meditation at www.cop.com/meditation.html.

Wisdom on a Larger Scale

This essay has focused on what I call life-centered wisdom—the wisdom that results in a happier, more productive personal life and more harmonious interpersonal relations. But there is also the big chaotic world out there that needs all the wise guidance it can get. I have written elsewhere about a variation on the wisdom theme that strikes me as particularly suited to the initiation of wise action in the political, economic, and biospheric arenas. I have called it deep understanding. In short, it involves coupling the wisdom development process just described with the acquisition of intellectual knowledge relevant to the world problematique. To come to grips with the major scientific, social, and economic issues that bear on the present world situation, we must all become more holistic knowers. The way I see it, we can deal effectively with humanity's problems only if we have a deep and comprehensive understanding of the context in which those problems are set. This includes knowledge of the systemic nature of the cosmos, the evolutionary process in its most general sense, consciousness, human cultures, economic systems, and some of the more important principles, laws, and regularities that underlie functioning in all these areas.

If this broader application of wisdom piques your interest, you might want to read the book *Matters of Consequence*; information about it can be found at mattersofconsequence.com. Also of possible interest is the essay "Deep Understanding: Wisdom for an Integral Age." It is available online in two places: www.cejournal.org/GRD/DeepUnderstanding.html and www.cop.com/deepundr.html.

© Copthorne Macdonald

Notes

[1] *From* Landscape, *Vol. 25, No. 1, Jan 1981.*

[2] *From Nicholas Maxwell's book* Is Science Neurotic?, *London: Imperial College Press, 2004, p. 119.*

[3] *From Roger Sperry's article* "Bridging science and values: A unifying view of mind and brain," American Psychologist, *April, 1977, p. 237.*

About the Author

Copthorne Macdonald is a writer, independent scholar, and former communication systems engineer. He writes about the nature and development of wisdom, new perspectives on mental and physical reality, and creating a sustainable future. Three of his seven books deal with wisdom: *Toward Wisdom, Getting a Life,* and *Matters of Consequence.* He has also written more than 130 published articles, scholarly essays, reviews, and column installments. He established and tends The Wisdom Page, a popular Internet-based compilation of wisdom-related resources. Additional details about his life and work can be found at www.cop.com.

A deep, inner, spiritual change is what has to happen. What is being called for at this time is to begin to live what all the great teachers have been telling us.

Peter Russell

Life is the only real counselor; wisdom unfiltered through personal experience does not become a part of the moral tissue.

Edith Wharton

There are seven things that will destroy us: Wealth without work; Pleasure without conscience; Knowledge without character; Religion without sacrifice; Politics without principle; Science without humanity; Business without ethics.

Mohandas K. Gandhi

What we need to know, we already know. It is not more knowledge that is needed, but more careful listening, more dreaming, more daring.

Jan Phillips

If we have had conscientious and "good" persons since the beginning of recorded history (the likes of Socrates), with much of their wisdom still available in the form of quotations, and if moral philosophy has carved out what is right and what is wrong for many decades, then what is the problem? If ancient philosophers in China were speaking of goodness and justice, why did an innocent person get executed in the last year?

Jason Merchey

Growth in wisdom may be exactly measured by the decrease in bitterness.

Friedrich Nietzsche

Perplexity is the beginning of knowledge.

Kahlil Gibran

The pursuit of truth shall set you free, even if you never catch up with it.

Clarence Darrow

COURAGE

DARING TO LIVE FULL

Katherine Martin

Ten years ago when I started writing about courage, I thought I knew all about it and set out to find people who had risked everything to do the seemingly impossible, putting themselves in great physical jeopardy. I was looking for the big courage of those who had conquered challenges against all odds. Legends. Heroes. The grand explorers, people who dared to do things that no one else had done, gone to the ends of the world and back. People who had broken down cultural barriers, stood up against injustice at great personal risk. I was looking for the headliner stuff, dramatic, wildly public.

That courage could arise from a grand exploration of the heart did not occur to me.

In pursuit of big courage, I met people like Fanchon Blake who was the first woman to sue the Los Angeles Police Department for discrimination against women and minorities, the first to break what she called a scary "code of silence." Her lawsuit lasted seven years and, at one point, she had to be put under federal protection. Because she stayed the course and dared to speak out when no one else would, over seventeen hundred women in Los Angeles have jobs on the force. That is the power of taking action when you know something isn't right. That is the power of being scared silly but being willing to be afraid - and to move ahead anyway.

Into the domain of these courageous people I traveled, feeling the utter magnitude of their stories, breathless with the dramatic turns in their lives and how they stepped up to meet those turns with a will of iron: "I will not back down." They embodied the best in us, they lived big. I wanted to be like them. I wanted to be fearless, confident, gregarious, willful, undaunted.

I had a great distance to go. I was a woman regularly visited by fear, unsubstantiated. I was shy. I did not cotton to making mistakes and would do just about anything to avoid them. This was not the profile of a woman on her way to courage.

And then along came Ann Bancroft.

Ann was the only woman on a North Pole Expedition where, she laughed, "even the dogs were male!" She returned a hero. There was the White House reception. The red carpet rolling out. The job offers. The marriage proposals from men she didn't even know. But Ann had a dream. And this dream would take her south. She wanted to lead the first all-women's expedition to the South Pole. Now, being the member of an expedition is a great deal different that being the leader, especially, when so many eyes would be on her; if she succeeded, she would make history for womankind. And it was this that caused her to say that "it would hurt all the more" if she failed.

A riveting interview generates heat, and this one was a scorcher. But, an odd and pregnant pause began to sink discernibly into the space between the end of the story and something unspoken. Finally, Ann confessed, "I really have to be honest with you…"

Ah, the story deepens, I thought, leaning forward, expecting a deepening of the story, an emotional stirring that every writer loves because it connects to one another, draws us into our humanity.

"…that wasn't courageous,"

I didn't quite catch her words…Say again?

"… it wasn't courageous, not for me…"

Hold on. She's just told me about a sixty-seven day journey on skis—no dogs and sleds and "mush, mush" for these women, they each pulled a two-hundred-pound sled against seventy-five-mile-an-hour winds in forty-below temperatures...and that wasn't courageous?

"Put me in those wild, open places and that's where I'm at home," she said beatifically. "That's where I find myself, where I'm at peace."

But, but, but...

"...but, if you want to hear about my courage, let me tell you about being dyslexic..."

At a time when there wasn't much known about it, Ann was in college, struggling toward a dream. She wanted to be an elementary school teacher. A great athlete, she wasn't a stellar student, and she knew that getting into the required teaching practicum would be a challenge. But when her college counselor suggested she get her BA and go on with her life because she'd never get into the practicum, Ann was stunned. Give up her dream?

"You don't understand, a BA means nothing to me if I can't teach."

When her counselor tried to convince her to give up sports and buckle down, hit the books, Ann could have relented. But, she stood her ground, because she knew that sports was the one place where she got the confidence she needed to face how difficult it was with the grades: "I won't give up sports," she said to the counselor.

Here was a woman who would go on to be inducted into the Women's Hall of Fame. A legend in her own time, having made history several times. An icon of courage. Perfect. And yet, her defining moment of courage was a quiet thing, a little moment.

This was not what I'd gone looking for. Not the bells and whistles, but a small, everyday moment of courage. It took several attempts but Ann got into the practicum and became an elementary school teacher. "My graduation was a pretty big deal," she told me. "My entire family came to the ceremony. I was our first college graduate. And, as it turns out, my learning disability and my struggle to get through school was great training that I would use later on when I needed perseverance. Standing in the bitter cold at the North Pole, I had the distinct thought, This is not worse than school. When I was having a bad day on the Arctic ice, that's what I would dredge up in my mind to keep me going: School was harder."

Talking with Ann was a turning point in my understanding of courage. Here was a woman whose true courage had nothing to do with the expeditions that turned her into a public heroine. Hers was much more personal and more perfect than I realized. I doubt that many of us can relate to being dropped at the edge of the continent of Antarctica, facing three months of nothing but white and ice and subzero temperatures with howling winds that make it impossible to hear the person next to us, all the while pulling a two-hundred-pound sled. But all of us can relate to standing in front of an intimidating authority figure who's trying to tell us what we should do or who we should be or that a dream we have will never come true.

After talking with Ann, I started to go deeper, to look beyond the obvious, to see the unexpected. She showed me that one of the most courageous things we do is to know ourselves, down at the bone where it really counts, and then to be true to that, to take a stand for who we really are, to walk our innermost talk. Not just for ourselves, but for those we love, our families, friends, and colleagues, and for the impact we have on our communities and the world at large when we show up fully for the living of our lives.

With everyday, practical courage, we can craft more meaningful and authentic lives, not waiting to do something dramatically courageous but doing it daily, awake to the desire of our true soul.

With my blinders off, I now saw courage all around me. Not just in the big dramatic moments but the quiet courage in the cracks and crevices of the everyday. I saw how thin had been my understanding. I had missed the courage in each and every one of us. I had missed the courage...in *you*.

My misconceptions began to show themselves in other ways.
* I thought I had to become fearless in order to be courageous.
* I thought I had to become gregarious and hugely self-assured before even thinking about doing something daring.
* I thought there were courageous people and then there were the rest of us.

What I've learned is this:
* Courage always comes with fear. Rather than trying to be fearless, strive to know your fear, be curious about it. What is it made of, what does it do to you, and how can you work with it? Is it contrived, something arising out of your imagination? Where did your fear come from, who gave it to you, do you want to keep it? Get up close to it. Don't be afraid to be afraid.
* Confidence is not always what it seems to be in a courageous moment. People who dare do not have confidence encoded in their DNA—an uncommon strand that enables them to take

374

risks that others wouldn't take. Their confidence is uncommon, yes, but in ways you might not expect, especially if your point of reference is the Webster dictionary where I found this definition: "A state of mind or a manner marked by easy coolness and freedom from uncertainty, diffidence, or embarrassment."

Not the case with courage. It may look cool and easy and certain, but underneath, it's hot. People often said to me, "I thought I was nuts..." or "People thought I was crazy..." or "It made no sense..." But. "But I did it anyway." It's in "but I did it anyway" where courage lives. When it comes to daring, confidence is not the absence of uncertainty, doubt, perspiration, fear, and even shyness, but rather the ability to act in spite of them.

> Doing battle with our insecurities only makes them bigger and more solid. Accepting them, letting them be a part of our character, disarms them.

Doing battle with our insecurities only makes them bigger and more solid. Accepting them, letting them be a part of our character, disarms them. A woman named Susan shared with me about embracing her nervousness in public. "Yesterday, I went out with my husband and didn't feel as nervous as usual. When my anxiety appeared, I floated with it until it went away. It felt great. I had control of my feelings and thoughts for a change."

Once disarmed, our insecurities can be broken down into human events and underlying causes. Why are we insecure? What event in our life caused us to retreat? What belief keeps us feeling small? Where did that come from? How does it weave together with a fear of rejection? What does the insecurity do for us? What do we gain from it? What would happen if we let it go?

Often, we simply need to get out of our own way.

Confidence is a straightforward appreciation of who you see in the mirror. An appreciation free of arrogance and self-aggrandizement. An appreciation filled with gratitude, humor, humility. Confidence is believing in yourself, imperfect, flawed, and yet good enough.

Too often, we think we're not good enough and it keeps us small. We're not smart enough, not gregarious enough, not witty enough, not savvy enough, not pretty enough, not educated enough, not clever enough, not romantic enough...endlessly not enough. When rooted in childhood, these feelings of being unenough can come—intentionally or unintentionally— from parents, teachers, and authority figures, from cliques we never belonged to or kids we wanted to be like or friends who dumped us. Somewhere inside us are dreams and desires we haven't made good on because a little gnat keeps buzzing around our heads, trying to convince us that, "You're not smart enough to do that," or "You're not clever enough," or "You're not experienced enough." What does your little gnat have to say?

What about you isn't good enough?

Who told you that?

What does it keep you from doing?

How would you feel if you knew it was just a belief?

What would you do if you knew you were enough?

Who would object to that?

What do you need to say or do to reassure that person or to dispel their influence over you?

Imagine what you could do if you knew, without a doubt, without a hesitation, that you were enough. Imagine that. What would you do? Who would you be? Imagine what you would do if you were willing to be out of your element, if you believed in yourself enough to sweat bullets. Imagine that you are enough even if you're shy and insecure. Imagine making mistakes and being fueled by what you learn. Imagine not being afraid of being afraid. Imagine yourself standing strong in a new brand of confidence. Imagine who you can be. Imagine...

Another misconception I had was that "courageous people" are a special breed set apart from the rest of us. In fact, on the one hand, we have courage. On the other, we have a person. Sometimes, they meet up, sometimes they don't. We are not always courageous all the time. But courage does live in each and every one of us. We all have a well of it from which to draw. Sometimes, we reach down deep for it. Sometimes, we don't.

As the first courage book took me places I hadn't expected to go, I saw that I would have to let go of my original agenda in order to follow the stories. I would have to open up to being surprised, to being fluid and flexible. Every interview, every story of courage was teaching me, revealing something that I personally needed to pay attention to, carrying me a little further across my own internal landscape...and closer to my true self. The experience was changing the way I saw myself, my place in my family, my place in my community, and my place in the world. I was stepping up and speaking out, I was being more authentic. It felt good.

The study of courage, in fact, would take me more personally, more intimately, more vulnerably into the meaning of the word than I had ever imagined. Not merely the telling of stories, this work would take a hold of me, rattle me, challenge me, wrest me free of little ideas, and demand of me that I be bigger. Not by climbing Everest, but in the way I lived my life every day. In the way I spoke up in a business meeting or responded to a project that was starting to head in the wrong direction. In the way I started to intentionally do things that made me nervous. In the way I opened myself to a deeper intimacy with my husband.

Emotional, mental, and spiritual courage can be as daunting as climbing Everest.

Sometimes, the most courageous thing we do is to say, "I love you" when it scares the pants off us. Sometimes, it's saying "I forgive you." To be emotionally vulnerable can cause our heart to beat in our throat. Inner courage, although not externally threatening, can be as scary as publicly loud courage. To say "I'm sorry" may be an emotional expedition of great magnitude. To face a marriage going stale is harrowing and to be willing to become more intimate can feel like we're splitting ourselves open.

Traveling the emotional landscape of the heart is a daring journey.

Facing the truth about who we are, how we're doing in this life with matters of conscience and love, with the substance of our greater purpose—these can be as frightening as slaying the dragon. Turning inward to assess requires that we risk seeing our emptiness, but also that we dare to see our fullness. As scary as it can be to face the truth about our weaknesses, facing the truth about our magnificence can be daunting. I've seen more people squirm at the suggestion that they're courageous, exceptional, inspiring. Who could be deserving of such big praise? To say so—to even think it—feels arrogant, narcissistic. I often heard, "Oh no, I'm just a…" —housewife, small-town person, regular kind of guy. Perhaps modesty is a way to ensure that we still belong as we step out, as we stand up, as we cross the boundaries of our familiar. "I'm only doing what anyone else would do," said many I interviewed.

Perhaps the responsibility of our bigness seems overwhelming. To be big is to have big impact. What will be expected of us? Will we become too visible, vulnerable to criticism? Will others become envious of us? Will we be able to sustain? Sometimes, we are attended by an amorphous fear that, if we admit our bigness, something terrible will happen and tragedy will strike.

We may have grown up with myths that make us hesitate at the threshold of our bigness. "It's lonely at the top." Or, "The higher you fly, the harder you fall." To do what we say we want to do, to be who we say we want to be, requires dismantling cultural myths, our own personal myths, and redesigning our beliefs.

Why do we fear our bigness? What are we afraid will happen if we live a life that matters? What beliefs hold us back from it?

"Our deepest fear is not that we are inadequate," writes Marianne Williamson in *A Return to Love*, "our deepest fear is that we are powerful beyond measure. It is our light, not our darkness, that most frightens us. We ask ourselves, 'Who am I to be brilliant, gorgeous, talented, and fabulous?' Actually, who are you not to be?"

Your playing small doesn't serve the world, Marianne says. "There is nothing enlightened about shrinking so that other people won't feel insecure around you. We were born to manifest the glory that is within us. And as we let our light shine, we unconsciously give other people permission to do the same. As we are liberated from our own fear, our presence automatically liberates others."

What will you do with your courage? How will you make your difference?

In claiming ourselves as the magnificent that we can be, in honoring ourselves at the deepest level, is courage. I will not be kept inside a box. My voice will not be muffled. My spirit will not be denied. I will be heard. I will use my life well.

From Those Who Dare, © *2004 by Katherine Martin. Excerpted with permission from New World Library, Novato, CA. 800-972-6657, ext. 52, or www.newworldlibrary.com.*

About the Author

Sadly, Katherine Martin passed away during the production of *Living a Life of Value*.

At one time the courage counselor at iVillage.com, Katherine started writing about courage with *Women of Courage*, a celebration of courageous moments—both loud and quiet—in the lives of modern women. *Women of Spirit* continued the telling of stories that inspire us to grab hold of life. Adapting her work to the stage, Katherine created the "Women of Courage theatre event," which has played to sold-out venues, standing ovations, and been called by one artistic director, "one of the most riveting, emotional, and ultimately inspiring pieces of theatre you are ever likely to see." As a public speaker, Katherine connected with the deep desire in each of us to make our lives matter, to make a difference—and she called upon us to live boldly and authentically.

Katherine co-authored the groundbreaking book, *Non-Impact Aerobics*, with fitness experts Debbie and Carlos Rosas, whose new book, *The Nia Technique*, was published by Broadway Books in January, 2005. Katherine has written for the *San Francisco Chronicle's* Sunday magazine, *Ms., Parents, Working Mother, Women's Sports & Fitness*, and numerous national magazines. An award-winning screenwriter, she co-wrote an original Showtime movie and an independent feature film.

A longtime student of the human potential, Katherine was the senior editor of *New Realities*, a cutting-edge, progressive thought magazine.

She is survived by her husband, Franc, and son, Benjamin.

Spirit has fifty times the strength and staying-power of brawn and muscle.

Mark Twain

Courage does not always roar. Sometimes it's the little voice at the end of the day that says, "I'll try again tomorrow."

Mary Anne Radmacher

Courage is contagious. When a brave man takes a stand, the spines of others are stiffened.

Billy Graham

We gain strength, and courage, and confidence by each experience in which we really stop to look fear in the face...we must do that which we think we cannot.

Eleanor Roosevelt

Everything I did in my life that was worthwhile I caught hell for.

Earl Warren

The ultimate measure of a man is not where he stands in moments of comfort and convenience, but where he stands in times of challenge and controversy.

Martin Luther King, Jr.

You can listen to what everybody says, but the fact remains that you've got to get out there and do the thing yourself.

Joan Sutherland

Why not go out on a limb? Isn't that where the fruit is?

Frank Scully

Fear left unchecked grows like a malignancy.

John A. Marshall

Bite off more than you can chew, then chew it.

Ella Williams

The cowards think of what they can lose; the heroes of what they can win.

J. M. Charlier

...principles have a way of enduring, as do the few irreducible individuals who maintain allegiance to them.

Christopher Hitchens

Great necessities call out great virtues.

Abigail Adams

True courage is not the brutal force of vulgar heroes, but the firm resolve of virtue and reason.

Alfred North Whitehead

Fear is the main source of superstition, and one of the main sources of cruelty. To conquer fear is the beginning of wisdom.

Bertrand Russell

The scars you acquire by exercising courage will never make you feel inferior.

D. A. Battista

Courage is the most important of all the virtues, because without it we can't practice any other virtue with consistency.

Maya Angelou

No coward soul is mine,
No trembler in the world's storm-troubled sphere;
I see Heaven's glories shine,
And faith shines equal, arming me from fear.

Emily Bronte

We rely upon the poets, the philosophers, and the playwrights to articulate what most of us can only feel, in joy or sorrow. They illuminate the thoughts for which we only grope; they give us the strength and balm we cannot find in ourselves. Whenever I feel my courage wavering, I rush to them. They give me the wisdom of acceptance, the will and resilience to push on.

Helen Hayes

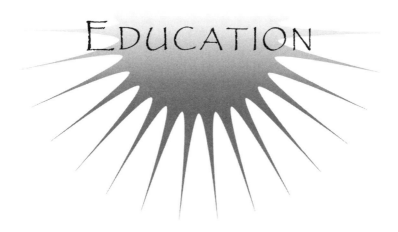

EDUCATION

LEARNING TO LIVE A LIFE OF VALUE

Nicholas Maxwell

Much of my working life has been devoted to trying to get across the point that we urgently need to bring about a revolution in the aims and methods of academic inquiry, so that the basic aim becomes to seek and promote wisdom rather than just acquire knowledge.

Early Experiences

To begin with, I wanted to understand the nature of the universe. When still a boy I became enthralled, mystified and horrified by theoretical physics—space-time curved, particles no more than waves of probability, the real world so utterly different from the way we ordinarily experience it. It was the mystery, the utter strangeness, of the physical universe that caught my imagination. None of this, by the way, should be taken to mean that I was horribly precocious. Not at all. In those far off days in England, eleven year olds had to take an exam which decided whether they would be able to go on to grammar school or not. Failure to pass this exam more or less condemned you to leaving school without qualifications (unless your parents could pay for your education). I failed this crucial exam, not once, but twice!

Then, with adolescence, I began to feel it was much more important to understand the hearts and souls of people, the way to do that being via the novel. Instead of reading Jeans, Eddington, and Fred Hoyle, I plunged into the worlds of Dostoevsky, Kafka, Stendhal, Chekhov, D. H. Lawrence, Virginia Woolf, and Flaubert. My real education began. I would become a novelist and dare to reveal dark secrets of the human heart no one before had uttered. I would depict worlds with such imaginative power that they would seem more real than reality itself. But my parents insisted that, first, I must go to University, to secure my future economically (of no significance to me at all at the age of seventeen). The educational system, fiercely classificatory in those days, had labeled me "science" and not "humanities." (And in any case I knew doing English at University would ruin any chance I might have of becoming a novelist.) I had read Eddington, who informed me that physics is really mathematics, and for a time, earlier, I had been dazzled by this invisible, esoteric world of mathematics. So off I went to University College London to do mathematics, convinced I could write my novels between and after lectures.

But I was miserable; I didn't know what to write about; and mathematics seemed both hollow and very difficult. It did not seem to be about anything. I passed all my exams but, abruptly, in my second year, my grant was stopped because I had not attended enough lectures.

So I did my National Service. I became a Sergeant in the Educational Corps. And then I went to Manchester University to do Philosophy. I had failed miserably as a physicist, and as a novelist, but I was interested in philosophical problems, so I would do that for three years, and then join the grey shuffle of ordinary, uncreative life (as I then saw it).

Visions and Confusion

But then, in the summer of 1961, while working in a factory during the day, I began to keep a diary, noting down my thoughts and feelings. And the outcome was a series of psychic explosions which tore me apart and changed the rest of my life. I decided that my earlier desire to be a great theoretical physicist and master the universe, and my desire to be a great novelist and master of human life, were both, when pushed to the limit, aspects of the desire to become God. Not only was this absurd; it was undesirable.

Far more desirable was to be something that, up to then, had seemed too insignificant to deserve any consideration at all: myself. This long-neglected, fragile, worthless scrap of almost nothing now seemed to me to be, for me, the most precious thing in existence, something holy and sacrosanct. But what was it? What was I? I had no idea. Having ignored myself, in some sense, for so long, in my striving to become acquainted with, identified with, some profoundly significant otherness (ultimate physical reality, ultimate human reality), my self had become a stranger to me. It felt like a young plant, fragile from neglect and lack of nourishment, needing attention and care to grow and flourish.

Our identity exists in the interplay between what lies within and without.

"When we are born," I wrote in the diary, "we do not know how to distinguish 'me' from 'not me:' there is just things happening. But then we do discover how to make the distinction, and we discover we are tiny and vulnerable in a vast, strange, and sometimes terrifying world. We falsely half remember the earlier state as a time when we were 'everything,' and our life project, in one way or another, becomes to return to this earlier, God-like state. One strategy is to try to convert the 'not me' into 'me,' by conquering it, knowing and understanding it, acquiring power over it, or even literally trying to swallow it. Another standard strategy is to do just the opposite: shrink the 'me' until it disappears, and there is only 'everything'. This is the strategy of the mystic who seeks mystical union with God; it is the strategy of the humble, and of those who commit suicide."

But both these conventional and absurd strategies rest on a mistaken view about the nature of the "me," the nature of personal identity. Our identity is not what is inside us. What lies within us is just as mysterious as what lies without us. Our identity exists in the interplay between what lies within and without. If the distinction between "me" and "not me" is depicted as a circle on a surface, the "me" is not, as we ordinarily assume, what lies within the circle; it is rather the line of the circle itself. We should not, ludicrously, try to increase the circle until, in the limit, everything is incorporated within it; nor should we, almost equally ludicrously, try to decrease the circle until it becomes a dot and disappears and there is just "everything": instead, we should "relax the muscles of identity" (as I wrote in my diary) so that the line of the circle becomes permeable, and there can be an easy interplay between what lies within and without, and we become our authentic selves, without striving to expand until, in the limit, we become everything, or shrink until we become nothing (and there is only everything).

My earlier projects to know and understand the nature of the universe by means of physics, and to know and understand humanity by means of literature, now seemed variants of the strategy to expand and expand the circle of identity. Pushed to the limits of absurdity, it was as if my ultimate aspiration had been to become God. But an infinitely more worthwhile goal lay before me, up till now neglected as worthless: to become myself. "The riddle of the universe," I wrote, "is the riddle of our desires." The fundamental question of philosophy is not, "How do I acquire knowledge?" but rather, "What do I want? How should I live?"

These ideas, which now seem to me somewhat absurd, exaggerated and dubious at best, were for me, at the time, the stuff of my life; they were experienced and lived. Before these "revelations," I had half believed in Descartes' picture of the self being the mind, linked to the brain but utterly different from anything physical, the whole experienced world being locked away within the prison of one's skull. This picture was shattered. What was within was just as much a mystery as what lay without: "I" was the region of interplay between these two mysteries. I became whatever I saw or experienced, my self being created and dying many times during the day. In one of his letters, John Keats spoke of becoming the bird he saw pecking on a path. That was how it now was with me. I would be whatever I experienced: seeing a blade of grass, I became that blade of grass; talking with a friend, I became that "talking with the friend." For six weeks it was as if I was high on some hallucinatory drug: visions of exhilarating and terrifying intensity came before breakfast, and throughout the day. I had become a prophet, and my prophecy was: be your own prophet, discover for yourself your own true self, what you really desire in life.

In the end I found having a great message for the world such a contradiction that I finally hit upon the idea: there are only stories or myths. One is that of science; another is that of personal experience. Not till I read Karl Popper did I free myself of this nonsense—so fashionable in some quarters.

I vowed that when I got back to Manchester University in the autumn, I would tell the Philosophy Department about my earth-shaking discoveries of the summer—especially, that philosophy should be about how to live, and not about how to acquire knowledge. I found I could not even open my mouth. Ecstasy gave way to persistent black despair.

Becoming a Professional Philosopher

The visions of the summer of 1961 had gone, but I continued, somehow, to believe I had discovered something of great significance, even though now I no longer knew what it was. I decided to devote my MA thesis to the question: How can the world of physics be reconciled with the world of experience, feeling and art? I was aware that I was grappling with the two worlds of my abandoned childhood megalomaniacal ambitions: to grasp the physical universe by means of science, and to grasp the human world by means of the novel.

In those days philosophy in England was dominated by "Oxford" philosophy, conceptual analysis in the manner of Wittgenstein, Ryle, and Austin, the sterility of which filled me with horror. However, I discovered the works of two contemporary philosophers which were of great help to me: Karl Popper and J. J. C. Smart. Here were two philosophers who took science seriously, and were concerned to tackle profound problems with intellectual integrity (not being content to dissolve pseudo-problems). I became a visiting graduate student at the London School of Economics and attended Popper's Seminars. I was profoundly impressed.

I was especially impressed by the following line of argument running through Popper's early work. In *The Logic of Scientific Discovery*, Popper defends falsificationism, the view that scientific knowledge is irredeemably conjectural in character, scientific theories being falsifiable, but not verifiable. According to this view, scientific knowledge grows by a process of conjecture and refutation. Conjectures are subjected to an onslaught of attempted empirical falsification. When a theory is falsified, we discover the need to develop a better theory, and it is this which drives science forward and makes scientific progress possible.

Falsificationism was then generalized by Popper to become critical rationalism. This holds that, quite generally, we cannot justify or prove our theories or beliefs. The best that we can do is subject them to sustained criticism, in this way giving ourselves the best chance of discovering error, where it exists, this making it possible for us to improve our theories and beliefs. In particular, we need to look critically at the capacity of our ideas to solve the problems they were invented to solve, and we need to consider whether rival ideas do better. Criticism demands that a number of rival ideas are available; criticism does not make sense unless there is the idea that the view being criticized is perhaps false, some other view being correct. Science is just a special case of all this, empirical falsification being just an especially devastating form of criticism.

Popper then applied critical rationalism to social and political problems, and problems concerning the nature of the social sciences in *The Poverty of Historicism*, and in his greatest work *The Open Society and Its Enemies*. In these books Popper mounts a ferocious criticism of the totalitarian doctrines of Plato and Marx, and sets out to demolish historicism—the doctrine that there are laws of historical development. But Popper also transforms the whole idea of what "the rational society" might be. Given pre-Popperian notions of rationality, the rational society could only be some kind of highly oppressive, rule-bound society dominated by reason, a kind of rational totalitarianism. But given Popper's new notion of critical rationalism, a rational society is one which sustains diversity of beliefs, values, ways of life, and one which values learning through criticism, criticism only being possible if there is a diversity of ideas around. The rational society is, in short, granted critical rationalism, one and the same thing as the open society. At a stroke, reason has ceased to have totalitarian connotations, and has become basic to liberalism.

University College London

Impressed by Popper's integrity and passion, I decided it might be possible after all to work inside academia with honor. I finished my MA thesis, taught Philosophy of Science for a year at Manchester University, and then joined the Department of History and Philosophy of Science at University College London as a Lecturer (later Reader). I taught and pursued my research at UCL for some twenty-eight years, taking early retirement in 1994, so that I could devote myself to my work.

To begin with, I published three papers extracted from my MA thesis: "Physics and Common Sense" (1966), "Can there be Necessary Connections between Successive Events?" (1968), and "Understanding Sensations" (1968). These papers were way ahead of their time and, as a result, failed to have the impact I hoped they would have. Together they tackled the problem of how the experiential world can exist embedded in the physical universe. Physics, I argued, is concerned only with a highly selected aspect of that which exists, namely that aspect which determines (perhaps probabilistically) the way events unfold. For all we know, physical reality may determine necessarily how events unfold: in so far as David Hume denied this, he was wrong. The silence of physics about the experiential is thus no grounds whatsoever for holding that the experiential does not exist. The experiential or mental aspect of a brain process is that aspect we become aware of as a result of having the process occur in our own brain. The experiential cannot, I argued, be reduced to the physical. In order to know what redness is one must oneself have experienced redness, but this is not the case as far as any physical feature is concerned (an argument made famous, some sixteen years later, by Frank Jackson in his paper "What Mary Didn't Know").

Dismayed by the lack of any response to these papers, I gave up publishing for a time, and concentrated on pursuing my interests. I began to appreciate that Popper had not done what he claimed to do, solve the problem of induction, not because he failed to show how theories can be verified, but because he failed to do justice to the scientific aim of discovering explanations for phenomena. This discovery led me back into the business of publishing papers. I spelled out the point in a paper that appeared in 1972 called "A Critique of Popper's Views on Scientific Method."[1]

A New Conception of Science

But then, with mounting excitement, even before the "Critique" paper was published, I realized that the implication of the argument was that we needed a whole new conception of science. In persistently only accepting unified, explanatory theories, to the extent of rejecting infinitely many theories more empirically successful but grossly disunified, science in effect makes a big, persistent, and highly problematic assumption about the universe: it is comprehensible, in the sense that it is such that explanations for phenomena exist to be found. The fundamental aim of science, in presupposing that the universe is comprehensible, is so profoundly problematic that it has been repressed and replaced with the apparently unproblematic aim of seeking truth, nothing being presupposed about the truth. But this latter view is hopeless; it creates the unsolvable problem of induction. Science is much more rational if big, problematic, implicit metaphysical assumptions concerning comprehensibility are made explicit, so that they can be criticized and, we may hope, improved. Science must be depicted as accepting, as a part of (conjectural) scientific knowledge, that the universe is comprehensible, more or less specific empirically untestable (and thus metaphysical) theses about how the universe is physically comprehensible being criticized and improved as scientific knowledge improves, associated methods being improved as well. There is something like positive feedback between improving scientific knowledge and improving aims and methods—improving knowledge-about-how-to-improve-knowledge—the methodological key to the ever-accelerating progress of modern science.

Problematic Aims

Then, walking home one day from UCL, it suddenly struck me: this idea of representing the real problematic aims of science in the form of a hierarchy, aims becoming increasingly unspecific and unproblematic as one goes up the hierarchy, in this way a framework of relatively unproblematic, fixed aims and methods being created within which more specific, problematic aims and methods can be improved as knowledge improves—all this has implications for any worthwhile human endeavour with problematic aims. Just as Popper had generalized and applied falsificationism, so too I could generalize and apply my much better conception of scientific method of aim-oriented empiricism. I could tread a parallel path to Popper's footsteps, starting from a radically improved initial view, and the outcome would be a radical improvement over what Popper had to say.

Even more striking, for me, was my realization that I had rediscovered my great explosive idea of the summer of 1961: philosophy should be about life; the riddle of the universe is the riddle of our desires. But my initial idea had been radically transformed. It was no longer just philosophy which should be concerned with our problems of living, but the whole academic enterprise. "The riddle of our desires" had become "the profoundly problematic character of our fundamental aims in life, both personal and institutional, including even the aims of science". The outcome of generalizing aim-oriented empiricism to form a general conception of rationality, aim-oriented rationality, and then applying this to the task of creating a better world, was an entirely new conception, not just of science, but of academic inquiry, with implications for all of life. I have even written a long paper (never published) called "Science as the Methodological Key to the Salvation of Humanity," the basic idea being that scientific method, when accurately captured as aim-oriented empiricism and properly generalized to become aim-oriented rationality, is indeed the methodological key to the salvation of humanity.

Initially, I wrote up an account of my new conception of science: this was published as a two part paper called "The Rationality of Scientific Discovery".[2] In the winter of 1972 I visited Pittsburgh University, and lectured for three hours (my watch had stopped) on my new conception of science. During the visit I had a long debate with Larry Laudan about my new aim-oriented empiricist conception of science; he held onto his problem-solving view (but later published views which showed the influence of my ideas).

Back in England I finished a manuscript called "The Aims of Science" setting out my new view. After years being considered for publication by Macmillan's it was finally rejected. Then, in three weeks, to meet the publisher's deadline, I wrote my first book, *What's Wrong With Science?*,[3] which takes the form of a debate between a scientist and a philosopher, and is perhaps the most vivid and accessible account of my overall view. At last a more thorough exposition of the whole argument appeared in my second book *From Knowledge to Wisdom*.[4] This got some terrific reviews, in *Nature* for example, and one by Mary Midgley, and a few less terrific reviews, mostly from uncomprehending philosophers. In the book I argue that there is an urgent need to bring about a revolution in the overall aims and methods of academic inquiry so that, instead of just seeking knowledge, the basic aim of inquiry becomes to seek and promote wisdom—wisdom being the capacity, and the active desire, to realize what is of value in life, for oneself and others, wisdom thus including knowledge and technological know- how, but much else besides. This revolution would affect every branch and aspect of the academic enterprise. The social sciences would become social philosophy, or social methodology (rather than social science), devoted to promoting more cooperatively rational solving of conflicts and problems of living in the world. Social inquiry, so pursued, would be intellectually more fundamental than natural science. The natural sciences would recognize three domains of discussion: evidence, theories, and aims. Problems concerning research aims would be discussed by both scientists and non-scientists alike, involving as they do questions concerning social priorities and values. Philosophy would become the sustained rational exploration of our most fundamental problems of understanding; it would also take up the task of discovering how we may improve our personal, institutional and global aims and methods in life, so that what is of value in life may be realized more successfully. Education would change so that problems of living become more fundamental than problems of knowledge, the basic aim of education being to learn how to acquire wisdom in life. Academic inquiry as a whole would become somewhat like a people's civil service, having just sufficient power to retain its independence and integrity, doing for people, openly, what civil services are supposed to do, in secret, for governments. These and many other changes all result from replacing the aim to acquire knowledge by the aim to promote wisdom by cooperatively rational means.

Quantum Theory

Having set out the case for a new kind of inquiry, rationally designed to help us learn how to live lives of value, I then plunged into the task of trying to develop a comprehensible version of quantum theory. Quantum theory may seem a far cry from wisdom, but in fact there is a connection. My new conception of science holds that science presupposes that the universe is physically comprehensible; furthermore, it provides us with a rational, if fallible, method for the discovery of new fundamental physical theories. Quantum theory is bafflingly incomprehensible; furthermore, because of the failure to solve the quantum wave/particle problem, the orthodox version of the theory is couched as a theory about the results of performing measurements. Orthodox quantum theory (OQT) is silent about what is going on physically when no measurement is being performed. But this has the disastrous consequence that OQT consists of two mutually incoherent parts: a quantum component, and a component made up of some part of classical physics for a treatment of measurement. OQT is, as a result, ad hoc, disunified, vague, ambiguous, non-explanatory, limited in scope, and resistant to unification with general relativity (as I have pointed out in a series of publications on quantum theory). It struck me that the transition from classical to quantum physics might be, in essence, the transition from determinism to probabilism. If so, what needed to be done was to develop a decent, unified, explanatory version of quantum theory was to specify precisely, in quantum mechanical terms, when probabilistic transitions occur. Electrons, atoms, and other quantum systems are neither waves nor particles: they are a new kind of probabilistic entity I dubbed the "propensiton." Propensitons interact probabilistically, I conjectured, when new so-called "particles" are created, new bound or stationary systems, as a result of inelastic interactions. All measurements that actually detect quantum systems invariably involve interactions of this kind, to leave a record of what has occurred. My new propensity version of quantum theory is free of the above defects of OQT, recovers all the empirical success of OQT, and furthermore is experimentally distinct from OQT, although the relevant crucial experiments, difficult to perform, have not yet been done. This work is recorded in papers in the *American Journal of Physics, Foundations of Physics, British Journal for the Philosophy of Science*, culminating with a paper published in *Physics Letters A* in 1994. An account of the work is also to be found in chapter 7 of my book *The Comprehensibility of the Universe*.[5]

My Campaign on Behalf of From Knowledge to Wisdom

Over the years I have written countless papers expounding the basic thesis and argument of *From Knowledge to Wisdom*. I have given endless lectures expounding the idea in different ways, in the UK, in Europe, the USA, and Canada. Much has changed since *From Knowledge to Wisdom* first appeared in the Orwellian year of 1984, but we are as far away as ever from putting wisdom-inquiry into academic practice. As I see it, there is hardly any more important task confronting us, as far as the long-term interests of humanity are concerned, than to bring about the revolution in aims and methods of our institutions of learning, so that the basic aim becomes to promote wisdom.

In 1994, I took early retirement from UCL because of horrible things going on in my Department. I retired to be able to get on with my work. For a time I was a visiting Academic at the London School of Economics. I have published three books since retiring: *The Comprehensibility of the Universe, The Human World in the Physical Universe*, and *Is Science Neurotic?* The first develops further aim-oriented empiricism and, most important, shows how the problem explicating what the simplicity or unity of physical theories is can be solved within this framework—a problem even Einstein was unable to solve, although he thought a solution should be possible. The second book sets out to solve the problem of how our human world, imbued with color and other perceptual qualities, consciousness, free will, meaning, and value, can exist embedded in the physical universe. In this book, I put forward a suggestion as to how it may be possible to explain correlations between sensations and brain processes. The book also reinterprets Darwinism so that evolution gives a better account of how human consciousness, free will, meaning, and value have evolved in the physical universe. *Is Science Neurotic?*

argues that science is neurotic because it represses problematic assumptions, associated with the aims of science, having to do with the comprehensibility of the universe, values. and politics. It is not just natural science that is neurotic; social inquiry and the humanities are, if anything, even more neurotic (neurosis being interpreted throughout as a methodological condition that arises when aims are repressed or misrepresented). Academic inquiry as a whole is neurotic in that it seeks to acquire knowledge rather than promote wisdom. This book updates and further develops the argument of *From Knowledge to Wisdom*.

Conclusion

Has this forty-five year effort to develop and communicate the idea that we need institutions of learning devoted to helping us realize what is of value in life been worth it? I am not sure. So far, by and large, I have failed even to get the idea across, let alone get it accepted—let alone help get it implemented in academic practice. Scattered about in the world there are individuals who see things more or less as I do—who believe, as I do, that we need to devote reason to acquiring wisdom. But they, like me, struggle with general indifference and incomprehension. Of course, in comparison with thousands of others in my lifetime who have struggled on behalf of humanity, my life has been blessed. I have not been imprisoned, tortured, or executed as so many others have been. I have had the incredible good fortune to be able to explore the problems that have preoccupied me, and I have been able to earn my living teaching and writing what has emerged from my passionate concern to understand—to understand, above all, how we can learn to create a better world. There have been times of great joy and exhilaration when problems, long struggled with, are suddenly resolved in an apparent flood of illumination, and new vistas seem to emerge. I am inclined to agree with Einstein when he says "The most beautiful experience we can have is the mysterious. It is the fundamental emotion that stands at the cradle of true art and true science." The search for understanding can have its own rewards. Nevertheless, I have failed, so far, to get what I see as my simple, profoundly important idea across, and this induces an immense sense of failure and shame. It is, of course, a mistake to identify the value of a life with the value of some life-project. And who knows, what I have devoted so much of my life working for, may gradually come to pass, and humanity may acquire what it so urgently needs, rational inquiry devoted to promoting wisdom. Perhaps I should feel proud to be associated with the effort to bring this about. In any case, few of us, perhaps, know where what is of most value in our life lies. It remains a mystery.

Notes

[1] Philosophy of Science *no. 39, 131-52.*

[2] Philosophy of Science *no. 41, 1974.*

[3] *Brans Head Books, 1976.*

[4] *Blackwell 1984, 1987 & 1988.*

[5] *OUP, 1998, 2003.*

About the Author

Nicholas Maxwell has devoted much of his working life to arguing that we need to bring about a revolution in academia so that it comes to seek and promote wisdom and does not just acquire knowledge. He has published five books on this theme: *What's Wrong With Science?* (Bran's Head Books, 1976), *From Knowledge to Wisdom* (Blackwell, 1984), *The Comprehensibility of the Universe* (Oxford University Press, 1998), *The Human World in the Physical Universe* (Rowman and Littlefield, 2001) and *Is Science Neurotic?* (Imperial College Press, December 2004). He has also contributed to a number of other books, and has published numerous papers in science and philosophy journals on problems that range from consciousness to quantum theory. For nearly thirty years he taught philosophy of science at University College London, where he is now Emeritus Reader in Philosophy of Science and Honorary Senior Research Fellow. He has given lectures at universities and conferences all over Britain, Europe and North America, and has taken part in the BBC Programme "Start the Week" on Radio 4. His Web site URL, where more information about his life and work may be found, is: www.nick-maxwell.demon.co.uk.

Men are born ignorant, not stupid. They are made stupid by education.

Bertrand Russell

People do not like to think. If one thinks, one must reach conclusions. Conclusions are not always pleasant.

Helen Keller

Learning without wisdom is a load of books on a donkey's back.

Zora Neale Hurston

Failure is the key to success; each mistake teaches us something.

Morihei Ueshiba

The teacher is like the farmer or the physician. The farmer doesn't produce the grains of the field; he merely helps them grow. The physician does not produce the health of the body; he merely helps the body maintain its health or regain its health. And the teacher does not produce knowledge in the mind; he merely helps the mind discover it for itself.

Mortimer J. Adler

What gives us the wisdom to choose to look for wisdom in the first place?

M. Scott Peck

When the Founders [of the United States of America] wrote "life, liberty, and the pursuit of happiness," they championed a life of value, not just property. But what constitutes a life of value? And how is such a life achieved?

Bob Kenny

As both Aristotle and Thomas Aquinas insisted, wisdom is to be contrasted with cleverness because cleverness is the ability to take right steps to any end, whereas wisdom is related only to good ends.

Philippa Foot

We have a hunger of the mind which asks for knowledge of all around us; and the more we gain, the more is our desire. The more we see, the more we are capable of seeing.

Maria Mitchell

Men and women must be educated, in great degree, by the opinions and manners of the society they live in. In every age there has been a stream of popular opinion that has carried all before it, and given a family character, as it were, to the century. It may then fairly be inferred, that, until society be differently constituted, much cannot be expected from education.

Mary Wollstonecraft

Arrogance, pedantry, and dogmatism...the occupational diseases of those who spend their lives directing the intellects of the young.

Henry S. Canby

Real education should educate us out of self into something far finer; into a selflessness which links us with all humanity.

Nancy Astor

In much wisdom is much grief: and he that increaseth knowledge increaseth sorrow.

Ecclesiastes 1:18

When you make a mistake, don't look back at it long. Take the reason of the thing into your mind and then look forward. Mistakes are lessons of wisdom. The past cannot be changed. The future is yet in your power.

Hugh White

He bids fair to grow wise who has discovered that he is not so.

Publilius Syrus

Living a life that's true to my values equals bliss.

Jan Phillips

IF WE DON'T TURN AROUND NOW...

Jason Merchey

The following is a recounting of an experience and dream that was written prior to the Abu Ghraib prison situation, back in early 2003. Naturally, it was also written before global warming and terrorism had claimed so many lives—or drawn as much sand out of humanity's hourglass. My intention is to heighten your attention to the moral and practical matters that I think are very important—and usually "left to those in power" to grapple with and fix. My interpretation of the dream, and the facts I juxtapose with it are, of course, open to debate. Think of it like my own impressionistic painting—it's not realism, but I am painting an impression of a landscape. You might not like painting, or you might think my subject matter, style, or symbolism is amateurish. If you believe I am overdoing it, or misinterpreting my dream, or foolishly partisan, I welcome you to engage me in dialogue. If my parable does touch you, or compel you, or challenge you, then I will be pleased.

Jason Merchey

jason@valuesofthewise.com

While jogging at sundown one day in April 2003, I had a very moving experience, one that may indeed have bridged my conception of the spiritual and the worldly. My wandering mind juxtaposed my impression of American Indian culture, spirituality, worldview, and morality with the current state of affairs and mentality in European-American culture. I experienced a combination of seemingly coincidental events that struck me as conveying great meaning: that we may come to face a startling reckoning for our legacy and lifestyle. For even if my people were absolved of the historical and continuing mistakes and atrocities that cling to us—not the least of which being our disrespect of American Indians—it is ironic that we long for something that our myopic forbearers systematically stamped out or overlooked in their approach to indigenous people and ancient wisdom. If spiritual and moral fulfillment can be achieved in this millennium, it will undoubtedly be due to a quantum leap forward in Americans' individual and collective dedication to a life of value.

Gazing at the sunset in the distance while a compelling American Indian tribal song played in my headphones, and with the second war in Iraq ever-present in the news, I experienced feelings of both reverence and regret, appreciation and shame. Though proud of the positive aspects of contemporary culture and values, I lamented the displacement of American Indian philosophical and spiritual perspectives for dubious "progress" and "globalization." Western lifestyle has replaced a profound appreciation for the divinity of nature, overall respect for the planet, and true community with a mechanized, profit-driven, staunchly individualistic lifestyle symbolized by our reverence for currency and respect for SUVs. I like to eat cake as much as the next lucky person, but I think there is much that is distasteful and unsatisfying about our typical level of consciousness and conscientiousness.

The wind against my face, the beauty of the sunset, and my release of endorphins must have enhanced the emotion of the experience. After the uphill finish, perspiration dripping from my face and heavy thoughts on my mind, I yielded to the novel urge to get down on one knee and, looking at the multi-hued sky, offer: "I'm sorry." To do so was an unusual departure from my more cerebral, conventional, and admittedly materialistic lifestyle. In what I characterize as a "moment of clarity," I attempted to connect with the pantheistic force that has spiritually guided non-Westerners for centuries and to make a sincere statement about the fact that we have sometimes acted so very wrongly, motivated to a large extent by greed and dominance, perpetrated by ignorance and unnecessary violence.

Just then, in what may seem like a coincidence to an onlooker, a conspicuous black bird landed on a nearby tree branch. As an elder was chanting and drums were sounding in my ears, and as the wind slowly moved the bright clouds in the distance, the bird seemed to be infused with a supernatural element. Believing its appearance to be more than just happenstance, I felt a similar depth of meaning in the experience as I did when I offered my feelings of regret seconds earlier. Later that evening, I watched a movie I had purchased the day prior, one that explored themes of courage, reckoning, and dedication. I went to sleep, having sunk back into my relatively pedestrian and self-centered lifestyle.

I was jolted awake by a poignant nightmare. Though it is difficult to describe the emotion and intuition present in a dream to the awake person, I gleaned meaning from it and wish to communicate some of the content and what I think it symbolizes. It was a representation of mainstream culture's intellectual and moral ignorance, as well as inhumanity, which in the dream becomes our undoing; the beauty of America tarnishing due to its decadence.

My nightmare elucidated much about America that is not fulfilling our highest potential: elitism, unsustainable values, posh luxury, and an inauthentic and unspiritual lifestyle. It exposed selfishness, ignorance, and corruption. Its denouement was pain and death; I awoke with a gasp following an ominous image of familiar faces being forced to choke down a reckoning of dire proportions: white bodies twisting on a rope from the ceiling of their marble-tiled bathroom. It harkened back to the dark song, "Strange Fruit": "…black bodies twisting in the Southern breeze." Breathing heavily and staring wide-eyed at the ceiling, I flashed to an image of Donald Rumsfeld, apparently my mind's personification of the darkness that rests where power meets politics and money and subterfuge, his visage superimposed on an image of the vile Nazi concentration camps, another representation of how far we humans can stray from our potential for greatness.

My dream signaled my disappointment in the fact that we are the wealthiest people in the history of the world, yet so many of our fellow human beings—even our kin—have unmet needs, representing the chasm between what is right and what is expedient. Institutionalized racism, the corporate juggernaut that pollutes water and does Machiavellian cost-benefit analyses on human life, environmental degradation for profit, and the inadequate funding and nominal importance of our educational system are indeed moral transgressions clinging to all who commit or ignore them. The drug problem seems intractable because we are looking for solutions in the form of tightening borders and heavily punishing drug providers. It is ironic that at the time of this writing we are engaged in a short-sighted war to remake the world, and the man debatably elected by our flagging voting system described it using such polarized rhetoric as, "good versus evil" and "crusade." My nightmare appeared to foretell a frightening and arresting collapse of our optimistic vision of the future of the planet—at least the American version of that vision. Wide awake at night during an Orange Terror Alert, thinking of humankind's age-old desire to dominate and destroy, I heard myself lament: "We're going to hang."

The land of opportunity—which is also the land of the all-you-can-eat buffet, the suburban Hummer, and the so-called USA Patriot Act—has made greater strides than perhaps any other civilization, but obviously, we are failing to seize the advantage of our unparalleled power to do right. If hegemony is what we want—fine—let's be a juggernaut for magnanimity as much as for our strength. However, I'm not proposing the mythical morality of the 1950s, I'm urging a creative fusion of ancient wisdom with progressive thinking.

Ironically, it is a Navajo saying that warns, "If we don't turn around now, we just might get where we're going," which, incidentally, is a favorite quote of the Middle East expert Thomas Friedman. I don't know that we're headed for a cataclysm, but if the omen proves true, and we feel the incessant pull of the coarse rope around our tender necks, we will know. If we don't think of regret—of change—before the noose is tightened, it will be too late. It may be extinction, or it may be Big Brother watching. To me, the result is the same. Rome was mighty and self-assured, and then Rome fell; it elevated humankind in many ways, but it was as infamous for slavery as it was notorious for megalomania and expansionism. The highly moral person might even consider the continued dishonor that is inherent in the quintessential Roman and American ways of life to be a figurative failure, even if the latter succeeds in preventing the rest of the world from physically harming it or storming the Bastille, as the former failed to accomplish.

Distrust those who claim that more military equals more safety; it is absurd. Furthermore, the unconstitutional surveillance and legal procedures that mark the USA Patriot Act would make America's founding fathers book passage back to England and ask the forgiveness of His Majesty, the King. Holding prisoners in an isolated camp without judicial review or other basic protections is a glaring example of the United States doing what is expedient rather than what is right. I'm not soft on terrorism; I'm strong on justice and responsibility, and against our policies that justifiably anger the rest of the world. Others are not just envious or respectful of our enormity; they feel humiliated and insulted by it.

> If my dream's dark message comes to pass, Americans are either dying a slow spiritual and moral death, or we will experience a grisly one in the form of blazing shrapnel or agonizing smallpox.

If my dream's dark message comes to pass, Americans are either dying a slow spiritual and moral death, or we will experience a grisly one in the form of blazing shrapnel or agonizing smallpox. Should such a scenario as my nightmare startle one into consciousness, the one thing he or she is going to be clawing at—begging the anthropomorphic vision of God for—is one more chance; a chance to make things right. For those who are having difficulty breathing because of the rope supporting their body weight, any place along humankind's path will not be too late. Remember the time when Columbus preyed on the gold- and slave-rich "New World," or the era that gave rise to Hitler, and our complacency, while he dominated Europe until the megalomaniacal Japanese leadership joined him in aspirations of world conquest? Would we not want to be in that lab of the first person to invent chemical weapons in order to try and derail that sin of science? Maybe the expensive Crusades to "take back the holy land" from the benighted Muslims. The Spanish Inquisition. Japanese internment camps. Enslavement of man and animal. Introducing syphilis into unwitting human subjects to study the effects. Maybe the final moments lived by the murderous religious zealots who executed their ignominious surprise attack on innocents working peacefully on September 11. How about the subsequent decision to ignore that dire warning, and instead move with unprecedented power and funding toward impulsive, unilateral, polarized rhetoric and action?

We will feel regret as we remember the past as countless missed opportunities to act to bring about significant change in ourselves and our culture. Any place along the road would be fine to us, the dying; any deal we can strike, just to go back from where we now realize we were headed all along. Our protestations about how we "have no quarrel with whoever did this" will be moot. We will be begging our own version of a higher force to mercifully grant us just one cellular phone call to say goodbye to our loved ones—for we would realize, in a panic, that our plane has long been hijacked. Our complacency was one of the main reasons that jet airplane flew below our radar.

The message I am conveying through this true story and the remainder of this book is broader and more ambitious than a single opinion about one foreign policy decision. I could just as well make this point if a centrist Democrat were in the White House. Furthermore, if the spiritual significance of the events and nightmare I described seem unbelievable, or if I appear to idealize American Indian and non-Western philosophies, I urge you to consider them mere representations to awaken creative and skeptical thought processes. I hope that we as a people wake up before we get where we're going.

© Jason Merchey

About the Author

Jason Merchey is a philosophical thinker, author, speaker, coach, poet, blogger, Internet radio show host, and, facetiously, "the Wise Guy." He was born in Southern California, but don't hold that against him! Raised Jewish in a Christian area somewhere between Hollywood and Disneyland and Orange County, his faith in organized religion and America as an ideal society faded at about the time that he gained critical thinking skills and his parents divorced. Growing up, Jason liked to catch butterflies and bugs, swim in the pool, and build with Legos. He was particularly fond of placing a beetle in a Lego boat and floating it in the pool...

Jason graduated from the University of California (Irvine) with highest honors, was inducted into Phi Beta Kappa, and earned a Master's degree in clinical psychology from California State University (Fullerton). He then high-tailed it from Orange County to San Diego where he put in 3,000 hours practicing psychotherapy and family therapy. He learned many things from his clients, and had some thrilling moments. However, he became so intrigued and satisfied studying wisdom, values, and ethics that he created the enterprise Values of the Wise™ rather than practice psychotherapy and family therapy.

Jason has always been intrigued by philosophy, existential thought, and ethics. These interests—combined with an affinity for language, progressive goals, and a humanistic perspective—inspired him to research, collect, and catalogue quotations from thousands of the world's greatest citizens, activists, and visionaries. Through his books, blog, radio show, website, and seminars, Jason offers individuals and groups ideas and methods for experiencing broader and deeper levels of thinking. His work provides the opportunity to synthesize ancient wisdom with progressive ideals to assist others to live "a life of value." He believes that folks can create greater awareness and fulfillment by clarifying and living their own values, and that such wisdom is what is going to save us—as a nation and a planet. As part of aspiring to a life of value, he has an active recreational life, including hanging out with his three pets, playing disc golf, driving his convertible, riding his mountain bike, being in the sun, and enjoying movies and music. He is most recently pursuing photography.

We are an adaptable species and this adaptability has enabled us to survive. However, adaptability can also constitute a threat; we may become habituated to certain dangers and fail to recognize them until it's too late.

Christopher Hitchens

There is an obligation that comes with wealth and power to use it in the right way for the benefit of humanity and not for personal whims.

Rushworth Kidder

Politics does not have to be about money and power games. Politics is about the improvement of people's lives. It's about lessening human suffering and it's about advancing the cause of peace and justice in our country and in our world.

Paul Wellstone

The fight must go on. The cause of civil liberty must not be surrendered at the end of one, or even one hundred defeats.

Abraham Lincoln

Democracy is a breeze during good times. It's when the storms are raging that citizenship is put to the test. And there's a hell of a wind blowing right now.

Bob Herbert

Use your mind, your money, your activism, your vote. Even the smallest act can make a difference.

Julia Hill

A great civilization is not conquered from without until it has destroyed itself from within.

Will Durant

The cure for what we face today is very simple: ethics and integrity in business are matters of the heart. The only way to bring about real change is to change the hearts of men and women.

Stephen G. Austin & Mary Steelman

If today I had a young mind to direct, to start on the journey of life, and I was faced with the duty of choosing between the natural way of my forefathers and that of the ... present way of civilization, I would, for its welfare, unhesitatingly set that child's feet in the path of my forefathers. I would raise him to be an Indian! We learned to be patient observers like the owl. We learned cleverness from the crow, and courage from the jay, who will attack an owl ten times its size to drive it off its territory. Above all of them ranked the chickadee because of its indomitable spirit.

Tom Brown, Jr.

Difficulties are meant to rouse, not discourage. The human spirit is to grow strong by conflict.

William Ellery Channing

It takes a multicontinental cataclysm-instantaneous, catastrophic, widely spread-to shake the world from its self-absorption.

Charles Krauthammer

The only Reconstruction worthwhile is a reconstruction of thought.

Charles Victor Roman

George W. Bush is not the problem. Nor is the high-spending Congress that oils the war machine. I'm the problem. I need to figure out how to be a better husband, a better father, a better writer, a better teacher.

Colman McCarthy

People who know how much is enough have everything they want and need to live a life defined by themselves as fulfilling and meaningful. They have a purpose for their lives larger than simply meeting their individual needs.

Vicki Robin

Man may burn his brother at the stake, but he cannot reduce truth to ashes; he may murder his fellow man with a shot in the back, but he does not murder justice; he may slay armies of men, but, as it is written, "truth beareth oft' the victory."

Adlai Stevenson

MAGNANIMITY

FOSTERING LOVE

Tammy Metz

When people discover that I am a foster parent they most often react in one of two ways: "You're such a wonderful person for taking in kids!" or, "I could never do what you're doing!" In the five years we have been a foster family I have not come up with an appropriate response for either of these reactions. Because, you see, my husband and I do not take children into my home because of what people may think of us. In fact, the reason why we foster children today is not why we began in the first place.

In our minds we had a very naïve idea of foster care. We had constructed a fantasy world where each child who came to our home would be grateful to be there. They would thrive and prosper under our love and support. They would be better off with us. We would be heroes.

We were wrong.

Things didn't exactly turn out how we had imagined it. In fact, things went quite the opposite way. Foster children didn't want to be in our home. They were angry for being separated from their parents. And when they should have been angry at their parents, or caseworkers, they turned their anger towards those in their face every day: us. They were afraid to be in a strange environment. They wanted to go home to where things were normal even if normal meant abuse and neglect. Despite our efforts to love them just as they were, to provide consistency for possibly the first time in their lives, and give them every opportunity they could imagine, they still wanted home. And when the children would allow themselves to care for us, just a little, or when they would get comfortable in our home, they would begin to hate us and act out.

The parents hated us too—understandably so. We had never considered the parent factor. We hoped that parents would just disappear so we could do our job of parenting and creating a lovely world for each child. We figured out that even though parents, for whatever reason, could not take care of them, they still wanted their children. Even more, they didn't want us to have them. If the parents couldn't have their children, they certainly didn't want anyone else to have them. This was especially true if the children fared well in their temporary home. Many times parents have prevented real growth in the children who came to our home. We have battled more than our fair share of parent/child head games.

Even more surprising, the caseworkers assigned to our foster children were not the advocates we had thought them to be. Some workers didn't have a child's best interests in mind. Many worked for the system helping to keep government costs to a minimum. That meant that children would go home before their parents were ready. We vowed we would never bounce a child from our home to another because things got difficult. Sometimes, despite our efforts to work things out with a child, the caseworker would move a child. This is most prevalent with teenagers who can voice themselves. Because when teens get too close, they will often find things wrong even (if they have to make them up). Caseworkers give in and the child is moved. Other workers would send a child home early to avoid paperwork or a review. And sometimes a child would be sent home because of money. Government constraints on the amount funded to DSS trickles down to when a child is ready to return home. A good caseworker, we discovered, has the child's safety at heart. These workers seldom last long and often move on to other careers. This was a sad finding. We began foster care with the very best of intentions on the assumption that those in the system would be like-minded.

There are three kinds of foster parents. Those who do it for the money, those who foster to increase their own families by adoption, and those who just foster. It was a great surprise to us to discover that, at times, we fell into all three categories. Most often we took any child for any amount of time. We have had children for one month, one day, and one hour. If a child's foster family were going out of town we would do respite for that child. We have loved weekend babies, runaways, HIV-positive babies, and pregnant teens. Yes, we once or twice took in children for the money. But make no mistake, it did not alter our parenting and love for them. As we gained experience and as our family grew, we no longer have the luxury of fostering any and all. We are selective in who we take now because we do not want the care of those at home to diminish. Bringing someone new into the home disrupts the family. The children we take in now will hopefully all become adopted.

Not all placement agencies are trustworthy. Some advertise in newspapers promising prospective foster parents thousands of dollars to take in a child. We have been blessed by choosing an agency that honors foster parents and supports the whole family.

Foster care is painful. The stories of abuse sadden me. The children we get think presents equal love. We can never, ever match up to their parents. These children would rather be with an abusive parent than in a warm, loving, supportive, consistent home. Very seldom do children want to leave their parents. Sometimes it is the child who is the cause of separation and not the parent. It is very hard for parents to take responsibility for the actions of their children in these cases.

I hadn't counted on the worry. Once a child is with us, they are part of our family for the rest of their lives. We have always been concerned with our former foster children. Are they okay? Are they safe? Happy? Do they think about us? A perfect scenario would be that each child goes home to healthy, dedicated parents and that they forget all about our family and the time they spent here. The pain of separation is something we would not want them to carry with them. A foster parent's goal is to not be needed any more. We would take any of them back if they needed a home.

How could we be a part of something so crooked? Foster care was certainly not all I had imagined it to be. Where were the grateful children with nothing but love in their eyes? I wanted to call the whole thing off. I hadn't signed up for the dishonesty, deceit, and anger. At times, when things seemed hopeless and negative, when the system was winning, when we were tired of fighting caseworkers, children, their parents, we wanted to quit. But something happened.

Foster care changed us.

We discovered all too well what our weaknesses as parents were. We are imperfect. It takes a certain kind of person to withstand all the pain. But after the pain is the joy. We discovered what was important: the children. Even though they might not return our love, we could allow ourselves to be blinded by the unconditional love towards these children. Yes, we might get hurt. God places children in our home, and for however long they stay, they will know love. We pray that someday, they can look back on this time as a model for their own lives. Each one of our children have touched us and changed us. They are etched into our hearts forever. We laugh and tell their stories honoring the role they played in our family. And in doing so, we realized that our idealistic dream was not so unrealistic.

Some children were better off in our home, but many parents stepped up to their parenting role. The dedication to their children came though when they got the support they needed to be better parents. And not all caseworkers are bureaucratic. Many have a fierce dedication to the very best they can give the children. We were champions for them. We stood up for them at school, to lawyers, to caseworkers, and even to their parents. We were on their side because we were by their side.

Among all the difficult times were times of joy, the kind of joy that comes from being a parent. Watching children grow, being a part of their accomplishments both large and small. We have seen children overcome giant obstacles. We have wiped their tears and cried along with them. We have cheered for them and laughed with them. We have had the honor and privilege of being a part of their lives if only for a short while. Our family has been graced by adoption of three children who we can call forever ours.

And what a blessing our family has been! Each new child is welcomed not only by us, but also grandmothers, grandfathers, aunts, uncles, cousins. All our foster children have been greeted with an openness that is warm and loving. They are included in whatever family activity we have planned. No one is left out. Our church family, likewise, have been welcoming. We would not have coped without them.

None of our foster children really leave. We keep them in our hearts. We ask about them and want to hear of their continuing successes and and their setbacks. We aren't the parents of six children, we are the parents of fifty...and the list keeps growing.

> None of our foster children really leave. We keep them in our hearts.

Foster care has most definitely changed us. We thought ourselves uber parents; super heroes. We would be the ultimate protectors. We laugh now at how silly we were.

So when people say that they just couldn't be a foster parent I just smile. And as for being wonderful, we are not. We have made mistakes, and will continue to make them, but our love for children has not, and will not, changed. It is innate in us.

We are blessed.

© Tammy Metz

About the Author

Tammy Metz is the mother of six, wife of one, and foster mom of many. She schools, writes, organizes, quilts, knits, volunteers, taxis children, and cleans. In her spare time she just tries to keep busy. Tammy resides in Pueblo, Colorado.

Verily the kindness that gazes upon itself in a mirror turns to stone, And a good deed that calls itself by tender names becomes the parent to a curse.

Kahlil Gibran

We must remember that those mortals we meet in the parking lots, offices, elevators, and elsewhere are that portion of mankind God has given us to love and to serve. It will do us little good to speak of the general brotherhood of mankind if we cannot regard those who are all around us as our brothers and sisters.

Spencer W. Kimball

How do we figure out what makes an action good? By forgetting about what it accomplishes. Indeed, moral philosopher Immanuel Kant believed that the consequences of our behavior should never enter the picture. So long as our intention is pure, then our actions will always have true moral worth--even if they happen to yield unfortunate results.

Judith Barad

There is no need for temples; no need for complicated philosophy. Our own brain, our own heart is our temple; my philosophy is kindness.

Tenzin Gyatso

My motto is not, "Live and let live," but, "Live and help to live."

E. Christian Neilsen

Deeds of kindness are equal in weight to all the commandments.

The Talmud

In Nicomachean Ethics, Aristotle argues that living the good life - the life of virtue - is our most important human activity.

Judith A. Boss

When I give to the poor they call me a saint. When I ask for food for the poor, they call me a communist.

Dom Heider Camara

Some people help others on the basis of duty, but I also think there are many people who do it because they experience joy and richness in giving. It's paradoxical: In the giving of self lies the unsought discovery of self.

Stephen Post

The most powerful lessons about ethics and morality do not come from school discussions or classes in character-building. They come from family life where people treat one another with respect, consideration, and love.

Neil Kurshan

Humans are the only animals that have children on purpose, with the exception of guppies, who like to eat theirs.

P. J. O'Rourke

Let us renew our resolution sincerely to be real brothers and sisters regardless of any kind of barrier which estranges person from person. In this holy resolution may we be strengthened, knowing that we are one family; that one spirit, the spirit of love, unites us; and that our work together for a more perfect and more joyful life leads us on.

Norbert Caper

Put together the lack of belief that your relationship to God matters, the breakdown of your belief in the benevolent power of your country, and the breakdown of the family. Where can one now turn for identity, for purpose, and for hope?

Martin E. P. Seligman

Children never owe their parents anything. No one asks to be brought into this often painful, lonely, and absurd life. Parents owe children everything they have, as long as they live.

John A. Marshall

I was born in a poor family, but I had the good fortune of having a mother who gave my brother, my sister, and me hope from the very beginning.

Herbie Hancock

MORALITY

A MINISTER FIGHTS BACK ON MORAL VALUES

Robin Meyers

I am minister of Mayflower Congregational Church in Oklahoma City, an Open and Affirming, Peace and Justice church in northwest Oklahoma City, and professor of Rhetoric at Oklahoma City University. But you would most likely have encountered me on the pages of the Oklahoma Gazette, where I have been a columnist for six years, and hold the record for the most number of angry letters to the editor.

I join ranks of those who are angry, because I have watched as the faith I love has been taken over by fundamentalists who claim to speak for Jesus, but whose actions are anything but Christian. We've heard a lot lately about so-called "moral values" as having swung the election to President Bush. Well, I'm a great believer in moral values, but we need to have a discussion, all over this country, about exactly what constitutes a moral value—I mean, what are we talking about? Because we don't get to make them up as we go along, especially not if we are people of faith. We have an inherited tradition of what is right and wrong, and moral is as moral does.

Let me give you just a few of the reasons why I take issue with those in power who claim moral values are on their side:

When you start a war on false pretenses, and then act as if your deceptions are justified because you are doing God's will, and that your critics are either unpatriotic or lacking in faith, there are some of us who have given our lives to teaching and preaching the faith who believe that this is not only not moral, but immoral.

When you live in a country that has established international rules for waging a just war, build the United Nations on your own soil to enforce them, and then arrogantly break the very rules you set down for the rest of the world, you are doing something immoral.

> We have an inherited tradition of what is right and wrong, and moral is as moral does.

When you claim that Jesus is the Lord of your life, and yet fail to acknowledge that your policies ignore his essential teaching, or turn them on their head (you know, Sermon on the Mount stuff—like that we must never return violence for violence, and that those who live by the sword will die by the sword), you are doing something immoral.

When you act as if the lives of Iraqi civilians are not as important as the lives of American soldiers, and refuse to even count them, you are doing something immoral.

When you find a way to avoid combat in Vietnam, and then question the patriotism of someone who volunteered to fight, and came home a hero, you are doing something immoral.

When you ignore the fundamental teachings of the gospel, which says that the way the strong treat the weak is the ultimate ethical test, by giving tax breaks to the wealthiest among us so the strong will get stronger and the weak will get weaker, you are doing something immoral.

When you wink at the torture of prisoners, and deprive so-called "enemy combatants" of the rules of the Geneva Convention, which your own country helped to establish and insists that other countries follow, you are doing something immoral.

When you claim that the world can be divided up into the good guys and the evil doers, slice up your own nation into those who are with you, or with the terrorists—and then launch a war which enriches your own friends and seizes control of the oil to which we are addicted, instead of helping us to kick the habit, you are doing something immoral.

When you fail to veto a single spending bill, but ask us to pay for a war with no exit strategy and no end in sight, creating an enormous deficit that hangs like a great millstone around the necks of our children, you are doing something immoral.

When you cause most of the rest of the world to hate a country that was once the most loved country in the world, and act like it doesn't matter what others think of us, only what God thinks of you, you have done something immoral.

When you use hatred of homosexuals as a wedge issue to turn out record numbers of evangelical voters, and use the Constitution as a tool of discrimination, you are doing something immoral.

When you favor the death penalty, and yet claim to be a follower of Jesus, who said an eye for an eye was the old way, not the way of the kingdom, you are doing something immoral.

When you dismantle countless environmental laws designed to protect the earth, which is God's gift to us all, so that the corporations that bought you and paid for your favors will make higher profits while our children breathe dirty air and live in a toxic world, you have done something immoral. The earth belongs to the Lord, not Halliburton.

When you claim that our God is bigger than their God, and that our killing is righteous, while theirs is evil, we have begun to resemble the enemy we claim to be fighting, and that is immoral. We have met the enemy, and the enemy is us.

When you tell people that you intend to run and govern as a "compassionate conservative," using the word which is the essence of all religious faith—compassion—and then show no compassion for anyone who disagrees with you, and no patience with those who cry to you for help, you are doing something immoral.

When you talk about Jesus constantly, who was a healer of the sick, but do nothing to make sure that anyone who is sick can go to see a doctor, even if she doesn't have a penny in her pocket, you are doing something immoral.

When you put judges on the bench who are racist, and will set women back a hundred years, and when you surround yourself with preachers who say gays ought to be killed, you are doing something immoral.

I'm tired of people thinking that because I'm a Christian, I must be a supporter of President Bush, or that because I favor civil rights and gay rights I must not be a person of faith. I'm tired of people saying that I can't support the troops but oppose the war.

I heard that when I was your age—when the Vietnam war was raging. We knew that that war was wrong, and you know that this war is wrong—the only question is how many people are going to die before these make-believe Christians are removed from power?

This country is bankrupt. The war is morally bankrupt. The claim of this administration to be Christian is bankrupt. And the only people who can turn things around are people like you—young people who are just beginning to wake up to what is happening to them. It's your country to take back. It's your faith to take back. It's your future to take back.

Don't be afraid to speak out. Don't back down when your friends begin to tell you that the cause is righteous and that the flag should be wrapped around the cross, while the rest of us keep our mouths shut. Real Christians take chances for peace. So do real Jews, and real Muslims, and real Hindus, and real Buddhists—so do all the faith traditions of the world at their heart believe one thing: life is precious.

Every human being is precious. Arrogance is the opposite of faith. Greed is the opposite of charity. And believing that one has never made a mistake is the mark of a deluded man, not a man of faith.

And war…war is the greatest failure of the human race—and thus the greatest failure of faith. There's an old rock and roll song, whose lyrics say it all: War, what is it good for? Absolutely nothing.

And what is the dream of the prophets? That we should study war no more, that we should beat our swords into plowshares and our spears into pruning hooks. Who would Jesus bomb, indeed? How many wars does it take to know that too many people have died? What if they gave a war and nobody came? Maybe one day we will find out.

Time to march again my friends. Time to commit acts of civil disobedience. Time to sing, and to pray, and to refuse to participate in the madness. My generation finally stopped a tragic war. Yours can too.

© *Robin Meyers. The above was Dr. Robin Meyers' speech during the November, 2004 Peace Rally at the University of Oklahoma.*

About the Author

Dr. Robin Meyers is senior minister of Mayflower Congregational UCC Church of Oklahoma City, professor of rhetoric in the philosophy department at Oklahoma City University, a commentator for NPR, and a syndicated newspaper columnist. His latest book, endorsed by Desmond Tutu, is *The Virtue in the Vice: Finding Seven Lively Virtues in the Seven Deadly Sins* (HCI Books, 2004). His next book, *Why The Christian Right Is Wrong: A Minister's Manifesto for Taking Back Your Faith, Your Flag, and Your Future*, is due out in the spring of 2006.

Selfishness is the only real atheism; unselfishness the only real religion.

Israel Zangwill

We've all seen the sleazy crook, the Enron guy, the financial guy bending the rules. In our zeal to win, we don't see how our competitiveness is contrary to Christian values.

Drew Crandall

America is polarized about values. The Christian fundamentalists try to own the entire field, by saying that their opponents are immoral or unethical. But those who are not Christian fundamentalists simply hold different values.

Peter Singer

I observe God's Golden Rule: treat others the way you want to be treated. If you want healthcare, ensure that every man, woman, and child has healthcare. If you want a home to call your own, ensure that everyone in the United States has home. You want to have enough to eat, then you have to ensure that every person has enough to eat. If this sounds like Socialism, it is not, it is Christianity at its core.

Donna Reuter

My problem with the Christian fundamentalists supporting Mr. Bush is not their spiritual energy or the fact that I am of a different faith. It is the way in which he and they have used that religious energy to promote divisions and intolerance at home and abroad.

Thomas L. Friedman

The Christians are right: it is pride which has been the chief cause of misery in every nation and every family since the world began.

C. S. Lewis

The best practical advice I can give to the present generation is to practice the virtue which the Christians call love.

Bertrand Russell

The greater the ignorance the greater the dogmatism.

William Osler

If Jesus came back and saw what's going on in his name, he'd never stop throwing up.

Woody Allen

I think it's crazy for us to play games with our children's future. We know what's happening to the climate, we have a highly predictable set of consequences if we continue to pour greenhouse gases into the atmosphere, and we know we have an alternative that will lead us to greater prosperity.

Bill Clinton

To swallow and follow, whether old doctrine or new propaganda, is a weakness still dominating the human mind.

Charlotte Perkins Gilman

Instead of waking each morning and defining myself as an impotent war protester in an America run by oil-worshipping thugs, I started waking up and thinking, "Okay. What small thing can I do today with love?"

David James Duncan

For the first time in a long time, I feel a surging momentum to return to real American values, progressive values, our values.

Ralph G. Neas

Poets, priests, and politicians
Have words to thank for their positions;
Words that scream for your submission,
And no one's jamming their transmission.

Gordon Sumner

In a time of universal deceit, telling the truth becomes an act of rebellion.

George Orwell

My moral value is based on the Golden Rule "do unto others as you would have done unto yourself." My moral values would not allow me to vote for a man who obviously does not live by that standard, and has the gall to call himself a Christian.

Genevieve Riquier

MEANING

LIVING FOR THE MOMENT

Crystal Montoya

I was married in August of 2003, and nine months later, I become the proud mother of an eight-pound immature teratoma. On my wedding day, I had no idea what a teratoma was or that they even existed. My vocabulary in the last year has broadened extensively. According to information presented by Cancer Research UK, "immature teratomas are often diagnosed in girls and young women, often younger than 18. These cancers are rare. They are called immature because the cancer cells look like cells from a developing fetus."

The first time I read this I was disgusted, for I had just had an eight-pound immature teratoma removed (along with my left ovary) and was left with a ten-inch scar down the middle of my previously-attractive abdomen. I was a new bride, and looking forward to becoming a mother. Now, I had to go out shopping for maternity clothes because my abdomen was so "distended" (another new word) from surgery.

As you may know, the news of cancer is very difficult to process. At first I was in a fog. My first question when I met my doctor a year ago was,

"Would I lose my hair," not, "Will I survive?" In those first days it just didn't occur to me that I might not survive.

It was after I went home and started reading on the Internet that I had the revelation that I could actually die from this. I remember drilling my wonderful husband that evening to find out exactly what the doctors had said about long-term survival rates (another new term). I had been in such extreme pain that I ended up in a drug-induced fog; I don't remember much about those days in the hospital. Sadly, my new husband had just sat beside his beautiful new bride for over a week in the hospital. I was in surgery for over four hours while my friends and family were calling him to find out what was happening. He had also just been given the news that I would need five rounds of chemotherapy, and I was badgering him about my chances of survival.

After talking further with my doctor and reading more about it, I became confident that most teratomas are cured. After the initial shock of the possibility I would not make it, I decided I had too much to live for, and that I would be one of the majority who does survive. I had decided I was going to be strong and to continue with "business as usual." I even considered going to an out-of-town meeting a week or so after my surgery wearing the maternity clothes I had purchased. My doctor advised against it as he handed me a tissue; I just couldn't stop crying. I asked him if he thought I might be depressed, and we chuckled.

I was devastated and went through periods of great despair. I knew I would survive, but I got very angry that I even had to deal with this. I hated my new, deformed body. I was distended for what seemed like forever, maybe a month. It was a strange time because I looked pregnant, and sometimes I'd look in the mirror for a moment and sort of fantasize I was.

Thinking about such absurdities, I laugh a lot. I crack myself up! I'm sure some of the things I laugh at seem inappropriate to others, but I just don't care. Laughter makes me feel really good. Cancer is a disgusting disease and sometimes disgusting jokes are the only way to deal with it. I thank God for giving me a sense of humor because I'm not sure I could handle it without one.

I didn't like chemotherapy, and it didn't take me long to discover that working wasn't working for me. I have the most gracious employers, who have treated me with care and genuine concern, and so I did not *have* to work; I feel so fortunate in so many regards.

Chemotherapy sucked. I know, I know, it saves lives, and it's a necessary evil. The hospital, doctors, and nurses did everything they could to make it as comfortable as possible—and they did an excellent job. I had five courses of BEP. The side effects of these chemo drugs are amazing. I mean, it's an array of lovely things: hair loss, nausea, fainting, numbness in your toes and fingers, fatigue, loss of appetite, changing of skin, developing another cancer, and on and on. These are just some of the side effects I experienced. I had a bad attitude about chemo: I'd cry in the morning and refuse to go to the hospital like a twelve-year-old. I'd always go, though; I never missed a day. I went five days in a row for seven or eight hours, depending on who was counting the drips. I'd have two weeks off and then I'd go back for five more days. Five rounds.

The days I was in chemo I crocheted. I couldn't read—I tried, but would read the same sentence over and over and not be able to process it. It was almost like I could weave all my anger, hostility, disbelief and discouragement into this blanket and that way the negativity wouldn't smother what little positivity I could feel. Some days I just couldn't find anything positive. Those were productive days for the blanket! I gave that blanket to a homeless man.

During the weeks I received chemo, I would go home and rant and rave like a lunatic. The steroids they gave me turned me into a Tasmanian devil. I was tired and didn't feel great, but I couldn't sit still. I was rude to my husband, I cleaned and paced, I was crawling out of my skin.

Every Friday of a chemotherapy week, I would pass out and have to be rushed to the hospital. The first time, I passed out three times before my husband finally talked me into calling my doctor. I was dehydrated. They pumped me full of so much fluid while I was getting chemo, it was unreal. I would go home and drink four liters of Gatorade, and still I was dehydrated. The other factor in the passing out episodes was that it always happened either on the way to use the bathroom, or while I was in the bathroom. I would lose control of my bowels. Here was my sweet husband, essentially changing my diapers a year after he married me. The last time it happened I was sitting on the toilet and just fell over sideways. When I landed, my front tooth made contact with the hardwood floor and chipped half of it off. Off to the hospital in an ambulance I went for more fluid. I was laughing at this point; I was a bald woman with half a front tooth! I felt like I was dressed up to play a hillbilly. It was awful, but humorous too. Sometimes I laughed when I looked in the mirror, and sometimes I cried.

The week following the chemo week, I was on the couch, lifeless. I felt sick and tired and uncomfortable. I got addicted to the stupid courtroom shows like *The People's Court.* The following week, I didn't feel so bad and I might even go out for a walk or two, but I knew the next week I had chemo and had to start all over again. Some people say their chemo experience wasn't that bad; I hated every minute of it.

Being bald was hard for me, as I'm sure it is for anyone. I had always had gorgeous hair, and I didn't want to lose it. I cut it short, and then my husband helped me shave my head when it really started coming out. Luckily, I'm not one of the rare people whose hair doesn't grow back. I think that's the only extremely rare thing that could possibly happen to me that hasn't! My hair is back now, and looking back, I think I made it a bigger issue than it was. I had beautiful scarves and wore hats and actually had a couple men confess to me that they thought bald women were sexy.

My chemo ended in October; everything looked good and I went back to work. I was still tired, but felt fairly well. I even was starting to feel better with each day when, all of a sudden, I just lost all motivation. I had zero energy, and I was discouraged.

My ability to read returned and I started reading a lot more about diet, cancer, nutrition, massage, and anything I could to make sure I stopped the cancer from coming back. Cancer doesn't seem to make a whole lot of sense; there are obvious cancer risks like smoking, stress, and fast food, but having spent more than ten years working in the property management industry, I've met a number of people who survive on nothing but those things and they don't get cancer. *You didn't give yourself cancer and you can't control whether it comes back.* I have to tell myself that a lot, because otherwise I could let frustration consume me.

I was sort of obsessed with gathering information. The Internet is a wonderful tool, but you have to be a responsible information consumer; it's a whole wide world of different ideas and opinions. I bought every book about nutrition I could find, and read most of them. While I would be reading a book, I'd share some of the strange things they said with my husband, and I'm sure he'd wonder what kind of food I'd be banishing from the house next! Then I just sort of realized that there was an overall consistency that I found in all of these books; they all pretty much gave me the impression that if you eat stuff that comes from the clean earth and has minimal processing, you should be okay. Things like vegetables, whole grains, and fruit. I've also been sold on organics, and I even use organic shampoo and conditioner. So now, instead of obsessing, I try to stick with that, and when I cheat, I don't let it eat at me all day, so to speak.

I was in for my blood work one week in early January, and my doctor decided they should look at my bone marrow. They did a bone marrow biopsy and found an abnormality—another new word: myelodysplasia. Myelodys…what!? "What the hell is this?" I angrily asked. My bone marrow wasn't producing enough mature cells and my immune system was compromised. I hung up the phone after getting this information and cried. My husband reminded me that I needed to keep a positive attitude. I was angry with him for saying that; I thought I had had a positive attitude already.

I had begun to see positive changes that cancer had provoked in me, and though I didn't feel well, I still had humor, and laughed as much as possible. I could get in touch with compassion, and an overwhelming desire to get closer to my family and friends—to nourish those relationships and develop new ones. I love people and I have a renewed, stronger desire to do things that contribute to the greater good of people. I don't get frustrated at slow people when they cross the street anymore; I admire them for walking. I decided that careers are overrated, and that having fun should be an absolute priority. I know how lucky I am for being able to make that choice.

I then became absolutely in awe of the mind-body connection. I listened to some books on tape by Bernie Siegel, a surgeon who discusses the traits that survivors share—positive attitude and involvement in treatment seemed to have yielded the best results. I strongly encourage you to read or listen to the audio version of *Love, Medicine and Miracles* by Bernie Siegel, as well as his other books; I've read a lot of good stuff that I would recommend, but if you are a cancer survivor this is particularly good.

The material I was reading about my new disease indicated there was no cure other than a bone marrow transplant. Rare; if nothing else, at least I'm unique! I never thought I would be the subject of the word *rare* so much in my life. If it's all so rare, why do I keep getting it!? I had very poor lung functioning to begin with—rare at my age, even in smokers, which I was. I was diagnosed with a very large immature teratoma, which is very rare. And then I developed myelodysplasia—even rarer. One doctor in Seattle told me

I was the exception to the exception to the exception of the rule. Well, I guess I should feel special.

I'm not an extremely religious person, but I absolutely believe there is a higher power or stronger force, and I will refer to that as *God*. God has been at work in my life in a major way. He gave me my husband just in time; he guided me into moving to California; and he gave me all the support I could possibly need while going through such a horrible experience.

I researched and studied all that I could, I went to a specialist here and I went to Fred Hutchinson in Seattle. I got the same general opinion from everybody. I needed a bone marrow transplant. He went to work again with regard to my new myelodysplasia diagnosis. My only true siblings, who are the best possibility for a bone marrow match, were put up for adoption when I was very young. I'll be darned if God didn't make them contact me right when I needed them. I got a phone call, and to make a long story short, my twin brothers had found me. They didn't actually find me, it was a meddling girlfriend who made contact, but I thank God for her, and eventually one of the boys called me directly.

So there was my long lost brother, with no idea that I had even existed—not even sure if he's ready for a relationship with his biological family—and I have to tell him that I have a terminal disease and he and his brother may be my best chance for survival. It took me a month to make that phone call to ask him if he and his brother were willing to get tested. Of course they were, and they did. Mark ended up being a perfect match. Even today, Mark still has never spoken to me; he sort of freaked out about having his biological family contacted without his knowledge and just isn't sure if he wants contact with us. But he was a perfect match and willing to go through the procedure. The relationship that I have been able to develop with my other brother, Adam, has been one of the greatest gifts I've ever received. Adam and I talk almost every week now, and he's a really neat person.

I received a blood transfusion, and that was the just thing I needed to start feeling better. I also listened to that Bernie Siegel book, and one of the things that stuck out most from it was his suggestion to "act as if"...Act as if you have the energy to go for a walk; act as if you feel well enough to cook dinner, etc. I took this to heart because I found that if I acted as if I could do it, I actually could. My husband and I even decided to act as if we had the money to go on a cruise through the Greek Isles and we booked it!

So at that point, I was planning on going on our cruise and then coming back for the bone marrow transplant that is going to provide me a cure for myelodysplasia. Otherwise, it will probably kill me in five years or fewer. The experts all gave me about a 50 percent chance of surviving the bone marrow transplant. The one last test I required was the pulmonary function test to see if my lungs were strong enough to handle the chemo drugs and the transplant procedure. My lungs weren't strong enough. The experts revised the 50 percent chance they gave me; I had about a 5 percent chance of making it through.

I've been feeling well. I've been feeling better than I have in months and months, so I asked myself, *Do I want to risk what's left of my life now for a 5 percent chance of surviving?* That just didn't make sense to me, so my husband, doctor, and I decided not to. I really do feel great and I have decided to take every moment I have and get the most out of it while I can. We went on our cruise through the Greek Isles and it was amazing! I hope we'll be able to act as if we can afford to see the rest of the world!

My blood work results have been stable, and I seem to continue improving. I try to stay away from fast food, stress, and other risk factors, but I refuse to live terrified. I planted a vegetable garden and I'm taking some classes at college. Cancer has entered my world and I have to live with it. I can choose to dwell on it, or I can choose to enjoy the time I've been given without losing hope that something will come along that offers me a cure. I choose to enjoy my time, and for me, that means nourishing my relationships with my husband, family, and friends. The things that used to be important to me, like climbing the corporate ladder, making money, and looking great while doing it, are no longer important. I feel this is a great lesson I've learned while there is still time to put my energy into more fulfilling endeavors.

I haven't needed repeated blood transfusions as many people with MDS do. I have been using a drug to keep my white cells boosted, but other than that, I'm using good, old-fashioned healthy food, exercise, love, and laughter. Statistics say that this method will eventually fail me, and that I will start to need more transfusions and eventually this disease will be my end. But I just refuse to believe it, and certainly while I feel great, I'm not going to worry about it.

I still read a lot and think that educating myself is the first step to getting better, but I spent a lot of time dwelling on all of the things that could go wrong before and it didn't get me anywhere. Now I refuse to think about those negative outcomes, and it seems to be working for me. When you're given a prognosis that has a time frame attached it, it is easy to dwell on the number and convince yourself you only have *five years*. I think if you take that approach, the possibility of that happening is much greater than if you choose to be one of the people who defies the odds. I've decided to be one of those people. I can't say how that decision will pan out, but I honestly believe I'll be here in twenty years to tell you about it.

I am a very fortunate person. Some people do not have understanding employers, support systems, insurance, homes, or any of the blessings I have had, and they have to go through the same thing I have (or worse). Everyone has only wanted to help and has done everything they can. People have been so wonderful throughout this experience and that has been one of the things that has helped me get through it all. My doctors and nurses are amazing. I have an amazing support system. I am thankful to my husband for being here and for taking such good care of me. He is wonderful and such a blessing. My friends, family, and even acquaintances have been so overwhelmingly kind. I had so many flowers in my hospital room that I had to have my husband move them to the car because I couldn't breathe. I still get cards and letters from people. The kindness that I have received from people has changed my life. My best friend drove from Las Vegas to my house twice during my chemotherapy to clean because I just couldn't muster the strength. I vaguely remember calling my dad the night I got out of surgery and telling him I needed to see him…when I woke up the next morning he was by my bed, in from Seattle.

> I have decided instead to live each moment and to make the most of all the moments I have.

I don't know why I got cancer. It's not fair, and it has been an extremely difficult journey…I don't know what the future holds for me, and I'm not going to worry about it. I have decided instead to live each moment and to make the most of all the moments I have. I hope you are able to do the same!

© *Crystal Montoya*

432

About the Author

Crystal Montoya was born and raised in the state of Washington. She began her career in property management after obtaining her G.E.D. at the age of seventeen. Having spent eight years polishing her skills as a management professional, she achieved the position of Director of Marketing and Education in the property management industry. Crystal has always been connected to the great outdoors and has spent a lot of time hiking through the rain forests of the Olympic Mountain range. She met her husband at a work convention in 2003, and moved to San Diego to get married and continue her career in property management. She was diagnosed with cancer in May of 2004, and thus began a path of seeking more value and meaning in her life, and for the lives of those around her. Crystal currently cares full-time for her thirteen-year-old nephew and spends time volunteering and helping her friends and family as much as possible. She is twenty-nine years old.

When the body sinks into death, the essence of man is revealed. Man is a knot, a web, a mesh into which relationships are tied. Only those relationships matter. The body is an old crock that nobody will miss. I have never known a man to think of himself when dying. Never.

Antoine de Saint-Exupery

I never saw a man who looked
With such a wistful eye
Upon that little tent of blue
Which prisoners call the sky...

Oscar Wilde

Birds sing after a storm; why shouldn't people feel as free to delight in whatever remains to them?

Rose Kennedy

Life is ours to be spent, not to be saved.

D. H. Lawrence

The meaning of life lies in the chance it gives us to produce, or to contribute to something greater than ourselves.

Will Durant

I postpone death by living, by suffering, by error, by risking, by giving, by losing.

Anais Nin

The young man looks to the future, the old man looks at the past, but only the present is real.

Leonard Leeman

How far that little candle throws his beams! So shines a good deed in a naughty world.

William Shakespeare

Action is the antidote to despair.

Joan Baez

But the essence of being human is that, in the brief moment we exist on this spinning planet, we can love some persons and some things, in spite of the fact that time and death will ultimately claim us all.

Rollo May

What is life? It is the flash of a firefly in the night. It is the breath of a buffalo in the winter time. It is the little shadow which runs across the grass and loses itself in the sunset.

Isapo-Muxika

Don't be afraid of showing your feelings, be afraid of regretting it when you don't.

Laura Springer

One day, years from now, if the planet is still inhabited by frail humanity, few if any will remember you. Your life is but a grain of sand on a beach of time. So live! Read what you have written. Listen to wonderful music. Remind yourself often of your goals. Say, "I have been hurt, and I'm going to be hurt by others in the future in all probability, but one thing is certain - either I can live, or fail to do so. I can grab life by the throat and move passionately, or I can be a prisoner to fear of the future and regret from the past. I can make it happen right now, even as I feel my pain, or I can yield to anxiety."

Jason Merchey

What love we've given, we'll have forever. What love we fail to give, will be lost for all eternity.

Leo F. Buscaglia

Dying is an art, like everything else.

Sylvia Plath

He who has the courage to laugh is almost as much master of the world as he who is ready to die.

Italian proverb

INTEGRITY

THE ETHICS SCANDALS OF OUR DAY

Tom Morris

One of the most interesting features of the business landscape in the past few years, and one of the most notable occurrences in the general culture, has certainly been the sudden emergence of ethical scandals on a grand scale, across industries, and involving corporations of almost every size. Because of all this, increasing numbers of sincere people tell me they've begun to wonder whether big business has suddenly become corrupt all over America. At times, it's seemed like there's been a new scandal almost every week—with Enron, Tyco, Global Crossing, WorldCom, Adelphia, ImClone, Xerox, Arthur Andersen, and others suddenly appearing in the glare of the malfeasance spotlight, and then being eclipsed by the next corporate malefactor—and the list keeps growing. People want to know what's going on and why. Has ethics been completely left behind in the contemporary pursuit of profit? Has the world of business become a slick and sophisticated front for the indulgence of unbridled greed? And why, suddenly, now?

The Ethical Challenge Now

The first thing to understand is that unethical behavior in the world of business, like unethical behavior more broadly, is of course nothing new. In the sixth century, BC, the philosopher Anacharsis once defined commerce in a distinctively pessimistic way. He said, "The market is a place set apart where men may deceive one another." Two centuries later, his spiritual descendent Diogenes was famously spotted carrying around a lighted lamp, up and down the city streets, in the middle of the day. Asked what he was doing, he replied, "Looking for an honest man." By the looks of many recent business headlines, it can indeed seem that in corporate America these days, he'd be burning the midnight oil as well, stalking the corridors of some of our biggest companies in a perpetual search for his elusive quarry. At the root of all our current business scandals are simply the classic and perennial human problems of greed, overweening ambition, pride, and massive self-deception. People have been vulnerable to these things since there was human life on earth. It's not that top executives, middle managers, and even a few frontline workers have suddenly become morally worse in American business, but that conditions have become ripe for the worst to come out and have major repercussions.

It's interesting to note that human nature hasn't really changed at all over the centuries, but the world of business has. There have always been corrupt business people and there always will be. But there have always been good and noble business people as well, and this continues to be true at every level. The current scandals of unethical behavior don't prove that rogues and rascals have secretly taken over modern American business in just the last few years. There are still plenty of ethical and honest people running companies of every size in America. I meet them all the time. The interesting difference now is that many businesses have grown in size and complexity to the extent that their structures and processes can leverage good actions into great results and bad actions into truly terrible consequences. It's a matter of scale and power. Globalization, technology, and the complexities of our markets have created new ways for people to exploit the system and cover their tracks, at least for a time, while doing incredible harm. It isn't that, suddenly, our leaders are worse than ever, just that the bad ones can do more damage than ever before, and on a spectacular scale.

In addition, I believe that the dot-com bubble economy of the 1990s, that "irrational exuberance" leading to and in turn further exacerbated by all the skyrocketing tech stock prices also created a lotto-land mentality roughly equivalent to a new gold rush. Senior executives in large corporations could easily be tempted to resent deeply all those savvy tech guys in their early- to mid-twenties who were starting up dot-coms and getting very rich overnight. I believe the whole bubble economy created tremendous new pressures to move and shake outside the ordinary boundaries, and people in a hurry began to take new risks and try new and dangerous things beyond the normal accounting and growth practices that were a tried and tested path in those larger companies. But the new boldness and creativity easily slid into impropriety as people rushed to get their piece of the pie just as quickly as the dot-comers had.

A Philosophical Misunderstanding

There any other changes in recent times that have helped to create our current climate, changes in addition to those having to do with the issues of size, power, and pressure I've just mentioned. Most important of all, I think many people have forgotten what ethics is really all about. Too many smart people in the world of business seem to think that ethics is really just about staying out of trouble. The mindset is that ethics involves creating lots of rules, and then following them to the letter, while encouraging others to do so as well, in booklets and memos—and all for the sake of staying out of legal and public relations trouble.

> Unethical success is always self-destructive over the long run.

But ethics has never been mainly about staying out of trouble. The best philosophers throughout history have seen into it all much more deeply. They have believed that ethics is all about creating strength—strong companies, strong relationships, and strong people. Ethical behavior creates the foundation for trust, and without trust there can never be effective, efficient partnerships and collaborations of any kind. When people come to think that ethics is just about staying out of trouble, they can easily be tempted to accept any other way of staying out of trouble as a functional equivalent—covering their tracks well, maintaining deniability, and manipulating accounting rules in complex ways—and that leads to disaster.

As we're currently seeing, ethical companies are stronger companies, all other things considered. Unethical success is always self-destructive over the long run. How many companies have to implode before we'll get the message that the great philosophers have always been delivering? Unethical behavior may sometimes hurt lots of people, but it always hurts the doer of the deed. Plato loved to say that other people can harm us only on the outside; only we are capable of harming ourselves on the inside—through the unintended consequences of our behavior. And that's exactly what we're seeing in all this unethical conduct on the part of some corporate leaders. Too many otherwise smart and technically well-trained people are completely self-destructing because they just don't get the lessons of the ages about ethics and success.

And, by the way, it's not just in the corporate world. In recent years, we've seen prominent football coaches caught lying on their resumes, well known historians found plagiarizing others' work, priests and leaders in the Catholic Church doing things and allowing things completely at odds with all the values and beliefs they espouse. Why? Because of greed, improper ambition, desire out of control, excessive pride, massive amounts of self-deception, and other universally operative forces in human life. But these forces have been allowed to prevail in a number of prominent people's lives for a diversity of reasons, and none of them have fundamentally and distinctively to do with the unique nature of business, corporate commerce, or capitalism as an economic process. This is amply demonstrated by the occurrence of similar and equally blameworthy conduct outside the bounds of all these structures.

Self-Deception and Unethical Conduct

Let's think for a second about the power of self-deception. People sometimes do things they know to be wrong because they convince themselves both that there is great benefit to be derived from whatever it is, and that they really won't get caught. We've seen the power of self-deception operative in the life of a sitting president in the White House, and in more than one way. The most visible man in the world in the most visible and scrutinized place in the world gets himself to believe that he can do whatever he wants and he won't get caught. As many great thinkers have pointed out, we're all masters at self-deception. We fool ourselves much more easily than we deceive others. And if we hadn't already fooled ourselves, we wouldn't even try to hoodwink the others.

In big organizations, people often are tempted to think they can cover their tracks and maintain deniability, regardless of what they do. They sometimes think they can get their pile of gold and be gone before anyone notices anything wrong, and that, because of this, they'll be able to leave the problems to their successors.

Even in small companies, there are sometimes individuals who just can't resist the temptation to cash out big and get out quick, not thinking for a second how their actions may affect and terribly harm other people. It's a fundamental misunderstanding of business to see it mostly as a matter of getting rather than giving. I know it sounds naïve to say that, but it's still true. There is a universal, cosmic law in life—we get in proportion to what we give. It's only those who have a mentality of giving, who are seeking to create and contribute, who will themselves benefit long-term in deeply satisfying and sustainable ways. Anything else is just a bad mistake.

Military Metaphors and Moral Mischief

There is also a misconception abroad in the land that, in some relevant sense, business is war, or else is at least a highly competitive mental contact sport, and that anything permissible in war or football is perfectly okay in corporate life as well, aside from, obviously, shooting or physically tackling people. Deception in war, for example, reduces casualties, and in a football game can make all the difference for a first down or a touchdown. Craftiness has always been seen as a warrior virtue, like courage, persistence, and focus. The quarterback who fakes out the defense can be a hero. But deception in business, rather than reducing harm, can have the absolutely opposite effect, as we've just been seeing. Surprising the competition can be completely acceptable, and even advisable in business, but there are certain sorts of surprises that neither Wall Street nor Main Street likes to see. Many of the warrior virtues, such as courage and persistence, do indeed apply in important ways to business. But others don't. And it's a failure to see the difference that has brought individuals and companies down. Business is a creative, humane endeavor that, for all its competitiveness, requires a level of honesty, public openness, and accountability that should never be compromised for the sake of the game or the win.

The Elements of Ethical Success

I've discovered, in the works of all the great thinkers across cultures and through the centuries, seven universal conditions for success in anything we do. When we understand these universals, we have a new framework for understanding the importance of ethical character in business. Let me introduce them simply, and comment on each briefly. In order to facilitate success in any endeavor, we need these seven things:

(1) A clear **CONCEPTION** of what we want to attain, a vivid vision, a goal clearly imagined. This mental conception that guides our actions should be rooted in proper self-knowledge and itself be directed by what we know is right.

(2) A strong **CONFIDENCE** that we can attain our goal. We can't be supremely confident concerning what we know is wrong, or wrong for us. Proper goals allow for great confidence, and confidence facilitates success.

(3) A focused **CONCENTRATION** on what it takes to reach that goal. The most successful people tend to be those who learn how to divide and conquer, setting intermediate and more immediate goals in support of their vision. Again, this process should be guided by a concern for what is right and proper.

(4) A stubborn **CONSISTENCY** in pursuing our vision, a determined persistence. Little things add up, day after day. The number one cause of failure in our time is self-imposed, self-sabotage—people acting inconsistently with their own goals and values.

(5) An emotional **COMMITMENT** to the importance of what we're doing. We need to be motivated by the noblest possible sense of what we're doing. The interesting thing to point out here is that, typically, you can't get the deepest possible commitment to goals that aren't right.

(6) A good **CHARACTER** to guide us and keep us on proper course. Integrity and conscience—that inner guidance system reported since the time of Socrates—should direct our paths. Bad characters can have success for a while, in a limited domain, and at the expense of what really matters, but over the long run,

unethical success is always self-destructive. That's just how life works.

(7) A **CAPACITY TO ENJOY** the process along the way. The best people in any field are people who love what they are doing. If we don't enjoy the process, we're unlikely to get the results we want to see.

These are **The 7 Cs of Success** that should guide all our enterprises. When we leave one or more out, we always suffer the consequences. Too many businesses have been hiring for intellect and skill without considering deeply enough the issue of character, our sixth condition of success. And we're now witnessing the consequences. When we understand the role of character within the overall framework of conditions for deeply satisfying, sustainable success, we come to a new appreciation of the part ethics is supposed to play in life. It's deeply connected to success and excellence.

A Long Term Prognosis

I've long enjoyed saying that the worse things get, the more of an optimist I become. But I'd better explain that. People can tolerate incredibly bad situations—the human spirit is so resilient, so capable of putting up with stuff, and the power of inertia is so strong—yet when things get bad enough, literally intolerable, it's a wake-up call to everyone, and we start making changes that, typically, are long overdue. I believe that the avalanche of ethical scandals we've been witnessing in recent years will serve as a vital wake up call to a lot of people. I've already seen it happening. We need new rules. We need new ways of monitoring corporate conduct. We need new procedures for corporate boards and new compensation schemes for top executives. But more deeply, we need a new understanding of ethics – one that happens, ironically, to be an ancient understanding – along with a new conception of what business is all about. Many people in the world of business have had warm and fuzzy positive feelings toward the topic of business ethics for quite some time, but we haven't been clear enough on what exactly ethics is and what exactly we need. The crisis we're going through now will serve to help us clarify many things we've been far too vague about. The wisest people in history had perspectives we can use now, and that we obviously need. As a philosopher, I love having the chance to point people in the directions of the ancient wisdom that's out there, and that can be more relevant to our modern business needs than absolutely anything else. Can a new understanding of ethics rid the world of scandal? Of course not, but it can help us to build up new safeguards with a new and deeper motivation to see that they work. The best understanding of ethics is an inherently motivational understanding. We all want success. The ethical way is the only way to get it right and to have a chance of sustaining it for the long haul.

© *Tom Morris*

About the Author

Tom Morris has become one of the most active business speakers and advisors in America due to his unusual ability to bring the greatest wisdom of the past into the challenges we face now. A native of North Carolina, Tom is a graduate of UNC and holds a PhD in both Philosophy and Religious Studies from Yale University. For fifteen years, he served as a Professor of Philosophy at the University of Notre Dame, where he quickly became one of their most popular teachers. He is now Chairman of the Morris Institute for Human Values (www.MorrisInstitute.com).

Tom's twelfth book, *True Success: A New Philosophy of Excellence*, launched him into a new adventure as a public philosopher and advisor to the corporate world. His audiences have included a great many of the Fortune 500 companies and many of the largest national and international trade associations. He is also author of the highly acclaimed book If *Aristotle Ran General Motors* and the big yellow book often seen in college dorms nationwide the night before final exams, *Philosophy for Dummies*. Recent books include *The Art of Achievement, The Stoic Art of Living, Superheroes and Philosophy*, and If *Harry Potter Ran General Electric: Leadership Wisdom from the World of the Wizards*.

To date, no corporate executive has been sent away for life after being caught three times polluting a river or ripping off its customers. In America, we reserve that special treatment for those who happen to be poor or African-American or fail to contribute to one of our fine political parties.

Michael Moore

Changing the social and cultural fabric of our society will be no easy thing. A focus on personal freedom and material well-being is deeply engrained in our national culture. There is nothing wrong with these traits – except when they grow too powerful: rationalizing our worst impulses and dividing people from each other.

David Callahan

It dawned on me that the way I'd been running [the huge carpet manufacturer] Interface was the way of the plunderer – plundering something that's not mine, something that belongs to all creatures on Earth. And I said to myself, The day must come when this is not legal, when such plundering is not allowed. Someday people like me will end up in jail.

Ray Anderson

Now is an extremely important time. For no matter how evil the Earl of Dungsbury was back in 1250 AD, he did not have the capacity to ruin lives as fully or elusively as a corporations of today does. If offending corporations are not checked by the citizenry, we all lose.

Jason Merchey

Right is right, even if everyone is against it, and wrong is wrong, even if everyone is for it.

William Penn

...individual and institutional investors can deploy a host of strategies including social and environmental screening to promote corporate social responsibility and more enlightened financial markets through their investment decisions. The process doesn't create perfect companies any more than voting creates perfect candidates or charitable giving creates perfect non-profits. But it is still worth doing. Over time, it can have a positive impact on companies, markets, and society as a whole.

Joseph Keefe

FULFILLMENT

COME ON, GET HAPPY

Wes Nisker

I f we are going to create a more relaxed and harmonious civilization, we have to investigate this thing called happiness. What is it, and how do we all get some?

"Happiness is a fatality," wrote the poet Rimbaud. I remember being somewhat puzzled when I first read that line, and then feeling a sense of ease and liberation wash over me. Turning the idea of happiness on its head had suddenly made me happy.

I would guess that happiness has ruined many a life since it was invented, which may not have been so long ago. It is doubtful that our pre-historic human ancestors had any idea of "happiness," distinct from what it felt like to satisfy basic needs. If the wolf was not at the door and there was enough food around for a few days, your ordinary Mr. or Ms. *Homo habilis* probably was quite happy, even by our standards. He or she just didn't know it. Being happy wasn't an issue. It wasn't on anybody's to-do list.

Now, we all want happiness. The American Declaration of Independence even proclaims that all humans have the right to pursue it, which implies, of course, that happiness is out there somewhere, and, for some reason is running away from us. But as the Taoist master Chuang Tzu says, "My opinion is that you will never find happiness until you stop looking for it."

Even though I know better now, I still catch myself believing that I catch happiness and take it home with me. I keep recognizing, hidden beneath my plans and fantasies, the assumption that if I can just get a hold of whatever I feel is lacking in my life at the moment—an empty mind, enough money, a great house—then I will "become" happy. And live happily ever after. I might as well wish for a magic carpet, special potion, or power ring.

> I would guess that happiness has ruined many a life since it was invented, which may not have been so long ago.

Maybe we aren't supposed to be happy. Scientists have done experiments on the standard mammalian (that's us) brain and found that it is not built for happiness. It functions so that, as neurologist Melvin Konner explains, "...the organism's chronic internal state will be a vague mixture of anxiety and desire—best described by the phrase 'I want, spoken with or without an object for the verb.'" Surely you are familiar with that brain, having seen it up close and personal.

It could be that nature is simply not selecting for happiness in mammals because it isn't useful for survival. At those times when you are feeling happy you won't be on the alert for trouble, and therefore your life will be in jeopardy. So if you feel as though you are an anxious person, just consider yourself one of the lucky, well-adapted ones, likely to live a long, unhappy life. And if you're feeling happy, maybe you should start worrying more.

My definition of happiness has changed over the years. When I was younger, I defined myself as happy when I was engaged in an activity that stimulated my nervous system and made my heart beat faster. We used to call that feeling "a rush." I was happy, therefore, at rock and roll concerts where the high audio decibel levels automatically caused my blood vessels to constrict. Recently I had a rock and roll concert experience, and the feeling was mainly one of irritation and discomfort. I have grown to enjoy "the slows" a little more than the rushes.

I have often confused pleasure with happiness, especially when I was younger. Pleasant sensations can accompany happiness, but what we call pleasure is a particular experience of the senses, which usually includes some kind of intensity. Pleasure is the feeling you get when you step into a shower or a hot bath, or when you first bite into something that tastes good. If you ask yourself, you may not be particularly happy at that moment, even though you are having pleasant sensations.

The act of sex is one of the most pleasurable experiences we can have, no doubt designed that way by evolution to keep us reproducing. When we have sex, many parts of our being—the nerve endings in our skin, the pleasure centers in the brain, the psyche, and maybe even our genes themselves—are all standing up and shouting, "Yes, go baby go, this is what you are alive to do! Go forth and multiply!" But as many will know, you can enjoy sex and still be sad.

Happiness may look different to people with certain temperaments. The reclusive types will feel happier alone, while those with a gene for "novelty seeking" will be happiest when on a quest for a new experience.

Those who have a need to accomplish will feel happiest when busy with their work. As Camus wrote about the ambitious ones, "The struggle toward the heights is enough to fill a man's heart. One must imagine Sisyphus happy."

How do you know when you are happy? What exactly does it feel like? That question is similar to the one asked by the cartoon character Zippy the Pinhead, "Are we having fun yet?" What does happiness feel like as a physical sensation? What is in your mind when you are happy? The better question may be to ask what is *not* in your mind.

These questions arose for me when I first began to meditate, which also started to alter my definition of happiness. Strange as it now seems to me, I was twenty-six years old before I first had an experience of the inner contentment that I would now call happiness. Before meditation, I had never experienced such moments and therefore had no way to measure them against pleasure or other degrees of happiness. Oh sure, there had been some post-coital, post-meal or post-work moments, when I felt a kind of self-satisfaction, but that kind of happiness usually did not last very long. In meditation, for the first time I felt the happiness of being at ease; I was released from the compulsions of those most primal of instincts as well as my individually conditioned demands on the world.

The Buddha says, "True happiness can only be found by eliminating the false idea of 'I' or self." The deepest ease and contentment comes when we have stepped out of our personal drama, perhaps because it involves letting go of the survival brain, which is perpetually twitching with "I want," and "I don't want." Only when we are free of that primal push and pull can we feel the "true happiness" that the Buddha describes. Of course, if you are no longer identified with yourself when you are happy, then there is no one home to enjoy the condition. Damn, it's always something!

I am not happy. Happiness arises in me from time to time, often regardless of my attempts to cultivate it. If I were truly in charge of my emotional life I would be happy all the time, but it turns out that I don't have much say in the matter of my moods, only in my reaction to them. But the Dalai Lama says that the purpose of life is to be happy, so the pressure is on. I don't want to blow the whole reason for living.

There is another feeling, one that I would distinguish from happiness, or add to it, and that is the experience of awe and wonder. The feeling is the same one that comes from seeing towering mountains or great natural beauty or sometimes from walking into a cathedral or mosque, or when we are watching a film about the enormity of the cosmos. The experience is one of selflessness but with a little rush to it, and it sometimes requires some reflection before it kicks in. There is no fear or desire in the mind, but the moment's presence includes an openness and lightness, sometimes tinged with the sense of being part of a great mysterious unfolding.

After a time of experimentation, I now regularly practice awe and wonder, doing a meditation that I call "Be Here Wow™." It involves feeling the energies in my body and occasionally recalling that it is composed of one hundred trillion cells all working together, or that the sun's energy is continually being transformed into my life's energy, or that my brain, according to recent calculations, is processing eleven million bits of information a second. All of that, and I hardly have to lift a finger!

Another way of sitting in awe is simply to come back to my breath or the experience of my basic aliveness, and sense the deep mystery of this life that moves through me. What is taking place here has not been explained by scientists or mystics, or even the Buddha. We have figured out some of the physics and chemistry that distinguish life from non-life, and some of us have realized that the constituents of body, mind, or personality are not "I" or "mine," but we still don't know whose they are, or why they came about, or why we got this incarnation. Okay, ignorance is to blame, but who thought of that? In the end, life is still a mystery, and dropping any concept or belief about it, and just sitting with this pulsing body and this enigmatic power of awareness can be both a calm and thrilling experience. Now, there's another type of happiness for you to pursue. Be sure to put it on your list.

To tell the truth, I don't really even know whether or not I am happy unless I ask myself the question. In other words, it's not an issue unless I check in to see what condition my condition is in. When I do check in, sometimes I find happiness, but more often I would just say, "I'm fine." And how are you? I find that invoking awe is a powerful antidote to suffering.

© Wes Nisker

About the Author

Wes "Scoop" Nisker is an author, radio commentator, Buddhist meditation teacher, and performer. His books include *The Big Bang, The Buddha, and the Baby Boom* (HarperSanFrancisco, 2003), the newly edited version of his national bestseller, *Essential Crazy Wisdom* (Ten Speed Press, 2001), and *Buddha's Nature* (Bantam, 1999). Mr. Nisker is also the founder and co-editor of the international Buddhist journal *Inquiring Mind*.

For over thirty years, Mr. Nisker has worked in radio, first as a news anchor, and more recently as a commentator, during his career winning the Billboard Magazine, Columbia School of Journalism, and San Francisco Media Alliance awards for excellence in FM radio programming.

Mr. Nisker has studied Buddhist meditation for three decades with teachers in Asia and America, and for the past fifteen years has been leading his own retreats and workshops in Buddhist insight meditation and philosophy at venues internationally. He is an affiliate teacher at the Spirit Rock Meditation Center in Woodacre, California, and does regular workshops at Esalen Institute and other venues.

His web site is www.wesnisker.com.

One time I got a letter from a woman complaining about some people who had just moved in next door. There was a guy with long hair and a couple of women with short hair. It was clear from her letter that these were gay people, and she wasn't happy about having them move into her nice neighborhood. She said, "We're disgusted with these types. What can we do to improve the neighborhood?" My answer was, "You could move."

Abigail van Buren

Genuine happiness is a byproduct of living in a way that is supportive of human flourishing. It is tied to excellence. Happiness comes from discovering who you are, developing your distinctive talents, and putting those talents to work for the overall benefit of others as well as yourself.

Tom Morris

And from the discontent of man
The world's best progress springs.

Ella Wheeler Wilcox

Recommend to your children virtue; that alone can make them happy, not gold.

Ludwig von Beethoven

You are forgiven for your happiness and your successes only if you generously consent to share them.

Albert Camus

The first and indispensable requisite of happiness is a clear conscience.

Edward Gibbon

A trait that makes you good at your profession does not always make you a happy human being.

Martin E. P. Seligman

To truly serve, purpose must be connected to our unique authenticity. That is why money cannot serve as our purpose. It can be a goal, but not a purpose.

Lenedra J. Carroll

We deem those happy who, from the experience of life, have learned to bear its ills without being overcome by them.

Juvenal

If a man insisted on being serious and never allowed himself a bit of fun and relaxation, he would go mad or become unstable without knowing it.

Herodotus

There is the difference between happiness and wisdom; he that thinks himself the happiest man really is so, but he that thinks himself the wisest is generally the greatest fool.

Charles Caleb Colton

The only Zen you find at the top of the mountain is the Zen you bring.

Robert Pirsig

Give me the young man who has brains enough to make a fool of himself.

Robert Louis Stevenson

There is only one way to happiness, and that is to cease worrying about things which are beyond the power of our will.

Epictetus

To be compassionate, knowledgeable, and kind is to be truly wise.

Will Travers

Nature has a funny way of breaking what does not bend.

Anonymous

Be happy while you're living because you're a long time dead.

Scottish proverb

We act as though comfort and luxury were the chief requirements of life, when all that we need to make us happy is something to be enthusiastic about.

Charles Kingsley

SOROKIN'S VISION OF LOVE AND ALTRUISM

Samuel P. Oliner and Jeffrey R. Gunn

The Russian-born Pitirim Sorokin (1889-1968) was a maverick in the field of sociology.[1] His abiding concerns in the last decades of his life were that sensate society, indulgent and materialistic, had led humanity to a crisis point. Recently, some scholars and commentators lament the fact that we find ourselves on the brink of spiritual bankruptcy. Sorokin's vision that only altruistic love will result in human consensus earned him the derogatory name of "philosopher of love," or "Christian anarchist" by mainstream sociologists in the 1950s. These positivistic sociologists were in turn accused by Sorokin as giving too much weight to their scientific method as the only way of knowing. He accused them of "quantophrenia" and "quantomania," and of indulging in the exercise of "fads" and "foibles."[2] Sorokin did not dismiss the scientific method, but felt that sociologists and sociological journals were filled with quantitative research that ultimately signified very little. Similar to Max Weber, he advocated a type of insightful understanding, a logico-meaningful approach to explain human behavior. In addition, Sorokin dared to argue that value-relativity was an elusive product of an overripe sensate mentality and a root cause of the crises of our age. He further dared to take a position of value-advocacy. He was particularly insistent on the need for humanity to recognize and propagate the value and process of altruistic love. In our view, Sorokin was a visionary who has not only described his contemporary world, but also foresaw what we are experiencing currently. A glance at any newspaper, journal, movie, or television will quickly remind us that the symptoms of human degradation and separation are pervasive.

If we accept Sorokin's premise that our human relations are in a state of worsening crisis that can only be averted by an increase in altruistic love, and if we are concerned about the future of society, then the promotion of altruistic love becomes imperative. Successful promotion, however, requires effective understanding, and our understanding of altruistic love today has not advanced much beyond Sorokin's initial conceptualization. Contemporary theories of altruism and prosocial behavior miss the point of altruistic love, and contemporary research methods may in part miss its essence.

The purpose of this paper is twofold: to renew Sorokin's vision of altruistic love and to present research on rescuers of Jews in Nazi-occupied Europe[3] that supports that view, having uncovered many living examples of this love, compassion, and courage. We hope to show that Sorokin's conceptualization means more than contemporary theories allow and that its understanding requires more than contemporary research methods can adequately yield. We also hope to show through examples that altruistic love is a tremendous force, which, if unleashed, could transform the character of human relations.

Sorokin's altruistic love is ideally boundless. It originates within itself and extends out to the cosmos. It makes no distinctions; it embraces all. It is unconditional and undaunted by disappointment and failure. It is compassionate and caring; it hurts when others hurt and suffers when they suffer. It is endlessly giving; it reaches out in the spirit of care, justice, and compassion. It is ennobling and exalted; it represents the highest in human potential, historically achieved by Buddha, the Dalai Lama, Christ, Gandhi, Albert Schweitzer, Mother Teresa, and many of the rescuers of Jews in Nazi Europe studied by the Oliners.[4]

Contemporary sociobiologists who attribute altruistic love to genetic programming miss the point. Sorokin's altruistic love is not the automatic "love" of the drone bee for its queen. Sorokin's love originates within itself and emanates from itself. It is not the barest of human predispositions but the highest of human achievements.

Contemporary psychologists who attribute altruistic love solely to developmental processes also miss the point. Sorokin's love does not depend on developed brain physiology or on the ability to differentiate self from others. It is not a Hobbesian egocentric love that occurs when the interests of self become identified with the interests of others. Altruistic love is a giving, sacrificial love; it often involves the sacrifice of very important interests, possibly one's life. Such sacrifices can never be based or justified on egocentric premises. As he said:

> No logical ego-centered ethics can urge the individual to transcend his ego(s)...to sacrifice his interests. The major premises of such logic forbid any plea for sacrifice. If it does present such a plea, it becomes self-contradictory: "For the benefit of your egos and your ego-centered I; for the benefit of your egos you have to sacrifice their very interests; for the benefit of your personal life you have to sacrifice your life." The second parts of these propositions deny what their first parts affirm.[5]

Sorokin's love is a selfless love attained by the primal human capacity to submerge self and others into a greater whole. He says:

> Love...annuls our individual loneliness; fills the emptiness of our isolation with the richest value; breaks and transcends the narrow walls of our little egos; makes us co-participants of the highest life of humanity and the... cosmos; expands our true individuality to the...boundaries of the universe.[6]

Sacrifice is encouraged, not contradicted, by this love. The individual who accepts the ontological primacy of the Whole does not have interests or life; he or she has existence that is bestowed by the living Whole, an existence that cannot subsist apart from the Whole. Such individuals do not sacrifice interests or life; rather, they sacrifice subsistence for life of the Whole. "Love tends thus to destroy death and to replace it with eternal immortality."[7]

Sorokin's altruistic love cannot be fully comprehended by the scientific method, nor is it likely to be found in the contrivances and manipulations of the social sciences' laboratories. Sorokin eschewed the scientific encapsulation of altruistic love. Though he did use reason and observation to outline some of its contours, he argued that love could not be adequately captured or confined within a tidy conceptual scheme; to do so would be to lose its manifold essence. Citing P. Tillich, Sorokin maintained:

> I have given no definition of love. This is impossible, because there is no higher principle by which it can be defined. It is life itself in its actual unity. The forms and structures in which love embodies itself are the forms and structures in which life overcomes its destructive forces?

Martin Buber had a similar view about love. Altruistic love can only be distorted, not encountered or actively known by scientific analysis. "It is not the law that is afterwards derived from appearance but in appearance itself that being communicates itself."[8] Love is also positively associated with forgiveness.[9]

Philosophers, poets, and novelists have been concerned over the centuries with the processes called love and loving. Several reflected Sorokin's notion that in any genuine psychological experience of love, the ego or "I" of the loving individual tends to merge with and to identify with a loved "Thee" and that love is the justification and deliverance of individuality through the sacrifice of egoism. Both Aristotle and Plato suggested that love is a motivating force that gives incentive to justice and moral action. A number of philosophers have addressed the issue that the love by God toward humankind is agape, a kind of altruistic love, which is eternally powerful. Agape love, which some say is divinely inspired, moves human beings to care and help other human beings. It also implies sympathy and compassion and the non-separation between self and others, as Max Scheler pointed out.[10]

Rescuers of Jews in Nazi-Occupied Europe

The authors have discerned clear manifestations of altruistic love envisioned by Sorokin in a study by Oliner and Oliner, "The Altruistic Personality,"[11] in which they interviewed a sample of rescuers of Jews, bystanders, and rescued survivors in Nazi-occupied Europe. Samuel P. Oliner and Pearl M. Oliner and their associates interviewed almost seven hundred people who lived in Nazi-occupied Europe. The sample consisted of authenticated Gentile rescuers, bystanders (a group of people who did not engage in rescue even though some were asked to help), and a group of rescued survivors. During the Nazi occupation, the respondents had lived in Poland, Germany, France, Holland, Italy, Denmark, Belgium, and Norway. The study sought answers to three key questions:

1. Was rescue primarily a matter of opportunity, that is, a question of external circumstances? If so, what circumstances?
2. Was rescue a matter of character, that is, personal attributes and values? If so, what attributes?
3. Were those attributes and values learned, and if so how?

The Oliners estimated that less than one percent of the population of Nazi-occupied Europe was engaged in the rescue of Jews during the Holocaust period. The rarity of this activity is somewhat understandable in view of its extreme danger. The occupied countries were saturated with Gestapo officers, German soldiers, and local collaborators. Persons caught sheltering or otherwise helping Jews were subject to arrest, torture, imprisonment, and/or death. One rescuer reported what he witnessed:

It started before the war…I was in Germany, where I visited a family—a very nice family—that had two boys. One boy was gone every night. The mother told me, "He is in a club. The club is unbelievable." The boy was in the Hitler Youth movement. It was a secret. In the evenings the boys took lessons and then they got an animal—a rabbit or a pig or a mouse or a rat. He had to kill that animal. He learned to kill, and he learned to see blood.

Another rescuer said:

I saw how they killed…I wanted flour for the bread. It was so quiet there, after-wards, I just saw in the street so many people killed—Jewish people. I was scared. I was really scared. I told my mother what I saw. My mother told me, "You are lucky they don't kill you."

Yet another said:

> Personal contacts were dangerous. A friend of mine was hung in a
> cell with a chain around his wrists. They hung him on the ceiling just
> so far from the floor. Then they killed him. I don't know if you have
> heard of the "bath" treatment—they put people underwater in a
> bath to suffocate.

Most of the rescuers knew the risks they were taking, and yet most of them
persevered for long periods of time. They had to provide transportation,
construct hiding places, avoid their neighbors and even some members of
their families, procure food, forge identification papers, and sometimes lie
and steal to carry out their rescues.

They lived in constant fear of detection. Many of the rescuers and their
homes were searched. Some of them were arrested and beaten or tortured.
Some lost loved ones who were also engaged in rescue. In Poland alone,
2500 Gentile Poles lost their lives when they were caught hiding Jews and
other victims of Nazi extermination. A Polish rescuer said:

> The Germans caught me and almost beat me to death. They
> grabbed me and threw me to the basement. I opened my eyes and I
> saw the man hanging in front of me. I sat with him like that for
> almost one week.

Yet another said:

> The S.S. came and they killed my husband and one of the Jews. They
> came with a dog… My husband wouldn't say anything so they set
> the dog on him. It bit off his hand...Then the dog ran upstairs.
> We had the hiding place upstairs. They went after the dog and took
> my husband up. The guy, Farber...he was the worst S.S. He was sit-
> ting with me with a gun in his hand and he ran upstairs after the dog.
> Somebody was shooting upstairs. The dog had found the hiding
> place...My little girl was crying because she wanted to go upstairs to
> Daddy—because Daddy was screaming.

The rescuers included both males and females. They were from all occupied countries, from all social class backgrounds, and from all levels of education. The rescuers held a variety of religious beliefs, while some held no
religious beliefs at all. They ascribed to various political ideologies; some

were politically indifferent. They represented a broad range of occupational specialties and some were housewives or too young to hold any occupation at all. No gender, country, social class, level of education, religious belief, political ideology, or occupational specialty was predominant in the sample.

The rescuers reported having learned a number of values as they were growing up. These values tended to cluster around care, compassion, empathy, honesty, religiosity, social responsibility, risk-taking and industriousness. The rescuers were interviewed using an open-ended questionnaire that included attitude scales measuring empathy, social responsibility, religiosity, self-esteem, and social control. They were not singularly located on any of these scales. The rescuers reported a variety of reasons or motives for their actions, and some reported they had no conscious reason or motive at all. In comparison to bystanders (non-rescuers) in our sample, the rescuers scored higher on the empathy and social responsibility scale. They were typically more psychologically attached to their family as well as being able to extend their responsibility to diverse other groups and included them in the universe of responsibility. They exhibited sympathetic concern, justice, Christian duty and, in a number of cases, prior friendship. Over 87 percent mentioned the ethic of caring for diverse others as a reason for helping.

The rescuers did exhibit two commonalties, both of which were emphasized by Sorokin. Most of the rescuers reported having been raised in a warm and loving family environment, and most showed a strong sense of attachment to their family as well as an extension of this attachment to others such as strangers, foreigners, and Jews.

While we cannot gain an active personal knowledge of altruistic love outside of the being of that love itself, we can catch a glimpse of that knowledge from those who have acted and lived that loving and caring reality. The rescuers of Jews saved lives. We discern the altruistic love of the rescuers from their stories. We provide excerpts from three stories. The first is from T.W., who lived in the Netherlands during the war. She was married and had five children, all less than ten years old in 1940. She told us that her father was the most influential person in her life as she was growing up. "From him, we learned that we were very poor, but if somebody knocked on the door, he would always give a few pennies. He told us to be kind to all people. Never point the finger." She related the following story:

When we first were occupied by the Germans we really did not think too badly of it. We were young, and we did not know. They were very friendly. It came so quick...My girl friend came and said to me, "Tia, I got here a little girl. Her father was shot to death, her mother fled with her brother, and she crunched her in a closet." Then the mother said—and that struck with me—"Christians will come and help you, but don't cry."

J.D., the second of these rescuers, also lived in the Netherlands during the war. He was married and had two children. J.D. was a coal miner, and his wife was a housewife. He regarded his mother as the most important person in his life while he was growing up. From her he learned, "We were not allowed to lie, not allowed to steal...You had to help little children and older people when they needed your help. When you didn't, you were in trouble with Mamma." When asked about his rescue activity, he told us the following:

It all started right in the beginning of the war. The Germans bombed Rotterdam pretty badly, and they sent children out. We ended up with a boy about my daughter's age...In 1942 they knew that we had a boy. So in 1942 a lady came. She heard we had a boy from Rotterdam, and asked if we would mind having another boy. My wife said, "Sure, we can have another boy." She said, "But he is Jewish." My wife said, "Then I will have to talk with my husband."

I was a coal miner at the time...It was about midnight when I came home. We talked it over. I said, "Sure. They are little human beings. When she comes back tomorrow you tell her to bring the little boy." And so she did. The boy was about three and a half years old. They called him Bobby...My wife says, "I am glad we got this little boy and not somebody else."

Then he talked about his little sister. I...found out where his little sister was. She was only a year and a half. I...went to the people. I asked, "May I come with the little boy sometime and visit her." That was granted.

That was only one visit. It was a really beautiful to see how pleased these little kids were and how happy they were to see each other again. Right then and there I made up my mind. Them kids should not go apart from each other...So I came home and I told my wife the story. She looked at me and said, "I think the same as you

462

do but it's risky for you. You are the head of the household." I said, "If they are going to shoot me for one, we may as well do two. It's the same bullet."

The next morning I got the little girl...After that they were always together. They grew up together. That time was a difficult time because there were so many Dutch people who moved over to the Germans. You didn't know who you could trust any more. So we didn't trust nobody...

The last couple they brought us was an elderly couple...They brought them over at one o'clock in the night.

After we were free this gentleman came back to thank us for what we did. My wife had chicken soup and we fed those people some warm food. And they had to have dry clothes. About three-thirty or four o'clock I had everything washed and dried for them. I laid down for an hour and got some shut eye. It was a trying time but it was forty years ago and I was so much younger. When you are young you don't feel it so much. I never knew who was coming with who.

We had a kind of a knock that we knew who was at the door. I did not open up when I didn't know who it was. There were four or five people who would bring Jewish people for us to hide. Most of the time we had our two little kids as well as adults.

We went through the war that way. Sometimes when it was dangerous we got a warning from the police. I had a friend who was a policeman. He was head of the police, we never met. I knew him and he knew me. When there was talk about a raid he told a friend of mine to come and warn us...

One night when it became very dangerous my wife was in the cell of the police station with the children. A cell was the safest place they could find. We put them in jail!

The father was picked up right in the beginning and was killed. The mother was underground in Belgium or the south of Holland. A Catholic priest came with the mother...

A third rescue took place in Krakow, the ancient capital of Poland. For purposes of space, we shall abstract the story. In Krakow in 1942, the S.S. guards were leading approximately a thousand Jews out of the ghetto toward a railroad station for trans-shipment to Treblinka death camp. Many among the marching Jews, which consisted of men, women, and children, had a premonition that they were going to their deaths. One marcher among the Jews was a woman with a small, infant boy. In desperation, she was thinking of a way of saving her child, when she noticed a blond, young Polish Catholic woman standing on the sidewalk among the other Poles who were simply onlookers to this tragedy. The Jewess sneaked away from the ranks of the marchers and rushed over to the Polish, Catholic woman and said to her, "Please, please, save my baby. I know that they are going to kill us." The woman on the curb took this infant into her arms and took it home. She was neither married nor pregnant, so the neighbors were curious how she got this Semitic-looking child.

Shortly thereafter, someone among the neighbors reported her to the local Krakow police, which was the Polish police in the service of the Nazis. Soon a Polish policeman came and arrested her, with the child. He sat her in a large room that contained at least a dozen desks, behind each sat a policeman. The captain walked in, sat down in front of the desk, and said to the woman, "This is not your child, is it? This is a Jewish child, isn't it? Do you know what the penalties for hiding a Jewish child are?" The woman burst into automatic, genuine tears, pounded the desk, looked the captain in the eyes and said, "You should be ashamed of yourself. Do you call your-selves Poles? Do you call yourselves gentlemen?" Then her eyes traversed the room and she said, "There is one among you who has fathered this child and who is willing to stoop so low, who is such a vicious human being, that he would rather see this child labeled as a Jew and have him exterminated than own up his responsibility and paternity in this matter." The captain proverbially straightened his tie, cleared his throat, looked around the room thinking who might be the father of this child, and let this woman go.

Many of the dozens of rescued survivors that the Oliners interviewed were asked the question, "Why do you think your people rescued you?" They responded that the rescuers "did it out of love, out of caring, out of compassion, and could not stand by and see the innocent die."

The rescuers' stories provide examples of a love that is neither deter-mined nor selfish. It is a love that reaches out to care for others, even to those who are strangers. It is a love directed by conscious choice, a choice by persons who are both motivated and existentially free to do otherwise. The great majority of people in Nazi-occupied Europe did do otherwise;

most people did nothing to help the Jews because of their fear or their indifference to the pain of others.

A salient concept derived from the Oliner study is the concept of extensivity, which has its roots partially in Sorokin's work on the dimensions of love. The rescuers, as they were growing up, felt attached to their family of origin in a psychologically healthy way. Their relationships with their families and also others deserving of their love and care, were not simply empty abstractions but involved action, and these relationships resulted in the motivation to aid and save others, often strangers. The Oliners assert that extensivity consists of several dimensions, including attachment to family of origin, inclusiveness of others, care, and so on.

> If altruistic love is neither self-interested nor determined, then what is it, and where does it come from?

If altruistic love is neither self-interested nor determined, then what is it, and where does it come from? It is more than anything a state of mind, a state of mind that cannot easily differentiate or separate self from the Whole, and where separation does occur. It is a state of mind that prompts action to be taken for the good of the Whole rather than for the good of the self. It regards all people as deserving of love. They feel responsible for all people, not just friends and family members.

We do not know exactly where this state of mind comes from. Most of the rescuers were raised in loving family environments, where caring for others was common practice. And most rescuers were taught to be tolerant, to regard everyone in the same caring light. But these environmental factors alone do not guarantee altruistic love, nor does their absence necessarily preclude it.

While the definition of love is complex, we can clearly discern its positive consequences. As Sorokin argued, altruistic love may be the most important key to the survival of humanity. In recent decades social science has opened new fields of altruism and love to its exploration and use. The probing into the subatomic world and the harnessing of atomic energy are but two examples. Perhaps the latest realm to be explored is the mysterious domain of altruistic love. Though now in its infancy, its scientific study is likely to become a most important area for future research. The topic of unselfish love has already been placed on today's agenda of history and may become its main business.[12] We see the field of social psychology, apology and forgiveness, positive psychology, evolutionary biology, and other disciplines have become interested in the nature of goodness that may lead to a more caring world.[13]

The Oliners, in their altruistic personality research, suggest that we must teach and tell the stories of altruistic heroes because our young people should use these rescuers and others as moral role models. The understanding and disseminating of altruistic love is the most important item on the agenda today. Fyodor Dostoyoevsky was once asked whether we should fight evil with force or with humble love. Humble love, he argued, is the most powerful force in the world, and was the only answer to evil.[14] Just as love is important in the survival of newborn babies, so it is crucial for the survival of the planet. Altruism and altruistic love may be the antidote to war and human antagonism. This was precisely Sorokin's vision.

© *Oliner and Gunn*

Notes

[1] *For further discussion of Sorokin's scholarship, see Ford, Richard, and Talbutt 1996.*

[2] *Samuel P. Oliner, "Sorokin's Contribution to American Sociology"* Nationalities Papers, *4 no.2 (1976): 125-151; Barry V. Johnston,* Pitirim A. Sorokin: An Intellectual Biography, *(University Press of Kansas, Lawrence, KS, 1995).*

[3] *Pitirim A. Sorokin,* The Ways and Power of Love: Types, Factors, and Techniques of Moral Transformation, *(Boston, MA: The Beacon Press, 1954); Pitirim A. Sorokin,* Fads and Foibles in Modern Sociology and Related Sciences, *(Henry Regnery Company, Chicago, IL, 1956).*

[4] *See Oliner and Oliner 1988, and Oliner 2003, 2005.*

[5] *Samuel P. Oliner and Pearl M. Oliner,* The Altruistic Personality: Rescuers of Jews in Nazi Europe, *(The Free Press, New York,1998).*

[6] *Pitirim A. Sorokin,* The Ways and Power of Love: Types, Factors, and Techniques of Moral Transformation, *(Boston, MA: The Beacon Press, 1954).*

[7] *Pitirim A. Sorokin,* The Ways and Power of Love: Types, Factors, and Techniques of Moral Transformation, *(Boston, MA: The Beacon Press, 1954).*

[8] *Pitirim A. Sorokin,* Explorations in Altruistic Love and Behavior: A Symposium, *(The Beacon Press: Boston, MA, 1950).*

[9] *Martin Buber,* I and Thou, *(Charles Scribner's Sons: NY, 1970).*

[10] *Samuel P. Oliner, "Altruism, Forgiveness, Empathy and Intergroup Apology," 2005.*

[11] *Max Scheler,* The Nature of Sympathy: Sorokin's Vision of Altruistic Love as a Bridge to Human Consensus, *(Yale University Press, New Haven, CT: 1954).*

[12] *1988*

[13] *Pitirim A. Sorokin, Pitirim, "The Mysterious Energy of Love." Transcripts of lectures recorded by Campus World, Inc., 1960.*

[14] *Samuel P. Oliner,* Altruism: Intergroup Apology and Forgiveness. *(In progress), 2006.*

[15] *Joseph Allen* Matter, Love, Altruism, and World Crisis: The Challenge of Pitirim Sorokin, *(Nelson-Hall Company: Chicago, IL.*

References

Buber, Martin. 1970. I and Thou. *New York: Charles Scribner's Sons.*

Johnston, Barry V. 1995. Pitirim A. Sorokin: An Intellectual Biography. *Lawrence, KS: University Press of Kansas.*

Matter, Joseph Allen. 1974. Love, Altruism, and World Crisis: The Challenge of Pitirim Sorokin. *Chicago, IL: Nelson-Hall Company.*

Oliner, Samuel P. 1976. "Sorokin's Contribution to American Sociology." Nationalities *Papers 4 (2): 125-151.*

Oliner, Samuel P. 2005. "Altruism, Forgiveness, Empathy and Intergroup Apology." Humboldt Journal of Social Relations. *29 (2): 8-39.*

Oliner, Samuel P. 2006. Altruism, Intergroup Apology and Forgiveness. *(In progress).*

Oliner, Samuel P. and Pearl M. Oliner. 1988. The Altruistic Personality: Rescuers of Jews in Nazi Europe. *New York: The Free Press.*

Scheler, Max. 1954. The Nature of Sympathy: Sorokin's Vision of Altruistic Love as a Bridge to Human Consensus. *New Haven, CT: Yale University Press.*

Sorokin, Pitirim A. 1950. Explorations in Altruistic Love and Behavior: A Symposium. *Boston, MA: The Beacon Press.*

Sorokin, Pitirim A. 1954. The Ways and Power of Love: Types, Factors, and Techniques of Moral Transformation. *Boston, MA: The Beacon Press.*

Sorokin, Pitirim A. 1956. Fads and Foibles in Modern Sociology and Related Sciences. *Chicago, IL: Henry Regnery Company.*

Sorokin, Pitirim A. 1960. "The Mysterious Energy of Love." Transcripts of lectures recorded by Campus World, Inc.

About the Authors

Jeffrey R. Gunn, MA, conducted research at the Altruistic Personality and Prosocial Behavior Institute in Arcata, California, and is a lecturer in sociology at Humboldt State University and associate faculty at College of the Redwoods in Eureka, California. He received his BA in History and Political Science from Claremont McKenna College, and his MA in Sociology from Humboldt State University. His research interests include the sociology of good and evil, altruism, the Holocaust, and the relationship between transnational capital and the spread of American-style democracy and where those trends may lead. He anticipates obtaining his PhD in the near future.

Dr. Samuel P. Oliner (PhD, University of California at Berkeley) is Emeritus Professor of Sociology at Humboldt State University and Founder and Director of the Altruistic Personality and Prosocial Behavior Institute. Dr. Oliner was awarded Scholar of the Year at Humboldt State University. He is founding editor of the *Humboldt Journal of Social Relations,* and is the author and co-author of several dozen publications on the Holocaust, altruism, prosocial behavior, and national and international race relations. Among his books are *Narrow Escapes: A Boy's Holocaust Memories and Their Legacy* (St. Paul, MN: Paragon House 1979), *Embracing the Other: Philosophical, Psychological, and Historical Perspectives on Altruism* (Co-editor, Pearl M. Oliner. New York: New York University Press. 1992), *Toward a Caring Society: Ideas into Action* (Co-author, Pearl M. Oliner. Westport, CN: Praeger Publishing. 1995), *Who Shall Live: The Wilhelm Bachner Story,* (Co-author, Kathleen Lee. Chicago, IL: Academy Chicago Publishers. 1996), *Race, Ethnicity and Gender: A Global Perspective,* (Co-editor, Phillip T. Gay. Dubuque, IO: Kendall/Hunt Publishing. 1997), *The Altruistic Personality: Rescuers of Jews in Nazi Europe* (Co-author, Pearl M. Oliner. New York: The Free Press. 1998), *Do Unto Others: Extraordinary Acts of Ordinary People* (Boulder, CO: Westview Press. Paperback published in 2004), "Altruism Forgiveness, Empathy, and Intergroup Apology" (Humboldt Journal of Social Relations 29:2), *Altruism, Intergroup Apology and Forgiveness* (in progress).

Nor can that endure which has not its foundation upon love. For love alone diminishes not, but shines with its own light; makes an end of discord, softens the fires of hate, restores peace in the world, brings together the sundered, redresses wrong, aids all, and injures none. And those who invoke its aid will find peace and safety and have no fear of the future ill.

Jadwiga Angevin

Love and compassion are necessities, not luxuries. Without them, humanity cannot survive.

Tenzin Gyatso

We must learn to love each other as brothers or perish together as fools.

Martin Luther King, Jr.

Wherever there is a human being, there is a chance for a kindness.

Seneca

What is called sympathy, kindness, mercy, goodness, pity, compassion, gentleness, humanity, appreciation, gratefulness, and service - in reality, it is love.

Pir-O-Murshid Hazrat Inayat Khan

Let us understand that poverty, racism, unemployment, lack of education, drug addiction, inadequate housing, hunger, and isolation contribute to criminal behavior. Let us be compassionate enough to believe that people change.

Leslie George

In spite of everything, I still believe that people really are good at heart. I simply can't build up my hopes on a foundation consisting of confusion, misery, and death. I see the world gradually being turned into a wilderness, I hear the ever-approaching thunder, which will destroy us too, I can feel the suffering of millions, and yet, if I look up into the heavens, I think that it will all come right, that this cruelty will end, and that peace and tranquility will return again.

Anne Frank

The day you feel hopeless, horrible, and worse, on that day get out of your room and ask people, "What can I do for you?" That service you have done that day will bring a revolution inside you.

Ravi Shankar

MODESTY

AFFLUENZA AND THE MYTH OF THE AMERICAN DREAM

Jessie H. O'Neill

ffluenza is a dysfunctional or unhealthy relationship with money or wealth or the pursuit of it. Globally, it is a back up of the flow of money resulting in a polarization of the classes and a loss of emotional and financial balance.

That's the "formal" definition. On a personal level, affluenza manifests itself in many insidious and obvious ways. It's the inability to delay gratification and tolerate frustration; the "I want what I want, when I want it" syndrome. And by God, I'll do anything to get it…now. It's a false sense of entitlement that touches everyone from the rich, who want to believe they are better than the rest, to the poor and bitter, who believe that they are entitled to take and steal from the rich. It's the loss of future motivation felt by so many, whether they've inherited money and don't have to work, or have the financial challenges of just making ends meet and are so overwhelmed that any extra "motivation" to succeed is squelched before it begins.

The less obvious results of affluenza, of a country drowning in it's own materialism, is the outrageous number of folks on antidepressants, the increase in alcoholism and drug addiction, the need to medicate a growing fear that our lives are meaningless, marching silently and in despair to the cultural tune that assures us that our value as a human being is measured by the bottom line on our bank statement. We have lost sight of the fact that we are human "beings," not human "doings."

> The less obvious results of affluenza, of a country drowning in it's own materialism, is the outrageous number of folks on antidepressants, the increase in alcoholism and drug addiction, the need to medicate a growing fear that our lives are meaningless, marching silently and in despair to the cultural tune that assures us that our value as a human being is measured by the bottom line on our bank statement.

Accompanying the low-grade depression, there is frequently a loss of affect; we are no longer able to respond in an emotionally appropriate way to the normal stimulus of everyday life. We need more, better, louder, faster...Our external senses have become saturated and our internal is dying. Bombarded with media stimuli assuring us that we "should" want anything they advertise; that, in fact, we will only be acceptable if we have the latest car, house, jewelry, clothes, gadget, etc., we grow more and more despondent as the credit card debt and number of bankruptcies increase all around us and in our own families. We do anything and everything to keep up with the Jones', judging ourselves and others for what their lives look like on the outside, rather than the person they are on the inside. We are a throwaway society, using more than 70 percent of the world's resources on an annual basis. We have lost ourselves and our souls, the very essence of who we are, to affluenza. And we are exporting it to other countries as fast as we can.

On an even more personal level, why have I, and others like me, taken up the banner to cure affluenza? How did a "trust fund baby," a "spoiled brat," someone who grew up with "a silver spoon" in her mouth, come to find her life's work in fighting the battle against affluenza? I ask myself that same question often, and can only answer that somehow my life experiences lead me to a place that pushed and prodded me down this path that I am now on. There seemed no other way to go, if I wanted to live with myself. As the journey has unfolded, I am able to look back and say, "Of course! Who better than someone who was born into "the American Dream" to debunk the myth? I scream, "Stop! Don't make the accumulation of wealth your primary life goal!" There is little but emptiness, loneliness, and isolation at the end; and the bitterness that comes with the knowledge that the goal was hollow and meaningless and that in our headlong rush to get "there," we have often lost that which truly makes life worth living: family, friends, community, spirituality, a sense of giving, not taking, from the world around us.

My knowledge of the journey chosen for me began at the age of forty on the lawn of Goddard College in Plainfield, Vermont, where I was going to get my master's degree in psychology and counseling. My mentor and teacher, Ellen Cole, was asking me what my thesis would be on. Having been involved in the twelve step programs for many years, I assumed it would be about self-help of some sort and that it would eventually become a book— a lifelong dream since my undergraduate work in English and creative writing. When Ellen began to dig a little deeper, asking me to tell her more about myself, I found myself talking about my confusion around what I have since come to call, "The Myth of the American Dream" —that money buys happiness. I had watched my famous grandfather, Charles E. Wilson or "Engine Charlie," become President of General Motors and then Secretary of Defense under Dwight D. Eisenhower, and the subsequent misery, chaos, and compulsive addictive behavior among most of his six children.

Growing up in the limelight of this powerful and brilliant man, I had vacillated between bragging, hiding who I was, and feeling somehow ashamed of all that I was given, when others had so little. I knew I hadn't earned it, and therefore I felt that I didn't deserve it. I have since learned that many inheritors feel the same way; it is as though the shame comes with the money. As a result I had become a closet wealthy person, hiding who I was and trying to fit in with the rest of the world. However, on that fateful day at Goddard, I shared my confusion and pain with Ellen. I remember clearly saying, "I don't understand why everyone thinks that money buys happiness, in spite of the fact that every tabloid, newspaper, and news shows are filled with stories of the rich and famous who are miserable." I spoke of the divorces, alcoholism, mental illness, abuse, and just plain unhappiness that existed within my own family tree; how people seemed to believe that the money should solve all the problems, that we should be happy. How dare we complain of unhappiness or depression when we had so much? Although the money helped to solve, or at least hide, many of the problems, it also created a host of its own issues that the non-rich, and certainly my rich family, refused to acknowledge. I remember Ellen looking at me and saying, "There's your thesis and there's your book." We both got "God" bumps and in that moment *The Golden Ghetto: The Psychology of Affluence* was born. Five years later, my book was published by Hazelden Publishing and Education. During that time I evolved from private practice to doing a workshop called "The Grace of Money" to doing speaking engagements, family consultations, individual and phone therapy, live and printed media appearances, and expert witness work in multi-million dollar divorce cases. Who would have thought? Certainly not me.

Although affluenza, at first glance, appears to be about the very rich, it is really about our entire culture. We have built a house of cards on a false foundation. In order for a real cultural shift to take place, rich and poor alike must be willing to look at the fact that making money is not the panacea it's made out to be. Some of the wealthy have come to realize that the joy of money is in the giving and we have great philanthropists among us, and outpourings of incredible generosity from even the poorest among us, during times of tragedy and need. However, many folks still spend their entire lives believing that if only...They die thinking that the only reason they weren't happy is because they weren't rich. What a travesty. What a waste of human potential.

Even our financial system encourages us to accumulate money and hoard it. There is very little incentive for giving or letting the money flow as it should and could. Little value is placed on other forms of currency, such as time spent. We have created a never-enough mentality, never stopping to ask ourselves, "What is enough? And when we get there, what are we going to do with the rest to make a difference in the world?" We jump on the financial treadmill and run faster and faster, never questioning whether it's time to get off. We expect the wealthy to save the world and yet, we disparage them, giving them little to no sympathy for the problems they have; a reverse snobbism called wealthism.

The bottom line is that if we admit that they are unhappy or have problems too, in spite of their wealth, then where does that leave us? We must then examine the very premise that many of our lives are built upon. We must find a new American dream, that is based on the values of giving, not getting; loving and nurturing, not fighting and imposing; honesty and integrity, not manipulation and lying; cooperation, not competition.

The cure for affluenza comes from a gentle turning inward to reacquaint ourselves with our souls. It has never been, and will never be, about what we look like on the outside or how much money we have. It will always be about who we are on the inside; what makes our heart sing, what brings true joy to our lives and to the lives of those around us.

When my children were little, during the holidays we always adopted a family at the Sojourner Truth House, a home for battered women and children in Milwaukee, Wisconsin. We would take gifts, a tree, food, and whatever else was needed to make a happy holiday for these children and their families. When my oldest daughter, Rebecca, was twelve years old, she asked me if we could adopt a second family. She wanted me to use the money I would normally spend on her. I was touched and curious about what motivated her to offer up her Christmas. She responded that she "wanted to feel the way I felt last Christmas when that little boy said, 'This is the best Christmas I've ever had!'" I came to call that the Joy Response and I believe that it is the highest emotion that we can feel as human beings. And true to our addictive, pleasure seeking personality structures, we will go back again and again to that which gives us pleasure, be it drugs, alcohol, sex, TV, shopping, gambling and, thank God…the joy of giving. As parents, and friends of children everywhere, it is up to us to instill in our kids that knowledge. It is an experiential type of learning that can only take place by happening. Create opportunities for the children of the world to learn the Joy of Giving. Let them experience the Joy Response.

The pull of affluenza is strong, the myth of the American dream runs deep within our culture. It will take a major shift to stop the rampage of greed and the destruction of our environment, the loss of our biodiversity, and life as we know it. Affluenza is only one name, one way of naming the disease that is destroying us. I don't care what we call it. I only care that we defeat it.

© The Affluenza Project, www.affluenza.com

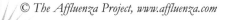

About the Author

Jessie O'Neill graduated Phi Beta Kappa with a Bachelor of Arts degree in English from the University of North Carolina at Chapel Hill and later earned a Master's degree in psychology and counseling. She is an entrepreneur, watercolor artist (JOVAGonline.com), and mother of two daughters.

As a result of extensive global media coverage of her research and professional work, O'Neill has emerged as the internationally-recognized authority on affluenza, sudden wealth syndrome, and psychological issues related to money. She is the author of *The Golden Ghetto: The Psychology of Affluence*, the definitive book on affluenza and how to better understand and reach the affluent.

He will always be a slave who does not know how to live upon a little.

Horace

Success has made failures of many men.

Cindy Adams

Do not store up for yourselves treasures on earth.

Matthew 6:19

The problem with capitalism is that it best rewards the worst part of us: the ruthless, competitive, cunning, opportunistic, acquisitive drives, giving little reward and often much punishment – or at least much handicap – to honesty, compassion, fair play, many forms of hard work, love of justice, and a concern for those in need.

Michael Parenti

It's strange, isn't it, that we can imagine solutions to global poverty - just as we can imagine the greatest buildings of civilization - but find that we can't "afford" them. Our imagination gives out when it comes to the simple matter of money.

Anita Roddick

People are only mean when they're threatened, and that's what our culture does. That's what our economy does. Even people who have jobs in our economy are threatened, because they worry about losing them. And when you get threatened, you start looking out only for yourself. You start making money a god.

Morrie Schwartz

Do not value money for any more nor any less than it is worth; it is a good servant but a bad master.

Alexandre Dumas

...our democracy, and I'm sorry to say this, in many ways is a democracy in name only. Big money now has so much control over the decisions in Washington.

Mark Hertsgaard

PROGRESSIVISM

MY WEIRD VALUES

Michael Parenti

S ince rather early in life I have been at odds with some of the mainstream values of this society. Which of us is the weird one? The dominant culture or I?

Take the fact that America has been described as a "car culture." The omnipresence of the automobile results from a national transportation system created and dominated by powerful oil and auto corporations. We did not ourselves create or choose this "car culture." Across the country in a score of cities, ecologically efficient, convenient, and less costly mass transit rail systems were deliberately bought out and torn up, beginning in the 1930s, by the automotive, oil, and tire industries. These corporations put "America on wheels," in order to maximize profits for themselves, with no regard for the costs to us and the environment.

I remember the people in my youth who used to talk about cars, comparing the different makes of automobiles, much the way men in earlier times must have talked about different breeds of horses. Misfit that I was, I did not join in because I never found automobiles to be cool or enticing. I always loathed their noise and stink and pollution and still do. And I hate all the danger and highway carnage caused by automotive vehicles, not to mention the endless pain of having to get the car paid for, registered, insured, serviced, repaired, fueled, parked, and dragged through perpetual traffic jams. I dislike the endless auto ads on television that portray cars as fast, devilish, beautiful, enhancing, and empowering, whipping around mountainous curves at homicidal speeds.

So is there something wrong with me and my values that I am so out of step with the car culture? I want high-speed monorails that can carry millions of people all over the country without injury and in great comfort, with less expense and minimal environmental damage.

There are other weird things about my values. I never thought it was important to devote my life to making large sums of money. And I was never interested in the more extravagant and elaborately gimmicky material goods that money can buy. However, while I disliked the preoccupation that some people had with making loads of money, I did always want to have enough money to get by. Coming from a poor family I knew that without enough money, an individual in this corporate dollar-driven society leads a life of constant anxiety, dreadful deprivation, and dangerous vulnerability.

I think there are a lot of people like me who want to live with some degree of comfort and security but who do not glorify vast wealth as some kind of great accomplishment. Now in my greying years I resent the idea of having to try to sock away large sums because there is no adequate communal system of human services and security in this free-market society. Eventually I will have to rely mostly on my own savings to survive. And if I get sick, I will have no health insurance other than Medicare, which does not cover everything and might eventually be taken away by the free-market reactionaries.

This is the way the social system is organized, forcing me and so many others into making "choices" that are not really choices of our own conception.

Here is another weird thing about my values. I never liked having to exercise authority over people. There are those who are enthralled with playing the kingpin and wielding organizational power over others. I never felt comfortable in that role, even though I am considered a strong personality and one who projects forth. When I do take the spotlight, it is to speak about urgent political matters. I try to become the instrument for a message of social justice. This is different from using the message as an instrument to project and elevate the speaker.

Whenever I have found someone kowtowing to me or deferring in some way for reasons having to do with that person's needs or vulnerability, I have never liked it. I taught at the college level for many years, and one of the nicest things I ever heard a student say to me was that I had a "democratic personality." She was referring to the way I was acting as faculty advisor to the student newspaper, encouraging the students to explore issues and make their own decisions, and supporting them when the dean started breathing censorship down their necks.

Lest there be any misunderstanding, I am not passing myself off as St. Frances of Assisi. I have a hot temper and my share of personal faults. But in the sociopolitical realm I don't like power for power's sake. I dislike power-mongers because they attempt to inflate themselves by diminishing others, and they have no dedication to social justice. Being hungry for power and privilege, they shine up to the powers that be, ready to serve the high and mighty as a way of advancing themselves, clawing their way up the greasy pole. It is what I call the Henry Kissinger Way of Life.

> I never wanted to live a life that was dedicated only to my self-advantage.

It was always an exciting thing for me to witness those occasions when people took things responsibly into their own hands in collective and coordinated actions, working together more or less as equals. I remember, during the Vietnam anti-war movement, watching young people organize to elect peace delegates to the Democratic Party state convention in Connecticut. I felt thrilled at how they planned for the tasks that needed to be done and acted in unison, operating with an unstudied dignity, with intelligence and quiet dedication. On other occasions I saw student protestors stand against state troopers with courage and spontaneous discipline. What a most beautiful and electrifying experience that always is for me, seeing people come into themselves, creating their own democratic impact, for one brief and shining moment taking control of their own destiny.

This gets back to another essential value. I never wanted to live a life that was dedicated only to my self-advantage. If this makes me a "do-gooder," I can only say, "Why is 'do-gooder' a term of scorn in the mouths of some." There are only two alternatives to doing good: 1) doing evil, serving the forces that do evil, and 2) doing nothing, living only for oneself in a narrow, atomized, hustling way, which sooner or later also serves the forces of evil.

Then there's the feeling I have long had about the environment. A half century ago, I used to be considered a little weird the way I worried about what was in my food and water. Well before it became fashionable, I began to have a concern for the environment and felt a connection to it. I was born and raised in East Harlem, an Italian working-class neighborhood, a street kid with no opportunity to cultivate a sensitivity to the natural environment because there was so little of it in New York City. But for some reason I do remember the few times I went into the countryside or to the seashore, and how I felt something come alive in me. How beautiful the natural world seemed to me, even though I was thoroughly addicted to the livelier city life.

We should recall what the level of environmental consciousness was a half century ago. When I was a young man in the 1950s, I would sometimes complain about the quality of the air in the city. People would smile patronizingly and say "What are you, a fresh air fiend?" Such was the quaint and monumentally ignorant expression of that day "fresh air fiend."

During the Vietnam War many of us were torn up about the death and destruction that was delivered upon Indochina by US forces. On one occasion I saw a slide show of how US planes and helicopters had sprayed tons of Agent Orange across the Vietnamese countryside, how a rich soil and fecund foliage were turned into a toxic moonscape. In this show there were no mangled bodies or burned villages, just ecocide, a bleached poison hardpan where once there had been living nature. It left me with a knot in my stomach and a weight on my heart. It was one of the most wrenching antiwar presentations I had ever seen.

Those who feel perfectly free to use Agent Orange in order to win a war are the same ones who, in times of peace, believe they have a right to all the earth's remaining natural resources, to use as they wish, transforming living nature into commodities and commodities into dead capital.

We hear the reactionaries mouth on about how they stand for values. They babble endlessly about personal values, family values, religious values, patriotic values, old-fashioned values of honesty and clean living, public service values, and all that. Yet their ranks are plagued with illicit scandals, unlawful scams, and massive corruption and corporate theft. They plunder the public treasure while posing as holier-than-thou patriots. And many beleaguered working folks, who need to believe that something in their world is right and trustworthy, give their uncritical allegiance to these "leaders."

These opportunistic, hypocritical value-mongers are no more honest and virtuous than anyone else. In many instances, they are far worse than the worst of us. They perpetrate monumental deceptions and crimes that most of us would never even imagine. They tirelessly tarnish their critics for being self-indulgent liberals and libertines who lack upstanding values.

But the truth is, if you are a progressive person then you have values, for peace and justice, for fair play, for environmental sustainability, for communal caring and power sharing rather than devoting yourself to plunder and privilege. Everyone has values, but ours are much better than theirs, not only because our values stand for far, far better things but because we really try to live by them.

© *Michael Parenti*

About the Author

Michael Parenti is an award winning author and activist who has published some 250 articles and 19 books, including: *Superpatriotism* (2004), *The Assassination of Julius Caesar* (2003), and most recently, *The Culture Struggle* (2006). For further information visit his website: www.michaelparenti.org.

Justice and freedom; discussion and criticism; intelligence and character - these are the indispensable ingredients of the democratic state. We can be rich and powerful without them. But not for long.

Robert M. Hutchins

Little progress can be made by merely attempting to repress what is evil; our great hope lies in developing what is good.

Calvin Coolidge

We can choose to use the wealth of our nation and the talents of our people for war, or we can use that wealth and talent to better the lives of men, women, and children in this country. We can continue being the target of anger and terrorism and indignation by the rest of the world, or we can be a model of what a good society should be like, peaceful in the world, prosperous at home.

Howard Zinn

When a just cause reaches its floodtide, whatever stands in the way must fall before its overwhelming power.

Carrie Chapman Catt

Laws and institutions must go hand in hand with the progress of the human mind.

Thomas Jefferson

When it comes to getting things done, we need fewer architects and more bricklayers.

Coleen C. Barrett

We must be active and positive about what can be done, or nothing is going to change. If we believe that nothing will change, it won't. If we tell ourselves we don't have power, then we don't have power.

Robert Reich

The greatest challenge of the day is: how to bring about a revolution of the heart, a revolution which has to start with each one of us?

Dorothy Day

Necessity is the plea for every infringement of human freedom; it is the argument of tyrants, it is the creed of slaves.

William Pitt

The millions of us who want to chart a different course for America must reclaim our power as citizens and overcome our doubts and fears - as well as the bad habits that have lessened our political effectiveness through the years.

Don Hazen

Now that the Soviets and the Nazis have disappeared from the world political scene, the nation's chief enemy, and by extension, the great enemy of Western civilization, is modern liberalism...

Marcus G. Raskin

The right-wing media tells us constantly that the problem with the mainstream media is that it has a liberal bias. I don't think it does. But there are other, far more important biases in the mainstream media than liberal or conservative ones. Most of these biases stem from something called "the profit motive."

Al Franken

The reporter, the editor, the producer and the executive producer all implicitly understand that their jobs depend in part on keeping their corporate parents happy.

Eric Alterman

A great civilization is not conquered from without until it has destroyed itself from within.

Will Durant

Throughout history, when the excesses of a corrupt establishment have gone too far, the American people have risen up and demanded reform of the political process to correct our nation's course.

Nancy Pelosi

SELF-CONFIDENCE

YOU ARE THE HELP

Jan Phillips

I pulled my car into the breakdown lane and grabbed my video camera. There was a flock of birds above Highway 194 that I couldn't keep my eyes off. There were hundreds of them performing a sky ballet that took my breath away. When I first looked, they were all white. Then they swooped down en masse, rolled over, and suddenly turned silver. When I looked again, they flew off in a new direction, and this time they all looked black.

Leaning up against my car hood, I turned on the camera and zoomed in on the flock. I had just focused in when I heard the sound of metal crashing into metal. Then everything became silent. I had one brief image of three things: my camera, my car, and myself flying through the air. Then everything went black.

When I came to, I was underneath my car, lying prostrate and facing the rear wheel. I lifted my head enough to see my outstretched arms and feared immediately that I was paralyzed. I tried to wiggle my fingers and was amazed when they moved. Then I tried my feet and my toes. They moved too. "I can get out of here," I thought. "I just have to shimmy out."

I tried to drag my body forward, but I couldn't move it. I was under the exhaust system, pinned to the ground, and the muffler was burning away my flesh. Now I realized I had to dig my way out. But it was high desert land, and with all my might, I could hardly make a scratch in the dry, hard dirt.

It was then I realized I was about to witness my own death. A great sorrow filled me at first when I thought of my mother, my family, and friends having to hear I was killed in a terrible accident. Next came the assessment of how I had done with the life I was given. Did I have regrets? No. Was anything unfinished, unforgiven? No. Was I proud of the wake I left behind? Had I done everything I could do to contribute my gifts? Had I given all my thanks to everyone I was grateful for? "Yes," I thought. "I did the best I could do. If there's anyone to report to, I'll be proud to report."

It was time then to let go, but how could I do this? I wanted to live. I started to fear, not so much the unknown, but the known coming to an end. Then I thought of what I'd heard about the Native American elders who went to the mountaintop when their time had come, and they calmly waited and peacefully released. And I thought about the Eskimos I'd heard of, who went off to lie in a drift of snow when they knew the transition was close at hand. "I can do this," I thought. "If they could do it, I can do it." And I closed my eyes, took one last deep conscious breath, and began to slip backward, into the silence, into the Source. I was going home.

Then I heard the frantic shouts, "Is anybody there? Is anybody alive?" Suddenly I was back under the car again. The voices continued to call, "Is there anybody there? Is anyone alive?"

"I'm here," I called back, in a voice barely audible. "I'm alive."

I heard the sound of running feet. "Where are you?"

"Under the car, by the back tire."

I looked up and saw their legs. Two men. "Oh my God!" they cried out. "Wait there! We'll go get help!"

"Don't go," I pleaded. "You are the help. Just lift up the car."

There was a terrible silence, broken by their fearful announcement.

"We can't! We need help!"

"Yes you can," I cried. "You can. Just lift it up...now."

And in one miraculous moment, they became the gods we are capable of being. They put their hands under the fender, and on the count of three, lifted the car as if it were an eagle's feather. Then two hands reached down to pull me out. They belonged to the man who had hit my car going seventy miles per hour.

The great gift that this event gave me was two-fold: first, it allowed me the chance to look at my life from a different perspective, to assess it as a whole and determine if I needed any mid-course corrections. Secondly, and most importantly, it taught me a great lesson—that we are the help.

> If I look at my life and find it lacking in adventure or challenge or joy, the solution to that is right inside me, dwelling as a potential, awaiting a decision, a decisive action.

When those men approached the wreckage, the first thing they experienced was their helplessness. They did not believe in their own powers and wanted to run off in search of help. They were caught in the story we've been told all our lives—that help is somewhere else, power and strength are somewhere else, the solutions are somewhere else, beyond us, outside of us. But when they heard that voice, "You are the help," some shift happened. Illusions dropped. Doubt was suspended. And in its place rushed a huge and mighty force, a new belief that rippled through every cell in their bodies and infused their beings with whatever strength was called for.

Whatever is needed at this time in history to right this world, to right our own personal and precious lives, we have these things within us. We do not need science and technology to save us. We do not need government and religion to save us. We do not need more information and faster computers to save us. What we need is to abandon our notions that solutions exist anywhere but in ourselves.

If I look at my life and find it lacking in adventure or challenge or joy, the solution to that is right inside me, dwelling as a potential, awaiting a decision, a decisive action. If I look at my business, my affiliations, my family and feel uninspired, unseen, or disconnected, the way to wholeness is inscribed on my heart, written on every cell in my body, waiting for me to look within and turn my ear to the Great Below.

No one becomes a visionary who does not first look within. And none of us can inspire another till we first learn how to inspire ourselves. Living a life of value means coming to grips with the power we have. It takes courage. It calls for reflection. It means letting go of the mediocre to create the magnificent. All those voices in your head—let them go like a bunch of balloons. Then remember those men coming upon the wreckage, thinking themselves powerless until they heard the voice coming up from below, and then lifted that car without a thought.

© 2006 Jan Phillips

About the Author

Jan Phillips is a multi-media artist, and an award winning writer and photographer. Jan recently completed a book entitled *The Art of Original Thinking: The Making of a Thought Leader* for The 9th Element Press. In this book, Jan describes the steps to becoming a thought leader, cites examples of thought leaders from all walks of life and discusses the impact of thought leaders in their workplaces, organizations, and communities.

Jan is the author of *Divining the Body* (SkyLight Paths, 2005), *God is at Eye Level, Marry Your Muse,* and *A Waist is a Terrible Thing to Mind.*

To realize the value of a minute, ask a person who has missed a plane. To realize the value of a second, ask someone who narrowly escaped a serious accident. Every moment of your life has value; make the most of your moments.

Holiday Mathis

Your spark can become a flame and change everything.

E. D. Nixon

Man is made or unmade by himself. In the armory of thought he forges the weapons by which he destroys himself. He also fashions the tools with which he builds for himself heavenly mansions of joy and strength and peace.

James Allen

Your future depends on many things, but mostly on you.

Frank Tyger

Commit yourself to being an example of the values you choose.

Richard M. Eyre & Linda Eyre

Go confidently in the direction of your dreams. Live the life you have imagined.

Henry David Thoreau

It is a very powerful experience to realize that there are choices—and that we can make them. It means that things do not have to continue along their current path; they can and may, but they do not have to. And, really, the choice is ours. But to choose in accord with our values, we must have good information.

Susan Meeker-Lowry

Even the smallest person can change the course of the future.

J. R. R. Tolkien

Skill and confidence are an unconquered army.

George Herbert

TOLERANCE

VILIFICATION AND VIOLENCE

Mark Potok

Are gay men and lesbian women "perverts"? Do they have "filthy habits" that lead inexorably to bestiality, incest, and prostitution? Are they intent on purposely spreading sexual diseases? Destroying Christianity? "Recruiting" youngsters in our public schools and "converting" them against nature to homosexuality?

The jihadists of the fundamentalist religious right say yes. These prominent Christian leaders, many of whom head gigantic ministries, are sure of it.

Moral Majority founder Jerry Falwell, who once raised funds off a "Declaration of War" on homosexuality, calls gays and lesbians "brute beasts" and says they are "part of a vile and satanic system [that] will be utterly annihilated."

Traditional Values Coalition founder Lou Sheldon, who once suggested isolating victims of AIDS in "cities of refuge," says they are "deviants" who "target children for recruitment" to gay sex, cross-dressing, and sex-change operations.

Christian Coalition founder Pat Robertson, who once warned of tornadoes and earthquakes hitting Orlando, Florida, if Disney World didn't cancel "Gay Day," says that allowing gays to serve in the military gives "preferred status to evil."

But science suggests these men are wrong.

The Straight Facts

Nothing in the legitimate scientific literature supports the notion that homosexuality is a "perversion" or a mental illness. The American Academy of Pediatrics, the American Counseling Association, the American Psychiatric Association, the American Psychological Association, the National Association of School Psychologists, and the National Association of Social Workers have all taken the position that homosexuality is not a mental disorder. It needs no cure.

> Even the notion that the Bible unswervingly condemns homosexuality is open to debate.

Similarly, there is absolutely no evidence—save the shrill and oft-repeated claims of the anti-gay movement's leaders—that homosexuals are more likely than heterosexuals to molest children. In fact, the best available science suggests that children raised by gay couples are no worse off, and in some ways may be better developed, than their peers in heterosexual households. The "studies" often cited by anti-gay leaders have been shown repeatedly to be based on junk science.

Even the notion that the Bible unswervingly condemns homosexuality is open to debate. Many scholars believe that several key passages actually are denouncing orgies and prostitution—or in the case of the town of Sodom, inhospitality—and not homosexuality. There are two Old Testament passages that do appear to condemn homosexual acts, one of them calling for the death penalty. But they both show up amid a long list of religious prohibitions, including eating pork and wearing mixed fabrics, that have been abandoned by almost all contemporary Christians.

Demonizing Gays

It's important for citizens to understand the religiously based crusade against homosexuals in America—a "thirty years war" that has intensified since the US Supreme Court struck down state anti-sodomy statutes in the

2003 Lawrence decision. Key points include the religious right's repeated use of bogus "science" and the bully-boy tactics of its leaders.

These leaders angrily rebut charges that their cruel name-calling—public descriptions of gays as "perverts," "child molesters," "deviants" and "evil" people—has led anyone to violence. They say they "hate the sin, but love the sinner."

That is a hard one to swallow. When perpetrators of hate crimes against gays use identical words to describe their victims, you have to wonder where it began.

When Lou Sheldon reportedly tells a journalist that if given the chance gay men will kidnap people's sons and convert them to gay sex, it's hard not to recall the infamous "blood libel" against the Jews—the accusation that Jews kidnap Gentile children, kill them and drain them of blood to be used in making matzohs.

When religious leaders describe gays as voracious sexual beasts trying to "recruit" in the schools, it's difficult to forget the way that nineteenth-century racists ranted about "lust-crazed" and "demonic" black men intent on raping white women.

Fundamentalist Christians have every right to their views of religion. But when they use that right to launch vicious personal attacks on an entire group based on characteristics that most scientists see as immutable, they poison the political debate and subject the objects of their scorn to the very real possibility of violence and even death. And that can only damage a healthy democratic society.

© Mark Potok

About the Author

As director of the Southern Poverty Law Center's Intelligence Project and editor of its award-winning *Intelligence Report* magazine, Mark Potok leads one of the most highly regarded operations monitoring the extreme right in the world today. In addition to editing the magazine, Potok acts as a key spokesman for the SPLC, a well-known civil rights organization based in Alabama, and has testified before the Senate, the United Nations High Commission on Human Rights, and in other venues. Before coming to SPLC in 1997, Potok spent almost twenty years as an award-winning reporter at newspapers including *USA Today*, the *Dallas Times Herald,* and *The Miami Herald*. While at *USA Today*, he covered the 1993 siege in Waco, the rise of militias, the 1995 Oklahoma City bombing and the trial of Timothy McVeigh. In 1996, his editors nominated him for a Pulitzer Prize for a series of stories on racism in Texas public housing. In his current position, Potok is regularly quoted by major media, scholars, and book authors in both the United States and abroad.

In modern humanism one finds a philosophy or religion that is in tune with modern knowledge, is inspiring, socially conscious, and personally meaningful. It is not only the thinking person's outlook, but that of the feeling person as well, for it has inspired the arts as much as it has the sciences, philanthropy as much as critique. And even in critique it is tolerant, defending the rights of all people to choose other ways, to speak and to write freely, to live their lives according to their own lights.

Frederick Edwords

We have just enough religion to make us hate, but not enough to make us love one another.

Jonathan Swift

Live and let live.

Dutch proverb

Self-confidence must be handled with some care, for it is either one's greatest asset or worst weakness.

John A. Marshall

It may well be that the soundest ethical basis for tolerance is to be found not in organized religion but in humanistic respect for others and their right to express themselves freely, so long as their expression does not harm other individuals or society.

Robert P. Ellis

The capacity for getting along with our neighbor depends to a large extent on the capacity for getting along with ourselves. The self-respecting individual will try to be as tolerant of his neighbor's shortcomings as he is of his own.

John Godfrey Saxe

True patriotism hates injustice in its own land more than anywhere else.

Clarence Darrow

America is a mix of every people in the world. What we are fixed by are our ideals. That's basically what America is. We are a set of principles. If we lose sight of those principles, then we lose sight of America.

Charles Swift

DEVELOPMENT

SOME THOUGHTS ON PARENTING

Marianne Preger-Simon

Love Without Strings

One day, my two-year-old granddaughter was heard talking to herself about herself: Touching each of her arms, she said: "This arm is named Love and that arm is named Scrumptious."

Where did such sentiments come from? They came from her sense of being just right the way she was, of being loved in every inch of her being. That is the feeling that comes from being loved unconditionally—the fertile soil in which children grow strong and sturdy, and in which adults also thrive.

Unconditional love doesn't mean a lack of standards or values, nor does it mean, "Anything goes."

It simply means, "No matter what, I love you. You don't need a different face or body or personality or higher grades or to become a doctor or a concert pianist, in order for me to love you. I love who you are (not who I wish you were) and I'm on your side. I will do all I can to help you become everything you can be, and want to be."

Looking and Listening

Newborn infants and their mothers look at each other a great deal of the time and listen to each other's voices. It's how they get to know each other. The infant soon recognizes her mother's face and voice, and the mother soon begins to decipher the meaning of the baby's different cries. These are all very instinctive responses, and help to create the bond between mother and child.

One of the things that is so irresistible about babies and young children is the wide-open way they have of looking at whomever comes into view. They have vast amounts of attention to focus on everyone and everything— that's how they learn so much, so quickly.

However, because we have more and more things pulling at our attention as we grow older, many of us have a harder time listening in a focused way than our young children do. So we need to be consciously intentional about our looking and listening, and reflective about what we are learning.

The Stamp of Legitimacy

Katya is three weeks old. She is lying in her mother's arms, her eyes glued to her mother's loving (though tired, of course!) face. Mama smiles at her, coos:

"Hi, my little one. I love you sooo much. You're just perfect in every way. You're the daughter I always dreamed of. You have such beautiful eyes, and such a sweet little nose, and your gurgles fill me with delight."

It is natural and easy for most people to notice, delight in, and admire their infants. As children grow and develop, it takes more thought and perceptiveness to grasp the significance of each of their forward steps, and to acknowledge those steps with some fanfare.

Rebecca, six, has been sitting on the trapeze bar, using it like a swing, for several months. Today, while sitting on it, she cautiously slides her hands down the ropes, letting her body drop backwards, til she is holding the bar with her hands and her knees, her head and body pointing down. She shrieks with pleasure. Her mother watches her and cheers:

"That's wonderful, honey! You're so brave and well co-ordinated! Congratulations! You're terrific!"

Mothers also need to take time to notice and acknowledge the particular qualities that make a child the unique person she is. Here is Elizabeth, age 11, cuddling with her mother, who says to her:

"I love being with you. I love talking with you. You're so smart and interesting, and you make me think about all kinds of different things that I ordinarily don't think about."

The appreciation, the validation, that Elizabeth's mother is giving her is not flattery—it's not generalized nor is it an empty cliché—it respects who Elizabeth is, and is about supporting her where she needs and deserves support.

All our lives we want to know that we are recognized as a special, remarkable, delightful person; that our existence matters; that we are worth being thought about and responded to; that we have a valid passport to being alive. When, as children, our elders reflect those realities to us, we gain strength and confidence. We can eventually carry those realities inside ourselves, even in the face of setbacks. And still, as adults, there are many times when we need to be reminded of our value and uniqueness, particularly in times of stress.

In order to validate another person, to give her that necessary stamp of legitimacy and approval, we have to pay attention to her, so that we can reflect back to her what we see and hear: her gifts, her passions, her unique qualities. This process begins from the first moments of life, and continues forever, as the anecdotes above exemplify.

Help Is at Hand

Mom is standing at the sink, cleaning up from breakfast. The dishwasher door is open and the upper basket is pulled out for loading. Sophia, fourteen months old, ambles over to the dishwasher and climbs onto the side of the door, hauling herself up by grabbing the upper basket.

Mom comes behind her and moves her gently around to the front, saying,

"You'll have more room to stand on the front." Mom stays behind her but does not impose her presence on Sophia's exploration.

When Sophia reaches for the dishes, Mom simply places china ones out of reach and puts plastic ones in front. Sophia moves the dishes around for a few minutes, then wanders off to another fascinating activity.

What has happened in this brief interlude is that Mom has seen what Sophia wants to do—imitate Mama loading the dishwasher—and has assisted her to do it successfully and safely.

> All our lives we want to know that we are recognized as a special, remarkable, delightful person; that our existence matters; that we are worth being thought about and responded to; that we have a valid passport to being alive.

What does it mean to assist someone? When we're taking care of another person, that question does—and should—come up with great frequency. The answer is different for each person—both for each care giver and for each care receiver, and it changes over time.

Sometimes the best assistance is support, as in the anecdote above; sometimes the best help is doing nothing; sometimes help is offered through a combination of allowing experience to be the teacher, while being actively connected; sometimes it occurs by following the other's lead; sometimes help means coming actively to the rescue.

Whatever decision we make, the outcomes we need to try for are pretty clear: communicating love and respect; helping expand confidence, competence, enjoyment and independence; and assuring safety (to the degree that we're able).

With You but Not of You

"AAAAAAAAAAAAAAOOOOOOOOOO!!!!!!" bawls my two-year-old granddaughter, when her mother, upon bumping into a table, has said, "ouch!". That is empathy. She is literally feeling her mother's pain. Her empathy comes from her profound bond with her mother.

Empathy is born from intimacy. Another source of empathy is experience—when you see someone feeling something that you have felt, you may share her feeling vicariously.

The value of empathy to a relationship is that it enables a person to understand another's feelings, and thus respond in ways that say,

"You are not crazy or weird to feel that way."

However, to be most helpful, empathy needs to be accompanied by objectivity (at two, my granddaughter is not yet capable of that)—by objectivity, I mean saying to oneself:

"I understand what you're feeling, but I am not in your situation, so I can think about it from outside of it."

Empathy can also be sought after, as in the following dialogue between myself and my daughter, who was four at the time:

Julianna, angrily: "Marla was mean to me. She called me lots of names. What should I do?"

Mom: "Why don't you just ignore her. She'll stop after a while."

Julianna shakes her head, "No."

Mom: "Tell her she's hurting your feelings, that you don't want her to do that."

Julianna sits there gloomily.

Mom: "Say, 'Sticks and stones can hurt my bones but names will never harm me.'"

Julianna frowns. Mom tries a few more suggestions, with no luck. Finally it dawns on Mom that she has to present a response that will reflect Julianna's anger, so she offers the grossest reply she can think of, that is just short of being off limits: "Tell her to go stick her head in the toilet and flush it!"

Julianna's eyes light up, she bounds off the chair and out the door. Mom hears no more about the problem, and Julianna doesn't complain again about being called names.

I had finally tuned in to my daughter's angry energy, and offered her something that was fierce enough to match her feelings, and thus validate them. Most likely, she never used that phrase aloud—she didn't have to, because she felt understood.

Letting Her Know

Every human being demands self-expression. At birth, the neonate expresses itself by sounds, gestures, physical activity, facial grimaces, eye contact. As the human matures, the complexity of self-expression becomes staggering. Here is a very incomplete list of ways humans express themselves: glances, sounds, physical activity and movement, gestures, words both spoken and written, smiles, frowns, withholding love or approval, hugs, laughter, weeping, tantrums, trembling, singing, creating images and music, cooking, decorating self and environment, worshipping, touching, sexual contact, teaching—you can add to the list.

The following anecdote illustrates a mother encouraging her daughter to express her feelings.

Diana, nineteen, is home from college during January break. Since she has been away from home, she has been recognizing how unhappy she was as a child, when her mom's attention was wrapped up in a difficult marriage, a divorce, and a re-marriage. She asks her mother, Yolanda:

"Will you sit down with me and have a 'heart to heart' talk?"

"Yes, of course, honey," replies her mother.

Diana's sadness and longing pour out, amidst many tears and along with some anger. Yolanda listens closely, acknowledges and accepts Diana's memories, observations, and feelings. Yolanda assures her daughter,

"My inattention was never because you were unlovable."

Yolanda takes lots of time with Diana, sits with her, and is affectionate while Diana weeps. Yolanda occasionally weeps with her, and expresses profound regret that things were not as they should have been.

"We can have a conversation like this again, whenever you want it."

Diana ends up feeling closer to her mom, less guarded around her, and more grounded in the reality of her experience.

Yolanda has already reflected deeply on her own feelings about those difficult events in her life, and on her guilt about how that affected her children, both through therapy and by writing in a journal. So she is able to pay attention to Diana's feelings, rather than to her own—she has already given herself the attention that she needed.

Courageous Love

"You never let me do what my friends do; it's not fair; no one else's mother is so strict," wails Alma, as she stomps into her room.

Alma, sixteen, is a warm and responsive young woman. She sometimes wanders through the house with eyes cast down, not looking at anyone, being unconnected and emotionally absent. Alma's mother, Ginny, has come to understand that at those times, Alma's full of uncomfortable feelings that she doesn't want to feel, doesn't want to pay any attention to, but that she can't shake off.

Usually, she'll try to get away from her feelings by asking to go out with her friends. But Ginny has also learned that if Alma does go out, it's as if she leaves at home the part of her that is feeling miserable, so when she returns, she gets right back in it—she's still sullen and inexpressive. What seems to be most helpful to her is when Ginny says "No" to her request to go out and then accepts Alma's eruption into a storm of protest and tears. Instead of going out, Alma "goes in" and feels all those uncomfortable feelings. After the storm, Alma seems fully restored to her usual interactive self.

It takes wisdom, courage and love to become a holding tank, a container, for a daughter's tumultuous or chaotic or miserable feelings; to maintain just the right amount of pressure, so that she has to notice what is going on in and around her; to arouse discomfort sometimes by expecting, and even insisting that she reach towards a goal that you know she deeply wants, but will come only with concentrated effort; to protect her from harm, while allowing her to face the consequences of her choices and actions.

This kind of interaction is the most complex of all—it includes all that are described in the preceding sections. It requires a mother to be sensitive, strong and flexible—much like the earthquake-proof buildings that hold together because they can "give" just the right amount in a temblor.

Daughters need their mothers to be such containers for them—it helps them develop an inner focus; it also helps them to build their own containers as they grow older. Occasionally, daughters can even be containers for their mothers, though that is not a useful long-term role for them when they are children. It can be, however, a reasonable role for an adult daughter.

Forever Connected

Every woman is a daughter, and every woman had a mother who birthed her.

The bonds between mothers and daughters are mysterious and profound. People can try to explain them biologically, psychologically, astrologically, energetically, relationally—but they remain beyond our capacity to fully grasp.

Those bonds can be tight, loose, peaceful, confused, conflictual, benign, malignant, erotic, uplifting, invigorating, liberating, stifling, imprisoning,—the full range of human relationships is possible between mother and daughter.

There are mothers and daughters who remain or become very close; there are others who remain or become distant or disconnected; whatever the outcome of that relationship, the essence of Mother and of Daughter is deep in all women's souls, and on some level both are eternally connected to each other.

Shifting Perspectives

It was ten minutes before the end of a workshop for mothers and daughters, and participants were writing in their journals. Suddenly Margaret burst out into loud sobs. Everyone became still, and waited to find out what had happened. All during the workshop, Margaret, who had attended the workshop without her mother, had described herself as a person who had been deprived of mothering in her childhood, and who still could not get close to her mother, or even touch her, even though she knew that was what her mother wanted. This situation was very distressing to her.

When she had calmed her weeping enough to speak, she told us that she had just recalled a memory from her childhood, one previously occluded. She was nine years old, at church with her mother, and she observed her mother and her mother's best friend holding hands with each other.

"You're queer," she said to her mother, not knowing what the word meant, but knowing somehow that it applied to this scene.

When they got home, her mother gave Margaret a lecture. Whatever the words her mother used, her facial expression and tone of voice conveyed embarrassment and discomfort. Suddenly Margaret felt very ashamed, and deep inside, below the level of thought, she drew the conclusion that it was wrong for women to touch each other. This decision remained with her and became a guiding principle in her life, depriving her of the capacity for intimacy and physical closeness with women, and especially her mother.

As she regained this memory, it dawned on her that her whole concept of her life story was turning upside down: she was not just a helpless victim of an unloving mother. She was an agent of her own destiny, and could therefore change it! It was she who had withdrawn from her mother's affection, because she had interpreted her mother's embarrassment as a condemnation of closeness between women. Now she was free to think consciously about that early unconscious decision. In doing so, she could begin the process of altering it, to one which could allow her to get what she wanted —some closeness with her mother, and all her women friends. She now would have the opportunity to stop blaming her mother for neglect in the past, and to stop blaming herself for her inability to get close to her mother in the present.

A shift in perspective can be triggered by a variety of events: a question someone asks, a book, a movie, a story someone tells, a comment someone makes, an observation of an interaction between people, a memory suddenly returning. If the time and situation are ripe and you are ready, the shift can come in a flash.

In that moment, it is as if the story you have been telling yourself all your life about why you feel and act the way you do, suddenly dissolves around you. In its place arises a new story, broader, more comprehensive, more liberating—one that allows you to notice more choices, to breathe in more love, and to breathe out more understanding—one that allows you greater freedom to create a greater life.

A Cry from the Heart

From earliest childhood, every daughter needs and wants her mother to be the ideal woman that the daughter rightly deserves: wise, loving, smart, competent, confident, strong, expressive yet capable of restraint and discretion, deeply feeling while at the same time optimistic and upbeat, holding high expectations yet completely accepting (clearly, to be all of this is almost impossible). Daughters need their mothers to demonstrate to them that it is safe to be a fully-dimensional human being.

Once daughters have navigated the adolescent struggle to feel their own independence and uniqueness, some may start to fight with their mothers in a new way. They will notice where aspects of their mothers' wholeness have strayed out of sight, and they will demand that their mothers reclaim the parts of themselves that have been abandoned or forgotten.

This fight comes from deep love and concern and also from deep yearning. It is a much more sophisticated expression of the two year old's urgent cry: "I want my Mommy!" It can be brutal, or it can be polite; it can be explicit or it can be in code; but the message is the same: "I love you and I demand that you be the woman that I know you really are."

Mothers of the world, when you encounter this fight, no matter how confusing or upsetting it is, murmur, "Thank you for telling me," because only your children will do that for you; then listen, reflect, and learn what you can.

Daughters of the world, don't give up unless and until you've tried many different approaches (if you keep trying the same one over and over, and it doesn't work, you're being a bit obstinate). If you see that she really can't engage, then it may be time to accept that she's doing the best she can and your energy would be better employed elsewhere.

The Impact of Mothers on Daughters

We mothers so often feel that we have little influence on our daughters, as they grow to be adolescents and adults. We wish they would heed our advice and our warnings, our alarms, our experience, our intuitions about what is best for them. We feel helpless to guide them any further. They have become headstrong, impatient for their own experiences, impatient with our intrusions into their quest for adventure, for love, for freedom. They want to swallow the world, and we want to caution them against indigestion.

Our daughters' determination to move in their own direction under their own steam blinds us to a glaring reality...we have had a huge impact on them, just by being their mothers. They absorbed our entire way of being in the world with every breath they took, from the moment they were born. That awesome drive to be on their own way is not a sign of our invisibility...on the contrary, it is a loud declaration that our impact has been so powerful, that to discover who they are and what is their unique way of being in the world takes fierce energy and single-minded focus.

Daughters seek their distinct place in the universe in many different ways: by fighting with us, by ignoring us, by challenging us, by questioning us, by sneering at us, by cutting us off, by distancing from us, by doing everything opposite from us; at the same time, they may also emulate us, love us, listen to us, ask our advice, become our friends and colleagues, even become dependent on us.

But, Mothers, do not be fooled. Your impact has been monumental. Be compassionate towards your daughter's goal, even if you do not like her means of getting there.

All of us, mothers and daughters alike, have a lifelong task—here are two similar descriptions of it from two disparate sources:

The Gnostic Gospel:
If you bring forth what is within you
What you bring forth will save you
If you do not bring forth what is within you
What you do not bring forth will destroy you

The poet Rumi:
There is a light seed grain inside.
You fill it with yourself, or it dies!

The above concepts are lifted from my anthology of stories and poems about the relationship between mothers and daughters. These are my introductions to each chapter. The book is entitled Heart By Heart: Mothers and Daughters Listening to Each Other.

© *Marianne Preger-Simon.*

About the Author

Marianne Preger-Simon leads mother/daughter workshops and is a psychotherapist in private practice in the Amherst-Northampton, Massachusetts area. She has published a book entitled *Heart By Heart: Mothers and Daughters Listening To Each Other*. Her experiences include being a founding member of the Merce Cunningham Dance Company, the first dance critic for *The Village Voice*, and a teacher at New Lincoln School (all of these in New York City). She was a folksinger in the Philadelphia inner-city public schools for three years, received her EdD from the University of Massachusetts, and taught there as a graduate student. She has led many workshops in values clarification all over the United States and in Canada; and has also led workshops in creativity and race relations. She also took a two-year internship in family therapy.

She is married and is a mother and grandmother, and is blessed with a large and affectionate extended family. Her website can be found at: www.mariannepregersimon.com.

What relationships are for is to bring out the better qualities within us.

David B. Wexler

You will not find the law of love shut out from the affairs of men after the feminine half of the world's truth is completed.

Anna Julia Cooper

To live with sensitivity in this age of limbo indeed requires courage.

Rollo May

In love there are no vacations...No such thing. Love has to be lived fully with its boredom and all that.

Marguerite Duras

Usually, if a person has work-confidence and love-confidence, we say he also has self-confidence. But this is not quite true. For self-confidence (or self-esteem, self-acceptance, or self-respect), when it truly exists, means that the individual fully accepts himself whether or not he thinks he is highly capable, and whether or not others approve of him.

Albert Ellis

Connections have a way of making us morally accountable. At a most basic level we behave better with people and places we see again and again. Some of the worst behaviors in America occur in airports and on interstates, places where we move among strangers.

Mary Pipher

Mature love is union under the condition of preserving one's integrity, one's individuality...In love the paradox occurs that two beings become one and yet remain two.

Erich Fromm

The person who tries to live alone will not succeed as a human being. His heart withers if it does not answer another heart. His mind shrinks away if he hears only the echoes of his own thoughts and finds no other inspiration.

Pearl S. Buck

Becoming responsible adults is no longer a matter of whether children hang up their pajamas or put dirty towels in the hamper, but whether they care about themselves and others – and whether they see everyday chores as related to how we treat this planet.

Edna Leshan

The dedicated life is the life worth living. You must give with your whole heart.

Annie Dillard

If we are regularly concerned with decency, intimacy, and self-direction within our own families, and if we encourage the introduction of courses in applied ethics in the educational system, we won't have to rely on politicians, athletes, comedians, and pious theologians to enlighten us about family values.

Earle F. Zeigler

Our ethic of caring - which we might have called a "feminine ethic" - begins to look a bit mean in contrast to the masculine ethics of universal love or universal justice. But universal love is an illusion.

Nel Noddings

Kind hearts are the gardens,
Kind thoughts are the roots,
Kind words are the flowers,
Kind deeds are the fruits,
Take care of your garden,
And keep out the weeds,
Fill it with sunshine:
Kind words and kind deeds.

Henry Wadsworth Longfellow

Feelings of worth can flourish only in an atmosphere where individual differences are appreciated, mistakes are tolerated, communication is open, and rules are flexible-the kind of atmosphere that is found in a nurturing family.

Virginia Satir

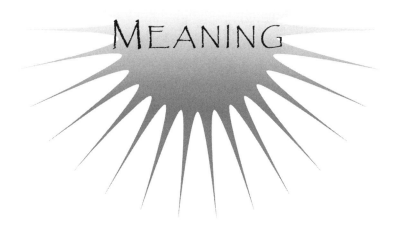

MEANING

THE VITALITY OF VALUES

Jenni Prisk

What is a value? You can't see it, smell it, touch it, or taste it. Yet a value can have a profound affect on you and your life. It can even shape your life.

When I look at the values in my life, they feel like verbs. That's because they play active roles in my life today. So, when Jason asked me to write a chapter for this book, I asked myself, what does a value look like when it is a noun? Here's what I came up with:

V
Vision
A
Attitude
L
Learning
U
Understanding
E
Emotion

So, let me begin with Vision. In this fast-paced world of ours, it's becoming increasingly important to have a vision—not only for a business or an organization, but for ourselves personally. I want to share the vision I have for Voices of Women (VOW) which I founded in 2001, following 9/11.

As I watched the news on TV during that savage time in our history, I found myself overwhelmed at the horror of all the lives being lost as the planes and the towers went down. All of those people who were killed were born of mothers, were loved by someone, and had probably done something worthwhile in their lives. My vision for the founding of VOW came from the painful realization that mothers' sons were killing mothers' sons and daughters. In other words, if you took away the killing, they were all the same.

Thirty like-minded women in San Diego agreed with me, and thus our journey began. Our mission is threefold. To educate ourselves and others about US and foreign policy as we attempt to understand the mythical or false facts that surround us. Secondly, we believe that through the understanding of diverse cultures we can, as a global community work towards non-military solutions for peace. And thirdly, we promote women as leaders in a worldwide campaign for peace.

This mission and vision helps me to consume bad news with hope...there is another side to every story; there is an opportunity to learn and understand; there is a hope for civility and communication.

Now, all of this requires a certain Attitude, my next value. We are constantly assailed by a barrage of TV, newspapers, internet, radio, and journal news—each source aiming for the biggest scoop or the biggest headline. How do we know if they are they true? If one contradicts another, what should we believe? If one story is coming from the White House and the other from the ground of a war-torn country, where is the truth? My attitude has to be that of asking: "Which story makes the most sense? What is consistent with my own head and heart? Who has nothing to lose by telling the truth? What aligns with our vision for Voices of Women?"

Those of us in VOW have to be constantly vigilant about our attitude towards others. We have agreed that all meetings and programs will be conducted in a spirit of peace and harmony. Therefore, we attune ourselves to listen without bias. The hardest thing can be to listen to the Bush administration without bias, and I admit there are times when I fail miserably!

Spinoza put it well: "Peace is not the absence of war; it is a virtue; a state of mind; a disposition for benevolence; confidence; and justice."

A finely tuned attitude allows breathing room for Learning, the third value. Socrates said: "The only wisdom is in knowing you know nothing." How I wish I could live by that simple saying every day! There is so much to be learned in this world that sometimes I panic knowing I don't have enough time to learn it all. But then I remember that life is not about knowing everything; it is more about learning important things well. Through the educational element of the Voices of Women mission, we endeavor to learn from those who live and work in different cultures. Universities, teachers, mentors, journals, and the Internet can teach us well, but there is nothing like learning from the source. The real life experiences of a person or people who can paint pictures and apply the imagery of their country, culture, or challenges are tantamount to gold. And the learning experience you can have by spending time in a foreign land is unparalleled.

> Listening to learn and learning to listen go hand in hand in the quest for understanding of our global community.

You can always tell when someone is a lifelong learner, because he or she is a good listener. Listening to learn and learning to listen go hand in hand in the quest for understanding of our global community.

And thus it is easy to move into the fourth value—Understanding. Adlai Stevenson, who was a Democratic candidate for President of the United States, made a wise observation: "Understanding human needs is half the job of meeting them." So much of daily human toil is focused on understanding, and being understood. As "sophisticated" beings we communicate with words and language in our endeavors to get our points across. A child will throw her hands into the air with a whoop of joy when she understands a complex puzzle. A teacher smiles when participants in a class understand the message he is conveying.

In order for us to understand another's point of view, we first have to wish to understand it. One of Webster's definitions of "understand" is "to gather." I like this definition because it conjures up an image of the coming together of ideas, people and communication. Carl Jung wasn't joking when he said: "Everything that irritates us about others can lead us to an understanding of ourselves." We are all intertwined. We are born of a woman, we

515

die when our heart stops. How incredible it would be if in between those two acts, we learned to understand each other.

And finally, I come to Emotion, one of my favorites. What is emotion? If it was spelled "e-motion" it would probably fit into a wireless device connected to the Internet. But instead it is connected to the greatest machine in the human body—the heart. Men, it is said, love with their heads, and women with their hearts, and I sure believe that!

Emotion makes us who we are. Emotion helps us to fall in love, welcome a baby, buy a home or a car, get angry, sad, or just plain happy. Emotion is what drove the founding of Voices of Women. Emotion is what keeps it going. Emotion is the ability to learn about another person's pain and to empathize with it to the point that action must be taken. Voices of Women asks this question at the conclusion of every event and program: "What can we do to change your plight, or make your life easier, or advise our government, or become your global partner?"

Life without emotion would be like a world without color. Life is so much richer because of the color of the sky, the land, and the people. As long as humans have the ability to feel emotion, there is hope on this planet. If we ever learn to respond to each other through emotionless chips in our brains, God help us.

Writing these words about Vision, Attitude, Learning, Understanding, and Emotion has helped me to understand my own values better. And I also realize that there is a greater need for me to live these values more fully. Living a life of value is a noble and worthy premise. It requires discipline and focus. It also means failing frequently. Yet, what else should we stand for if not for a life of value? I believe everyone is born for a purpose. Or fate if you prefer, but that always sounds fatalistic to me! During our lives we shape, and are shaped, by actions and reactions. When we love, we are often rewarded with love in return. When we think well of others, the chances are they will treat us well. If we live for greed and envy, then eventually we will pay the price.

Values are invaluable. They are stars that guide us, signposts that lead us, and catalysts for change within us. The Dalai Lama put it this way: "Open your arms to change, but don't let go of your values." I say amen to that.

© Jenni Prisk

About the Author

An award-winning motivational speaker, communications coach, and trainer, Jenni Prisk founded Prisk Communication in 1989. Her mission is to provide comprehensive and outstanding training in public speaking and communication skills that will remove the associated risk and fears, engendering confidence, effectiveness and positive results.

Her diverse background includes working in the newspaper industry where she received four writing awards, two from the San Diego Press Club. In 1994, she received the *San Diego Business Journal's* Award for Women Who Mean Business, and was nominated in 2000. In 1995, Jenni was a finalist in Bank of America's first Enterprise Award Program, as well as an honoree in the Women Together Awards. In 1999, she was honored as a regional finalist in *Working Woman* magazine's first Entrepreneurial Excellence Award Program.

Following the September 11th terrorist attacks in 2001, Jenni founded Voices of Women (VOW), an international forum for non-military solutions, to foster global peace, justice and equality around the world. For more information, please visit www.voicesofwomen.org.

Jenni resides with her husband, Kim, in the Sorrento Valley area of San Diego.

We often use the word "meaning" in relation to personal feelings and emotional significance. It then reveals and sometimes declares our highest values. It manifests ideals that we cherish and pursue...

Irving Singer

The finer things in life are fine, but the meaningful things in life are more meaningful.

Jason Merchey

A person's life is limited, but serving the people is limitless. I want to devote my limited life to serving the people limitlessly.

Lei Feng

Live all you can; it's a mistake not to. It doesn't matter so much what you do in particular, so long as you're living your life. If you haven't had that, what have you had?

Henry James

To love what you do and feel that it matters - how could anything be more fun?

Katharine Graham

Man is simply here; he has to make what he can of a universe that is not even hostile but strange and uncertain. Man is never given a purpose or mission; he must devise them for himself, knowing that their fulfillment has no external justification or reward-altogether and absurd situation.

Jacques Barzun

Happy are they who dream dreams and are ready to pay the price to make them come true.

Leon J. Suenens

We cannot live only for ourselves. A thousand fibers connect us with our fellow men; and among those fibers, as sympathetic threads, our actions run as causes, and they come back to us as effects.

Herman Melville

Hatred is a feeling which leads to the extinction of values.

José Ortega y Gasset

Americans need to talk today more than ever, especially about politics. We don't need more diatribes or name-calling. We need meaningful conversations with people who agree - and disagree - with our views and values.

Leif Utne

Those Americans who drew the short straw and live in poverty are systematically shut out of the blessing of American society, Horatio Alger success stories notwithstanding. Talk is cheap in Washington, and talk about "values" is cheaper still. If we really valued work, then the janitors and garbage collectors and sweatshop workers and the rest of the hardworking poor would be able to put food on the table. If we really valued children, we'd make sure that the poorest of our children weren't taught in hallways and broom closets or in shifts and we'd guarantee that they all had textbooks and qualified, well-paid teachers.

Nydia M. Velázquez

It's not the circumstances you come from; it's the values you fight for.

John F. Kerry

He who values principles and exercises control,
Faces the omnipresent threat of adversity.
Perceived as odd, foolhardy, and droll,
Despite the failure of respect from his society,
By crushing the dice rather than letting them roll-
He can sleep at night sure of his integrity.

Jason Merchey

If I have included visibility in my list of values to be saved, it is to give warning of the danger we run in losing a basic human faculty: the power of bringing visions into focus with out eyes shut, of bringing forth forms and colors from the lines of black letters on a white page, and in fact, of thinking in terms of images.

Italo Calvino

KNOWLEDGE

PHILOSOPHY AND THE SPARKLING LIFE

Peter B. Raabe

I'm both a professional philosopher and philosophical counselor. I teach a third year course titled "Philosophy for Counsellors" at the University College of the Fraser Valley (UCFV) in Abbotsford, British Columbia, Canada. And I also work with non-students who come to me for philosophical counseling. To understand what I do, and what role values play in what I do, it's necessary to first of all understand what philosophy is all about.

Philosophy is very useful in every facet of life, whether in individual life decision making, corporate problem solving, or in international policy making. On a personal level philosophy is an examination of the reasons you have for the values you hold as good and the beliefs you hold as true so that you can free yourself from simply following tradition, obeying the dictates of authority figures, or acting on your feelings. In philosophical counseling I help others to examine the reasons they have for their values, beliefs, and assumptions. With this definition in mind, there is no clear separation between academic philosophy and clinical philosophy, and between the classroom and the counseling room.

The practice of philosophy is neither the transference of knowledge from expert to novice, nor simply the memorization of ancient wisdom. Philosophy is an activity, and philosophical counseling involves a philosopher having a discussion with a client about that client's issues or concerns. The philosopher will draw on a number of different fields, such as critical and creative thinking (good reasoning), politics (making group decisions that are ethical), metaphysics (reality, being, existence), feminism (equality, care, relationships), religion (God, meaning of life, spirituality), psychology (function of the mind), ethics, and more. The last issue—ethics—is often misunderstood. I have often heard people say that being moral or ethical means following principles or rules of some sort. If this were true then being moral would simply be a matter of memorizing and following rules. But experience has shown us that it's impossible to make rules for every imaginable situation, to memorize them, and then to live by following all of them. A much more reasonable way to think about morals and ethics is that being moral or ethical has to do with trying to avoid harm to others when making a decision about what to say or do. Some philosophers suggest that we should also always try to benefit others, but this is not generally a requirement. In order to be moral, it's enough that you have the sort of values which lead you to act in such a way that you don't hurt others. But this raises the question, what exactly is a value, and how do I know what my values are?

> The practice of philosophy is neither the transference of knowledge from expert to novice, nor simply the memorization of ancient wisdom.

A value is something you believe is important, something you hold dear, something that you take into serious consideration when making meaningful decisions. You can value an object, such as a diamond, but morals and ethics are not based on valuing objects. The values underlying morals and ethics are things like truthfulness, kindness, charity, patience, and so on, all reflecting who you are, all conducive to living an ethical life, both in terms of avoiding harm to others and living a good life for oneself. The values that influence our morals are generally not related to objects; they're non-material qualities. You might say, "But I know someone who values money. Isn't that valuing a kind of object?" Although it may seem like valuing coins and dollar bills is valuing objects, what that person actually values is what money represents, namely security, status, power, or whatever.

Human beings are what I call "meaning creatures," we see meaning in objects and we create meaning with our words and actions. You can discover your values if you are observant because your values are present not only in your words and actions, your values are reflected back to you by those things you believe to be meaningful. But it's not always obvious to us what our values actually are. For example, you could be the sort of person who tries to always tell the truth, and feels very bad when you tell the occasional fib, yet you may not be able to say what values are reflected in your behavior. This is where a philosopher can be of help to you. To a philosopher and a philosophical counselor, your speaking truthfully and feeling bad about fibbing would indicate that you value truthfulness and honesty. Of course values aren't always this easy to spot.

In philosophy and in philosophical counseling I help individuals discover first their values and then to evaluate their values in order to be able to decide which values to keep and which to get rid of. Philosophy can help an individual to come to an understanding of why they value those things they believe to be meaningful. If they're struggling with a troubling issue they can't seem to resolve I help them to examine which of their values might be in conflict and therefore preventing its resolution. For example, a person might be trying to decide how to end a relationship. This person may value both truthfulness and kindness at the same time, and the question arises, "Should I tell the truth—that I want to end the relationship—knowing it will hurt my friend, or should I avoid the truth in order to be kind?" Which value should take precedence, truthfulness or kindness? Philosophy can help this person answer this question. Another example is the situation where an individual values equally both her professional development and time spent with her family. The question for this person is, "How should I decide how to spend my time?" I often hear these sorts of questions, regarding seemingly contradictory values, in my philosophical counseling practice. My response is never to tell this person what to do, but rather I help her to examine her values, to look behind those values to find out what it is she finds most meaningful, and then to decide on a course of action, perhaps in the form of an acceptable compromise. With philosophy I help her to make an ethical decision, based on what is most meaningful to her, so that she can pursue the course in life she values the most, while at the same time remaining true to herself.

Life is clearly our most valuable possession, but what we do with our lives will determine how much value it ultimately holds for ourselves, and how much of value we will be giving to others. Like a diamond in the rough each of us is responsible for the cutting and polishing that makes life shine. Philosophy is an important tool, that, when used with even minimal skill, can help us to live a sparkling life of great value.

© *Peter Raabe*

About the Author

I was born in 1949. I have a BA (Honors) and an MA in philosophy, and a PhD in philosophical counseling from the University of British Columbia (UBC). I'm currently professor of philosophy at the University College of the Fraser Valley (UCFV) in Abbotsford, and seeing clients in private philosophical counseling practice. I'm the author of *Philosophical Counselling: Theory and Practice* and *Issues in Philosophical Counselling* (both published by Praeger/Greenwood), and the editor of *The Unconscious Philosophical and Counselling* (Trivium Press). I've published a number of papers in peer reviewed professional journals, and given presentations at various national and international conferences. I have experience in both group work and individual counseling with both students and non-academics of all ages, as well as in addition recovery counseling. For eight years I hosted a monthly philosophy café discussion group, and I've done philosophy with young school children. I'm married, and the father of one (somewhat philosophical) son.

In philosophy an individual is becoming himself.

Bernard Lonergan

Philosophy recovers itself when it ceases to be a device for dealing with the problems of philosophers and becomes a method, cultivated by philosophers, for dealing with the problems of men.

John Dewey

Moral philosophy is the study of the values and guidelines by which we live, as well as the justification of these values and guidelines.

Judith A. Boss

Philosophy, though unable to tell us with certainty what are the true answer to the doubts it raises, is able to suggest many possibilities which enlarge our thoughts and free them from the tyranny of custom. Thus, while diminishing our feeling of certainty as to what things are, it greatly increases our knowledge as to what they may be...

Bertrand Russell

How freely we live life depends both on our political system and on our vigilance in defending its liberties. How long we live depends both on our genes and on the quality of our health care. How well we live – that is, how thought- fully, how nobly, how virtuously, how joyously, how lovingly – depends both on our philosophy and on the way we apply it to all else. The examined life is a better life...

Lou Marinoff

Philosophy did not find Plato already a nobleman; it made him one.

Seneca

We actually have no choice of whether to have a philosophy or not, of whether to be philosophers or not. We inevitably operate out of some philosophical worldview, however well formed or incomplete it might be. Our choice is between bad philosophy - unreflectively absorbed from the culture around us and the prejudices of our time - or good philosophy, built on critical questioning and sustained thought.

Tom Morris

THE CONFLICT OF RESOLUTION

Marcus Raskin

The task of conflict resolution is just beginning, for we are caught in wars, barbarism, torture, and every manner of misery in the world. In the United States we are faced with increasing legal and paralegal forms that are aimed at narrowing civil liberties. We are expanding spy technology into every aspect of a person's life. None of this is surprising. War narrows civil liberties and free speech—exactly those instruments that conflict resolution depends on.

How should one think about the work of those who undertake conflict resolution? And how should we think of conflict resolution in general? Is it a scientific discipline, an art? Is it a skill which can be tailored to different situations from the small group level to the international level? Is a good practitioner one who, like the lawyer, keeps his values and opinions to himself or herself? It is these, and other, questions that need airing, not only in conflict resolution theory and practice, but in the social sciences in general. For those who practice conflict resolution, the struggle is daunting—as we have learned in Israel, Ireland, and the Balkans. It is an uphill battle for peace makers in a world dominated by those who eschew cooperation with others and who see any form of consensus and compromise as fatal weaknesses.

There is another side as well: knowing where disagreement is—not among equals, but where the colonizer and the oppressor seek to use dominant power to avoid recognizing the humanity of the oppressed. Here the mediator must ask how inequality should be recognized in the resolution of disputes. It is in these situations that those who practice conflict resolution include their notions of justice. It is an idea that has developed throughout history. It is a sense of empathy between people that recognizes equality, dignity, and fairness not only as goals to be achieved, but sentiments to be unlocked in each person.

> Human rights in the United States became a popular fig leaf for the country to believe that it continued on the high road of self-worth and certitude after the moral and political disaster of Vietnam.

Is it true that conflict resolution is a normative science with a hidden agenda beyond wanting to keep the peace? So the conundrum is that the skills of the mediator, that of keeping or achieving event transient settlements, is not highly credited among us. The proof of this is in how little is taught about this skill, about nonviolence, and about peace research and peace studies in our universities. Unfortunately, what is taught in the modern university is taught through the prism of violence, and perpetuates the kind of security which asserts dominance over others. It is the coercion and violence of the kind one finds in the philosophers of yore who could not escape blowing the war bugle as exercises in manliness or leaders who have seen war and its preparations as their right and ticket to greatness. Such notions retain their hold within the United States, and just as the United States is a leader in many things, its position as a state is that of a leader in the belief in war and violence as conditions to be bent for their own purposes. It is painful to say that the assumptions of various "think-tanks" operate in the coordinates of power, violence, and war and that they are often taken very seriously as advisors to the palace court. And it is astonishing how universities rejected the kinds of research and inquiry that would understand and then transcend man's organizational failures to ensure peace and a modicum and economic and social justice.

This state of affairs was not inexorable. Quite the contrary, especially for those who believed in enlightenment, human progress, reason attached to action, experience, and passion. It is one of the curious things in American universities that the pragmatist sense of social scientists of the 1930s understood the acquisition of knowledge as a means (perhaps the most important means) of fulfilling, of achieving, and of sustaining those rights that came to be recognized because they were central to what humanity, and humanity's potential, was. This was not an easy road to travel in American life, nor has it been easy for those who believed that their knowledge and understanding were part of their moral system and demanded they take action in the world for their studies and beliefs. For pragmatists, this notion later took the form of recognizing cultural rights beyond political boundaries. Not only did this mean recognition of the worth of the individual, it also meant the organization of a society where an individual had not only the right to privacy, but also guaranteed rights of participation. But what did these words mean in practice? Certainly there was ample evidence to show that states, and especially the United States, as the sole superpower the pundits described American power to be, would be bound to the covenants of human rights. But the slogan had a more profound value.

Human rights in the United States became a popular fig leaf for the country to believe that it continued on the high road of self-worth and certitude after the moral and political disaster of Vietnam. Behind the fig leaf, preparation for war and torture seemed boundless. The pain which we see on peoples' faces whether from war, disease, or starvation seems to be invariant. Certainly in the twentieth century we have witnessed sufficient destruction to prove this point. Peace was only a prelude to war where heroes are made, destruction is tolerated (if not applauded), and the fragile fabric of human existence is destroyed or so badly damaged that millions have no control over their lives to live, if not well or decently, at least adequately. But even that is denied to millions.

The bar of existence is very low indeed. It is hardly surprising that people hope for a better world once they are dead, or that they hope for a wonder cure for their dis-ease, or for the next ideological and scientific fashion—be it faster computers, or free markets, or socialism as the final cure. Our technologies, certainly without much moral understanding, prove our superiority and that this superiority is the redemption of our civilization.

The victory of American and western civilization is our own redemption and justification for empire. But nuclear weapons and missiles can hardly speak well of our civilization. Gandhi was once asked what he thought of Western civilization. He replied, "I think it would be a good idea [if they tried it]."

Some think of peace as stability. It may not matter whether or not it has an element of justice about it, whether it is the stability of a rigid class system, or a prison, just so long as there is quiet and the comfortable can go on unaffected by what is around them: give very little to keep everything in place and keep everything as it was. The specialist in conflict resolution was silent. Problems could fester much the way they did in the United States before the civil war, or as we see how poverty can seethe as we walk past beggars, avert our eyes from them, own civil responsibilities, and our consciences.

As long as there is no commotion, no revolution, no attempts at rights, the situation is said to be stable. One of the lessons of the civil rights movement showed that an injustice which is deep, which is out of character with the cumulative ideals of a society, demands fundamental change. And the good conflict resolver will be unhesitant in either taking sides or reflecting what the underlying principles are that must be fulfilled in practice. King understood this basic point when ministers sought him to mediate in Birmingham, Alabama between the civil rights movement and the city on tokenism. He understood that there was no defusing the conflict even as a short term solution. So off to jail he went. He understood that conflict resolution would fail because the interest in the mediators was pacification. This cannot be the purpose of those committed to conflict resolution. They must reach to the moral innateness of the others and themselves. There is a moral sense, a capacity underneath the anger and hatred which must be reached; this capacity is one in which the self has identified with the other in an empathic way. This is not so easy to do, and one of the tasks of those involved in conflict resolution is to find ways of nurturing that moral affection in themselves and others. People must be seen behind their social roles, not as a mass without power and lacking common humanity.

There was a moment in twentieth century history where recognition seemed to be given to a new civilization with plural cultures. After the Second World War there was a belief reflected in the UN declaration, the covenants of a moral sense. However imperfectly, such ideas gave hope to hundreds of millions of people throughout the world. That in many cases they were betrayed does not change the fact that that sentiment remains.

Admittedly, this reflection of the moral sense is now challenged again by forces of resentment that have been unleashed all in the name of doing good. Beware the leader who speaks of victory, who believes God speaks through him, and who has no time for ideas. These are masks for continued oppression. But what can be done by conflict resolution specialists?

There are skills to be thought about and taught:

One is an early warning qualitative social analysis which does not begin from risk assessment but from the application of legal and moral boundaries that were developed through the introduction and linkage between empathy (the moral capacity), cohesion, identification with the other beyond the social role, and recognition that stability built on oppression merely hides more fundamental problems, such as the organization of power, and resentment for the past passed on from one generation to the other. Here there is no forgetting unless new conditions prevail that reach to the humane sensibility. In that case, the scholar of conflict resolution has to be the defender of humane values, and the underlying notions of progress and universalism. It means that you will be called to choose sides in certain circumstances. In many cases this will mean keeping a neutrality between the parties, but in those instances that go to the very essence of humanity there is no question where you will have to stand. You must defend the values in which you believe, always analyzing your own reasons and feelings as well the context of the situation in which you are drawn to. You will be called upon in some cases to make it clear that this is the master/slave relationship in its modern form, and it is untenable. You will be called upon to show great courage. We have terrifying problems, which require reason and include shedding shyness and false modesty. It demands occupying the public space with new inquiries about the nature of humanity and the social, political, and economic organizations that will help humanity survive.

In the process of social transformation, the question in conflict resolution is: which way is that transformation moving, and does it walk on the path of political equality, social justice, and non-violence? If not, this is a dangerous path and a wrong one. Non-violence is an answer to injustice. War, however, is a failure of reason, justice, and humanity. But what are our tools? The first is courage greater than any soldier's, commanders, or suicide bomber's. The second is listening and recognizing that in a period of profound social transformation it is more important than ever to listen and find the kind of conversation that captures new meanings and possibilities. It is shedding the skin of what needs to be discarded from the past. This is no mean feat in a period where people feel threatened or have been privatized—where we care nothing for the other and close our minds, believing that the world is revealed only to believers while non believers are dispensable. It is no mean feat to uphold human rights when one's own culture cares little or nothing about them. This places more pressure on your work and your own integrity.

There will be those of you who want to follow a more research-oriented and scholarly direction. But even here, there will have to be activism in order to get information from governments—something that is notoriously difficult and has been worse since 2001. Secret information of this kind, once made available, will help give you the tools to move further on a path that will enable you to better comprehend the world you live in, work in, and in which you will make your mark.

There is one last point to be made. It is that now is the time to think seriously about a sort of Hippocratic oath for those who practice conflict resolution. What would that oath be? Let's begin that conversation!

© *Marcus Raskin. Excerpted from a speech given by Marcus Raskin commemorating the new building of the Conflict Resolution Center at George Mason University, September 18, 2004.*

About the Author

Marcus Raskin is the co-founder of the Institute for Policy Studies and professor in the School of Public Policy at George Washington University. He is an author and editor of eighteen books on political theory, international and national security affairs, and politics. He is also the general editor of a series called "Paths for the Twenty-First Century." As well, he is on the editorial board of *The Nation* magazine. During the Kennedy administration, he was a member of the special staff of the National Security Council and White House Consultant on Education. He was a member of the Boston 5 antiwar trial and acquitted. His two latest books are *Liberalism, The Genius Of American Poltics;* and *In Democracy's Shadow: The Secret World of National Security* (co-edited with Carl Levan).

Non-violence leads to the highest ethics, which is the goal of all evolution. Until we stop harming all other living beings, we are still savages.

Thomas Edison

The fundamental idea in the concept of justice is fairness.

John Rawls

Activism is my rent for living on this planet.

Alice Walker

Liberty, as we all know, cannot flourish in a country that is permanently on a war footing, or even a near-war footing. Permanent crisis justifies permanent control of everybody and everything by the agencies of the government.

Aldous Huxley

Peace is not the absence of conflict, but the presence of creative alternatives for responding to conflict - alternatives to passive or aggressive responses, alternatives to violence.

Dorothy Thompson

What else are you doing that is more worthy of your efforts than trying to establish the moral principles of fairness, justice, and equality for all?

Jim Hightower

I am convinced that the truest act of courage, the strongest act of manliness is to sacrifice ourselves for others in a totally non-violent struggle for justice.

César Chávez

It's the shame of American schools that the young are not taught even the basics about pacifism and nonviolence. We raise our children in a culture saturated with violence and then wonder why individuals, groups, and nations keep opting for fists, guns, and bombs as the way to settle differences.

Colman McCarthy

WISDOM

STUMBLING ONTO THE PATH TO ENLIGHTENMENT

Nicholas Ribush

I had it all…or so I thought. Wonderful family and friends, beautiful girl-friend, great career, excellent prospects, good health, reasonable looks! And a fantastic piece of land, 240 acres just north of Brisbane, where I worked as a physician in the renal unit of a large teaching hospital. I was smart, irreverent, and hip; I knew what was going on.

So why was it, I wondered, as I lay on my bed at the farm one weekend morning in 1970, that I had this gnawing, empty feeling inside? What was missing?

Then it struck me. Travel. Apart from a brief trip to New Guinea once, I'd never really left Australia. The world was out there and I hadn't seen any of it. Of course; that was it.

Now although I had this blossoming career, I had become a little disillusioned with the practice of medicine. It's a longer story than I have time to tell here, but basically, in my seven years of mainly hospital practice, it seemed that well over half the patients I'd been seeing were sick directly or indirectly as a result of the abuse of tobacco, alcohol, and over-the-counter medications, and all we doctors were doing was patching them up and sending them back into the very circumstances that made them ill in the first place. It seemed insane to me that not only were these toxic substances freely available, but they were also heavily advertised. But when I looked at what I, as a doctor, whose main interest was supposed to be people's health, could do to improve this situation, I realized that I'd have to get out of medicine and into politics. That was such a distasteful option I couldn't even consider it.

So, a little disenchanted with medicine, I was open to change, and the prospect of world travel found no objections in my mind or in my girlfriend's, either—she was into it as well.

Accordingly, in May 1972, we flew to Bali, our airline tickets indicating that we were planning to stepping-stone the Pacific Rim: Jakarta, Singapore, Kuala Lumpur, Manila, Hong Kong, Taipei, Seoul, Tokyo, and over the ocean to Vancouver. Actually, we had a four-year plan. From Vancouver we were going to go by train across Canada to Toronto, where some of my doctor friends were engaged in graduate studies. We were then going to travel overland through the United States and Central and South America, get a boat from the bottom of Argentina to Cape Town, and travel overland up through Africa to London. There we'd stay and regroup, work in a hospital for maybe six months (my girlfriend was a nurse), and then take off across Europe, the Middle East into India, down into Southeast Asia and finally, four years later, back to Australia. That was the plan.

What actually happened was somewhat different.

In the couple of months we spent on Bali's Kuta Beach we met many Europeans and Americans who had come overland all the way through Asia on their way to Australia to work, earn some money, and go back home. Our conversations with these travelers soon convinced us it would be more fun to stay in the East than go back to the West so soon, so we cashed in our tickets and changed our plans.

Hitch-hiking and busing our way north, we finished up in Thailand, a Buddhist country where I saw for the first time the external manifestations of Buddhism—monks, stupas, temples, and Buddha statues. More as a dutiful tourist than a spiritual seeker, I thought I'd better get a book that explained what Buddhism was all about. And since we were on our way to India, I got books on Hinduism and Islam as well.

However, not only was I not at all interested in religion, I was openly scornful of it. My family was Jewish, but not in the least observant, and I was educated at private Christian schools. When I was in my teens and a couple of friends tried to convert me to Christianity, my mother—a card-carrying atheist—panicked and gave me Bertrand Russell's *Why I Am Not a Christian* to read. I guess it worked; I didn't become a Christian.

I don't think I actually thought of myself as anything. If I did it, I was a non-believer—a scientific materialist. The universe had arisen through the chance interaction of atoms and molecules; life was a random occurrence that, when it crawled out of the protoplasmic slime, had no purpose other than to survive. As we evolved we added having a good time to mere survival. And when we died, that was it...oblivion forever. The idea of a creator God was preposterous.

So, as I read my first Buddhist book something strange happened. My heart stirred and, after a couple of passages, a voice inside me said, "This stuff's true"—true not in the factual sense of an anatomy textbook, but something deeper. Well, I noted the feeling but was certainly not motivated to act upon it—at least, not then. I also noted that the author mentioned the indispensability of meditation in Buddhism but I didn't know what that was and, again, didn't feel particularly motivated to find out—at least not then, either.

However, a couple of months later, having traveled more extensively through Thailand, as well as Laos and Burma, been exposed to more signs of Buddhism, and reading a bit more about it, we found ourselves in Kathmandu to meet this Danish guy to whom we'd lent money. No sooner had we stepped off the bus than José, a Brazilian friend from Bali and Bangkok who was hanging around the bus stop for some unknown reason, joyfully took us under his wing and proceeded to show us around town: where to stay, where to eat, who has the best pie, where to listen to music, where to buy dope and, "If you're interested in Buddhist meditation, there's a one-month course starting at a small Tibetan monastery just out of town."

Buddhist meditation? Wasn't that what I was supposed to find out more about at some point? Was now the time? The Danish guy was nowhere to be seen so we headed up to Kopan Monastery to find out about the course.

Kopan sits on the top of a little hill in the Kathmandu Valley, about a half hour's walk through beautiful rice paddies (well, they were rice paddies then, now it's all houses) from the great stupa of Boudhanath, one of

Kathmandu's great Buddhist landmarks. We found out that the course start-ed in less than a week's time and would be taught by a young Tibetan monk called Lama Zopa Rinpoche. It would also cost less to stay at Kopan and do the course than it would to wait for the Danish guy in town, so the deal was clinched. We'd do the one-month course.

> The spiritual way of life is completely different from the worldly, but unless you find a spiritual path you can never make the choice of which to follow.

There we were, about fifty out-of-control Westerners from all over the world, strangers stuck together for a month, most of us listening to Buddhist teachings for the first time. We were up at five in the morning, out into the cold, to sit cross-legged for an hour and a half's guided meditation. A one-hour break for breakfast, then the morning discourse until lunchtime. After lunch, a group-dis-cussion period followed by the afternoon discourse. Chai at five, more med-itation at six, dinner at eight, bed at ten. This went on relentlessly for thirty days. For the last two weeks we even skipped breakfast and dinner and got up an hour earlier. Most of us had never disciplined ourselves that much before. Most of us enjoyed it immensely.

The spiritual way of life is completely different from the worldly, but unless you find a spiritual path you can never make the choice of which to follow. Thus meeting my teacher, Lama Zopa Rinpoche, and the teachings of the Buddha made attending the Kopan course the most important event of my life. And from the opening discourse, which was an introduction to the meditation course and the first of about fifty that Rinpoche would deliv-er over the next month, we were confronted with a vast array of revolution-ary new concepts. Revolutionary to a Western mind, at least.

The subject was Dharma, or the teachings of the Buddha. Lama Zopa's definition of Dharma was "that which keeps you out of suffering." But to the Buddha, suffering wasn't only the pain, illness, loss, and mental problems that I'd always taken suffering to be. It went much deeper than that. There were innumerable different sufferings and many levels of it. Even igno-rance—not knowing something, even if you didn't know you didn't know it—was suffering. Ignorance, in fact, was the fundamental suffering and all others arose from it. No matter, then, that you felt good. As long as you were prone to experience any kind of problem in the future you were still in a state of suffering.

I could see that. Say a person has lung cancer but doesn't know it and feels perfectly well. In the early stages, the disease may be asymptomatic and detectable only by X-ray. You can't say that the person is healthy. But then the Dharma takes it one step further back. Even if you don't have cancer, as long as you're susceptible to it, you're suffering–even though you might be singing and dancing and having a good time. Furthermore, if that good time you're having is going to stop, that's another form of suffering. Having a good time is suffering? That was a new one for me.

The Dharma concept of happiness was also very different from the usual one because it taught two levels: temporary and ultimate. Temporary we all knew and it was all we knew. But ultimate happiness–that state beyond suffering–was not something most of us would have considered seriously. But in the face of much supportive evidence and the challenge to prove logically that such a state did not or could not exist and that the experience of countless meditators should be ignored, at Kopan, we had to consider it.

To understand how it was possible to attain everlasting happiness it was necessary to understand how one could last forever. Thus came the teaching on the beginningless and endless nature of mind and what is commonly called rebirth or reincarnation. All of us knew there was no such thing. But when called upon to prove it we were unable to do so.

This was one of the most striking features of the course and Buddhism in general you didn't have to accept or believe anything the Buddha taught, but you were expected to know clearly what you believed and why. And if you wanted to reject the teachings you were expected to be able to refute them with common sense and logic.

The Dharma explains all existence—describes, categorizes, classifies. Even if we didn't want to accept the Buddhist view of things, at least the analytical way it considered all phenomena gave us a framework for thinking about them. There wasn't a question that could not be asked and no answer was unobtainable. Suddenly there was no excuse for avoiding further the hitherto joke questions such as "What is the meaning of life?" that most of us tacitly accepted as being futile. We were told clearly what the Buddha saw as life's purpose and it was up to us to find a better alternative. A difficult task, for the purpose of the teachings was to bring all universal beings to the very highest state of mental development and happiness. It was extremely hard to ignore these teachings, although it might have been more comfortable to do so.

The main thing the Dharma addresses is the mind—its nature and the different kinds of positive and negative minds. Suffering and happiness were states of mind, and all beings wanted to experience happiness and avoid suffering. But why was our search for happiness endless, and why was the happiness we found so fleeting and so poor? Why did we always experience suffering instead pain, worry, frustration and loss? Why were we never satisfied with what we had? We had to experience all this because we didn't know what the true causes of happiness and suffering were and therefore didn't know what to do and what not to do to create them.

Thus, Rinpoche made clear what he felt was one of the main points of the Dharma teaching—that the cause of suffering is not in the external conditions, it is in the mind; and therefore the method to eradicate the cause of suffering has to primarily affect the mind, not the environment or other beings. Hence it was necessary to understand and practice Dharma, the inner method, if we were to escape from suffering and give value to our lives.

The root of suffering was ignorance; the ultimate cure was wisdom. Ignorance and wisdom were mental factors. As Dharma brought the highest wisdom and totally destroyed the cause of suffering, it led to permanent freedom from suffering and everlasting happiness. And, in contradistinction to external methods of finding happiness, there were no unpleasant or dangerous side effects from the Dharma. Its practice brought only better and higher happiness. Further, all the different Dharma methods could be integrated into one path leading to the very highest state, enlightenment, which all of us had the potential to experience. All we had to do was to create the cause of it in our own minds.

But most of us lead lives that are nothing but a series of disjointed attempts to experience the ephemeral pleasures we call happiness, and most of the time we spend doing the things we "have to" we're wishing we were doing the things we liked instead.

However, it is impossible to relate the details of that one month's teachings here.[1] The clear descriptions of the mind and life we received from Lama Zopa Rinpoche made it sound as if he knew each of us individually better than we knew ourselves. We were encouraged to listen to the teachings as a mirror for our mind, and when we checked our minds and lives against the teachings most of us saw ourselves clearly for the first time. After each discourse we practiced analytical meditation, subjecting the teachings we had just heard to the scrutiny of logic and reflecting upon our own experience to see if those teachings were in accordance with it.

There was also another kind of meditation—that designed to make the mind stable and calm—concentration meditation. This was when we got a really good view of what the lamas called the mad elephant mind—wild, uncontrollable, and dangerous. Until we sit down and try to still our mind we never realize just how restless it is. It doesn't matter how much a person is told that his mind is out of control; until he tries to control it, he'll never understand.

At first it seemed a hopeless task, but during the month of the course under its relatively ideal conditions, some of the students gained a little experience of tranquility of mind. Although I didn't have any such experience myself, I was encouraged to know that there was a tried and true method of seeing, understanding and developing the mind that would work for those who practiced it properly.

By the end of the course I knew that I had to investigate all this much more and that this was the most important thing to do. There were many things I found difficult to accept—such as the beginninglessness of mind—but I had gained enough wisdom, or suppressed enough arrogance, to be open to the possibility that any difficulty in comprehension came from my own ignorance rather than from some intrinsic flaw in the teachings. And I remember lying in my bed the night the course ended thinking, "It's all true," trembling slightly at the devastating consequences of such a thought should it still be with me the next morning.

The thought remained and so did I—at Kopan. I had decided that I wanted to devote my life to "practicing Dharma," but the question then was how. There were two possibilities—as a layperson or a monk. It would be at least six months and another meditation course before I seriously entertained the latter option.

In the summer of 1973 I was studying Lama Zopa Rinpoche's teachings on the perfect human rebirth—the state of being human with all the freedoms and endowments necessary to practice Dharma perfectly. At one point, Rinpoche stressed that it was very rare to find the chance to take ordination as a monk or nun but that it made practicing Dharma much easier and more profitable. At this point I was totally into practicing Dharma but even more into making it easy and profitable.

Furthermore, I couldn't find even one reason not to get ordained. Some people said that by taking robes you impaired your ability to communicate with others, but I didn't believe it then, and I now know through experience that the reverse is true. Since my ego was unable to produce any convincing arguments against becoming a monk and since the benefits were indisputable, I took novice ordination from His Holiness Ling Rinpoche at Bodhgaya in January 1974...as did my girlfriend.

Well, all that was more than thirty years ago and I can now look back on the road I've traveled since then to see if the life-changing decisions I made in my early thirties were sensible or not. At the time I was thinking that I was definitely into practicing Dharma full time, I was also wondering how I would support myself. I asked this question of Anila Ann McNeil, the Canadian nun who had assisted Lama Zopa Rinpoche with the course, and she looked at me as if I were a bit simple and said, "Oh, if you give yourself to the Dharma the Dharma will always look after you." So I was like, "Oh, Okay..." and went for it.

The question, of course, is how much I've truly given myself to the Dharma. I must be one of the worst practitioners the Buddha has known. Nevertheless, I have tried my best to follow the main principles of Mahayana Buddhism: respect and follow your teacher, study and meditate on the teachings, develop a good heart and never stop working for the happiness of others; always consider others' happiness to be more important than your own.

My little bio outlines my feeble attempts to give myself to the Dharma these past three decades, mainly founding and running meditation centers and Buddhist publishing houses. I lasted only twelve years as a monk— "only" because I had intended to remain ordained my whole life (my ex-girlfriend remains a nun to this day). All my teachers were monks and I had become one because I wanted to be like them, to help others as they did, as they had helped me. I thought this would mean a life of study, meditation, and teaching but that was not to be.

In 1977, Lama Yeshe, the head lama at Kopan and Lama Zopa Rinpoche's main teacher, sent me to New Delhi to start a meditation center and in 1983 to London to take over Wisdom Publications, the Buddhist publishing company we had co-founded at Kopan in 1975. All this running businesses in two of the world's largest cities—especially London—was too much for my frail, deluded mind and, as bad habits awoke with renewed vigor in response to the seductive environment, I realized that if I wanted to remain a monk I would have to retreat to a monastery, and if I wanted to continue publishing books I would have to disrobe. Figuring that developing Wisdom Publications would be of greater benefit than hiding in a monastery, I disrobed and carried on.

In 1989 we moved from London to Boston, where I remain. That same year, at Lama Zopa Rinpoche's request, I established Kurukulla Center for Tibetan Buddhist Studies in Boston and in 1996 left Wisdom to establish the Lama Yeshe Wisdom Archive.

How does all this qualify, at least in my mind, as a life of value? Karmically speaking, the main thing that determines whether what we do is beneficial or not is our motivation for doing it and, as much as I've been able to muster it, my motivation for doing what I've done since I met the Dharma has been the happiness of others; not just ordinary happiness but the highest happiness of all—that of enlightenment; and not just a few others but all beings everywhere throughout the infinitude of space.

Where does happiness come from? Good karma. Where does that come from? It comes from Dharma practice. Where does that come from? It comes from knowing about it. Therefore, in dedicating myself to the spread of Dharma by various means and the establishment of centers where people can study Dharma wisdom and learn to put it into practice, I feel that I have added great value to not only my life but to the lives of many others.

Furthermore, in turning my back on the normal conventional realities of family, job, career, reputation, wealth, and so forth and not having to work for money, I have been able to integrate that great dichotomy of modern life: work and leisure. I am free to channel all my energy in one direction: to the attainment of enlightenment for the sake of all sentient beings.

© Nicholas Ribush

Note

[1] *Transcripts of Lama Zopa Rinpoche's teachings at many of the Kopan courses may be found at www.LamaYeshe.com.*

About the Author

Dr. Nicholas Ribush, MB, BS, is a graduate of Melbourne University Medical School (1964) who first encountered Buddhism at Kopan Monastery in 1972. Since then he has been a student of Lama Yeshe and Lama Zopa Rinpoche, and a full time worker for the FPMT. He was a monk from 1974 to 1986. He established FPMT archiving and publishing activities at Kopan in 1973, and with Lama Yeshe founded Wisdom Publications in 1975. Between 1981 and 1996 he served variously as Wisdom's director, editorial director, and director of development. Over the years he has edited and published many teachings by Lama Yeshe and Lama Zopa Rinpoche, and established and directed several other FPMT activities, including the International Mahayana Institute, Tushita Mahayana Meditation Centre, the Enlightened Experience Celebration, Mahayana Publications, Kurukulla Center for Tibetan Buddhist Studies and now the Lama Yeshe Wisdom Archive. He currently sits on the board of three FPMT centers and was a member of the FPMT board of directors from its inception in 1983 until 2002.

Some people are suffering from lack of work, some from lack of water, many more from lack of wisdom.

Calvin Coolidge

It is difficult to overcome one's passions, and impossible to satisfy them.

Marguerite de La Sabliere

If we could see the miracle of a single flower clearly, our whole life would change.

Siddhartha Gautama

The only medicine for suffering, crime, and all the other woes of mankind is wisdom.

Thomas Huxley

Should those of us who are privileged to live in relative plenty forgive ourselves if we do not do everything we can to alleviate the preventable suffering that is all around us?

Christopher Phillips

One reason we cannot get "back to the garden of simplicity" - to that vision we all hold of a balanced life - is that we have forgotten that money is just a tool we invented. We now believe that without money we won't survive...

Vicki Robin

To be ignorant of one's ignorance is the malady of ignorance.

A. Bronson Alcott

Our scientific power has outrun our spiritual power. We have guided missiles and misguided men.

Martin Luther King, Jr.

There is a penalty for ignorance. We are paying through the nose.

W. Edward Deming

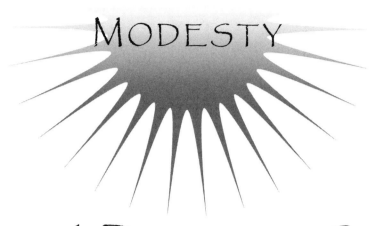

MODESTY

A DIFFERENT SENSE OF SECURITY
Sometimes the Past Holds the Key to Our Future

Kimberly Ridley

My father grew up on a subsistence farm, where his family scratched out a living from ten bony acres of pasture and forest. Because they had very little cash, they bartered for the few things they couldn't produce themselves. "We were so poor, we didn't even notice the Great Depression," my dad says.

They had no indoor plumbing or electricity. My grandmother cooked on a stove fed with wood my grandfather cut and split by hand. She canned mountains of vegetables and fruit to get her family through the long, cold Maine winters, and stashed the jars in a root cellar filled with potatoes and beets, carrots and onions, and apples from the family's little orchard.

As I stand in my own kitchen peeling potatoes from our garden, I marvel at how hard my father's family must have worked just to feed themselves. If my husband and I had to live on what we grow, we'd starve long before spring. I call my father and tell him this. He laughs.

"How did you manage, dad?" I ask. "Weren't you exhausted?"

"No," he says. "We had time to enjoy ourselves every day, and we never hurried to get things done."

His reply stuns me. I ask him, how was leisure time possible in the midst of a life filled with the basic tasks of survival? Neighbors helped each other with big jobs like haying the fields, he says, and work stopped when darkness fell. In the evenings, people read, played games, and told stories by lantern light. The main entertainment was "visiting" with family and friends.

> As I stand in my own kitchen peeling potatoes from our garden, I marvel at how hard my father's family must have worked just to feed themselves.

As I listen to my father's stories, it strikes me that he grew up the way many people in the world still live and have lived for centuries—linked to the land and thriving in the embrace of an interdependent community. Of course, it wasn't perfect or easy. Farm chores were strenuous, the closeness of a small community could grate on you, and women's lives were much more confined.

I'll be the first to admit that I love the comfort of modern conveniences. Yet in these troubled times, I think it's worth revisiting the ways my father's family sustained themselves during another tumultuous period in modern history. While thousands lost their livelihoods and homes, my father's family enjoyed a kind of security that had nothing to do with money. Although they were poor by material standards, they were rich in the things that are disappearing from our over-stuffed lives: free time, the knowledge and skills to provide for ourselves, and strong bonds of community.

Sometimes the past holds the key to the future—even if that future appears increasingly dark as global crises loom. In *The Long Emergency*, James Howard Kunstler writes of massive social breakdown he sees coming with the end of cheap fossil fuel. He also describes the qualities of the places he thinks have the best chances of emerging from the ensuing chaos. "The successful regions in the twenty-first century will be the ones surrounded by viable farming hinterlands that can reconstitute locally sustainable economies on an armature of civic cohesion," he writes.

Kunstler's vision bears striking similarities to the way my father's family—and so many others like them—thrived in difficult times. Perhaps it's time to re-examine some of the ways of life that have served humanity well for millennia, and explore how we might weave aspects of them into our everyday lives today. The experts are all around us—organic farmers, urban gardeners, and villagers around the world who have lived sustainably and happily in the same place for generations. We need only to listen to people like my father to learn how to live a sane, sustainable, and loving life.

© *Kimberly Ridley*

About the Author

Kim Ridley writes about positive social change. She is co-editor of *Signs of Hope: In Praise of Ordinary Heroes* and a contributing editor to *Ode* magazine.

I was born upon the prairie, where the wind blew free, and there was nothing to break the light of the sun. I was born where there were no enclosures, and where everything drew a free breath ... I know every stream and every wood between the Rio Grande and the Arkansas. I have hunted and lived over that country. I lived like my fathers before me, and like them, I lived happily.

Ten Bears

I was attracted to "small c" communism because, in theory, it sought to harness technology to solve human needs, give us less work and more leisure, and free us all to create, invent, explore, love, relax, and enjoy life without the want of the basic necessities of life.

Robin D. G. Kelley

Many companies are beginning to recognize their responsibility to the world around them. Their premise is simple: corporations, because they are the dominant institution of the planet, must squarely face and address the social and environmental problems that afflict humankind.

William J. McDonough

Look around, believe in what you see. The kingdom is at hand; the promised land at your feet. We can and will become what we aspire to be, if heaven's here on earth, if we have faith in humankind.

Tracy Chapman

Now that the United States and the rest of humanity have begun to confront the natural limits to our resources, we are in need of a new vision - a vision of a sustainable economy.

Herman E. Daly

Let's not talk anymore of capitalism and socialism; let's just talk of using the incredible wealth of the earth for human beings. Give people what they need: food, water, clean air, pleasant homes to live in, trees, some grass! Some hours of work; more hours of leisure. Don't ask "Who deserves it?" Every human being deserves it.

Howard Zinn

There is no greatness where there is not simplicity, goodness, and truth.

Leo Tolstoy

Throughout history, humans have lived on the Earth's sustainable yield - the interest from its natural endowment. But now we are consuming the endowment itself. In ecology, as in economics, we can consume principal along with interest in the short run, but in the long run it leads to bankruptcy.

Lester Brown

When the media produce pap, it's because those are the covers that sell and the programs that spike the Neilsens. When companies manufacture junk and junk food, it's because that's what we buy.

Anna Quindlen

Open your arms to change, but don't let go of your values.

Tenzin Gyatso

Many CEOs run their businesses like a one-night stand. People are buying from nameless global corporations with low prices. There's no feeling of intimacy or community, just of loneliness, separateness. We have lost our sense of place.

Judy Wicks

I used to think that as societies got richer they would quiet down. Instead, they seem to have got more frenetic. I used to think that wealth would make people nicer and more tolerant. Instead they became more competitive and more protective of what they had.

Charles Handy

We are in a war against a radical, violent stream of Islam that is fueled and funded by our own energy purchases. We are financing both sides of the war on terrorism: the U.S. Army with our tax dollars, and the Islamist charities, madrasas and terrorist organizations through our oil purchases.

Thomas L. Friedman

COURAGE

THE COURAGE TO CHALLENGE

Anita Roddick

The big dilemma about courage is that you never think anything you do is remarkable when it's instinctive. I can tell you what I've done that's been really controversial, what's put me on a brink. But one of the scariest things I've done was around the time of the Gulf War. It was a stand I took that could have cost me my company.

I was in America on business at the time, visiting my stores in Boston. I felt strongly that we, as a company, should be supporting the notion of United Nations sanctions against Iraq because I simply felt that we should be doing anything other than supporting military engagement. We were not alone in demanding development of the sanctions—the U.S. churches and labor unions supported sanctions. The idea of going to war was so obscene to me, especially to go to war in a repressive country and not for a moral issue but because of the commercial implications of oil production in Kuwait. I initiated a big sanctions campaign in England that was at the U.K. government and the major players: George Bush and Saddam Hussein. We had people writing letters and phoning. We gave customers the fax numbers of Margaret Thatcher, Bush, and Hussein and asked them to send a personal message. We plied our customers with the message, "Keep the Sanctions Going." At this stage, especially in Britain, there was a huge obsession, fueled by the media's gung ho approach, with going to war. Mrs. Thatcher favored going to war, and for the rest of us, there was no chance to be asked, to debate the issues.

I had billboards put up in Littlehampton, home base of The Body Shop. Quotes from Jesus Christ. From Gandhi. From some of the great warmongers, who were actually pacifists five minutes before they died. I put them up without any permission. We took a clear stand, and the town was confused. Littlehampton is a blue-collar town. Most of the grandparents have probably experienced war, but the kids have no notion of it. The English, in general, were just gung ho for the war: forty thousand kids off to the Gulf in nanoseconds. What I was doing wasn't very popular. It riled people up, and it riled up my company, split it right down the middle, male and female—and I think because of the male myths surrounding the war. One of the board members rang me up in America and said, "We've got to take these billboards down." And I said, "Over my dead body. They come down and I leave. This is not negotiable."

I came back to the U.K. and closed down the offices for an afternoon, and we held a huge intercompany debate. We had staff come down from our sites in London to join in the discussions at our headquarters where we had hundreds of people working. And as we debated, I thought, What if the whole company says, "Anita, stop this. We have to follow government policy." What would I do? If I endorse the democratic process, I have to follow democratic minds. And I just knew, absolutely knew, I would be out of the company like a bat out of hell. I would have to leave my own company. The tension for me was huge. And I remember thinking, very fleetingly, What would it be like if I didn't have my baby? I birthed it. I shaped it for all those years. And I hadn't yet done all that I wanted to do with it. Yet, I was willing to leave it on an issue of principle. I had my heart in my mouth thinking, Oh, God, they know I'm antiwar, but I'm not going to be able to persuade anybody that this campaign, this stand we're taking, is right.

And then, I don't know, something amazing happened. Some time ago, I had spent about a week with a group of our employees, a guy who drove a truck, a guy who packed the boxes, a woman who filled the bottles, and others, about twenty of them. I had them up to my house, just talking about life. (I used to do this, take twenty people, spend three, four days and just listen to them.) That particular time, we had talked about war and we had talked about violence. One man had been in the Falkland Islands and another had served in Northern Ireland during the Irish troubles. They said that, in reality, actions change your values. The experience of participating in the Falklands War and serving in Northern Ireland had changed their whole notion about war absolutely. And it was those guys who stood up during the debate and eloquently spoke. They told what was war like, the reality of it, who benefits and who doesn't, and it was as if two guardian angels had plopped down—and I didn't need to say anything.

I didn't leave the company, but the experience brought me to a scary brink. Very few people, maybe a dozen close colleagues, knew what was going on with me, what would have happened—that I would have left the company. It was such a personal, private decision. And the strange thing is that when something like that happens, you have no options. Either you don't have the time to think—and so what comes through you is instinctive, and therefore, the most honest expression of who you are—or you just know you have no alternative. I don't know if it's courage, but there's a clarity of purpose when nothing is negotiable.

I felt that same clarity during my face-off with Shell Oil. No question, that took courage. That took incredible courage.

In *Our Agenda*, a publication of political and social issues supported by The Body Shop, we speak about this campaign, about Ken Saro-Wiwa, the Ogoni people, and Shell Oil: "On 10 November 1995, the Nigerian military dictatorship shocked the world by executing innocent writer and human rights activist Ken Saro-Wiwa and eight other environmentalists for their involvement in a long and peaceful campaign about homelands polluted by the oil-drilling activities of Royal Dutch Shell and other multinational companies over thirty years."

Although I never met him, Ken Saro-Wiwa became a good friend, through his letters, his family, and colleagues. Saying his name still makes me stop in grief that he's gone. He was an environmental activist and writer, one of the most popular in Nigeria. When he visited The Body Shop offices in the U.K., he said he wanted to go back to Nigeria, and when I heard this, I just knew he was going to be arrested. In his last speech to the military court in Nigeria, he said, "Shell is here on trial...The company has ducked this particular trial, but its day will surely come and the lessons learnt here may prove useful to it for there is no doubt in my mind that the ecological war the company has waged in the Delta will be called to question sooner than later and the crimes of that war be duly punished."

I tried desperately to stop that ecological war in the Ogoni. We lobbied members of Parliament. We demonstrated at the Nigerian Embassy. We protested outside the headquarters of Shell. We organized letter writing and brought the Ogoni issue to the attention of the media. When you challenge another company on a moral issue, or an issue of human sympathy or behavior, you set yourself up for assault, unlike when you challenge for a market share, in which case you can be as mean and dirty as you like. On the Shell issue, I contacted a number of companies belonging to the socially responsible business movement and basically said to them: "You've got to help us on this one. We need to have international outrage about what the Nigerian military dictatorship and Shell have done. What Shell has done in Nigeria would be banned in the Western world." Some offered support, while others said they couldn't because they never challenge another company. Others excused themselves by saying they were not perfect as a company either. Well, neither am I perfect, but that shouldn't keep your sense of outrage in a straight jacket. There's so much outrage that's tempered and squashed and watered down in business because of these strange myths that you can't be political, that you can't challenge the system.

We challenged Shell in a very honorable way. I have learned a lot from tribal peoples, and one lesson is that you change by shaming. Gordon, my husband, spent a lot of time with top officials of Shell in England. We offered to collaborate with them. We have a very strong, very bright group of academics who work with us on environmental issues. We offered to put together the assessments on pollution, social impact, environment, and so forth. We would do all the homework, all the strategizing, all the academic stuff. And we'd plop it in their laps so they' know what to do. But no, they wouldn't touch it.

Working with the Ogoni community in Nigeria—doing ads, standing up and speaking out—was not easy. In England, activism by women is seen either as shrill or as marketing. People never support you because you care passionately about something. They cut you off and ridicule you. Standing in this huge courtyard outside the Shell building with a microphone and hundreds of people looking at me and, in a very studied and diplomatic way, talking about what was happening—it wasn't easy. I love storytelling, but standing up there against one of the biggest multinationals in the world and challenging them...scary. Scary in a physical sense, certainly, but what was even scarier was how Shell officials simply looked on passively at the demonstrations against them, taking no action on the plight of the Ogoni. In the end, that corporate passivity has cost them. The constant public outcry about their conduct in Nigeria has forced them to invest heavily in reputation management.

I think whatever bravery I have in me came from my mother. We were one of a handful of Italian immigrant families in the seaside town of Littlehampton on the English Channel, and Mummy begrudgingly sent us to Catholic Mass conducted by a priest whom she hated. When my father died young of a heart attack, the priest came knocking on the door and said, "Mrs. Perella, we know your husband was an atheist, and you're lucky we're going to bury him at St. Catherine's Church." Mummy took a bucket of dirty water and threw it at him. Now there was a courageous act.

Sacred cows were shattered early, and I learned a rebel's brand of courage.

The four of us Perella children attended school at the local convent. Mummy would squash garlic between our fingers to fight the incense and there we'd be, all four of us lined up and smelling down the place. When the nuns told the Perella children to put on skirts, Mum said, "No, it's cold, wear trousers." Sacred cows were shattered early, and I learned a rebel's brand of courage.

I've done things that, when I look back on them, I wonder, "Why ever did I do that—it was crazy." I travel six months out of the year to learn from indigenous tribes, and I've known at times, in the blink of an eye, we shouldn't be someplace, that we were in danger. That's the bit I don't understand, the nonnegotiable, the driven part. George Bernard Shaw said, "Life is no brief candle...it is a sort of splendid torch which I've got hold of for a moment, and I want to make it burn as brightly as possible before handing it on to future generations." Anyone who does a courageous act passes it on. We learn from them. I guess, in a way, that's what I'm doing with this life of mine.

Reprinted with permission by New World Library from Women of Courage, *edited by Katherine Martin.*

About the Author

Dame Anita Roddick is an activist and entrepreneur passionately committed to issues of fair trade and human rights. Roddick founded The Body Shop in 1976. The first shop was opened in Brighton, England, and has grown world-wide. Roddick is passionately committed to issues of fair trade and human rights. She was named a Dame of the Order of the British Empire in 2003. To read more about Anita Roddick visit her Web site at www.anitaroddick.com.

It is noble to fight wickedness and wrong; the mistake is in supposing that spiritual evil can be overcome by physical means.

Lydia Maria Child

There's no honorable way to kill, no gentle way to destroy. There is nothing good in war. Except its ending.

Abraham Lincoln

No matter what the fight, don't be ladylike! God almighty made women and the Rockefeller gang of thieves made the ladies.

Mary Jones

There is little place in the political scheme of things for an independent, creative personality; for a fighter. Anyone who takes that role must pay a price.

Shirley Chisholm

I know there are military moms who view the war in Iraq through different ideological lenses than mine. Sometimes I envy them. God, how much easier it must be to believe one's son or daughter is fighting a just and noble cause!

Teri Wills Allison

Nothing could be worse than the fear that one had given up too soon, and left one unexpended effort that might have saved the world.

Jane Addams

Politicians and religious icons often fail to be authentic leaders who have the people's interests in mind. But we do need true leadership to help Americans find our way before it's too late. Each of us has potential for leadership, for developing ourselves, and chipping in. We are all responsible for moving stones from the quarry to the site where we're building this chapel of ours, and some of us are sleeping on the job, while others are stealing the stones and selling them at market. If I take time to go counsel, expose, or defeat the lollygagger or the thief, then who's doing my work!? It's an awful position for humans to be in.

Jason Merchey

CREATIVITY

ESCAPING THE CAGE

Christine Rose

The culture in which we are raised is a tricky thing. We are conditioned to believe that the values it supports are good and what it does not embrace is bad, or, at best, weird. Most people seem to live their entire lives without seriously questioning this conditioning, much of which are useful to a great extent, such as at least seven of the Ten Commandments. But what happens when over time they are misinterpreted for bad reasons? "Thou shalt not kill," seems straight forward enough, but since the founding of our country, soldiers have been sent to do just that. Sometimes it is done for noble purposes, but more often it is done simply to increase this country's wealth and control of the world's resources. It is difficult for a person to break free of this cultural trap, because one must first examine the foundations of their belief system, and breaking these down could destroy one's view of world and self. Their perception of reality would literally change. They would be cast adrift in an unknown universe.

For me, breaking away was a long and painful process. There are still times I feel as if I'm not meant for this world, this life. My opinions and perceptions are so very far from "the norm."

I was raised in the prison town of Huntsville, Texas, literally "The Execution Capital of the World." Throughout High School, I prided myself on being a "hippie" and talking about peace and love. As you can imagine, that went over well with the local east Texas mentality! Needless to say, I wasn't a popular girl.

> We are conditioned to believe that the values it supports are good and what it does not embrace is bad, or, at best, weird.

At twenty, while attending Sam Houston State University, I came across a PETA pamphlet on campus. This was the first turning point in my life. It was the first time I became aware that there were horrible things going on "behind the scenes." As I read in horror about animal testing and factory farming, I said to myself, *If people only knew, they would stop this!* Ah, young naiveté! I took it upon myself to tell everyone I could, but I quickly realized that people didn't want to know. They wanted to stay in the dark, and they certainly didn't want to be preached to about their food or their lifestyle.

So, surrounded by the beef-eating population who consider ketchup a vegetable and actual vegetables a garnish, I became a vegetarian. Alone and quite often ridiculed, it was a difficult struggle; one which I never quite overcame until I moved to Northern California in my twenty-seventh year. There, I met others with like minds, discovered there was something called the Green Party, and recycling was done at the curb! I felt like I had come home for the first time in my life. I quickly joined the Green Party and subsequently ran for local office. I sat on the County Council in two different counties during my time in California.

It was also in California that I met my husband, and we could not be more perfectly suited for each other. Ethan, a general contractor, had been long interested in alternative energy and building techniques. He enjoyed Renaissance Faires, swing dancing, magical fiction, progressive politics, and he was a vegetarian. After our wedding, we bought our first solar panel and were well on the way to being off-grid and living lightly on the land.

That was five years ago.

Now, somewhere in the wilds of the Bly Mountain Region in Southern Oregon—beyond the reach of power lines and phone lines—my husband, a menagerie of cats and dogs, and I quietly live and work on my third feature length film.

Before becoming a filmmaker, I spent many years as an activist working with local progressive political organizations. To my dismay, I gradually realized that these organizations were overburdened with organizers and had a decided lack of people who were prepared to buckle down and do the necessary work to accomplish the larger goals they kept setting for themselves. The most effective people seemed to be those who took the responsibility upon themselves and quietly worked away at it.

After seeing *Bowling for Columbine*, being impressed by the inspiration it engendered in so many people, I decided that movies were the way to reach people. Michael Moore's film so contrasted with the mainstream media's unresponsiveness and misrepresentation of what was happening in the world; I knew that people were hungry for this kind of information.

When I began my first film, *Liberty Bound*, I was still teaching myself the process of movie-making. The one thing I failed to learn was that it couldn't be done without financing, celebrity connections, and expensive equipment. I simply knew that making movies was what I wanted to do.

Starting with basic business knowledge, a desktop computer, and a consumer-grade camcorder, I set off to make my first film. The greatest resource I had was my determination to make a great film and to tell the truth as I saw it. This sustained me, despite my doubts that I'd be able to successfully fund distribution. I soon learned that getting my movie before an audience would be a much more costly and time-consuming enterprise than making the film itself. Since I was working virtually alone, I handled both tasks simultaneously. I familiarized myself with the filmmaking process by making several short films, including one about a large peace march in San Francisco, which even the *local* media failed to cover. At the same time, I reached out over the Internet to other people in the film community. Once again, I met many people who talked a lot about their plans and ideas without doing much, but I learned quite a bit and occasionally met a rare individual eager and willing to help. One such person was Lorraine Evanoff, who was a tremendous help in marketing and eventually selling the film.

I researched people whose civil rights had been violated and set up interviews with them, as well as leaders of the liberal community such as Howard Zinn and Michael Parenti.

Once I had outlined a plan of action, I set off by train across the country, conducting interviews and gathering information. While on the train, I witnessed the interrogation of a fellow passenger by police officers. The passenger had made a comment about the inappropriateness of President Bush's response to 9/11 in a private conversation, and had been overheard and reported to the police by another passenger. I quietly put my headphones on and pressed "record," later incorporating it into her movie. It remains the most compelling part of the film to this day.

When I returned home, I began cataloguing footage and editing it into shape. Since I lacked the resources to do extra filming, I purchased stock footage & licensed news footage; however, I used public domain footage whenever possible to keep costs down. It was a long process involving months of working late into the night. David Petergnana, another crew member I had met on the Internet, agreed to write the music for a deferred fee, and when it was finally finished, Lorraine Evanoff offered to take it with her on her trip to the Cannes Film Market. To my astonishment and delight, I received a call from Lorraine two days later. She shouted into my disbelieving ear, "We sold the film! We sold the film!"

Take Off, a French distributor, expressed interested in acquiring the Foreign Distribution rights and providing finishing funds. I was flown to Paris for final post-production and again for the Theatrical Premiere at Place Saint-Michel in June 2004, just across from Notre Dame Cathedral, but there was still a great deal of hard work ahead.

My first two feature documentaries, *Liberty Bound* and *Internationally Speaking*, were shot primarily with a consumer grade camcorder. I have since upgraded to a Panasonic DVX100A, which I was able to purchase when I was hired by local organizations to shoot their own projects. This includes a fire safety video (PSA) narrated by Gary Burgoff ("Radar" from *M*A*S*H*), the only famous actor with whom I have ever worked.

Now on my third film, *Nesting Habits of the Feral Hippie*, a mockumentary which pokes fun at documentaries and reality shows, I work without phone lines, using power generated onsite with solar panels and a windmill. My husband and I are the subjects of the film, while three actors play the research team who documents the building of the environmentally friendly house.

Just as our commitment to conservation inspired us to build our house with alternative and recycled material gathered locally, we also save money on sets and travel by bringing that same resourcefulness to our movie-making process. We make full use of the situations and material available to us. Since my husband, a general contractor by trade, is also a talented writer, we have a very funny script produced at the cost of a package of legal pads and a few cases of beer.

Through example and work I have taught more than I ever could've by lecturing in an academic setting. Due to the subject matter, I continually meet other people (like Howard Zinn) whose lives are a continuing inspiration to me. It's a wonderful circle, and we must continue to recharge each other's batteries, because it's not easy living a life outside the cage.

© *Christine Rose*

About the Author

Christine Rose is a director-writer-producer who started making films out of a deep desire for an artistic outlet that merged her creative core with her technological talents. Focusing mainly on political and controversial themes, her work has been viewed around the world. She has relentlessly pursued diverse and litigious issues that are at the crux of social and political life in the United States. Her films range from staged parodies to raw Cinéma Vérité documentaries.

Rose received a BA in English Literature from Sam Houston State University in 1992 and earned a Master's in English from Texas Woman's University in 1996. She has received no formal filmmaking training, but has been a committed and tireless activist since her days as a student. She participated in the recent worldwide anti-War movement, worked passionately for animal advocacy groups, volunteered for Peace & Justice Centers, served as a county-level elected political official and defended civil liberties and democratic rights during the Bush Regime. As a filmmaker, she has recently completed her second feature-length documentary.

Films by Christine Rose:

Magdalen Trailer (2002) – promotional trailer
Real Terrorists (2002) – short
Corporate Nation (2002) – short
SF Protest A20 (2002) – short
Evolve! (2002) – animated short
Wally Wally (2003) – short
Liberty Bound (2003) – feature documentary
Internationally Speaking (2005) – feature documentary

Founder of Blue Moose Films, Christine lives in Oregon with her husband Ethan.

The only thing worse than being blind is having sight but no vision.

Helen Keller

The greatest danger for most of us is not that our aim is too high and we miss it, but that it is too low and we reach it.

Michelangelo

In a way, I feel like Johnny Appleseed. I'm planting seeds all over this country: seeds of peace, seeds of hope. At some point, maybe years from now, there will be orchards. So in a sense, it's about more than this election. It's about more than politics. It's about envisioning a new America.

Dennis Kucinich

First they came for the Jews. I was silent. I was not a Jew. Then they came for the Communists. I was silent. I was not a Communist. Then they came for the trade unionists. I was silent. I was not a trade unionist. Then they came for me. There was no one left to speak for me.

Martin Niemoller

Adapt or perish: now as ever is Nature's inexorable imperative.

H. G. Wells

How will I know what lies over the next ridge, beyond the next trail's turning, along a creek, in the corners of my mind, if I don't give myself permission to wander?

Cathy Johnson

No matter what anybody tells you, words and ideas can change the world.

Thomas Schulman

If you work at that which is before you, following right reason seriously, vigorously, calmly without allowing anything else to distract you, but keeping your divine part pure, as if you might be bound to give it back immediately; if you hold to this, expecting nothing, fearing nothing, but satisfied with your present activity according to nature...you will be happy. And there is no man who is able to prevent this.

Marcus Aurelius

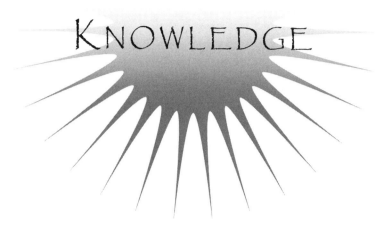

KNOWLEDGE

THE SCIENTIFIC METHOD AND VALUE JUDGMENTS

Andreas Rosenberg

The word "value" stands for a quite complex, abstract concept as you cannot see, hear, or touch a value. It measures the position of the consequences of some event or act on a quite arbitrary scale, established by a group of people. High value is desirable to this group and low value is definitely something to be avoided. Economics is a prescriptive system of acts, all designed to produce outcomes of high value on a monetary scale. An act has a high value in such a system if it produces credit for those acting! It is a simple system, and nobody disputes that science, whether it be used in economics or technology, plays a large role in creating such value.

When we go to another common value scale, that of *moral* value, the situation becomes immediately more complex. On the moral value scale, we grade acts and events as to their effect on the members of the group that established the value scale. Without a group around the act or event, there is no need for this scale. A hermit on some island has no need for moral values—unless he ponders his past before becoming a hermit. As economic values are related to our material possessions, where do moral values belong?

We seem still to be suffering from the dualism introduced in antiquity: body and soul. Moral values are relegated to the soul, whereas science, technology, and all learned knowledge ultimately can be reduced to observations and thus belong to the spheres of the body. It is popular even among scientists to talk about two different magisteria: one associated with weekdays and the work required in producing the food, shelter, and the entertainment that we feel we are entitled to; the second associated with Sundays when we are supposed to gather and evaluate on the moral scale the deeds we carried out during the week. The practitioners of this Sunday evaluation build their norms on other grounds than those used by the workers during the week, thereby asserting their superiority and the superiority of the soul over the body. It became immensely popular to stress this separation by referring to the so-called two culture model of C. P. Snow—the shabby curate of poetry, theology, arts, music, and history against the mundane world of mathematicians, statisticians, chemists, and astronomers. The scientists and the technicians created the Maxim gun, but whether we should massacre or not our opponents with it was decided in the realm of the moral soul.

> We seem still to be suffering from the dualism introduced in antiquity: body and soul.

There is something definitely artificial in this separation. Albert Einstein's well-known admiration of the incredible beauty of the regularity of the universe is still assigned to the scientific, technical edifice and to the observations by our senses, whereas when in the movie *Patton* the general orders his chaplain to pray for good weather so the bombings could commence. Does this represent an act in the realm of morals?

It is not only artificial; it's wrong! All value scales, including the economic and moral, are based on the basic assumption of a world driven by causality. The expression "if A then B" characterizes not only a logical relation, but it is what we observe with our senses every day. Both the illustrious representative of the soul, Thomas Aquinas, and the lowliest of chemists use the same arguments based on the irrefutability of causality. If their arguments both have wings and both say, "Quack, quack," they are both ducks.

You cannot separate ducks saying thatone wing flaps for the soul and the other for the benefit of the body.

If we add to causality the condition of the irreversibility of time, we have a common foundation for all human experience, value scales included. Science and morality, consequently, have a common foundation.

The question is: how do we establish our value scales when we are dealing with morality and not with counting money? In the last case, it was quite simple. More is better than less! Morality, however, deals with acts and their consequences. Human deeds form a tapestry of events tied together in strings of causality. How do we judge such sequences of events on a moral scale? We just declared science to grow from the same ground as morality. If this is so, how do they relate to each other?

We can approach the problem historically. We record the past; in fact, there is but the past to record. The deeds of Kublai Khan, Mahatma Gandhi, and Albert Schweitzer all represent sequences of events, each of which is a cause for some subsequent event as well as being itself caused by something preceding. It is a wonderful, meandering path in time and space—maybe verifiable, maybe not. However, it is also a colored thread in the tapestry of the total history of mankind; it is now nothing independent that can be extracted from the tapestry. We see a picture in the tapestry and we convert the progress of the threads forming a pattern into a story.

The travels of the lost warriors of Greece after the Trojan War become the epic tale of Odysseus. The shadows of the past also form patterns in the tapestry. We fellow tribe members or towns gather, listen, and decide then what patterns in the stories or myths are attractive, desirable, and have consequences that we appreciate. They are the same stories our parents heard and appreciated. So through generations, we form a value scale for *our* acts recorded in our mythology. Let us make it clear that calling a story a mythological yarn does not mean that it is necessarily a fantasy. The real past has been reduced, idealized to essentials retold in poetic form. Washington's crossing the Delaware, a true military operation, is rapidly changing into a colorful picture of flags, heroics, and leadership—not false, but probably neither entirely correct. With time, reality retreats and symbolic acts replace the real ones. Moses carries down tablets from Mount Sinai and parts the Red Sea. These are acts quite far from what we can stretch ourselves to believe. The causal pattern of rules presented within the frame of the story remains and forms part of the basis for one possible moral value scale.

The retelling of the narrative is the principal method which our liberal arts education uses today to counsel us and judge the acts of others. Prose, poetry, history are the fields where value judgments are formed. Our *moral* values grow out of our past. Fine, but where does science enter the picture, or has it been left wayside?

Of course, there is indeed another way to look at the progress of time ,and thus our past—the scientific method. At this point, the practitioners in the circle of the First Culture stridently assert that the sciences, servants of our senses, have no place in this discussion. They often declare that the proposal about the common root of causality for science and morality is not relevant. Since David Hume, the argument has been that sciences talk about events and observations using "is" and "is not" in propositions verifiable by our senses. You cannot derive from such propositions new propositions of obligatory nature containing expressions such as "ought" and "ought not." To do so is to commit the so-called natural fallacy.

This argument represents a curious illusion both about science and the origin of norms for moral values. First, the moral values originate in our past and represent the presence of a lexicon of values assigned by our tribe or town to different acts and their consequences. The norms derived from these observed consequences can, and should, be examined with scientific methods because history deals with events recorded by our senses and those are amenable to the scientific method. The propositions defining the historical record, the source of all our myths and narratives, can be expressed in terms of "is" or "is not." History records the sequence of events A, B, C, etc. without bias and explanation. Mythology sees in this sequence a pattern that is common to many such event sequences and interprets it metaphorically. This operation transfers patterns of causality to vastly more general relationships between facts and concepts.

We know from detailed analysis of documents that the 1765 question of British taxation of the American colonies, necessary for their own defense, led to a series of successive events, the Boston tea party and the Boston massacre among them, and each representing a complex conflict of economic and political interests. These events eventually led to war and independence now form, however, a beautiful legend from which acts of courage and treason have defined the patriotic value scale in America. The patterns so produced, now abstract in their nature, become the models for valued or not-valued actions of individuals.

The metaphoric transfer of actual patterns of events takes time and is more pronounced in the older legends, such as the narrative forming the backbone of Christian theology.

If we admit that the myths and legends used in establishing value scales all have their ultimate source in real history and thus are accessible for analysis by scientific methods, where do the so-called normative propositions originate?

The proposition containing the expression "ought" has its origin in teaching. Children are taught, using normative sentences of the type "You should not do this" and textbooks record these expressions—the aim of which is not to define moral behavior but to train children. The statement, "You should turn your body when delivering a forehand in tennis" is in no way a proposition dealing with the realm of the soul but, nevertheless, can not be derived from propositions based on the use of "is" or "is not." It is based on the consequences observed for past forehands. There is no difference in a teaching process used for tennis or for morality. When I throw a brick at my window one hundred times and the glass breaks each time, the suggestion to my son "you should not throw bricks at windows" is directly derived from observations by the scientific method, although it cannot be derived by classical logical procedures. The frequency of the consequence of past actions defines the probability of them repeating themselves in the future. The perceived natural fallacy is a result of applying classical logical structure to propositions linked by the concept of probability, a concept unknown to classical logic.

We have thus restored the role of science into morality as an instrument of investigation and examination. We have to make very clear the difference of science as a compilation of propositions dealing either with stars and space or molecules in a plastic material and the scientific method of examination applicable to all areas of human endeavor. The compilation of facts in any area of science is intentionally framed in a way that relates ultimately to the observations we make of the objects we study, be they stars or molecules. However, if we study the foundations of morality, we have to study the record of human behavior to establish the rules by which the game of life has been played.

The human race is a conglomerate of individuals sharing knowledge, storing it, and transferring it from generation to generation. The thoughts of Aristotle, Spinoza, the mathematics of Leibniz, and the poetry of Frost all form a cohesive, incredibly colorful tapestry. Tracing the threads of thought and action by scientific method, we recognize and discover patterns. Value scales and morality are no different from patterns of stars in the sky or patterns of molecules in the compounds we analyze; they are but another aspect of reality where the objects and their relationships are not directly observable but definitely conceivable. It is the ultimate satisfaction to recognize a shape that maybe never has appeared to anybody before. It is here that the great challenge for the mind lies, never ending oceans of thought to explore and adventures to discover. A life of value is an examined and examining life.

© *Andreas Rosenberg*

About the Author

Andreas Rosenberg is an Estonian by birth who, due the turbulence of the war, received his education in Sweden. After graduating from the University of Lund with a degree in physics and chemistry he moved to the University of Uppsala, Sweden where he was awarded both PhD and a doctorate of science in biochemistry. He was invited 1961 by the University of Minnesota to participate in a research program financed by National Science Foundation. He continued his research in protein chemistry at the University of Minnesota for the next forty years, during which time he became professor of laboratory medicine and pathology, as well as of biochemistry and biophysics. He was also on a parallel track of studying the philosophy of science at the Humanist Institute of Minnesota and New York. After becoming professor emeritus, he joined the Osher Institute of Lifelong Learning at the University of Minnesota as lecturer.

He has published about 150 scientific papers in his field and about fifteen chapters and articles about science, philosophy, and religion.

Where would we be without prophets, visionaries, nonconformists, ironists, and dissenters? The great ethical traditions, both religious and secular, as well as literature and the arts, are filled with eccentrics – complex characters who challenge, inspire, and irritate those around them. They flaunt conventional wisdom, stubbornly champion new and unsettling ideals, love those whom others deem unlovable, or are themselves considered strange and unlovable.

Elizabeth Kiss

The significant problems we have cannot be solved at the same level of thinking with which we created them.

Albert Einstein

We are sometimes tempted to think of Einstein and other physicists as coldly analytical men because they expressed their thoughts through mathematics – a universal and precise language that is completely lacking in passion. Yet when we peek behind the equations to look that these scientists' personal experiences and insights, we find that they were deeply moved by the music of the cosmos.

Thomas J. McFarlane

To discover my own questions required wandering in a self-created void, allowing each question to push me to the next. The process permitted me to see what my "teachers" had missed, not because I was smarter or had more data, but because I listened to my own questions and let them take me where they would.

Frances Moore Lappé

We are continually faced with a series of great opportunities brilliantly disguised as insoluble problems.

John W. Gardner

Genius is nothing but continued attention.

Claude A. Helvetius

Every revolution was first a thought in one man's mind.

Ralph Waldo Emerson

SELF-CONFIDENCE

BE YOUR OWN GURU

Douglas Rushkoff

My good friend Jody Radzik—the guy who first introduced me to raves, actually—started up a blog this year. Jody is about the most loving and optimistic person I've ever known. That's why I was surprised that instead of touting a new spiritual or cultural phenomenon, Radzik had decided to bash one.

Guruphiliac.com is dedicated to exposing the profoundly manipulative legions of grifters preying on the spiritually hopeful, as well as those teachers who simply go around letting people think they're God, one guru at a time. It's is an entertaining website, to be sure (for those of us who enjoy watching false messiahs unmasked) but it's also important ongoing work. And the more I think about it, the more guru-bashing is starting to look like a form of optimism, in itself.

We all have gurus of some sort, whether we realize it or not. Even just for brief moments during the day. Haven't you felt yourself regress to a childlike state, say, when talking to the auto mechanic about your car, the doctor about your test results, or your bartender about which Scotch to drink? In those moments—for an instant—the person becomes something of trusted authority in whose hands you trustingly place yourself. He will take care of me; he has my best interests at heart.

And in most cases, there's of no great negative consequence to relinquish that authority. It's just a drink, after all. And while we may want to self-educate a bit before undergoing surgery, we don't need to learn how to remove an appendix in order to have one taken out. Unless we're chronically ill, the doctor doesn't remain our guru.

Even in situations where we're learning to do something—say hang-gliding or building a campfire—it can be helpful to surrender authority to the teacher. Certainly in their area of expertise, and for the duration of the lesson, the teacher is the master.

Where it gets tricky is when we assume that our protector's expertise in one area makes him or her, somehow, better than us in all in all things. The Outward Bound leader knows how to build a fire and eat nettles—so in the context of the wilderness, he's certainly got a leg up on you. But does this mean the little life lessons and platitudes he drops on you during difficult moments on the trail are universally valid teachings? They sure seem so in the moment, and they may occasionally be applicable to some other situation. But they're just the musings of some guy.

Yes, it's terrific to be able to surrender to the unassailable mastery of your cello teacher. She has stories to tell, techniques to share, and a holistic understanding of her instrument and music that you'd be well to emulate. And focusing on her brilliance, holding her phrases in your head like a mantra while you're running your scales can make those interminable hours of practice more bearable and even productive.

But nowhere does there exist a genuine Bagger Vance or Horse Whisperer. There are no shrinks like Judd Nelson in *Ordinary People* or Robin Williams in *Good Will Hunting*. Sure, there are great golf pros, horse trainers, and therapists. But they're just people. The successful therapeutic ending is not surrendering to the loving embrace of a psychologist, however much we may feel the need for a parental substitute or emotional surrender. In the trade, they call this transference, and at best it's a means, not an ends.

It's also a terrific technique for engendering loyalty. Back in the 90s, I did some studies on coercive tactics. From the CIA Interrogation Manual to one of Toyota's sales handbooks, I found the same basic strategy: confuse or disorient the subject until they regress to a childlike state, then step in as a parent figure and offer relief by accepting a confession or sale.

The guru operates the same way. At the end of the post-modern era, those brave souls courageous enough to see through the religions they may have grown up with emerge frightened and confused. An ex-orthodox Jew or a "recovering" Catholic is also a disoriented, vulnerable person. Although the latest cool bumper sticker says "Eastern religions suck, too," it's hard to go through the world suddenly without a ready system and someone to administer it. So, like people who end up in the same bad relationship time after time only with partners with different color hair, people who liberate too quickly or angrily from one system often end up adopting the next one that comes along.

The path of devotion offered by gurus is also a natural fit for those of us who are fed up with the relativistic haze of a world where there are no discernible rules, yet equally disillusioned by institutional religions that appear to have sold out to American consumerism. The guru offers absolutism. Certainty. A point of focus.

As one slick guru, chronicled on Guruphiliac explains on his website: "When you meet a master, you have two choices. Transform or walk away. You cannot be in his presence and remain the same." Uh, yeah. In other words, conform to his reality or scram.

The guru is the starting place from which all other decisions are to be made. You start with the guru as the one perfect point in the universe, and from there everything else can fall into place. If the guru has instructed you to eat a certain food or do a certain practice, then—according to the logic of gurudom—everything else you have to do for this to happen is part of the perfection. Slowly but surely, surrender to the guru requires you to reject pretty much everything that doesn't fit whatever model of the world he's offering you.

But, honestly, that's what the devotee was after in the first place. An excuse to do or not do all that other confusing stuff in life like encounter people with different ideas, wrestle with the questions of existence, and accept that nobody really knows what happens when we die.

Most of us who have had gurus eventually see something awful—like sexual exploitation, financial abuse, or faked magic—that turns us off. (If we see the guru as perfect, then those blowjobs and false claims get justified: perhaps the guru is testing us, or breaking our hang-ups, at least for a while.)

Or we decide that this guy is just too much of an asshole to really be enlightened. Or we simply tire of the idea that "enlightenment" is around the corner, and decide that life is just fine without enlightenment. And getting to that point is a beautiful thing in itself. If an experience with a guru really teaches one the futility of aspirational spiritual quests, then it can even be worth the time, money, and humiliation.

The biggest spiritual victim in the equation is the guru, himself. He's just a person, after all, who probably had a profound spiritual or psychedelic experience and began to speak or write about it romantically. Charismatically. And this invites admirers and would-be devotees. The guru-in-waiting may not even mean to attract this sort of attention—at least not at the beginning. It's just the kind of positive reinforcement that naturally comes to a person who speaks passionately about something. I've felt shades of it myself, especially when I'm doing a book tour or a lecture about a transcendental topic. Wide-eyed audiences, especially those in areas where don't get many weird authors, gobble up every word. College students want to hang out late into the night, talking over drinks (or better) about alternate realities, magick sigils, or the nature of time. How hard it is not to speak about magick in a magickal way?

And it feels good to give people answers—something to chew on for a while, even if, like a Zen koan, it eventually turns out to be little more than a puzzle to keep them occupied and less afraid of death or existence for a while. To accept this path of the guru, though, however tempting, is certain doom for the artist, writer, or philosopher. It turns his existence from a question into an answer, from flux to certainty—from a life into a death.

Most of the generation of weird sages above my peers and me has died. So now we're the ones invited to run workshops at places like Esalen and Omega, to speak to groups of young spiritual people or counterculturalists, and to share our insights on the occult, psychic realms, and religious practices.

Lucky for me, I've been on the receiving end of the guru dynamic, so I know how and why to avoid doing it, myself. Avoidance usually entails deconstructing an event before it begins, decrying the self-help bias of America's spiritual community, and then teaching in the most straightforward manner possible, even at the expense of mystery. (I'm married with a daughter, now, so the temptation to succumb to the consequence-free fringe benefits of retreat weekends has diminished, anyway.)

But as I look around me, I see other members of my generation claiming to see the weirdest things, to be enlightened, or to be able to offer access to energies from alternate realms. And it makes me sad and just a bit angry. The insights, such as they are, get lost in fiction. Even if a few of us do happen to be carrying some fragment of real wisdom, the object of the game is to get out the way so the wisdom can be shared. I mean, if I really thought I was channeling something or someone, I'd do it over the radio, anonymously.

The answer, of course, is for all of us to get over our need for gurus. Remove the demand and the supply should dwindle, too. I mean, most of us have already endured one set of parents. Why go

The truth about the great spiritual quest of our species is that it just can't work with followers and leaders.

through that again? The stuff they didn't do right simply cannot be corrected. Mourn what you missed and move on. (Meanwhile, if it's magic you're after, go to Vegas and see a show. No one can teach you how to walk on water or be in two places at once. And if you do get awakened someday, whatever that means, you'll realize this very need to talk to God or see the light is what's been getting in the way of your clarity the whole time. Besides, is it really magical abilities and transcendent experiences you're after, or merely escape from the pain of everyday experience?)

The truth about the great spiritual quest of our species is that it just can't work with followers and leaders. There's way too much duality built-in to such a scheme. Hierarchies are fun, but they're a construction. I've been around the spiritual block more times than I care to mention, and have read the work of the very best teachers and philosophers I can get a hold of. And as I've come to see it, there is no such thing as awakening. It's a ruse. Think about it: the whole concept of reaching enlightenment is so steeped in dualism, expectation, and obsession with self. The word "enlightenment" may sell books and earn devotees, but it doesn't refer to anything real. It doesn't exist. The true spiritual path may just be a matter getting over that fact, and in the process, learning to express and enact as much compassion as you can. That's why I see guruphiliac.com as an optimistic effort; it assumes we're ready to let all this go.

If you've got to start with some perfect point in the universe, start with yourself. There's no path to take, no one else to follow. And you don't need anyone to tell you this for it to be true. All the places you might get to are equally valid, because everyone is just as lost as you are. The sooner we all admit this, the sooner we can begin to orient to one another as siblings and partners in the great adventure.

© *Douglas Rushkoff*

About the Author

Winner of the first Neil Postman award for Career Achievement in Public Intellectual Activity, Douglas Rushkoff is an author, teacher, and documentarian who focuses on the ways people, cultures, and institutions create, share, and influence each other's values. He sees "media" as the landscape where this interaction takes place, and "literacy" as the ability to participate consciously in it.

His ten best-selling books on new media and popular culture have been translated to over thirty languages. They include *Cyberia, Media Virus, Playing the Future, Nothing Sacred: The Truth about Judaism,* and *Coercion,* winner of the Marshall Mcluhan Award for best media book. Rushkoff also wrote the acclaimed novels *Ecstasy Club* and *Exit Strategy* and the graphic novel, *Club Zero-G.* He has just finished a book for HarperBusiness, applying renaissance principles to today's complex economic landscape, *Get Back in the Box: Innovation from the Inside Out.*

Rushkoff graduated magna cum laude from Princeton University, received an MFA in Directing from California Institute of the Arts, a post-graduate fellowship (MFA) from The American Film Institute, and a Director's Grant from the Academy of Motion Picture Arts and Sciences. He has worked as a certified stage fight choreographer, and as keyboardist for the industrial band PsychicTV.

He lives in Park Slope Brooklyn with his wife, Barbara, and daughter Mamie.

Discard all theologies and belief...the whole principle that someone else knows and you do not know, that the one who knows is going to teach you.

Jiddu Krishnamurti

Values helped to guide me in a precarious world and during times of tenuous family and God support. I lost God as an eleven year-old; I went to the temple to talk to the Rabbi about whether God existed, and how this Jesus, whom my society venerated, figured into the picture. I received no satisfactory answers. And my search has been inconclusive since.

Jason Merchey

Follow not me, but you.

Friedrich Nietzsche

Trust yourself; then you will know how to live.

Johann Wolfgang von Goethe

No morality can be founded on authority, even if the authority were divine.

A. J. Ayer

Every head must do its own thinking.

Jabo proverb

That fear created the gods is perhaps as true as anything so brief could be on so great a subject.

George Santayana

A person must live in a self-directed way. You must make your own decisions. Don't let anybody tell you how to play the hand you get dealt; poker players don't listen to other people about how to play their hand. And make no mistak— everyone you come in significant contact with is playing the same game at the same table. Poker players don't have advisors, and they don't count on the beneficence of their fellow players. I'm not advocating a harshness or thick-headedness - just noting that you're a loser to the degree that you let another tell you how to play this game of life.

Jason Merchey

SELF-AWARENESS

THE EVOLUTION OF CONSCIOUSNESS

Peter Russell

Before we can begin to consider the evolution of consciousness, we have to ask when consciousness first arose. Are human beings alone conscious, or are other creatures also conscious? Is an animal such as a dog, for example, conscious?

Dogs may not be aware of many of the things we are aware of. They are not conscious of much beyond their immediate world, the world defined by the span of their senses. They know nothing of lands beyond the oceans, or the space beyond the earth. Nor can dogs be aware of much beyond the present time. They know nothing of the course of history, or where it might be headed. They are not aware of their inevitable death in the same way that we are. They do not think to themselves in words, and they probably do not reason as we do. And they do not seem to have the self-awareness that we do; they certainly do not get caught up in concern for their own self-image, with all the strange behaviors that engenders. But this does not mean that dogs have no awareness at all.

Dogs experience the world of their senses. They see, hear, smell, and taste their world. They remember where they have been. They recognize sounds. They may like some people or things, and dislike others. Dogs sometimes show fear, and at other times excitement. When asleep, they appear to dream, feet and toes twitching as if on the scent of some fantasy rabbit. They clearly are not just a biological mechanism, devoid of any inner experience. To suggest that they are not conscious is absurd—as absurd as suggesting that my neighbour across the street is not conscious.

Where dogs differ from us is not in their capacity for consciousness but in what they are conscious of. Dogs may not be self-aware, and may not think or reason as we do. In these respects they are less aware than we are. On the other hand, dogs can hear higher frequencies of sound than we do, and their sense of smell far surpasses our own. In terms of their sensory perception of the world around, dogs may be considered more aware than humans.

A useful analogy for understanding the nature of consciousness is that of a painting. The picture itself corresponds to the contents of consciousness; the canvas on which it is painted corresponds to the faculty of consciousness. An infinite variety of pictures can be painted on the canvas; but whatever the pictures, they all share the fact that they are painted on a canvas. Without the canvas there would be no painting.

The pictures that are painted on the canvas of consciousness take many forms. They include our perceptions of the world around, our thoughts, our ideas, our beliefs, our values, our feelings, our emotions, our hopes, our fears, our intuitions, our dreams and fantasies—and more. But none of this would be possible if we did not in the first place possess the capacity for consciousness. Without it there would be no subjective experience of any kind.

> A useful analogy for understanding the nature of consciousness is that of a painting. The picture itself corresponds to the contents of consciousness; the canvas on which it is painted corresponds to the faculty of consciousness.

Are All Creatures Conscious?

If dogs have the faculty of consciousness, then by the same argument so must cats, horses, deer, dolphins, whales, and other mammals. Why else would we require veterinarians to use anesthetics?

If mammals are conscious beings, then I see no reason to suppose birds are any different. Some parrots I have known seem as conscious as dogs. If birds have the capacity for consciousness, then it seems natural to assume that so do other vertebrates—alligators, snakes, frogs, salmon, and sharks. What they are conscious of may vary considerably. Dolphins "see" the world with sonar; snakes sense infrared radiation; sharks feel with electric senses. The pictures that are painted in their minds may vary considerably; but, however varied their experiences, they all share the faculty of consciousness.

Where do we draw the line? At vertebrates? The nervous systems of insects may not be as complex as ours, and they probably do not have as rich an experience of the world as we do. They also have very different senses, so the picture that is painted in their minds may be totally unlike ours. But I see no reason to doubt that insects have inner experiences of some kind.

How far down do we go? It seems probable to me that any organism that is sensitive in some way to its environment has a degree of interior experience. Many single-celled organisms are sensitive to physical vibration, light intensity, or heat. Who are we to say they do not have a corresponding degree of consciousness?

Would the same apply to viruses and DNA? Even to crystals and atoms? The philosopher Alfred North Whitehead argued that consciousness goes all the way down. He saw it as an intrinsic property of creation.

Consciousness and Biological Evolution

If all creatures are conscious in some way or other, then consciousness is not something that evolved with human beings, or with primates, mammals or any other particular degree of biological evolution. It has always existed. What emerged over the course of evolution were the various qualities and dimensions of conscious experience—the contents of consciousness.

The first simple organisms—bacteria and algae—having no senses, were aware in only the most rudimentary way: no form, no structure, just the vaguest glimmer of awareness. Their picture of the world is nothing but an extremely dim smudge of colour—virtually nothing, compared to the richness and detail of human experience.

When multicellular organisms evolved, so did this sensing capacity. Cells emerged that specialized in sensing light, vibration, pressure, or changes in chemistry. These cells formed sensory organs, and as they developed, the ability to take in information increased. Eyes are not only sensitive to light; they react differently to different frequencies, and can tell from which direction the light is coming. The faintest smudge of the bacterium's experience had begun to take on different hues and shapes. Forms had begun to emerge on the canvas of consciousness.

Nervous systems evolved, processing this data and distributing it to other parts of the organism. Before long, the flow of information required a central processing system, and with it a more integrated picture of the world appeared. As brains evolved, new features were added to consciousness. With reptiles the limbic system appeared, an area of the brain associated with emotion. Feeling had been added.

In birds and mammals the nervous system grew yet more complex, developing a cortex around it. With the cortex came other new abilities. A dog chasing a cat around a corner holds some image in its mind of the cat it can no longer see. Creatures with a cortex have memory and recognition; they can pay attention and show intention.

With primates the cortex grew into the larger, more complex neo-cortex, adding yet more features to consciousness. The most significant of these was the ability to use symbols. Not only did this ability enable simple reasoning, it also led to a new form of communication—symbolic language.

Chimpanzees and gorillas may not be able to speak as we do, but this is not because they lack something in their brains; they lack a voice. They have no larynx, or voice-box, and cannot move their tongues as freely as we can. But they can use other forms of symbolic language. When taught sign language, such as that used by the deaf, they show a remarkable ability to communicate. Coco, a gorilla in California, now has a vocabulary of more than a thousand words, and composes sentences in sign language.

Language and Consciousness

For one reason or another, human beings evolved slightly differently. We have a well-developed voice-box, and after the first year of life the tongue frees up, permitting the complex sounds necessary for speech. With these two seemingly small advances, everything changed.

Being able to speak allows us to share our experiences with each other. Whereas a dog learns principally from its own experience, and builds up its knowledge of the world from scratch, we can learn from each other. We can build up a body of collective knowledge and pass it on from one generation to another—the foundation of a cohesive society.

This new ability has expanded our consciousness in several ways. Our experience of space expanded as we learnt of events beyond our immediate sensory environment. And as we learnt of events that had happened before our own lives, our experience of time expanded.

As well as using speech to communicate with each other, we can also use it to communicate with ourselves, inside our own minds. We can think to ourselves in words. Of all the developments that came from language, this has probably been the most significant.

Thinking allows us to conjure up associations to past experiences. When we think of the word "tree," images of trees readily come to mind. Or if we think of a person's name, we may find ourselves remembering past experiences with that person. Other creatures may well experience associations to past experiences, but their associations are almost certainly determined by their immediate environment; what is out of sight is out of mind. Thought liberated human beings from this constraint. We can deliberately bring the past back to mind, independently of what is happening in the present.

In a similar way, thinking expanded our appreciation of the future. We can think about what might or might not happen, make plans and take decisions. A new inner freedom had been born—the freedom to choose our future and so exercise a much greater influence over our lives.

Thinking in words opened our minds to reason. We could ask questions: Why do stars move? How do our bodies function? What is matter? A whole new dimension had been added to our consciousness—understanding. We could form hypotheses and beliefs about the world in which we found ourselves.

We could also begin to understand ourselves. We could think about our own conscious experience. We became aware not only of the many aspects and qualities of our consciousness, but also of the faculty of consciousness. We are aware that we are aware—conscious of the fact that we are conscious.

Consciousness could now reflect not only upon the nature of the world it experienced, but also on the nature of consciousness itself. Self-reflective consciousness had emerged.

Self-consciousness

As we reflect upon our own consciousness, it seems that there must be an experiencer—an individual self that is having these experiences, making all these decisions, and thinking all these thoughts. But what is this self? What is it really like? What does it consist of?

Questions such as these have intrigued and puzzled philosophers for centuries. Some, like the Scottish philosopher David Hume, spent much time searching within their experience for something that seemed to be the true self. But all they could find were various thoughts, sensations, images and feelings. However hard we look, we never seem to find the self itself.

Not finding an easily identifiable self at the core of our being, we look to other aspects of our lives for a sense of identity. We identify with our bodies, with how they look, how they are dressed, and how they are perceived by other people. We identify with what we do and what we have achieved; with our work, our social status, our academic qualifications, where we live and who we know. We derive a sense of who we are from what we think, our theories and beliefs, our personality and character.

There is, however, a severe drawback to such a sense of self. Being derived from what is happening in the world of experience, it is forever at the mercy of events. A person who draws a strong sense of identity from their work may, on hearing that their job is threatened, feel their sense of self is threatened. Someone else, who identifies with being fashionably dressed, may buy a new set of clothes every time the fashion changes, not because they need new clothes, but because their sense of self needs to be maintained. Or if we identify with our views and beliefs we may take a criticism of our ideas to be a criticism of our self.

Any threat to our sense of self triggers fear. Fear is of great value if our physical self is being threatened. Then we need to have our heart beat hard, our blood pressure rise, and our muscles tense. Our survival may depend on it. But this response is totally inappropriate when all that is being threatened is our psychological self.

Having our bodies repeatedly put on full alert is a principal cause of stress. We can easily end up in a permanent state of tension, opening us up

590

to all manner of physical illnesses. Our emotional life may suffer, leading to anxiety or depression. Our thinking and decision making can likewise deteriorate.

Fear also leads to worry. We worry about what others might be thinking of us. We worry about what we have done or not done, and about what might or might not happen to us. When we worry like this, our attention is caught up in the past or the future. It is not experiencing the present moment.

Perhaps the saddest irony of all is that this worry prevents us from finding that which we are really seeking. The goal of every person is, in the final analysis, a comfortable state of mind. Quite naturally, we want to avoid pain and suffering, and feel more at peace. But a mind that is busy worrying cannot be a mind that is at peace.

Other animals, not having language, do not think to themselves in words, and do not experience many of the worries that we do. In particular, they do not experience all the worries that come from having a vulnerable sense of self. They are probably at peace much more of the time. Human beings may have made a great leap forward in consciousness, but at our present stage of development we are no happier for it—quite the opposite.

Transcending Language

There is, it would appear, a downside to language. Language is invaluable for sharing knowledge and experience—without it human culture would never have arisen. And thinking to ourselves in words can be very useful when we need to focus our attention, analyze a situation, or make plans. But much of the remainder of our thinking is totally unnecessary.

If half my attention is taken up with the voice in my head, that half is not available for noticing other things. I don't notice what is going on around me. I don't hear the sounds of birds, the wind, or creaking trees. I don't notice my emotions, or how my body feels. I am, in effect, only half-conscious.

Just because we have the gift of being able to think in words does not mean that we have to do it all the time. Many spiritual teachings seem to have recognized this. In Buddhism, for example, students are often advised to sit with a quiet mind, experiencing "what is" without naming it in words or putting it into some category—to see a daffodil as it is, without the labels "daffodil," "flower," "yellow," or "pretty." To see it with the mind in its natural state, before language was added to our consciousness.

Sat Chit Ananda

Returning the mind to this simple pre-linguistic state of consciousness is not easy. A lifetime of conditioning makes it hard to stop thinking and let go. This is why many spiritual teachings include practices of meditation designed to quieten the voice in the head, and bring us to a state of inner stillness. In Indian philosophy, this state is called samadhi, "still mind."

Furthermore, it is said that when the mind is still, then one knows the real self, and the nature of this self is, according to the ancient Vedic teachings, sat-chit-ananda.

It is sat—"the truth, unchanging, eternal, being." It is always there, whatever our experience. It never changes. It is not a unique self; it has no personal qualities. It is the same for everyone. It is the one undeniable truth—the fact that we are conscious.

It is chit–"consciousness." It is not any particular form or mode of consciousness, but the faculty of consciousness. It is that which makes all experience possible.

And it is ananda—"bliss." It is the peace that passeth all understanding, that lies beyond all thought. It is the state of grace to which we long to return; from which we fell when we began to fill our minds with words.

This is the self that we have been seeking all along. The reason we have had such difficulty finding it was that we have been looking in the wrong place. We have been looking for something that could be experienced—a feeling, a sense, an idea. Yet the self cannot be an experience. It is, by definition, that which is experiencing. It is behind every experience, behind everything I see, think, and feel.

What the mystical traditions around the world seem to be saying is that the self, that sense of I-ness that we all feel, but which is so hard to pin down or define, is actually consciousness itself. The pure self is pure consciousness—the faculty of awareness common to all sentient beings.

Moreover, when we come to know this to be our true essential nature, our search for identity ends. No longer is there any need to buy things we don't really need, say things we don't really mean, or engage in any other unnecessary and inappropriate activities in order to reinforce an artificially derived sense of self. Now we discover a deeper inner security, one that is independent of circumstances and events. Here is the peace we have long been seeking. It is right here inside us, at the heart of our being. But as with the self, we have been looking for it in the wrong place—in the world around.

Our Evolutionary Imperative

With the advent of human beings, the awakening of consciousness took a huge leap forward. Consciousness began becoming aware of itself. But at present this leap is only partially complete. We may be self-aware, but we have not yet discovered the true nature and potential of consciousness. In this respect our inner evolution has some way to go.

Throughout history there have been those who have evolved inwardly to higher states of consciousness. They are the saints and mystics who have realized the true nature of the self. Such people are examples of what we each have the potential to become. There is nothing special about them in terms of their biology. They are human beings, just like you and me, with similar bodies and similar nervous systems. The only difference is that they have liberated themselves from a limited, artificially derived sense of identity and discovered a greater peace and security within.

In the past the number of people who made this step was small, but the times we are living through make it imperative that many more of us now complete our inner evolutionary journey into full wakefulness.

The many crises that we see around us—global warming, desertification, holes in the ozone layer, disappearing rainforests, polluted rivers, acid rain, dying dolphins, large-scale famine, a widening gap between the "haves" and the "have nots," nuclear proliferation, over-exploitation, and a host of other dangers—all stem in one way or another from human self-centredness. Time and again we find decisions being made not according to the merits of the situation at hand, but according to the needs of the individual or special interest groups. Governments strive to hold on to power, businesses seek to maximize profit, leaders want to retain their status, and consumers around the world try to satisfy their own needs for identity and security. In the final analysis, it is our need to protect and reinforce an ever-faltering sense of self that leads us to consume more than we need, pollute the world around, abuse other peoples, and show a careless disregard for the many other species sharing our planetary home.

Even now, when we recognize that we are in great danger, we fail to take appropriate remedial action. We continue driving our cars, consuming dwindling resources, and throwing our waste into the sea because to do otherwise would inconvenience ourselves.

The global crisis now facing us is, at its root, a crisis of consciousness. The essence of any crisis, whether it be a personal crisis, a political crisis, or, as in this case, a global crisis, is that the old way of functioning is no longer working. Something new is being called for. In this case the old way that is no longer working is our mode of consciousness. The old mode is destroying the world around us, and threatening the survival of our species. The time has come to evolve into a new mode. We need to wake up to our true identity, to make the step that many saints and mystics have already made, and discover for ourselves the peace and security that lie at our core.

With the advent of human beings, evolution has ceased to be a blind affair governed by random genetic mutations. A new degree of freedom has appeared; we can think ahead and determine our own future. Our further evolution is now in our own hands—or rather, in our own minds.

Our next step is to rise beyond the handicaps that came with the gift of language and discover who we really are. Then, free from the need to reinforce an artificially derived sense of identity, we will be able to act in accord with our true needs—and with the needs of others and the needs of our environment.

Relieved of unnecessary fears, we will be in a much better state to cope with the many changes that we will undoubtedly see over the coming years. Liberated from unnecessary self-centeredness, we will be free to care for each other, to offer others the love we so much want for ourselves. And we will be in a much better position to build a new world—one that is not so driven by this halfway stage in the unfolding of self-consciousness.

Our task is to manifest this change on earth, now—both for our own sakes and for the sake of every other creature.

© *Peter Russell*

594

About the Author

Peter Russell is a fellow of the Institute of Noetic Sciences, of The World Business Academy and of The Findhorn Foundation, and an honorary member of The Club of Budapest.

At Cambridge University (UK), he studied mathematics and theoretical physics. Then, as he became increasingly fascinated by the mysteries of the human mind he changed to experimental psychology. Pursuing this interest, he traveled to India to study meditation and eastern philosophy, and on his return took up the first research post ever offered in Britain on the psychology of meditation.

He also has a post-graduate degree in computer science, and conducted there some of the early work on three-dimensional displays, presaging by some twenty years the advent of virtual reality.

In the mid-seventies Peter Russell joined forces with Tony Buzan and helped teach "Mind Maps" and learning methods to a variety of international organizations and educational institutions.

Since then his corporate programs have focused increasingly on self-development, creativity, stress management, and sustainable environmental practices. Clients have included IBM, Apple, Digital, American Express, Barclays Bank, Swedish Telecom, ICI, Shell Oil and British Petroleum.

His principal interest is the deeper, spiritual significance of the times we are passing through. He has written several books in this area—*The TM Technique, The Upanishads, The Brain Book, The Global Brain Awakens, The Creative Manager, The Consciousness Revolution, Waking Up in Time,* and *From Science to God.*

As one of the more revolutionary futurists, Peter Russell has been a keynote speaker at many international conferences, in Europe, Japan, and the USA. His multi-image shows and videos, *The Global Brain* and *The White Hole in Time* have won praise and prizes from around the world. In 1993 the environmental magazine *Buzzworm* voted Peter Russell "Eco-Philosopher Extraordinaire" of the year.

The next great advance in the evolution of civilization cannot take place until war is abolished.

Douglas MacArthur

The real social revolution is the switch from a life largely organized for us...to a world in which we are all forced to be in charge of our own destiny.

Charles Handy

We have proof that life has a way of avoiding demise, that water erodes rock, and that earthquakes reshape the land inches every decade. Humanity has so many weaknesses that get played out over and over again, be it in the theatre of war, the form of domestic violence, or the shape of white-collar crime. But we have the ability to invent language, to fly, and to grasp incredible virtues such as responsibility and magnanimity, and this is evolution.

Jason Merchey

The world of learning is so broad, and the human soul is so limited in power! We reach forth and strain every nerve, but we seize only a bit of the curtain that hides the infinite from us.

Maria Mitchell

Humans have the ability to act consciously, and collectively, [exercising foresight to] choose their own evolutionary path. In our crucial epoch we cannot leave the selection of the next step in the evolution of human society and culture to chance. We must plan for it, consciously and purposefully.

Erwin Lazlo

Man as we know him is a poor creature, but he is halfway between an ape and a god, and he is traveling in the right direction.

William R. Inge

Global economic justice is not just ethical; it is key to reversing the demise of our ecosystems, our spirituality, our connection with nature, our health, our children's future, and humanity itself.

Juliette Beck

If I create from the heart, nearly everything works; if from the head almost nothing.

Marc Chagall

Musicians must make music, artists must paint, poets must write if they are to be ultimately at peace with themselves. What humans can be, they must be. They must be true to their own nature.

Abraham Maslow

All we have in the end is the dignity and integrity of our person. But this is enough.

Kristen Renwick Monroe

We all live with the objective of being happy: our lives are all different and yet the same.

Anne Frank

When we finally know we are dying, and all other sentient beings are dying with us, we start to have a burning, almost heartbreaking sense of the fragility and preciousness of each moment and each being, and from this can grow a deep, clear, limitless compassion for all beings.

Sogyal Rinpoche

When humans participate in ceremony, they enter a sacred space. Everything outside of that space shrivels in importance. Time takes on a different dimension. Emotions flow more freely. The bodies of participants become filled with the energy of life, and this energy reaches out and blesses the creation around them. All is made new; everything becomes sacred.

Sun Bear

In the evening I go out to the desert where you can see the world all around, far away. The hours I spend each evening watching the sun go down-and just enjoying it-and every day I go out and watch it again. I draw, and there is a little painting, and so the days go by.

Georgia O'Keefe

RESPECT

COLLATERALS

Robert Shetterly

For the past few months, at the same time that I've been painting the Americans Who Tell the Truth portraits, I've been working on a series of little portraits that I call "collaterals." They exist as a kind of dark star to the Truth Tellers. The name refers to collateral damage, the term given to civilian individuals killed in a military action who were not "intentionally" targeted. These paintings are fictions. One rarely sees the face or knows the identity of a collateral. It's a virtual and abstract category in which the victim is never a real person, a kind of discarded ghost. Such is the magic of language and of denial. When you come to think of it, there is probably no more obscenely immoral term than the one that dismisses the importance of other people or animals or plants as collateral damage when their deaths become incidental to the achievement of some military or economic objective. As collateral, the individuals bear the same value as sawdust to a carpenter.

The obvious assumption is that our goals and our lives have more significance than theirs, and, further, that we therefore have the right to murder them with no consequence. Precisely because there is no penalty, it must be a right. But what kind of right is it? An inalienable right? A human right? A legal right? Moral right? No, it's really a right of entitlement. Similar to the right we exercise when we build a road through a forest and then run over the raccoon that crosses it. They, the civilians, the raccoons, are the necessary fatalities for our notion of progress.

So, the collaterals have been obligated, in effect, to become martyrs for the indiscriminate power that killed them for its own higher cause, martyrs not for their own beliefs, their own right to life, their own volition, but ours. It is as though, by the very fact of their deaths, they are subsumed into a sub-legal category of existence, the category of martyrdom by default. And, as sub-legals, their killers are obligated not to feel remorse. On TV we see their surviving kin weep and wail and shout revenge, but we think they will get over it when they realize their loved ones have been sacrificed for their own good.

It should be self-evident that anyone who professes to believe in any of the democratic ideals of this country, such as respect for the essential equality and rights of all individuals, could not possibly utter the words "collateral damage" without shame or cynicism. Interestingly, during the Vietnam War, Henry Kissinger and Robert McNamara used the term "integers" to describe civilian deaths that they preferred objectified to the abstraction of numbers rather than the reality of flesh. At least, though, the term "integer" implies the act of counting. Collaterals are not counted. Their numbers are denied and suppressed along with their identities, their places in their communities, families, their sexes, ages, jobs, who loved them and whom they loved, what stories they told, their favorite foods, how they laughed and cried, what achievements they aspired to, what hopes, what dreams. The fact that the current US administration keeps no count of the Iraqis murdered as collateral damage mocks any claim they may have to bringing democracy and freedom to that country. What would lead anyone to believe that a country which doesn't count the innocent dead would actually respect the votes of the living?

Civilians killed incidental to the progress of war are collateral; those killed purposefully are victims of terrorism. Sometimes it's very hard to tell the difference. Governments do one and call it the other, but get the desired effect. In other words, if an attack on a civilian population is called "Shock and Awe," isn't it really terrorism, even if you later call the dead collaterals.

The notion of collateral damage has larger ramifications than just that of civilians run over in the way of military or economic objectives. Western civilization is based on a linear idea of progress that requires the euphemistic "development of resources." Blowing the tops off mountains, grinding up the great forests, depleting the seas of fish, creating a mass extinction by habitat destruction, poisoning the earth, air and water, injecting a toxic brew of chemicals into the body of every living creature in the world, this is the collateral damage of a culture of consumption and increasing profit.

So, in the paintings I made up the faces. Some anguished. Some simply bearing witness to the immense amoral disregard in the face of which they are powerless. They are the blur created by the momentum of our rush to get where we are going. But they must be brought into focus. For, in that focus is not only the truth about the nature of the killer's behavior, but also the key to survival on a sustainable earth. Hypocrisy about the value of other lives is no longer something about which an otherwise decent person may be negligent or cynical; that hypocrisy is tantamount to suicide. By placing economic expansion, resource depletion, and increased consumption

> Collateral damage is the same whether it's a term for Iraqi children or our own drinking water, Mayans in Guatemala or the plague of breast cancer, Africans dying in the hold of a slave ship or global warming.

before the wisdom of sustainability, which is the wisdom of the earth, we become our own collateral damage.

This is what Malcolm X meant after the assassination of President Kennedy when he said that the chickens had come home to roost. That is, if we live by power, violence, and exploitation, by disrespect for other people's lives, it will come back to haunt us. The snake will bite its own tail. No one wanted to hear it then, and they don't now.

But collateral damage is the same whether it's a term for Iraqi children or our own drinking water, Mayans in Guatemala or the plague of breast cancer, Africans dying in the hold of a slave ship or global warming. It's really a term for a mentality, a conscience, a system profoundly out of balance. Perhaps it would be a good idea to show the picture on world-wide television each night of one mother or one little girl or one little boy or one father, one pine warbler, one right whale, one mahogany tree targeted for the next day's collateral damage, and let the world agonize, as it is did about Terry Schiavo, whether this life should be taken.

There are times when it is hard to know what is the wise thing to do, especially when the conflict is between competing empathies, competing compassions. But it is not hard at all when the conflict is between the self-interest of power, profit, and exploitation on the one hand and compassion on the other. We are, however, learning that wisdom, if wisdom means sustainable, just existence for all life on this earth, demands eradication of the notion of collateral damage, and eradication of the denial of empathetic perception that allows it. For, that wisdom is the basis of our self interest.

© Robert Shetterly

About the Author

Robert Shetterly was born in 1946 in Cincinnati, Ohio. He graduated in 1969 from Harvard College with a degree in English Literature. At Harvard he took a couple of courses in drawing which changed the direction of his creative life—from the written word to the image. Also, during this time, he was very active in Civil Rights and in the Anti-Vietnam War movement.

For twelve years he did the editorial page drawings for the *Maine Times* newspaper, illustrated National Audubon's children's newspaper *Audubon Adventures*, and more than thirty books.

Now, his paintings and prints are in collections all over the U.S. and Europe. A collection of his drawings and etchings, "Speaking Fire at Stones," was published in 1993. He is well know for his series of seventy painted etchings based on William Blake's *Proverbs of Hell*, and for another series of fifty painted etchings reflecting on the metaphor of the Annunciation. For the past four years he has been painting the series of portraits (numbering now over ninety) called "Americans Who Tell the Truth." The show has been traveling around the country for two years and is scheduled for the next two. In 2005, Dutton published a book of them by the same name.

Say you'll never try to paint what is rotten with a sugarcoat. Say you'll talk about the horrors you're seen and the torment you know. And tell it like it is.

Tracy Chapman

As one whose husband and mother-in-law have both died the victims of murder assassination, I stand firmly and unequivocally opposed to the death penalty for those convicted of capital offenses. An evil deed is not redeemed by an evil deed of retaliation. Justice is never advanced in the taking of a human life. Morality is never upheld by legalized murder.

Coretta Scott King

Little boy of three sitting on the floor Looks up and says, "Daddy, what is war?" "Son that's when people fight and die." Little boy of three says, "Daddy, why?"

Johnny Cash

It is true that I came of age at a place and in a time when pacifism was a ruling principle, and it has become a part of my character. Perhaps it has gone deeper now that I am a mother and am therefore obliged to picture my own children as cannon fodder and Iraqi children as collateral damage.

Anna Quindlen

Pat [Tillman, my son, the professional football player turned Army volunteer, who died in Pakistan by "friendly fire" in 2004] had high ideals about the country; that's why he did what he did. The military let him down. The [George W. Bush] administration let him down. It was a sign of disrespect. The fact that he was the ultimate team player and he watched his own men kill him is absolutely heartbreaking and tragic. The fact that they lied about it afterward is disgusting.

Mary Tillman

Here is the other question that I have been leading toward, one that the predicament of modern warfare forces upon us: How many deaths of other people's children by bombing or starvation are we willing to accept in order that we may be free, affluent, and (supposedly) at peace? To that question I answer: None. Please, no children. Don't kill any children for my benefit.

Wendell Berry

DEDICATION

WORK AS SERVICE

Justine Willis Toms and Michael Toms

In the Indian Classic, *Bhagavad Gita*, Krishna says to Arjuna, "Look at me Arjuna! If I stop working for one moment the whole universe will die. I have nothing to gain from work; I am the sole Lord. But why do I work? Because I love the world." This is compassion in action and serves as the basis of the Eastern tradition known as Karma Yoga, the practice of work without attachment to the results, and service for the sake of the other.

We live in an interdependent world. Wherever we are, whatever we do, we must keep this global perspective in the forefront of our minds. Joanna Massey, author of World as Lover, World as Self, writes, "Everything is interdependent and mutually conditioning—each thought, word, and act, and all beings, too, in the web of life." Just as health care advocates expound on the mind-body link and how our physical condition affects our thinking, so each of us influences the world, and the world in turn has an impact on our personal life.

So, too, are nations interdependent. A rebellion of peasants in Mexico affects the stock market in New York. A contract to build airplanes in China causes workers to lose jobs in the United States. No nation can operate in a vacuum within such a world. Neither can we function without a recognition that our personal behavior is inseparable from our behavior as participants in society. The bad news is that each of us contributes in some measure to the problems in the first place. The good news is that once we realize our link to the problems of the world, we become empowered to contribute toward alleviating them. As we change behavior and perception patterns, so too will the world.

As we move toward a global society, becoming ever more aware of the sufferings and struggles of the peoples of the Earth, there is more and more reason to recognize the social responsibility each of us has and respond to it. Life is too brief not to. As you're able to do this in daily life, then others may be influenced and inspired to do the same. It's the way the world changes, and each of us makes it happen through what we do.

> As we move toward a global society, becoming ever more aware of the sufferings and struggles of the peoples of the Earth, there is more and more reason to recognize the social responsibility each of us has and respond to it.

All of the world's spiritual traditions have stressed the value of compassionate service to alleviate suffering and grow spiritually. Not only does service relieve the suffering of others, it also transforms self-centeredness. In today's world, socially responsible activism and spirituality are becoming more aligned as engaged forms of spiritual practice become more prevalent.

When social and political activism are rooted in spiritual practice, you have the energy and vision to persevere and do whatever is necessary. Though your service may manifest in the external world, this is not an outward path. It is a path guided from within, so that your work becomes like a meditative practice, and your contribution for the benefit of others burns away egocentric motivations. The more you wake up, the more effective your work becomes.

The paradox is the more active you are in the world, giving freely of yourself, the deeply you can go into yourself. Gradually, through this process of engagement, you become less attached to whether the results of your actions are successful. As you stay in the present moment and perform your work without imagining a goal in the future, you become more relaxed and less anxious. Success and failure no longer have a hold on you. You are at one with your work and can offer it without any thought of return.

We all want to contribute, to make a positive difference with our lives. Research and polls have revealed that people who live into their eighties, nineties, and even past a hundred, stay healthy and vital because they are doing something meaningful and feel they are making a contribution to others. It is this generosity of spirit we need to carry into our actual work. When our work is motivated by the deep calling to make a contribution, then it is life-affirming and imbued with love. Such work is powerful and compelling. In the giving is the receiving. It's a circle—the energy returns and enables us to continue doing the work.

R. Buckminster Fuller, in his autobiographical book, *Critical Path*, writes, "The larger the number for whom I work, the more positively effective I became. Thus, it became obvious that if I worked always and only for all humanity, I would be optimally effective."

Most of us are conditioned to believe that the helper is bestowing some beneficent act on the helped. The fact is that spiritual teachers have always spoken of the true benefit of giving; the real beneficiary is the giver. Swami Vivekananda suggests that we express gratitude for the opportunity to help: "We must remember that is a privilege to help others...It is not the receiver who is blessed, but it is the giver. Be thankful that you are allowed to exercise your power of benevolence and mercy in the world."

There is so much to be done; the opportunities are limitless. What do you want to give to the world? What moves you? Where do you feel inspired to serve? Listen to your inner voice and pay attention to the world around you. You have very special gifts to offer. Use your imagination and intellect to discover what they are.

You will discover your passion by uncovering your compassion, your own sense of connection to others. The word compassion means "with passion." Compassion is a deeply felt resonance with humanity and the natural world. With it comes purpose, and the two combine to create work as service.

Whatever work you are doing or may choose to do in the future, remember always that you are connected to the world and even the smallest act makes a difference. Gandhi said, "What you do may seem insignificant, but it's very important that you do it." Just as mathematicians have shown that the flapping of a butterfly's wings in Japan can affect the weather in New York, so too does your work affect the rest of the planet. How you do your work matters to all of us, and especially to yourself. You alone are the creator of true work.

Excerpted with permission from True Work: Doing What You Love and Loving What You Do *by Justine and Michael Toms Bell-Tower/Crown Publishers 1998.*

About the Authors

Michael Toms has been described as the "Socrates of radio" and is well known for his uncanny skill at consistently eliciting great depth and creative thinking in his dialogues. For more than a quarter of a century, Michael Toms has been exploring personal, social, and spiritual transformation through his work as an electronic journalist, editor, and writer. He is the founding President of New Dimensions Foundation, co-founder of New Dimensions Radio, and Chief Executive Officer of the New Dimensions World Broadcasting Network. He serves as the Executive Producer and principal host of the award winning, widely acclaimed "New Dimensions" internationally syndicated radio series, dialogues addressing "the history of the future." He is Board Chairman Emeritus of the California Institute of Integral Studies. He also was an editor of "The Inner Edge," a newsletter for enlightened business practice and is the bestselling author of *A Time for Choices: Deep Dialogues for Deep Democracy, At the Leading Edge, An Open Life: Joseph Campbell in Conversation with Michael Tom,* and co-author of *True Work: Doing What You Love and Loving What You Do.*

Justine Willis Toms is the co-founder and managing producer of New Dimensions World Broadcasting Network and New Dimensions Radio, a nonprofit educational organization. She has produced many award winning radio series including "Deep Ecology for the 21st Century," and "Bioneers: Revolution From the Heart of Nature." She also serves as guest host of New Dimensions, which is distributed world-wide and is primary host of the thirteen-part radio and CD series, "In Her Company: Deep Dialogues with Women of Wisdom." Besides her radio work, she leads workshops on "Living Life On Purpose." She is co-author with *Michael Toms of True Work: Doing What You Love and Loving What You Do.*

I have devoted most of my working life to finding new ways of doing business, and the last ten years at least looking for ways for business to take a lead in making the world a better place.

Anita Roddick

There is no exercise better for the heart than reaching down and lifting people up.

John Andrew Holmes

The goal is not to have but to be, not to own but to give, not to control but to share, not to subdue but to be in accord.

Abraham Joshua Heschel

When people are serving, life is no longer meaningless.

John W. Gardner

It is high time the ideal of success should be replaced with the ideal of service.

Albert Einstein

How is it that so many wealthy, capitalistic, suburban-dwelling, golf-playing individuals decry the merit of trying to change the world, while at the same time work so hard and are so successful in their particular occupation? Imagine how the world would be in twenty years if they dedicated themselves to service as surely as they now do profit, perfection, and popularity.

Jason Merchey

Find something you like to do. Learn to do it well, and do it in the service of the people.

Karlene Faith

How simple it is to make a difference in the lives of others.

Jack Canfield and Mark Victor Hansen

Continuity of purpose is one of the most essential ingredients of happiness in the long run, and for most men this comes chiefly through their work.

Bertrand Russell

MEANING

A SHORT TALE ABOUT THE LONG WAY TO BUDDHALAND

Hawley Trowbridge

Jason asked me to participate in this book, noting that he intended it to be a "look at the practical ways people are implementing the challenge of living a value-based life on a daily basis." I'll get to the practical part in a moment, but first, the challenge for me has not been to live a value-based life, but to discover the implications of my original commitment, and to be faithful to that priority. Long ago I made a decision to pursue a life that, to me, was of utmost value; but I had little idea of what this would involve. While this life has allowed me to respond to what feels deepest in my nature, it has meant an often erring best estimate of what that is. Years have been spent wandering down paths that now seem to have contributed little but loss of time to the quest. Ultimately, everything contributes to the fullness of existence; and yet, there is a difference between gold and dross—and no extra credit for overfondness of the latter. Living this value-based life has meant foregoing many experiences most people take for granted. Mainly it meant ceaseless effort. Companions and guides have been few.

It is hard to know now what the values were that impelled me to such a life. Circumstances contributed to the formation of my values and commitment more than personal virtue, and perhaps the sources were negative as much as positive—certainly anger and pride as well as a religious upbringing in which service and love were emphasized. From an early age I was sensitive to others. It hurt me to see another person or animal suffering. Almost from the time I could write, I felt a need to express myself in writing, and create little newspapers for the family or stories for myself. For some reason I was prepared to ignore all other goals and focus on accomplishing one, and to push myself to continue another hour or two at the end of the day, day after day for decades. The only value that made a real difference was the sense that there was something I needed to bring forth from within. That was the gold, but its gleam was vanishing faint, and surrounded by much that I mistakenly believed was a part of the gold. And when I momentarily encountered the truth or true path, it was still impossible to stay with it. It occurred to me years ago, for example, that overcoming haste is the key. Yet knowing this—feeling deeply the truth that the unhurried, mindful perspective opens up a different perceptual dimension, a closer view of the essence, and gives one the confidence that comes from being centered—was of no help. There was always more I had to learn, and I couldn't slow down until accomplishing the minimal task of "reading around the perimeter," of having traversed the fields of knowledge until arriving at the place where, I felt certain, there is no more initial surveying to do, and I could proceed to explore and cultivate the land within.

> The word "efficient" has a soulless, industrial sound, but there is nothing wrong with sound planning.

Perhaps human maturation requires prior construction of some sort of framework, whether it be making one's place in the outer world as Jung describes the task of the first half of life, or making a framework of understanding such as I was compelled to put together. Still, when I was twenty-two, in the early phase of this work, the only mentor I have had told me that I had done enough in this regard, that I was "spinning my wheels" and should get on with living.

Over thirty more years were to pass before I could establish a new balance and enter the perimeter. There were few days in this long process not enlivened with enthusiasm and enjoyment. This journey filled my life, and I avoided marriage and a career in order to stay day and night with this obsession. And still I wasted so much time, engaging in study of trivialities and not pursuing the more difficult path efficiently.

The word "efficient" has a soulless, industrial sound, but there is nothing wrong with sound planning. Perhaps increased effectiveness too is a natural result of maturation. For several years my method was almost wholly intuitive. The thought crossed my mind that I was learning about just those things that naturally interested me, and allowing myself to be led to a large extent by serendipity. Yet I didn't take the next step, of asking myself, *Is there a better way?* I never explicitly considered the ultimate goal. I read what I enjoyed, looking for the consecrated authors, and those who gave me a feeling of hidden realms, of divine treasure. Developing the metacognitive ability to observe my thoughts and learning processes, and to direct them effectively was a lesson slow to ripen.

The decision to give my life to a powerful but faint vision was made when I was thirteen. Important for making this possible was being told when I was ten that I had the ability to become whatever I wanted. I had always excelled in school, and took it as natural that I was the best. This permission to choose my future provided the impetus to consider how I might use my life. When I was in the eighth grade, a boy gave me a paperback copy of Irving Stone's biography of Jack London: he said his mother thought I might enjoy it. We weren't friends or even classmates. From the time that I read this book I knew what I wanted to do with my life—to be a writer. It wasn't simply that I wanted to write, there was something in particular I needed to express. Something tantalizing that would draw me on like a drug for almost half a century.

In any case, books had been always with me, familiar and dear, from before the time I could read; and while I happily sought out lists of great books, even at thirteen I was confident that I knew what was worthwhile, no matter critical opinion. Fifteen years of unsuccessful efforts passed before I realized I could not write like Dostoevsky or Dickens, and I discovered my form: simply to record the world as I observed and reflected on it, without the clothing of fictional plot and characters.

Yet as soon as I figured this out, I felt a need to begin a second long course of study. I began to read or read again the authors who seemed most to exemplify the form and content that I needed to express. Solzhenitsyn,

Henry Miller. And then I thought I needed to be familiar with literature in a language other than English. My German was fair, but it seemed more important to return to the study of ancient Greek begun in high school. This would mean work on Latin as well, as I really enjoyed reading, or trying to read, Latin.

The method was too random, and even until I was forty I lacked the ability to understand difficult material. I lingered with the popularizers and only gradually began to enter into the realms of history of civilization. And even until I was fifty, it was mainly the popularizers I found. Maybe it is an inevitable error for one who shuns the guidance of academia.

It should be clear that the message I felt it my mission to articulate may not have importance for anyone else. And as much as I want to give myself to a righteous cause in great efforts to improve the world, this is not my path. While I have been involved in nonprofit work and humane issues for years, my contribution is at the level of frontline worker, not as a leader. And even in that role, my heart has always been with my own quest more than with the cause: to finish going around the perimeter, and enter within.

Even though I knew that the key was to overcome haste, the task of reading around the perimeter kept me from doing so and from being fully present in the Now, and from reflecting on experience. It seemed that before slowing down, I had to acquire an adequate orientation. And while there were a few times I told myself that I had arrived at a natural end, that it was alright to stop hurrying, to encounter the present situation fully, enriched by all that I had learned, I was soon off and running for another year or more, to fill another gap in my knowledge. I agreed that dissatisfaction is a primary delusion, that the gold lies in simply embracing the present moment—but how can a person understand reality without having a basic idea of cosmology, or of the history of the human species, or the nature of life? Or of the current world situation and the epochal changes of our time? Or of what the most insightful psychologists have to say about the interpretation of dreams? And so on. Even though it seems likely that answers to these questions will change fundamentally before too long, I still needed this orientation. Another mistake?

And so I took up Greek and left Manhattan. During the thirteen years I dedicated to this study I wrote, among other things of little interest, a novel, a novella, the first draft of a translation of Diogenes Laertius' *Lives of the Philosophers*, and the first version of a biography of my Grandmother. I didn't try to publish anything, partly because I was discouraged by stories of how difficult it is to be published, but more because what I wrote didn't come close to expressing what was within the perimeter. The novella, *Freedom of Speech*, was meant to break through to that message. It didn't succeed, so I put down the Greek and changed my job to become more involved with basic human experience. I learned Spanish and returned to school to get a master's degree.

This third period, lasting about fourteen years, was a time of filling in more gaps in my knowledge of history and the modern problematique. Toward the end, I felt that I had connected with the message, through coming across the Rule of St. Benedict, which led me back to mystic diaphanics. I tried to work out a program for systematically cultivating human potentials, all of them: physical, mental, social, and spiritual; and I rewrote my Grandmother's biography, making it five times as long as the original booklet.

By then, I felt ready to return to school for a doctorate. A friend told me it would be a shame to stay in school all my life, that I should try to establish my program for cultivating human potentials for a year, and if that didn't succeed, then go back. After two years I began preparing for doctoral studies, and through these studies I finished traipsing around the perimeter, arriving at a sort of culmination of my value-based life. Some three years into the program, the dean approved my dissertation proposal with a single comment: "Research question requires a more narrow focus." This statement brought me to the end of the journey.

Upon entering these studies I was undecided between a) a project to develop my program for "training athletes of human potentials," a research-based method for maximizing full human abilities; or b) working out a flourishing Earth philosophy, a rationale for creating a world where all people will be able to flourish in a flourishing natural environment. The proposal criticized by the dean inclined toward the former. Through the summer I meditated on his statement, first thinking of narrowing the focus to a program for training higher-order cognitive skills such as memory, critical thinking, metacognition, concentration, and self-observation, until, upon waking one morning, it occurred to me that it would be better to concentrate on only one higher-order mental function: wisdom.

This meant taking a deep breath and setting out along another bulge in the perimeter, as my knowledge of wisdom and the wisdom tradition was slight. After a while I realized that the perimeter had closed, the journey was finished. A call from a person interested in having me promote *transletix*, the methodical cultivation of human potentials, drew me back—almost. But by then, the feeling of peace and freedom from haste was too great, or I had simply reached my limit. It was the land within the perimeter that interested me now.

After so many years involved with preliminary tracing of the borders, this surveying mode had become a habit and it was difficult to live any other way. Life within the borders is qualitatively different, as different as reflection is from reading the daily news. Some serendipity helped me change my approach; for example, coming across Bernadette Roberts' explanation that the life of no-self is for the most part mundane. Why had similar Zen statements not had the same effect? Maybe they prepared the ground, and at last, understanding this principle, I was able to stay within the borders of Buddhaland even when the magic seemed to dissolve into the real (as described by the morning paper) world.

Here is where practical techniques implemented on a daily basis became golden. These are my solutions, every person will find hir[1] own. Maybe these can help. I fill my life with reminders. One is "centering before entering." Whenever I enter a building I take a moment to bring myself back to mindfulness and recollect my purpose. Before getting out of bed in the morning I recite Ken Keyes' "twelve pathways to higher consciousness," and on retiring let thoughts of them drift through my mind.

Before starting the day I sit over coffee to let thoughts arise and pass. Over thirty years ago I attended the New York Zen Center on West 81st Street, and while my practice of zazen has been spotty, lessons in meditating and observing the mind have become a part of my perspective, the second nature that shapes unreflected on the first nature. Sitting in the small meditation room facing the wall in long periods of silence, I found that by sitting quietly, letting thoughts and feelings pass without holding on to any, or spinning out lengthy (usually mindless) monologs or scripts, eventually deeper thoughts appear, and thoughts that integrate more of the isolated, atomistic, experiences. Awareness of these thoughts is necessary for knowing ourselves.

This time in the morning helps carry the process forward. I note insights in a little book I carry around—I have over a hundred eighty of these books now—and I transcribe the contents of enduring interest into various files in the computer, for further consideration.

Writing for me has a centering power, particularly since my writing became a recollective-introspective-observational exercise, around the time I began to attend the Zen center. Writing this essay is a reminder, a help toward living a value-based life at a period of history when old values are crumbling, where "things fall apart and the center cannot hold." The center can hold, but it has become a new, living, and always changing center. The flowers faded and the grass withered, but the word of the Lord remains forever. But it is now a meta-logos.

I spend a lot of time in fast food restaurants. Sitting outside if the weather permits, otherwise inside by a window. I put earplugs in to block the music, and if necessary put rifle-range ear protectors over them. It is in such settings, bent over my notebook or a piece of blank paper, that thoughts from the center are likely to sound. Some people recommend thinking or writing indoors where there are no distractions, no windows, but I need to see the outdoors. It is often the sight of a plant, or hopping sparrows, as I contemplate them, that connects me with a thought that creates a path for deeper messages to wend their way from within.

Simplicity is essential for going beyond haste. The principle seems to be to minimize involvements so that those encountered receive adequate attention and reflection. This is a difficult matter of discernment. Simultaneously, it seems essential to be open to whatever appears in the present moment. The path of striving for more seems to lead in the wrong direction. Or maybe not. This is where my need for orientation got me on the racecourse around the perimeter in the beginning.

At any rate, unlimited experience provides too much—too much to make sense of. The task necessary for reaching the center is not, however, to make just any meaning, and not to discover the meaning either. It seems likely that there is no final conclusion to arrive at, but rather the goal is to find a method, a way of looking at things.

Simplicity and poverty don't have to go together, but I have always lived on the edge of poverty. When I mention how long I have been without health insurance, people look sympathetic; but at times, other financial needs are so great that the lack of health insurance is low on my list of concerns. This is one of the less desirable results of living my value-based life, but part of the package.

Dealing well with negative feelings is pretty important. I have come to use them as messages that something needs to be addressed. It took me quite a while to figure out that in interpersonal relations, negative feelings are challenges to find a positive response rather than signs of threat appropriately followed by automatic defense. Negative feelings are signals to attend to rather than triggers for fleeing or fighting. I struggle to catch a reflex response of impatient annoyance, one of the aspects of my personality that pleases me least—a venial sin, but not to be overlooked.

A special, conscious effort needs to be made to maintain awareness of the full context—my place in the world of two hundred nations, six billion people, and millions of animal species, on a small planet with major challenges, in the midst of endless space and time. This context is hard to feel but is as real as the table on which I am writing: I will be dead before long. In a world that is 4,540,000,000 years old, I may have thirty more years to live. And the world will then go on for another four billion years and everything about me will be forgotten before my ashes have dispersed.

There is so much to think about. We are thrown into this world with no idea of what it means. Whether positivistic scientist or devout religious believer, we are deeply concerned with the question, "What is this existence?" To claim to know more than we do is to fool only ourselves, even if we have authoritative communities supporting our stand. The ultimate condition for humans is uncertainty, but not everything is uncertain or equal. In this chaos, choices, and responsibility for our choices, are unavoidable. Meanwhile, there is enormous suffering, much of it caused by human ignorance and folly, and remediable. The present moment offers opportunities, if we have awareness and imagination. Suffering and folly, love and wisdom. Imminent death. The question, "What really matters?" The responsibility to see and to choose, the possibility of nurturing full healthy development. We come across each of these every day. How does it all fit into Buddhaland?

© *Richard Hawley Trowbridge*

618

Note

1 Note on gender-inclusive language: for the generic use of pronouns with human referents, "hir" is sometimes used here. We are fortunate that in English it is easy to make our language gender inclusive. There is no reason not to do so, and every reason not to postpone doing so. To use hir is as simple as to use 'Ms.' to refer to any woman (Miss or Mrs.); and in speaking, the pronunciation is the same as the currently used feminine pronoun "her." The term hir dates back to Chaucer, though he used it as a plural (their).

About the Author

Richard Hawley Trowbridge is currently completing a doctoral program in human development at Union Institute & University, and teaching a course surveying the literature on wisdom in the West. He lives on the New York side of Lake Ontario with his partner Alice McAdam.

His dissertation, "The Scientific Approach to Wisdom," is available at www.cop.com/TheScientificApproachtoWisdom.doc, and his website, www.flourishingearth.org, contains more material and information about transletix, the systematic cultivation of full human potential.

The shortest and surest way to live with honor in the world is to be in reality what we would appear to be; all human virtues increase and strengthen themselves by the practice and experience of them.

Socrates

Once we commit to a life of excellence, meaning, purpose, nothing can get in the way. We find the joy and purpose we're seeking because we're acting in accordance with our values.

Jan Phillips

A man is truly ethical only when he obeys the compulsion to help all life which he is able to assist, and shrinks from injuring anything that lives.

Albert Schweitzer

Let go of others' values. Take only what your church, family, and society inculcated in you that is authentic, rational, and feels right. Spend the time it takes to find out what you value, what you cherish, and why. Socrates heralded the process of really inquiring about values, and he made a massive impact. I value his method.

Jason Merchey

The dedicated life is the life worth living. You must give with your whole heart.

Annie Dillard

If you want to be a follower of Socrates, that means thinking for yourself and, if necessary, departing from ideas and areas that Socrates had marked out as his own.

Miles Burnyeat

I believe life is constantly testing us for our level of commitment, and life's greatest rewards are reserved for those who demonstrate a never-ending commitment to act until they achieve. This level of resolve can move mountains, but it must be constant and consistent.

Anthony Robbins

What is necessary to change a person is to change his awareness of himself.

Abraham Maslow

Joy is but the sign that creative emotion is fulfilling its purpose.

Charles Du Bos

The good life is one inspired by love and guided by knowledge.

Bertrand Russell

The universe is full of magical things, patiently waiting for our wits to grow sharper.

Eden Philpotts

By using reason to weigh the consequences of overindulging, as well as to avoid those pleasures that cause more pain than others, the wise hedonist comes to experience the greatest pleasure of all - tranquility.

Judith Barad

If reason and empirical observation steer the course of discovery, and the passion for truth supplies the fuel, it is intuition that provides the spark.

Frances Vaughan

All truths are easy to understand once they are discovered; the point is to discover them.

Galileo Galilei

The Wright brothers flew right through the smoke screen of impossibility.

Charles F. Kettering

To live content with small means; to seek elegance rather than luxury, and refinement rather than fashion; to be worthy, not respectable, and wealthy, not, rich; to listen to stars and birds, babes and sages, with open heart; to study hard; to think quietly, act frankly, talk gently, await occasions, hurry never; in a word, to let the spiritual, unbidden and unconscious, grow up through the common - this is my symphony.

William Henry Channing

MORALITY

RATIONAL ETHICS
Moral Principles for Optimal Living

Peter Voss

E
thics, or morality, is a system of principles that helps us tell right from wrong, good from bad. This definition, by itself, tells us nothing about the standard by which we establish or measure right and wrong. The centuries have seen many different approaches to ethics; none seem to be satisfactory. The terms "ethics," and even more so, "morality" carry heavy emotional baggage. Traditional approaches to morality are confused and contradictory. While supposedly telling us what is "right" or "good" for us, they variously imply sacrificing our lives to some Greater Good, restrict beneficial sexual conduct, oppose our legitimate desire for personal happiness, or offer supposedly ideal, but impractical solutions.

I consider these views to be distortions of what ethics really has to offer—given a rational approach. Ethics should and can give real and practical guidance to our lives—our best rational interests—without sacrificing others. The system that I'm proposing is a workable personal guide to acquiring virtues that promote optimal living, both for the individual and, by extension, for society. It is designed for self-motivated individuals who seek a rational system of principles that will help them both define and achieve ever improving character and living. It is a system that we can enthusiastically pursue, not from duty or primarily to please others, but for personal benefit and from personal conviction.

Why Do We Need Ethics?

Morality is often used by various leaders and organizations to control society—sometimes benevolently, but usually bringing about self-sacrifice and human suffering. There are, however, far more fundamental and legitimate reasons for ethics: to provide purpose and meaning to our lives by helping to define goals in our lives—and then to help guide us to achieve them.

The most basic need for ethics lies in the fact that we do not automatically know what will benefit our lives and what will be detrimental. We constantly face choices that affect the length and quality of our lives. We must choose our values: where to live, how to spend our time, whom to associate with, whom to believe. We must choose what to think about, and how to go about achieving our goals. Which character traits to acquire, and which to eliminate. By what criteria to judge others, and on what basis to interact with them. We must proactively think about these issues and deliberately direct our lives. To the extent that we default on this, we are at the mercy of social and emotional factors that may be far from optimal—a drifting boat, at the mercy of the currents and winds.

Ethics is about the choices that we make—or fail to make. We are aware of our conscious thoughts and of our ability to make informed, intelligent choices; that is what we call free will. We are aware that the choices that we make have consequences, both for ourselves and for others. We are aware of the responsibility that we have for our actions. But, we do not have reliable inherent knowledge or instincts that will automatically promote our flourishing. We have an inherent emotional desire to survive and avoid pain, but we do not have innate knowledge about how to achieve those objectives. A rational, non-contradictory ethic can help us make better choices regarding our lives and well-being. Issues not subject to our choice—unknown to us or outside of our control—are not moral issues.

Most moral systems concern themselves primarily with social interactions: *what effect do my actions have on others?* This puts the cart before the horse. How can we hope to judge what is good for others, good for society, before we have determined what is good for the individual? What is good for me? The answers to these questions—personal morality—can, and must, form the foundation to social morality, political and legal systems. Judging the morality of social norms, public policy and laws can only be done with reference to what is good for the individual. After all, social morality is supposed to benefit the individuals who make up a given society. Furthermore, each individual really only controls his own morality. Others can be influenced to think and act morally, but they cannot ultimately be forced to do so.

The other key feature of ethics is living by principles. But, why live by principles? Why not just make the "right" rational decision as we go along? Aren't principles limiting and, in any case, old-fashioned? Disregarding the fashionability of principles, let's look at two major advantages of living by principles:

Firstly, the scope of our knowledge and cognitive abilities is always limited. We are never fully aware of all the factors influencing the outcome of any given choice, and thus make our decisions based on limited information. In addition, our reasoning ability is limited both in time and complexity in any given situation. Principles—generalized rules that have wide applicability—help us make better decisions in complex situations; the best decision "all other things being equal." Principles can give us useful guidance in a wide range of situations.

Secondly, generalized principles can be automatized. Consistently living by rational, non-contradictory principles will tend to make principled thought and behavior habitual: principles give birth to positive character traits, virtues. This subconscious assimilation leads to automatic emotional responses that are in harmony with our explicit conscious values. Our virtues mobilize our emotions to encourage moral choices, judgments, and actions. Furthermore, our virtue-based subconscious evaluations help us make better complex, split-second decisions.

Automatic and instantaneous guidance can be immensely beneficial if— and this is a big if—we learn and automatize the correct principles. If we, for example, automatize self-hatred, superstition, or a victim-mentality, then this is surely detrimental. If, on the other hand, we acquire the virtuous habit of seeking self-knowledge, then automatic internal warning bells are likely to alert us to any attempts of evading or disowning our actual emotions or actions.

Morality Today

Morality is an endangered species: global communications and travel, cultural upheaval, plus massive changes in lifestyles and technology are increasingly exposing contradictions and practical limitations in traditional systems. Unable or unwilling to live by hopelessly flawed dogma, we have all but abandoned systems of morality. Some resort to explicit amorality, others to a "pragmatic" approach of "what one can get away with," many simply do what feels right—more or less. Hypocritical behavior by spiritual and political leaders, rampant dishonesty in others, and the anonymity of urban life further encourage this rejection of traditional ethics.

> Morality is an endangered species: global communications and travel, cultural upheaval, plus massive changes in lifestyles and technology are increasingly exposing contradictions and practical limitations in traditional systems.

However, all of these factors cannot hide our desperate need for guiding principles. Modern life offers additional freedoms that impose increasingly numerous, difficult and far-reaching choices on our lives—choices about relationships, children, education, careers, politics, wealth, health, and even death. We can alter genes, synthesize life, and will soon create artificial intelligence. Our decisions have more profound consequences than ever before—ultimately effecting mankind's very survival. This trend continues to escalate, yet "progress" will not wait for us to sort out our values.

In summary, a rational, personal morality is both a conscious, as well as subconscious, aid to defining and achieving our goals and happiness. A guide to our own flourishing—a guide to how to live optimally.

What could be more important?

Traditional Sources of Moral Principles

Traditional systems of morality comprise a mix of four separate, but interrelated, sources:

- Social rules or customs that are either agreed on by the majority or enforced by some kind of law.

- Some authority, usually claimed to be "divinely inspired," that establishes an absolute dogma.
- Intuitive, emotional "knowledge" of what is right and wrong— a personal moral compass.
- Rational or common sense rules and principles aimed at achieving a given objective.

Let's explore each of these sources in some detail:

Social rules and customs are, in themselves, a mix of religious or philosophical dogma, "what feels right," and common sense. They evolve by various random forces impinging on them: an influential philosopher, a charismatic spiritual leader, economic factors, disease, wars, immigration, art. The resulting morality is usually recognized as being relativist—its subjectivity being rather obvious. For example, one society believes that having more than one child is immoral, while another sees contraception as depraved. Unfortunately, this relativism does not usually prevent people from trying to force their views on others, even killing and dying for it in its name.

Religious, spiritual, or cultish ethics claim to possess absolute knowledge—divinely inspired—and therefore not subjective. From an outsiders point of view its relativism is apparent. Who has the direct line to God or to some platonic Eternal Wisdom? How would we know? Conflicting claims of authenticity cannot be resolved rationally. Opponents are "persuaded" either emotionally or physically. "Divine" morality is frequently used by religious and cult leaders—alone or cahoots with kings and governments—to control people, claiming a preferential relationship with Divinity, they can trade "salvation," "absolution," and "godly knowledge" for their followers' obedience and sacrifice. Many wars and vast amounts of human suffering have their roots in this kind of "morality"; though, granted, many systems are not consciously malevolent.

We all judge morality intuitively to some extent. We tend to have deep emotional convictions about certain issues; be it euthanasia, gay marriages, abortion, or the "need" for mothers to stay at home to raise their children. Some philosophers believe that intuition is the only valid source to knowing right from wrong. For the reasons mentioned under "morality as an endangered species" many people today reject religious and social morality and rely primarily on their own personal moral compass. In one sense, this is exactly what we have to do—automatized principles are essential for coping with the myriad of complex decisions we face. However, without explicit, conscious selection of the principles that we internalize, our emotions are unguided missiles. Slavery, racism, or treating women as second class citizens may feel very right—as it has, and still does, to many people. Intuition is no guarantee of morality. Our moral compass needs to be calibrated and checked to ensure that our intuition guides us to desired destinations.

What we need is an explicit system of ethics to serve as a reference to the programming of our subconscious values. Without this reference, intuitive morality remains a hodgepodge of various religious, social, and rational ideas picked up during a lifetime: a persuasive idea gathered here, a powerful emotional lesson retained there, added to the comfortable social and religious norms of our childhood. The overwhelming preponderance of adults retaining their own parents' social and religious values is proof of these influences. However, the fact that many of us do break away from our childhood influences attests to the possibility of reprogramming ourselves. We do have free will—we can choose to review and change deeply held beliefs.

Everyone uses reason, the fourth source of moral knowledge, to some extent. Even the most narrow-minded, emotional, or dogmatic person occasionally uses reason to try to resolve moral conflicts—and the traditional approaches certainly provide plenty of contradictions and conflict: communists reason about the practical contradictions in communal ownership and personal motivation. Catholics decide to use birth control as they realize the folly of that restriction. Entrenched racists often go color-blind with people they personally know well. Reality eventually impinges upon irrational beliefs. But we can go much further in utilizing rationality to establish principles for living—we can proactively seek to systematically eliminate contradictions, detrimental beliefs, and inappropriate emotional responses. But is there really such a thing as objective knowledge, especially with regard to moral issues?

Reason and Objectivity

Reason is the mental faculty that integrates our perception of reality while eliminating contradictions. Reason seeks to obtain as accurate a representation of reality as possible. This model includes knowledge of external reality, as well as knowledge of our own thoughts and emotions. Reasoning consists of conscious and subconscious processes. For example, intuition and induction, which are partly subconscious, are used in integration and conceptualization. Information obtained by these subconscious means must be double-checked by conscious processes to establish its accuracy. Because of limits in our cognitive ability (we are not infallible or omniscient), we need to systematically test our data and reasoning against other minds (explain, debate, learn) and against reality (gathering empirical evidence to test our conclusions).

Reason does not provide absolute, acontextual certainty. All objective knowledge—knowledge of reality obtained by rational means—is subject to context and subject to future revision and clarification. Some objective knowledge is beyond doubt; we have no reason to doubt it. That knowledge we call "certain." It is certain within the context of our experience, knowledge, and cognitive ability.

Objective, or rational, ethics provides principles that will practically achieve a desired purpose. A given principle's truth is measured by its general effectiveness. We call a principle "good" if it's good at accomplishing its goal. In this sense, we can call this a scientific approach to ethics. Rational morality is an integrated, non-contradictory, reality-based system of goals and principles. But how do we establish the ultimate goal—the standard of what constitutes good and bad, right and wrong, true and false principles?

Good and Bad

Two crucial questions represent the key to understanding the moral meaning of good and bad. Yet, moral philosophers have frequently ignored these questions, or have grossly underestimated their importance. Some prominent philosophers don't even seem to be aware of them: Good for whom? Good to what end?

For some reason, we have come to accept that there exists some independent Platonic "Good"—some absolute meaning of good not related to any other standard. We will say "it is good to speak the truth," meaning, somehow, good in itself—not because of some beneficial consequence. Were we to ask "why?" we would get a paternal "because...because you should." Ethics is rife with this meaningless categorical imperative "should." "Should" only has meaning in the context of "should in order to..." An ethics is only as rational as its standard of value is—its standard of good and bad.

Good to what end? The purpose of ethics is to help us make decisions, to help us define and achieve our goals. If we have multiple goals, then ethics must also help us reconcile and prioritize these. Some claimed objectives of ethics are: "getting to heaven," "doing our duty," "clearing our karma," "filling our evolutionary purpose," "pleasing others," "achieving wealth," "maximizing our own pleasure," or "living a full and healthy life." Having concluded that a rational approach to ethics is the only meaningful and practical one, we can eliminate all the irrational options—goals that are not reality based. On the other hand, money or pleasure, by themselves, are not sufficiently comprehensive long-term goals. Anyone who seeks life-long guidance—and moral principles and virtues are by their very nature not quick fixes—needs to cast his moral net wider.

In the most general form, our goal comes down to defining and achieving a good life: physical, emotional, mental, and spiritual health—a fulfilled life. There are objective measures of health: physical—living a full life-span (within the limits of current medical knowledge) as free as possible from physical impairments; emotional—generally free from depression and emotional conflicts, high self-esteem, and the ability to experience joy; mental—cognitive competence including intelligence, memory, and creativity; spiritual—the ability to enjoy literature, art, friendships, and love. This list is not exhaustive and is open to debate, but few people would argue about the importance of these basic qualities of human life. The particular manifestations of a good life—the specific level and choices of health, relationship, productive work, artistic enjoyment—will vary from person to person and from time to time. This general description of the good life I call "Optimal Living," and take as the standard of good and bad, right and wrong. More about this later.

Good for whom? Living optimally requires holding certain moral values, setting and pursuing personal goals, and acquiring rational virtues. None of these can be done for someone else. We cannot make others think rationally, make them have a proactive or optimistic outlook, or give them self-esteem. We may encourage others to think and act morally, but we can really only make those choices for ourselves. We can take most responsibility for our own lives because we have most control over it. We also have maximum motivation for expending the effort to live a principled, moral life when we are the primary beneficiary. In short, we cannot live someone else's life for them.

This does not mean that what is good for us is necessarily detrimental to others—life is not a zero-sum game. Fortunately, many rational moral principles benefit both ourselves and others. Examples of these virtues are rationality, productiveness, integrity. Later I will show why these are indeed selfish virtues.

On the other hand, attempting to base morality on what is good for others, a selfless ethic, is doomed to failure. Apart from the reasons given above, altruism invariably entails that we force others to do what we think is good for them—indeed it is our duty to do so. People can be expected to make all sorts of sacrifices claimed to be to the "public good." This destructive belief also reduces the individua's moral motivation, responsibility, and authority by making them shared issues. A morality based on society's well-being is inherently detrimental to many individuals in the group because it imposes the subjective values of some of the group on the rest.

Having outlined the nature and purpose of this practical and personal rational ethic, let us take a closer look at its goal—Optimal Living—and at the processes and virtues that help achieve it.

The Goal: Optimal Living

There our two fundamental, but interrelated, aspects to Optimal Living: becoming the best possible person and living the best possible life. The first allows us to achieve the second—the second entails the first. Living a healthy, flourishing life on an ongoing basis necessitates an appropriately virtuous character. Both of these aspects can, in turn, be seen both from an abstract, generic ideal and from a specific personal context. Rational moral principles guide us towards general as well as specific values. For example, the generic value of seeking good physical health, and the specific value of discovering a diet-exercise regimen appropriate to our age and life-style. Or, identifying the general principles and virtues, and discovering particular personal character traits that require development.

Ethics should help us define, prioritize and achieve our values—general as well as specific ones.

I want to stress an important aspect of Optimal Living: discovering and defining the exact nature of what it means to live optimally, what integrated personal health and well-being entails, is itself subject to a dynamic, ongoing process. We cannot start out with absolute immovable parameters that cast Optimal Living in concrete. However, we do start out with a pretty

good idea of the sort of things essential for an objectively healthy life: free
from unnecessary disease, poverty and trauma; mental competence; sharing
our life with people important to us; being able to experience joy. Many of
these values will turn out to be universally recognized and valid, others that
we discover may surprise us. The key is: acquiring knowledge and fundamental virtues improves our ability to dynamically define Optimal Living.

The values that make up the basket of Optimal Living occasionally compete for priority. Objective resolution of these trade-offs is sometimes difficult—they do not always have a useful common standard for comparison.
Examples include: short-term versus long-term goals; physical versus pre-
dominantly mental aspects of well-being; quantity versus quality of life.
Prioritizing competing aspects of Optimal Living may, at times, be difficult,
but it is far from impossible. A natural hierarchy of values helps us to determine priorities. Survival is a prerequisite for flourishing; long-term existence
presupposes short-term survival; physical suffering impairs mental functioning; successful human relationships require adequate emotional health.

In any case, Optimal Living is not one single, "perfect" version of life.
In addition to a fulfilled life being a conglomeration if values, it also frequently offers several equally attractive alternatives: choice of professions,
places to live, friends, holidays. Optimal Living gives us a general bearing
rather than a specific single destination. It points us in the right direction;
towards survival and flourishing—away from suffering and death.

Optimal means "best or most favorable under a given set of circumstances." Optimal is, by definition, contextual and dynamic—not absolute or
static. Optimal is judged against what is actually possible—what is possible
in reality. For example, optimal health takes into account our actual medical
history. It does not postulate some abstract, ideal genetic and environmental conditions. Our optimal spouse is not faultlessly perfect, but the best
possible kind of partner given our own limitations and reality constraints.

The circumstances and contexts of our lives are also in a continual state
of flux. Specific values optimal to one person at a given time may be detrimental in a different context: a mother may legitimately devote the bulk of
her time and effort to rearing her children—provided that they are not forty
years old! A focus on increasing wealth may be appropriate to a happy couple planning a home and family, not to a discontented billionaire.

Our quest for an ever improving personal and life-experience is a
dynamic, life-long process—an iterative, but hopefully increasingly success-

ful journey. We seek an optimal state of personal physical, cognitive, and emotional well-being. Optimal within the context of who and what we currently are; optimal within the context of what is possible. Living a moral life does not imply guaranteed abolition of disease, stress or unhappiness—even assuming the best ethics and its ideal implementation. Not everything is under our control. Ethics concerns itself with factors potentially under our control. Many factors not directly under our control—other people's actions, nature, and random chance—variously help or hinder our well-being.

Paraphrasing a well-known motto: Ethics—give me the strength to change the things I can, the serenity to accept those I can't, and the wisdom to know the difference. What is likely to give us that strength, serenity, and wisdom? We will return to this question a little later.

Knowledge, Goals, Action

The strategy for discovering and acquiring the virtues for Optimal Living can usefully be depicted as a triangle of knowledge-goals-action.

The amount and quality of pertinent knowledge that we acquire is crucial; it directly affects the suitability of the goals that we choose, and the effectiveness of our actions. We need knowledge both of ourselves, and of other aspects relevant to our lives. Self-knowledge, a frequently overlooked moral value, is crucial to discovering personally satisfying goals, assessing the state of our virtues (and vices), and deciding on particularly effective action strategies. The virtues of rationality, curiosity and honesty embody this love of true knowledge. On the other hand, the vices of mystical thinking, logical inconsistency, evasion, and deceit undermine our ability to effectively understand and deal with reality.

The second corner of our triangle—goal-setting—is another underdeveloped moral concept. Without passionate, but achievable goals, life has little meaning. All the knowledge, productiveness and integrity in the world are wasted without a meaningful focus for them. Yet, discovering optimal goals and sub-goals is no trivial task. Two of the virtues associated with goal-setting are self-awareness and self-responsibility.

Action—the third corner of our strategy triangle—is the "simple" act of getting down to implementing our plans. We sometimes get stuck at this level: we have a passionate goal and know, more or less, how to achieve it, but we don't—be it laziness or fear; or be it just lack of practice. Maybe we need to become aware of the virtues needed for this essential step. They include: integrity, productiveness, discipline, and dynamic optimism.

Before we explore a more comprehensive list of virtues that make up rational ethics, let us investigate two important aspects of Optimal Living: relationships and psychology.

The Importance of Relationships

Optimal Living is impossible without harmonious human relationships. Successful social interactions are an integral part of our lives and flourishing—from the most fundamental act of our conception to the glorious interplay of a romantic union. People can benefit each other in so many ways!

So, what principles and virtues foster beneficial human interactions? The basic personal virtues of rationality, awareness, self-knowing, honesty, productiveness, and integrity form a solid basis for reaping benefits from other—as they benefit from us. We prefer to deal with moral, principled people because they are productive and dependable. They represent a value, not a threat.

A uniquely social principle is that of voluntary, mutually beneficial interaction. It recognizes the merit of individuals trading value for value; not giving or taking undeservedly; not squandering value on others or defrauding them. This has elegantly been termed the Trader Principle. This principle rejects the notion that human interaction is a zero-sum game. Interactions can, and should be profitable to all parties. Exchanges that are voluntary are inherently deemed beneficial to all concerned, otherwise they would not engage in them. This is true not only for commercial transactions, but equally—and possibly even more importantly—for primarily emotional, psychological trades: friendships.

A healthy friendship is a mutually beneficial exchange of value—values such as positive character traits, skills, knowledge, intelligence, beauty, and emotional support. We don't keep literal scorecards of these values traded, but once they become substantially lopsided, the relationship suffers. One person sacrifices, the other loses independence—both undermine their self-esteem.

Understanding the potential and actual value of interacting with others on the basis of the Trader Principle encourages such virtues as justice, respect, tolerance, and benevolence.

This morality encourages social virtues not as "a price to be paid" for personal security or simply "because one should," but as a direct extension of personal virtues. Moral social interaction cannot be based on self-sacrifice—sacrifice to family, society, or nation. They must be based on the individuals' rational self-interest. Rational social principles foster our own Optimal Living—as well as that of others. It also advances diversity; yet it reduces social conflicts by providing a means of resolving them. A shared rational personal ethic forms the basis of social conduct, law and politics—conflicts are resolved using reason, not force.

A Smorgasbord of Rational Virtues

Virtues—the habitual application of specific moral principles—form a complex network of interrelated guidelines.

Below follows a listing of most of Rational Ethics' virtues. Because this system must help us now and in the future to optimize our lives, it must include virtues relating specifically to modern living; virtues pertaining to psychology, technology, and finances. Ethics is not (or should not be!) primarily of academic interest: "This is life, this is not a rehearsal."

Knowledge virtues previously mentioned: respecting reality, cognitive competence, rationality, curiosity, creativity, independent thinking, wisdom, honesty, and a love of knowledge. In addition we have: creativity, as learned skill, not as "innate" talent; wisdom, which can be described as seeking and possessing practical knowledge pertaining to human life and, in particular, knowledge of human nature and relationships; and honesty, which is a love of, and commitment to, the truth—truth about our selves and other aspects of reality. Honesty is an essential part of cognitive competence—maximizing our effectiveness by rejecting fabricated "realities."

Goal virtues: self-responsibility, rational self-interest, goal-directedness, purpose-seeking, dynamic optimism, principled living, respecting value itself, love of the good. All of these virtues support discovering and valuing personal goals. Principled living—as does discipline (listed below) —recognizes the long-term nature of many of our goals. It is, of course, also the quality that recognizes the fundamental benefits of virtuous character.

Action virtues: integrity, productiveness, independence, decisiveness, discipline, love of money and financial knowledge, love of technology and progress, health-consciousness. Integrity means acting in accordance with your beliefs and values. Productiveness is the ability and propensity to create the physical and spiritual (psychological) values needed for Optimal Living. These values may be for direct personal use or, more likely, to be traded with others. Love of money does not refer to some trivial mindless worship of accumulated assets, but to an important concrete sub-goal; the means of achieving other goals. It is also a rejection of the notion that money and wealth are inherently evil. The same applies to the love of technology.

Psychological virtues: self-curiosity, pride, valuing self-esteem, valuing psychological knowledge. Seeking self-knowledge entails truly getting in touch with our feelings. It necessitates seeking objective knowledge of our strength, weaknesses, and desires—seeking this knowledge irrespective of what we would like to find. As we practice this virtue, as we begin to realize its benefits, it will please us to learn more and more about ourselves—good and bad. We will understand that knowledge is a prerequisite for change, and that rational change leads to improved living. We will get a kick out of knowing ourselves, instead of fearing it.

Relationship virtues: valuing trade, respect for the autonomy of others, justice, empathy, benevolence, tolerance, courtesy, communication, and social skills. Virtuous people are of value to us—as we are to them. They represent an opportunity for enhancing our lives—not a threat. Recognizing this, and the fact that personal virtues are universal, that they are potentially beneficial to every individual, provides the basis for respecting the rights of others. Valuing personal autonomy reflects in our recognition of the universal right of individuals to self-ownership and to pursue their own goals. Social virtues, derived from personal ones, form the basis for developing workable social, legal, and political systems—and for judging existing ones. Workable systems built on rational principles are also moral ones.

Empathy is our ability to rationally and emotionally relate to another's point of view. Being tolerant means to put up with others' contrary tastes or with their shortcomings. This tolerance is justified in the context of more important values arising from the relationship or the potential of a valuable relationship developing later. Benevolence is the empathetic well-wishing of others—valuing the happiness of others. Depending on circumstances, benevolence may involve both moral and material support. A related virtue is valuing and supporting justice, even in cases where we are not directly involved. These, plus the other social virtues, all help to maximize benefits of human relationships. They help ensure that, overall, people are a value to each other, and not a burden or threat.

To return to the motto quoted earlier, we now have a better idea of how ethics, rather than God, can help us live our lives. Appropriate knowledge of life and people gives us wisdom; rationality yields serenity; self-esteem, goal-directedness, and dynamic optimism provides the strength.

Let us now turn to some principles or beliefs that are considered virtues by many, but that are actually quite detrimental to Optimal Living.

Examples of Specific Detrimental "Moral" Beliefs

One of the most disabling, and thus immoral, beliefs that has long been a cruel tool of suppression is still causing untold self-inflicted suffering. It is an essential part of religion, mysticism, and superstition but has also found its way into the secular theory of determinism. It is the belief that our lives are subject to some unknown or inexorable master plan or master planner: "It's my karma...," "If it was meant to be, I'll....get married, find a job, lose weight," "I'm just a product of circumstances," "There must be a reason...that we suffered this tragedy," "It is probably for the best," "It is written....in the stars," "It is God's will—He works in mysterious ways." These beliefs encourage us to abdicate self-responsibility, they paralyze us. They also undermine our self-esteem by casting doubt on our efficacy.

Religions have, of course, always used this ploy to control us. Self-appointed leaders claim to have a direct line to God or some "cosmic consciousness." Some of them are self-deluded and act in "good faith." No matter what their motivation, the effect is the same. We waste our time and energy following their advice, while doubting our own ability to take charge of our lives. A more subtle form of this handicap are social standards and peer pressure. "Act your age," "Accept your station in life," "That's not the done thing," "All good people go to church."

My criticism of Karma and Fate should not be confused with the legitimate acknowledgment of cause-and-effect. "What goes around comes around" is a popular expression of this aspect of causation. It recognizes that our actions have consequences—that, more likely than not, good actions will have good consequences; bad actions bad effects. On the other extreme, there are countless random chance events that impinge on our lives. Some will have significant effect on our lives, but none are causally connected to our actions in any meaningful way. We can call that luck, without ascribing any spiritual or cosmic meaning or intent to them.

All you need is love; from Buddha to Christ to 60s hippies. Love everyone. Unconditional love. Don't judge others.

Dangerous advice. Love means cherishing, valuing. Un-judged, unconditional, indiscriminate love is no love at all. We judge something or someone to be valuable—that is the root of our love. To a large extent this positive evaluation is subconscious; sometimes it is unwarranted. Love manifests itself in two ways: how we feel and how we act. We may feel love for someone, yet not act in a loving way—and vice versa. This dichotomy indicates incomplete integration of our explicit values. An important aspect of optimal living is to bring conscious values and emotions into harmony. Reason usually provides the most reliable assessment, however, occasionally our emotions know better. Carefully exploring our emotions and motivations will help us to resolve these kinds of conflicts.

This does not mean that love is a moment to moment evaluation of our friends and lovers. The justified love that we have for someone is based on who and what the whole integrated person is. This may change over a period of time—and so should our love. It may grow or diminish. True love is not motivated by duty or commitment. Do we really want to be "loved" by someone because "they promised"? Even love for our children cannot be unconditional. We may love the memory of who they were, or visions of who they might have been; we may still have many of the feelings, but we cannot consciously value a child turned mass murderer.

"Don't judge others," a judgment we hear frequently. Do we really want to live by that code? Will any ole' person do as a business partner, a baby sitter, a spouse? I doubt it. "Love everyone equally" is another gem. You might just as well choose to marry your neighbor, the tax-collector, or the local child-molester. "There are no good or bad cultures—just subjective preferences." Tell that to some poor soul murdered for providing insufficient dowry. These bromides may be meant as harmless expressions of benevolence. However, anyone trying to live by them—and many are—will harm not only themselves, but others too. Let's not confuse kindness, or lack of prejudice, with the self-contradictory concept of "universal love."

To live, never mind optimally, we must judge. Judge people, cultures, laws, governments. Judge, not pre-judge. We need to know if things are good or bad, pro living or pro suffering. It is detrimental loving someone who abuses and hurts us. We are right to love political, economic and social freedom; it promotes life and happiness.

638

Furthermore, I yearn to be objectively judged by others. I want them to recognize my virtues, skills, strength. I also want them to reject my moral weaknesses. I don't want others to encourage any of my detrimental behavior or beliefs. That would make them accessories.

The lack of judgment, combined with a rejection of personal responsibility, leads to the unfortunate modern phenomenon of "the right to be helped." The belief that a need by one person (the have-nots) automatically imposes an obligation on another (the haves), undermines the concepts of justice and charity. It also encourages victimhood and abdication of personal responsibility. Charity is not a right or obligation. Moral charity is the voluntary assistance given to an appreciative recipient. The donor can, and should, set the terms of his assistance to ensure that the charitable gift will not be wasted or end up being counterproductive.

A major factor perpetuating this perversion of charity is the common acceptance of self-sacrifice as a virtue. Self-sacrifice—acting against your own values—is a vice. Doing things for others—our children, our partner, our community, our country—is only moral to the extent that it promotes our personal values. In that case there is no sacrifice, just selecting—often painfully—priorities among different values. Forgoing a tropical vacation to pay for our children's schooling is no more a sacrifice than paying our rent—provided that we value having educated children. It is only when the motivation is not to protect or foster our rational values that we sacrifice. Such sacrifice may be motivated by a foolish sense of duty or by irrational goals, such as heaven.

What will such sacrifice achieve? If we regard it as moral to sacrifice our lives to our children, then what do we expect of them? To sacrifice theirs? And their children? Who ever gets to live? At a national level, blind, self-sacrificing patriotism has provided much unnecessary cannon fodder. I suspect that the concept of Original Sin, or its more modern Freudian derivative of an inherently evil human nature, are largely responsible for the popularity of self-sacrifice. If we are born guilty, then we sure have a lot to pay for.

Many life-enhancing values have been perversely misidentified as vices or disvalues. These include reason, knowledge, technology, business, wealth, pride, pleasure, our bodies, and sex. Christianity has played a large part in spreading and entrenching these unfortunate moral misconceptions in societies around the world. Another by-product of a misguided morality can be seen in a number of popular false dichotomies: the moral cannot be practical; what is good and moral differs from what we want to do; self-interest invariably undermines social order and well-being; reason and emotion are opposing forces; worthy research and art are incompatible with money and business. Correctly identifying values and virtues, and rejecting these false dichotomies, is an important aspect of living a truly moral life.

Finally, the individual, personal dimension: to live, explore, and enjoy ethics. Being a living, shining example of the benefits of our ethics is its best promotion. As we live our ethics, we gain a deeper understanding; as we learn more about it, we get more out of life. It must never become a duty or obligation. If it does, then we have slipped back into an obsolete view of morality. Rational ethics is a practical tool to help us live and enjoy life. Once it fails to do that, we must stop to reevaluate. Our selfish goal is to become the best person possible—because that person will live the best possible life.

This is an abbreviated version of an essay available at:
http://www.optimal.org/peter/rational_ethics.htm. The full version includes additional examples and references, plus sections on other moral systems, limitations and objections, and psychological considerations.

© *Peter Voss*

About the Author

Peter Voss is an entrepreneur with a background in electronics, computer systems, software, and management. He has a keen interest in cognitive science and the interrelationship between philosophy, psychology, ethics, and computer science.

Peter spent several years studying philosophy and ethics, which led to developing his theory of Rational Ethics. He founded the (now dormant) nonprofit Institute for Optimal Living to promote these ideas.

For the past few years he has been researching artificial general intelligence, and started Adaptive A.I., Inc., with the goal of developing a highly adaptive, general-purpose AI engine. He considers himself an Extropian, and is actively involved in futurism, free-market ideas, and extreme life-extension.

He lives (happily) in Los Angeles.

Rarely, if ever, do we stop to reflect on what we truly want in life, on who we are and want to become, on what difference we want to make in the world, and thus on what's really right for us. That is the unexamined life...You pay a big price for living such a life. What is the price you pay? What's the cost? Socrates identified it when he stated that this form of life, the unexamined life, is not worth what you have to pay for it - that this form of life simply is not worth living.

Tom Morris

We are discussing no small matter, but how we ought to live.

Socrates

A virtuous person feels pleasure in doing a virtuous act, and pain when he or she is unable to do good.

Judith Barad

The good life is one inspired by love and guided by knowledge.

Bertrand Russell

We do not resolve moral issues by checking the law books or taking a hand count.

Judith A. Boss

I think of a hero as someone who understands the degree of responsibility that comes with his freedom.

Bob Dylan

Our enlightenment, our joy, our feelings of passion, our meaning, are byproducts of living a committed and ethical life.

Jan Phillips

We should each ask ourselves: what place does ethics have in my daily life? In thinking about this question, ask yourself: what do I think of as a good life, in the fullest sense of that term? This is an ultimate question. To ask it is to ask: what kind of a life do I truly admire, and what kind of life do I hope to be able to look back on, when I am older and reflect on how I have lived? Will it be enough to say: "It was fun"?

Peter Singer

EDUCATION

EVERY LIFE OF VALUE
Humane Education for a
Peaceful and Sustainable World

Zoe Weil

What if, by the time they had completed eighth grade, all children were aware of and concerned about the people who make their sneakers, T-shirts, and electronics in factories around the globe, and realized that their money and choices represented their vote for working conditions throughout the world? What if they understood the relationship between the food in their cafeteria, growing obesity rates and ill-health, water pollution and soil erosion, and the suffering of farmed animals, so that with their teachers and school administrators they were able to influence the food service to offer healthy, organic, humanely-produced meals?

What if, by the time these students graduated from high school and college, they could readily identify sustainable practices in various industries that were not only ecologically sound but also profitable, and this model became their personal standard as they forged their own careers? These young men and women would be so fully and naturally aware of the connections between their own actions and the future of the world that no matter what field they pursued—healthcare, engineering, computer technology, architecture, business, journalism, politics, law, the arts—their education would have prepared them thoroughly for their pivotal role as successful agents of positive change.

What if, in essence, we raised a generation to care—to know that what they do matters, not just to themselves but also to everyone their lives touch; to understand the connections between both their personal and cultural choices and the fate of other people, other species, and the Earth, and to take responsibility for creating a better world?

> The education I'd stumbled upon was something quite different—it was humane education, that is, education that seeks to create a truly humane world.

Humane education will help us raise that generation by inspiring young people to identify the values that will guide them through life, and then teaching them the process of embodying these values in the face of complex problems and needs. The times we live in call upon us to make the acquisition of relevant knowledge, skills, and commitment to living ethically, sustainably, and peaceably on this planet the very purpose of education. We must make the curricula that we offer students—from kindergarten through graduate school—evolve fluidly from this purpose so that we teach the next generation what we ourselves are struggling now to learn.

In 1987, when I was twenty-six years old, I taught several week-long summer courses to seventh graders through a program offered at the University of Pennsylvania. One of the courses was on environmental preservation, another on animal protection. Each course included field trips, traditional sharing of information, hands on activities, debate, discussion, and brainstorming for creative actions. I watched in amazement as the students in these classes were transformed in a week. Many made specific changes in their food and shopping choices. Some became activists. One boy who learned about cosmetic testing on animals on Wednesday came to class on Thursday with a pile of leaflets that he'd made the night before. During our lunch break he stood on a street corner handing them out to passersby. A few went on to start clubs at their school and then formed a Philadelphia-area student group that eventually inspired hundreds of young people to develop and participate in positive acts for change.

That summer I realized that I'd found my life's work. Until then I had felt stymied by the question of what I would do with my life. What was going to make the biggest difference? After teaching these courses I discovered that something as ordinary and ubiquitous as education held the key to a peaceful and sustainable future. But it wasn't going to be just any sort of education, and certainly not schooling as it's practiced today with high stakes testing held out as the Holy Grail for a competitive society seeking ever more growth at the expense of the biosphere, other species, and all people. The education I'd stumbled upon was something quite different—it was humane education, that is, education that seeks to create a truly humane world. What exactly do I mean by humane? The word literally means, "having what are considered the best qualities of human beings." Thus, humane education seeks to instill humanity's best qualities in students of all ages in an effort to create a world in which people live in accordance with their most humane values.

To live with compassion, kindness, courage, honesty, and wisdom (to name a few "best qualities") as our guiding values requires a commitment to seeking new knowledge and perspectives, dedication to making examined, deliberate choices with your ethics foremost in mind, and a solution-oriented attitude to destructive systems. While humane education begins by inviting students to identify their values, it does not stop there. Quality humane education uses a four-element approach that includes:

- Providing accurate information about the interrelated issues of human rights, environmental preservation, animal protection, and culture.
- Teaching critical thinking so students can discern fact from opinion and resist forms of manipulation, whether from advertising, media, peers, or social norms.
- Inspiring the 3 Rs of reverence, respect, and responsibility so students will have both the passion for, and the commitment to, bringing about positive change.
- Offering choices for both individual decision-making and group problem-solving so that students can become part of a growing effort to develop sustainable, peaceful, and humane systems by which to live.

Our world faces a host of problems, from genocide, escalating worldwide slavery, and extreme poverty to pollution, resource depletion, and the loss of this planet's biodiversity to widespread institutionalized animal cruelty in our food, fur, and research industries. Young people are neither educated to be aware of more than a few of these problems (and usually only in the vaguest sense), nor are they taught about the connections between them or inspired to come up with viable social and personal solutions. Nor are they prepared to take their place as citizens, future job-holders, and professionals whose role will be to change systems of oppression and destruction into new systems that are healthy, humane, and just.

Yet the problems mentioned above will confront our children all too soon, and we do them a grave disservice if we do not prepare them to be practical and creative changemakers in whatever careers they choose. While it's important that we don't offer children a laundry list of disasters and lay upon them the burden of solving problems that generations before them created, it's imperative that we make surviving well and humanely into the coming centuries the centerpiece of education and help students develop the skills for innovative responses to global challenges. Our children deserve no less than real preparation for the real world and inspiration for an exciting journey toward restoration and peace. I can't think of any educational approach as relevant and as exhilarating as this. Humane education provides the knowledge, the inspiration, and the tools to create a caring generation of powerful and empowered citizens that won't simply perpetuate destructive, oppressive, and habitual systems, but will, in fact, create systemic change for the good of all. This may well be the most revolutionary and effective effort that we as a society can undertake to create a peaceful and just world.

What does humane education actually look like in practice? In the humane education classroom, young children in the early grades are offered not only the tools for learning—the ability to read, reason, and compute—but are also given plenty of opportunities for experiencing reverence and respect, whether outdoors in nature, by meeting and learning from wise members of the community, or by hearing stories about heroic, compassionate historical figures. In the older grades and through college, students are taught how to analyze products, advertisements, and the media so that they can discern truth from hype and news from public relations, and then make truly informed choices. They are not only provided with accurate information about the challenges that confront us, but are also given the opportunity to meet visionary inventors and leaders who are creating sustainable technologies and systems to meet those challenges, and they are encouraged to work together to generate their own realistic solutions to problems as well. Ultimately, these students learn to take individual responsibility for creating a life of value that contributes to the creation of a humane world.

In terms of specific subjects, math classes offer word problems for learning not only arithmetic and algebra, but also for understanding how numerical equations, statistical analysis, and algorithms can be applied meaningfully to solve real-life concerns. Teachers of language arts choose books in which empathy, courage, integrity, and generosity enable protagonists to successfully prevail over adversity and injustice. History becomes far more than memorizing facts and dates, and, for example, might explore such books as Jared Diamond's *Collapse: How Societies Choose to Fail or Succeed,* in order to understand how and why cultures crumble or thrive and explore methods for achieving a sustainable and peaceful society on a global scale.

In a humane education school the categorization of subject disciplines might itself disappear as students are taught to see anthropology, ecology, geography, social studies, literature, history, art, and philosophy as wholly interconnected. In this way, *Cradle to Cradle*, a book written by architect William McDonough and chemist Michael Braungart that explores cutting edge products and systems that are non-polluting, regenerative, and ultimately civilization-saving, might become the high school text for a semester-long unit on creating a viable future that interweaves technology, engineering, environmental science, physics, chemistry, and social studies. Another unit might be simply titled "Food" (surely a subject worthy of discussion in that none of us can survive without it) and would examine food and its myriad effects through economics, nutrition, history, government, mathematics, marine science, political science, anthropology, psychology, law, health, ecology, genetics, and ethics, to name some of the subjects connected to food. A year-long course could be spent examining a fast food meal in an effort to both unravel a web of interconnected problems and to determine dietary choices and farming practices that are actually sustainable, humane, and healthy.

Humane education is not an educational reform movement; it is an educational revolution that places all of the challenges of our time under one umbrella, refusing to separate and segregate problems—a common approach which too often perpetuates single-issue fixes that don't lend themselves to the reparation of whole systems. By raising these interwoven issues under the rubric of "humaneness"—that is, as part and parcel of being a human endowed with the capacity to live a meaningful and moral life—humane education nurtures the healthy unfolding of both the whole self and all of society. Were humane education to offer only an academic examination of world problems and an intellectual approach to solving them, I suspect it would not succeed in its goal of creating a humane world. But humane education is not simply cerebral; it cultivates empathy, kindness, and integrity. In the humane education classroom, students and teachers look inward to grapple with their personal beliefs, hopes, and values, and the challenges of living their lives as compassionate and responsible citizens. The path inward and the path outward are inextricably entwined and equally essential making humane education both "soft" work and "hard" work; philosophical and practical; deeply traditional and profoundly radical; ancient and brand new.

Whether or not you are not a classroom teacher or college professor, you are still part of this endeavor. If you are a parent, a friend, a colleague, a neighbor, or a family member, you are also a teacher, and the most significant way in which you teach is through your example. While what you say matters, what you model matters more. Just as humane education lays the mantle of responsibility upon the shoulders of young people to identify and then live according to their values, so, too, is each of us responsible for embodying the values we seek to instill in others and working toward the creation of a just and sustainable world. We need more than traditional teachers and professors to take upon themselves the goals of humane education. We need everyone who cares.

© Zoe Weil

About the Author

Zoe Weil is the co-founder and president of the International Institute for Humane Education (IIHE). IIHE trains individuals to be effective humane educators and offers the only Master of Education degree in humane education, through an affiliation with Cambridge College, in the US. IIHE also offers humane education weekend workshops throughout the US and Canada. Zoe is the author of *The Power and Promise of Humane Education* and *Above All, Be Kind: Raising a Humane Child in Challenging Times.*

America's future will be determined by the home and the school. The child becomes largely what he is taught; hence we must watch what we teach, and how we live.

Jane Addams

No one can simply read about ethics and become ethical. It's not that easy. People have to make many decisions under economic, professional, and social pressure. Rationalization and laziness are constant temptations. But making ethical decisions is worth it, if you want a better life and a better world.

Wes Hanson

Personally, for the last 25 years I have always stayed one step away from partisan politics. Instead, I have been partisan about a set of ideals: economic justice, civil rights, a humane foreign policy, freedom and a decent life for all our citizens.

Bruce Springsteen

A Humanist Code of Ethics: Do no harm to the earth, she is your mother. Being is more important than having. Never promote yourself at another's expense. Hold life sacred; treat it with reverence. Allow each person the digity of his or her labor.

Arthur Dobrin

Character education is no panacea. By itself, it will not repair disintegrating schools, neighborhoods, or families; dry up the drug trade; or create jobs. But it can be an important part of efforts to invest in our children's development and well-being.

Elizabeth Kiss

We need to try to save the Earth at least as fast as it's being destroyed.

David Brower

Many still don't see any relationship between driving a large vehicle and global-warming gas emissions or rising consumption of paper and the loss of ancient forests. We must help people make these kinds of associations.

Betsy Taylor

Out of the Indian approach to life there came a great freedom, an intense and absorbing respect for life, enriching faith in a Supreme Power, and principles of truth, honesty, generosity, equity, and brotherhood as a guide to mundane relations.

Black Elk

The highest result of education is tolerance.

Helen Keller

To repeat what others have said, requires education, to challenge it, requires brains.

Mary Pettibone Poole

What would [business] look like if instead of being growth centered - with people treated as a means to growth - it were people centered, with people being both the purpose and the primary instrument?

David Korten

Intelligence comes into being when the mind, the heart, and the body are really harmonious.

Jiddu Krishnamurti

And to others of good will, who want to help make a better world, I recommend strongly that they consider science – humanistic science – as a way of doing this, a very good and necessary way, perhaps even the best way of all.

Abraham Maslow

The goal is not to have but to be; not to own but to give; not to control but to share; not to subdue but to be in accord.

Abraham Joshua Heschel

Money may be the husk of many things, but not the kernel. It brings you food, but not appetite; medicine, but not health; acquaintances, but not friends; servants, but not faithfulness; days of joy, but not peace and happiness.

Henrik Ibsen

ALTRUISM

NEVER TOO GOOD TO BE TRUE

Ruth Westreich

Theoretically I should have fallen through the cracks of life and no one would have been the wiser or cared. Why didn't that happen to me? Even to this day in the fall of my fifty-eighth year, I still don't have the answer.

I think the thing I missed the most growing up was a mentor. Not that I knew what a mentor was or what a mentor did, but I always longed for someone to give me some sage words of advise or to share their aspirations and accomplishments. Eventually, I realized that I had to be my own mentor. So many of my early lessons were spent reinventing the wheel. There were people who came in and out of my life at some point and they had great impact on me. Most of them never knew that. They shared a word or situation or a compliment and it gave me hope. So in my daily life, I try to make everyone's life better for having come in contact with me. I guess you can call it magnanimity. Sometimes, it's a smile, a laugh, a helping hand, a bit of advice, or letting them in front of me on the freeway. I have the joy of having people tell me that I have brightened their day and, in many cases, changed their lives. The only thing I ever ask in return is that they help someone when they get the chance.

I have a zest for life that cannot be quenched. Everyday I can't wait to learn more. The more I know, the more I can share with others. Growing up, I instinctively knew that anger hurts everyone, especially oneself. Anger and jealousy (a product of ignorance) were a way of life for my family, so, many years ago, I made a conscious decision not to hold anger for people who had been unkind or deliberately hurt me. I made a conscious decision to value education and learning.

I grew up in a home with no books, no one ever asked if my homework was finished, asked so see my report cards, or showed up for back to school nights. No one ever graduated from college (in fact, I have aunts and uncles that never learned to read or write) and when I announced that I would like to go to college that decision was met with disbelief and a bill for room and board, due weekly after my high school graduation.

My mother sometimes worked in a lotion factory and my dad, when not off binge drinking for weeks at a time, was a gasoline distributor for the now defunct Anchor Oil Company. They shared a small two-bedroom duplex with my aunt and rage-a-holic uncle. My mom, already forty at the time, learned she was pregnant for the third time. By the time she learned this in her second trimester, however, it was too late to obtain an abortion as she had done for the other two. She knew, because of her dysfunctional existence with my dad, that she wasn't willing or prepared to be a mom.

So after I arrived, she suffered a "breakdown" of sorts that lasted for a couple of years. That explains why in my first few years of life, I was always with my aunt and uncle in pictures. My mom and dad, conspicuously absent, began to show up occasionally after the third year.

In my fifth year, after a month of drinking, my dad and two illustrious Las Vegas showgirls were killed in a horrible automobile accident that made all the papers, invited lawsuits from the families of the dead girls, and so my destitute mom and I were sent to live with my childless aunt and her husband in the south central suburb of South Gate that borders the now famous Watts area in Los Angeles. From the time we moved in with them, my aunt spent much of her time trying to break my spirit by locking me out of the house all day while my mom worked at a local dry cleaners'. I became one of those children that ran in the streets all day and showed up about the time my mom came home from work.

Survival was a challenge, to say the least, but survive, I did. I wasn't really sure why I needed survive but the more my aunt focused on making my life intolerable, the more determined I was not to let her.

Somehow I knew I must create my own toolbox and fill it with tools to insure my survival. I didn't seem to have an angry disposition and was pretty resilient to the exterior things happening around me. I didn't know exactly why, but I always did well in school and studying came easy for me. I won praise from my teachers, but doing well in school was really frowned on by my peers, so here began another conflict. I was pretty popular, so after a while they just accepted that I would get good grades and it gradually became less of an issue.

I never thought about what I would do after school. I didn't have a burning desire to have a career. In the sixties, in my blue-collar town, girls concentrated on getting married and having children. I think that life just happened to most of us back then. We functioned in a reactive mode until life's events propelled us into a more conscious, proactive mode.

I thought I was quite the success when I married a doctor from the other side of town, but would never in my wildest dreams have been prepared for what the next twenty years of my life would hold for me. By this time, of course, I was the sole support of my mother who had been in ailing health since I was nine. I immediately got pregnant and had a child within a short period of time. At twenty-five, I thought I'd finally come to a place in my life where I could relax because I'd found a partner to go over life's bumps with me. Little did I know that my husband suffered from chronic depression, chronic anxiety, and was addicted to prescription drugs. He went to his office one sunny morning and by twelve o'clock, he came home with the assistance of medical professionals and didn't leave the house for eighteen months. This was my life for the next eighteen years.

With my ailing, aging mother, raising my children, and caring for my depressed, anxious husband, I was experiencing the "sandwich generation" before they coined such a word. Years of my life went by with me in a reaction mode. I probably wasn't doing a great job at any of it, but I got through it. It never occurred to me that I had any other choice.

I began to take stock of my life when my mother died at eighty-three. I was forty-three years old and all I can ever remember is taking care of people who couldn't take care of themselves. I had the feeling I was at a turning point in my life. I could either stay, or continue to take care of my chronically ill husband until he died or, more likely, I died, or I could move forward in my life not knowing what lay before me. The little voice inside kept telling me to move ahead. All the other voices creating guilt and uncertainty were telling me to stay. Did you ever know you were in the wrong place but too afraid to make a move? I finally got the nudge I needed in the form of my own health crisis, severe chronic ulcers, brought on by constant stress. In those days you just took antacids and hoped for the best, never thinking about the source of the disorder…never considering moving on being a healing option.

Well, eventually, I did move on. I was middle aged, but not quite over the hill, and I somehow knew I could create a life that worked for me. I read somewhere to "never give up before the miracle." It played over and over in my mind and I just didn't give up. I became proactive in my own self-development, empowerment, and creativity.

> I don't know if there was that one defining moment in my transformation, but I truly feel that the guiding force in my life was to survive.

The life I created and enjoy today is one that, in my wildest dreams, I could never have imagined. I didn't know how to have dreams that big. I guess I would have called them fairy tales. I brought into existence the person I had always wanted to be and she just keeps growing. I am in awe of the people that I have drawn into my life—amazing human beings who empower and inspire me, but that's another story.

I am in the very rare position to do great good in the world. I don't take it lightly and on a daily basis I thank the universe for entrusting me with this great honor. My not-so-new husband and soul mate has endowed a foundation, of which I am the president, and I have the privilege of helping many people and causes. I have to admit that I ponder, "Why me?" I guess it is not important that I know the answer to this question, but to constantly be in awe of what is before me.

I don't know if there was that one defining moment in my transformation, but I truly feel that the guiding force in my life was to survive. I didn't know why, but I knew it was important.

Now I know that I survived to do this work in the world: I make sure every day that the world is a better place because I am here. The life that I value, and gratefully live, is guided by magnanimity and altruism. Fortunately, the universe has supported me by giving me the resources and spirit to be of service and make all those around me happier because I'm in the world. Because I never gave up, the miracle finally came.

© *Ruth Westreich*

About the Author

Ruth Westreich brings over thirty years experience as a creative marketing communications director and strategic marketing director in both the corporate and nonprofit sectors. Ruth is a visionary and big picture person with particular expertise in helping nonprofits move forward by stabilizing revenue generation to insure future legacy. Her contagious enthusiasm and tireless focus help individuals and groups achieve their highest potential. Ruth is also a talented mixed-media fine artist for which she has won national awards and continues to pursue her passion every chance she gets.

She works tirelessly in the area of nonprofit to move the sector forward. She is one of the founders of the University of San Diego's Applied Center for Non-Profit Research under the auspices of the university's Non-Profit Leadership and Management master's program. Her vision for the nonprofit sector, which is the sixth largest economy in the world, is to have the nonprofit sector be held to the same best practices that we hold the for-profit sector, and to have the same level of education and expertise in the nonprofit sector that is demanded in the for-profit sector.

She works hands-on with battered and abused women and children, children at risk, mentoring programs, and literacy.

Those who are driven by a burning desire or higher purpose usually achieve great deeds. This purpose transcends money, security, or status. It is the knowledge that they are part of something worthy, right, and valuable.

David Dibble

If we have the opportunity to be generous with our hearts, ourselves, we have no idea of the depth and breadth of love's reach.

Margaret Cho

I've never known any human being, high or humble, who ever regretted, when nearing life's end, having done kindly deeds. But I have known more than one millionaire who became haunted by the realization that they had led selfish lives.

B. C. Forbes

Resolve to be tender with the young, compassionate with the aged, sympathetic with the striving, and tolerant with the weak and wrong. Sometime in life you will have been all of these.

Bob Goddard

Our responsibility as privileged human beings is to pay back for the opportunities we've received.

Kathryn Anastos

I have found that among its other benefits, giving liberates the soul of the giver.

Maya Angelou

The secret of success is to realize that the crisis on our planet is much larger than just deciding what to do with your own life, and if the system under which we live - the structure of western civilization - begins to collapse because of our selfishness and greed, then it will make no difference whether you have one million dollars when the crash comes, or just $1.00. The only work that will ultimately bring any good to any of us is the work of contributing to the healing of the world.

Marianne Williamson

Life's most persistent and urgent question is, "What are you doing for others?"

Martin Luther King, Jr.

For me, heroes are the people who have made money and then used it as a platform for service.

Mark S. Albion

Morality is not properly the doctrine of how we may make ourselves happy, but how we may make ourselves worthy of happiness.

Immanuel Kant

There are eight rungs in charity. The highest is when you help a man to help himself.

Moses Maimonides

Happiness is a form of courage.

Holbrook Jackson

The places I have been emotionally have helped to make me who I am today, as fire is needed to bend steel. The values that move me came into focus for me in part because of the duress of pain I have gone through – such is life.

Jason Merchey

Psychoanalysis is concerned with the past; while one is analyzing the past one is missing the challenges of the present.

Jiddu Krishnamurti

All we have in the end is the dignity and integrity of our person. But this is enough.

Kristen Renwick Monroe

Nobody can give you freedom. Nobody can give you equality or justice or anything. If you're a man, you take it.

Malcolm X

INTEGRITY

TAKING THE HIGH ROAD IN BUSINESS

Stanley Westreich

In late spring of 1997 my company, Westfield Realty, was in the process of completing the renovation of a twelve-story office building in Rosslyn, Virginia. We had an agreement in principle that a major aerospace company would lease two-thirds of the building. This had been accomplished during a thirty-day negotiation that culminated in a face-to-face meeting where a non-binding letter of intent was to be executed.

This letter of intent was quite voluminous and contained all the language that would normally be in a lease agreement. Just before the signing of the document, I said to my counterpart, who was the head of real estate for the aerospace company, "My father often remarked that he knew hundreds of ways to break a contract, but he had never figured out how to break a handshake." I then extended my hand and said, "Even though this letter of intent is non-binding until a lease is executed, I am prepared to be bound by it. If you are ready to make the same commitment, then shake my hand. If you are not ready, I fully understand and we will shake hands when you a ready." He looked at me and said, "I am ready," and shook my hand. We then signed the letter of intent.

Over the next few days I prepared a lease and sent it to him. Two weeks went by without hearing anything. This was not a good sign, for I have learned that these agreements have a certain period of gestation and once that period goes by, the agreement usually dies.

> When you take the high road in business you have established a reputation that will precede you, and thus set the stage for all future business dealings. Your reputation in business is your most valuable asset.

The next day I read in the newspaper that this aerospace company has announced a merger with one of its rivals. I also knew that this rival company has just leased a significant amount of space in an office building next to our building, and the problem is that this other building still had a great deal of space still vacant. I now believed that my deal was dead because it made no sense to have space in two buildings when a consolidation was easily achieved.

Two days later, I receive a call from my counterpart, the head of real estate, in which he told me in a very sheepish voice that he had absolutely no knowledge of the merger and he had negotiated with me in good faith. I responded that I believed him, and told him that I understood and was going to release him from his handshake. I could hear a sigh of relief at the other end of the phone as if someone had magically removed the Sword of Damocles from over his head. I then told him that I fully understood why he should locate in the other building and that perhaps one day in the future we could do business together. He thanked me for my understanding and assured me that he too hoped for the same result.

Six weeks passed and one day I received a call from him. He stated he would be in town the next day and could we get together to reopen negotiations for the building. I told him I would be delighted but asked him, since neither of us needed any more practice in negotiating, what his purpose was. His response was that he was unable to come to terms with the other building owner and would like to try to conclude a lease with me.

We met and he agreed that for the obvious efficiencies, the space should be consolidated and he was going to move out of the other building and sublease that space. With that he said, "I want to lease your entire building."

In the next few weeks we concluded a long-term lease for the entire building.

The moral here is that my conduct enabled him to make that second call to me. If I had taken a different approach and tried to claim that we had a deal once we had shaken hands, we never would made the deal because he would never have made the final telephone call—being either too angry or too embarrassed to place the call.

When you take the high road in business you have established a reputation that will precede you and thus set the stage for all future business dealings. Your reputation in business is your most valuable asset.

© Stanley Westreich

About the Author

Stanley I. Westreich, a New York City native, spent most of his varied career as a real estate developer in Washington, DC. He is currently a member of the Board of Directors for Capital One Financial. He now resides in Rancho Santa Fe, California with his wife, Ruth.

There is no poverty where there is virtue and no wealth or honor where virtue is not.

Chinese proverb

One can pay back the gift of gold, but one dies forever in debt to those who are kind.

Malayan proverb

Mankind's true moral test, its fundamental test (which lies deeply buried from view) consists of its attitudes towards those who are at its mercy.

Milan Kundara

Choose being kind over being right, and you'll be right every time.

Richard Carlson

What is a man profited if he shall gain the whole world, and lose his own soul?

Matthew 16:26

If there be any truer measure of a man than by what he does, it must be by what he gives.

Robert South

The reputation of a thousand years may be determined by the conduct of one hour.

Japanese proverb

True victory is not defeating an enemy. True victory gives love and changes the enemy's heart.

Morihei Ueshiba

It is not what a lawyer tells me I may do; but what humanity, reason, and justice tell me I ought to do.

Edmund Burke

Character building begins in our infancy, and continues until death.

Eleanor Roosevelt

Nobility of soul is more honorable than nobility of birth.

Dutch proverb

I know of hundreds of ways to break a contract, but I never found a way to break a handshake.

Al Westreich

Conscience is a mother-in-law whose visit never ends.

H. L. Mencken

What's a man's first duty? The answer's brief: To be himself.

Henrik Ibsen

The conscientious moral agent is someone who is concerned impartially with the interests of everyone affected by what he or she does; who carefully sifts facts and examines their implications; who accepts principles of conduct only after scrutinizing them to make sure they are sound; who is willing to "listen to reason" even when it means that earlier convictions may have to be revised; and who, finally, is willing to act on the results of this deliberation.

James Rachels

Two things fill the mind with ever new and increasing admiration and awe, the oftener and more steadily we reflect on them: the starry heavens above and the moral law within.

Immanuel Kant

Honor is much dearer than money.

Yiddish proverb

How you decide to define success and other material measures/results will determine to a large degree what kind of business and life you'll have.

Mark S. Albion

STRENGTH

WHEN GOOD MEN BEHAVE BADLY
Change Your Behavior, Change Your Relationship

David B. Wexler

Odysseus, Relational Heroism & Imaginary Crimes

Despite the cultural pressure to stay emotionally hidden or react strongly to perceived injuries to your sense of self, you probably know of remarkable exceptions. Exceptions in others and exceptions in yourself. Every day, men are heroes—not only in the conventional sense of rescuing people from burning buildings or making tough decisions in the workplace, but also by behaving in relationships in ways that are profoundly counterintuitive. For many men, good relationship behavior requires a tremendous act of will, and choosing the counterintuitive behavior is truly heroic.

To help you understand this concept of heroism, let me introduce the term relational hero from Terrence Real's 1997 book *I Don't Want to Talk About It*. Real defines relational heroism this way:

Relational heroism occurs when every muscle and nerve in one's body pulls one toward reenacting one's usual dysfunctional pattern, but through sheer force or discipline or grace, one lifts oneself off the well-worn track toward behaviors that are more vulnerable, more cherishing, more mature. Just as the boyhood trauma that sets up depression occurs not in one dramatic incident, but in transactions repeated thousands of times, so, too, recovery is comprised of countless small victories.

Odysseus the Hero

I find it very valuable to use the story of Odysseus as a parable about personal maturity and relational heroism. Not the whole story, of course, for reasons of time management, but one particular episode from Odysseus's long journey homeward after fighting the Trojan War. After his success as a warrior in the Iliad, Odysseus spends ten years making his odyssey navigating his ship through troubled waters, enduring hardship and adventure. In this classic Greek tale of man's search for self-discovery, Homer's Odyssey, each challenge makes Odysseus stronger and wiser, fostering his development as an evolved and mature man. He is forced to develop as a psychological hero after his many years as a physical hero in the Trojan War.

Odysseus and his men encounter the sorceress Circe, a female creature with enticing and evil powers. She has the power to cast a spell over any man. She welcomes Odysseus's men and offers them wild pleasures, then turns them into swine. However, she takes a liking to Odysseus and spends a year frolicking with him on her island. When they finally realize that it is time for him to resume his journey, she offers him a gift. This is a gift of knowledge that will save the lives of Odysseus and his men. She warns him of the next island that he will encounter, the island of the Sirens.

Like Circe, the Sirens are capable of enticing men. The sound of the Sirens' music is so alluring to men that they can never resist heading toward the source. The Sirens, however, with bodies of birds and heads of women, tear apart any men who succumb to the sounds. Odysseus and his men would be prime candidates to succumb to the Sirens, except that Circe has warned Odysseus. As they approach the island of the Sirens, he orders all of his men to plug their ears with beeswax so they cannot hear the sounds. Odysseus, however, the ambitious seeker, wants it all. He insists on hearing the Sirens himself, so he does not put wax in his own ears, but he demands that his crew tie him to the mast of the ship so that he cannot yield to the seduction. He cautions his men not to release him under any circumstances, no matter how desperately he pleads, cries, or threatens. Thus prepared,

Odysseus and his men continue successfully on their epic journey. His men note his writhing attempts to become free (although they cannot hear his words) but, following orders, continue to row until they are out of range of the Sirens. In despair, the Sirens kill themselves—proving that if you do not succumb to destructive temptations, they wither away.

The moral of the story is this: If you are aware of what temptations or struggles lie ahead, you can transform them, or at least meet them head-on. If you have no context or understanding, then you are doomed to simply react. Be a hero, like Odysseus. Get conscious. Prepare yourself for situations that you know may seduce you into destructive behaviors, and come up with a plan to handle them differently. If you know that hearing your kids arguing makes you start criticizing your wife, come up with a plan to prepare for this so you do not go there. Be a hero, man!

Acts of Relational Heroism

Rick was mentioned in chapter two of my book and passed on the legacy of emotional cruelty to his son. Rick was the man who kept hearing the mantra. "Nobody ever brought me fucking lunch when I was a kid!" whenever his son needed something from him.

Rick's past gripped him and insisted that he withhold from his son. He couldn't bear to offer Stephen more than he himself had received. In fact, offering more to Stephen would only serve to highlight the pain that Rick had endured; keeping the legacy going allowed Rick to pretend that he himself had not actually suffered much.

But when Rick's wife asked him to bring lunch to Stephen, Rick found a way to go counterintuitive. In making that decision, Rick entered the Hall of Fame for relational heroes. And there was nothing earth-shattering or dramatic about his actions. No newspaper would ever report it and no real Hall of Fame would ever take note. Rick simply brought Stephen lunch. And he did it with a positive attitude. Stephen looked at him, shocked and pleased, and gave Rick a look of appreciation he did not quickly forget. Rick told me, "After I did it, I felt really good about it!"

Rick had grabbed himself by the collar, thrown himself against the wall, and told himself that there was something bigger at stake and that he had better avoid just slipping into his default behavior. He sucked it up and became a hero. His son noticed, although few others would. The payoff for Rick was that the new behavior actually felt good and made him feel proud of being a different kind of man. As a footnote, Rick told me that he had been sick recently. Stephen, very uncharacteristically, fixed him a bowl of soup and took care of him. Rick told me, "In the back of my mind, I wondered if he was treating me generously because he remembered the time I brought him lunch, and maybe a few other nice things!"

Another story from chapter two of my book, of Luke confronting his father, also moved me to tears and qualified for Hall of Fame consideration. I watched Luke, usually so composed and slick, crying, snot running from his nose. Yelling "Fuck you!" at his father, revealing long-repressed emotions—and his father taking it. Not only taking it, but obviously moved by it and even encouraging it. Even when he did not have the right responses (he would give advice, he would slip into platitudes), Luke's dad was open to this feedback about what his son needed from him. I did not know who was the greater relational hero, Luke or his dad! They were co-MVPs. When Luke's dad, in response to what must have felt like bitter condemnations and resentments, started talking about what a son of a bitch his own father had been, and how he had tried (with moderate success) to offer Luke something different, I did not hear a man trying to escape responsibility, but rather trying to take it. He wanted Luke to be able to tell him these things, which he never would have been able to say to his own dad. I think he wanted to model for Luke how a stand-up guy can take the truth and learn from it. When the dust had settled, I told them both, "If this trend continues, with each generation trying to be even more evolved than the one before, Luke's son is going to be one hell of a man!"

In one of my men's groups, Brantin described another one of those Hall of Fame moments that the casual observer might not notice. He and his wife had separated after months of tension and discord. By mutual consent, she had taken their six-year-old daughter with her to stay with her family in another state for a couple of months. She and Brantin decided they were ready to give the relationship another try.

When his wife and daughter arrived back in town on a Greyhound bus, Brantin met them at the station. His little girl came running up to him, yelling "Daddy, Daddy, Daddy!" with the kind of gusto that only little kids can generate. He swept her into his arms and hugged her tight, then turned to his wife, who was walking more slowly toward him, to embrace her. She turned away and said she was hurt because she should have been the one he hugged first.

Brantin's self-talk? To put it as he told me, "What a bitch! What am I supposed to do, not hug my own daughter? I can't believe this shit!" But instead of retaliating or pouting, he chose to react differently this time. He stayed calm. He told his wife that he was sorry, that he didn't mean to hurt her feelings, and that he was really glad to see her. He reassured her that he really loved her.

She paused for a second, then smiled and said okay. She reached out for him, and it was over. He had passed a test. Maybe she shouldn't have tested him like that, but that's the reality of it. Sometimes your wife or girlfriend, like you, will be insecure and will do something to check out whether or not you really care. You can either dig in your heels and tell yourself that you're not going to put up with it, or you can try and find some way to soothe her. Brantin found a way, and it brought out the best in both of them. He was a hero.

Preston, another man I worked with, was in the midst of a very rocky period in his marriage when the future was very much in doubt. He began talking to his wife about a vacation he was hoping they could take almost a year later. She looked at him and said, half-joking and half-serious, "Well, you're assuming a lot, aren't you?" Preston's commentary about his own reaction was this:

> Sharice made that crack about how I was assuming too much, and I just shut down, like I always do. I just felt so hurt. Same old stuff. But it didn't take me too long before I turned to her and told her that her comment had really hurt me, and I asked her, sort of nicely, why she had said it. And we actually had a conversation about the whole thing.

> I guess that's sort of the relational hero thing we've been talking about, isn't it? I guess I'm doing pretty well.

Rob, the main character in Nick Hornby's 1995 novel *High Fidelity,* is another man who becomes a relational hero. He has a long history of failed relationships and a long history of selfish, neurotic, immature behaviors that contribute to these failures. He makes a practice of preparing compilation tapes of carefully selected songs for each woman he is interested in, but his tragic flaw is that he selects songs based on his own very snobbish criteria of what the woman should be listening to. He always misses the mark, because he is never able to see her as she really is, only as he wants her to be.

Finally, after more and more errors and grief, he matures and has a breakthrough. About the love of his life, Laura, he says, "I start to compile in my head a compilation tape for her, something that's full of stuff she's heard of, and full of stuff she'd play. Tonight, for the first time ever, I can sort of see how it's done." The task is so simple, yet it took him years to prepare for. And again, the actual behavior is not bold and dramatic to the outside observer, but bold and dramatic nevertheless.

Exercise: Daily Appreciation

Expressing appreciation is one way to test the waters of relational heroism. No twenty-four hour period should go by without you telling your partner or kids something that you really appreciate about them. It can be something rather trivial, like, "You really helped me out when you made those phone calls for me, something major, like You are such a great mom! I love watching how you handle things with the kids," or something in between, like "Hey, I really appreciate that you left me alone for a while tonight when I was in a bad mood. I really need that sometimes."

> No twenty-four hour period should go by without you telling your partner or kids something that you really appreciate about them.

Expressing yourself this way is a habit like any other. Couples who are in a good groove with each other just do this naturally. If things are not going well with you and your partner, or if there are ongoing tensions with you and your kids, you may have gotten out of the habit. Starting it up again may feel a little awkward and insincere at first, but it won't for long if you find things to say that you genuinely feel.

In your notebook or journal, prepare a chart for each day with a column for each family member. At the end of the day, check the spaces for the daily appreciations you have offered. If there are holes in your chart, make an effort to fill them the next day.

A tip: It is almost always helpful to tell your partner that you are doing this exercise. She is more likely to genuinely appreciate your intentions than she is to discount the appreciations because they are "just an exercise."

And one more tip: Just because your kids act like they don't care or don't even notice, don't be an idiot—they do.

Copied with permission from New Harbinger Publications; Oakland, CA; David Wexler, PhD; When Good Men Behave Badly: Change Your Behavior, Change Your Relationship, www.newharbinger.com.

About the Author

David B. Wexler, PhD, is a clinical psychologist in private practice in San Diego, specializing in the treatment of relationships in conflict. He is the Executive Director of the Relationship Training Institute, which provides education and treatment internationally for relationship development and the prevention and treatment of relationship violence. Dr. Wexler has trained thousands of community professionals, military personnel, and law enforcement officials through extensive training seminars on the Domestic Violence 2000 model throughout the world. The California Psychological Association has also designated Dr. Wexler as a Master Lecturer and he received the Distinguished Contribution to Psychology award at their annual convention in 2003.

Dr. Wexler is the author of *When Good Men Behave Badly: Change Your Behavior, Change Your Relationship*, and his newest book, *Is He Depressed or What?: What to Do When the Man You Love is Moody, Irritable, and Withdrawn*. Dr. Wexler has been featured on the *Dr. Phil* show and the *TODAY* show, in the *Washington Post*, *"O"* magazine, *Cosmopolitan, Redbook, Men's Health*, and on dozens of radio and TV programs throughout North America to help educate the public about relationships in conflict and how to resolve them.

Laws control the lesser man. Right conduct controls the greater one.

Chinese proverb

Tenderness and kindness are not signs of weakness and despair, but manifestations of strength and resolutions.

Kahlil Gibran

Courage is what it takes to stand up and speak; courage is also what it takes to sit down and listen.

Winston Churchill

There are two ways of exerting one's strength; one is pushing down, the other is pulling up.

Booker T. Washington

Man who man would be, must rule the empire of himself.

Percy Bysshe Shelley

We do not pray not to be tempted, but not to be conquered when we are tempted.

Origines Adamantius

Most of us look at our ideals, say, how far we are from them, and get depressed. But it is heroic simply to say, "Here are my ideals," state them before the world, and then spend your life trying to live up to them.

Keshavan Nair

Courage is not the towering oak that sees storms come and go;
It is the fragile blossom that opens in the snow.

Alice M. Swain

It is the character of a brave and resolute man not to be ruffled by adversity and not to desert his post.

Cicero

There is nothing wrong with admitting that you have problems. It is your struggle that makes you worthy, not your perfection.

Jason Merchey

Courage is doing what you're afraid to do. There can be no courage unless you're scared.

Eddie Rickenbacker

Nothing is easier than self-deceit. For what each man wishes, that he also believes to be true.

Demosthenes

There's right and wrong. Do one and you're living. Do the other and you may be walking around, but you're as dead as a beaver hat.

Davy Crockett

I think self-awareness is probably the most important thing to being a champion.

Billie Jean King

One must raise the self by the self
And not let the self sink down,
For the self's only friend is the self
And the self is the self's one enemy.

The Bhagavad Gita

Men weren't really the enemy - they were fellow victims suffering from an outmoded masculine mystique that made them feel unnecessarily inadequate when there were no bears to kill.

Betty Friedan

...I swear I will not dishonor my soul with hatred, but offer myself humbly as a guardian of nature, as a healer of misery, as a messenger of wonder, as an architect of peace...

Diane Ackerman

PASSION

CONSUMED BY EITHER FIRE OR FIRE
Journeying with T.S. Eliot

Margaret Wheatley

For too long, I have lived in the world wanting to change it. This has been an impossible stance. It intensifies normal desires to contribute something to the human condition into crusades that are doomed to disappoint. I have gradually weaned myself from this posture, I think, because it is just too exhausting and unsatisfying to maintain.

As I've traveled on this road that I made hard, I've had many essential friends. Including T.S. Eliot. I cannot avoid him. Time and again I get absorbed in the relentless weaving of paradox and imagery in Four Quartets. Many times I have used Eliot to provoke my own experience-to understand what I've learned about this work of wanting the world to be different, better. Eliot shines brilliant beams of light on the path I've been exploring. He names sensations that now lie deep in my body, sensations I experienced as I discovered how best to direct my energy and passion. Sensations that began as pain or wonder, that now sometimes sleep quietly within as wisdom gained, questions answered.

As I was reading him yet again recently, I began copying those passages that always leap out at me. Certain lines endure as an meaningful chronicle of my experience, expressed in his voice far beyond my own capacity for expression. I became engaged in a dialogue with myself (undoubtedly the easiest kind to have) about why these lines keep attracting me.

> We create ourselves by what we choose to notice.

I know that we notice what we notice because of who we are. We create ourselves by what we choose to notice. Once this work of self-authorship has begun, we inhabit the world we've created. We self-seal. We don't notice anything except those things that confirm what we already think about who we already are. But I've always appreciated the thought of I. A. Richards who described a good reader as "a mind paying attention to itself." Using the terms of his field of semantics, he speaks of what meditative traditions call the observer self. When we succeed in moving outside our normal processes of self-reference and can look upon ourselves with self-awareness, then we have a chance at changing. We break the seal. We notice something new.

So I'm wondering now what newness I might notice as I go back into The Four Quartets. If I contemplate those descriptions of his world that I chose to notice, will I then see mine differently? I want to follow Eliot's lead on this journey. I want to enter the endless spiral of his paradoxes to see what I will see. And from this, I hope to enlarge the paradoxes I embrace as I draw the circle of self.

You say I am repeating
Something I have said before. I shall say it again.
Shall I say it again? In order to arrive there,
To arrive where you are, to get from where you are not,
You must go by a way wherein there is no ecstasy.
In order to arrive at what you do not know
You must go by a way which is the way of ignorance.
In order to possess what you do not possess
You must go by the way of dispossession.
In order to arrive at what you are not
You must go through the way in which you are not.
And what you do not know is the only thing you know

And what you own is what you do not own
And where you are is where you are not.

East Coker III

I choose to begin with this passage not because of its profound paradox, but because it begins with humor and frustration. I want to appreciate
these emotions that are frequent companions of paradox. I relate to his repetition, because I find myself on many different podiums, repeating myself.
And I'm frustrated with repeating myself (I shall say it again. Shall I say it
again?) because I know I'm saying things that have been said by others, over
and over. I'm giving voice to ideas that have been expressed by mystics, martyrs, philosophers, scientists, and everyday people. For millennia. Is anybody
listening?

I lose my patience. I wonder where all the learning is going, why it isn't
showing up in new beliefs, new practices. Patience is my greatest challenge.
(Well, actually, the challenge is compassion, from which patience arises.) So
I try to relearn patience from the true exemplars, those spiritual teachers
past and present who spend their whole ministries being repetitious. They
never accuse us of being stupid or stubborn. These teachers so love the
truth of what they say that they seem to enjoy repeating themselves. I think
this must be the key. Loving truth so much that no repetition is tedious.
Feeling truth new and vibrant each time it is voiced. Loving people so well
that giving voice energizes the speaker long past normal human endurance.

Well, maybe.

What are the truths that Eliot must keep repeating? He follows with a
timeless description of the path by which truth is obtained. Pure paradox, a
path that jostles us continually with its demands. A path that requires no less
than the total loss of certainty and identity. "A condition of complete simplicity, (Costing not less than everything)" he says at the very end of the
Quartets. The way of no ecstasy, the way of ignorance and not-knowing, the
path of dispossession and the dissolution of self that opens us to life.

Many years ago when I was first beginning to write of new science, I
was well-guided. In one trenchant phrase, the journey ahead was described
to me as a journey "of wonder and not-knowing." I have remained clear
about that, and perhaps in contradiction to Eliot, I have found that wonder-
ment, which opens us to new truth, is often accompanied by something a
bit like ecstasy. Astonishment is fun; people love the experience. Wonder

seems to return us to our innocence. We enter into a state of delight-show us something else strange and preposterous so that we can laugh and exclaim. In this innocent state, we are willing to give up our self-concepts and glimpse into the unknown with new eyes. Ever since I began noticing the effects of wonder, I've tried to lead people to a place where they could encounter this astonishing world and grin with delight. If I could do that, I learned they would willingly follow me elsewhere in thought.

But the rest of the journey is just as Eliot describes it. He is, after all, repeating the paradoxes of Jesus, of Buddha, of Lao Tzu. If you would save your life, you must lose it. If you would thrive in the new world, you must dissolve your old form. Letting go is the only path to safety. Surrounded by so much truth, it's a puzzle how we ever came to deny it. Did we ever really believe we could proceed through life by growing all the time, new and improved at every turn? How did the shadow disappear from our pursuit of the light? When did we forget that "there must be opposition in all things." When did we stop acknowledging the great space for discovery that is created by the opposing poles of paradox?

I said to my soul, be still, and wait without hope for hope
would be hope for the wrong thing; wait without
love

For love would be love of the wrong thing; there is yet faith
But the faith and the love and the hope are all in the waiting.
Wait without thought, for you are not ready for thought:
So the darkness shall be the light, and the stillness the dancing.

East Coker III

Eliot extends his hand and asks us to dance into the emptying stillness that truth places on our path. We cannot approach truth from who we are. We think too small. We are confined and confining in our beliefs. A few years ago, feeling imprisoned by the beliefs I was promulgating passionately to myself and to the world, I imagined creating a year-end ritual. I've never done it in all the glorious pomp and pageant I imagined, but the ritual is "The Bonfire of Beliefs." At least once a year, can I take those ideas and beliefs I most cherish and try to see the world without them? "For hope would be hope for the wrong thing. . .for love would be love of the wrong thingÉ" Give up what I believe-these truths are too small for me to perceive what I truly seek. Open to something much wilder, although that too will become tame. Do this over and over, until I ring inside from hollowness and emptied faith. Except the faith I learn in the waiting. Real faith.

We must be still and still moving
Into another intensity
For a further union, a deeper communion
Through the dark cold and the empty desolation,
The wave cry, the wind cry, the vast waters
Of the petrel and the porpoise. In my end is my beginning.

East Coker V

The journey is the accumulation of stillness. Patience. Emptiness. The union that I seek is not of my creation. The self I have created impedes union. Stillness must be learned, and the endless time in which I learn it is filled with doubts and desolations. Stillness often feels like abandonment. Why isn't Spirit communicating with me? What have I done to deserve such a stony, cold silence? How do I avoid filling with new terrors the emptiness that terrifies me?

Yet the wave cry and the wind cry want to fill the silence. Life is our comforter. When I stop the self-absorption, when I can pause a moment to gaze on what's around me, I experience this comfort. I feel the movement of forces that exist beyond me, but which willingly carry me with them. I don't experience nature's elemental energies of wind, movement, or mountains cast high into the sky as hostile. In that, I may be lucky-never to have been overwhelmed by gales or floods. When I lift my head into the wind, or commune with a mountain, I do so as a participant. I feel this planet as an expression of the life that moves in me and everyone. Often, Nature is my most comforting companion. She invites me to remember that I am necessary to creation.

But only if I discipline myself to stop looking inward. Only if I remember that the communion I seek is everywhere around me, waiting for me to notice its presence. It is another intensity and it cries out for us.

> And what you thought you came for
> Is only a shell, a husk of meaning
> From which the purpose breaks only when it is fulfilled
> If at all. Either you had no purpose
> Or the purpose is beyond the end you figured
> And is altered in fulfillment.

Little Gidding I

Here is Life's great gift-unending surprise. And it's other gift-Life's inherent orderliness. We are not adrift in a purposeless universe. We are not the byproduct of a Darwinian accident that felt lucky because we were the ones to survive. I used to challenge MBA students with the question, "Do you think your life's purpose is something you create or discover?" They always wheedled out of it by answering, "Both." This may be true, but I feel that Viktor Frankl was right when he said that "meaning precedes being." I know we each have a unique contribution that is necessary for the whole of us to thrive. I know our gifts are required. I don't know where these gifts originate, but I know what they feel like. I feel joyful when I yield to their expression.

Yet Eliot cautions us about something I also know to be true. We so want to know our purpose that we too quickly determine what we think it is, and we kill ourselves in the process. We turn from stillness and listening to earnest action, and Spirit disappears. After a while we find ourselves expired-we played God with our lives and lost the source of all inspiration, the breath of life.

This is a real dilemma. How do we attend to our purpose while holding the humility that we do not create it? Once we catch a glimmer of what it might be, how do we avoid taking over as creator? It gets even more complicated. How do we avoid getting ego-seduced by the specific manifestation of our gifts? Is it possible to live in the humility of knowing that our purpose, as clearly as we self-define it, is but "a husk of meaning"? The task is really to become superb listeners. Heidegger wrote that waiting, listening, was the most profound way to serve God.

Can we live into the presence of purpose, never hoping for a straight-forward answer but inviting in always the great mystery that gives rise to our questions?

You are not here to verify,
Instruct yourself, or inform curiosity
Or carry report. You are here to kneel
Where prayer has been valid.

Little Gidding I

To this place, listening carries us. Whatever we conceive our work to be, in the end we know that we are only, infinitely, serving the place of prayer. I used to believe my work was about organizations and life inside them. Then a bit later I thought I was charged with changing the dominant world-view of Western thought. Notice how my scope increased as my ego gained a surer footing. Then one day, in a sunny patch of jungle in the Yucatan, I leaned against a small but perfect Mayan ruin while my two sons swam in a shadowy cave pool. Faced with jungle growth and sun, and the cold stones of yet another attempt at civilization, I knew that my work was, as is every-one's, about reclaiming Life. All of us are struggling together toward a time when the human spirit can find more room for itself in the societies we cre-ate. We are all participating in enlarging the spaces in which we together dwell, so that they might hold more of the greatness of each of us.

Who then devised the torment? Love.
Love is the unfamiliar Name
Behind the hands that wove
The intolerable shirt of flame
Which human power cannot remove.
We only live, only suspire
Consumed by either fire or fire.

Little Gidding IV

I lose my breath reading this passage. Do I experience the demands of Love as an intolerable shirt of flame? I know I feel there is no escape from this path, but I don't yet know that this path leads only to fire. I do, more and more, feel as my companions those from all centuries who followed the blinding path of Love, who willingly donned the shirt of flame and wore it to their martyrdom. Recently I've been reflecting on how strange we are, my generation, to believe we can help birth a new world without it affecting our career progress. I'm aware of how little courage our lives have required of us. But Life keeps raising the stakes.

When I thought the opposition to my work was in the person of a controlling boss, it seemed I might maneuver my way past him or her. When I thought the opposition originated from a lack of evidence for how much we all benefit from inclusive, inviting workplaces, it seemed I might create change by rational argument. When I thought the work was about shifting a world view and welcoming in life's great creative capacities to our human lives, it seemed I had a lot of support from the planetary community of living beings. They were making their case-I needed merely to direct attention to what they were doing.

But Love is not satisfied by logic. It may be that we'll accomplish this latest revolution with grace, that we'll marshal the powers of non-violence and people will willingly surrender their ideas and their power because they too are tired of the violence and the impotence. But maybe not. Maybe the only route to Love is fire, or fire. I don't know this, but I do know that I have had to surrender to this as the great possibility. I have had to confront whether I am willing, if asked, to forego the life that holds me so securely and comfortably. And I don't know what I have answered, because Life hasn't yet asked me. I believe I have recognized the shirt of flame, but will I be asked to wear it?

But Eliot has moved past my question. He has put my queries to rest. He has illuminated my path and assured me of the journey. I have learned what we are engaged in and how we must be together.

> There is only the fight to recover what has been lost
> And found and lost again and again: and now, under conditions
> That seem unpropitious.
> But perhaps neither gain nor loss.
> For us, there is only the trying. The rest is not our business.

East Coker V

This is the knowing that resolves paradox, that puts an end to questions. Shall I say it again? I shall say it again. We do what we are called to do because we feel called to do it. We walk silently, willingly, down the well-trodden path still lit by the fire of millions. And the rest, I know now, is not our business.

© *Margaret Wheatley*

About the Author

Margaret Wheatley writes, teaches, and speaks about radically new practices and ideas for organizing in chaotic times. She works to create organizations of all types where people are known as the blessing, not the problem. She is president of The Berkana Institute, a charitable global leadership foundation serving life-affirming leaders, and has been an organizational consultant for many years, as well as a professor of management in two graduate programs.

Her newest book, *Finding Our Way: Leadership for an Uncertain Time*, will be released in January 2005. Her book, *Turning to One Another: Simple Conversations to Restore Hope to the Future,* (January 2002) proposes that real social change comes from the ageless process of people thinking together in conversation. Wheatley's work also appears in two award-winning books, *Leadership and the New Science* (1992, 1999) and *A Simpler Way* (with Myron Kellner-Rogers, 1996,) plus several videos and articles. She draws many of her ideas from new science and life's ability to organize in self-organizing, systemic, and cooperative modes. And, increasingly her models for new organizations are drawn from her understanding of many different cultures and spiritual traditions.

Her articles and work can be accessed at www.margaret-wheatley.com, or 801-377-2996 in Utah, USA.

What is to give light must endure burning.

Viktor Frankl

With time and patience the mulberry leaf becomes a silk gown.

Chinese proverb

Your vision will become clear only when you can look into your own heart... Who looks outside, dreams; who looks inside, awakes.

Carl Jung

Not hammer strokes, but the dance of the water singes the pebbles into perfection.

Rabindranath Tagore

Sometimes a person has to go back, really back - to have a sense, an understanding of all that's gone on to make them - before they can go forward.

Paulie Marshall

The opened mind can be relaxed and playful. It is filled with curiosity and wonder. There is something childlike about it. It loves to get off the beaten track, to explore paths that are not the ones taken by social convention.

F. Barron, A. Montuori & A. Barron

The majority of men prefer delusion to truth. It soothes. It is easy to grasp.

H. L. Mencken

Each needs to develop the sides of his personality which he has neglected.

Alexis Carrel

There lives more faith in honest doubt - believe me - than in half the creeds.

Alfred Tennyson

Dare to be yourself.

Andre Gide

A single event can awaken within us a stranger totally unknown to us. To live is to be slowly born.

Antoine de Saint-Exupery

Trust yourself. You know more than you think you do.

Benjamin Spock

What I am is good enough if I would only be it openly.

Carl Rogers

As you become aware of your feelings, thoughts, and actions - and can observe them - you reach a most powerful place: the place of choice.

David Dibble

The only thing that can save this world is the reclaiming of the awareness of the world. That's what poetry does.

Allen Ginsburg

Man as a scientist has come to know a great deal, but as human being, knows and feels intuitively love and ambition, poetry and music. The heart and mind reaches deeper than the power of reason alone.

Jacques Barzun

What a man knows at fifty that he did not know at twenty is for the most part incommunicable.

Adlai Stevenson

Yet the deepest truths are best read between the lines, and, for the most part, refuse to be written.

Amos Bronson Alcott

Fiction is a piece of truth that turns lies to meaning.

Dorothy Allison

RESPONSIBILITY

DISPATCHES FROM THE GLOBAL ASSEMBLY LINE
New Millennium, Same Challenges

Heather White

I am often asked by people concerned about possible sweatshops behind the clothes and consumer products they buy, "What brands are sweatshop-free?" and, "Where can I shop with a good conscience?"

Having worked for the past ten years as a social auditor and advocate for workers' rights and protections in factories producing for the world's global companies, and having seen that nearly all companies doing business in developing countries operate in environments which foster violation and exploitation at some level, I regret that there is no single answer to these questions. For example, do we wish to reward companies that have made a public commitment to requiring good standards by their overseas suppliers, but then do nothing to ensure or verify that the standards are being met? Do we want to support companies that have thousands of overseas factories they purchase from annually, but claim there is no way to check on more than 5 percent of them to determine they are not operating sweatshops?

How a concerned American consumer makes purchasing decisions regarding products made in the world's poorest regions ultimately depends on her (or his) values. I've taken several approaches over the years in terms of my own personal consumption choices, ranging from trying to only buy brands that I personally knew, from Verite's audit experience, were making a good effort to address human rights issues in their factories, to avoiding all products made in certain countries (which I still do to some extent, avoiding everything from Myanmar/Burma). I avoid mass-produced consumer items from Pakistan and Bangladesh because I know that the working con-

> How a concerned American consumer makes purchasing decisions regarding products made in the world's poorest regions ultimately depends on her (or his) values.

ditions in the factories producing items such as canvas bags, baseball caps, and generic garments are among the worst found in global supply networks. That being said, I do buy labor-intensive handmade craft items from those two countries, or those with fairly traded labels. The issues of underpayment of wages, physical abuse by supervisors, and excessive overtime are so severe in almost every factory audited by Verite in those two countries that I do not want to contribute to continuing systems of exploitation. Bangladesh (one of the lowest GDP countries) is raising a generation of children born in the past ten years who are not being breastfed because their mothers work excessively long hours in factories with no support for nursing their babies. The impact on the overall health of the children in that country, and the complicity of the companies that operate there cannot be overstated. Labels stating "Made in Cambodia" also raise serious issues for me, having overseen audits of factories where workers collapsed from heat exhaustion, reported the murder of their colleagues by factory management, and where journalists reported to us their efforts to follow up on the allegations led to their being warned away by local police. Combined with the fragility of the government, and a local environment that has seen violent confrontations at factories where women workers have been killed for protesting low wages and mistreatment, I do not feel comfortable buying products made in Cambodia unless they carry a fairly traded label.

So, which companies do I buy from, and who do I recommend based on my knowledge of their overseas suppliers' practices? I will provide a list below, but first I'd like to point a few more issues that need to be consid-

ered by consumers, and encourage everyone who is purchasing manufactured goods made in developing countries to be in regular email contact
with the merchandisers and retailers that they purchase from, making clear
their expectations that the products they buy need to provide some assur-
ances they were produced under safe and humane working conditions.

For wealthy consumers on the winning side of the growing global
divide, per capita consumption has risen at a steady annual rate of 2.3 percent over the last twenty-five years. According to UN development studies,
the upper fifth of those living in high-income countries account for 86 percent of all of the world's private expenditures on consumption. Yet for the
vast majority of residents in the countries which produce the (arguably
largely unnecessary) goods that constitute this growing consumption, life is
a daily preoccupation with obtaining safe water, rudimentary health care, living wages, and sufficient nutrition.

Sadly, it has been my firsthand experience to observe that workers in the
factories which serve the world's largest brands are often dealing with issues
of basic survival, despite the fact that the global corporations purchasing
from the factories are experiencing record high profits. When doing a social
audit for one of these high-end brands at an apparel factory in Indonesia
that produces for US retailers, my colleagues from a local NGO found that
the drinking water in the factory was turned off for several hours daily, preventing workers from drinking during their twelve-hour shifts, despite temperatures exceeding 90 degrees Fahrenheit inside the factory. That these
workers were also barefoot, and not allowed to purchase any of the garments they made, added to the overall indignity of the working environment. When we asked the workers what was the most important thing they
would first change about the factory, assuming we could even deliver on any
of the long list of legally mandated upgrades, workers said they wanted to
be treated respectfully and as human beings by factory management. These
comments reflect what we were told everywhere, in sixty countries, by workers in every hemisphere, working in some cases under the most horrendous
of circumstances. They want to be treated as human beings and given the
respect they deserve for making what we as Americans would view as a
superhuman commitment to ensuring their employers' financial success—
which, in the case of the CEOs of several US brands, is an annual salary that
would take workers in the Indonesian and Thai factories over 10,000 years
to earn at their current wages levels.

The desire expressed to be treated with respect by management, and the expectation that management should be accountable for their actions, was underscored closer to home when New York-based Pico Products, Inc. closed, without warning, an electronics factory near Seoul in 1989 after workers formed a union and gained a collective bargaining agreement. Three hundred workers, mostly women assemblers, were left jobless. When a settlement finally offered a cash pay-out to workers but no admission of wrongdoing on the part of the company the workers refused, stating "We'd rather get no money and a final judgment that the company broke the law," they said, "than twice the money due us and this 'non-admission' clause."

Despite increasing awareness of global labor issues by American corporations, negative trends continue to keep pace with efforts to bring more countries' laws and individual factories into compliance with international standards. To list a few examples:

Colombia: steadily increasing rates of fatalities at work resulted in a deterioration of the country's conditions of work rating by the state of California's employee pension fund, placing it at risk for overseas investment. (China, with somewhere between 10,000 and 40,000 deaths annually in the workplace, is already on CalPERS prohibited list. Colombia and Coke-a-Cola have also been the target of student boycotts and international grassroots campaigns regarding the murder of eleven Coke employees in Colombian factories.)

Thailand: growing (not decreasing) reports of children (often from Cambodia or Burma) found in indentured servitude in domestic service and of children and young women in situations of forced labor in underground sweatshops.

Philippines: the Philippine government intervened in a sugar mill workers' strike, leading to police and military actions, which resulted in the deaths of fourteen people in November 2004.

India: the Indian government has been increasing the difficulty for international human rights groups to enter the country. As the world's largest democracy, efforts by the government to limit the role of civil society organizations' ability to operate threaten protections for workers during a technology boom.

I do not wish to create too negative a picture, however, and acknowledge that since 2003 there have also been some notable developments among developing countries with respect to labor practices:

Egypt: abolished the use of hard labor as a criminal penalty. This was progress for Egypt, which had proved to be nearly impossible for us to conduct social audits beginning in 2002 with the arrest of our local NGO (nongovernmental organization) partner in Cairo, Saadeddin Ibrahim director of the Ibn Khaldoun Institute, who was arrested with twenty-seven of his staff as he prepared to monitor the upcoming national elections. Ibrahim's arrest was decried by human rights activists worldwide, who declared that Egyptian civil society had suffered a major setback with the arrest of a well-respected internationally known scholar. The government also shut down groups that had accepted grants and financial support from the EU and major international advocacy organizations. Working with NGOs in the Middle East in general often proves to be a challenge, due to fear on the part of the local non-profit groups of government reprisals.

India: in February 2004, the government of India—together with the US Department of Labor and the International Labor Organization—launched a $40 million project to combat exploitive and hazardous child labor. Child labor in India continues to be an ongoing serious problem, particularly in labor-intensive industries, despite the technology boom led by global software firms. A recent Indian government report estimates there are 100 million children working illegally in the country.

Sri Lanka: over 160,000 tea estate Tamils were granted full citizenship by the Government of Sri Lanka. Other major exporting countries, in addition to Sri Lanka, such as Thailand and Cambodia, continue to deny full citizenship to indigenous peoples within their borders. In many cases indigenous groups are advocating for the preservation of natural resources and protection from internationally-funded exploitative development at the same time as they experience the loss of their traditional lifestyles due to expropriation of their land. As they lose their land to corporate development projects, such as free trade zones meant to attract foreign investment, indigenous peoples are migrating to urban areas in search of employment, where they then experience a pull-effect by the global assembly line into factories, which, in many cases, offer them illegally low wages, excessively long work hours, and a new, unfamiliar lifestyle.

Is there anything consumers can do about the global trafficking issue? Where should consumers be placing pressure? Throughout the world, illegal activities—such as the trafficking of women and children for the sex trade—are of significant human-rights concern and gaining more attention in the media and by lawmakers. However, based on the research we conducted at Verite, the impact of trafficking upon labor conditions in aggregate, in any particular country, is minimal; its scale and range are difficult to document; and its direct relevance to international trade and investment is seen to be small. Moreover, the absence of accurate numbers makes any assessment of such industries unreliable. Consequently, due not only to the unreliability of data regarding employment in informal or illegal industries but also to their limited impact upon foreign investment, the ability of consumers to address these issues directly is currently limited. Where consumers can exert more direct influence is as shareholders, engaging in shareholder resolutions to require the companies whose stock they hold to comply with higher standards. In my experience, the shareholder activist movement has had a profound influence on the responsiveness of US corporations regarding sweatshop and global labor issues. For example, in 2001 a social research study I designed for CalPERS, the $150 billion California pension fund, which evaluated the social and human rights performance of twenty-seven emerging market countries resulted in a loss of eligibility for investment by Thailand, the Philippines, Malaysia, and Indonesia. In response, the labor and finance ministries of those countries sent delegations to the US to learn about the performance expectations required by CalPERS and how they could reinstate themselves in the portfolio.

The recent phenomenon of a global migrant labor force, which sends workers legally from the poorest countries to wealthier nations, also continues to be a major source of concern. While contract labor arrangements are often framed as ways of increasing a country's global competitiveness and stimulating economic growth, the actual employment arrangements often subvert existing collective bargaining agreements, weaken or break unions, and pay employees less than the minimum wages and overtime compensation normally required by law. Migrant Chinese workers in Korea, for instance, have to work for twenty-nine months on average, in order to repay the recruitment fees they paid for the privilege of "purchasing" their factory jobs.

A 2004 Verite unpublished study found that over 70 percent of workers were also denied maternity benefits and freedom of movement by factory management, and sometimes locked into factories to complete production runs, or locked into dormitories. It is difficult to imagine that most American consumers would purchase products that they knew came from factories with illegal or unsafe working conditions, yet such practices are closer to the norm than the exception. A legal effort by several anti-sweatshop groups and unions to address the issue of sweatshops in the US Commonwealth of Saipan led to the then-largest class action suit in US history, and then to a legal settlement whereby the defendant companies paid $20 million to settle several lawsuits. Sadly, the women workers themselves only received $120 total compensation, having paid, in many cases, up to $6000 to purchase a job which demanded nine-six-hour workweeks, but paid them for only forty hours, insisted they have abortions if they became pregnant, and locked them in the factories under twenty-four-hour surveillance by male security guards. The pièce de résistance was the legal bill for expenses submitted by the pro bono lawyers for the workers, which claimed over $6 million total in "reimbursable expenses." (Fortunately the judge did not allow all of the expenses). The defendant companies which paid into the settlement fund included: Abercrombie and Fitch, the Gap, Polo Ralph Lauren, the Limited, Sears, Nordstrom's, Talbot's, and JC Penney. Wal-Mart managed to be excused from the litigation by claiming that no one could prove the company had purchased products directly from Saipan. One of the plaintiffs in the suit called me to ask if I could recommend a strategy that would successfully keep them in the litigation. As a former sourcing agent I was well aware of how nearly impossible it can be to assign ownership through morasses of supply chains when a single importer is buying from trading companies, agents, private label companies in addition to its own brand merchandise. Admittedly, it was a brilliant strategy utilized by a retailer to successfully avoid inclusion in the litigation. The brands, however, would have had difficulty in making the same claim.

So where does one buy from with a relatively clear conscience? I make my purchasing choices based on the companies where I personally know the individuals responsible for the social compliance programs, have read their factory social audits reports or been to their factories myself, and worked on the development and remediation plans for improving conditions for workers in their contracting factories. This list is not comprehensive and does not imply that every factory in these companies' supplier networks is problem-free.

Some on the list were named in the Saipan litigation mentioned above, yet still meet my criteria because I personally know, have either worked with or otherwise trust the individuals trying to make things better at their companies, and I believe they are devoting credible resources and efforts toward improving their social performance. I also think it is important to be realistic; most Americans are going to be going to a Home Depot or major department store at some point every year, and would like to know which major companies ($300 million and above) are doing better on these issues than others. Even anti-sweatshop activists make purchases on a regular basis that do not come from fair-trade boutiques.

What this list means is that, having worked with over three hundred companies on these issues over the past decade, the corporations below have met my criteria for making an ongoing good-faith effort to ensure that their overseas factories are not sweatshops and are working to meet international standards:

Tommy Hilfiger
New Balance Athletic Shoe
Federated Department Stores (Macy's)
Eileen Fisher
Reebok
Target
Adidas-Solomon
Levi Strauss Co.
Nautica Enterprises, Inc.
Sears Roebuck and Co.
Pentland Group UK (Sketchers)
The Gap

All of the companies listed here have staff working full-time exclusively on supplier standards and labor issues. I'm not saying they are doing a perfect job. I wish the list were longer. Some companies came close to making it but didn't for lack of sufficient critical mass devoted to eliminating labor violations. Some companies' supply chains are simply too huge to be fundamentally under control at any given point in time without devoting hundreds of thousands of dollars more to the effort annually. I hope I will be able to provide a longer list in the near future. In the meantime I welcome questions and inquiries from anyone wishing to assess the performance of their favorite brand merchandisers or retailers who were not included here. I can be reached at heatherhsw@gmail.com.

P.S. I have never been in a Wal-Mart.

About the Author

I grew up in Boston, Mass. during the 1960s, and was groomed by my father, who was a scholar and activist, to become a socialist revolutionary in the New China. Both my parents were active in the civil rights movement, with a particular interest in Mao's proletarian revolution. I've managed to stay on the original course they set me on for most of my professional life, with just a few detours. The detours came about mostly because China, in the 1970s, began to pursue an entirely new course, moving steadily toward a capitalist economy in recent years. Yet somehow I ended up somewhere fairly close to my parents' vision, working with Chinese factories for the past twenty-five years, spending the last ten years supporting Chinese worker rights through monitoring the country's factories to identify labor violations.

Once identified, I develop remediation solutions to bring the factories into compliance with local laws and international standards. I graduated from Harvard with a degree in Chinese Politics in 1980 and set off for China soon after to spend the next fifteen years working with former communes and worker collectives seeking to do business with US companies in the new era of export-oriented trade and industrialization.

The early 90s were spent getting an MS from MIT in international political economy. I spent three years doing research on globalization and its impact on women workers in China and Southeast Asia.

Within a few months I developed a concept for an NGO focused on increasing transparency in international trade relationships and monitoring factories' working conditions throughout the developing world. I created Verite (which is an acronym for Verification in Trade and Ethics and means "truth" in French) eleven years ago to address those issues, as well as some others on the global sweatshop continuum.

I recently left Verite to work independently on projects focusing on women worker's labor rights. My work in China and elsewhere continues through a global network of colleagues and NGOs also working on these issues, called New Standards.

Human rights are not a reward of development. Rather, they are critical to achieving it.

Amartya Sen

Out there, everywhere, there is somebody or some group of somebodies who are lighting little prairie fires of rebellion against this economic and political exclusion.

Jim Hightower

Too much focus on profit is no good; neither is too much social activism while ignoring profit. Capitalism for the common good, community action for economic strength – two sides of one coin. That's what nourishes me and my business.

Judy Wicks

Cultural institutions that prompt us to see the world from a "having, desiring, possessing, consuming" perspective aren't leading us in the direction of wisdom, inner peace, and deeply-felt contentment.

Copthorne Macdonald

The success of the European [justice for garment workers] campaigns suggest that comparable progress is possible on this side of the Atlantic as well...If we can educate consumers and mobilize activists, we can "clean" the American closet. Doing so would be a substantial step toward a sustainable, but also fashionable, planet.

Juliet B. Schor

If the focus on You has yet to make you happy, the logic of the consumer machine is simply to get something more. Surely it will do the trick - and if not, then the next thing. Surely.

Bill McKibben

Clothes are a great window into the global economy, getting consumers to think about who makes their clothes. Are people who make their clothes being treated fairly? Some of the most heinous human rights abuse occurs in factories where our clothes are coming from.

Juliette Beck

We are learning once more - as leaders like Teddy Roosevelt learned a century ago - that our noblest aspirations for America cannot be realized when we allow economic competition to grow too harsh.

David Callahan

History has a long-range perspective. It ultimately passes stern judgment on tyrants and vindicates those who fought, suffered, were imprisoned, and died for human freedom, and against political oppression and economic slavery.

Elizabeth Gurley Flynn

This is the true face of the global economy: labor has been erased. Wal-Mart is larger than the economy of 161 countries...It was 104 degrees in the factory...housed in rat-infested dormitories. The real face of Wal-Mart is this thirteen-year-old girl in Bangladesh. She only had two days off in the last four months. She's never ridden a bicycle. Seven cents an hour!

Charlie Kernaghan

The economic logic of the machine age predicted that only good would come from the relentless pursuit of self-interest. Most of these [business] executives didn't realize, when they were climbing their way to the control tower, that they were taking charge of a machine responsible for environmental destruction or human exploitation.

Elizabeth Debold

Capitalism is unethical at its very heart. I don't think it has to be; I don't think it's been developed enough. I do believe that if we put our great minds together, we could develop, perhaps, a kind of "higher level capitalism" that does not thrive on the abuse of people, and that does not put profit over people.

Jan Phillips

Low prices reflect democracy. Brand names represent our search for a better life. And designer boutiques embody the promise of an ever-improving self. Yet Americans have made a Faustian deal with the culture of shopping, and especially with bargain culture. The retail prices may be low, but the social costs are high.

Sharon Zukin

WILL

ROSES OR DIAMONDS
Choosing a Life of Value

Ona Rita Yufe

L iving a life of value...what does that mean? How do I define the value of my life? Or the value in my life. In today's hectic and sometimes frantic world, it often feels as if things are not considered valuable unless they have a price tag. Can my life be translated into monetary terms? That's a strange notion—to imagine that a life of value could be reduced to dollars and cents. I don't want to lose sight of what I consider truly worthwhile, those intangibles that have value but no price tag. I don't want to be seduced by gadgets, acquisitions, stuff.

My goal has been to live an ethical life based on honesty, balance, and integrity. When I reflect on the wide variety of experiences I've had, I realize that my search for value led me to make choices and decisions prompted by the situations I lived through. These choices may not always have proven the easiest, but through the decades they have helped me behave in ways that had substance, and allowed me the freedom and courage to change my mind.

Although I've met positive role models whom I've attempted to emulate, I believe I've learned more difficult and meaningful lessons from encounters with some who "did me wrong" and left me wondering where I had missed the boat, where I had gone astray. I came to understand that it wasn't me—it was them—and thus I learned from the wrong-doers how *not* to behave.

This is the story of some of the events that have shaped my life and the outcomes that enhanced my quest for value. It is a story of joy and sorrow, hope and despair, tranquility and turmoil, love and anger, faith and patience and grace. It is a story that may resonate with others, it may invoke in them a feeling of "Ah-ha—so *that* explains it," but, ultimately, it's all mine. If I walk alongside other seekers of value, I embrace them with kindness and encouragement as we travel together on this parallel path.

Some memories:

I'm seven or eight years old, walking the short distance to Garfield Elementary School and passing the parochial school a few blocks from home. A bunch of kids in the playground spot me and start yelling "Dirty Jew" and "Christ Killer"—I'm so shocked I stop short. Then the rocks start flying and I'm hit squarely on the nose. Sticks and stones *do* break my bones (in my nose) and names do really hurt me. My father diplomatically confronts the school's principal, who promises to lecture about hatred and its consequences. Dad's obviously upset, but never loses his temper. My choices: I will never verbally or physically hurt someone simply because that person is different. I may not understand but I will try to accept those who seem to hate me. I will speak up for justice, calmly and persistently.

When I'm ten, my parents finally save enough money to buy our first property. There are two houses on the lot—we will live in the front house and the back house will be rented. Then the "unthinkable" happens. The tenants are a black family, and they will be living on a "white" street. People actually send us messages that threaten all kinds of mayhem, which my parents ignore. Instead, my father introduces us to the tenant's children and, like kids usually do, we start playing together in the yard. I'm taunted at school and ask my father why so many kids are saying nasty things about my new friends being "colored." My Dad replies with words I remember vividly even now: "Ona, we're all colored, but some of us are pinker than others." I decide that I will not choose friends based on other people's guidelines. I will look beneath the surface to see what an individual is all about. I will have patience with those who cannot accept differences. If someone doesn't look like me but we're having fun playing together—let the games proceed.

In high school I befriend an older boy who, like me, loves the arts and especially classical music. We sit together in his room listening to recordings by various musicians—and offer our own critiques about which artist is best. I know that my friend is homosexual, but it has no effect on our passion for good music and great performing. (Besides, it's not entirely new to me. My mother's very best friends are Aunt Min and Aunt Pearl, a couple we kids adore because they're attentive and loving and always bring us presents when they come to visit.) One day, my friend is found by a family member with another young man in a compromising situation. Fearful of repercussions based on the "standards" of the time that would severely condemn his son's "unspeakable" behavior, the professional father quickly moves the family out of town. His son is forbidden from contacting any of his old friends and I never hear from him again. As a result of this pain, I decide I want to accept how people live even (or especially) if it's outside the "mainstream" and evaluate them by the quality of their spirits. I realize that there are those who will not be able to accept the reality of alternative lifestyles. I will miss my friend, and hope he finds happiness.

Sexism rears its ugly head in my early working life. After a year at college, with no money to pay for my continued education, I'm at home and working at my first real job at the daily newspaper in my New Jersey home town. I love it! After almost four years of excellent work as a reporter and editor, I apply for a reporter's job at a competing daily in a nearby town, a newspaper with an outstanding reputation. There's another applicant, a reporter I know well from my current job. I know him well because he's not a very good writer and frequently seeks me out to help him with rewrites. The editor of the other paper calls to tell me they're hiring my colleague. You're much more qualified, he says, but after all "John" is a married guy with a family to support. Sorry. Sorry? I bite the proverbial bullet.

So I job search in New York City, where I really want to be, and find a position as the editorial assistant to the CEO of a national organization. My first assignment: research and compile a program guide for member chapters. I dive in with enthusiasm and several months later the project is completed. I eagerly await the debut of the publication. And wait. And wait. And one day I happen to see a copy of the book on a colleague's desk. *My* book.

Except my name is nowhere to be found. Rather, the CEO has listed himself as the author and editor and when I build up enough courage to ask him about it, he freely admits having omitted my name because, after all, I'm just a young girl and really can't expect to take credit for his idea. He's actually serious (the only thing he gets right is that I *am* female and young), so I quietly tell him I quit, take my few personal items, walk out and never look back. Age will not matter for me. Gender will not matter for me. Personal glory will not matter for me. Fairness *will* matter. So will honesty, reliability, determination, and grit.

In the years to come I confront many more perplexing life situations; two stand out as particularly disturbing, yet enlightening:

The first: for twenty-four years I'm married to an abusive man who cannot take responsibility for his battering. It's all my fault. Or the fault of my being too smart for my own good. Or the fault of my big mouth. Or the fault of Women's Lib. And in stereotypical fashion, I accept his explanations and spend endless hours trying to figure out how to change myself and please him so the abuse will stop. I believe it's my job to make him happy and make the marriage work. I fool myself into thinking I'm protecting my children, and although he never beats them, they are profoundly affected by the violence in the home. When the time finally comes that I'm "strong" enough and "wise" enough to walk away, it takes me more than a year to feel even a modicum of personal safety. (During the marriage I was active in my community and known by many people, but from the time I leave and for many years to come I never hear from a single friend—although they all know where I am.) In the meantime, and before the actual divorce, my former husband is already starting a new family with the woman who will become Wife Number Two.

I rebuild my life, remake my image, finish my education (including a master's degree), and pursue a twenty-five-year career as a manager of volunteer services in social service and nonprofit agencies. Although it is typically an under-recognized and poorly-reimbursed profession, I'm completely committed to its core values of empowerment, leadership by example, and service. Volunteering is a family tradition and working with volunteers dovetails well with my personal goals. Slowly I build a reputation as an expert in the field and offer trainings, advice, and support locally, nationally, and internationally.

The second situation: my last job, for fifteen years, is with the hospice component of a large healthcare organization. When I start in this position, management is eager to acknowledge who I am and what I can offer. Unfortunately, new people later come in to run the department and decide to revise all systems to align with their own limited viewpoint. Among other slights, they fail to recognize the value of the volunteers and consider the volunteer administrator position similar to a clerical job. They actually tell me that managing volunteers (I supervise eighty-five people) requires no special skills or expertise. So I speak up for the program, the position, and myself. I point to fifteen years of success that reflect positively on the organization. Then, after handing me a negative performance evaluation (my first one ever), management tells me that they've "restructured" and my position is eliminated. There's a "new" position I can apply for. They must believe I'm naïve enough to think the contrived performance evaluation will not come up in an interview. No thanks, I tell them, and choose retirement instead.

After these life-altering events, I contemplate the consequences for me based on how I decide to react. Do I seek revenge? *No—I do not,* although that might be seen as a valid response. Viktor Frankl wrote that "What is to give light must endure burning." And South African author Alan Paton noted that "there is a hard law…that when a deep injury is done to us, we never recover until we forgive." When I have been wronged, I have forgiven. Trying to figure out why it happened is a waste of time. (One of my favorite cartoon strips from "Hagar the Horrible" shows Hagar on a hillside being fiercely assaulted by all manner of weapons as he cries out "Why me?" And from the heavens on high comes the response, "Why not?") Things happen. The valuable lessons I learn are that I will never treat another human being the way I was treated, and that focusing on the past is debilitating. The true question then becomes "Now that it has happened, what do I do about it?" I forgive—and I go on.

Where have I gone? Have I lived a life of value? What have I done to turn setbacks into triumphs, pain into passion, obstacles into growth?

After divorcing and returning to the work force, I join the staff at the first shelter for battered women in San Diego. Without judging, I approach the residents and hotline clients with compassion and insight based on my own experiences, but also grounded in nurturing and love, and the strong conviction that they are worthwhile human beings no matter how they choose to go on with their lives. To this day women approach me: "You're Ona, aren't you? I remember you from the shelter. You helped me change my life." (I continue to do trainings on domestic violence issues. It helps me keep a healthy perspective and contributes to my growth and healing.)

A few years pass, and I'm working at the San Diego AIDS Project, a fledgling organization committed to raising awareness and providing service as the epidemic spreads through the area. This insidious disease, a virtual death sentence at the time, cruelly erodes any semblance of normalcy among its victims. I find myself in the role of loving, accepting acquaintance to so many young men who must "confess" to their families that not only are they gay, but they're dying of AIDS. I do this willingly, at the same time recognizing and addressing my own emotional upheaval whenever a friend becomes sick and dies. HIV claims so many—it is indeed an equal opportunity destroyer. The lessons I learned through the years help me navigate these treacherous waters and maintain equilibrium and

> And so we tell our stories—the treasures of our hearts, the tales and words and rhythms that help us create a reality where everything is possible, where we endure and succeed and transcend and ultimately discover that it's only one story after all.

my usual sense of humor. When a friend on his deathbed smiles broadly at me and says "Remember, Ona, that the brownies in the frig are mine, but you can eat them after I'm gone," I know that I've nurtured his sense of the absurd and ridiculous and he's okay expressing it even at the end of his life. All of us at the bedside are soon laughing and munching on brownies, celebrating this legacy. The nature of the disease and treatments change and improve over time; my involvement is ongoing. I've become a long-time volunteer at a summer camp in New York State for HIV families. It's another piece of living where I get far more than I give. It's another step on my road towards serenity and fulfillment.

What motivates me to live an ethical and value-based life? I believe that I (like many others) am compelled to move through this existence in a way that creates peace and beauty and joy for those around me. That I am not concerned with the color of your skin, or the language you speak, or how much money you make, or how you worship, or whom you love, but rather care about your compassion, your contribution, your commitment. I need not know the details of your struggles but can touch your pain and courage, and mine, and together reach out for and demand more of life. I can ask of your hopes, your dreams, your experiences, and then realize that enlightenment and understanding may come not only through your answer, but with the posing of the question itself.

And so we tell our stories—the treasures of our hearts, the tales and words and rhythms that help us create a reality where everything is possible, where we endure and succeed and transcend and ultimately discover that it's only one story after all. And we make our choices. Emma Goldman, a notable, uncompromising anarchist with a powerful value system, said that she'd "rather have roses on my table than diamonds on my neck." A bit of fragrance always clings to the hand that gives roses, according to an old Chinese proverb. I believe that the sweet scent clings and lingers for a while, but the memory of it remains intact forever. I have roses—they grow in my garden.

I also have diamonds: I have family members who have challenged adversity with trust and hope, chosen their battles, and prevailed. I have colleagues who find words of praise for what I've accomplished, pat me on the back, and urge me to never give in or give up. I live in a house full of books (many still waiting to be read), and music, and a graceful old piano that I play daily. I am a short distance from the ocean, where I walk to the end of the pier and marvel at the magnificence of the night sky, or watch in wonder as a school of dolphins skim gracefully through the waters. I sit quietly and do not disturb the hummingbirds and caterpillars exploring my garden. I grip the hand of a young child at camp after telling a "ghost" story at campfire, and he looks up at me and says "That was *so* scary—do it again!" My world is surrounded by gems!

I look forward to each sunrise as it brings me to a day I have never seen before. I fill with awe facing this wondrous enigma we call life and nurture my sense of belonging and attachment, the feelings of connection and refuge that continue to support me on my journey of discovery. My imagination has free rein. An inner strength sustains my soul, along with the hope that at some time and some place the value of my life will be questioned and the answer will be: *priceless!*

And at the end of this magnificent adventure, when at last I reach Home, I will look back and shout out for all to hear:

"I did good! Darn—I did good!"

© *Ona Rita Yufe*

About the Author

I am a work in progress. My life has taken many twists and turns as I steer a course of inquiry, introspection, imagination—and I still have many roads to travel. From an early age I knew that I wanted to learn, to teach, and to serve. With my inquisitive mind, I was always passionate about school and gathering knowledge. After an early career in journalism, I returned to the workforce years later—filled with experiences as a mother and homemaker—and was employed for twenty-five years in social service and non-profit agencies as a manager of volunteer resources. Here I found ample opportunity to help others. I learned from every person I met and every situation I encountered, and shared what I learned; thus my passion for teaching was satisfied. And to be of service I volunteered, delivering meals to homebound AIDS patients, leading a troop of Brownie Girl Scouts, nurturing fledgling volunteer managers through local and national professional organizations, assisting in my children's school library, offering encouragement to hurricane survivors who came to my city, training volunteers and staff at a summer camp for HIV families, facilitating a support group for battered women—and so much more. Value accumulates in my life and my spirit soars the more I reach out, look beyond my own needs, welcome change, embrace diversity, enjoy a hearty laugh. What a ride—and it isn't over yet!

Within yourself deliverance must be searched for, because each man makes his own prison.

Edwin Arnold

Resentment is like drinking poison and waiting for the other person to die.

Carrie Fisher

...find meaning not in possessions or positions, but in personal commitments to ideals bigger than our own needs. And the ideals that seem to consistently provide this kind of meaning are ideals of service-of acting for the common good and overcoming whatever risks and obstacles may lie in the way.

John Graham

Forgive those born beneath an angry star, lest we forget how fragile we are.

Gordon Sumner

Never does the human soul appear so strong as when it forgoes revenge, and dares to forgive an injury.

E. H. Chapin

There is no revenge so complete as forgiveness.

Josh Billings

Although the world is full of suffering, it is full also of the overcoming of it.

Helen Keller

To take the difficulties, setbacks, and sorrows of life as a challenge to overcome which makes us stronger - rather than unjust punishment which should not happen to us - requires faith and courage.

Erich Fromm

We all have limitations we are trying to overcome. That is what being human is about.

Raymond W. Novaco

INTEGRATION

GROWING UP CLASS-CONSCIOUS

Howard Zinn

I was in my teens when I wrote this poem:

Go see your Uncle Phil
And say hello.
Who would walk a mile today
To say hello.
The city freezing in the snow?
Phil had a news stand
Under the Black El.
He sat on a wooden box
In the cold and in the heat.
And three small rooms across the street.
Today the wooden box was gone,
On top the stand Uncle Phil was curled,
A skeleton inside an Army coat.

He smiled and gave me
a stick of gum
With stiffened fingers, red and numb.
Go see your Uncle Phil today
My mother said again in June
I walked the mile to say hello
With the city smelling almost sweet
Brand new sneakers on my feet.
The stand was nailed and boarded tight
And quiet in the sun.
Uncle Phil lay cold, asleep,
Under the black El, in a wooden box
In three small rooms across the street.

I recall these lines, certainly not as an example of "poetry," but because they evoke something about my growing up in the slums of Brooklyn in the thirties, when my father and mother in desperate moments turned to saviors: The corner grocer, who gave credit by writing down the day purchases on a roll of paper; the kind doctor who treated my rickets for years without charging; Uncle Phil, whose army service had earned him a newsstand license and who loaned us money when we had trouble paying the rent.

Phil and my father were two of four brothers, Jewish immigrants from Austria, who came to this country before the First World War and worked together in New York factories. Phil's fellow workers kept questioning him: "Zinn, Zinn—what kind of name is that? Did you change it? It's not a Jewish name." Phil told them no, the name had not been changed, it was Zinn and that's all there was to it. But he got tired of the interrogations and one day had his name legally changed to Weintraub, which from then on was the name of that branch of the family.

My father, looking to escape the factory, became a waiter, mostly at weddings, sometimes in restaurants, and a member of Local 2 of the waiters Union. While the union tightly controlled its membership, on New Year's Eve, when there was a need for extra waiters, the sons of the members, called juniors, would work along side their fathers, and I did too.

I hated every moment of it: the ill-fitting waiter's tuxedo, borrowed from my father, on my lanky body, the sleeves absurdly short (my father was five-foot-five and at sixteen I was a six-footer); the way the bosses treated the waiters, who were fed chicken wings just before they marched out to serve roast beef and filet mignon to the guests; everybody in their fancy dress, wearing silly hats, singing "Auld Lang Syne" as the New Year began and me standing there in my waiter's costume, watching my father, his face strained, clear his tables, feeling no joy at the coming of the New Year.

When I first came across a certain E.E. Cummings poem, I didn't fully understand why it touched me so deeply, but I knew it connected with some hidden feeling.

> my father moved through dooms of love
> through sames of am through haves of give,
> singing each morning out of each night
> my father moved through depths of height

712

His name was Eddie. He was always physically affectionate to his four boys, and loved to laugh. He had strong face, a muscular body, and flat feet (due, it was said, to long years as a waiter, but who could be sure?), and his waiter friends called him "Charlie Chaplin" because he walked with feet splayed out—he claimed he could balance the trays better that way.

In the Depression years the weddings fell off, there was little work, and he got tired of hanging around the union hall, playing cards, waiting for a job. So he became at different times a window cleaner, a pushcart peddler, a street salesman of neckties, a W.P.A. worker in Central Park. As a window cleaner, his supporting belt broke one day and he fell off the ladder onto the concrete steps of a subway entrance. I was perhaps twelve and I remember him being brought, bleeding, into our little flat. He had hurt himself badly. My mother would not let him clean windows again.

All his life he worked hard for very little. I've always resented the smug statements of politicians, media commentators, corporate executives who talked of how, in America, if you worked hard you would become rich. The meaning of that was if you were poor it was because you hadn't worked hard enough. I knew this was a lie, about my father and millions of others, men and women who worked harder than anyone, harder than financiers and politicians, harder than anybody if you accept that when you work at an unpleasant job that makes it very hard work indeed.

My mother worked and worked without getting paid at all. She was a plump woman, with a sweet, oval Russian face—a beauty, in fact. She had grown up in Irkutsk, in Siberia. While my father worked his hours on the job, she worked all day and all night, managing the family, finding the food, cooking and cleaning, taking the kids to the doctor of the hospital clinic for measles and mumps and whooping cough and tonsillitis and whatever came up. And taking care of family finances. My father had a fourth grade education and could not read much or do much arithmetic. My mother had gone as far as seventh grade, but her intelligence went far beyond that; she was the brains of the family. And the strength of the family.

Her name was Jenny. Toz and I sat with her in our kitchen one day when she was in her seventies and had her talk about her life, with a tape recorder on the table. She told of her mother's arranged marriage in Irkutsk, of how "they brought a boy home, a Jewish soldier stationed in Irkutsk, and said, This is who you'll marry."

They emigrated to America. Jenny's mother died in her thirties, having given birth to three boys and three girls, and her father—against who she boiled with indignation all her life—deserted the family. Jenny, the eldest but only a teenager, became the mother of the family, took care of the rest, working factories, until they grew up and found jobs.

She met Eddie through his sister, who worked in her factory, and it was a passionate marriage all the way. Eddie died at sixty-seven. To the end he was carrying trays of food at weddings and in restaurants, never having made enough money to retire. It was a sudden heart attack, and I got the news in Atlanta, where Roz and I had just moved. I remembered our last meeting, when my father was clearly upset about our little family moving south, so far away, but said nothing except "Good luck. Take care of yourself."

My mother outlived him by many years. She lived by herself, fiercely insisting on her independence, knitting sweaters for everybody, saving her shopping coupons, playing bingo with her friends. But toward the end she suffered a stroke and entered a nursing home.

As a child I was drawn to a framed photograph on the wall, of a delicate-faced little boy with soft brown eyes and a shock of brown hair, and one day my mother told me it was her firstborn, my older brother, who died of spinal meningitis at the age of five. In our tape recording she tells how when he died they'd been in the country for a brief, cheap vacation, and how she and my father held the boy's body on the long train ride back to New York City.

We lived in a succession of tenements, sometimes four rooms, sometimes three. Some winters we lived in a building with central heating. Other times we lived in what was called a cold-water flat—no heat except from the coal cooking stove in the kitchen, no hot water except what we boiled on that same stove.

It was always a battle to pay the bills. I would come home from school in the winter, when the sun set at four, and find the house dark—the electric company had turned off the electricity, and my mother would be sitting there, knitting by candlelight.

There was no refrigerator, but an icebox, for which we would go to the "ice dock" and buy a five- or ten-cent chunk of ice. In the winter a wooden box rested on the sill just outside the window, using nature to keep things cold. There was no shower, but the washtub in the kitchen was our bathtub.

No radio for a long time, until one day my father took me on a long walk through the city to find a second-hand radio, and triumphantly brought it home on his shoulder, me trotting along by his side. No telephone. We could be called to the phone at the candy store down the block, and pay the kid who ran upstairs to get us two pennies or a nickel. Sometimes we hung out near the phone to take the call and race to collect the nickel.

And yes the roaches. Never absent, wherever we lived. We'd come home and they'd be all over the kitchen table and scatter when we turned on the light. I never got used to them.

I don't remember ever being hungry. The rent might not paid (we moved often, a step ahead of eviction), no bills might be paid, the grocer might not be paid, but my mother was ingenious at making sure there was always food. Always hot cereal in the morning, always hot soup in the evening, always bread, butter, eggs, milk, noodles and cheese, sour cream, chicken fricassee.

My mother was not shy about using the English language, which she adapted to her purposes. We would hear her telling her friend about the problem she was having with "very close veins," or "a pain in my crutch." She would look in the dairy store for "monster cheese." She would say to my father if he forgot something, "Eddie, try to remember, wreck your brains."

My brothers—Bernie, Jerry, Shelly—and I had lots of fun over the years recalling her ways. She would sign her letters to us, "you mother, Jenny Zinn." We laughed at those memories even while standing by in the hospital room where she lay in a coma, kept "alive" by a tangle of tubes, her brain already damaged beyond repair. We had signed that terrible order, "Do Not Resuscitate," shortly after which she coughed up her breathing tube and died. She was ninety.

We four boys grew up together—sleeping two or three to a bed, in rooms dark and uninviting. So I spent a lot of time in the street or the schoolyard, playing handball, football, softball, stickball, or taking boxing lessons from a guy in the neighborhood who had made the Golden Gloves and was our version of a celebrity.

In the time I did spend in house I read. From the time I was eight I was reading whatever books I could find. The very first was one I picked up on the street. The beginning pages were torn out but that didn't matter. It was *Tarzan and the Jewels of Opar* and from then on I was a fan of Edgar Rice

715

Burroughs, not only his Tarzan books but his other fantasies: *The Chessmen of Mars*, about the way wars were fought between Martians, with warriors, on foot or on horses, playing out the chess moves; *The Earth's Core*, about a strange civilization in the center of the earth.

There were no books in our house. My father had never read a book. My mother read romance magazines. They both read the newspaper. They knew little about politics, except that Franklin Roosevelt was a good man because he helped the poor.

As a boy I read no children's books. My parents did not know about such books, but when I was ten, the New York Post offered a set of the complete works of Charles Dickens (of whom they had never heard, of course). By saving coupons cut out of the newspaper, they could get a volume every week for a few pennies. They signed up because they knew I loved to read. And so I read Dickens in the order in which we received the books, starting with *David Copperfield*, *Oliver Twist*, *Great Expectations*, *The Pickwick Papers*, *Hard Times*, *Tale of Two Cities*, and all the rest, until the coupons were exhausted and so was I.

I did not know where Dickens fitted into the history of modern literature because he was all I knew of that literature. I did not know that he was probably the most popular novelist in the English-speaking world (perhaps in any world) in the mid-nineteenth century, or that he was a great actor whose readings of his own work drew mobs of people, or that when he visited the United States in 1842 (he was thirty), landing first in Boston, some of his readers traveled two thousand miles from the Far West to see him.

What I did know was that he aroused in me tumultuous emotions. First, an anger at arbitrary power puffed up with wealth and kept in place by law. But most of all a profound compassion for the poor. I did not see myself as poor in the way Oliver Twist was poor. I didn't recognize that I was so moved by his story because his life touched chords in mine.

How wise Dickens was to make readers feel poverty and cruelty through the fate of children who had not reached the age where the righteous and comfortable classes could accuse them of being responsible for their own misery.

Today, reading pallid, cramped novels about "relationships," I recall Dickens' unashamed rousing of feeling, his uproariously funny character, his epic settings—cities of hunger and degradation, countries in revolution, the stakes being life and death not just for one family but for thousands.

Dickens is sometimes criticized by literary snobs for sentimentality, melodrama, partisanship, exaggeration. But surely the state of the world makes fictional exaggeration unnecessary and partisanship vital. It was only many years after I read those Dickens novels that I understood his accomplishment.

For my thirteenth birthday, my parents, knowing that I was writing things in notebooks, bought me a rebuilt Underwood typewriter. It came with a practice book for learning the touch system, and soon I was typing book reviews for everything I read and keeping them in my drawer. I never showed them to anyone. It gave me joy and pride just to know that I had read these books and could write about them—on a typewriter.

From the age of fourteen I had after-school and summer jobs, delivering clothes for a dry cleaner, working as a caddy on a golf course in Queens. I also helped out in a succession of candy stores my parents bought in a desperate attempt to make enough money so my dad could quit being a waiter. The stores all failed, but my three younger brothers and I had lots of milkshakes and ice cream and candy while they existed.

> I was a radical, believing that something fundamental was wrong in this country—not just the existence of poverty amidst great wealth, not just the horrible treatment of black people, but something rotten at the root.

I remember the last of those candy store situations, and it was typical. The six of us lived above the store in a four-room flat in a dirty old five-story tenement on Bushwick Avenue in Brooklyn. The street was always full of life, especially in spring and summer, when everyone seemed to be outside—old folks sitting on chairs, mothers holding their babies, teenagers playing ball, the older guys "throwing the bull," fooling with girls.

I read something called the Brown Book of the Nazi Terror, which described what was happening in Germany under Hitler. It was a drama beyond anything a playwright or novelist could imagine. And now the Nazi war machine was beginning to move into the Rhineland, Austria, Czechoslovakia. The newspapers and radio were full of excitement: Chamberlain meeting Hitler at Munich, the sudden, astonishing nonaggression pact of the two archenemies, Soviet Russia and Nazi Germany. And finally, the invasion of Poland and the start of the Second World War.

The Civil War in Spain, just ended with victory for the Fascist general Franco, seemed the event closest to all of us because several thousand American radicals—Communists, socialists, anarchists—had crossed the Atlantic to fight with the democratic government of Spain. A young fellow who played street football with us—short and thin, the fastest runner in the neighborhood—disappeared. Months later the word came to us: Jerry has gone to Spain to fight against Franco.

There on Bushwick Avenue, among the basketball players and street talkers, were some young Communists, a few years older than me. They had jobs, but after work and on weekends, they distributed Marxist literature in the neighborhood and talked politics into the night with whoever was interested.

I was interested. I was reading about what was happening in the world. I argued with the Communist guys. Especially about the Russian invasion of Finland. They insisted it was necessary for the Soviet Union to protect itself against future attack, but to me it was a brutal attack of aggression against a tiny country, and none of their carefully worked out justifications persuaded me.

Still, I agreed with them on lots of things. They were ferociously antifascist, indignant as I was about the contrasts of wealth and poverty in America. I admired them—they seemed to know so much about politics, economics, what was happening everywhere in the world. And they were courageous—I had seen them defy the local policeman, who tried to stop them from distributing literature on the street and to break up their knots of discussion. And besides, they were regular guys, good athletes.

One summer day they asked me if I wanted to go with them to "a demonstration" in Times Square that evening. I had never been to such a thing. I made some excuse to my parents, and a little bunch of us took the subway to Times Square.

When we arrived it was just a typical evening in Times Square—the streets crowded, the lights glittering. "Where's the demonstration?" I asked my friend Leon. He was tall, blonde, the ideal "Aryan" type, but the son of German Communists who were also nature worshippers and part of a little colony of health-conscious German socialists out in the New Jersey countryside.

"Wait," he said, "Ten o'clock." We continued to stroll.

As the clock on the Times tower struck ten, the scene changed. In the midst of the crowd, banners were unfurled, and people, perhaps a thousand or more, formed into lines carrying banners and signs and chanting slogans about peace and justice and a dozen other causes of the day. It was exciting. And nonthreatening. All these people were keeping to the sidewalks, not blocking traffic, walking in orderly, nonviolent lines through Times Square. My friend and I were walking behind two women carrying a banner, and he said, "Let's relieve them." So we each took an end of the banner. I felt a bit like Charlie Chaplin in Modern Times, when he casually picks up a red signal flag and suddenly finds a thousand people marching behind him with raised fists. We heard the sound of sirens and I thought there must be a fire somewhere, an accident of some kind. But then I heard screams and saw hundreds of policemen, mounted on horses and on foot, charging into the lines of marchers, smashing people with their clubs.

I was astonished, bewildered. This was America, a country where, whatever its faults, people could speak, write, assemble, demonstrate without fear. It was in the Constitution, the Bill of Rights. We were a *democracy*.

As I absorbed this, as my thoughts raced, all in a few seconds, I was spun around by a very large man, who seized my shoulder and hit me very hard. I only saw him as a blur. I didn't know if it was a club or a fist or a blackjack, but I was knocked unconscious.

I awoke in a doorway perhaps a half-hour later. I had no sense of how much time had elapsed, but it was an eerie scene I woke up to. There was no demonstration going on, no policemen in sight. My friend Leon was gone, and Times Square was filled with is usual Saturday night crowd—all as if nothing had happened, as if it were all a dream. But I knew it wasn't a dream; there was a painful lump on the side of my head.

More important, there was a very painful thought in my head: those young Communists on the block were right! The state and its police were not neutral referees in a society of contending interests. They were on the side of the rich and powerful. Free speech? Try it and the police will be there with their horses, their clubs, their guns, to stop you.

From that moment on, I was no longer a liberal, a believer in the self-correcting character of American democracy. I was a radical, believing that something fundamental was wrong in this country—not just the existence of poverty amidst great wealth, not just the horrible treatment of black people, but something rotten at the root. The situation required not just a new president or new laws, but an uprooting of the old order, the introduction of a new kind of society—cooperative, peaceful, egalitarian.

Perhaps I am exaggerating the importance of that one experience. But I think not. I have come to believe that our lives can be turned in a different direction, our minds adopt a different way of thinking, because of some significant though small event. That belief can be frightening or exhilarating, depending on whether you just contemplate the event or *do* something about it.

The years following that experience in Times Square might be called "my Communist years," but that phrase would be easy to misunderstand because the word "Communist" conjures up Joseph Stalin and the gulags of death and torture, the disappearance of free expression, the atmosphere of fear and trembling created in the Soviet Union, the ugly bureaucracy that lasted seventy years, pretending to be socialism.

None of that was in the minds or intentions of the young working-class people I knew who called themselves Communists. Certainly not in my mind. Little was known about the Soviet Union, except the romantic image, popularized by people like the English theologian Hewlitt Johnson, the Dean of Canterbury. In his book The Soviet Power, distributed widely by the Communist movement, he gave idealists disillusioned with capitalism the vision they longed for, of a place where the country belonged to "the people," where everyone had work and free health care, and women had equal opportunities with men, and a hundred different ethnic groups were treated with respect.

The Soviet Union was this romantic blur, far away. What was close at hand, visible, was that Communists were the leaders in organizing working people all over the country. They were the most daring, risking arrest and beatings to organize auto workers in Detroit, steel workers in Pittsburgh, textile workers in North Carolina, fur and leather workers in New York, longshoremen on the West Coast. They were the first to speak up, more than that, to demonstrate—to chain themselves to factory gates and White House fences—when blacks were lynched in the South, when the "Scottsboro Boys" were being railroaded to prison in Alabama.

My image of "a Communist" was not a Soviet bureaucrat but my friend Leon's father, a cabdriver who came home from work bruised and bloody one day, beaten up by his employer's goons (yes, that word was soon part of my vocabulary) for trying to organize his fellow cabdrivers into a union.

Everyone knew that the Communists were the first antifascists, protesting against Mussolini's invasion of Ethiopia and Hitler's persecution of the Jews. And, most impressive of all, it was the Communists, thousands of them, who volunteered to fight in Spain in the Abraham Lincoln Brigade, to join volunteers from all over the world to defend Madrid and the Spanish people against the army of Francisco Franco, which was given arms and airplanes by Germany and Italy.

Furthermore, some of the best people in the country were connected with the Communist movement in some way, heroes and heroines one could admire. There was Paul Robeson, the fabulous singer-actor-athlete whose magnificent voice could fill Madison Square Garden, crying out against racial injustice, against fascism. And literary figures (weren't Theodore Dreiser and W.E.B. Du Bois Communists?), and talented, socially conscious Hollywood actors and writers and directors (yes, the Hollywood Ten, hauled before a congressional committee, defended by Humphrey Bogart and so many others).

True, in that movement, as in any other, you could see the righteousness leading to dogmatism, the closed circle of ideas impermeable to doubt, and intolerance of dissent by people who were the most persecuted dissenters. But however imperfect, even repugnant, were particular policies, particular actions, there remained the purity of the ideal, represented in the theories of Karl Marx and the noble visions of many lesser thinkers and writers.

I remember my first reading of *The Communist Manifesto*, which Marx and Engels wrote when they to were young radicals; Marx was thirty, Engels twenty-eight. "The history of all hitherto existing society is the history of class struggle." That was undeniably true, verifiable in any reading of history. Certainly true for the United States, despite all the promises of the Constitution ("We the people of the Unites States..." and "No state shall deny...the equal protection of the laws").

The analysis of capitalism by Marx and Engels made sense: capitalism's history of exploitation, its creation of extremes of wealth and poverty, even in the liberal "democracy," of this country. And their socialist vision was not one of dictatorship or bureaucracy but of a free society. Their "dictatorship of the proletariat" was to be a transitional phase, the goal a classless society of true democracy, true freedom. A rational, just economic system would allow a short work day and leave everyone freedom and time to do as they liked—to write poetry, to be in nature, to play sports, to be truly human. Nationalism would be a thing of the past. People all over the world, of whatever race, of whatever continent, would live in peace and cooperation.

In my teenage reading, those ideas were kept alive by some of the finest writers in America. I read Upton Sinclair's *The Jungle*; work in the Chicago stockyards was the epitome of capitalist exploitation, and the vision of a new society in the last pages of the book is thrilling. John Steinbeck's *The Grapes of Wrath* was an eloquent cry against the conditions of life wherein the poor were expendable and any attempt on their part to change their lives was met with police clubs.

When I was eighteen, unemployed and my family desperate for help, I took a much publicized Civil Service examination for a job in the Brooklyn Navy Yard. Thirty thousand young men (women applicants were unthinkable) took the exam, competing for a few hundred jobs. It was 1940, and New Deal programs had relieved but not ended the Depression. When the results were announced, four hundred of the applicants had gotten a score of 100 percent on the exam and would get jobs. I was one for them.

For me and my family it was a triumph. My salary would be $14.40 for a forty-hour week. I could give my family $10.00 a week and have the rest for lunch and spending money.

It was also an introduction into the world of heavy industry. I was to be an apprentice shipfitter for the next three years. I would work out on "the ways," a vast inclined surface at the edge of the harbor on which a battleship, the USS *Iowa*, was to be built. (Many years later, in the 1980s, I was called to be a witness at the Staten Island trial of pacifists who had demonstrated against the placement of nuclear weapons on a battleship docked there—the USS *Iowa*.)

I had no idea of the dimensions of a battleship. Stood on end, it would have been almost as tall as the Empire State Building. The keel had just been laid, and our job—thousands of us—was to put together the steel body and inner framework of the ship. It was hard, dirty, malodorous work. The smell caused by cutting galvanized steel with an acetylene torch is indescribable—only years later did we learn that the zinc released in such burning also causes cancer.

In the winter, icy blasts blew from the sea, and we wore thick gloves and helmets, and got occasional relief around the little fires used by the riveters.

They heated their rivets in these fires until the rivets were glowing globules which they then pulled from the fire and pounded into the steel plates of the hull with huge hammers driven by compressed air. The sound was deafening.

In the summer, we sweated under our overalls and in our steel-tipped boots, and swallowed salt pills to prevent heat exhaustion. We did a lot of crawling around inside the tiny steel compartments of the "inner bottom," where smells and sounds were magnified a hundred times. We measured and hammered, and cut and welded, using the service of "burners" and "chippers."

No women workers. The skilled jobs were held by white men, who were organized in A.F. craft unions know to be inhospitable to blacks. The few blacks in the shipyard had the toughest, most physically demanding jobs, like riveting.

What made the job bearable was the steady pay and the accompanying dignity of being a workingman, bringing home money like my father. There was also the pride that we were doing something for the war effort. But most important for me was that I found a small group of friends, fellow apprentices—some of them shipfitters like myself, others shipwrights, machinists, pipefitters, sheet-metal workers—who were young radicals, determined to do something to change the world. No less.

We were excluded from the craft unions of the skilled workers, so we decided to organize the apprentices into a union, an association. We would act together to improve our working conditions, raise our pay, and create a camaraderie during and after working hours to add some fun to our workaday lives.

This we did, successfully, with three hundred young workers, and for me it was an introduction to actual participation in a labor movement. We were organizing a union and doing what working people had done through the centuries, creating little spaces of culture and friendship to make up for the dreariness of the work itself.

Four of us who were elected as officers of the Apprentice Association became special friends. We met one evening a week to read books on politics and economics and socialism, and talk about world affairs. These were years when some fellows our age were in college, but we felt we were getting a good education.

Still, I was glad to leave the shipyard and join the Air Force. And it was while flying combat missions in Europe that I began a sharp turn in my political thinking, away from the romanticization of the Soviet Union that enveloped many radials (and others, too), especially in the atmosphere of World War II and the stunning successes of the Red Army against the Nazi invaders.

The reason for this turn was my encounter, which I described earlier, with an aerial gunner on another crew who questioned whether the aims of the Allies—England, France, the United States, the Soviet Union—were really antifascist and democratic.

One book he gave me shook forever ideas I had held for years. This was *The Yogi and the Commissar,* by Arthur Koestler. Koestler had been a Communist, had fought in Spain, but he had become convinced—and his factual evidence was powerful, his logic unshakable—that the Soviet Union was a fraud. (After the war, I read *The God That Failed,* in which writers whose integrity and dedication to justice I could not question—Richard Wright, Andre Gide, Ignazio Silone, and Koestler, too—describe their loss of faith in the Communist movement and the Soviet Union.)

But disillusionment with the Soviet Union did not diminish my belief in socialism, any more than disillusionment with the United States government lessened my belief in democracy. It certainly did not affect my consciousness of *class*, of the difference in the way rich and poor lived in the United States, of the failure of the society to provide the most basic biological necessities—food, housing, health care—to tens of millions of people.

Oddly enough, when I became a second lieutenant in the Army Air Corps I got a taste of what life was like for the privileged classes—for now I had better clothes, better food, more money, higher status than I had in civilian life.

After the war, with a few hundred dollars in mustering—out money, and my uniform and medals packed away, I rejoined Roz. We were a young, happy married couple. But we could find no other place to live but a rat-infested basement apartment in Bedford-Stuyvesant ("rat-infested" is not a figure of speech—there was that day I walked into the bathroom and saw a large rat scurry up the water pipe back into the ceiling).

I was back in the working class, but needing a job. I tried going back to the Brooklyn Navy Yard, but it was hateful work with none of he compensating features of that earlier time. I worked as a waiter, as a ditch-digger, as a brewery worker, and collected unemployment insurance in between jobs. (I can understand very well the feeling of veterans of Vietnam War, who were important when soldiers, coming back home with no jobs, no prospects, and without the glow that surrounded the veterans of World War II—a diminishing of their selves.) In the meantime, our daughter, Myla, was born.

At the age of twenty-seven, with a second child on the way, I began college as a freshman at New York University, under the G.I. Bill of Rights. That gave me four years of free college education and $120 a month, so that with Roz working part-time, with Myla and Jeff in nursery, with me working a night shift after school, we could survive.

Whenever I hear that the government must not get involved in helping people, that this must be left to, "private enterprise," I think of the G.I. Bill and its marvelous nonbureaucratic efficiency. There are certain necessities— housing, medical care, education—about which private enterprise gives not a hoot (supplying these to the poor is not profitable, and private enterprise won't act without *profit*.)

Starting college coincided with a change in our lives: moving out of our miserable basement rooms into a low-income housing project in downtown Manhattan, on the East River. Four rooms, utilities included in the rent, no rats, no cockroaches, a few trees and a playground downstairs, a park along the river. We were happy.

While going to NYU and Columbia I worked the four-to-twelve shift in the basement of a Manhattan warehouse, loading heavy cartons of clothing onto trailer trucks which carry them to cities all over the country.

We were an odd crew, we warehouse loaders—a black man, a Honduran immigrant, two men somewhat retarded mentally, another veteran of the war (married, with children, who sold his blood to supplement his small pay check). With us for a while was young man named Jeff Lawson whose father John Howard Lawson, a Hollywood writer, was one of the Hollywood Ten. There was another young fellow, a Columbia College student who was named after his grandfather, the socialist labor leader Daniel DeLeon. (I encountered him many years later; he was in a bad way mentally, and then I got word that he had laid down under his car in the garage and breathed in enough carbon monoxide to kill himself.)

We were all members of the union (District 65), which had a reputation of being "left-wing." But we, the truck-loaders, were more left than the union, which seemed hesitant to interfere with loading operation of this warehouse.

We were angry about our working conditions, having to load outside on the sidewalk in bad weather with no rain or snow gear available to us. We kept asking the company for gear, with no results. One night, late, the rain began pelting down. We stopped work, said we would not continue unless we had a binding promise of rain gear.

The supervisor was beside himself. That truck had to get out that night to meet the schedule, they told us. He had no authority to promise anything. We said, "Tough shit. We're not getting drenched for the damned schedule." He got on the phone, nervously called a company executive at his home, interrupting a dinner party. He came back from the phone. "Okay, you'll get your gear." The next workday we arrived at the warehouse an found a line of shiny new raincoats and rain hats.

That was my world for the first thirty-three years of my life—the world of unemployment and bad employment, of me and my wife leaving our two- and three-year-olds in the care of others while we went to school or to work, living most of that time in cramped and unpleasant places, hesitating to call the doctor when the children were sick because we couldn't afford to pay him, finally taking the children to hospital clinics where interns could take care of them. This is the way a large part of population lives, even in this, the richest country in the world. And when, armed with the proper degrees, I began to move out of that world, becoming a college professor, I never forgot that. I never stopped being class-conscious.

I note how our political leaders step gingerly around such expressions, how it seems the worst accusation one politician can make about another is that "he appeals to class hostility...he is setting class against class." Well, class has been set against class in the realities of life for a very long time, and the words will disappear only when the realities of inequity disappear.

It would be foolish for me to claim that class consciousness was simply the result of growing up poor and living the life of a poor kid and then the life of a hard-pressed young husband and father. I've met many people with similar backgrounds who developed a very different set of ideas about society, and many others, whose early lives were much different from mine but whose world-view is similar.

When I was chair of the history department at Spelman and had the power (even a *little power* can make people heady!) to actually hire one or two people, I invited Staughton Lynd, a brilliant young historian, graduate of Harvard and Columbia, to join the Spelman faculty. (We were introduced at a historian's meeting in New York, where Staughton expressed a desire to teach at a black college.)

The summer before Staughton Lynd came south, we met in New England and decided to climb a New Hampshire mountain (Mt. Monadnock) together and get acquainted. My two children, Myla and Jeff, came with us. They were thirteen and eleven. When we reached the summit, tired and hungry, we found the remains of a pack of cigarettes, and the four of us—all nonsmokers, it is fair to say—sat down cross-legged and puffed silently, pretending we were characters in *Treasure of the Sierra Madre*.

That mountain-climbing conversation was illuminating. Staughton came from a background completely different from mine. His parents were quite famous professors at Columbia and Sarah Lawrence, Robert and Helen Lynd, authors of the sociological classic *Middletown*. Staughton had been raised in comfortable circumstances, had gone to Harvard and Columbia. And yet, as we went back and forth on every political issue under the sun— race, class, war, violence, nationalism, justice, fascism, capitalism, socialism, and more—it was clear that our social philosophies, our values, were extraordinarily similar.

In the light of such experiences, traditional dogmatic "class analysis" cannot remain intact. But as dogma disintegrates, hope appears. Because it means that human beings, whatever their backgrounds, are more open than we think, that their behavior cannot be confidently predicted from their past, that we are all creatures vulnerable to new thoughts, new attitudes.

And while such vulnerability creates all sorts of possibilities, both good and bad, its very existence is exciting. It means that no human being should be written off, no change in thinking deemed impossible.

© Howard Zinn

About the Author

Howard Zinn is a historian, playwright, and social activist. He was a shipyard worker and Air Force bombardier before he went to college under the GI Bill and received his PhD from Columbia University. He has taught at Spelman College and Boston University, and has been a visiting professor at the University of Paris and the University of Bologna. He has received the Thomas Merton Award, the Eugene V. Debs Award, the Upton Sinclair Award, and the Lannan Literary Award. He lives in Auburndale, Massachusetts.

He is best known for his landmark history book, *A People's History of the United States*. Also remarkable are *You Can't Be Neutral on a Moving Train*, his autobiography, and recently (with Anthony Arnove) *Voices of a People's History of the United States*, a collection of original writings from a diverse group of activists and thinkers that stretches all the way back to the time of Christopher Columbus.

This is how we were warned it would be. President Reagan told us from the very beginning that he believed in a kind of social Darwinism - survival of the fittest - government can't do everything we were told, so it should settle for taking care of the strong and hope that economic ambition and charity will do the rest. Make the rich richer, and what falls from the table will be enough for the middle class and those who are trying desperately to work their way into the middle class.

Mario Cuomo

The golf [courses] lie so near the mill
That almost every day
The laboring children can look out
And see the men at play.

Sarah Cleghorn

The next phase or epoch is already discernible; it is the fight to extend the concept of universal human rights, and to match the "globalization" of production with the globalization of a common standard for justice and ethics.

Christopher Hitchens

Philanthropy is commendable, but it must not cause the philanthropist to overlook the circumstances of economic injustice, which makes philanthropy necessary.

Martin Luther King, Jr.

While there is a lower class I am in it, while there is a criminal element I am of it; while there is a soul in prison, I am not free.

Eugene V. Debs

Questioning the system is the height of loyalty. The American system differs from other systems in that my loyalty is to defend the Constitution, not to follow orders. Our loyalty is to fairness.

Charles Swift

America must finish what we started in the Declaration of Independence and the Constitution and go all the way until we assure liberty and justice for the millions of children of all races and incomes left behind in our society today despite national leaders who seek to turn us back to the not-so-good old days of race and class and gender divisions.

Marian Wright Edelman

The revolution of our hearts does not require new wisdom—but new seriousness and dedication.

Erich Fromm

INDEX

Y

Z